T0389675

Christian-Muslim Relations
A Bibliographical History

History of
Christian-Muslim
Relations

VOLUME 39

Christians and Muslims have been involved in exchanges over matters of faith and morality since the founding of Islam. Attitudes between the faiths today are deeply coloured by the legacy of past encounters, and often preserve centuries-old negative views.

The History of Christian-Muslim Relations, Texts and Studies presents the surviving record of past encounters in a variety of forms: authoritative, text editions and annotated translations, studies of authors and their works and collections of essays on particular themes and historical periods. It illustrates the development in mutual perceptions as these are contained in surviving Christian and Muslim writings, and makes available the arguments and rhetorical strategies that, for good or for ill, have left their mark on attitudes today. The series casts light on a history marked by intellectual creativity and occasional breakthroughs in communication, although, on the whole beset by misunderstanding and misrepresentation. By making this history better known, the series seeks to contribute to improved recognition between Christians and Muslims in the future.

A number of volumes of the *History of Christian-Muslim Relations* series are published within the subseries *Christian-Muslim Relations. A Bibliographical History*.

The titles published in this series are listed at *brill.com/hcmr*

Christian-Muslim Relations
A Bibliographical History

Volume 14. Central and Eastern Europe
(1700-1800)

Edited by
David Thomas and John Chesworth

with Stanisław Grodź, Emma Gaze Loghin,
Radu Păun, Mehdi Sajid, Cornelia Soldat

BRILL

LEIDEN · BOSTON
2020

Cover illustration: This shows the mosque in the gardens of Schwetzingen Palace in the state of Baden-Würtemburg, Germany. It was built by Nicolas de Pigage between 1779 and 1795, following the model of the mosque in Kew Gardens, London, built by William Chambers, and the designs of Johann Fischer von Erlach. Stock photo ID: 1086438212

The Library of Congress Cataloging-in-Publication Data is available online at http://lccn.loc.gov/2009029184

Typeface for the Latin, Greek, and Cyrillic scripts: "Brill". See and download: brill.com/brill-typeface.

ISSN 1570-7350
ISBN 978-90-04-42226-1 (hardback)
ISBN 978-90-04-42317-6 (e-book)

This book is printed on acid-free paper and produced in a sustainable manner.

CONTENTS

German and Habsburg states

South-Eastern Europe

Poland and Lithuania

Russia

FOREWORD

David Thomas

Christian-Muslim relations. A bibliographical history volume 14 (*CMR* 14) is the third of the three that cover relations between followers of the two faiths through the 18th century. It includes nearly all the works from Central and Eastern Europe, including Russia, that are known from this period, all by authors who called themselves Christians or came from a Christian background, and they cast light on Christian attitudes towards Islam and Muslims from this region in the period 1700-1800. Some attest to influence from changing western European attitudes towards Islam as a faith, others relay themes and prejudices that are familiar from former times, and a great number reflect the accumulated resentment and hatred resulting from the incessant atrocities committed by Ottoman invaders. A substantial number represent direct experience of Islam, sometimes of Shīʿī Islam from travellers in Iran, though mostly of Sunnī Islam from travellers and merchants in the Ottoman Empire, and from ambassadors and their entourages resident in Istanbul or engaged in peace negotiations. This was a period of rapid redressing of power balances, as the Ottoman Empire gradually lost the invincibility for which it had been feared and European courts competed for influence with officials who governed the vast Ottoman domains in the sultan's name.

Many of the themes that are found in works on Islam from western Europe in the 17th and 18th centuries are also evident in the works from further east that are analysed in this volume. Central and Eastern European authors either made use of many of the same sources as their counterparts further west, as in the case of Greek Orthodox authors writing within the Ottoman Empire, or borrowed them from western writings that came to them in translation, as in the case of many German Pietist authors preparing works for mission among Muslims. Thus, the works analysed here show little divergence from the inherited attitude towards Muḥammad as a self-promoting fraud, and minimal interest in the details of early Islamic history, which they frequently got wrong. But there are also signs of a similar growing fascination with the Ottoman world, its history, society, customs and rulers, to that in the west, though deriving from a much wider and longer direct encounter, accompanied by an understandable concern to emphasise the ungodliness of the Islamic faith and the callousness of its people in the way they maltreated Christians who had been taken prisoner and reneged on treaties after showing every sign of friendship with the people who had signed them. Questions about the religious aspects of Islam seem to have engaged no more than a handful, and while translations of the Qur'an were made, and some study of it was pursued, this was less often out of scholarly interest than in preparation for disavowal. In the great majority of portrayals, Muslims remained the stock other, though an exception is Russia, where legal measures passed under Catherine the Great accorded Muslims within the empire a definite legal status alongside Christians, without regard for their moral or religious standing.

The overall intention of the *CMR* series is to provide full accounts of all the known works that were written by Christians and Muslims about the other and against the other throughout the world in the period 600-1914. As in earlier volumes, here the team of editors (listed on the back cover) have been generously helped by scholars both new and well-established. These have often written at length and in considerable detail, and in many instances they have produced entries that not only sum up past and present research but also take it forward.

Like its predecessors, *CMR* 14 starts with introductory essays that treat details of the political, cultural and religious situation in 18th-century Central and Eastern Europe. Following these come the entries that make up the bulk of the volume. Again, the principle has been to choose works written substantially about or against the other faith, or containing significant information or judgements that cast light on European Christian attitudes towards Islam. By their very nature, apologetic and polemical works are included, while letters, religious treatises and works of travel and history also often qualify. Sometimes the reason for including a work may not seem obvious because its direct references to Islam are few, though time and again it emerges that the work attests to particular attitudes in the way it is structured or its information has been selected, or occasional insults about Islam point to its author's prejudice. Everything is present that has been judged to contribute in any significant way towards conveying the information about the religious other that was possessed by 18th-century Eastern and Central Europeans, and towards constructing the impressions about the religious other that they generally held to be true.

In most cases, this principle is easily applicable, though it proves difficult in some instances. The approach has therefore been inclusive, especially regarding works that may contain only slight though insightful details or appear to touch only obliquely on relations. Another principle is that inclusion of works within this volume, like its predecessors, has been decided according to the date of their author's death, not the date when the works themselves appeared. The adoption of this approach has led to evident anomalies at either end, where authors were mainly or almost entirely active in one century but died at the beginning of the next. Other principles could have been adopted, such as an author's most active period, though while this could have worked for some, it would not have helped at all for many others.

Each entry is divided into two main parts. The first is concerned with the author, and it contains biographical details, an account of their main intellectual activities and writings, the major primary sources of information about them, and scholarly works on them that have appeared since the mid-20th century. A small number of entries are concerned with clusters of authors writing on the same theme who were active in the same period, or anonymous works on the same theme that appeared at about the same time, in which case they are situated in the sequence of entries as appropriate. Without aiming to be exhaustive in biographical detail or scholarly study, this section contains enough information to enable readers to pursue further points about the authors and their general activities.

The second part of the entry is concerned with the works of the author that are specifically devoted to the other faith. Here the aim is completeness. A work is named and dated, and then in two important sections its contents are described, with particular emphasis on its attention to Islam, and its significance in the history of Christian-Muslim relations is appraised, including its influence on later works. There follow sections that list publication details (manuscripts where known, and then editions and translations, except in cases of famous authors where a selection of the most significant editions and translations is listed) and studies from roughly the middle of the 20th century onwards. Both these sections are intended to be fully up to date at the time of going to press.

With this coverage, *CMR* 14 provides information to enable a work to be identified, its importance appreciated, and editions and the latest studies located. Each work is also placed as far as is possible together with other works from the same region written at the same time, though this grouping should be regarded as more a matter of organisational convenience than anything else. Proximity between entries is definitely not an indication of any direct relationship between the works analysed in them, let alone influence between them (though this may sometimes be discernible). In this period, just like any other, it is as likely that an author would be influenced by a work written in another country or century as by a work from their immediate locality or time.

The task of bringing together *CMR* 14 has involved numerous contributors, and it is gratifying to note that they have often undertaken to write entries readily, and have sometimes produced compositions that will remain authoritative accounts of a work and its author for the foreseeable future. Under the direction of David Thomas, the work for this volume was led by John Chesworth (Research Officer) and Emma Loghin (Research Associate) in the Birmingham office, Stanisław Grodź (Poland and Slavonic neighbours), Radu G. Păun (South-east Europe), Mehdi Sajid (Germany and Austro-Hungary) and Cornelia Soldat (Russia). These are members of a much larger team that comprises 26 specialists in total, covering all parts of the world. Other scholars gave time and attention to identifying relevant material, finding contributors and generally lending their expertise. Without their help and interest, the task of assembling the material in this volume could not have been completed. Among many others, special gratitude goes to Gwyn Bourlakov, Nikolaos Chrissidis, Marek Dospěl, Lucien Frary and Alastair Hamilton. In addition, Carol Rowe copy-edited the entire volume, Phyllis Chesworth compiled the indexes, Cai Lyons worked on the illustrations and Louise Bouglass prepared the map. We are deeply indebted to everyone who has contributed to bringing this volume into being.

The project is funded by a grant from the Arts and Humanities Research Council of Great Britain, and this is acknowledged with gratitude.

Extensive efforts have been made to ensure the information in the volume is both accurate and complete, though in a project that crosses as many boundaries of time, place, language and discipline as this it would be unrealistic and presumptuous to claim that these have succeeded. Details must have been overlooked, authors and whole works could have been ignored, new historical works may have come to light, new dates and interpretations may have been put forward, and new editions, translations and studies published. Therefore, corrections, additions and updates are warmly invited. They will be incorporated into the online version of *CMR*, and into any further editions. Please send details of omissions and corrections to David Thomas at d.r.thomas.1@bham.ac.uk.

LIST OF ILLUSTRATIONS

MAP

ABBREVIATIONS

BL
British Library

BNF
Bibliothèque nationale de France

BSOAS
Bulletin of the School of Oriental and African Studies

DİA
Turkiye Diyanet Vakfı İslam Ansiklopedisi, Ankara, 1988-2013

DNB
Dictionary of National Biography, Oxford, 1885-1996; https://www.oxforddnb.com/

ECCO
Eighteenth Century Collections Online; https://www.gale.com/intl/primary-sources/eighteenth-century-collections-online

EI2
Encyclopaedia of Islam, 2nd edition

EI3
Encyclopaedia of Islam Three

EIr
Encyclopaedia Iranica; http://www.iranicaonline.org

ESTC
English Short Title Catalogue; http://estc.bl.uk

ICMR
Islam and Christian-Muslim Relations

JAOS
Journal of the American Oriental Society

MW
Muslim World

ODNB
Oxford Dictionary of National Biography, Oxford, 2004- ; http://www.oxforddnb.com

Q
Qur'an

VD18
Das Verzeichnis Deutscher Drucke des 18. Jahrhunderts; https://gso.gbv.de/DB=1.65/

Introduction: Central, Eastern and South-Eastern Europe

Stanisław Grodź, Radu G. Păun and Cornelia Soldat

In the 18ᵗʰ century, the region covered in this volume – Central Europe, Eastern Europe and South-Eastern Europe – was controlled by the Habsburg Empire, the Russian Empire, the Polish-Lithuanian Commonwealth and the Ottoman Empire, though with strong Swedish involvement.

Of the four powers, the Habsburg and Russian Empires were gaining in prominence, while the Polish-Lithuanian Commonwealth and the Ottoman Empire were in decline. At the beginning of the century, the Habsburgs and the Russians were supporting each other against the 'Ottoman threat', though each was also wary of the growing strength and expansionist interests of the other. Russia was in the more advantageous situation, having the Ottomans as their only main adversary and the Habsburg Empire as an ally, although one that needed to be watched. Neighbouring states, with the exception of Prussia, were not strong enough to withstand Russian expansion during the course of the century. The Habsburgs, apart from keeping guard along their eastern frontier with the Ottomans, also had to watch their western borders, where France was often the main challenger to their interests. In the course of the century, the position of the Habsburgs in the German-speaking part of Central Europe was increasingly contested by Prussia, which gradually gained strength and prominence under King Frederick II (r. 1740-86) and rose to become a major political player in Central Europe, replacing Sweden. The other German-speaking lands were divided into a number of comparatively small political entities. The death of Charles II of Spain in 1700 led to the war of the Spanish Succession, which brought the Habsburg Empire and the Holy Roman Empire[1] into contention with France.

---

[1] Lands in Western and Central Europe ruled first by Frankish then German kings between 800 and 1806. With the passing of time, the title of emperor became largely honorary, though various German rulers still strove to acquire it. During the 18th century, it was held by the Habsburg rulers (with the exception of Charles VII of the House of

Central Europe

The beginning of the century in the region was marked by the Treaty of Karlowitz (1699), which curbed Ottoman expansion in Europe. The Ottomans resented it, but they were unable to reverse the balance of power, even though they managed to regain some areas for a time as the century progressed.

The Great Northern War (1700-21) put an end to Swedish military domination in Central Europe, when the Russians defeated the Swedish army at Poltava (today in Ukraine) in 1709. The wounded King Charles XII (r. 1697-1718) and the remnants of his army crossed into Ottoman territory and were detained there; Charles only returned to Sweden in 1714.[2] Swedish diplomats in Istanbul continued to undermine the position of one of Charles's adversaries, Augustus II the Strong, prince-elector of Saxony (r. 1694-1733) and king of the Polish-Lithuanian Commonwealth (1696-1704, 1709-33), and pressed support for his rival, Stanisław Leszczyński (r. 1704-9, 1733-6). The Ottomans stepped into the Great Northern War in 1710 on the side of the Swedes and surrounded the pursuing Russians at the River Prut. The defeated Russians managed to negotiate a truce by conceding their earlier gains (1711).[3]

The War of the Spanish Succession came to an end in 1714 with a series of treaties concluded over successive years that are jointly known as the Treaty of Utrecht.[4] In 1715, King Louis XIV of France (r. 1643-1715), a powerful long-time adversary of the Habsburgs, died. At this point, war between the Ottoman Porte and the Republic of Venice broke out in consequence of the Ottomans' indignation at being deprived of the Morea in the Treaty of Karlowitz. The Habsburgs came to the support of Venice, and defeated the Ottomans and captured Belgrade. The war ended with the Treaty of Passarowitz (1718), which secured Habsburg territorial gains

---

Wittelsbach, r. 1742-5). See P.H. Wilson, 'The Empire, Austria and Prussia', in P.H. Wilson (ed.), A companion to the eighteenth century, Chichester, 2014, 260-75, pp. 261-6.

  [2] K.A. Roider, *Austria's eastern question, 1700-1790*, Princeton NJ, 1982, pp. 35-6.

  [3] V. Aksan, *Ottoman wars, 1700-1870. An empire besieged*, Abingdon, 2014, pp. 90-8.

  [4] 'The Treaty of Utrecht of 1714, which ended Louis XIV's drive for European hegemony, was the last international peace to refer to the continent as the Republic of Christendom. Pacts that followed referred simply to "Europe", particularly in agreements struck with the Porte' (P.S. Fichtner, *Terror and toleration. The Habsburg Empire confronts Islam, 1526-1850*, London, 2008, p. 88).

in South-Eastern Europe for some 20 years. Among Habsburg subjects, this war was looked on as an echo of the crusades.[5]

The years 1703-11 were marked by a Hungarian uprising against the Habsburgs until the forces of Ferenc Rákóczi (1676-1735), the leader of the uprising, were defeated and he was compelled to leave Hungary. Finding support in neither Poland, England or France, he ended up as an exile in the Ottoman Empire.[6]

Attacks by Barbary coast pirates against the ships of the Ostend Company in 1723 led the Habsburgs to conclude treaties that safeguarded trade with the rulers of Tunis, Tripoli and Algiers.[7]

In the 1720s, the Ottomans were involved in wars with the Hotaki Afghans over the control of Persian territories that the declining Safavid dynasty could no longer hold. Despite military defeat in 1726, the Ottomans managed to seize the western and north-western parts of the Safavid state, though the subsequent military engagement in Persia between 1730 and 1736, although it brought initial victories, ended with defeat.[8] Ottoman military weakness encouraged the Habsburgs first to assist the Russians, who persistently sought to acquire the northern shores of the Black Sea, and then to take direct military action against the Ottomans. This was despite bad experiences during the War of the Polish Succession that broke out in 1733 after the death of Augustus II, the Strong. The Habsburgs supported Augustus's son, Augustus III (r. 1733-63), who was

---

[5] Roider, *Austria's eastern question*, pp. 49-50; Aksan, *Ottoman wars*, pp. 100-2. Two works by Christian Augustin Pfaltz ab Ostriz (1629-1701) from the end of the 17th century may give the background to this attitude: *Abominatio desolationis Turcicae – Der türckische Verwüstungs-Grewel durch unsern Herrn und Heiland Iesum Christum vorgesagt: Wann ihr sehen werdet den Grewel der Verwüstung, dass er steht an dem heiligen Orth (Matth. 24, V. 15.) Bei diesen bedrangten, elenden letzten Zeiten, sambt desen Ursachen und Beifügung heilsamen Trosts vom Türcken-Fall, mit theologischen, sittlichen und historischen Discursen der werthen Christenheit erkläret und vorgestellt*, Prague, 1672; and the anti-Turkish sermon *Krieg- und Siegs-Predigt, in Theatrum Gloriae. Das ist Schau-Platz der Ehren oder Lob-Predigten von denen heiligen, ausserwählten glorwürdigen Patronen des hochlöblichen Königreichs Böheimb, mit Ehren-Preiss ihres gottseeligen Wandles, rühmlichen Verdienst und herzlicher Wunderthaten aus böhmischen Geschichten historico-moraliter verfasset, in Göttlicher Schrifft und heiligen Vätern gegründet; mit Theologischen Fragen und Concepten gezieret; An deren heiligen, hohen Fest-Tagen, bei Gegenwart Volckreicher Versamlung in der Ertz- Stuhl- und Haupt-Kirchen S. Viti in Prag auffgerichtet [...]*, Alt-Stadt Prague, 1691.

[6] D.M. Luebke, 'Participatory politics', in P.H. Wilson (ed.), *A companion to the eighteenth century*, Chichester, 2014, 479-94, p. 486.

[7] Roider, *Austria's eastern question*, pp. 59-61; D. do Paço, 'The political agents of Muslim rulers in Central Europe in the 18th century', in *CMR* 14, 39-55, highlights further diplomatic contacts.

[8] U. Ryad, 'Introduction. The Ottoman and Persian Empires in the 18th century', in *CMR* 12, 3-14, pp. 3-5.

married to a Habsburg princess, but his election to the throne was only possible with the support of the Russian army. His rival to the throne, Stanisław Leszczyński (the father-in-law of Louis XV of France), who had been elected a few weeks earlier by the Polish nobles, formally gave up his rights in 1736 and became the Duke of Lorraine (1737-66).

The new war with the Ottomans showed that the Habsburg forces could not find an adequate replacement for their long-time military commander, Prince Eugene of Savoy (1663-1736). Potential allies refused to get involved: Augustus III did not want to risk his shaky position, and the Venetians were indignant at the treatment they had received from the Habsburgs. Only Pope Clement XII (r. 1730-40) came to their side, assisting them financially and ordering church bells to be rung each morning to remind the people to pray for victory (*Türckenglocken*), apparently the last time such a 'religious' element was included in any war against the Ottomans.[9] As a result of this war, which lasted from 1736 to 1739, the Habsburgs lost their territorial gains along their border with the Ottoman Empire, including the fortress of Belgrade, and showed themselves vulnerable to attacks on other fronts.

The death of Charles VI, Holy Roman Emperor and Archduke of Austria, in 1740 without a male heir led to the War of the Austrian Succession (1740-8). To the surprise of the European monarchs, the Ottoman sultan offered to mediate between the competing sides. The sultan also demanded an end to hardships inflicted on the Jews in Bohemia for their welcome of the Bavarian forces during a brief occupation of Prague. This offer of mediation was declined, and in return for lenience to the Jews in Bohemia, the Habsburg Empress Maria Theresa (r. 1740-80) asked the sultan to end restrictions against the religious practices of Armenian Catholics in the Ottoman Empire.[10]

In the mid-18th century, Frederick II of Prussia (r. 1740-86), for whom religion was a political tool and religious officials were mainly rival political players, and who had earlier seemed to share Voltaire's critical perspective on Muḥammad and Islam, sought closer contacts with the Ottomans. He needed them to keep at bay both the Austrians and the Russians, who from their side were trying to prevent Prussia from gaining too much power. When Austrian diplomacy in Istanbul succeeded in

---

[9] Roider, *Austria's eastern question*, pp. 77-8.
[10] Roider, *Austria's eastern question*, pp. 94-8.

frustrating all the Prussian attempts, Frederick sought contacts with the Crimean Tatars.[11]

The Seven Years War (1756-63) had widespread consequences, and almost put an end to the rising power of Prussia. Frederick suffered heavy defeats in 1759 and managed to stay in power only because of the withdrawal of the Russians from the conflict. Peter III (r. 1762), the new Russian tsar, was an admirer of Frederick II and signed a peace treaty with Prussia immediately after his accession to the throne. After he was assassinated, his wife and successor Catherine II, the Great (r. 1762-96), upheld the peace with Prussia. During the war, the Russian armies were active within the territory of the Kingdom of Poland, which under the reign of Augustus III was in fact a Russian protectorate. When Augustus died in 1763, Catherine II secured the election of one of her favourites, Stanisław August Poniatowski, a member of the Commonwealth nobility, as king of Poland (r. 1764-95). This growing Russian influence caused resentment on the part of the Polish nobles who tried to oppose it. They established the Bar Confederation in 1768 (see more below), causing a civil war that spilled over the border into the Ottoman Empire and ignited a new conflict between the Ottomans and Russians (1768-74). Poland suffered the first partition of its territory, between Russia, Prussia and the Habsburg Empire in 1772.

Frederick II of Prussia died in 1786 and was succeeded by his nephew Frederick William II (r. 1786-97). The century ended with two further partitions of Poland, and the country ceased to exist as a sovereign state until 1918.

The role of religion in decision-making

The first half of the 18th century continued to be marked by the problem of captives and slaves held by the Ottomans. Embassies sent to Istanbul usually included agents (often members of religious orders) who sought to ransom them. Others also pursued this goal for various reasons, as the example of Salomea Regina Pilsztynowa, a self-established physician in

---

[11] J. Croitoru, *Die Deutschen und der Orient. Faszination, Verachtung und die Widersprüche der Aufklärung*, Munich, 2018, pp. 14-55; Roider, *Austria's eastern question*, pp. 102-4.

Illustration 1. James Gillray, 'Taming of the shrew …'. Catherine II of Russia, supported by France and the Habsburgs, cowers away from Prime Minister William Pitt, who appears as both Petruchio, and Don Quixote, supported by Prussia and Holland, with Selim III kneeling in obeisance

the Ottoman Empire, shows. Slaves and captives were still being freed as late as the 1780s.[12]

Several entries in the present volume refer to the Institutum Judaicum et Muhammedicum ('Jewish and Muhammedan Institute') run in Halle by the German Pietists between 1728 and 1792 with the purpose of providing materials and preparing missionaries who sought to convert Jews (especially in Europe) and Muslims.[13] Missionary work was also carried out by groups of Catholics. The beginning of the century was still marked by so-called *Türckentaufen* (baptisms of Turks) in the Habsburgs' domains (present day Austria, Czech Republic, Slovakia, Poland and southern Germany).[14] The fate of the Ottoman prisoners of war in European countries should perhaps be more fully explored.[15] At the beginning of the century, works were written as textbooks for (potential) converts, such as Michał Ignacy Wieczorkowski's *Breve compendium fidei catholicae turcico textu* ('A brief digest of the Catholic faith written in Turkish') and *Katechizm.*[16] Jesuits were sent to Persia sometimes in the role of royal envoys (e.g. Wieczorkowski), though, rather than attempting to make conversions among Muslims, they generally worked among local Christian populations and engaged in scholarly works (e.g. Tadeusz

---

[12] Roider, *Austria's eastern question*, p. 16; in n. 20 (pp. 198-9), he refers to K. Jahn, *Türkische Freilassungserklärungen des 18. Jahrhunderts (1702-1776)*, Naples, 1963, with published copies of documents attesting to the freeing of slaves and serving as passports for the return journey home. The Polish-Lithuanian records are referred to in J. Reychman, *Znajomość i nauczanie języków orientalnych w Polsce XVIII wieku*, Wrocław, 1950, p. 20. See A.S. Nalborczyk, 'Salomea Regina Pilsztynowa', in *CMR* 14, 516-24.

[13] J. Chesworth, 'Johann Heinrich Callenberg', in *CMR* 14, 128-39; R. Elger, 'Jonas Korte', in *CMR* 14, 151-6; S. Grodź, 'Michał Bogusław Ruttich', in *CMR* 14, 451-5.

[14] The last of these ceremonies took place in 1746; see Fichtner, *Terror and toleration*, p. 69; M. Friedrich, 'Türkentaufen. Zur theologischen Problematik und geistlichen Deutung der Konversion von Muslimen im Alten Reich', in M. Friedrich and A. Schunka (eds), *Orientbewegungen deutscher Protestanten in der Frühen Neuzeit*, Frankfurt, 2012, 47-74.

[15] A. Hamilton, '"To rescue the honour of the Germans". Qur'an translations by eighteenth- and early nineteenth-century German Protestants', *Journal of the Warburg and Courtauld Institutes* 77 (2014) 173-209, p. 179 n. 32, refers to an article by O. Spies, 'Schicksale Türkischer Kriegsgefangener in Deutschland nach den Türkenkriegen', in E. Gräf (ed.), *Festschrift Werner Caskel. Zum siebzigsten Geburtstag 5. März 1966 gewidmet von Freunden und Schülern*, Leiden, 1968, 316-35.

[16] B. Podolak, 'Michał Ignacy Wieczorkowski', in *CMR* 14, 456-64. Reychman, *Znajomość i nauczanie języków orientalnych*, p. 81, refers to what was probably a similar work by the son of Salomea Regina Pilsztynowa that was burned during the destruction of Warsaw in 1944, *Teo Muza albo nauka wiary Chrystusowej z polskiego na turecki język wytłumaczona dla tym łatwieyszego objaśnienia przystępującym Turkom do wiary katolickiej przez Stanisława de Pichelstein* ('Teo Muse or learning of the Christian faith, translated from Polish into Turkish as an easier explanation to Turks joining the Catholic faith, by Stanisław de Pichelstein).

Juda Krusiński).[17] When it comes to the Jesuits' reports, perhaps attention should be given to the contents and function of two periodical publications, *Lettres édifiantes et curieuses*, 1702-76, and *Nouveax mémoires de la Compagnie de Jésus dans le Levant*, 9 vols, 1715-55.[18]

Knowledge of Oriental languages proved to be even more crucial in the 18th century than earlier. The Habsburgs started with the training of so-called *Sprachknaben* (boys learning languages) in Istanbul but transferred the emerging school to Vienna in 1754, laying the foundations of the *Orientalische Akademie* (Imperial Royal Academy for Oriental Languages).[19] Its staff were also concerned with giving the students and the wider public insight into Ottoman religious culture, as is attested for instance by the stage play *Godefroi de Bouillon*.[20] The rulers of the Polish-Lithuanian Commonwealth attempted a similar scholarly enterprise, though it never developed into a full-blown institution.[21]

The German-speaking inhabitants of states that did not have direct contact with the Ottomans also developed interests in Oriental languages. This was particularly so at German universities under the impetus of biblical studies, leading to translations from Arabic and other Eastern languages, especially the Qur'an, where competition with the Latin translation by the Roman Catholic Lodovico Marracci and similar works provided a strong impetus.[22]

Increasing numbers of works of all kinds published in German during the 18th century made reference to Islam, typically repeating older tropes about Muḥammad and the faith. Research on the following would undoubtedly provide fuller details about the way in which Islam was viewed and the use to which it was put in a range of genres: M.G. Schröder, *Muhammed testis veritatis contra se ipsum Turcis verax, qui mendacia admittat, Christianis mendax, qui veritatem dicat utrinque ex locis Alcorani utrisqve demonstratus*, Leipzig, 1718; Wilhelm Haller,

---

[17] M.P. Borkowski, 'Tadeusz Juda Krusiński', in *CMR* 14, 494-504.

[18] They were partly or entirely republished in German (*Neuer Welt-Bott*, a journal published for the German-speaking Christians [Catholics] by Joseph Stöcklein SJ) or Polish translations (*Listy różne ku chwalebnej ciekawości i chrześcijańskiemu zbudowaniu służące*, Warsaw, parts 1-3 [1756], part 4 [1767], by F. Bohomolec and M. Juniewicz SJ).

[19] Fichtner, *Terror and toleration*, pp. 121-30.

[20] Ç. Sarıkartal, 'Josef Franz', in *CMR* 14, 171-7.

[21] Reychman, *Znajomość i nauczanie języków orientalnych*, pp. 56-7.

[22] A. Ben-Tov, 'Central European encounters with the Muslim world in the 18th century', *CMR* 14, 23-38 provides an overview on these issues. See also e.g. Hamilton, '"To rescue the honour of the Germans"', pp. 175-82.

Mochammads Lehre von Gott aus dem Koran gezogen, Altenburg, 1779; G.L. Bauer, *Was hielte Mohammed von der christlichen Religion und ihrem Stifter? Aus der Urkunde beantwortet*, Nuremberg, 1782; anonymous, *Leben und Meinungen Mahomeds, des Propheten der Muselmänner, und Stifters einer großen Monarchie. Nebst der Geschichte Arabiens*, Lausanne, 1789; J.W.L. Gleim,[23] *Halladat oder Das rothe Buch*, Hamburg, 1774; Ferenc Szdellar, *Itinerarium peregrini philosophi Turcia (Graecia) definitum*, Trnava, 1721; Stephan Schultz,[24] *Die Leitungen des Höchsten nach seinem Rath auf den Reisen durch Europa, Asia und Africa*, 5 vols, Halle, 1771-5.

Lexical publications should also be taken more fully into account, as their contents often shaped the perception of other religions and their believers.[25] Other works often overlooked by scholars researching Christian-Muslim encounters include a short *disputatio* by Theophilus Lessing (1647-1735), the grandfather of Gotthold Ephraim Lessing, on religious tolerance. He wrote it in 1669 when he was a law student, though it was not published until 1881 (and republished with a German translation as G. Gawlick and W. Milde [eds], *De religionum tolerantia. Über die Duldung der Religionen*, Göttingen, 1991).

Knowledge of Islam was an integral element in the so-called 'Fragments controversy', which started when Gotthold Ephraim Lessing published excerpts from Hermann Samuel Reimarus's (1694-1768) manuscript *Apologie oder Schutzschrift für die vernünftigen Verehrer Gottes* ('An apology for, or some words in defence of, reasoning worshippers of God'); see the entries on Gottfried Arnold, Gotthold Ephraim Lessing, Johann Christoph Döderlein and Gottfried Less.[26]

During the century, a change can be observed in the attitude of the Christian population of various areas of Central Europe towards the

---

[23] See A. Hamilton, 'Friedrich Eberhard Boysen', in *CMR* 14, 210-15, for references to Gleim; cf. Croitoru, *Die Deutschen und der Orient*, pp. 171-6, 230-40, 247-9, 262-5, 304-6.

[24] See R. Elger, 'Jonas Korte', in *CMR* 14, 151-6, for references to Schultz; cf. J. Schmidt, 'The journey of Stephan Schultz, Protestant missionary from Halle, in the Ottoman Empire 1752-1756', *Oriens* 39 (2011) 17-57.

[25] For the Polish-Lithuanian Commonwealth, see D. Dolański, 'The image of Muslims and Islam presented in the 18th-century geographical and historical compendia', in *CMR* 14, 540-53). For the German-speaking lands, at least two works could be taken as generic: Johann Franz Buddeus (Budde, 1667-1729), *Allgemeines historisches Lexicon*, Leipzig, 1709, and Johann Heinrich Zedler (1706-51), *Großes vollständiges Universal-exicon*, 60 vols, Leipzig, 1732-50 (vol. 19 contains the entries 'Mahomet' and 'Mahomedischer Glaube').

[26] C. Tauchner, 'Gotthold Ephraim Lessing', in *CMR* 14, 216-24; S. Grodź, 'Gottfried Arnold', 'Johann Christoph Döderlein' and 'Gottfried Less', in *CMR* 14, 98-104, 225-30, 237-43.

Ottomans. Despite the popular 'crusading spirit' in the Habsburg Empire, in the first half of the century, 'neither the Church nor the state had ever made anti-Turkish propaganda an end in itself. Officially-sponsored denunciations of Islam were political manoeuvres, not critical theology.'[27] The centenary of the siege of Vienna in 1783 was also celebrated without any recourse to demonising the Ottomans.[28] Similar changes of attitude are apparent in Poland as the century progressed,[29] though this growing sympathy towards the Ottomans did not prevent the spread of prophecies about the fall of the Ottoman Empire, especially in the 1770s (at the end of the disastrous war with Russia).[30] Although during the second part of the century anti-Ottoman propaganda would have been seen in the Polish-Lithuanian Commonwealth as pro-Russian, it was criticised not only on political but also on humanistic (Enlightenment) grounds (in Poland, the ideals of the Enlightenment were propagated by a number of Roman Catholic clergy).[31] Piotr Świtkowski in his newspaper *Pamiętnik historyczno-polityczny* (published 1782-92) mocked a call to war against the Ottomans, indicating that incitement against them on apparently religious grounds was ridiculous, because 'the Turk in his mosque worships God similarly to what other people around the world do', as he wrote elsewhere. According to Świtkowski, there was also no point in comparing 'the Mochamedans' to e.g. the Poles, and reproaching them for being different (in that way one could reproach English horses for not being Arabian horses). He also criticised the Westerners who went to the East in search of imagined happiness but found the reality quite different, and came back calling the Turks barbarians and criticising all they had seen in Ottoman lands.[32] Świtkowski's may have been an isolated voice, but it should be kept in mind that Eastern Europeans were

---

[27] Fichtner, *Terror and toleration*, p. 73.

[28] J.G.K., *Ein Soldaten Jubiläum über die Belagerung von Wienn und der dabey den 12ten Sept. 1683 über die Türken erfochtene Sieg*, Prague, 1783; G. Uhlich, *Geschichte der zweyten Türkenbelagerung Wiens*, Vienna, 1783. See Fichtner, *Terror and toleration*, pp. 111-12, also p. 142. In that context, a work by Kaspar Pilat, *Christliche Betrachtung über den gegenwärtigen Krieg des Erzhauses Österreich mit der Ottomanischen Pforte*, Prague, 1788, should perhaps be included.

[29] M. Bałczewski, 'Zmiany w ocenie Turcji w opinii polskiej XVIII w.', *Acta Universitatis Lodziensis. Folia Historica* 22 (1985) 91-108, p. 96, indicates reports of the Austrian and Russian ambassadors in Warsaw signalling a growing sentiment for the Ottomans already from 1738.

[30] Bałczewski, 'Zmiany w ocenie Turcji', pp. 97-8.

[31] B. Grochulska, 'The place of the Enlightenment in Polish social history', in J.K. Fedorowicz et al. (eds and trans), *A republic of nobles. Studies in Polish history to 1864*, Cambridge, 1982, 239-57; Dolański, 'Image of Muslims'.

[32] Bałczewski, 'Zmiany w ocenie Turcji', p. 107 n. 52.

not only consumers and appropriators of ideas and trends coming from the West (though that evidently took place). The 'Orientalisation' of the everyday life of the nobility in the Polish-Lithuanian Commonwealth, shown in their dress, interior decoration, weapons, horse trappings and so on, was already evident in the second part of the 17th century and extended into the first half of the 18th century (also as part of reaction against Western European influences).[33]

South-Eastern Europe

Before the 18th century, South-Eastern Europe had long been a disputed borderland, with territories changing hands between Venice, the Habsburg Empire and the Ottoman Empire (with occasional meddling by the Polish-Lithuanian Commonwealth). During the 18th century, Russia entered the scene as a political actor and became the most serious rival of the Ottoman Empire in the region. In these conditions, peoples under Ottoman rule became more ready to break away and to seek external support.[34]

The general situation in the area has often been overlooked as a consequence of attention being focused on the main centres of power. In a survey of events through the 18th century, it is helpful, following Gilles Veinstein, to divide the Ottoman Europe into three zones or concentric circles.[35] The outermost of these, which was the most difficult for the government in Istanbul to control, comprised the territories north of the Danube and Sava rivers, namely Central Hungary, the Banat of Temesvár (Timişoara), Slavonia (the regions between the Sava and Drava) and parts of Croatia. These areas were Ottoman provinces proper, though they displayed their own distinctive local features because of their distance from the centre, their relatively late integration into the Ottoman system and their status as a border zone. The Muslim population living

[33] R.T. Mańkowski, *Sztuka islamu*, Warsaw, 1959, pp. 163-4; Bałczewski, 'Zmiany w ocenie Turcji', pp. 106-7. See M. Kuran, 'Anti-Turkish literature in the Polish-Lithuanian Commonwealth, 1575-1733', in *CMR* 14, 471-93; Dolański, 'Image of Muslims', 540-53.

[34] See P. Sugar, *Southeastern Europe under Ottoman rule, 1354-1804*, Seattle WA, 1977; B. Jelavich, *History of the Balkans. Eighteenth and nineteenth centuries*, Cambridge, 1983; G. Castellan, *History of the Balkans. From Mohammed the Conqueror to Stalin*, trans. N. Bradley, Boulder CO, 1992.

[35] G. Veinstein, 'Ottoman Europe. An ancient fracture', in J. Tolan, G. Veinstein and H. Laurens (eds), *Europe and the Islamic world. A history*, trans. J.M. Todd, Princeton NJ, 2013, 149-63.

in the area, composed mainly of Islamised Bosnians, represented only a relatively small group of administrators, soldiers, merchants and artisans, confined to the main cities (Buda, Pécs, Szeged, etc.). The countryside and a good part of the urban settlements remained mostly Christian and were largely autonomous.

In addition to these provinces, which had been incorporated completely into the empire, there were the autonomous tributary principalities of Wallachia, Moldavia and Transylvania (the last only between 1541 and 1699). The first two acknowledged Ottoman suzerainty (though not without military resistance), Wallachia at the end of the 14th century and Moldavia in 1456.[36] They were allowed to retain their own administration, political structures, religion and local rulers, but in exchange paid a tribute to the sultan.[37] Also, and very importantly, Muslims were not allowed to settle or build mosques in Wallachian and Moldavian territory. The twin principalities were therefore integrated into the category of 'tamed enemies', non-Muslim tributaries depending on the Sublime Porte. This privileged status allowed Wallachian and Moldavian rulers to act as protectors of Christian Orthodoxy in the Balkans until the first decades of the 19th century. Orthodox believers south of the Danube were able to look on the two principalities as an oasis of freedom, in profound contrast to the situation within the empire proper. This was notably the case with many Orthodox Church hierarchs, who spent long periods of time at the princely courts in Bucharest and Iaşi.

The second circle, called by Veinstein 'a transitional zone', was bordered by the Danube and Sava rivers in the north and by northern Bulgaria and the Vardar valley in the east. It covered continental and Aegean Greece, Serbia, Montenegro, Albania, Bosnia-Herzegovina and the tributary republic of Ragusa (Dubrovnik). While they were completely integrated into the Ottoman administrative system, these lands had borders with Venetian and Habsburg territories. The Muslim population there

---

[36] For a recent discussion, see A. Pippidi, 'Taking possession of Wallachia. Facts and interpretations'; and Şt.S. Gorovei and M.M. Székely, 'Old questions, old clichés. New approaches, new results? The case of Moldavia', both in O.J. Schmitt (ed.), *The Ottoman conquest of the Balkans. Interpretations and research debates*, Vienna, 2016, 189-208 and 209-42, respectively.

[37] The standard work on this topic is V. Panaite, *Ottoman law of war and peace. The Ottoman Empire and tribute payers from the north of the Danube*, Leiden, 2019. For the period under scrutiny here, see V. Panaite, 'Wallachia and Moldavia from the Ottoman juridical and political viewpoint, 1774-1829', in A. Anastasopoulos and E. Kolovos (eds), *Ottoman rule and the Balkans, 1760-1850. Conflict, transformation, adaptation*, Rethymno, 2007, 21-44.

was confined to certain urban centres located along the former routes of Turkish penetration or on old border lines. The different regions within this circle did not share the same administrative status. Areas such as northern Albania, the Mani Peninsula in the south of the Peloponnese, the districts of Suli in Epirus and of Agrapha in the Pindus mountains enjoyed extensive *de facto* autonomy because they were not easily accessible and did not produce significant revenues. The 'monastic republic' of Mount Athos on the Chalcidice Peninsula also enjoyed a special status, as well as Montenegro, a small province under the authority of the Orthodox bishop (*vladika*) residing in Cetinje. The lands north of the Black Sea, neighbours to the Crimean Khanate and the Tatar steppes, namely the *sančak* (later the *eyālet*) of Kefe (Italian, Caffa; Greek, Theodosia; present-day Feodosiia) and Akkerman (Italian, Moncastro; Romanian, Cetatea Albă; present-day Bilhorod-Dnistrovskyï), which were aggregated around the commercial ports conquered by the Ottomans in the second half of the 15th century, also belonged to the same second circle.

The last and innermost circle of Ottoman Europe included the territories that had been conquered earliest and were closest to the two successive capitals, Edirne and Istanbul, namely Bulgaria, Thrace, Thessaly, Macedonia and Dobrogea. This was Rumelia in the strict sense of the term, a part of the empire without any common borders with other countries. In these regions the Muslim population, Turkish migrants from Anatolia as well as converts, was predictably greater in size, mainly in some urban centres (Skopje, Niğbolu [Nikopol], Kyustendil and Trikkala).

Muslims were always numerically in the minority within the European part of the empire. Even in the 18th century, when the spread of Islam in the Balkans reached its peak, they hardly exceeded one third of the total population. Furthermore, the Muslim population was not homogenous: apart from the Sunnī majority, groups of Shī'ī *Kızılbaşi* also existed, as well as various Sufi brotherhood networks.[38]

The mass of the Balkan population that had once belonged to the 'Byzantine Commonwealth' remained Orthodox throughout the entire Ottoman period. Communities of Roman Catholics were settled mostly in the north-western part of the region, including parts of present-day Bosnia, the Dalmatian coast and northern Albania and Croatia, as well as in the Aegean islands taken from Venice and Genoa. Catholic presence

---

[38] For examples of this diversity, see I. Aščerić-Todd, 'Religious diversity and tolerance in Ottoman guilds', in *CMR* 12, 29-42.

was further fostered by missionaries (notably Franciscans).[39] Western merchants, both Catholic (French and Italian) and Protestant (English and Dutch) were generally settled in the large commercial centres of the empire. They were granted the status of *müste'min*, being under the protection of their respective consuls.[40] Jewish populations of various backgrounds lived in relatively small communities (18th-century Thessaloniki, for instance).[41] So did the Armenians,[42] who only became a noticeable religious minority in the 17th century, mainly in some eastern Balkan towns.

As is made evident from this description, the Ottoman Europe was a multicultural and multi-confessional area, a patchwork of ethnic, linguistic and confessional groups. These groups interacted constantly in various fields of daily life, regardless of their religious (or ethnic) affiliation.[43] On the other hand, various political and military events (internal troubles, wars, etc.) often forced local populations to move away from their homeland, and therefore to become subjects of new rulers, which changed the religious and ethnic structure of the areas concerned. Another factor that contributed significantly to this change was Islamisation or, to be more accurate, conversions to Islam.[44]

---

[39] The standard (but largely outdated) work on this topic is C. Frazee, *Catholics and sultans. The Church and the Ottoman Empire 1453-1923*, London, 1983. See now R.-A. Dipratu, 'Catolici în Imperiul otoman în prima jumătate a secolului XVII. Diplomația protectoratului religios', Bucharest, 2017 (PhD Diss. University of Bucharest; an English version will be published soon).

[40] V. Panaite, 'Being a Western merchant in the Ottoman Mediterranean. The evidence of a Turkish manuscript from Bibliothèque nationale de France', in S. Kenan (ed.), *ISAM papers. Ottoman thought, ethics-law-philosophy-kalam*, Istanbul, 2013, 91-135.

[41] On this topic, see among others, S.J. Shaw, *The Jews of the Ottoman Empire and the Turkish Republic*, New York, 1991; W.F. Weiker, *Ottomans, Turks and the Jewish polity*, Lanham MD, 1992; M. Rozen 'The Ottoman Jews', in S.N. Faroqhi (ed.), *The Cambridge history of Turkey*, vol. 3. *The later Ottoman Empire, 1603-1839*, Cambridge, 2006, 256-71 (with large bibliography).

[42] K. Bardakjian, 'The rise of the Armenian Patriarchate of Constantinople', and H. Barsoumian, 'The dual role of the Armenian *amira* class within the Ottoman government and the Armenian *millet* (1750-1850)', both in B. Braude and B. Lewis (eds), *Christians and Jews in the Ottoman Empire. The functioning of a plural society*, vol. 1, New York, 1982, 89-100 and 171-84, respectively.

[43] See, for instance, E. Gara, 'Conceptualizing interreligious relations in the Ottoman Empire. The early modern centuries', *Acta Poloniae Historica* 116 (2017) 57-92.

[44] A large part of the literature devoted to this topic is listed in G. Grivaud, *Les conversions à l'islam en Asie Mineure et dans les Balkans aux époques seldjoukide et ottomane. Bibliographie raisonnée (1800-2000)*, Athens, 2011. See also T. Krstić, *Contested conversions to Islam. Narratives of religious change in the early modern Ottoman Empire*, Stanford CA, 2011; O.J. Schmitt, 'Islamisierung bei den Albanern. Zwischen Forschungsfrage und Diskurs', in R. Lauer et al. (eds), *Osmanen und Islam in Südosteuropa*, Berlin, 2014, 243-68; N. Antov, 'Emergence and historical development of Muslim communities in the

During the 18th century, Christian authors from various parts of South-Eastern Europe continued to write about life under Islamic rule. Some of them openly approached the subject of religious differences between Christianity and Islam, e.g. Anastasios Gordios[45] and Krsto Pejkić.[46] In addition to a comprehensive history of the Ottoman Empire, the Moldavian Prince Dimitrie Cantemir composed an entire treatise on the Muslim religion,[47] while Chrysanthos Notaras the Patriarch of Jerusalem (d. 1731) wrote about Muslim central cultic places in his *Peri tēs Mekkas kai Medinas* ('About Mecca and Medina'), which was never published (MS Athens, National Library – Metochion tou Panagiou Taphou 441). The interest in the history of the Ottoman power is also indicated by the relatively important number of works that circulated in manuscript form.[48] Aware of the major conflicts happening in Europe, authors looked for support from fellow Orthodox rulers in Russia.[49]

Authors from the Western Balkans produced a relatively rich literature on the Ottoman power and the situation of the Christians within the empire.[50] These included Jerolim Kavanjin (1641/47-1714) from Split, a poet and member of the Illyrian Academy, whose 32,000-line *Povijest vandjelska bogatoga a nesrećna Epuluna i uboga a čestita Lazara* ('The history of the rich but miserable Epulun and the poor but happy Lazarus'; after 1700) reveals a strongly Dalmatian and anti-Turkish view of history.[51]

Franciscan monks wrote histories too.[52] Filip Grabovac (c. 1697-1749), from Vrlika, wrote *Cvit razgovora naroda, i jezika iliričkoga, alliti rvackoga*

Ottoman Balkans. Historical and historiographical remarks', in Th. Dragostinova and Y. Hashamova (eds), *Beyond mosque, church and state. Alternative narratives of the nation in the Balkans*, Budapest, 2016, 31-56.

[45] A. Argyriou and C. Karanasios, 'Anastasios Gordios', in *CMR* 14, 298-303.

[46] I. Manova, 'Krsto Pejkić', in *CMR* 14, 290-7.

[47] O.-V. Olar, 'Dimitrie Cantemir', in CMR 14, 304-22.

[48] M. Païzē-Apostolopoulou, 'Gnōsta kai agnōsta historika erga tēs Tourkokratias se heirographo kōdika tou Nikolaou Karatza', *Ho Eranistēs* 28 (2011) 193-210; Radu G. Păun, 'Ianache Văcărescu', in CMR 14, 364-81.

[49] V. Makrides, 'Eighteenth-century Greek Orthodox contacts with Russia', in *CMR* 14, 403-34; M. Hatzopoulos, 'Eighteenth century Greek prophetic literature', in *CMR* 14, 382-402.

[50] D. Dukić, *Sultanova djeca. Predodžbe Turaka u hrvatskoj književnosti ranog novovjekovlja*, Zadar, 2004; D. Dukić, 'Das Türkenbild in der kroatischen literarischen Kultur des 18. Jahrhunderts', in B. Schmidt-Haberkamp (ed.), *Europa und die Türkei im 18. Jahrhundert / Europe and Turkey in the eighteenth century*, Göttingen, 2011, 109-20.

[51] J. Kavanin, *Poviest Vandjelska*, ed. J. Aranza, Zagreb, 1913; J.V.A. Fine, *When ethnicity did not matter in the Balkans*, Ann Arbor MI, 2006, pp. 285-8; Z. Kravar, art. 'Kavanjin, Jerolim', in *Hrvatski biografski leksikon*, 2009; http://hbl.lzmk.hr/clanak.aspx?id=196.

[52] V. Kursar, 'Nikola Lašvanin', in *CMR* 14, 331-9.

('The flower of discourse among the Illyrian or Croatian people and language'; 1747);[53] Andrija Kačić-Miošić (1704-60), who began and ended his career at the monastery of Zaostrog, near his birthplace, also spending a decade teaching in Šibenik, wrote *Razgovor ugodni naroda slovinskoga* ('Pleasant conversation of Slavic people'; 1756,[54] translated into Latin by Emerik Pavić (1715-80). Pavić also published *Nadodanje glavni dogadaja Razgovoru ugodnom naroda slovinskoga* ('A major event, added to a pleasant conversation of Slavic people'; 1768).[55] These works sought to show the historical importance of the area and its pan-Slavic links in a call for support against the Muslim oppression of Christians.

Matija Antun Reljković (d. 1797), an army officer, wrote *Satir iliti divji čovik* ('The satyr or wild man'; 1762, expanded edition 1769), a long poem in which he blames the Turks for the under-developed state of the Slavs and their society.[56] In addition, works by two priests, Joso (Josip) Krmpotić (1750/55-c. 1797) from Barlete, and Antun Ivanošić (1748-1800), should be included here. Krmpotić served as court chaplain in Vienna from 1788 and wrote several poems, including *Katarine II i Jose II put u Krim* ('Catherine II and Joseph II's journey to the Crimea'; 1788); *Pjesma Crnogorcem* ('Montenegran's song'; 1788) and *Pjesma voevodam austrijanskim i rosijanskim* ('Song to Austrians and Russians'; 1789).[57] In *Vindicatio orthographiae Illyrico-Slavonicae* ('Vindication of Illyrian-Slavonic orthography'; 1785) he states that 'Muḥammad holds in prison the Slavic kingdoms. [...] Let all these peoples with one thought rise up, with sword and spear, let all these peoples whom a Slavic mother bore, together with the Hungarians and Germans march under Joseph [II Habsburg] and Catherine [the Great] and conquer Tsargrad [Constantinople].' His style, like that of Jerolim Kavanjin, is influenced by Dživo Gundulić (1588-1638).[58] Ivanošić attended Jesuit schools, pursued further education in Vienna and Bologna, and served as a parish priest then a military chaplain. He composed *Pieszma od junàchtva vitéza Peharnika* ('Poem on

---

[53] Fine, *When ethnicity did not matter*, pp. 347-50; S. Botica, art. 'Grabovac, Filip', in *Hrvatski biografski leksikon*, 2002; http://hbl.lzmk.hr/clanak.aspx?id=13.

[54] Fine, *When ethnicity did not matter*, pp. 288-300; D. Dukić, art. 'Kačić Miošić, Andrija', in *Hrvatski biografski leksikon*, 2005; http://hbl.lzmk.hr/clanak.aspx?id=267.

[55] Fine, *When ethnicity did not matter*, pp. 511, 517, 520; art. 'Pavić, Emerik (Mirko)', in *Hrvatska Enciklopedija*, n.d.; http://www.enciklopedija.hr/natuknica.aspx?id=47121.

[56] Fine, *When ethnicity did not matter*, pp. 507-11; art. 'Reljković, Matija Antun', in *Hrvatska enciklopedija*, n.d.; http://www.enciklopedija.hr/Natuknica.aspx?ID=52390.

[57] Fine, *When ethnicity did not matter*, pp. 526-8; T. Rogić Musa, art. 'Krmpotić, Joso', in *Hrvatski biografski leksikon*, 2013; http://hbl.lzmk.hr/clanak.aspx?id=11295.

[58] See Z. Zlatar, 'Džino Gundulić', in *CMR* 10, 221-30.

the heroism of the knight Peharnik'; 1788) and *Pisma od uzetja Turske Gradiške iliti Berbira grada* ('Letters on the capture of Turkish Gradishka or Berber city'; 1789), both with anti-Turkish themes, in a style that shows the influence of Pavao Ritter Vitezović's poem *Odiljenje Sigetsko* ('Siget's farewell').[59]

The Russian Empire

From the end of the 17th century, the old Muscovite regime was gradually changed by the reforms of Peter the Great (r. 1682-1725) into an effective absolutist state in which geopolitical development was supported by economic development. In the 18th century, Russia changed from a local power of the steppe region into an empire stretching from the Pacific Ocean to Central Europe between the Baltic and Black Seas, and in the south towards the Caucasus and the Asian steppes. Victories over the Ottomans (the capture of Azov, 1695-6) and the Swedes (Poltava, 1709) were also due to the reform of the army that had been initiated by Peter. His military success in defeating the Swedes led him to pursue the dream of freeing the Balkans from Ottoman power and capturing Constantinople. But his army suffered defeat against the Ottomans at the River Prut in 1711 and the dream had to be abandoned, while the Ottomans regained Azov.[60]

Taking advantage of the fall of the Safavids, the Russians and the Ottomans fought for control over parts of Persian territory and signed a treaty on that matter in Constantinople in 1724.[61]

The first half of the 18th century saw various minor wars between Russia and the Ottomans. Many generals, e.g. C.H. Manstein (1711-57) and B.C. Münnich (1683-1767), both Germans in Russian service, wrote war memoirs and accounts of their experiences with the Muslim Turks.[62] In their search to acquire full access to the Black Sea, the Russians again engaged the Ottomans militarily in the 1730s. They managed to invade

---

[59] Fine, *When ethnicity did not matter*, pp. 505-6; S. Marijanovic, art. 'Ivanošić, Antun', in *Hrvatski biografski leksikon*, 2005; http://hbl.lzmk.hr/clanak.aspx?id=8730. See also N. Budak, 'Pavao Ritter Vitezović', in *CMR* 14, 255-61.

[60] L. Hughes, *Russia in the age of Peter the Great*, New Haven CT, 1998, p. 239.

[61] F. Kazemzadeh, 'Iranian relations with Russia and the Soviet Union, to 1921', in W.B. Fisher and P. Avery (eds), *The Cambridge history of Iran*, vol. 7, Cambridge, 1968, 314-49, p. 320.

[62] C.H. Manstein, *Zapiski Manshteina o Rossii*, St Petersburg, 1875; B.C. Münnich, *Zapiski fel'dmarshala grafa Minikha*, St Petersburg, 1774.

Ottoman-controlled Moldavia in 1735, but after defeats suffered by Austria, their main ally, in battles with the Ottomans, the ensuing Treaty of Belgrade (1739) brought the Russians no significant territorial gains.

From the mid-18th century, there was a Russian ambassador in Constantinople. In his account of his time there, the first permanent ambassador, P.A. Tolstoi, emphasised his role as the protector of Orthodox Christians in the Ottoman Empire.[63] I.I. Bulgakov (1743-1809) gave an account of his journey to Constantinople in 1775-6 as a negotiator working to implement the Treaty of Küçük Kaynarca (Kuchuk-Kainarji). Later, as ambassador in Constantinople (1781-9), he wrote a description of court ceremonial that was published by the Russian Academy of Science. This was intended to project an official image of Russo-Turkish relations, though it also provides important information about the reasons for Russian annexation of the Crimea.[64]

A major war with the Ottomans began in 1768 as an offshoot of the political problems in Poland. In an attempt to demonstrate his power, the Russian ambassador in Warsaw, Nicholas Repnin, enforced the so-called Perpetual Treaty of 1768 between Poland and Russia. This caused general dissent on the part of the Polish nobility, and an armed confederation in the fortress town of Bar near the Ottoman border was created in February 1768. The Russian army easily defeated the confederates and captured Bar in July 1768, though the dissent turned into partisan fighting, and some of the confederates fled to Ottoman territory. The Russian troops followed them and razed the Ottoman town of Balta, and in response the staff of the Russian embassy in Constantinople were imprisoned in October 1768, giving rise to war. During the ensuing military actions, the Russians captured Azov, the Crimea, Bessarabia and Moldavia. The Russian fleet that was sent to the Mediterranean (with the consent of the British) defeated the Ottoman Aegean fleet at Chesme (1770).[65] These Russian victories raised concern among other European powers, who were not keen to see the Ottoman Empire fall at the hands of the Russian armies. The war ended with the Treaty of Küçük Kaynarca in 1774.[66] The Ottoman Empire was spared because the Russians acquired a substantial eastern part of the Polish state during the so-called first

---

[63] See L. Frary, 'Petr Andreevich Tolstoi', in *CMR* 14, 586-91.

[64] I.I. Bulgakov, *Rossiskoe posol'stvo v Konstantinopole*, St Petersburg, 1777.

[65] I. de Madariaga, *Russia in the age of Catherine the Great*, New Haven CT, 1981, pp. 208-9.

[66] See C. Soldat, 'Treaty of Küçük Kaynarca', in *CMR* 14, 662-8.

partition in 1772, but its weakness became fully apparent. The Russians extended their territorial control to the river Buh and were now able to maintain a fleet on the Black Sea, while the Crimean Tatar Khanate achieved independence from the Ottomans (in fact it fell under unofficial Russian control). Russia also asserted for itself vague rights to protect the sultan's Christian subjects in the Balkan region.[67]

The Russians pursued their interests in the Crimean Peninsula and supported the pro-Russian faction in the conflict that broke out in the ruling Giray family. The Russian troops were again sent to Bakhchisarai in 1776. Finally, Catherine decided to annex the Crimea in 1783.

A second major war with the Ottomans broke out in 1787, in which the Habsburgs assisted the Russians until 1791. The war ended with the Treaty of Jassy (Iași) in 1792, as a result of which the entire western Ukrainian Black Sea coast was allocated to Russia.

Russian politics regarding Muslims in the 18th century

Although from the time of Ivan IV (r. 1533-84) Muslim communities had maintained a relatively autonomous status within Muscovy, and Muslim elites were integrated into the government system, the Orthodox Church hierarchy continued to look on Muslims with suspicion. From the middle of the 16th century, high-ranking Muslim officials in the Russian service were induced by tax-exemptions and other benefits to convert to Christianity.

By 1680, Russian-controlled territory in the south-western part of the empire extended into Ukraine as far as the left-bank of the Dnepr, and Kazan' ceased to be a frontier region. The relatively tolerant policies towards Muslims changed during the time of Tsar Peter the Great. Financial incentives for the conversion of animists and Muslims became law, as in 1681 the tsar decreed that land belonging to Muslim Tatars might be seized and given to newly baptised Tatars.[68] Peter the Great strove for russification in his newly built empire, especially in the province of Kazan'. He also supported Orthodox missions, which employed material incentives and outright coercion. In 1713, Peter promised converts three

---

[67] B.L. Davies, *The Russo-Turkish War, 1768-1774. Catherine II and the Ottoman Empire*, London, 2016, pp. 16-48.

[68] M. Romaniello, 'Orthodox communities on Russia's frontiers', *Canadian-American Slavic Studies* 51 (2017) 137-41, pp. 139-40. See also M. Romaniello, 'Mission delayed. The Russian Orthodox Church after the conquest of Kazan', *Church History* 76 (2007) 511-40.

years' exemption from taxes and military obligations, and also decreed that land-owners who refused to convert would be deprived of their land and their Christian serfs. He turned the Muslim Tatars who did not convert into state peasants, while the minority who did convert became part of the Russian nobility. By the end of Peter's reign in 1725, about 40,000 Tatars in the Kazan' region had been baptised.[69]

In the 1720s, Feofan Prokopovich, a Russian-Ukrainian theologian, churchman and politician (probably the most influential Orthodox cleric of the era of Peter the Great), wrote an ode on Peter's fateful anti-Ottoman campaign in which the tsar suffered defeat on the River Prut (1711). The poem carried a messianic, anti-Islamic message and promised final vengeance against the enemy. It circulated widely in both manuscript and book forms as a witness to the popularity of the messianic attitude of the growing Russian Empire.[70]

During the time of Peter the Great, the first attempts were made to deal systematically with Islam. This took the form of a translation of the Qur'an from French into Russian by P.V. Postnikov in 1716, and a systematic description of the Muslim faith by the Moldavian statesman and ally of Russia, Dimitrie Cantemir.[71] Concomitantly, the foundation of the Academy of Science in 1724 gave rise to new scientific explorations of Russia. The Empress Anna Ivanovna (r. 1730-40) supported Vitus Bering's second Kamchatka expedition in 1733-43. Gerhard Friedrich Müller, a young historian, and Johann Georg Gmelin, a naturalist, botanist and geographer – both of German descent, like most of the Academy members – took part. Their German descriptions of the Russian East as far as the Pacific give noteworthy insights into the attitude towards Muslims of German Protestants they encountered.[72]

Empress Anna Ivanovna did not change Peter's policy towards the Tatars. She established a baptism commission in 1731 that organised conversions and also grants of clothing, money and crosses to converts. This strategy proved fruitful in quantitative ways. By 1742, 17,000 new converts were reported, and whole villages of animists were baptised. In 1730, the government began a missionary campaign in the Volga region. About

---

[69] R.P. Geraci, *Window on the East. National and imperial identities in late tsarist Russia*, Ithaca NY, 2001, p. 20.

[70] See E. Grishin, 'Feofan Prokopovich', in *CMR* 14, 600-4.

[71] See C. Griffin, 'Pyotr Vasilevich Postnikov', in *CMR* 14, 605-7, and Olar, 'Dimitrie Cantemir', in *CMR* 14, 304-22.

[72] See G. Bourlakov, 'Gerhard Friedrich Müller', in *CMR* 14, 640-6, and 'Johann Georg Gmelin', in *CMR* 14, 628-31.

8,000 Muslims were forcefully converted to Christianity in Kazan' and Nizhnii Novgorod, and most of the mosques there were destroyed.[73]

Empress Elizabeth (r. 1741-62) continued this approach. A policy of encouraging the religious homogeneity of communities was implemented in 1756, expelling Muslims from villages that were composed of more than ten percent baptised Russians. It also enforced the evacuation of converts when they made up less than ten percent of the population of a village.[74]

In the 1740s and 1750s, anti-Muslim policies intensified. Between 1742 and 1744, 418 mosques out of 536 that had been built in Kazan' were destroyed. After a fire in Kazan', two churches were built in the Muslim area, because the bishop held Tatars responsible for the fire. Missionaries were sent to the Tatars, while the converting of animists and Christians to Islam was forbidden. This approach towards the Muslim Tatars was very unsuccessful, because forced Christianisation led to deeper roots in the Muslim faith.[75]

Catherine the Great ended these policies of repression. She stopped repressive assimilation and Orthodox missionary activity in 1764, and began a policy of toleration and integration of the Muslim population into the realm, nominating Muslim officers and implementing religious structures within the Islamic population.[76] These policies led to a blossoming of Muslim institutions and in particular the multiplying of mosques, Muslim schools and the appearance of a dynamic Muslim nobility and commercial bourgeoisie in the Volga-Ural region in western Siberia. Lively discussions about religious, social and political innovations in their communities developed among the Muslim elites, employing traditional Islamic literary genres.[77]

This decree of toleration was a part of the general administrative reform, but also a means by which the government could secure administrative influence over the Muslim population, leading to a firmer attachment of the Muslim borderlands to Russia. In this way, thanks to Enlightenment ideas, the Muslim faith was treated according to its usefulness to the state.[78] The investiture of official state institutions for all

---

[73] V. Bobrovnikov, 'Islam in the Russian Empire', in D. Lieven (ed.), *The Cambridge history of Russia*, vol. 2. *Imperial Russia, 1689-1917*, Cambridge, 2006, 202-23, pp. 204-5.

[74] Geraci, *Window on the East*, pp. 20-1.

[75] S. Tornow, *Handbuch der Text- und Sozialgeschichte Osteuropas. Von der Spätantike bis zum Nationalstaat*, Wiesbaden, 2011, pp. 376-7.

[76] Geraci, *Window on the East*, pp. 21-3.

[77] Bobrovnikov, 'Islam and the Russian Empire', pp. 209-10.

[78] E. Grishin, 'The 1773 decree on religious toleration', in *CMR* 14, 653-8.

religious communities brought most subjects under state supervision. In 1784, Muslim military and religious elites were granted noble status and privileges in exchange for military or civil service. However, they were still not allowed to own Christian serfs.[79]

After the annexation of the Crimea and the north-western Caucasus in 1783, and Dagestan and eastern Transcaucasia in 1796, the Russian army as well as loyal Muslim elites fought against militaristic Islamic movements, especially in the north Caucasus.[80]

In the 18th century, Muslim landowners were pressed to accept Russian Orthodox Christianity or to give up their estates for religious rather than ethnic or cultural reasons; baptised Tatars did not have to give up their ethnic and cultural distinctiveness. Vladimir Bobrovnikov therefore suggests that the relationship between Christians and Muslims in the Russian Empire should not be seen according to the Orientalist prejudice that Islam is a monolithic and unchanging entity that opposes all non-Muslim cultures. It should rather be seen as a part of the Russian Empire, where peaceful interaction took place more often than conflict.[81]

Historians agree that the forced conversions of the first half of the 18th century created a community of newly baptised Tatars who were not sincere in their beliefs. Enforced Christianisation lived for long in the memory of the newly baptised. In the second half of the 19th century, their descendants were the first to revert to Islam as soon as they thought the tsar had given them freedom to do so.[82]

---

[79] Bobrovnikov, 'Islam in the Russian Empire', pp. 206-7.
[80] Bobrovnikov, 'Islam in the Russian Empire', p. 205. Conflicts with Muslims became common in the area during the 19th century.
[81] Bobrovnikov, 'Islam in the Russian Empire', p. 202.
[82] A.N. Kefeli, *Becoming Muslim in imperial Russia*, Ithaca NY, 2017, p. 29.

Central European encounters with the Muslim world in the 18th century

Asaph Ben-Tov

In 18th-century Central Europe one need not have been a traveller to the Near East to encounter aspects of the Islamic world, nor need one have been a trained Orientalist or even a well-informed layman, to have entertained an opinion about it. While much of what Central Europeans recognised as Oriental, Turkish, or Muslim was a European representation, often far removed from historical authenticity, there were plenty of opportunities to experience facets of the Muslim world that were genuine. The 'Orient' appeared in diverse cultural, ideological and religious contexts for Central Europeans, and acquired equally diverse meanings. Many of these were part of broader European interests, and their manifestations in the Holy Roman Empire or the Polish-Lithuanian Commonwealth were often the fruit of French or Italian influences, rather than of a direct encounter with Muslim or Ottoman phenomena. At the same time, some responses to the Muslim world (both real and imagined) took place within distinctly Central European contexts.

A new balance of power

Most attempts at periodisation have an element of arbitrariness to them, and all are a form of interpretation. In considering Central European attitudes towards the Muslim world, it is fair to ask whether the 18th century provides a meaningful historical framework. As the following suggests, I believe it does, despite significant continuities stretching back into the 17th century and extending well into the 19th century. Central European encounters with the Muslim world (both real and imaginary) occurred within numerous contexts. While these were not all related to military encounters, such confrontations were pivotal for Central European experiences of the Muslim world in the early modern period. Since the 16th century, the Habsburgs had been engaged in a series of wars with the Ottoman Empire. So a good starting point for a consideration of Central European attitudes toward the Muslim world is offered by the dramatic events of 1683.

In this year, Ottoman forces led by the Grand Vizier Kara Mustafa Pasha laid siege to Vienna. This second Ottoman attempt to conquer the Habsburg city[1] was thwarted on 12 September at the Battle of Kahlenberg (Battle of Vienna). Unlike the Holy League's naval victory over the Ottomans at Lepanto in 1571, the Ottomans' defeat in 1683 had significant long-term consequences for their empire and its European adversaries. After disrupting the siege, the Holy League – a Habsburg-Papal-Venetian-Polish alliance, which was joined by Russia in 1687 – engaged in a protracted offensive war against the Ottomans in South-Eastern Europe, known as the Great Turkish War (*Der Große Türkenkrieg*). Reversing most of the Ottoman territorial gains in Europe (especially in the wake of the 1526 Battle of Mohács), Buda was taken by the League in 1686 together with most of Hungary, followed by Belgrade in 1688 (later reconquered by the Ottomans) and other territories that had been conquered by the Ottomans in the 15th and 16th centuries. The war ended with the Treaty of Karlowitz in 1699 and marked a decisive power shift between the Habsburgs and their allies and the Ottomans.[2] A further armed conflict ended with the Habsburgs completing their conquest of Hungary.

Wars with the Ottomans in the 18th century resulted in further Habsburg gains in South-Eastern Europe. Though the Ottomans were occasionally victorious on the battle-field, the general trend was apparent. A momentous development came with the ascent of Russia as a military and political power in eastern Europe and its expansion at the expense of the Ottoman Empire. The Turco-Russian War of 1768-74 ended in Ottoman defeat and was followed by the Treaty of Küçük Kaynarca (1774), which sealed the Ottoman loss of suzerainty over the mostly Muslim Crimea.[3] This decline in the relative power of the Ottoman Empire and its loss of former territories gave rise to the 'Eastern Question'. From the perspective of Habsburg foreign policy Ottoman decline was often viewed with ambivalence. While the decline of a formerly formidable foe was in itself welcome, there was a growing concern over the ascendancy of Russia and the need to avoid its domination of the remnants of the Ottomans' European possessions, which could prove a threat to Habsburg monarchy.[4]

---

[1] The first Ottoman siege of Vienna was in 1529.

[2] For an overview, see M. Hochedlinger, *Austria's wars of emergence 1683-1797*, London, 2003, pp. 153-67, and C. Ingrao, *The Habsburg monarchy, 1618-1815*, Cambridge, 2000, ch. 3.

[3] Annexed by Russia in 1783.

[4] See Ingrao, *Habsburg monarchy*, and A. Roider, *Austria's eastern question 1700-1790*, Princeton NJ, 1982. The Eastern Question, according to Roider, had been on Habsburg

Present-day students of Ottoman history caution against framing the long period between the Treaty of Karlowitz and the breakdown of the Ottoman Empire in the First World War as a linear tale of inexorable decline. The Ottomans were still an important presence in the 18th century and would occasionally defeat European powers – and continue to trade with them. However, from the point of view of Central European political and military history, the Ottoman Empire in the 18th century was becoming the object of plans by European powers, rather than a considerable player, with some European powers attempting to carve out portions of it for themselves and others on occasion supporting its integrity for their own purposes.[5] A third siege of Vienna was not forthcoming, and most 18th-century Europeans were aware of this. The 'Turks' could still be loathed and admired, as they had been since the late Middle Ages, and yet, as the new century ran its course, ever fewer inhabitants of Central Europe felt they had cause to fear them. On the occasion of the centenary of the Battle of Kahlenberg, celebrated in Vienna in 1783, an observer could remark contemptuously that the 'Turkish cowards' were no longer worthy of the gunpowder the Viennese were setting off in memory of their historic victory a century earlier.[6] The fear of the Turks (*Türkengefahr*), with both its rational and fantastic elements, which had been a significant part of the Central European worldview, was rapidly slipping into the past.[7]

Turquerie *and* alla turca

One indication of this shift is the fascination with Turkish style in 17th- and 18th-century Europe known as Turquerie.[8] Instances varied in their relation to actual Ottoman art and fashion, some being very loose European elaborations of what was taken to be a Turkish style. Turquerie

---

minds since the early 18th century, decades before the Treaty of Küçük Kaynarca in 1774. See C. Soldat, 'Treaty of Küçük Kaynarca', in *CMR* 14, 662-8.

[5] See C.K. Neumann, 'Political and diplomatic developments', in S.N. Faroqhi (ed.), *The Cambridge history of Turkey*, vol. 3. *The later Ottoman Empire, 1603-1839*, Cambridge, 2006, 44-62.

[6] L. Wolff, *The singing Turk. Ottoman power and operatic emotions on the European stage from the siege of Vienna to the age of Napoleon*, Stanford CA, 2016, p. 146.

[7] See P.S. Fichtner, *Terror and toleration. The Habsburg Empire confronts Islam, 1527-1850*, London, 2008.

[8] See A. Bevilacqua and F. Pfeifer, 'Turquerie. Culture in motion, 1650-1750', *Past & Present* 221 (2013) 75-118, and H. Williams, *Turquerie. An 18th-century European fantasy*, London, 2014.

was not a Central European invention and was in vogue in the 17th and 18th centuries in affluent circles in England, France and Italy. It is worth noting that the vogue for Turquerie, though attested in the Habsburg lands before 1683, seems to have mainly flourished in Central Europe after the Ottomans' military decline. A case of an ornamental representation of Turks in Central Europe is offered by the so-called *Türkenköpfe* ('Turk-heads'), which were put in place to adorn many edifices in Vienna after 1683. As the 18th century progressed and for most Viennese the violent encounter with the Ottomans had become a thing of the past, we find further (and less belligerent) uses of Ottoman ornaments as well as *Türkenköpfe* to decorate clocks and other artefacts.[9] Similar trends are evident in other parts of Central and Eastern Europe.[10]

An intriguing and distinctly Central European adoption of what was perceived as a Turkish fashion is found in the Sarmatian movement, which was widespread among the nobles of the Polish-Lithuanian Commonwealth until the later 18th century – an Oriental self-fashioning as part of Polish-Lithuanian nobles' perceived Oriental descent.[11] Recently described as a 'lived orientalism', it was an appropriation of various outward aspects of the Orient which coexisted with staunch Catholicism and opposition to the Ottoman Empire and all it represented to the ruling class of the Polish-Lithuanian Commonwealth.[12]

Though much of this Turkish vogue had more to do with European fantasy than with genuine Ottoman art and fashion, we should not underestimate the impact of encounters with actual Ottomans. After

---

[9] R. Witzmann, 'Türkenkopf und Türkenkugel. Einige Türkenmotive und Bildvorstellungen der Volkskultur aus dem 17. und 18. Jahrhundert', in R. Waissenberger (ed.), *Die Türken vor Wien. Europa und die Entscheidung an der Donau 1683*, Vienna, 1982, 291-303.

[10] See e.g. A. Petrová-Pleskotová, 'Das Türkenthema in der slowakischen Kunst des 17. und 18. Jahrhunderts', in Waissenberger, *Die Türken vor Wien*, 273-83.

[11] See A. Koutny-Jones, 'Echoes of the East. Glimpses of the "Orient" in British and Polish-Lithuanian portraiture of the eighteenth century', in R. Unger (ed.), *Britain and Poland-Lithuania. Contact and comparison from the Middle Ages to 1795*, Leiden, 2008, 401-19, and D. Uffelmann, '"Here you have all my stuff!" Real things from a mythical country. Ottoman "Sarmatica" in Enlightened Poland', in B. Neumann (ed.), *Präsenz und Evidenz fremder Dinge im Europa des 18. Jahrhunderts*, Göttingen, 2015, 323-38. See M. Długosz and P.O. Scholz (eds), *Sarmatismus versus Orientalismus in Mitteleuropa. Sarmatyzm versus Orientalizm w Europie Środkowej*, Berlin, 2013; also K. Schneiderheinze, 'Between Orient and Occident. The Polish nobility in the Early Modern age', in R. Born and A. Puth (eds), *Osmanischer Orient und Ostmitteleuropa. Perzeptionen und Interaktionen in den Grenzzonen zwischen dem 16. und 18. Jahrhundert*, Stuttgart, 2014, 185-205.

[12] P.O. Scholz, 'Sarmatismus als ein Sonderweg des polnischen Orientalismus. Skizzen und Bemerkungen', in Długosz and Scholz (eds), *Sarmatismus versus Orientalismus*, 93-114, pp. 112-13.

the Treaty of Karlowitz, the Sublime Porte sent more diplomatic delegations to Europe. The pomp and ceremony of the occasions of their arrival fascinated European spectators. Some of the Ottoman diplomats, such as Mehmed Efendi (d. 1732) and his son Mehmed Said Efendi (d. 1761), deeply impressed their European counterparts and wider circles of European elites, who were taken by the sophisticated Ottoman emissaries. Diplomatic encounters also fostered an interest in Turkish military music. An important role was played here by Janissary bands (*mehter*), presented as the sultan's gift at European courts, most famously at the Dresden court of Friedrich August of Saxony (from 1697 also August II of Poland). The Saxon ruler used them extensively, as well as other real and mock Turkish elements in his pageantry.[13] This craze for Turquerie reached its zenith in Dresden with the elaborate 'Turkish' celebrations surrounding the wedding in 1719 of Friedrich August II (August III of Poland) and Maria Josephina of Austria, the Habsburg Emperor's daughter.[14] Thus, when Ahmed Resmi Efendi, the Ottoman emissary arriving in Vienna in 1758 at the height of the Seven Years' War, was shown ballets on Turkish themes, he is reported to have approved of their accuracy, while the Janissary band he heard in Berlin five years later failed to impress him.[15]

Turkish influence and mock Turkish *alla turca* went far beyond bands at European courts. *Alla turca* was an easily recognisable musical style, involving what 17th- and 18th-century composers and audiences would immediately identify as Turkish (however remote many of these musical elements were from genuine Turkish music), and *mehter* percussions often found their way into European orchestras. It is today best remembered in works such as the final movement of Mozart's A major piano sonata (K 331), known as the *rondo alla turca*, the final movement of his fifth violin concerto in A major (K 219), also known as the Turkish concerto, the Turkish march and Dervish choir (1811) in Beethoven's

---

[13] E.A. Bowles, 'The impact of Turkish military bands on European court festivals in the 17th and 18th centuries', *Early Music* 34 (2006) 533-59, pp. 546-50. See also J.B. Stockigt, 'The court of Saxony-Dresden', in S. Owens, B.M. Reul, and J.B. Stockigt (eds), *Music at German courts, 1715-1760*, Woodbridge, 2011, 17-49.

[14] Bowles, 'Impact of Turkish military bands', pp. 549-50.

[15] Wolff, *Singing Turk*, pp. 112-14. On Ahmed Resmi Efendi's embassy, see V.H. Aksan, *An Ottoman statesman in war and peace. Ahmed Resmi Efendi 1700-1783*, Leiden, 1995, ch. 2.

Illustration 2. Portrait of Resmi Ahmed Efendi

music for August von Kotzebue's *Die Ruinen von Athen* (opus 113),[16] and, of course, numerous 'Turkish' operas. Here too, Central European artists and their patrons who commissioned these operas, were following Italian and French trends. Some of the best known 18th-century examples of such operas were Christoph Willibald Gluck's *La rencontre imprévue ou les pèlerins de la Mecque* (1764), which was first performed at the Viennese *Burgtheater*,[17] Joseph Haydn's *L'incontro improvviso* performed at the Eszterháza in 1775, and Mozart's *Die Entführung aus dem Serail*, first performed in Vienna in 1782. The Russo-Turkish War (1768-74), which ended in a decisive Russian victory, coincided with numerous operas on Turkish subjects in the Habsburg territories. Mozart's opera was originally planned as entertainment for the visit of the Russian heir to Vienna. Earlier operas on Turkish, even contemporary themes are attested in earlier works such as Johann Wolfgang Franck's two-part opera *Cara Mustapha*

---

[16] On a more serious note, Beethoven also employed a 'Turkish march' in the final movement of his ninth symphony.

[17] See R.P. Locke, *Music and the exotic from the Renaissance to Mozart*, Cambridge, 2015, ch. 13.

(named after the ill-fated Grand Vizier whose failed siege of Vienna had such historic consequences for Europe and the Ottoman Empire – and terminal consequences for himself), first performed in Hamburg in 1686, three years after the lifting of the siege.

The study of Oriental languages

The academic study of Oriental languages in the Holy Roman Empire was usually aimed at ancient texts, mostly in the context of confessional biblical studies.[18] In addition to Hebrew, the early modern period saw the burgeoning of the study of Aramaic, Syriac, Arabic, Samaritan, Coptic and Ethiopic. The 18th century inherited this broadening of Oriental studies from the 17th century, and thus witnessed non-theological approaches to the study of Arabic, championed by the great Leipzig Arabist Johan Jacob Reiske (1716-74), who famously advocated the study of Arabic and Muslim civilisation as an art of the 'geography of the human spirit' rather than as an auxiliary discipline of biblical studies.[19] Reiske, though lionised in later times, was fairly isolated in his day, and the works of most German Arabists of his time remained embedded within the framework of theologically oriented scholarship. The academic study of Turkish[20] and Persian was a relative rarity.

Central Europeans in the 18th century also had other opportunities to study Oriental languages and other reasons for doing so. Apart from merchants and adventurers travelling to the Near East, another important group were diplomats – in the present context mostly Habsburg diplomats. It is here that the 18th century witnessed a new start. Since the mid-17th century, the Habsburgs had trained so-called *Sprachknaben*, young

---

[18] A. Ben-Tov, 'The academic study of Arabic in seventeenth- and early eighteenth-century Protestant Germany. A preliminary sketch', *History of Universities* 38 (2015) 93-135.

[19] Reiske formulated this programme in his *Prodidagmata ad Hagji Chalifae librum memorabilem rerum a muhammedanis gestarum exhibentia introductionem generalem in historiam sic dictam orientalem* (1747), printed in J.J. Reiske (ed.), *Abulfedae Tabula Syriae cum excerpto geographico ex Ibn Ol Wardii geographia et historia naturali*, Leipzig, 1766, 215-40. See J. Loop, 'Kontroverse Bemühungen um den Orient. Johann Jacob Reiske (1716-1774) und die Orientalistik seiner Zeit', in H.-G. Ebert and T. Hanstein (eds), *Johann Jacob Reiske. Leben und Wirkung*, Leipzig, 2005, 45-85; J. Loop, 'Johann Jacob Reiske', in *CMR* 14, 192-209.

[20] On the study of Turkish, see F. Babinger, 'Die türkischen Studien in Europa bis zum Auftreten Josef von Hammer-Purgstalls', *Die Welt des Islams* 7 (1919) 103-29.

stipend holders trained in Ottoman Turkish in Constantinople.[21] By the mid-18th century, there were increasing misgivings in Vienna about the efficiency of this arrangement, and, following the advocacy of the Jesuit scholar Josef Franz, this training was replaced by the *Kaiserlich-Königliche Akademie für orientalische Sprachen* (the Imperial-Royal Academy for Oriental Languages), which was founded in Vienna in 1754 with the aim of training future Habsburg diplomats to the Ottoman Empire.[22]

Several of the Academy's alumni were to distinguish themselves as scholars and translators of Turkish and Persian literature. Thus, for example, Thomas Chabert, from a family of dragomans in Pera, Istanbul, who studied and later taught at the Academy, wrote a short Turkish grammar for Habsburg officers at the outbreak of the Austro-Turkish war of 1789,[23] as well as translating into German the 16th-century poets Latifi and Aşık Çelebi.[24] The best-known alumnus of the Viennese academy was the Orientalist Joseph Hammer, later Freiherr von Hammer-Purgstall (1774-1856), known for his history of the Ottoman Empire (appearing in ten volumes, 1827-33) and his German translation of Hafez's poems (1812-13), which inspired Goethe's late masterpiece *West-östlicher Divan* (1819).[25] In his autobiography, Hammer-Purgstall gives a vivid account of his years as a student at the Academy (1789-99).[26] Apart from the demanding course of study, this provides a glimpse of the excitement aroused by Ottoman delegations to Vienna, such as the large delegation of 1792.

---

[21] C. Balbous, *Das Sprachknaben-Institut der Habsburgermonarchie in Konstantinopel*, Berlin, 2015, pp. 48-70.

[22] V. Weiss Edlem von Starkenfels, *Kaiserlich-königliche orientalische Akademie zu Wien, ihre Gründung, Fortbildung und gegenwärtige Einrichtung*, Vienna, 1839; F. Gall, 'Türkisch-österreichische Beziehungen in der Geschichte der Wissenschaft', in *Internationales kulturhistorisches Symposium Mogersdorf 1969 in Mogersdorf. Österreich und die Türken*, Eisenstadt, 1972, 85-93. See Ç. Sarıkartal, 'Josef Franz', in *CMR* 14, 171-7.

[23] [T. Chabert], *Kurze Anleitung zur Erlernung der türkischen Sprache, für Militär Personen*, Vienna, 1789.

[24] T. Chabert, *Latifi oder biographische Nachrichten von vorzüglichen türkischen Dichtern, nebst einer Blumenlese aus ihren Werken. Aus dem Türkischen des Monla Abdoul Latifi und des Aschik Hassan Tschelebi*, Zürich, 1800. See Weiss Edlem von Starkenfels, *Kaiserlich-königliche orientalische Akademie zu Wien*, pp. 56-7.

[25] E.D. Petritsch, 'Die Anfänge der Orientalischen Akademie', in O. Rathkolb (ed.), *250 Jahre. Von der Orientalischen zur Diplomatischen Akademie in Wien*, Innsbruck, 2004, 47-64; E.D. Petritsch, 'Erziehung in *guten Sitten, Andacht und Gehorsam*. Die 1754 gegründete Orientalische Akademie in Wien', in M. Kurz et al. (eds), *Das Osmanische Reich und die Habsburgermonarchie. Akten des Internationalen Kongresses zum 150-jährigen Bestehen des Instituts für Österreichische Geschichtsforschung. Wien, 22.-25. September 2004*, Oldenburg, 2005, 491-502.

[26] J. Freiherr von Hammer-Purgstall, *Erinnerungen aus meinem Leben 1774-1852*, ed. R. Bachofen von Echt, Vienna, 1940, pp. 22-34.

On this occasion, Hammer-Purgstall and his fellow students were able to hone their Turkish and assist as interpreters. The young student was also impressed by the fact that lemonade and almond-milk were served instead of wine – a not uncommon courtesy shown to high-ranking Ottoman visitors.[27] An older 18th-century Habsburg diplomat who had studied Oriental languages before the Academy was founded, and was to make a name for himself as a connoisseur of Persian poetry, was the Hungarian nobleman Karl Emmerich Alexander von Reviczky von Revisnye, whose Latin (and highly classicised) *Specimen poeseos persicae* (1771) was translated into both German and English.

The Orient and 18th-century belles lettres

Of course, interest in Middle Eastern literature and a literary interest in the Middle East in Central Europe preceded the 18th century. A good example is Adam Olearius' German translation of Saʿdī's *Gulistan* (1654), which was reissued in 1660, 1697 and again as late as 1775. In this last edition, the anonymous editor added a German translation of Luqman's Fables. A milestone in European literary interest in the Middle East came with Antoine Galland's French rendering of the *Arabian nights* (*Mille et une nuit*, 1704-17).[28] Galland's version was soon translated into German by August Bohse (under his nom de plume Talander).[29] As with other European languages, we find countless echoes of the *Arabian nights* in 18th-century German literature, from the heights of Goethe's work[30] to exotic characters in long-forgotten comedies and libretti. Interest in the *Arabian nights* seems to have peaked in Germany in the 1770s and 1780s.[31] Johann Heinrich Voss, best remembered today for his masterful translation of the *Iliad* and the *Odyssey*, published his German rendering of the *Arabian nights* (1781-5), which he made from Galland's French.

---

[27] Hammer-Purgstall, *Erinnerungen*, pp. 25-6.

[28] Or rather *Thousand and one nights*, as the collection is called in Arabic and in other translations. See F. Bauden, 'Antoine Galland', in *CMR* 13, 529-47.

[29] *Die Tausend und Eine Nacht, Worinnen Seltzame Arabische Historien und wunderbare Begebenheiten, benebst artigen Libes-Intiguenm auch Sitten und Gewohnheiten der Morgenländer, auf sehr anmuthige Weise erzehlet werden; erstlich vom Hrn. Galland, der Königl. Academie Mitgliede, aus der Arabischen Sprache in die Französische, und aus selbiger anitzo ins Teutsche übersetzet*, Leipzig, 1711-37.

[30] K. Mommsen, *Goethe und 1001 Nacht*, Berlin, 1960.

[31] Mommsen, *Goethe und 1001 Nacht*, pp. 30-6.

The Orient played various roles in the literature of the day – and here too, much of what Central European poets and novelists had to say about the Muslim world was indebted to broader European literary trends and genres. Oriental rulers, both historical figures as well as made-up caricatures such as August von Kotzebue's Persian Sultan Wampum,[32] served as accentuated despotic figures opposed by a hero (or heroine), often a fellow Muslim who would be strikingly akin to 18th-century Europeans. Many of these 'orientalised' works of literature were not intended as profound commentaries on the Middle East.

The 18th century offers a plethora of literary caricatures of Oriental cruelty and other stereotypes. Some authors merely use an Oriental setting, historical or fantastic, as a convenient backdrop for their ideas, a good example for which is the pensive hero of Friedrich Maximilian Klinger's *Geschichte Giafars des Barmeciden* (1792-4), a lengthy exposition of Enlightenment themes on an Oriental stage. Another literary use of the European inventory of Oriental figures was meant as an acceptable way of indirectly criticising what the author considered to be malaises of his own society. Often, the hypocritical, wine-guzzling dervish in 18th-century plays performed in Vienna was a thinly veiled mockery of Catholic clergy. These characters betrayed widespread contemporary perceptions of the Middle East and helped perpetuate them. As Nina Berman has argued: 'Whereas Turkish characters are conceptualized as being capable of transforming themselves to correspond to new ethical standards, their cultural context is identified with outdated and objectionable norms and ethics.'[33]

Johann Wolfgang Goethe (1749-1832), the towering figure of 18th- and early 19th-century German letters, is known for his lifelong and profound interest in Islam and the portions of Islamic literature that were available to him in European translations.[34] While he could not read either Arabic or Persian, he was, from early on, an avid reader of the Qur'an in translation. His engagement with Islamic literature is attested repeatedly in his vast oeuvre, most famously in the *West-östlicher Divan* (1819) mentioned above, a poetic dialogue with the 14th-century Persian poet Hafez, whom Goethe had read in Joseph von Hammer-Purgstall's German translation.

---

[32] August von Kotzebue, *Sultan Wampum oder. Die Wünsche*, Leipzig, 1794.

[33] N. Berman, *German literature on the Middle East. Discourses and practices, 1000-1989*, Ann Arbor MI, 2001, p. 134.

[34] See esp. Mommsen, *Goethe und 1001 Nacht*; K. Mommsen, *Goethe und die arabische Welt*, Frankfurt, 1988; Mommsen, *Goethe und der Islam*, Frankfurt, 2001.

The Qur'an and Islam

There were several approaches to Islam in 18th-century Europe, each usually closely related to its champion's approach to his own religion and society. Whether one detested Islam as an anti-Christian aberration, or derided it as a form of religious enthusiasm, whether one admired it for its rejection of the Trinity or celebrated it as a manifestation of rational monotheism, it was never a pursuit conducted *sine ira et studio*. As in the 17th century, the academic study of Oriental languages in the 18th century was still mostly theologically motivated. The geographical and cultural heartland of Islam was also the cradle of Christianity, and a study of Arabic was undertaken by many Central European scholars as part of their attempt to better understand the language and historical setting of the Old Testament. Reiske, who championed the study of the East liberated from theological and exegetical concerns, did not evince great interest in the Qur'an or the systematic study of Islam. His great contemporary, the Göttingen Orientalist and Old Testament scholar Johann David Michaelis (1717-91), embodied both the more typical intellectual continuities with earlier academic Oriental studies as well as dramatic new departures in the 18th century within the broad framework of a biblically-oriented study of Oriental languages. This embeddedness in biblical studies had its limitations, but in no way did it imply an ossified form of scholarship. Michaelis, who, unlike Reiske, was immensely influential in his own day, is famous for, among other things, initiating a scientific expedition to the Middle East with the aim of conducting systematic empirical observations to enable a better understanding of the historical reality behind the Bible. The sole survivor of this expedition (1761-7), which in many ways took on a route and agenda that greatly differed from Michaelis' original design, was Carsten Niebuhr, who later published an account of the Arabian Peninsula and also a valuable travel account.[35]

Eighteenth-century thinkers in Central Europe, as elsewhere in Europe, entertained both positive and negative views of Islam. More traditional anti-Muslim invectives and earnest attempts at understanding this

---

[35] C. Niebuhr, *Beschreibung von Arabien aus eigenen Beobachtungen und im Lande selbst gesammleten Nachrichten abgefasset*, Copenhagen, 1772; C. Niebuhr, *Reisebeschreibung nach Arabien und andern umliegenden Ländern*, 2 vols, Copenhagen, 1774-8. On Niebuhr and the expedition, see J. Wieshöfer and S. Conermann (eds), *Carsten Niebuhr (1733-1815) und seine Zeit*, Stuttgart, 2002, as well as M.C. Carhart, *The science of culture in Enlightenment Germany*, Cambridge MA, 2007, ch. 1.

religion and its followers' convictions and practices can be found shoulder to shoulder throughout the century, and many of the most interesting and influential arguments about Islam came from writers who were not themselves trained Orientalists.[36] To name but two prominent and very different examples, Henri de Boulainvilliers's *La Vie de Mahomed* was available both in the original (1730) and in a 1747 German translation, and Voltaire's play *Le fanatisme ou Mahomet le prophète* (1741) was reluctantly translated into German by Goethe in 1800.[37] Also, scholars with Orientalist training could portray Islam in radically different ways. Thus, we find at the beginning of the century German translations of Humphrey Prideaux's mordant (and popular) biography of Muḥammad (1699),[38] as well as a German translation of the well-informed and non-polemical account of Islam by the Dutch Orientalist Adriaan Reland (1716), which was a landmark in the early modern European study of Islam.[39]

At the beginning of the 'long 18th century' of Central European engagement with the Muslim world, we find the pioneering edition of the Arabic text of the Qur'an by the Hamburg Lutheran pastor Abraham Hinckelmann in 1694, which was shortly followed by the publication of a landmark edition of the Qur'an accompanied by a Latin translation and commentaries by the Roman Catholic priest Ludovico Marracci in 1698.[40] Both these achievements were preceded by decades of European study of the Qur'an. For the broader Central European public of non-specialists, the Qur'an had been available in print in Latin since 1543,[41] and in a

---

[36] See e.g. A. Hamilton, 'Western attitudes to Islam in the Enlightenment', *Middle Eastern Lectures* 3 (1999) 69-85; J. Israel, *Enlightenment contested. Philosophy, modernity, and the emancipation of man 1670-1752*, Oxford, 2006, ch. 24; M. Mulsow, *Die drei Ringe. Toleranz und clandestine Gelehrsamkeit bei Mathurin Veyssière La Croze (1661-1739)*, Tübingen, 2001.

[37] Mommsen, *Goethe und die arabische Welt*, pp. 218-38.

[38] Humphrey Prideaux, *Das Leben Mahomets*, Leipzig, 1699. The English original first appeared in 1697 and was followed by numerous editions.

[39] Adriaan Reland, *Zwey Bücher von der Türckischen oder Mahommedischen Religion*, Hannover, 1716. The Latin original first appeared in Utrecht in 1705.

[40] For German studies and translation of the Qur'an from the late 17th to the early 19th century, see A. Hamilton, '"To rescue the honour of the Germans". Qur'an translations by eighteenth- and early nineteenth-century German Protestants', *Journal of the Warburg and Courtauld Institutes* 77 (2014) 173-209.

[41] A revised version Robert of Ketton's 12th-century translation published in Basel by Theodor Bibliander and Johannes Oporinus, *Machumetis saracenorum principis, eiusque seccessorum vitae, ac doctrina, ipseque Alcoran*, Basel, 1543; see H. Bobzin, *Der Koran im Zeitalter der Reformation. Studien zur Frühgeschichte der Arabistik und Islamkunde in Europa*, Stuttgart, 1995, 159-275.

1616 German translation by the Nuremberg pastor Salomon Schweigger.[42] Revealingly, this first German translation was made from an Italian rendering of the Latin version. This derivative nature was typical of numerous early modern Qur'an translations. Thus, David Nerreter's 1703 German version was made from Marracci's Latin version.[43] The influential English translation of the Qur'an by George Sale[44] was the source of a further German version published in 1746 by Theodor Arnold.[45] Arnold, like Schweigger and Nerreter before him, did not read Arabic (nor did he claim to), but it was his translation in which the young Goethe immersed himself.

Arguably, some of the most significant 18th-century German writers to influence the broader educated public's interest in Islam could not themselves read Arabic. The first German Qur'an translation made directly from the original was published 1772 by the Lutheran theologian and orientalist David Friedrich Megerlin.[46] It was not well received. A more successful direct translation into German appeared the following year, this too the work of a Lutheran theologian, Friedrich Eberhardt Boysen.[47] While the appearance of German Qur'an translations and scholarly works in German and mostly Latin on the Qur'an and Islam are very much a continuation of 17th-century scholarship, there is an important development in one aspect of interest in the Qur'an and the expectations of an educated lay readership in the 18th century. This was a growing appreciation for the Qur'an as a work of poetry.[48] Within the realm of German letters, this realisation reached its apex in the early 19th century with

---

[42] S. Schweigger, *Alcoranus Mahometicus: das ist, der Türcken Alcoran, Religion und Aberglauben*, Nuremberg, 1616. On Schweigger, see A. Schunka, art. 'Salomon Schweigger', in W. Kühlmann et al. (eds), *Frühe Neuzeit in Deutschland 1520-1620 Literaturwissenschaftliches Verfasserlexikon*, vol. 5. *Paganus, Petrus – Seusse, Johannes*, Berlin, 2016, 590-7.

[43] Published in D. Nerreter, *Neu eröffnete Mahometanische Moschea*, Nuremberg, 1703. See D. Cyranka, 'David Nerreter', in *CMR* 14, 105-11.

[44] On Sale's translation and its indebtedness to Marracci's Latin translation, see A. Bevilacqua, 'The Qur'an translations of Marracci and Sale', *Journal of the Warburg and Courtauld Institutes* 76 (2013) 93-130.

[45] T. Arnold, *Der Koran, oder insgemein so genannte Alcoran des Mahommeds*, Emden, 1746.

[46] D.F. Megerlin, *Die türkische Bibel*, Frankfurt, 1772. See A. Hamilton, 'David Friedrich Megerlin', in *CMR* 14, 187-91.

[47] F.E. Boysen, *Der Koran, oder das Gesetz für die Moslemer, durch Muhammed den Sohn Abdall*, Halle, 1773. A revised edition appeared in 1775. See Hamilton, '"To rescue the honour of the Germans"', pp. 182-201. See A. Hamilton, 'Friedrich Eberhard Boysen', in *CMR* 14, 210-15.

[48] J. Loop, 'Divine poetry? Early modern European Orientalists on the beauty of the Koran', *Church History and Religious Culture* 89 (2009) 455-88.

Friedrich Rückert's masterful (though incomplete) translation – both a considerable scholarly achievement and a poetic masterpiece.[49]

A deeply ambivalent view of Islam and the Qur'an is evident in the writings of the late 18th-century philosopher, theologian and poet Johann Gottfried Herder (1744-1803).[50] His characterisation of the Qur'an in his *Ideen zur Philosophie der Geschichte der Menschheit* ('Reflections on the philosophy of the history of mankind', 1784-91) as 'this extraordinary mixture of poetry, rhetoric, ignorance, wisdom, and pretension' epitomises the ambivalence of his times.[51] Herder also stressed the civilising role of Islam in converting pre-Muslim pagans. Muḥammad's religion, he writes in the same work, had both admirable and woeful effects on its believers and their society. It allowed them true peace of mind and 'unity of character', which Herder sees as both a great asset and potentially dangerous. His disapproval of Muslim polygamy is a *locus classicus* of Christian critique; more typical of his day is his claim that Islam's 'ban on scrutiny of the Qur'an, and the despotism which it enforces in matters spiritual and temporal, cannot but have evil consequences'. Yet Herder the philosopher and poet could not help admiring the language of the Qur'an. This appreciation for the Qur'an as a work of Arabic poetry and what Herder took to be its roots and profound historical significance are laid out in his 1778 essay *Über die Wirkung der Dichtkunst auf die Sitten der Völker in alten und neuen Zeiten* ('On the effect of poetic art on the ethics of peoples in ancient and modern times'). In his view, the spirit of Arab poetry had also exercised a decisive influence on European culture and mores in the Middle Ages.

By way of conclusion, the last word goes to Johann David Michaelis, who elaborated his views on Islam in a lengthy review of Boysen's Qur'an translation (1774). His portrayal of Islam exemplifies both lines of continuity with earlier European attitudes and also the emergence of new approaches that were intimately related to evolving attitudes to Christianity and religion in Central Europe in the later 18th century:

---

[49] Written in the 1820s, it appeared posthumously in 1888.

[50] The literature on Herder is vast. For a concise overview of his (and Johann David Michaelis') Oriental scholarship, see S. Marchand, *German Orientalism in the age of empire. Religion, race, and scholarship*, Cambridge, 2009, ch. 1.

[51] J.G. Herder, *Ideen zur Philosophie der Geschichte der Menschheit*, Riga, 1784-91, vol. 4, book 19, ch. iv: *Sein Koran, dies sonderbare Gemisch von Dichtkunst, Beredsamkeit, Unwissenheit, Klugheit und Anmaßung, ist ein Spiegel seiner Seele, der seine Gaben und Mängel, seine Neigungen und Fehler, den Selbstbetrug, und die Notbehelfe, mit denen er sich und andere täuschte, klärer als irgend ein anderer Koran eines Propheten zeiget.*

It is evident that after the religion which the Bible teaches, none is so sensible as the Mohammedan, which retains Natural Religion almost in its entirety, especially in its teaching about a sole, omnipotent, and eternal God, an eternal life, in which one will be punished and rewarded, and its great merit for having toppled idolatry and introduced the worship of the true God, acknowledged by Christians, Jews, Mohammedans, and Deists alike, into such expansive territories (only too often with the aid of arms, yet without religious coercion).[52]

Michaelis goes on to celebrate the political effects of Islam: 'It was this religion which forged the Arabs within the span of three generations into a great nation. The Arabs' fortitude which allowed them to conquer lands which the Greek and Roman before them had never reached they owed to their new religion, and once their vast empire was established it was Islam which leant it cohesion.' Yet for all this admiration, Michaelis was writing centuries after the heyday of the 'Abbasid Empire and the flourishing of al-Andalus, and a century after the Ottomans' decisive defeat at the Battle of Kahlenberg. Viewing Muslim history from the standpoint of a Göttingen professor in the late 18th century, Michaelis also saw in Islam itself the seeds of political decline: the subversion of rulers and the failure to establish long-lasting political entities. Nowhere in the Islamic world, he continued, could one find freedom and prosperity. Not a single Muslim state was flourishing or even powerful in his day.[53] In a lengthy footnote,[54] he offers his explanation for the detrimental influence of Islam on Muslim commonwealths, the thrust of which is the ban on a

---

[52] J.D. Michaelis, Review of Boysen's Qur'an translation, *Orientalische und exegetische Bibliothek* 8 (1775) 30-98, p. 31.

[52] Michaelis, Review of Boysen, pp. 33-4: *Aber eben diese Religion hatte auch so schädliche politische Folgen: ewige Umstürze von Staaten, und die immer mit Unglück der Völker verbunden, nichts so bleibendes, als wir in Europa kennen, nirgends eigentlich Freyheit und Glück der Völker, ungeachtet viel ungebundene Frechheit und Gesetzlosigkeit war, jetzt sehen wir keinen einzigen Muhammedanischen Staat glücklich, ja nicht einmahl mächtig, ungeachtet sie die weiten Länder in sich fassen, in denen sonst alle Macht der Welt beysammen wart: den Türkischen Staat, der noch immer der mächtigste unter allen ist, vergleiche man einmahl mit dem Preußischen, und das nach den drey von der [p. 34] unabhängigen politischen Dimensionen der blossen Länder, Quadratmeilen, Lage und Fruchtbarkeit, und denn ihre Macht, wiederum nicht die in der Qualität der Armeen, sondern nur die ihrer Grösse, und in den Einkünften des Staats bestehende so wird man doch merken, daß etwas in der Muhammedanischen Religion seyn müsse, daß den Staaten zuletzt nachtheilig wird. Wäre das einzige Kleinasien bey einer viel importanten Lage, und grösseren Fruchtbarkeit, in anderen Stücken eben das, was der Preußische Staat ist, so müßte es ja allein überaus viel mächtiger seyn. --- Sollte einer nicht auf eine Religion die so sonderbahre politische Wirkungen hat, aufmerksahm seyn.*

[54] Michaelis, Review, pp. 34-5, n. i.

rational (historical) scrutiny of the Qur'an (analogue to his own biblical scholarship).

Islam, which he admired as an almost perfect incarnation of natural religion, is thus for him also a religion riddled with enthusiasm, which was not only intellectually unsound but also politically dangerous. And so, perhaps unwittingly, Michaelis offers both poles of the 18th-century perceptions of Islam among learned Europeans: it was both a rational, unitary religion (a sentiment at which his great contemporary and occasional adversary Gotthold Ephraim Lessing must have nodded approvingly)[55] and at the same time a dangerous form of religious enthusiasm. Revealingly, for Michaelis, it was not Oriental despotism that constituted a central point of criticism (as it had been, for example, for Montesquieu, whom he had read carefully), but weak government and the lack of a religious teaching inculcating obedience to the ruler. Fatalism and the lack of political obedience were the bane of contemporary Muslims. Having died in Göttingen in 1791, Michaeilis did not live to learn of Napoleon's invasion of Egypt in 1798, but it is fair to guess that, had he been granted a prophetic premonition of it, he would not have been surprised.

---

[53] S. Horsch, "'Was findest Du darinne, das nicht mit der allerersten Vernunft übereinkomme?' Islam as natural theology in Lessing's writings and in the Enlightenment', *Edinburgh German Yearbook* 1 (2007) 45-62.

The political agents of Muslim rulers in Central Europe in the 18ᵗʰ century

David Do Paço

The history of early modern European diplomacy is heavily dependent on studies focussed on the Peace of Westphalia of 1648. The treaties that were signed in Münster and Osnabrück have been portrayed as the foundations of a 'European diplomatic culture' based on international law and a new order established among Christian powers, that of proto-nation states. This order was reinforced by the regular practice of multilateral negotiations at congresses that followed the numerous wars fought during the reign of Louis XIV (r. 1643-1715). The study of 'the order of Westphalia' has allowed us better to understand the importance of protocol in political communication between powers, the sociability and culture of ambassadors and those who by default we call 'diplomats'.[1] Nevertheless, these studies have also created a distortion of European history that favours a Western Europe seen as dominant and ignores political activity between empires in Central Europe that crossed boundaries, both cultural and religious.

By analysing the political activities of Muslim rulers in Central Europe and the practices of their agents, this essay underlines the existence of a diplomatic order between empires whose foundations were laid between representatives of the Habsburg Empire, the Republic of Venice and the Ottoman Empire in 1718 at the Congress of Passarowitz. This order was characterised by a form of diplomacy based on the trans-imperial structures (such as commercial networks, aristocratic families, religious orders) that had predated diplomatic processes. It was embodied by agents who operated across political, linguistic and religious borders, and offered their personal economic and social resources for the service

---

[1] T.A. Sowerby and J. Hennings (eds), *Practices of diplomacy in the early modern world*, London, 2017; N.F. May, *Zwischen fürstlicher Repräsentation und adliger Statuspolitik: das Kongresszeremoniell bei den westfälischen Friedensverhandlungen*, Ostfildern, Stuttgart, 2016; D.H. Nexon, 'Westphalia reframed', in D.H. Nexon (ed.), *The struggle for power in early modern Europe. Religious conflict, dynastic empires, and international change*, Princeton NJ, 2009, 265-88; D. Croxton, *Westphalia. The last Christian peace*, New York, 2013; H. Duchhardt, *Der Westfälische Friede. Diplomatie – politische Zäsur – kulturelles Umfeld – Rezeptionsgeschichte*, Munich, 1998.

of public affairs. Far from being focussed in the person of an ambassador, the diplomacy of Muslim rulers in central Europe is characterised by the diversity of regulations backed by official and non-official agents, whose personal interests were in line with those of the sultan, bey or dey they served. Although the Ottoman sultan was the most active diplomatically, the 18th century is marked by a variety of Muslim rulers represented at the imperial court in Vienna and also in Berlin and Warsaw. The sultan regarded Vienna as one of the most favoured objectives of his foreign affairs, and the Mediterranean powers of Algiers, Tunis and Tripoli were also represented there. In 1783, the Moroccan ambassador singled himself out by the ease with which he was able to join in the life of the Viennese court and to conduct his activities there – he preferred Vienna to Venice. In this, he competed with the agents of the Ottomans and the familiarity they had developed with the court, the nobility and the town of Vienna since the 17th century. In another connection, the growing power of the Kingdom of Prussia prompted Mustafa III (r. 1757-74) and Selim III (r. 1789-1807) to send their agents to Berlin. There, they discussed such matters as the expansion of Russia to the Black Sea, the conditions for Ottoman merchants trading at the Leipzig fair and the fate of Poland.[2]

The study of the political agents of the Islamic powers in the Christian monarchies leads to the discussion of a historiography that makes them into brokers in negotiations between Christian and Muslim powers.[3] These 'agents of empires' are often presented as 'trans-imperial subjects', according to the precise definition given by E. Natalie Rothman, and are characterised by linguistic and social skills that allowed them to move between many worlds. In the modern era, this knowledge gained institutional recognition, enabling them to seek positions as interpreters, chancery secretaries, chancellors, consuls and ambassadors. Their experience of interculturality made dialogue and negotiation possible between different cultural, linguistic and confessional areas.[4] This approach assumes that the incommensurability of cultural areas, or the empires they

---

[2] D. Do Paço, *L'Orient à Vienne au dix-huitième siècle*, Oxford, 2015, pp. 65-9.

[3] 'Cross-confessional diplomacy and diplomatic intermediaries in the early modern Mediterranean', a special issue of *Journal of Early Modern History* 19/2-3 (2015).

[4] E.N. Rothman, *Brokering empire. Trans-imperial subjects between Venice and Istanbul*, Ithaca NY, 2011. M. Kaczka, 'Pashas and nobles: Paweł Benoe and Ottoman-Polish encounters in the eighteenth century', Florence, 2019 (Ph.D thesis, the European University Institute).

represented, remained a fundamental issue that could only be resolved through intermediaries.

While the focus here is on the diversity of the political agents of the Islamic powers in central Europe, we would also like to shed light on the relations between empires that depended not on intermediaries but on social worlds that crossed these empires and were deeply rooted in each of them, as diverse and dissimilar as they were. The political agents of the Islamic powers in 18th-century Central Europe participated in the interlocking of empires and, more broadly, their integration.

The diplomatic system of Ottoman agents in central Europe

When he visited Vienna in 1664, the dervish Evlyia Çelebi, who was officiating as the *divan efendi* (legation secretary) of Kara Mehmet Paşa, recounted in his travelogue that the town had been handed over in 1529 to Süleyman I (r. 1520-66). Moreover, the 'German padishah' (German emperor) was required to install a golden globe on the top of the cathedral and had regularly to pay a tribute to the Sublime Porte as a sign of his submission. In the aftermath of the Treaty of Vasvár of 1664, which followed the Austrian victory at the Battle of St Gotthard, Çelebi reminded Mehmed IV (r. 1648-87) of the vastness of the world he had inherited, thereby symbolically reducing Austria to the status of a subordinate province with no more significance than the principalities of Wallachia and Moldovia.[5] Nevertheless, the Treaty of Vasvár propelled Habsburg-Ottoman relations into a new era, whose logic seemed to be outside the dervish's conservative expectations. Far from crystallising the antagonism between them, the treaty instigated regular trade arrangements along the Danube between Vienna and the *pashalik*s of Buda and Serbia.[6]

The aim of the Ottoman siege of Vienna in 1683, in the wake of the Franco-Ottoman alliance, was to force the Habsburg emperor to concentrate on his eastern front at a time when Louis XIV was embarking on the War of the Reunions against Spain (1683-4). The defeat of the Ottomans at the Battle of Vienna on 11 September 1683 allowed Habsburg troops

---

[5] K. Teply, *Türkische Sagen und Legenden um die Kaiserstadt Wien*, Vienna, 1980, pp. 90-2.

[6] R.-T. Fischer, *Österreich im Nahen Osten. Die Grossmachtpolitik der Habsburgermonarchie im Arabischen Orient, 1633-1918*, Vienna, 2006, pp. 13-22; P.S. Fichtner, *Terror and toleration. The Habsburg Empire confronts Islam, 1526-1850*, London, 2008, pp. 89-90.

quickly to enter the *Pashalik* of Buda and regain control of the principal towns of the former kingdom of Hungary, including Pest in 1684, Buda in 1686 and Belgrade in 1688. However, far from being seen as a liberator, the Habsburg army divided the Hungarian nobility into supporters of the emperor and of the sultan. The former saw this conquest of Ottoman Hungary as an opportunity to extend their land and to rule a reunified kingdom, while the latter feared the creation of an absolute monarchy that would challenge the economic, political and religious privileges that Ottoman sultans had regularly confirmed since 1526.[7]

The victory of the Habsburg army was confirmed in 1699 by the Treaty of Karlowitz, in which Mustafa II (r. 1695-1703) recognised the first defeat of the Ottoman Empire by a Christian army by ceding the *eyalets* of Buda, Eğri, Kanije, Uyvar and Varat, and the Principality of Transylvania, former territories of the Kingdom of Hungary. Moreover, the Treaty of Karlowitz was accompanied by a commercial treaty, which strengthened the common desire of Vienna and Istanbul to encourage economic exchanges and movement between the two empires. These treaties included freedom of movement for Catholic merchants. In 1718, Article XIII of the Treaty of Passarowitz stipulated that 'The merchants of both sides shall follow their commerce, freely, securely and peacefully in the dominions of both empires', regardless of their religion.[8] The 1739 peace and trade treaties of Belgrade set customs duties at five percent of the value of imported products, and finally, in 1791, the Treaty of Sistova allowed almost total liberalisation for major trade between the Habsburg Empire and the Ottoman Empire.[9]

This evolution of Habsburg-Ottoman relations can be seen to emerge from works that challenge two dominant historiographies. The first is focused on the conflict between the Habsburg and Ottoman forces, searching for the origins of the so-called 'Eastern question' through the bias of a classic conception of diplomacy based on a study of the official negotiations between the agents of the two rulers.[10] The second

---

[7] R.J.W. Evans, *Austria, Hungary, and the Habsburgs. Central Europe c. 1683-1867*, Oxford, 2008, pp. 3-16, 56-74.

[8] *A general collection of treatys of peace and commerce, manifestos, declarations of war, and other publick papers, from the end of the reign of Queen Anne to 1731*, vol. 4, London, 1732, p. 408.

[9] M. Pittioni, 'Österreichisch-Osmanische Wirtschaftsbeziehungen', in I. Feigl et al. (eds), *Auf den Spuren der Osmanen in der österreichischen Geschichte*, Frankfurt, 2002, 145-54.

[10] K.A. Roider, *Austria's eastern question 1700-1790*, Princeton NJ, 1982; B. Lewis, *The Muslim discovery of Europe*, New York, 2001.

concerns trading diasporas, and notably the Greek diaspora, presenting the development of trans-imperial trade as the simple fact of a specific, ethno-confessional community operating almost independently between Central Europe, the Balkans and the Mediterranean.[11]

The new diplomatic history, such as the one notably promoted by Christian Windler and Hillard von Thiessen, invites interest in a variety of actors, their economic and social resources, and their networks, leading to a reinterpretation of the history of relations between the Habsburg Empire and the Ottoman Empire in the 18th century.[12]

The correspondence of Prince Eugène of Savoy during the Hungarian War of 1684-99 shows the variety of the interlocutors whom the generals of the Habsburg army met, as well as the relationships they developed with officials, merchants and Ottoman scholars. The occupation of Belgrade from 1688 to 1690 and in 1717 was, for Habsburg officials, an opportunity to develop connections within the Ottoman world and to govern the fortress by bringing together various players in Hungary and Ottoman Serbia. The network of influence that Prince Eugène established during the Hungary campaign led to his appointment as president of the Aulic Council of War (*Hofkriegsrat*) in 1706 by the Emperor Joseph I (r. 1705-11) with responsibility for managing the diplomatic and commercial affairs of the House of Austria with the Ottoman Empire. Prince Eugène managed these relations personally, mobilising his clients in the service of the emperor.[13]

One of the most striking examples of this governance system of Habsburg-Ottoman relations established by Prince Eugène was embodied in the career of Heinrich Penckler.[14] Protected by Prince Eugène, Penckler was sent to Istanbul in 1719 to learn Oriental languages under the *internuncio* (the emperor's representative) in Pera. He studied particularly under Osman Efendi, a former *sipahi* originally from Temesvár who had been captured in Vienna in the 1690s. In the service of Prince

[11] O. Katsiardi-Hering and M.A. Stassinopoulou (eds), *Across the Danube. Southeastern Europeans and their travelling identities (17th-19th c.)*, Leiden, 2016.

[12] H. von Thiessen and C. Windler (eds), *Akteure der Außenbeziehungen Netzwerke und Interkulturalität im historischen Wandel*, Cologne, 2010. 'Transformation of intercultural diplomacies. Comparative views on Asia and Europe (1700-1850)', a special issue of *The International History Review* 41/5 (2019).

[13] E. Zöllner and K. Gutkas (eds), *Österreich und die Osmanen. Prinz Eugen und seine Zeit*, Vienna, 1988.

[14] R. Zedinger, 'Vom "Sprachknaben" zum Internuntius Freiherr Heinrich Christoph von Penckler (1700-1774) im diplomatischen Dienst an der Hohen Pforte', in U. Tischler-Hofer and R. Zedinger (eds), *Kuppeln - Korn – Kanonen. Unerkannte und unbekannte Spuren in Südosteuropa von der Aufklärung bis in die Gegenwart*, Innsbruck, 2010, 215-42.

Schallenberg in Vienna, Osman Efendi had unquestionably been associated with Prince Eugène and, when he returned to the Ottoman Empire at the start of the 1700s, he retained contact with the emperor's agents in Istanbul as well as advising the *reisülküttab* (the Ottoman minister in charge of foreign affairs) on Central European matters. Penckler was recalled to Vienna in 1726 following the appointment of a *shahbender* (consul general) of the Ottoman merchants, Ömer Ağa, himself an active Ottoman merchant in Vienna who had profited from the commercial treaties of 1699 and 1718 and had been protected by the Tulip Era reformist, the Grand Vizier Nevşehirli Damat Ibrahim Paşa. In the service of Prince Eugène, Penckler was an interpreter and intermediary between Ömer Ağa and the *Hofkriegsrat*, and the *shahbender* himself was accompanied by an interpreter who was none other than Osman Efendi.[15]

Austro-Ottoman relations were based on a system of mutual knowledge between actors, and also on their common interests in the sound management of relations between the two empires.[16] Thus, the Ottoman merchants in Vienna quickly denounced Ömer Ağa's authoritarian attitude and the tax burden he imposed on them. Through Osman Efendi, these merchants turned to Penckler and placed themselves under his protection. By passing on the merchants' complaints and by defending their cause, Penckler gradually replaced Ömer Ağa until the latter was recalled from the consulate in 1731 by the Ottoman ambassador, Tavukçubaşı Mustafa Efendi, when he was on an official visit to Vienna. In the report that he prepared for his superiors, Tavukçubaşı Mustafa Efendi showed how important Prince Eugène was to the Viennese court, and emphasised the relationships he himself had developed with the nobility and with the young Penckler. Thanks to his experience in Vienna, Tavukçubaşı Mustafa Efendi was also able to negotiate the Peace of Belgrade in 1739 with Penckler.[17] In 1740, Penckler was appointed the Habsburg Resident in Pera, and then promoted to the rank of *internuncio*

[15] H. Wurm, 'Entstehung und Aufhebung des Osmanischen Generalkonsulats in Wien (1726-1732)', *Mitteilungen des Österreichischen Staatsarchivs* 42 (1992) 152-87; F. Hitzel (ed.), *Osmân Agha de Temechvar, Prisonnier des infidèles. Un soldat dans l'empire des Habsbourg*, Arles, 1998.

[16] Do Paço, *L'Orient à Vienne*, pp. 169-72. See also, M.W. Kaczka, 'The gentry of the Polish-Ottoman borderlands: the case of the Moldavian-Polish family of Turkuł/Turculeţ', *Acta Poloniae Historica* 104 (2011) 129-50; and M. Wasiucionek, *The Ottomans in Eastern Europe. Borders and political patronage in the Early Modern world*, London, 2019.

[17] F. Sanaç, 'Der Gesandtschaftsbericht Mustafa Efendis über die Gesandtschaftsreise nach Wien im Jahre 1730/31', Vienna, 1992 (PhD Diss. University of Vienna). See also V.H. Aksan, *An Ottoman statesman in war and peace. Ahmed Resmi Efendi, 1700-1783*, Leiden, 1995, pp. 24-9.

in 1748, a position he held until he was recalled to Vienna in 1755. On his return to Vienna, Penckler wrote two voluminous reports in which he detailed the Austrian diplomatic system established in Pera, and the multiple scholarly, political and merchant circles in which he had gradually gained acceptance.[18]

Ottoman diplomacy in central Europe also profited greatly from a network strengthened by family ties. Following his mission to Vienna, Tavukçubaşı Mustafa Efendi became *reisülküttab* in 1736. His *sefâretnâme* (mission report) had the appearance of a genuine treatise on European affairs and an accurate description of the affairs of the House of Austria. In 1747, he again wrote a report on the new Emperor Francis I (r. 1745-65), and thus prepared the way for his protégé Mustafa Hattî Efendi, who was sent to Vienna in 1748 to congratulate the emperor on his election. Mustafa Hattî Efendi in turn produced a *sefâretnâme* that clarified and updated the information given by his master. As Penckler would do in 1755, Tavukçubaşı Mustafa Efendi presented himself as essential in the conduct of the sultan's affairs because of his exceptional political knowledge concerning Vienna. In other respects, the *reisülküttab* strengthened his position by developing his patronage of young servants of the sultan. Mustafa Hattî Efendi came under his protection in 1737, having arrived in Istanbul in 1734. He married the daughter of Tavukçubaşı Mustafa Efendi in 1747, and appeared to be his legal and political heir. In turn, Ahmed Resmi Efendi came to prominence for his knowledge of the European political system, and continued his master's work after Tavukçubaşı Mustafa Efendi's death in 1749. Ahmed Resmi Efendi's mission to Vienna in 1758 equipped him to clarify the importance of the Austro-Prussian conflict to Mustafa III (r. 1757-73) and to prepare his mission to Berlin in 1763. Ahmed Resmi Efendi's reports stressed above all the necessity of keeping a check on the political life of the Holy Roman Empire, of which the House of Austria was a part, and therefore of engaging with the emperor's principal competitor, Frederick II of Prussia (r. 1740-86).[19] The opening up of Ottoman diplomacy towards Prussia also occurred in a family setting, as Ahmed Resmi Efendi was accompanied in 1763 by his brother-in-law, Ahmed Azmi Efendi, who had married a daughter of

---

[18] 'Succincter Bericht meines Pencklers Aufenthalt bey des Ottomanischen Pforte von Anno 1740 bis inclusive 1755', MS Vienna, Oesterreichisches Staatsarchiv (OeStA), Haus-Hof- und Staatsarchiv (HHStA) – Saatenabteilungen, Türkei V, 15.

[19] V. Aksan, 'An Ottoman portrait of Frederick the Great', *Oriente Moderno* 18/79 (1999) 203-15.

Mustafa Efendi and led the second Ottoman mission to Berlin in 1790, using networks established by Ahmed Resmi.[20]

The compartmentalisation of Ottoman diplomacy into family networks, in this respect very close to the system developed by the House of Austria, gradually left less space for informal agents than is recorded for the 17th century. Nevertheless, Ottoman ambassadors in Berlin established their diplomatic system by relying on the Latin, Jewish and Orthodox diasporas, and by involving in their delegation numerous Ottoman agents from different religions in order to expand the scope of their engagement and to ensure their resources were sufficient. Connected to the merchant world and serving as brokers of language, information and social links, Phanariots (members of prominent Orthodox families from the Phanar district of Istanbul) played a central role in the conduct of Ahmed Azmi's mission. These intermediaries were not, however, free agents, but were part of the patronage of Istanbul's Christian families, which was conducted as much through Christian ambassadors as through Ottoman dignitaries. The interpreter Constantine Karatzas, who served Ahmed Azmi in Berlin in 1790, was the son-in-law of John Fragopoulos, who had himself served as an interpreter to Ahmed Resmi Efendi in Berlin in 1763. All were heirs of the diplomatic system established by the *reisülküttab* Tavukçubaşı Mustafa Efendi.[21]

Vienna as the centre of Ottoman diplomacy in Europe

It was due to the multiple circles of belonging of which Ottoman political agents were part that Vienna became the centre of the Sublime Porte's diplomacy in Europe, in the second half of the 18th century. Until 1797, the 'imperial and royal court' was the place to which Ottoman embassies were sent for the ratification of a new peace treaty, to announce the

---

[20] Aksan, *Ottoman stateman*, pp. 24-6, 70-1. A.İ. Savaş, 'Der Gesandtschaftsbericht des Mustafa Hatti Efendi über die Gesandtschaftsreise nach Wien', Vienna, 1989 (PhD Diss. University of Vienna); G. Karamuk, *Ahmed Azmi Efendis Gesandtschaftsbericht als Zeugnis des osmanischen Machtverfalls und der beginnenden Reformära unter Selim III*, Frankfurt, 1975. See also, V. Aksan, 'Ottoman political writing, 1768-1808', *International Journal of Middle Eastern Studies* 25 (1993) 53-69.

[21] I. Fliter, 'From delegates to diplomats. The Ottoman diplomatic office in Prussia, 1763-1808', Tel Aviv, 2016 (PhD Diss. University of Tel-Aviv); C.A. Minaoglou, 'Entertainment instead of negotiations? The Ottoman embassy in Berlin (1791)', in G. Barth-Scalmani, H. Rudolph and C. Steppan (eds), *Politische Kommunikation zwischen Imperien. Der diplomatische Aktionsraum Südost- und Osteuropa*, Innsbruck, 2013, 275-88.

succession of a new sultan, or to congratulate a new sovereign.[22] Vienna
still competed with the courts of the King of Poland and the Elector of
Saxony, where Mehmed Efendi, Hacı Ali Ağa, and Şehid Osman Efendi
were respectively received in 1730, 1755, and 1757-8 to announce officially
the successions of Mahmud I (r. 1730-54), Osman III (r. 1754-7) and Mustapha III (r. 1757-74). However, the Seven Years' War (1756-63) relegated
Warsaw to a subsidiary place behind Vienna, St Petersburg and Berlin/
Potsdam.[23]

In 1741, the British ambassador in Vienna, Thomas Robinson, was
able to attract the attention of his minister in London, Lord Harrington,
regarding Janibi Ali Paşa's information networks:

> Turks need not have recourse to the Princes of Moldavia and Wallachia
> for constant informations of what is passing in Europe; there are other
> canals [channels] enough, and I know that the Swedes at the Porte have
> assured the Swedish Resident here that he may safely commit to the care
> of the Turkish Ambassador all that he has to write to them at Constan-
> tinople, and Monsr. Vincent [French agent] will not be wanting, I sup-
> pose, to make use of so sure a canal. That ambassador received not long
> ago from thence a Servant, whom he had dispatched upon the Emperor
> [Charles VI]'s Death, and having Letters by the same occasion from M.
> Höpken and Mr Carlson from Mr. Pingwigt [Swedish agents], the Turkish
> Interpreter, accompanied with about 20 Turks, waited publickly upon the
> Swedish Resident with them. They were dated so long ago as the 10th of
> December [...] the Day after Sir Guerard Fawkener wrote by Count Uhle-
> feld [the *internuncio*]'s former Courier, and confirmed the same advices, as
> if the Turks would suspend acknowledging the Queen till they should see
> what European Courts would do, particularly Sweden and France, which
> last Circumstance makes the long expected Letter from France of the more
> importance, as what, if once in the hands of this Court, might be made a
> good use of by Count Uhlefeld with the Turks.[24]

At the beginning of the War of the Austrian Succession (1740-8), the
Ottoman Empire's neutrality allowed Austria and its British ally to hope

---

[22] D. Do Paço, 'Trans-imperial sociability. Ottoman ambassadors in 18th-century
Vienna', in T.A. Sowerby and J. Hennings (eds), *Practices of diplomacy in the early modern
world*, London, 2017, 166-84. See also, Lewis, *Muslim discovery of Europe*, pp. 279-94.

[23] G.R. Berridge, 'Diplomatic integration with Europe before Selim III', in A.N. Yur-
dusev (ed.), *Ottoman diplomacy. Conventional or unconventional?*, London, 2004, 114-30;
V. Panaite, 'Islamic tradition and Ottoman law of nations', in Hasan Celâl Güzel et al.
(eds), *The Turks*, vol. 3. *Ottomans*, Ankara, 2002, 597-604; S. Yerasimos, 'Explorateurs de la
modernité. Les ambassadeurs ottomans en Europe', *Genèses* 35 (1999) 65-82.

[24] MS London, British National Archives – State Papers 80/144 (Thomas Robinson to
Lord Harrington, Vienna, 11 February 1741).

for a reversal of the conflict after the invasion of the Kingdom of Bohemia in 1740 by Prussia and Bavaria with France's support. The Ottoman
envoy who arrived in Vienna to confirm the Treaty of Belgrade in 1739
found himself facing a war of succession following the sudden death of
Charles VI (r. 1711-40) and the controversial claims of his daughter Maria-
Theresa to the crowns of Bohemia and Hungary.[25]

The daily reports written by the captains of the Habsburg guard on
Janibi Ali Paşa's activities show how the Ottoman delegation had become
part of Vienna's political and social life. From January to May 1741, the
delegation received the most influential European ambassadors, including those from France, Britain and Venice. Also mentioned were the
numerous representatives of German princes involved in the conflict,
and notably the agents of the Electors of the Palatinate, of Mainz and of
Saxony. Janibi Ali Paşa maintained Ottoman neutrality during the conflict by receiving both the emperor's supporters (the envoys of the Electors of Mainz and of Saxony) and those from Prussia and Bavaria (the
envoy of the Elector of the Palatinate). From Vienna, he also maintained
diplomatic ties with the envoys of the United Provinces and Venice.
From March onwards, meetings between the members of the Venetian
and Ottoman delegations were held weekly.[26]

Contrary to what the *sefâretnâme*s may imply, Ottoman diplomacy
actually relied on a variety of actors with very specific functions, as is
shown by the increasing size of the Ottoman embassies in Vienna. In
1718, there were close to 300 individuals, while in July 1740 the number
500 was mentioned in *La lettre historique et politique*. Joseph von Hammer-Purgstall gives more moderate figures, citing 100 people in 1748 and
only 50 in 1755, which also corresponds to the number of dignitaries
who served Hacı Ali Ağa in Warsaw the same year. Ahmed Resmi Efendi
was served by about 60 officials when he arrived in Vienna in December 1757, and by more than 70 'servants' when he left for Berlin in 1763.
The number of Ottoman agents in positions of responsibility who made
up the official delegation should, of course, be distinguished from the
number in the full delegation, including all the individuals in their service. The *Wienerishes Diarium* on 11 May 1774 lists an Ottoman delegation
in Vienna consisting of 69 people with functions linked to the catering

---

[25] B. Stollberg-Rillinger, *Maria Theresia, die Kaiserin in ihrer Zeit. Eine Biographie*,
Munich, 2017.
[26] 'Ein Journal über die Turkische Gesandschaft der Botschaftens Gianibi Aly Pasha
nach den Belgrader Frieden', MS Vienna, OeStA, HHStA – Türkei IV, 13.

trade, music or horse riding, making it far from easy to ascertain the group of assistants who served them.[27]

In such a company, the daily life of the delegation was not managed by the ambassador himself. In 1741, because of his military connections, the *chiaja* (marshal) appeared to be the preferred intermediary of the agents from the Vienna court. However, from 1755 it was the *divan efendi* who carried out the formal mediation between the Ottoman delegation and the court. In particular, he played an important role in the organisation of the ambassador's quarters and of official ceremonies. On these occasions, he was regularly accompanied by the embassy's imam, who ensured that the ceremonies conformed to Islam. In 1792, the *divan efendi*, Mustafa Bey, even became the preferred interlocutor of the agents of the Viennese court, relegating the ambassador Ebubekir Ratîb Efendi to a representative role. In comparison, the legation secretary of the Moroccan ambassador in Vienna in 1783 also appeared to be the most active diplomatic agent of the delegation, doubtless due to his linguistic capabilities. This evolution echoed the role played in 1791 by the dragoman Constantine Karatzas in Berlin. In place of the ambassador, he accompanied the *divan efendi* in his meetings with the Prussian Minister of Foreign Affairs.[28] This permanent reconfiguration of the Ottoman delegation partially reflected the movements of agents from one delegation to another, and depended on the specific skills of a particular agent. For example, the *divan efendi* of Ahmed Azmi Efendi was none other than Mustafa Bey. Other Ottoman dignitaries played a central role throughout the 18th century as treasurers, who in Vienna, as in Berlin, were in daily contact with Ottoman merchants throughout central Europe, as well as with local merchants and craftsmen. This activity shows how economic diplomacy was becoming increasingly important, which is particularly well illustrated by the Viennese sources dealing with the embassy of El Hajj Halil Efendi in 1755, the official purpose of which was to announce the accession of Sultan Osman III.[29]

The day-to-day activities of El Hajj Halil Efendi's delegation are well-documented in the report of the interpreter of Oriental languages at the

[27] S. Yerasimos, 'Le Turc à Vienne ou le regard inversé', in B. Rupp-Eisenreich and J. Stagl (eds), *Kulturwissenschaft im Vielvölkerstaat. Zur Geschichte der Ethnologie und verwandter Gebiete in Österreich, ca. 1780-1918*, Vienna, 1995, p. 33; Do Paço, *L'Orient à Vienne*, pp. 193-4; H. Topaktaş (ed.), *Lehistan'da Bir Osmanlı Sefiri. Ziştovili Hacı Ali Ağa'nın Lehistan Elçiliği (1755)*, Ankara, 2015; Aksan, *Ottoman stateman*, pp. 47, 70.

[28] J. Caillé, 'Une ambassade marocaine à Vienne en 1783', *Hespéris-Tamuda* 3 (1962) 35-42, p. 37; Minaoglou, 'Entertainment instead of negotiations?', p. 277.

[29] Do Paço, *L'Orient à Vienne*, pp. 194-6.

Viennese Court, Anton Seleskowitz-Binder. Although Ottoman ambassadors in Vienna and Berlin claimed to be relatively isolated – such as Ahmed Resmi Efendi when he left Berlin for Potsdam in 1763 – Seleskowitz allows us to reassess the actual activities of Ottoman diplomats in the cities they visited, including the patronage they exerted over the merchants of the Sublime Porte. By choosing to stay in the Viennese suburb of Leopoldstadt, rather than in a palace in the old town, El Hajj Halil Efendi made clear the priority of his embassy upon his arrival, which was to defend Ottoman merchants' interests, in parallel to participating in official negotiations. Seleskowitz emphasises this repeatedly. El Hajj Halil Efendi did not miss an opportunity to renew the petitions of merchants whom he himself supported or who were under the protection of Ottoman dignitaries such as the *paşa* of Belgrade. These merchants were not only Muslims but also Orthodox Christians, Jews and Armenians who had settled in Vienna following the Treaties of Karlowitz and Passarowitz and remained subjects of the Ottoman sultan. Seleskowitz emphasises further that even after his final official audience, the ambassador refused to leave Vienna before all the petitions that had been passed to him had been examined by the Austrian administration. As it turned out, the requests put forward by El Hajj Halil Efendi were almost always successful. The Viennese court even benefited from that year's Bayram celebrations to justify *ex gratia* the exceptional nature of its negotiations in favour of merchants from the Sublime Porte and at the expense of subjects of the emperor – such as Viennese merchants – or of the Imperial Treasury.[30]

Above all, the success of Ottoman diplomacy in the Habsburg court was mostly due to the ability of the principal members of the delegation to become part of Vienna's social circles. Together with this, the mediation of the Liechtenstein princes was essential in the 1740s. The Liechtensteins made up for Maria Theresa, by livening up the social life of the *Residenz*. According to the daily reports of the captains of the imperial guard, between the beginning of March and the beginning of May 1741 the Liechtenstein princes met Janibi Ali Paşa and the principal dignitaries around him 18 times. These meetings ranged from simple courtesy visits to walks in the gardens, from hunting parties to sessions in which

---

[30] 'Journal Oder Haupt Bericht Über alles das jenige, was sich mit dem von der Ottomanischen Pforte an des Kaÿserl : König : Hof-Laager im Jahr 1755 abgeschickten Gesandten El Hage Halil Efendi[...]', MS Vienna, OeStA, HHStA – Türkei IV, 3.

each tried riding the other's horses and learning the other's way of riding.[31]

Other evidence of this cross-cultural sociability can be found in Vienna and other central European cities throughout the 18th century. In 1755, the Ottoman ambassador in Warsaw, Hacı Ali Ağa, was entertained by the Polish aristocracy before returning to Wschowa, halfway between Warsaw and Dresden, where the king of Poland-Lithuania lived as the Elector of Saxony.[32] In Leopoldstadt, Ottoman dignitaries would stay until 1755 in the suburban palace of Count Ötting, a protégé of the Liechtenstein princes.[33] In 1792, Ebubekir Ratîb Efendi even stayed for some days in the Liechtensteins' garden palace, in Rossau suburb.[34]

The inclusion of Ottoman delegations in the life of the imperial palace was just like that offered to an ambassador from a Christian monarchy, and the Ottomans were neither excluded from the society of the court nor marginalised. The impression still regularly given by historians, that Ottoman ambassadors were isolated in the Vienna and Berlin courts, was essentially nourished by the *sefâretnâme*s, in which almost nothing about the social life of the embassies was noted. But the private papers of members of Ottoman embassies in Berlin in 1791, just like the reports of interpreters in Oriental languages from the Vienna court, show a degree of participation in society comparable to what was common for Vienna. In many respects, visits to palaces, universities, academies, churches, theatres, gardens and factories brought the social life of Ottoman agents in Vienna and Berlin close to that of young European aristocrats taking the Grand Tour.[35]

---

[31] MS Vienna, OeStA, HHStA – Türkei IV, 13; Do Paço, 'Trans-imperial sociability', pp. 173-6.

[32] Topaktaş, *Lehistan'da Bir Osmanlı Sefiri*.

[33] Do Paço, *L'Orient à Vienne*, pp. 194-6.

[34] MS Vienna, OeStA, HHStA – Türkei IV, 3.

[35] I. Fliter, 'The diplomats' debts. International finance disputes between the Ottoman Empire and Prussia at the end of the eighteenth century', *Osmanlı Araştırmaları / The Journal of Ottoman Studies* 46 (2016) 399-416; Do Paço, 'Trans-imperial sociability', pp. 173-81; Minaoglou, 'Entertainment instead of negotiations?', pp. 279-80.

The variety of Muslim diplomatic delegations

In addition to embassies from the Ottoman Empire, in the 18th century envoys from Muslim rulers in the Mediterranean also habitually travelled to Central European courts, notably from the regencies of Algiers, Tunisia and Tripoli, and from the Sultanate of Morocco.

The Mediterranean regencies have too readily been considered as vassal states of the Ottoman Empire, starting with Viennese diplomacy itself, which held the sultan responsible for the failure of North African privateers to comply with treaties. Although each of these regencies was linked in a personal and particular way to the Sublime Porte, it only exercised its authority over them to ensure they demonstrated their loyalty by paying taxes. Moreover, these regencies appear in practice to have been free to negotiate their own peace and trade treaties with foreign courts. It was in the middle of the 18th century, and in part due to Penckler's initiative, that envoys from Tunisia, Tripoli and Algiers came to Vienna in 1732, 1750 and 1758. The challenge for Charles VI and Maria Theresa was to enforce the imperial flag in the Adriatic and the Mediterranean in order to allow the development of the free port established in Trieste in 1719. For the Regencies, interest in negotiating with Vienna lay in opening up the ports at Trieste and Fiume to their trade, but also at Livorno, and in the North Sea at Ostend and Nieuwpoort. This trade economy was intended to be more attractive than open competition.[36]

The envoys of the Maghreb rulers were not all Muslims. For example, Hatschi Demeter Marcachi, who represented the Dey of Algiers in Vienna in 1758, was described by the *Wienerisches Diarium* of 25 October 1758 as a 'Greek by birth'. When he landed at Livorno on the west coast of Tuscany (of which Francis I, the Holy Roman Emperor, was Grand Duke) on 28 May, he was accused of being a renegade, though he was for the most part a merchant who had grown rich through trade between Algiers, Livorno and Trieste, following the implementation of a trade treaty in 1747 between the House of Austria and the Mediterranean Regencies. When he arrived in Vienna, Marcachi was 'dressed in Oriental Greek clothing, and instead of a turban, he wore a sable hat on his head'. His followers were Greek merchants from Livorno (including his cousin officiating as treasurer), who followed him 'on foot in Oriental Greek clothing'. He 'made his speech in the Turkish language'.[37]

---

[36] Do Paço, *L'Orient à Vienne*, pp. 202-5.
[37] Österreichische Nationalbibliothek, *Historische österreichische Zeitungen und Zeitschriften, Wiener Zeitung*, 25 October 1758, p. 9-10.

Just like Ahmed Resmi Efendi in Berlin the same year, Marcachi represented to Vienna the interests of both the Dey of Algiers and those of the Greek merchant diaspora to whom the dey had delegated a part of his trade and diplomatic activities. On his return to Livorno, Marcachi became the consul of the Greek nation, but he also became a client of the Habsburgs, from 1765 receiving an annual pension of 200 florins from Maria Theresa and her younger son Pietro Leopoldo of Tuscany. Maria Theresa justified this by citing 'the zeal which Marcachi had shown, [...] an honest and loyal minister', who worked for peace 'as much on the Barbary Coast as in the whole of the Levant'.[38]

In this way, the representatives of the Mediterranean regencies in Vienna acted as trans-imperial agents, whose sociability was similar to that of the Ottomans. Their embassies were official and followed the same protocol as the ambassadors of the Sublime Porte, with the exception that they were not officially received by the emperor, since that would amount to recognising their independence from Istanbul. If in 1750 the dey of Tripoli's envoy, Hassan Efendi, complained about not having an opening audience with Francis I, he was compensated by an unannounced visit by the emperor and empress to his theatre box. This box being easily visible to the audience, the public witnessed this meeting *incognito*, which maintained protocol without offending either the dey of Tripoli or the sultan of Istanbul.[39] Following the example of the Ottoman ambassadors in Vienna, Warsaw and Berlin, the envoys of the Regencies to the imperial court in Vienna were also welcomed into the circles of aristocratic and ministerial Viennese society, and visited the most prominent attractions, from the gardens to the baths in Baden via the theatres.[40]

The Moroccan embassy of 1783 led by Muḥammad ibn ʿAbd al-Malik was completely different in character. The ambassador, recognised as such, was in this case the governor of Tangier and the brother-in-law of Muḥammad III (r. 1757-90) – again, family structured foreign affairs.

[38] C. Piazza, 'L'agente dei Algeri a Livorno (1758-1765)', in C.L. Jacono (ed.), *Scritti in memoria di Paolo Minganti*, Cagliari, 1983, 475-512.

[39] 'Bericht vorinnen umständlich angemerkt was sich beÿ Gelegenheit des im Jahr 1750 an dem Kaiserlichen Hof-Lager gewesenen Tripoliner Gesandter Hasan Efendi', MS Vienna, OeStA, HHStA, Obersthofmeisteramt – Tripoliner Gesandschaft am Kaiserlische Hof, 1750, p. 37.

[40] S. Suner, 'Of messengers, messages and memoirs. Opera and the eighteenth-century Ottoman envoys and their *Sefâretnâmes*', in M. Hüttler and H.E. Weidinger (eds), *Ottoman empire and European theatre*, vol. 2. *The time of Joseph Haydn. From Sultan Mahmud I to Mahmud II (r.1730-1839)*, Vienna, 2014; Minaoglou, 'Entertainment instead of negotiations?', p. 285.

His mission was to open trade between Tangier and the Netherlands, and also the Adriatic ports under Habsburg control. More widely, the embassy was part of the Moroccan policy of opening up the country to trade. In 1778, Muḥammad ibn ʿAbd al-Malik established a first connection with the House of Austria during a visit to Livorno, from where he returned with a first trade treaty between the Moroccan sultanate and Pietro Leopoldo. The matter of the embassy in Vienna was developed in 1780, when the governor returned to Tangier. Arriving at the beginning of January 1783 in Trieste, Muḥammad ibn ʿAbd al-Malik was supported by Emmanuel Isidore Tassara, former Resident in Pera between 1777 and 1779 and brother-in-law of the *internuncio*, with links to the Austrian minister of foreign affairs. The Moroccan ambassador was therefore supported by agents of the family of the vice-chancellor of state, Philipp von Cobenzl.[41]

Muḥammad ibn ʿAbd al-Malik's stay in Vienna gained a very positive response, and it was partly due to this that he was received by the finest families of the city. The *Gazette d'Amsterdam* on 18 March 1783 reported:

> The reigning Prince of Liechtenstein threw a magnificent Ball to all the nobility and which the Moroccan Ambassador and more than 500 people attended. The rooms were magnificently illuminated; there was a sort of elevated stage, where the ambassador was sitting [...]. The dinner was served at midnight on twenty different tables.[42]

A slightly earlier issue of the *Gazette* stresses Muḥammad ibn ʿAbd al-Malik's liking for 'the European way of living', as 'he ordered that the apartments reserved for him be furnished with chairs, sofas, high tables and beds in the French style'.[43] The *Courrier de l'Europe* emphasises that:

> The ambassador of Morocco is now what concerns us the most in this capital: it is difficult to be more sensitive and more affable to the good practices of this African minister, who despite the opposition of our customs to his, is open to all with the ease of a man of wit and even a courtier. We can see moreover every day that this lord is very commendable by his principles of morality, and that his acquaintances go beyond expectations for the country he lives in. He is particularly excited about our arts which

---

[41] Caillé, 'Une ambassade marocaine', pp. 35-42; D. Do Paço, 'A social history of transimperial diplomacy in a crisis context: Herbert von Rathkeal's circles of belonging in Pera, 1779-1802', *International History Review* 41 (2019) 981-1002; M. Fendri, 'Nouveaux documents sur l'ambassade marocaine à Vienne en 1783 dans la presse européenne', *Hespédis-Tamuda* 52 (2017) 287-339.

[42] *Gazette d'Amsterdam*, 18 March 1783, supplément.

[43] *Gazette d'Amsterdam*, 14 March 1783.

inspired him to make some very fine observations which demonstrated great insight.[44]

Entering the circles of Viennese sociability was planned and encouraged by the imperial court, but it was also made possible by the Moroccan ambassador's entourage, notably his legation secretary, the merchant Muḥammad Mahdī l-Ḥajj, and other followers, Christians and Jews converted to Islam and speaking Italian.[45]

Conclusion

By the end of the 18th century, agents of Muslim delegations who were working closely with the ambassador, officially or otherwise, had become the preferred interlocutors of the Christian courts. They embodied the ability of a delegation to operate in multiple social circles. This evolution also characterised a clearer division of roles between representation and negotiation. These agents mobilised the resources from their different circles of influence at the service of the ambassador and the ruler they served and represented. They also conducted diplomacy in the interest of their own career or affairs. These resources comprised contacts who possessed linguistic, social, political and cultural knowledge, and with the expertise and capacity to access information. They were drawn from diplomatic, aristocratic, scholarly, religious and merchant circles. The 18th century was also marked by a stronger institutionalisation of the agents' function, with roles that could be more informal than in the previous century. They were rewarded with titles and ranks, and they helped the delegations fit into the societies they encountered without giving up their primary and principal activity as merchant or scholar. Through their activities, these agents of empire demonstrated an integration of political societies in different religious frameworks. Such integration characterised the social space on which the empires' diplomacy rested and which developed throughout the century from 1718. The history of the diplomatic agents of Muslim rulers in central Europe invites us to write the history of another Europe, which continues to be too artificially reduced to its Christian component only.

---

[44] *Courrier de l'Europe*, 4 April 1783.
[45] Caillé, 'Une ambassade marocaine', p. 36.

Ottoman influences on European music, part 2

A. Yunus Gencer

Introduction

This is a continuation of the essay entitled *Ottoman influences on European music* in *CMR* 10, which briefly examines the history and characteristics of Turkish music and focuses on the influence of the Ottomans on European music to the mid-18th century. This second part covers the period from the mid-18th to the early 20th century. During this time, there was a crescendo, followed by a decrescendo, in the frequency and intensity of Ottoman-related concepts being utilised by European composers, with a climax occurring in the works of Wolfgang Amadeus Mozart (1756-91). After Mozart's death, as Europeans came into contact with various other 'exotic' cultures, and as Ottoman power declined further in the 19th century, *Ottomania* slowly but steadily died away. As it was dying, a reverse influence began, this time Europe being the influencer, and the 'eternal state' being the influenced. The reigns of reforming sultans such as Mahmud II (r. 1808-39) and Abdülaziz (r. 1861-76) saw increasing interest in European culture and music, as well as the reforming of the military bands (Janissary *mehteran*), which were the main element that had influenced European composers in the first place. Following the collapse of the empire, the succeeding Turkish Republic made considerable efforts to Westernise the music scene in the country. It not only founded new conservatoires and orchestras solely devoted to teaching and playing European classical music, but went so far as to forbid Turkish classical and folk music education in its music institutions from 1926 to 1976.

Alla turca *in the classical period*

The creative application of Ottoman themes in French baroque music[1] was followed in Vienna by a well-known composer of the early classical period, Christoph Willibald Gluck (1714-87). He employed

---

[1] In the works of J.B. Lully and J.P. Rameau.

Ottoman-influenced material in his *La rencontre imprévue* ('The unex-
pected encounter'), composed in 1763,[2] which may have been one of the
most Turkish-sounding operas until Turks themselves started composing operas. First, in this work all the main characters have Middle Eastern names, such as Ali, Balkis, Amine and Osmin: the character Osmin
is the servant of the protagonist Ali, who is trying to save his beloved
Rezia from the sultan's harem. Ali and Rezia plan to escape from the
harem disguised as pilgrims to Mecca, which hints at the original title
of the libretto of the opera.[3] Second, there is extensive use of piccolos,
triangles and other percussion instruments, and of 'left... left... left, right,
left' rhythms. Third, Gluck ventures into the world of scale manipulation
as he aims to create a Turkish sound, which is truly extraordinary for
his time. For example, in the melodic line in the aria *Castagno, cast-
agna – je vous demande pardon*, he uses many G-sharps descending from
B-flats, and C-sharps descending from E-flats, forming melodic lines with
a diminished 3rd interval, which is the defining characteristic of some of
the most used *makam*s in Turkish music, including one of the daily calls
to prayer. The raised 4th interval occurs in two pentachords that are used
to make up *makam*s; both *nikriz* and *pencgah makam*s constitute a raised
4th interval, while the first also has a flat 3rd. It is possible to lay *hicaz* tet-
rachord over the *nikriz* pentachord to come up with a scale very similar
to what Gluck was using. So could it be possible that he heard this scale
in a diplomatic ceremony, or in some way obtained solid information
about the characteristics of Turkish music? Furthermore, the orchestra
plays completely in unison at the beginning of the aria, mimicking the
monophonic (or heterophonic) texture of Turkish music. It is fascinating
to see how dedicated Gluck is in creating a Middle Eastern flavour.

Joseph Haydn (1732-1809) also composed music for the same subject as Gluck's opera, using the Italian version and naming it *L'incontro
improvviso* (1775).[4] Haydn was one of the first composers to notate the
percussion parts properly in the score.

Like Gluck, Antonio Salieri (1750-1825) played with pitch alteration
in his overture to *Axur, re d'Ormus*,[5] composed and premiered in 1787.
He raises the G to G-sharp in a D major setting, thus using a raised 4th
degree. This, according to American musicologist Thomas Bauman, is

---

[2] Its libretto was written by the French librettist Louis Hurtaut Dancourt.

[3] Alain-René Lesage's 1726 *comédie en vaudevilles* with the title *Les pèlerins de la
Mecque* ('The pilgrims to Mecca') was adapted into an opera libretto by Dancourt.

[4] It was translated to Italian by the Austrian librettist Karl Frieberth.

[5] *Axur* is a reworked Italian version of *Tarare*, which is in French.

one of the important elements in mimicking Turkish (non-tonal) sound for the European composer.[6] In the overture to the same opera's French version, which is titled *Tarare*, Salieri composes a melodic line that starts from C and descends from B to A-flat, creating an augmented 2nd interval. This is also reminiscent of various *makam*s. Lastly, there is a lot of spoken speech in this opera-comique which points to the *Singspiel* genre. *Singspiel* was very popular in *Burgtheater*,[7] and Mozart composed a few such works, including *Die Entführung aus dem Serail*, which is important in understanding his approach to *alla turca*.

Mozart seriously flirted with *alla turca* in his Fifth Violin Concerto in A Major (K. 219) of 1775. In the middle section of the third movement, the metre changes from 3/4 to 2/4, preparing for the quintessential rhythmic structure of the Janissary music that is to come. At this point, the key changes to A minor, cellos and double basses start playing *col legno*,[8] and unison chromatic crescendos empower the tension. The shift in this sequence of the concerto forms a great contrast to the preceding and following sections.

In *Die Entführung aus dem Serail*, Mozart explores further clashes between cultures through music. From his correspondence with his father, it is known that he was familiar with Gluck and his music,[9] and there is a possibility that the revival of Gluck's *La rencontre imprévue* in 1780 may have motivated Mozart to write this *Singspiel*.

The subject of slavery was very important in operas featuring Turkish characters in the 18th century (e.g. *Die Entführung*). The main reason for this would have been the Barbary corsairs,[10] Muslim pirates who were especially active in 16th and 17th centuries and, according to historian Robert C. Davis' estimate, between 1530 and 1780 captured and enslaved about 1,250,000 Europeans.[11] The Barbary States were mainly present-day

---

[6] See T. Bauman, *W.A. Mozart. Die Entführung aus dem Serail*, Cambridge, 1987, pp. 62-5.

[7] Austrian National Theatre.

[8] Mozart's actual indication on the score is *coll'arco al rovescio*.

[9] See R. Spaethling, *Mozart's letters, Mozart's life*, New York, 2006, pp. 293, 302, 346.

[10] Two of the most notorious corsairs who operated under the Ottoman Empire were Hızır Hayreddin Barbarossa and his brother Oruç Barbarossa.

[11] See art. 'British slaves on the Barbary Coast' on the website of the BBC – History by R.C. Davis, http://www.bbc.co.uk/history/british/empire_seapower/white_slaves_01. shtml. For a more comprehensive work on the topic, see R.C. Davis, *Christian slaves, Muslim masters. White slavery in the Mediterranean, the Barbary Coast, and Italy, 1500-1800*, Basingstoke, 2004. As Davis hints in his BBC article, the chorus section of *Rule Britannia*, a famous British patriotic song by Thomas Arne composed in 1740, is of

Tunisia, Algeria and Libya, at the time vassals of the Ottoman Empire, and also Morocco. Slaves captured and taken to the Barbary towns would often be taken on to some of the biggest cities in the Empire, such as Constantinople, so the operas were actually based on fact. What is fascinating though, is that most of them are comedies and they do not completely condemn the Turks, and even find good in some of them.

In *Die Entführung*, Mozart uses bass drum, cymbals, triangle and piccolo for the Turkish sound and, as Haydn did before him, notates them properly on the score. Salieri in his *Tarare* (1787) utilises the same setting in the overture, with the exception of piccolo – an instrument he loathed.[12] In *Die Entführung*, the overture and Janissary choir are set in the key of C major, the major key relative to A minor. Osmin's aria *Solche hergelau'fne Laffen* begins in F major but ends in A minor (*Erst geköpft, dann gehangen*), and at the end, when he interrupts the vaudeville, he again sings in A minor. Osmin's repetitive and vigorous melodies may be intended to signify the stubborn and unyielding nature of the Middle Eastern man in Mozart's mind.

In addition to *Die Entführung*, maybe Mozart's best-known Turkish-influenced piece is the last movement *alla turca* (Turkish march) of his Piano Sonata no. 11, composed in 1783. The substantial Turkish element in this piece is the *mehter* marching rhythm. At the time, some pianos enabled the utilisation of Janissary stops to enhance the percussive quality of the sound. These stops created a bell-like sound, and were popular from the late 18th to the mid-19th century. Mozart starts the piece in A major, as he had in his violin concerto, but when he arrives at the Turkish-influenced section he changes the key to A minor.

C.F.D. Schubart (1739-91) in his *Ideen zu einer Ästhetik der Tonkunst*[13] writes: 'F major and B-flat major seem to be the favourite keys of the Turks because the range of all their instruments coincides best in these keys. Meanwhile, we Germans have also made successful experiments

---

historical importance in relation to the events that were taking place in the Mediterranean because, among other things, the lyrics also signify British defiance against the Muslim corsairs.

[12] As the Paris Opera was reviving *Tarare* in 1818, Salieri wrote a letter to the director of the Opera, Louis-Luc Loiseau de Persuis, stating: 'Above all, do not allow the piccolo, music's shame, to be played in my operas, not even in foreign dance airs'; see J.A. Rice, *Antonio Salieri and Viennese opera*, Chicago IL, 1998, p. 393.

[13] T.A. DuBois, 'Christian Friedrich Daniel Schubart's *Ideen zu einer Ästhetik der Tonkunst*, an annotated translation', Los Angeles CA, 1983 (PhD Diss. University of Southern California).

with D major and C major from which the great importance of Turkish music becomes apparent.' It is intriguing to see that Mozart may have connected in his mind the key of A minor (relative of A major) and Turkishness as well. It is probable that he imagined the clash of Eastern and Western cultures as the clash between A major and A minor keys. Using C major in the Janissary choir section at the end of *Die Entfüh-rung* might constitute the 'good Turk's' attributes, especially embodied by Bassa Selim. Schubart's claims are supported further by Beethoven's choice of the key of B-flat major for his *Turkish march*, and a short section of the last movement of the Ninth Symphony, which has a Turkish flavour. Also, Gluck's choice of A major for the overture of *La rencontre imprévue* strengthens the idea that European composers of the time were inclined towards picking a tonic (centre) in that area for Turkish-inspired compositions.

Seeing Mozart's output with numerous Turkish-influenced pieces might be thought to support the notion that he listened to actual Turkish music. However, there is disagreement among musicologists on this issue and, according to the German musicologist Kurt Reinhard, who specialised in the field of Turkish music, Mozart's biographers do not say whether he listened to Turkish music.[14] Reinhard went further in his research to refine and summarise the characteristics of Turkish music, and he came up with 14 of them: continuity of duple metre, marked accents on strong beats, loud dynamics, simple rhythmic patterns and repeated notes in the accompaniment, rudimentary harmony, repetition of sounds that creates a *bordun* effect,[15] doubling of the sung melodic line by octaves, Oriental ornaments, thirds as melodic outline, sequences in the melody, creation of pockets of scales as a result of these sequences, short motifs, multiple repetitions of motifs, and duple/triple sequences created by the repetition of motifs. The Israeli musicologist Benjamin Perl argues that the aria *Fin ch'han dal vino* from Mozart's *Don Giovanni* 'has ten of these fourteen characteristics', and writes 'odd as it may sound, Don Giovanni's aria is in a sense more "Turkish" than most compositions recognized under this label'.[16] This is important, for it shows how these

---

[14] K. Reinhard, 'Mozarts Rezeption türkischer Musik', in H. Kuhn and P. Nitsche (eds), *Bericht über den internationalen musikwissenschaftlichen Kongress Berlin 1974*, Kassel, 1980, 518-23.

[15] Repeatedly playing the 1st and 5th, while omitting the 3rd of a specific chord.

[16] B. Perl, 'Mozart in Turkey', *Cambridge Opera Journal* 12 (2000) 219-35.

'Turkish' elements are merged into composers' creational processes even without any obvious Turkish subject-matter.

The Haydn brothers[17] Joseph and Michael both dived into Turkish musical conventions in their respective creative worlds. Joseph Haydn's Symphony no. 100 (1793), nicknamed 'the military symphony', has a distinctive *alla turca* sound in its second movement, for which he uses triangle, cymbal and bass drum for the first time. Furthermore, the C major key at the start changes into C minor when the percussion instruments start playing, after which he experiments with them in major sections as well. Just before the conclusion of the symphony, in the fourth movement, percussion instruments return for a powerful and effective ending. Joseph's younger brother Michael composed a *marcia turchesca* which is in cut time (duple metre) and in C major, using cymbals and drum, and maintaining the strong 'left... left... left, right, left' beat structure almost throughout. This marching rhythm structure is a common denominator of the 'Turkish' atmosphere in many classical works.

Originally composed for the piano as one of the themes in his six *Variations on an original theme* in 1809, Beethoven's orchestral arrangement of the *Turkish march* was then used as incidental music in the play *The ruins of Athens* in 1811.[18] Beethoven also uses piccolo, triangle, cymbals and bass drum, along with the Janissary march rhythm. He makes use of the same instrumentation in *Wellington's victory* (1813) and in the last movement of the Ninth Symphony ('*Froh, wie seine Sonnen*'), showing that by this time the characteristics of Janissary music were absorbed into European culture and could easily be used in different contexts. It should also be mentioned that in *Froh, wie seine Sonnen* Beethoven uses 6/8 metre, which is still duple but differs from 2/4 in having two groups of triplets. This is an imaginative reframing of the by this time long-lasting tradition of using duple metres in *alla turca* sections.

---

[17] Haydn's paternal grandparents were nearly killed by the invading Ottoman army in Hainburg in 1683; most of their fellow-citizens did not survive the attack. See G. Feder and J. Webster, art. 'Haydn, (Franz) Joseph', in S. Sadie and J. Tyrell (eds), *The new Grove dictionary of music and musicians*, London, 2001.

[18] The Turkish marches of Mozart, Haydn (Symphony no. 100, second movement) and Beethoven have grace note figures that are part of the principal melody. It may be that they were trying to project the uncommon pitch elements and/or the heterophonic quality in Eastern music.

The fading of Ottomania *and reverse influence*

The Age of Discovery and the Enlightenment provided Europeans with 'others' who came from places different from the vast Ottoman Empire to the east. This was the first blow to the Turkish vogue in Europe. The second was the progress of science and social reforms in Europe, and the failure of the Ottomans to keep up with them, which would eventually make the empire 'the sick man of Europe'. The industrial revolution pushed Western civilisation even further ahead, forcing other cultures into a passive state, unable to compete, and downtrodden both physically and culturally. It is clear from historical accounts and the actual deeds of some of the Ottoman sultans that they felt this way, and understood the need to reform. The first sultan who made this attempt was Selim III (r. 1789-1807). He ignited the torch of progress, but in the end he paid the ultimate price at the hands of revolting Janissaries. Although the conservative establishment successfully installed a reactionary sultan, Mustafa IV (r. 1807-8), on the throne, his reign ended in failure after only one year, and another reform-minded ruler, Mahmud II (r. 1808-39), succeeded.

It was especially during Mahmud's reign that true and long-lasting steps were taken towards Westernisation. The conservative Janissary corps was abolished in 1826, and the *mehteran* was disbanded in 1828. In its place a new, European-style military band was founded with the name of *mızıka-ı hümayun*,[19] and Italian composer Giuseppe Donizetti[20] was invited to oversee its training. Along with this job, Donizetti Pasha played a significant role in Westernising the music scene in the palace and among the high society of Constantinople. Furthermore, he played host to prominent virtuosi from Europe, including Franz Liszt, Leopold de Meyer, Eugene Vivier, Henri Vieuxtemps, Augute d'Adelburg and Elias Parish Alvars. Their visits and performances were made possible by the support of the Sublime Porte. Following Donizetti's death in 1856, another Italian composer, Callisto Guatelli, was invited to take his place. Guatelli also stayed in charge of *mızıka-ı hümayun* until his death in 1899, with an interim between 1858 and 1868.

Another important change occurred in musical notation in the 19th century. As previously discussed in Part 1 of this essay, music was taught

---

[19] The sultan's musical band.
[20] For a comprehensive biography of the composer, see E. Aracı, *Donizetti Paşa. Osmanlı sarayının İtalyan maestrosu*, Istanbul, 2006.

orally through *meşk*, and performers rarely used notation. When they did use it, it was just to remind themselves of the main sections of a piece they already knew. The first system to be used was the *ebced* notation system, which dates back to Abū Yūsuf Ya'qūb al-Kindī in the 9th century.[21] Over a long period of time, other notation systems were developed by various composers such as Ali Ufkî Bey, Kantemiroğlu, and Hampartsum Limondjian. It was Limondjian's *Hamparsum* notation (named after himself)[22] that Donizetti had to learn when he arrived in Constantinople, though he continued to employ European notation in his compositions. Eventually, towards the end of the 19th century, standard Western notation became the norm, and it was fully adopted in the conservatoires of the new republic in the 20th century.

The fervour of reform endured through the reigns of the succeeding sultans Abdulmejid I (r. 1839-61), and Abdülaziz (r. 1861-76), so much so that the empire entered into a period called *Tanzimat*, which would pave the way for the first constitutional era in 1876. Although the reforms to democratise the country were stopped and an absolute monarchy was reintroduced with the ascension of Abdul Hamid II (r. 1876-1909) to the throne, the need for European expertise was indisputable. So, Abdul Hamid kept educational reforms going and founded the *Darülfünun* in 1900 (later known as the University of Istanbul). He had founded the *Sanâyi-i Nefîse Mektebi* in 1882 (later known as Mimar Sinan Fine Arts University), the first fine arts school in the country, and he appointed the distinguished painter Osman Hamdi Bey as its director. Both these schools have conservatoire departments which still provide some of the best musical education in Turkey. Abdul Hamid II, was personally fond of *alla franga* (European style) music, and commanded operas to be performed in his palace.

The empire declined even further during the Balkan Wars and the Great War. Eventually, the Turkish War of Independence was fought and the new Turkish Republic was founded. Its founder, Mustafa Kemal Atatürk, initiated a series of reforms that were aimed to push the country 'above the level of civilised nations'. In the field of music, *mızıka-ı hümayun* was restructured into a full symphony orchestra in 1924 and took the name Cumhurbaşkanlığı Senfoni Orkestrası (CSO, 'Presidential Symphony Orchestra'), making it one of the oldest orchestras in

---

[21] See A.H. Turabi, art. 'Kindî, Ya'kub b. İshak', in *DİA*.
[22] Read from left to right, as opposed to earlier notations.

the world.[23] The new Westernised 'symphonic Turkish sound' was pioneered by composers who had been educated in Europe, the Turkish Five,[24] Ahmet Adnan Saygun, Cemal Reşit Rey, Ulvi Cemal Erkin, Hasan Ferit Alnar and Necil Kazım Akses. Most of them taught in conservatoires. Furthermore, to organise and institutionalise musical education, the government invited the German composer Paul Hindemith to Turkey in 1934, and the first state conservatoire was founded in Ankara in 1936.[25] In 1948, the government enacted a statute to send exceptionally gifted young people to Europe to receive education there. At the same time, talented and well-educated Jewish scholars and musicians who had escaped from Nazi Germany and were granted asylum further improved musical education in Turkey. In the second half of the 20th century, decisions taken in these years would yield many Turkish composers and performers, such as İdil Biret, Suna Kan, Gürer Aykal and İlhan Usmanbaş, instructed in Western music and renowned all over the world.

Conclusion

When it comes to tracing Turkish musical influences in Europe, it is possible to say that there is a line to be followed. It might be a little vague at some points, but it is definitely there: from Lully, to his heir Rameau, to French-enthusiast Gluck, to Haydn, who basically copied Gluck before he reached the point of writing his Symphony no. 100, to Mozart, who was connected with both Gluck and Haydn and knew their music very well, to Beethoven and beyond. The role played by Gluck in bringing this line to Vienna and showing creative minds that it could be successful is immensely important. His approach was both progressive and innovative, opening up numerous possibilities in terms of mixing sounds from different origins and different worlds in the name of drama.

It is important to note that it was in the Turkish sections of their music that European composers almost exclusively took risks, whether in Osmin's interruption of the vaudeville towards the end of *Die Entführung* or in Gluck's first act of *Iphigenie* ending with only one short divertissement in *alla turca* style. This was because these sections let the

---

[23] See art. 'History' on the website of the Presidential Symphony Orchestra, https://www.cso.gov.tr/history.html.

[24] See Y. Aydın, *Türk Beşleri*, Istanbul, 2003; Ü. Deniz, *Milli Musiki ve Türk Beşleri*, Istanbul, 2015.

[25] Béla Bartok also came to Turkey for ethno-musicological research and toyed with the idea of settling there.

composers think of the dramatic qualities of the sound as well as its tim-bre. The world they were picturing opened up new doors for their cre-ativity rather than bowing to the mundane. The mystery of the unknown allowed them to give free rein to their capabilities.

Obviously, European composers in the classical period were not com-posing genuine Turkish music. They were creating sounds that are *alla turca*, Turkish inspired, or it may be better to say, Middle-Eastern, Otto-man-inspired, since at that time they called everyone from that region a Turk. A pinch of Middle Eastern flavour added a lot of imagination, creativity and wonder to their work, invigorated the sound they created, and helped carry it to eternity.

Works on Christian-Muslim relations

1700-1800

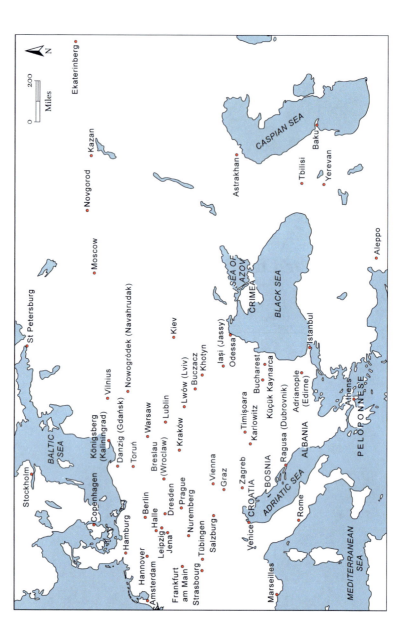

Map. Central and Eastern Europe

German and Habsburg states

Gottfried Wilhelm Leibniz

DATE OF BIRTH 1 July 1646
PLACE OF BIRTH Leipzig
DATE OF DEATH 14 November 1716
PLACE OF DEATH Hannover

BIOGRAPHY

Widely considered to be one of the greatest thinkers in modern Euro-pean philosophy, Gottfried Wilhelm Leibniz spent the first 20 years of his life in his native Leipzig, acquiring a degree in law at the university there before eventually leaving it to embark upon a career of public service – working at the courts and offices of various electors and aristocrats, most notably the Duke of Brunswick at the House of Hannover, where Leib-niz would spend the remaining 40 years of his life. Famous for so many ideas and inventions – his notion of the 'Monad', his contribution to the invention of calculus, his various attempts to construct a universal language, not to mention the 'best-of-all-possible-worlds' argument for which Voltaire would mock him in *Candide* – Leibniz travelled widely throughout Europe and conversed with some of the finest minds of his age – Spinoza, Newton, Malebranche and the mathematician Huygens.

Although Leibniz only really dedicated one text wholly to the Islamic Orient, his *Consilium Aegyptiacum* ('Egyptian plan') of 1671, a wide array of remarks and references to Islam and Muslims throughout his life occur in his letters, tracts and essays. These generally fall into three categories: a political interest in Islam, a philological curiosity, and a theologically-motivated concern.

Politically, Leibniz's interest in the Ottomans grows as Mehmed IV's (1648-87) armies lay siege for the last time to Vienna – and fades as Otto-man power recedes from the region. Leibniz's remarks in this period (really ending in 1692) not only see the Turks as a generally backward, proletarian, anti-intellectual rabble, but also (strikingly) fail to comment for the most part on the Islamic faith of the Ottomans. In terms of theol-ogy, Leibniz – as a believing Christian – saw Islam initially in quite nega-tive terms, but as time goes on (certainly by the time of the *Théodicée* in 1710) he appears to concentrate on the aspects of Islam (such as anti-idol-atry) that overlap with Christianity. Leibniz's desire, in particular, to find a translation of the Qur'an made by a layman, not by a priest, reflects a theological curiosity in Islam which seems gradually to overshadow an initial antipathy to the rival religion. Again, this more neutral attitude only starts to emerge after 1697 – once the Ottomans are no longer a major presence in the Balkans.

The final aspect of Leibniz's interest in Islam – his philological approach – is perhaps the most interesting. It is tied to his search for the 'Adamic' language; by the end of the 1690s, we find him conversing with Orientalists such as the Swede Johan Gabriel Sparwenfeld to try and get versions of the Lord's Prayer in Arabic, Persian and Turkish, and to obtain more information about the Islamic Orient in general – for example, on the genealogy of Muḥammad or the *oeuvre* of Arab scholars such as Ibn Khallikān and Ibn Khaldūn. It runs in some ways parallel to an interest in China that he had started to develop, even though his expectations of an interaction between China and Europe far exceeded what he thought Europeans might learn from the Islamic world.

MAIN SOURCES OF INFORMATION

Primary

G.W. Leibniz, *Sämtliche Schriften und Briefe*, ed. Deutsche Akademie der Wissenschaft, Berlin, 1923

G.W. Leibniz, 'Quelques reflexions sur la guerre', in *Sämtliche Schriften*, vol. 4, pt 2, p. 613

G.W. Leibniz, *Philosophical writings*, ed. G.H.R. Parkinson, London, 1973

G.W. Leibniz, *Gottfried Willhelm Leibniz*, ed. F. Heer, Frankfurt, 1958

P.J. Riley (ed.), *Leibniz. Political writings*, Cambridge, 1988

P. Remnant and J. Bennett (eds), *New essays on human understanding*, Cambridge, 1989

G.W. Leibniz, *Philosophical papers and letters*, ed. L.E. Loemker, Dordrecht, 1989

G.W. Leibniz, *Theodicee*, Berlin, 1996

Secondary

J.E.H. Smith, *Divine machines. Leibniz and the sciences of life*, Princeton NJ, 2011

I. Almond, *History of Islam in German thought from Leibniz to Nietzsche*, New York, 2010, see esp. pp. 6-29

I. Almond, 'Leibniz, historicism and the "Plague of Islam"', *Eighteenth-Century Studies* 39 (2006) 463–83

F. Perkins, *Leibniz and China. A commerce of light*, London, 2004

N. Jolley (ed.), *The Cambridge companion to Leibniz*, Cambridge, 1995

A.P. Coudert, *Leibniz and the Kabbalah*, Dordrecht, 1995

D.J. Cook, 'Leibniz's use and abuse of Judaism and Islam', in M. Dascal and E. Yakira (eds), *Leibniz and Adam*, Tel Aviv, 1993, 283–97

E.J. Aiton, *Leibniz. A biography*, Bristol, 1985

WORKS ON CHRISTIAN-MUSLIM RELATIONS

Consilium Aegyptiacum
'Egyptian plan'

DATE 1671-2

ORIGINAL LANGUAGE Latin

DESCRIPTION

Leibniz's *Consilium Aegyptiacum* ('Egyptian plan') is a tract of nearly 200 pages, written in Latin, divided into three sections (*Regi Christianissimo, Justa dissertatio* and *Breviarium*), which attempts to persuade the French King Louis XIV (r. 1643-1715) to attack Ottoman Egypt instead of his European neighbours. It was written by Leibniz at the age of 24, and is a surprisingly well-prepared and considered argument for an invasion. Although Leibniz says at the beginning that his proposal is 'to the profit of Christendom' (*pro profectu religionis Christianae*), what follows is a material analysis of the region – although scholars have disputed the various motivations Leibniz had for proposing an invasion of Egypt (see Strickland, 'Leibniz's Egypt plan'). Religion and a very worldly desire for power are blended together. Cynically, one could say the *Consilium Aegyptiacum* is a treatise that begins with a promise to Christianise the East, ends with the declaration that 'never was God's honour and our own more narrowly intertwined', and spends large amounts of text in between describing naval facilities, army sizes, grain stores and trade routes. In the second part, it is clear that part of Leibniz's hopes in a French invasion would be to create a sense of Christian solidarity among the (currently) warring European nations. Leibniz also hopes to bring Christianity back to Asia and Africa, and ease the oppression of Christians already there, even cultivating the hope that Christians in Ottoman lands will rise up against the empire there.

His description of Turkish and Egyptian believers is not flattering; in some parts of the *Consilium* he seems to suggest the Orientals do not have any religion at all (*Sämtliche Schriften und Briefe*, vol. 4, pt 1, p. 393): 'It will be necessary to wave a bag of booty to persuade the Arabs to join our side', for 'it is foolish (*stultum*) to believe that these people are guided by religion' (p. 395). The plan is quite detailed: Leibniz describes the Turks' armies and the Egyptian soldiers, detailing their in/efficiency and their motivations to fight, and then goes on to describe the effects such a war would have on France's European neighbours. In the final section, the emphasis seems to shift onto the ecumenical benefits of combatting the Turks, rather than the actual destruction of the Ottomans themselves.

SIGNIFICANCE

The *Consilium Aegyptiacum* throws an interesting light on a number of points in Leibniz's attitude towards the Islamic East and the Christian Europe he juxtaposed to it. Most obviously, it shows how even at an early age, he was actively engaged in the research of non-European cultures. Some fairly detailed (albeit exaggerated) descriptions of Ottoman intrigues, Middle Eastern geography and Arab resentment against their Turkish masters attest to an already extant familiarity on the young Leibniz's part with travel accounts and ambassadorial reports. The conscious use of history in the *Consilium* as a pragmatic tool of legitimation is also striking. 'This project', Leibniz tells us, 'has always been attractive to the greatest and wisest men as the sole means of re-establishing (*restaurandum*) the interests of Christianity in the Orient' (*Sämtliche Schriften und Briefe*, vol. 4, pt 1, p. 383). The word *restaurandum* is instructive; Leibniz is careful to contextualise historically his proposal partly to be able to supply precedents such as Caesar and Alexander the Great, but more importantly to sell the *Consilium* not as an invasion but a restoration.

PUBLICATIONS

Gottfried Wilhelm Leibniz, *Consilium Aegyptiacum*, 1671

Gottfried Wilhelm Leibniz, *Consilium aegyptiacum. Mémoire sur la conquête de l'Égypte*, trans. A. Vallet de Viriville, Paris, 1672 (French trans.)

Gottfried Wilhelm Leibniz, *A summary account of Leibnitz's Memoir, addressed to Lewis the Fourteenth: Recommending to that monarch, the conquest of Egypt, as conducive to the establishing a supreme authority over the governments of Europe*, London, 1803 (abridged English trans.)

Gottfried Wilhelm Leibniz, *Mémoire de Leibnitz, à Louis XIV, sur la conquête de l'Égypte*, Paris, 1840 (French trans.)

Gottfried Wilhelm Leibniz, *An account of the 'Consilium Aegyptiacum', written by Leibnitz: under the auspices of the elector of Mayence, and presented to Louis XIV*, London, 1850 (abridged English trans.)

Gottfried Wilhelm Leibniz, *Leibnitii De expeditione Aegyptiaca: Ludovico XIV Franciae Regi proponenda scripta quae supersunt omnia adjecta praefatione historico-critica*, ed. O. Klopp, Hannover, 1864

Gottfried Wilhelm Leibniz, *Consilium Aegyptiacum*, in *Sämtliche Schriften und Briefe*, ed. Deutsche Akademie der Wissenschaft, Berlin, 1923, vol. 4, pt 1, 220-399

Ahmed Youssef, *La fascination de l'Egypte. Du rêve au projet*, Paris, 1998 (includes the text of 1672 edition of *Consilium Aegyptiacum*)

STUDIES

L. Strickland, 'Leibniz's Egypt plan (1671-1672). From holy war to ecumenism', *Intellectual History Review* 26 (2016) 461-76

Almond, *History of Islam in German thought*

I. Budil, 'Gottfried Wilhelm Leibniz and the idea of conquest of Egypt in the context of the emergence of the European world economy', in A. Skřivan (ed.), *Prague papers on history of international relations*, Prague, 2009, 65-86

P. Ritter, *Leibniz' Aegyptischer plan*, Darmstadt, 1930

Ian Almond

Abraham a Sancta Clara

Ulrich Megerlin; Ulrich Megerle; Johann Ulrich Megerlin;
Johann Ulrich Megerle

DATE OF BIRTH   Before 3 July 1644
PLACE OF BIRTH   Kreeheinstettin, Swabia
DATE OF DEATH   1 December 1709
PLACE OF DEATH   Vienna

BIOGRAPHY

Abraham a Sancta Clara was born in 1644 as Johann Ulrich Megerlin
(Megerle) in the village of Kreeheinstetten in Swabia. He received his
early education at the Latin school in nearby Mösskirch. Probably with
the assistance of his uncle, canon of Altötting and court composer to the
archbishop of Salzburg, Ulrich continued his studies at the Jesuit school
in Ingolstadt from 1656 to 1659 and at the Benedictine *gymnasium* in
Salzburg from 1659 to 1662. In 1662, he arrived in Vienna and became a
novice at the Discalced Augustinian monastery at nearby Mariabrunn.
In 1663, he made his vows as a member of the order and took the name
'Abraham a Sancta Clara'. After travelling to Prague and Ferrara, he
returned to Vienna in 1665 and was ordained priest in 1666. Sent by his
order to Taxa, a pilgrimage site near Augsburg, from 1670 to 1672, Abraham gained favourable attention for his preaching. Returning to Vienna,
he gained the title of Doctor of Divinity prior to his appointment as a
preacher at the court of Emperor Leopold I (r. 1658-1705) by 1677.

Despite his position and his access to the imperial family, Abraham
seems to have avoided participation in court politics or policymaking.
He became prior of his monastery in Vienna in 1680, but he left Vienna
for Graz by early 1683 and became prior there in 1686. He served as provincial of the Discalced Augustinians from 1689, and became subprior of
the Mariabrunn monastery near Vienna in 1694. Abraham returned to
the Discalced Augustinian monastery in Vienna in 1695, and delivered
his last sermon nine months before his death in Vienna in 1709.

Abraham a Sancta Clara was known as one of the most prominent German Catholic preachers and writers of his time. He was fluent in Latin,
had some knowledge of Hebrew and Greek, and delivered occasional

guest sermons in Italian in his later years. Several of his works praised the Habsburgs, including the sermons *Astriacus Austriacus* (1673) and *Prophetischer Willkomm* (1676). He frequently criticised the morals of all ranks of society, illustrating his sermons and publications with numerous colourful stories, rather than focusing on social or political reforms. His preaching followed traditional rhetorical patterns rather than creating new styles, although he was credited with deploying the German language very effectively to move his noble and common audiences.

His work *Mercks Wienn* (1680) commemorated the severe plague of 1679 and admonished the Viennese to better morals. Abraham was in the city for the initial outbreak, although he lived the last five months of the epidemic in the palace of a government official. He was in Graz during the Ottoman campaign against Vienna in 1683, but his major publication on Islam and the Ottoman Turks, *Auff auff ihr Christen!*, appeared just prior to the siege. Other major works included the four volumes of *Judas der Ertz-Schelm* (1686-95), a review of the pilgrimage site of Taxa, *Gack, Gack, Gack, Gack à Ga* (1685), and *Huy! und Pfuy! der Welt* (1707).

MAIN SOURCES OF INFORMATION

Secondary

A.P. Knittel (ed.), *Unterhaltender Prediger und gelehrter Stofflieferant. Abraham a Sancta Clara (1644-1709)*, Eggingen, 2012

P.S. Fichtner, *Terror and toleration. The Habsburg Empire confronts Islam, 1526-1850*, London, 2008

J. Schillinger, *Abraham a Sancta Clara. Pastorale et discours politique dans l'Autriche du XVIIᵉ siècle*, Berne, 1993

F.M. Eybl, *Abraham a Sancta Clara. Vom Prediger zum Schriftsteller*, Tübingen, 1992

M. Arndorfer, *Abraham a Sancta Clara. Eine Ausstellung der Badischen Landesbibliothek und der Wiener Stadt- und Landesbibliothek*, Karlsruhe, 1982

W.F. Scherer, 'Through the looking glass of Abraham a Sancta Clara', *Modern Language Notes* 85 (1970) 374-80

F. Maurer, *Abraham a Sancta Claras "Huy! und Pfuy! der Welt". Eine Studie zur Geschichte des moralpädagogischen Bilderbuches im Barock*, Heidelberg, 1968

R.A. Kann, *A study in Austrian intellectual history. From late Baroque to Romanticism*, New York, 1960

WORKS ON CHRISTIAN-MUSLIM RELATIONS

Auff, auff Ihr Christen!
'Arise, arise you Christians!'

DATE   July 1683
ORIGINAL LANGUAGE   German, with some Latin

DESCRIPTION

Auff, auff Ihr Christen! is Abraham a Sancta Clara's most extensive pub-
lication related to Islam and the Ottoman Turks (its full title is *Auff, auff
Ihr Christen! Das ist: Ein bewegliche Anfrischung der Christlichen Waffen
Wider Den Türckischen Bluet-Egel; Sambt Beygefügten Zusatz vieler her-
rlichen Victorien und Sieg wider solchen Ottomannischen Erb-Feind;
Wie auch andere Sittlicher Lehr- und Lob-Verfassung der Martialischen
Tapfferkeit*, 'Arise, arise you Christians! which is: a moving re-invigora-
tion of the Christian weapons against the Turkish bloodsucker, together
with an accompanying supplement of many glorious victories against the
said Ottoman hereditary enemy; also other noteworthy and praiseworthy
moral conditions of martial courage'). The Viennese printer Johann von
Gehlen dated the 181-page work on 8 July 1683, just prior to the Ottoman
siege of Vienna. Abraham had been in Graz since the beginning of the
year and must have completed the work there, away from the main theatre of conflict. It was printed at least in Vienna and Salzburg in 1683 and
again in 1684, with a subsequent printing in Salzburg in 1687. Abraham
included the treatise in his collected works, published in 1684 and 1687.
Numerous figures endorsed it, including members of the theology faculty
and the rector of the University of Vienna, the consistory of Salzburg, and
Abraham's superiors in the Discalced Augustinian order. He dedicated
the work to the nobles of Styria, praising them for being on the front line
of the Habsburg war effort.

Abraham divided the treatise into 12 sections, usually ten to 15 pages
each, of which the first and 11th sections are most pertinent for his discussion of Islam. In the first section, Abraham gives a biographical description of Muḥammad in traditional Christian polemical terms. He describes
him as the son of a sorcerer and a Jewess, who poisoned his master in
order to inherit his business, and then conspired with a Nestorian monk
named Sergius, an Arian named John, and some Jews to construct the
Qur'an. Abraham clearly disapproves of some of Muḥammad's teachings,
especially on marriage, and he mocks the death of Muḥammad, claiming
that his corpse was torn apart by dogs.

In the 11th section, he characterises Islam as a heretical mix of Judaism, Christianity, Arianism and Nestorianism, yet he favourably describes Islamic practices such as ritual washing, devotion in prayer, almsgiving and fasting. He does not give a comprehensive account of Islam, but uses these points to comment on the morals and piety of Christians. For example, he praises the strict fasting practised by Muslims, and bemoans the numerous exceptions to the fasting rules manipulated by Christians. Turkish temperance is contrasted with German loose living.

The second, third, fifth, sixth, and eighth sections discuss the Ottoman Turks most directly, particularly regarding previous wars between Christians and the Ottomans. Abraham lists several medieval and early modern wars, including the fall of Constantinople, the conquest of Famagusta (in Cyprus) and the battle of Lepanto, and also comments on the brutality of Ottoman armies and their reliance on Christian disunity. Rather than providing a strict account of events, he refers to them briefly to make a larger point about Christian sinfulness.

Illustration 3. Title page of Abraham a Santa Clara, *Auff, auff Ihr Christen!*

The discussion of historical events is often meandering and not always in chronological order. Occasional praise of Ottoman administration is given, such as when Abraham notes how the Ottomans punished injustice in their lands. Remaining sections of the work consider what Christians could do to support the military effort against the Ottoman Turks.

Auff, auff Ihr Christen!, only one small item in Abraham a Sancta Clara's published corpus, introduces little new information about Islam or the Ottoman Turks. When citations are provided, they display his rather conventional knowledge of Islam and the Ottoman Turks, drawn from medieval and early modern accounts and themes. The same can be said about his comments. He relies on traditional histories such as Laonicus Chalcocondyles, Martin Crusius, Leonicus Cuspinianus and Gregory of Tours. In addition, he uses the first-hand 16th-century accounts of the captive Bartholomaeus Georgievicz and the diplomat Ogier de Busbecq, neither of which was new in the *Turcica* genre in the late 17th century.

Despite this, the work is important for demonstrating larger themes in Abraham's output. Significantly, it lacks the harsh confessional polemic towards Protestants that marked the Turkish works of earlier Catholic preachers in Austria. Whereas late 16th- and early 17th-century preachers regularly linked Islam to Protestant teachings as well as to Judaism, Abraham fails to do so in a systematic or even overt manner, despite his strong Catholicism and the anti-Judaism expressed in his other works. Rather than focusing on Protestant errors, he uses the Ottoman threat to promote his moral programme. Christian sin has allowed the Muslims and the Ottoman Turks to conquer so many lands, he remarks; just like B following A, the T of the Turks follows the S of sin. Abraham dedicates an entire section to the morality of soldiers, urging them to live good lives in order to have success against the Ottomans. This campaign for improved morals was a hallmark of Abraham's preaching and writing.

Auff, auff Ihr Christen! also displays Abraham's emphasis on astrology. In addition to using the preface to refer to signs foretelling the downfall of the Islamic and Ottoman Empires beginning in 1683, Abraham uses an entire section to review the signs preceding various wars with the Ottomans. Finally, he also uses the opportunity of the Ottoman threat to bolster support for the Habsburg dynasty, noting the past leadership of the Austrian house in fighting Islam and urging Germans, Austrians and Hungarians to rally under the Habsburg sceptre and behind the true Church.

SIGNIFICANCE

The work did have some impact on German authors. Eberhard Werner Happel used it in his *Ungarische Kriegs-Roman* of the late 1600s, and it also formed the basis for a section of Friedrich Schiller's play *Wallensteins Lager*. Schiller even modelled one of his characters in the play on the Discalced Augustinian. It is also highly likely that later authors used the book as a source of historical information, as they did Abraham's other works. In the preface, Abraham specifically remarks that he has attempted to be as historically accurate as possible.

PUBLICATIONS

Abraham a Sancta Clara, *Auff auff Ihr Christen*, Vienna, 1683; bsb10457504-5 (digitised version available through *MDZ*)

Abraham a Sancta Clara, *Auff auff Ihr Christen*, Salzburg, 1683

Abraham a Sancta Clara, *Auff auff Ihr Christen*, Salzburg, 1684; 2BZ157704705 (digitised version available through Österreichisches Nationalbibliothek)

Abraham a Sancta Clara, *Reimb dich/ oder ich liß dich/ das ist: allerley materien/ discurs, concept, und predigen/ welch bißhero in underschidlichen tractätlen gedruckt worden*, Salzburg, 1684 (Abraham a Sancta Clara's collected works containing *Auff auff Ihr Christen*)

Abraham a Sancta Clara, *Auff auff Ihr Christen*, Salzburg, 1687; 2BZ1559835002BZ157704705 (digitised version available through Österreichisches Nationalbibliothek)

Abraham a Sancta Clara, *Reimb dich/ oder ich liß dich/ das ist: allerley materien/ discurs, concept, und predigen/ welch bißhero in underschidlichen tractätlen gedruckt worden*, Salzburg, 1687 (Abraham a Sancta Clara's collected works containing *Auff auff Ihr Christen*)

Abraham a Sancta Clara, *Auff auff Ihr Christen*, ed. A. Sauer, Vienna, 1883

STUDIES

Fichtner, *Terror and toleration*, pp. 61-4

Schillinger, *Abraham a Sancta Clara*, pp. 240-7

Eybl, *Abraham a Sancta Clara*, pp. 277-82

Kann, *Study in Austrian intellectual history*, pp. 74-6

Paul Strauss

Matthias Friedrich Beck

DATE OF BIRTH   23 May 1649
PLACE OF BIRTH   Kaufbeuren (in modern-day Bavaria)
DATE OF DEATH   2 February 1701
PLACE OF DEATH   Augsburg

BIOGRAPHY

Matthias Friedrich Beck was born in 1649 in the small Swabian free imperial town of Kaufbeuren, where his father, Matthias Beck served as a pres-
byter. He attended the Latin school in nearby Memmingen and in 1660
moved to the Latin school in Augsburg. Beck enlisted at the University of
Jena in 1668, where he studied, among others, with Johannes Frischmuth
(a former student of the Altdorf Orientalist Theodoricus Hackspan) and
engaged in a study of Arabic and Persian. Having graduated as *magister
atrium* in 1670, he returned to Augsburg and then back to Jena in 1673 to
pursue his studies and work as an adjunct teacher in the philosophical
faculty. In 1677, he was appointed Lutheran minister in Augsburg, and
this was followed by a series of ecclesiastical appointments in the city,
where he would spend the rest of his life. In 1682, Beck married Rosina
Kaltschmidt, who was to survive him. The couple had nine children, of
whom three daughters and two sons survived their father.

Even by the standards of his day, Beck was a versatile and prolific
scholar. He mastered Hebrew, Arabic, Aramaic, Syriac, Samaritan, Ge'ez,
Persian and Turkish, and was best known to contemporaries for his
achievements as an Orientalist. Apart from his annotated edition of two
Qur'an suras, discussed below, his oriental interests included the ancient
Aramaic translation of the Old Testament (*Paraphrasis Chaldaica I &
II*, 1680/3), Jewish epigraphy in Augsburg (*Monumenta antiqua judaica*,
1686), and Persian calendars (*Ephemerides Persarum*, 1695). To these
can be added his work on medieval ecclesiastical chronicles (*Martyrolo-
gium ecclesiae germanicae*, 1687). Eighteenth-century sources claim that
among his unpublished papers could be found further works pertaining
to oriental scholarship, as well as an unpublished edition he had prepared of the famous travel account of the 12th-century Iberian Jew, Benjamin of Tudela, and a Russian-Latin lexicon. Beck received a pension
from the Prussian King Friedrich I (r. 1701-13).

While the breadth of Beck's learning was remarkable, the fact that a respected Orientalist such as he should pursue an ecclesiastical career was not. Beck was among several one of numerous notable Orientalists who were also Lutheran ministers, including his contemporaries August Pfeiffer, Andreas Acoluthus and Abraham Hinckelmann.

MAIN SOURCES OF INFORMATION

Primary

J.B. Luhn, *Matthiae Friderici Beckii, V.D.M. apud Vindelicos vita munereque sancti tou nunen hagiois memoria*, Wittenberg, 1703

G. Jöcher, *Gelehrten-Lexikon*, Leipzig, 1750

G.A. Will, 'Nachricht von den Schriften Matthias Friedrich Becks', *Literarisches Museum* 2 (1780) 376-417

Secondary

J.F.L.T. Merzdorf, art. 'Beck, Matthias Friedrich', in *Allgemeine Deutsche Biographie*, Leipzig, 1875, vol. 2, p. 218

WORKS ON CHRISTIAN-MUSLIM RELATIONS

Specimen arabicum
'An Arabic sample'

DATE   1688

ORIGINAL LANGUAGE   Arabic and Latin

DESCRIPTION

Beck published his *Specimen arabicum*, the Arabic text of Sura 30 (*al-Rūm*, 'the Romans', or 'Byzantium') and Sura 48 (*al-Fatḥ*, 'The victory') in 1688, under the full title *Specimen arabicum, hoc est, bina capitula Alcorani xxx. De Roma & xliix. De Victoria, e iv. codicibus mss. Arabice descripta, latine versa, & notis animadversionibusque locupletata. His nostris temporibus, quibus Imperium Romano-Germanicum Victorias contra Muhammedanos prosequitur, accommodatum argumentum* ('An Arabic sample, i.e. two short chapters from the Qur'an, 30 "Rome" and 48 "Victory", transcribed in Arabic from four hand-written codices, translated into Latin and adorned with notes and comments. An apt argument in these our times, in which the Roman-Germanic Empire is pursuing victories against the Mohammedans'). Owing to the lack of Arabic printing type, the qur'anic text was produced in Hebrew transliteration – a not uncommon typo-graphical solution at the time. Like several other 17th-century Arabists who published samples of the Qur'an, Beck presented here the text of a small portion accompanied by a Latin translation and commentary. Though several translations of the Qur'an were available in print at the time (most of them not made from the original Arabic), the text of the entire Qur'an would only become available in print in the 1690s (Hinck-elmann, 1694 and, more importantly, Marracci, 1698).

For this work, Beck used four Qur'an manuscripts that were available to him in Augsburg. Like other qur'anic *specimina*, his was a work writ-ten in Latin by a scholar for fellow scholars, although it stands out for its visible embeddedness in current affairs, namely the Great Turkish War, which was raging at the time – the clash between the Habsburg-led Holy League and the Ottomans, which witnessed the second siege of Vienna

Illustration 4. Matthias Friedrich Beck, *Specimen Arabicum*, the beginning of the Arabic text of *Sūrat al-Fatḥ* in Hebrew characters, with Latin translation

(1683) and the decisive victory of the Holy League, which changed the balance of power between the Ottoman Empire and the European powers.

Beck's native Swabia contributed to the Habsburg war effort, sending soldiers and officers from Augsburg, who supplied Beck with Ottoman manuscripts and artefacts they had seized. Thus, the year before publishing the *Specimen arabicum*, Beck had published *Abbild- und Beschreibung deß Türckischen Haupt-Fahnens* (1687), a short work on an Ottoman flag seized by Swabian forces in the successful siege of Nové Zámky (Neuhäusel) in southern Slovakia. This Ottoman flag was inscribed with the opening verse of Sura 48, which is included in Beck's *Specimen*. At least rhetorically, Beck advertised his work as a scholarly contribution to the war effort. Just as the imperial forces were opposing the 'Turkish tyrant', so should Christian scholars wage a war of the intellect against Muḥammad and the Qur'an. But while there are numerous polemical comments in Beck's commentary, his *Specimen* is by no means restricted to anti-Muslim polemics.

It is hardly surprising that *Sūrat al-Rūm*, in which a future victory of the Roman Empire (Byzantium) is foretold at the outset, suggested itself for translation at a time when the Holy Roman Empire was waging war against its Ottoman adversary. This being said, Beck is careful to provide the 7th-century context of the set-back suffered by the East Roman Empire in its prolonged struggle with the Sassanids, blaming the ambiguous syntax of the opening verse on sophism, a Delphic equivocation meant to guarantee the truthfulness of the pretended prophecy, whatever the outcome. The monotheistic solidarity this sura offers fails to impress the Augsburg minister.

Beck's learned commentary on both suras makes patent his indebtedness to the availability of Ottoman manuscripts brought back to Augsburg as spoils. Thus, for example, in discussing *subḥāna llāhi* ('praise be to God') in Q 30:17, apart from referring readers to Jacob Golius's Arabic lexicon, he also refers to a parallel use of the phrase in a Turkish prayer book recently seized in Buda, which was placed at his disposal by a Catholic nobleman in Augsburg. Augsburg was a biconfessional Lutheran and Catholic city, and, despite his being a Lutheran minister, some of his prized informants were Catholics.

In commenting on Sura 48, *al-Fatḥ* (The victory), Beck is only marginally interested in the original historical context (the Treaty of al-Ḥudaybiya between Muḥammad and the pagan Meccans). As with Sura 30, in his commentary here he gives numerous references to previous Western scholarship, most notably to Robert of Ketton's 12th-century translation of the Qur'an and Nicholas of Cusa's 15th-century *Cribratio Alcorani*, as well as to the 17th-century Orientalist Johann Heinrich Hottinger. Noting that Robert of Ketton numbered this as Sura 58 (rather than 48), Beck quotes Nicholas of Cusa in pointing out the discrepancy in chapter division between the Eastern and Western (i.e. Iberian) Muslims.

Interestingly, Beck translates the term *sakīna* (Q 48:4) not as safety or tranquillity, as his predecessors had done, but as *Spiritus Dei*, corresponding to the Hebrew *shekhina*, which he claims was adopted into Arabic from the Hebrew or Aramaic. This, to Beck's mind, vindicates the Christian teaching on the three distinct persons of the Trinity, as in this verse (the indisputable author of which for him is Muḥammad) God claims to have bestowed the Holy Spirit on believers. A further instructive polemical note is struck in Beck's comment on Q 48:23, where the qur'anic text stresses the immutability of God's way (*sunnat llāh*). For Beck, this is no less than a diabolical mimicry of Isaiah 40:8 ('the word of our God shall stand forever'). Muḥammad, Beck fulminates, was mimicking his masters, the Jewish scholars, who wished to portray Mosaic Law as immutable. This condemnation of Muḥammad's claim ends with a damning quote from the ninth of Maimonides' *Principles of faith*, in which the medieval Jewish philosopher postulates the immutability of Mosaic Law. This demonstrates how entangled anti-Jewish and anti-Muslim polemics were in the minds of many early modern Christian Orientalists. As with Beck's Hebrew and Jewish scholarship, so with Arabic and the Qur'an his accomplished scholarship was an intrinsic part of a polemical culture. However, this presented no impediment to his studies, which by the standards of his day, were highly accomplished and went far beyond inter-faith polemics.

A decade after Beck's *Specimen*, Ludovico Marracci's milestone Qur'an appeared. The famous scholar Gottfried Wilhelm Leibniz himself expressed hopes for a Qur'an translation undertaken by a Protestant scholar, and for a while it seemed that Beck might be the person to carry out this task (Hamilton, 'Lutheran translator'). This was not to be.

SIGNIFICANCE

While the basic approach of Beck's work to the Qur'an and Islam follows the tradition of inter-faith polemics and relies on earlier works such as Nicholas of Cusa's *Cribratio Alcorani*, it is also indicative of the expanding horizons of European knowledge about the Qur'an and the Muslim world in general. In addition, it illustrates the immediate historical context, the

Great Turkish War (1683-99) and the interest in Islam it helped foster among broader circles of non-specialists, who provided Beck with manuscripts. This work is an example of the scholarly uses and resonances of Oriental manuscripts circulating in early modern Europe, acquired as spoils of the wars with the Ottoman Empire. Beck's command of Arabic was impressive by the standards of his day, although his Arabic scholarship was still traditionally tied to that of Hebrew – not only in producing the qur'anic text in Hebrew transliteration for lack of Arabic type, but also through his Hebraising understanding of certain Arabic terms such as *sakīna*. His censure of Muslim teaching in his commentary is closely associated with his rejection of Jewish teaching. Both the polemics and the genuine curiosity and expanding knowledge about the Muslim world here form an integral part of the traditional, theologically directed Oriental studies, of which, despite the paucity of his published writings, Beck is an impressive representative.

PUBLICATIONS

Matthias Friedrich Beck, *Specimen arabicum, hoc est, bina capitula Alcorani xxx. De Roma & xliix. De Victoria, e iv. Codicibus mss. Arabice descripta, latine versa, & notis animadversionibusque locupletata. His nostris temporibus, quibus imperium Romano-Germanicum victorias contra Muhammedanos prosequitur, accommodatum argumentum*, Augsburg, 1688; 4 A.or. 415 (digitised version available through *MDZ*)

Luhn, *Matthiae Friderici Beckii, V.D.M.* [...] *memoria*; 4 Diss. 172#Beibd.6 (digitised version available through *MDZ*)

Will, 'Nachricht von den Schriften Matthias Friedrich Becks'; Eph.lit. 151-2 (digitised version available through *MDZ*)

STUDIES

A. Hamilton, 'A Lutheran translator for the Quran. A late seventeenth century quest', in A. Hamilton, M.H. van den Boogert and B. Westerweel (eds), *The republic of letters and the Levant*, Leiden, 2005, 197-221

Asaph Ben-Tov

Sebastian Gottfried Starck

DATE OF BIRTH	1668
PLACE OF BIRTH	Brand near Freiberg, Germany
DATE OF DEATH	1710
PLACE OF DEATH	Berlin

BIOGRAPHY

Sebastian Gottfried Starck (or Starcke) was born in 1668 in the village of Brand, where his father was the Lutheran preacher. From the age of 12, he studied at the Fürstenschule in the nearby city of Meissen, and then spent four years at the University of Leipzig, where he defended his thesis in 1690. He subsequently travelled to Holstein, where he had been appointed tutor to two young noblemen whom he was to accompany to France. The departure was delayed, however, and he made instead for Hamburg. There, on the recommendation of the influential Leipzig jurist Friedrich Benedict Carpzov, he encountered Abraham Hinckelmann, the pastor of the St Katharinenkirche, who was preparing an edition of the Qur'an in Arabic. Starck remained with him for two years, learning Arabic, describing Hinckelmann's library, which included some 70 Arabic codices and over 50 Persian ones, as well as material in Hebrew, Ethiopic, Russian and Japanese, and assisting him with his edition of the Qur'an, which appeared in 1694.

Hinckelmann, who died in 1695 at the age of 43, was impressed by Starck. He praised him highly in the introduction to his Qur'an, dwelling on the integrity of his character, his precocious knowledge of literature, and his competence as an Arabist. He thus ensured for him a name in the republic of letters.

Starck published his catalogue of Hinckelmann's oriental manuscripts and, on the advice of the scholar and diplomat Ezechiel Spanheim, moved to Berlin. In 1696, he was instructed to catalogue the Arabic manuscripts in the electoral library and was authorised to lecture on Hebrew, Greek and Arabic and on other cultural topics. In the following year, he issued a bilingual edition, in Greek and in his Latin translation, of the collection of fables attributed to Bidpai and known in the Arab world as *Kalīla wa-Dimna*. The text, which originated in India, was translated first into Persian and Arabic – Hinckelmann possessed a copy of the Arabic version – and Starck had laid his hands on a Greek version that had once belonged to the antiquarian Lucas Holstein. He dedicated his *Specimen sapientiae Indorum veterum* to Frederick III, Elector of Brandenburg, and pleaded in his introduction for a greater knowledge and appreciation of the fables of the East. His reputation in the republic of letters was thus further consolidated. Leibniz had already mentioned him as one of the most promising young German Arabists in a letter to the Swedish orientalist Johann Gabriel Sparwenfeld in January 1697, and in December, after reading Starck's edition of *Kalīla wa-Dimna*, he remarked on it in a letter to the Italian scholar Antonio Magliabechi. In 1698, Starck was appointed principal of the Berlin Gymnasium zum Grauen Kloster, and in the same year he published a specimen translation of Sura 19 of the Qur'an, *Maryam, Specimen versionis Coranicae, adornatum in Caput XIX*, which he had started to prepare some four years earlier when he was staying with Hinckelmann.

In 1701, the elector of Brandenburg was crowned Frederick William I, King of Prussia (r. 1713-40). Starck, who had been elected to the newly founded Sozietät der Wissenschaften, completed his description of oriental manuscripts in the royal library, and in 1705 was accorded the title of royal librarian. He was also given the chair of oriental languages at the Swedish university at Greifswald. He married in Greifswald, but three years later, in 1708, he left the university, where he had never had many students, and was appointed head of the Ritterschule in Brandenburg. His health, however, was declining. He consequently returned to Berlin to take up his appointment as librarian, but died on 20 June 1710.

Starck was noted for his piety and for his habit of studying the Bible every morning in his spare time. In 1697, however, he revealed a considerable pettiness when he savagely slandered a fellow scholar, Andreas Acoluthus, whom Spanheim had also set to work on a description of the electoral manuscripts, and whom Starck feared as a rival. Starck thereby forfeited Spanheim's favour and incurred the disapproval of the republic of letters whose rules of courtesy he had infringed. Yet, even if the poor quality of his sample Qur'an translation led contemporaries such as the Dresden librarian Siegmund Gottlob Sebisch to dismiss him as an Arabist, his reputation as a scholar remained high and he continued to exhibit his versatility. Shortly before his death, he translated John Locke's *Some thoughts concerning education* (1693) into German. He also prepared an unpointed edition of the Hebrew Old Testament, apparently intended for prospective students of rabbinic literature and of Samaritan. It was published in 1711, the year after his death, by the court preacher Daniel Ernst Jablonski, who paid tribute to Starck's 'literary merits'.

MAIN SOURCES OF INFORMATION

Primary

A. Hinckelmann, *Al-Coranus S. Lex Islamitica Muhammedis, filii Abdallae Pseudoprophetae*, Hamburg, 1694, sigs. u1v.-2r

[S.G. Starck], *Bibliotheca manuscripta Abrahami Hinckelmanni, Doctoris theologiae, de Ecclesia Christi reque literaria, dum viveret, optime meriti, sicuti pleraque ex parte constat ex codicibus orientalibus*, Hamburg, 1696

S.G. Starckius, *Specimen sapientiae Indorum veterum, id est liber ethico-politicus pervetustus, dictus arabice, Kalila wa-Dimna, Graece Stephanitēs kai Ichnēlatēs*, Berlin, 1697

S.G. Starckius, *Specimen versionis coranicae, adornatum in Caput XIX. quod inscribitur Caput Mariae*, Cölln, 1698

D.E. Jablonski (ed.), *Biblia Hebraica non-punctata*, Berlin, 1711

J.H. Zedler (ed.), art. 'Starcke (Sebastien Gottfried)', in *Grosses vollständiges Universal-Lexicon aller Wissenschafften und Künste* [*Zedler's Universal lexicon*], Leipzig, 1744, vol. 39, col. 1245

C.H. Tromler, 'Leben und Schriften des Hrn. Andreas Akoluth, weil. Predigers und Professors zu Breslau, und der Königl. Preuß. Akad. der Wissenschaften Mitglieds', *Neue Beyträge von Alten und Neuen Theologischen Sachen, Büchern, Urkunden, Controversien, Anmerkungen, Vorschlägen etc. zum Wachstum der Theologischen Gelehrsamkeit*, Leipzig, 1761, 414-71, pp. 456-8

G.W. Leibniz, *Allgemeiner politischer und historischer Briefwechsel*, Berlin, 1987, vol. 13, p. 546

G.W. Leibniz, *Allgemeiner politischer und historischer Briefwechsel*, Berlin, 1993, vol. 14, p. 800

Secondary

A. Hamilton, 'A Lutheran translator for the Quran. A late seventeenth-century quest', in A. Hamilton, M.H. van den Boogert, and B. Westerweel (eds), *The republic of letters and the Levant*, Leiden, 2005, 197-221

K. Tautz, *Die Bibliothekare der Churfürstlichen Bibliothek zu Cölln an der Spree. Ein Beitrag zur Geschichte der Preussischen Staatsbibliothek im siebzehnten Jahrhundert*, Leipzig, 1925 (= *Zentralblatt für Bibliothekswesen*, Beiheft 53/1925, repr. Nendeln-Liechtenstein/Wiesbaden 1968), pp. 187-91, 217-18

G. Siegfried, art. 'Starcke. Sebastian Gottfried', *Allgemeine Deutsche Biographie*, Leipzig, 1893, vol. 35, p. 467

WORKS ON CHRISTIAN-MUSLIM RELATIONS

Specimen versionis Coranicae adornatum in Caput XIX quod inscribitur Caput Mariae
'Latin translation of Sura 19'

DATE 1698
ORIGINAL LANGUAGE Latin

DESCRIPTION

Starck's specimen translation of Sura 19 of the Qur'an ('Mary', *Maryam*) is a brief work consisting of 26 pages, six of which contain a prefatory address to the reader. Published in Cölln in Brandenburg (now part of Berlin) by the electoral typographer Ulrich Liebpert, it only gives a Latin translation of the text, though the extensive notes occasionally contain words in Arabic.

Starck informs us in his preface that he had started working on his specimen four years earlier, when he was staying with Hinckelmann in Hamburg and was preparing the edition of the Arabic Qur'an. He thus depended mainly on Hinckelmann's own library, though he later made additions to the notes, mentioning material contained in the electoral library. Aware of the importance of a *tafsīr*, an Islamic commentary, in order to understand the Qur'an, Starck drew heavily on the 15th-century *Tafsīr al-Jalālayn* by the two Egyptian scholars, Jalāl al-Dīn al-Maḥallī and Jalāl al-Dīn al-Suyūṭī. This was the commonest and most easily available commentary in the Arab world at the time, and Hinckelmann had a copy. For a dictionary, Starck used Golius's *Lexicon Arabicum-Latinum* (Leiden, 1653), by far the best in existence. Of the works he later discovered in the electoral library, he quoted chiefly the world history by the 14th-century historian Abū l-Fidā' Ismāʿīl ibn ʿUmar ibn Kathīr, *Al-bidāya wa-l-nihāya*.

After the praise expended on him by Hinckelmann, Starck's translation of the relatively brief sura, consisting of 98 verses, is disappointing. It contains mistakes that could easily have been avoided, if only by consulting earlier translations of the Qur'an such as that by André du Ryer. The third verse, *idh nādā rabbahu nidā'an khafiyyan*, 'when he called upon his Lord in secret', is translated by Starck as *Quum is invocavit Dominum suum, precando et manifestando desideria sua* ('When he called upon his Lord, by appealing and making known his wishes') The idea of silence and secrecy contained in *khafiyyan* is thus entirely lost. In verse 24, Mary is told that the Lord has placed a stream at her feet. The word for 'stream' is *sariyyan*. Starck, however, translates it as 'prince', *princeps*. This error can be explained by a misuse of the dictionary since the word *sarī* does indeed have two different meanings – one is 'stream' and the other is 'nobleman'. In his dictionary, Golius gives both meanings, but the *Tafsīr al-Jalālayn* states clearly that the meaning in the Qur'an is *nahr mā'*, a 'stream of water'. In the next verse, Starck makes another mistake. The Arabic runs *wa-huzzī ilayki bi-jidh'i l-nakhlati*, 'shake the trunk of the palm tree towards you', so that, the text continues, ripe dates will fall from it. Starck gives an entirely different translation: *Et ariditas juxta te est in stipite palmae,* literally 'sterility is next to you in the trunk of the palm tree'. Like his translation of the previous verse, this is wrong and makes little sense. In a note, however, Starck does indeed suggest the correct translation, but justifies his own by claiming that he could not find *huzzī* in Golius's dictionary. In fact, Golius gives the root *hazza*, 'to shake', but not the form *huzzī*, which a better Arabist than Starck would have recognised as the feminine imperative. Starck then goes on to quote the *Tafsīr al-Jalālayn*, where the commentators, like al-Zamakhsharī earlier, do indeed describe the palm tree as being sterile, *yabisa*. The reader's confidence in Starck as an Arabist is further shaken by the misprints of Arabic titles. Ibn Kathīr's *Al-bidāya wa-l-nihāya*, for example, is printed in Arabic as *Bidāyir al-nihāyir*. The impression of superficiality and carelessness is confirmed both in his catalogue of Hinckelmann's library and in the list of oriental manuscripts in the electoral library.

In his notes, which retain the anti-Islamic tone of the preface, Starck is keen to point out the use of the Bible made by the 'pseudoprophet' in his 'hodge-podge' of sources, and his misunderstanding of the Old and New Testaments. The statement in verse 7, that the name of John had never been used before John the Baptist, is one of the easier targets. Starck's main contribution to the existing commentaries on the sura is his use of Ibn Kathīr as an indication of Islamic beliefs. In his preface, he also refers to a copy of Abū Manṣūr 'Abd al-Qāhir ibn Ṭāhir al-Baghdādī's *Al-farq bayn al-firaq* in the electoral library. Starck's interest in this study on the Muslim sects is one of the very few indications of a desire to explore Islam in any depth.

SIGNIFICANCE

Ever since Luther and Melanchthon had made known their approval of the first printed translation of the Qur'an, Theodor Bibliander's edition of the medieval Latin version by Robert of Ketton, *Machumetis Saracenorum principis, eiusque successorum vitae, doctrina, ac ipse Alcoran*, published in Basel in 1543, German Protestants had not only taken an interest in the text but had developed something of a proprietorial attitude towards it, but this was a continual source of frustration. For many years, no German Arabist seems to have been capable of translating the Qur'an directly from the Arabic, and the German reading public had to be content with translations of translations. By the 1680s, moreover, alarming reports were entering Germany: a major new translation of the entire text of the Qur'an, containing the Arabic, a Latin translation, and abundant annotations, was about to appear, but it was the work of the Italian Ludovico Marracci, once confessor to Pope Innocent XI (r. 1676-89), a member of the Congregation of the Index and of the missionary organisation De Propaganda Fide, in short one of the most orthodox representatives of the Church of Rome. The German scholars were deeply concerned. Was there not a single German Protestant who could compete with Marracci and actually publish a satisfactory edition of the Qur'an? By the last decades of the 17th century, a number of young German Orientalists seemed determined to enter the lists, and their chances were assessed by Leibniz and his friends. The only one who actually produced an edition of the Qur'an was Hinckelmann, but his edition was solely of the Arabic text, with neither a translation nor a commentary. The others never seem to have got so far. All they published were small specimens of individual suras which suffered from the same drawback, namely the shortage of *tafsīr* works in the German libraries. One of these young Orientalists was Sebastian Gottfried Starck.

Starck was particularly unfortunate where his timing was concerned. His edition of Sura 19 came out in the very same year as Marracci's text of the entire Qur'an. Marracci's version was infinitely more satisfactory than Starck's. Not only were there no mistakes, but Marracci, who had access to a greater variety of commentaries than anyone in Germany and who quoted them extensively both in Arabic and in a Latin translation, gave a far richer idea of the manifold meanings of the text. Had Starck waited to publish his specimen, he might have been able to take issue with Marracci on certain points as Andreas Acoluthus would, but, as it stands, his translation was already outdated when it appeared in print.

Starck's contribution to qur'anic scholarship is thus limited to the assistance he provided to Hinckelmann. As an Arabist he suffered from the polymathy so fashionable at the time, never concentrating sufficiently on Islam or Arabic studies, but publishing in too great a variety of domains. His most important achievement is his edition of *Kalīla wa-Dimna*, for it was he who introduced the Greek translation to a Western readership and who thus helped to promote a text the Arabic version of which would soon be attracting some of the greatest Arabists in Europe.

PUBLICATIONS

S.G. Starck, *Specimen versionis coranicae, adornatum in Caput XIX. quod inscribitur Caput Mariae*, Colonia Brandenburgica [Cölln], 1698; 4 A.or. 427 (digitised version available through *MDZ*)

STUDIES

A. Hamilton, '"To rescue the honour of the Germans". Qur'an translations by eighteenth- and early nineteenth-century German Protestants', *Journal of the Warburg and Courtauld Institutes* 77 (2014) 173-209
Hamilton, 'A Lutheran translator for the Qur'an'

Alastair Hamilton

Constantinopolitan- oder Türckischer Kirchen-Staat

'The Constantinopolitan or Turkish church-state'

DATE 1699
ORIGINAL LANGUAGE German

DESCRIPTION

Constantinopolitan- oder Türckischer Kirchen-Staat (in full, *Constanti-nopolitan- oder Türckischer Kirchen-Staat: In welchem Die vornemste[n] Glaubens-Puncten des Alcorans, wie nicht weniger der gantze Mahometa-nische Gottesdienst nebst des falschen Propheten Mahomets Leben, in einer kurtz-gefaßeten doch gewissen und deutlichen Erzehlung vorgestellet wird,* 'Constantinopolitan or Turkish church-State, in which the most import-ant beliefs from Alcoran, as well as all the Mahometan cultic practices and the life of the false prophet Mahomet, will be presented in a short but definite and clear narrative') was published in Leipzig in 1699 by Friedrich Groschuff, and also (according to D. Cyranka, *Mahomet*, pp. 49-50, 62) by Thomas Fritsch, another Leipzig publisher, in the same year. No author's name is given in the work itself, but Martin Bircher (*Deutsche Drucke des Barock 1600-1720. Katalog der Herzog August Biblio-thek Wolfenbüttel*, vol. 20, Munich, 1992, p. 348) attributes it to Johann Georg Priz (Pritius; 1662-1732), a preacher at St Nicolas' Church, Leipzig (*Nikolaikirche*; 1690-99), and formerly a fellow-student of August Her-mann Francke in Leipzig. However, J. Croitoru (*Die Deutschen und der Orient. Faszination, Verachtung und die Widersprüche der Aufklärung*, Munich, 2018, p. 18) identifies it as a German translation of Pride-aux's *The true nature of imposture fully display'd in the life of Mahomet* (London, 1697).

The author uses the term 'church' (*Kirche*) in the sense of a 'sect', or an organisational unit. A series of books with similar-sounding titles about various religious groups was issued by the same publisher at the end of the 17th century.

The book contains 188 pages. An adaptation of a picture from J.U. Wallich's *Religio Turcica* (1659) appears as the frontispiece. It contains a turbaned figure of a man with a dove on his left shoulder; he points at a book with the title ALCORAN in Latin script; the book rests on a stand in the shape of a tree-trunk, flanked by a double-bladed sword and a torch; an ox approaches the stand from the right-hand side; a crescent moon shines in the sky - all features of medieval European ideas about Muḥammad's claims to have received revelation.

The preface of 16 pages, with a dedication to Frederick Augustus I, Elector of Saxony (known also as Augustus the Strong; d. 1733) on his election and coronation as king of the Polish-Lithuanian Commonwealth (1697), is followed by a few lines of rhymed text and a page containing the genealogy of Muḥammad ('the false Arab prophet'). In the first chapter (pp. 1-113 in the Groschuff edition), the principles of the Islamic faith, rituals and customs are presented, including a lengthy description of the *ḥajj* and discussion about it. This includes numerous passages from the Qur'an. The role of 'mufti, priests, monks and hermits' is discussed in the second chapter (pp. 114-39). Ch. 3 contains a description of the life and death of Muḥammad (pp. 139-68).

With his accession to the Commonwealth throne, Frederick Augustus brought Saxony into direct contact with the Ottoman Empire. The author of the work signals the threat still posed to Western countries by the Ottomans and Islam, and expresses the opinion that it is good to know more about Islam. In the preface, Augustus is presented as a direct adversary of Muḥammad and at the same time as the epitome of the winner, while Muḥammad is depicted as the conquered one. Islam, Muḥammad and the Ottoman Empire seem to be used synonymously to mean a general enemy.

The work is a compilation of extracts from *Chronica Turcica*, printed by Wilhelm Serlin in Frankfurt am Main in 1664, and *Thesaurus exoticorum*[...], itself a compilation made by Eberhard Werner Happel (1647-90) and published in Hamburg in 1688. The author adds his own notes and comments to both texts, adding negative implications, so that, for example, 'the book' (i.e. the Qur'an) becomes 'the book of lies', and Muḥammad (the author spells the name in seven different ways) is presented as the 'false prophet' (*der Lüge-Prophet*) who concocted a new religion in Arabia from the various sectarian Christian, Jewish and Arab beliefs.

Compiling the passages from his sources, the author does not pay too much attention to harmonising them, seeming to be more eager to present them negatively, and on such a note he ends the chapter on Muḥammad with a venomous epitaph. The author also makes clear his desire for the fall of the Ottoman Empire (*das Türkischen Reich*).

SIGNIFICANCE

Fuller information concerning the work itself and its impact is still required.

PUBLICATIONS

Constantinopolitan- oder Türckischer Kirchen-Staat: In welchem Die vornemste[n] Glaubens-Puncten des Alcorans, wie nicht weniger der gantze Mahometanische Gottesdienst nebst des falschen Propheten Mahomets Leben, in einer kurtz-gefaßeten doch gewissen und deutlichen Erzehlung vorgestellet wird, Leipzig: Groschuff, 1699; PPN781524911 (digitised version available through Deutsche Digitale Bibliothek)

Constantinopolitan- oder Türckischer Kirchen-Staat, Leipzig: Fritsch, 1699

STUDIES

D. Cyranka, *Mahomet. Repräsentationen des Propheten in deutschsprachiger Literatur des 18. Jahrhunderts*, Göttingen, 2018, pp. 49-62

Stanisław Grodź

Gottfried Arnold

DATE OF BIRTH   5 September 1666
PLACE OF BIRTH   Annaberg im Erzgebirge, Saxony
DATE OF DEATH   30 May 1714
PLACE OF DEATH   Perleberg, Brandenburg

BIOGRAPHY

Gottfried Arnold was the son of a Latin teacher. After completing his education at a school in Gera, he studied in Wittenberg. Quite early in his life, he made contact with the Pietists. Ph.J. Spener helped him to obtain a teaching post in Dresden (1689-93), then Quedlinburg (1693-96), where he found the time and interest to research themes in Church history. In his book *Die erste Liebe, Das ist: Wahre Abbildung der ersten Christen* (1696), he presented the early Christians as the lasting ideal. This work earned him a position as professor of Church history in the Pietist university at Gießen (1697-8).

Dismayed by the 'secularised' academic life and influenced by like-minded radicals, he gave up the post a few months later and returned to Quedlinburg. There, he lived withdrawn from worldly and wider church affairs (1698-1701), studying medieval and early modern mysticism. He was highly influenced by the heritage of Jacob Böhme (1575-1624) and his disciples (as witnessed in Arnold's book, *Das Geheimnis der göttlichen Sophia* (Leipzig, 1700, repr. 1963). His open separatism involved him in various conflicts with the Church.

Then, surprisingly, in 1701 he married Anna Maria Sprögel and took up a position as a court preacher in Allstedt (1702-5). After this, he worked as a parish priest and inspector (*Pfarrer und Inspector*) in Werben/Altmark (1705-7) then in Perleberg (1707-14) in Brandenburg. He retained his convictions, though somewhat modified.

Unparteyische Kirchen- und Ketzer-Historie (1699-1700, 1715[2], 1729[3] [repr. 1967], 1740[4]) was a thoughtful result of Arnold's long historical studies. He continued to write during his time as a parish priest, and published *Historia et descriptio theologiae mysticae* (Frankfurt am Main, 1702), on mystical theologians, a work on Pietistic pastoral theology, collections of sermons and biographies. Some of his writings appeared under the pen name Christophorus Irenaeus.

MAIN SOURCES OF INFORMATION

Primary

G.P. Busch and E.H. Campe (eds), *Seel.Hn. Gottfried Arnold's, Ehemals Professoris Historiam etc., Gedoppelter Lebenslauf, wovon der eine von ihm ihm selbst projectiret und aufgesetzt worden*, Leipzig, 1716

Anonymous, *Certain queries, with their respective answers; by way of introduction to the Reverend Mr. Godfrey Arnold's impartial history of the church and hereticks.: From the commencement of the New Testament, to the year of our lord, 1688. Faithfully translated, in a concise manner, from the High-Dutch*, London, 1744 (proposal for an English trans., includes a biographical sketch, pp. 3-6)

Secondary

A. Missfeldt (ed.), *Gottfried Arnold. Radikaler Pietist und Gelehrter*, Cologne, 2011

W. Raupp, art. 'Arnold, Gottfried', in H.F. Klemme and M. Kuehn (eds), *Dictionary of eighteenth-century German philosophers*, London, 2010, vol. 1, pp. 34-6

W. Raupp, art. 'Arnold, Gottfried (Pseudonym: Christophorus Irenaeus)', in *Biographisch-bibliographisches Kirchenlexikon*, vol. 20, Nordhausen, 2002, cols 46-70 (extensive bibliography in cols 51-70)

D. Blaufuß and F. Niewöhner (eds), *Gottfried Arnold (1666-1714). Mit einer Bibliographie der Arnold-Literatur ab 1714*, Wiesbaden, 1995

H. Schneider, art. 'Arnold, Gottfried', in W. Killy (ed.), *Deutsche biographische Enzyklopädie*, vol. 1, Munich, 1995, 187

G. Dünnhaupt, art. 'Gottfried Arnold', in G. Dünnhaupt, *Personalbibliographien zu den Drucken des Barock*, vol. 1, Stuttgart, 1990, 314-52

P. Meinhold, art. 'Arnold, Gottfried', in *Neue Deutsche Biographie*, vol. 1, Berlin, 1953, 385-6

E. Seeberg, *Gottfried Arnold. In Auswahl herausgegeben*, Munich, 1934

F. Dibelius, art. 'Arnold, Gottfried', in *Realenzyklopädie für protestantische Theologie und Kirche*, vol. 2, Leipzig, 1897[3], 122-4

G. Frank, art. 'Arnold, Gottfried', in *Allgemeine Deutsche Biographie*, vol. 1, Leipzig, 1875, 587-8

WORKS ON CHRISTIAN-MUSLIM RELATIONS

Unparteyische Kirchen- und Ketzer-Historie, vom Anfang des Neuen Testaments Biß auf das Jahr Christi 1688
'Impartial history of the Church and heretics, from the start of the New Testament to the year of our Lord 1688'

DATE   1699-1700
ORIGINAL LANGUAGE   German

DESCRIPTION

This work appeared in Frankfurt am Main in two volumes, in 1699 and 1700. The first volume consist of two parts, the first comprising 15 chapters (each chapter describing the events of one century) and running to 422 double-column pages, and the second, comprising only two chapters, covers the period 1500-1688 in 728 double-column pages. Matters concerning Muḥammad and Islam cover only three pages (five columns), in part 1, ch. 7, pp. 275-7.

Muḥammad, Arnold says, was God's punishment for non-Christians (*Unchristen*; he must mean Christians) and did more harm to them than anyone else. His followers completely overran the heartlands of Christianity in the East. He was at first a camel driver, and was uneducated but naturally intelligent. He first proclaimed his message in Mecca, the home of the Quraysh, where some people were inclined to take up novelties and had already abandoned idolatry and worshipped only one God, practised circumcision as the followers of Ishmael, believed in resurrection, gave alms, prayed and lived better lives than Christians. Threatened with imprisonment by the rulers of Mecca, Muḥammad fled with his followers to Medina in 622. More people joined him there, where he prepared some parts of his Qur'an. He captured Mecca eight years later.

Muḥammad was against any form of idolatry. Finding only empty words in Christian teaching, abhorring pagan wisdom and being even less impressed with the miserable condition of the Jews, he invented his own religion. Christian historians maintained that he was instructed by Christians in Arabia, identifying John of Antioch, an Arian, Sergius, a Nestorian monk, and Bairam, a Jacobite, all of them heretics. In addition, two Jews, Phineas and Abdias, also taught him. Arnold supports this by demonstrating that, whenever Muḥammad shows any similarity to Christianity in his teachings, it is always to Christian heretics. He sees some of the main reasons for Muḥammad's success as the prohibition against arguing about his religion under the penalty of death, permission to marry more than one wife, and the promise of a sensual paradise. Daniel Cyranka (*Mahomet*, pp. 117-18) argues that, despite his efforts to rectify the image of Muḥammad, Arnold presents him as a crook, impostor and fraudster (*Betrüger*), mainly proved by his desire for people to believe him without any deep scrutiny of his teaching.

Arnold is critical about the sources available to him, noting that the Turks tell fabulous stories about Muḥammad, while the Christians, especially the 'gossiping Greeks', denigrate him as though nothing good was in him. The Christians were so bitter against Muḥammad because he often accused them of corruption and godlessness in his Qur'an.

Arnold accuses the authors of the sources on Islam of inventing bad things about Muḥammad only as part of their refutations of him, though they also admit that he lived a more pious life than the Christians, who bitterly fight against one another.

SIGNIFICANCE

Arnold's intention was to present the history of various Christian groups impartially and not apologetically. He inserts Muḥammad among them not as a solitary figure, but together with like-minded Christians as a non-conformist who was acting against the establishment (Cyranka, *Mahomet*, p. 122). This was in line with Arnold's own dislike of institutionalised religion, which he saw as a sign of decay – the Church had been in such a state from the time of the Roman Emperor Constantine. For him, individual forms of piety and not confessional orthodoxy were the appropriate kinds of belief (Schneider, 'Arnold, Gottfried', p. 187). Thus, he shows Muḥammad as a searcher for God within the framework of the history of the Church, and he shows his sympathy for him by calling him 'poor Muḥammad' because of the difficulties he encountered. This was a surprisingly new attitude in the German-speaking milieu.

Some critics accused Arnold of showing too much sympathy for the various 'heresies' he includes in his work, and rejected his view that he could still consider himself a 'Lutheran'. The contemporary critic Ernst Salomon Cyprian wrote that Arnold 'could also call himself a Muslim (*sich auch Muhammedisch nennen*) because there are also things in the Qur'an which he takes as true' (*Allgemeine Anmerckungen*, p. 138).

Arnold responded in *Supplementa* (1703), arguing that hostile criticisms arose from misunderstandings of his intention to be impartial. *Supplementa* was included in the second and third editions of *Unparteyische Kirchen- und Ketzer-Historie,* and in the 1740 edition it was brought into the main body of the book. This accusation against Arnold of being 'a Muhammedan' seems to have played only a marginal part in debates about his book.

PUBLICATIONS

Gottfried Arnold, *Unparteyische Kirchen- und Ketzer-Historie von Anfang des Neuen Testaments biß auff das Jahr Christi 1688,* vol. 1, Frankfurt am Main, 1699; 2 H.eccl. 21-1/2 (digitised version available through *MDZ*)

Gottfried Arnold, *Unparteyische Kirchen- und Ketzer-Historie von Anfang des Neuen Testaments biß auff das Jahr Christi 1688,* vol. 2, Frankfurt am Main, 1700; 2 H.eccl. 21-3/4 (digitised version available through *MDZ*)

Gottfried Arnold, *Supplementa, Illustrationes und Emendationes zur Verbesserung der Kirchen-Historie,* Frankfurt am Main, 1703; 4 Th H 166 (digitised version available through *MDZ*)

Gottfried Arnold, *Unparteyische Kirchen- und Ketzer-Historie von Anfang des Neuen Testaments biß auff das Jahr Christi 1688,* Frankfurt am Main, 1715[2]; 2 H.eccl. 22-3/4 (digitised version available through *MDZ*)

Gottfried Arnold, *Unparteyische Kirchen- und Ketzer-Historie von Anfang des Neuen Testaments biß auff das Jahr Christi 1688,* Frankfurt am Main, 1729[3], repr. Hildesheim, 2008); 4 Th H 168 -3/4 (digitised version available through *MDZ*)

Gottfried Arnold, *Historie der kerken en ketteren van den beginne des Nieuwen Testaments tot aan het jaar onses Heeren 1688,* 3 vols, Amsterdam, 1701-29 (Dutch trans.); KW 357 D 57 [-58] (digitised version available through Koninklijke Bibliotheek)

Gottfried Arnold, *Unpartheyische Kirchen- und Ketzer-Historie, vom Anfang des Neuen Testaments biß auf das Jahr Christi 1688, bey dieser neuen Auflage, An vielen Orten, nach dem Sinn und Verlangen, Des seel. Auctoris, Verbessert, vermehret, und in bequemere Ordnung gebracht, und mit dessen Bildnus und Lebens-Lauff gezieret,* Schaffhausen, 1740; 2 H.eccl. 23-1 (digitised version available through *MDZ*)

Gottfried Arnold, *Unpartheyische Kirchen- und Ketzer-Historie, Dritter Band. In welchem so wohl die von den verschiedenen Gelehrten gegen die Arnoldische Historie herausgebene Bedencken, Anmerckungen, Untersuchungen und andere dergleichen Schrifften, Als auch die theils von dem seel.Verfasser selbst, theils von seinen Freunden ans Licht gestellte und zur Erläuterung der Kirchen-Historie dienende Vertheidigungs-Schrifften Ingleichem verschiedene nützliche Zusätze mitgetheilet werden. Nebst einer Vorrede und unpartheyischen Einleitung in die Historie der Arnoldischen Strittigkeiten wie auch Einem allgemeinen und vollständigen Register über alle drey Bände*, Schaffhausen, 1742; 2 H.eccl. 23-3 (digitised version available through *MDZ*)

STUDIES

D. Cyranka, *Mahomet. Repräsentationen des Propheten in deutschsprachiger Literatur des 18. Jahrhunderts*, Göttingen, 2018, pp. 114-23

D. Fleischer, *Zwischen Tradition und Fortschritt. Der Strukturwandel der protestantischen Kirchengeschichtsschreibung im deutschsprachigen Diskurs der Aufklärung*, Waltrop, 2006, pp. 23-69

K. Greschat, 'Gottfried Arnolds "Unparteiische Kirchen- und Ketzerhistorie" von 1699/1700 im Kontext seiner spiritualistischen Kirchenkritik', *Zeitschrift für Kirchengeschichte* 116 (2005) 46-62

A.U. Sommer, 'Geschichte und Praxis bei Gottfried Arnold', *Zeitschrift für Religions- und Geistesgeschichte* 54 (2002) 210-43

Blaufuß and Niewöhner, *Gottfried Arnold*

Schneider, 'Arnold, Gottfried'

H. Schneider, 'Der radikale Pietismus im 18. Jahrhundert', in M. Brecht et al. (eds), *Geschichte des Pietismus*, vol. 2, Göttingen, 1995, 107-97

H. Schneider, 'Der radikale Pietismus im 17. Jahrhundert', in M. Brecht et al. (eds), *Geschichte des Pietismus*, vol. 1, Göttingen, 1993, 390-437

I. Martin, 'Der Kampf um Gottfried Arnolds Unpartheyische Kirchen- und Ketzerhistorie. Vornehmlich auf Grund des dritten Bandes der Schaffhaiserner Ausgabe von 1740-42', Heidelberg, 1972 (PhD Diss. Heidelberg)

E. Seeberg, *Gottfried Arnold, Die Wissenschaft und die Mystik seiner Zeit. Studien zur Historiographie und zur Mystik*, Darmstadt, 1964[2], Meerane, 1923

H. Dörries, *Geist und Geschichte bei Gottfried Arnold*, Göttingen, 1963

E. Beyreuther, 'Die Gestalt Mohammeds in Gottfried Arnolds

Kirchen- und Ketzerhistorie', *Theologische Literaturzeitung* 84
(1959) 255-64

E.S. Cyprian, *Allgemeine Anmerckungen über Gottfried Arnolds Kirchen-
und Ketzer-Historie, Worinnen bescheidentlich und gründlich erwiesen wird, daß Arnold vermöge seiner vergefaßten Meynungen,
nothwendig partheyisch schreiben, seine Klagen wider die Kirche
auff schwache Gründe bauen, und einiger Scribenten Meynung so
gar verdrehen müssen, daß auch nur in einem halben paragrapho
der Sinn und die Worte Augustini, denen Donatisten zum Behuff,
über sechsmahl verfälschet worden. Zum Drittenmahl gedruckt, Und
sowohl mit einer Antwort auff alle dagegen edirte Schrifften, als Vor-
bericht von Arnolds Religion, wie auch ferneren Aumerckungen von
deßen historischen Verfälschungen und Fehlern vermehret*, Frankfurt, 1701, pp. 129-49

Stanisław Grodź

David Nerreter

DATE OF BIRTH 1649
PLACE OF BIRTH Nuremberg
DATE OF DEATH 1726
PLACE OF DEATH Stargard, Pomerania (today Poland)

BIOGRAPHY

David Nerreter had his family roots in Nuremberg. He studied in Alt-dorf and Königsberg, where he finally presented his dissertation on philosophy in 1672. In 1670 he earned the *poeta laureatus* prize, and was admitted to Pegnitz Flower Society in Nuremberg (*Societas Florigera ad Pegnesum; Pegnesischer Blumenorden*, a German literary society founded in 1644, and still active) under the name 'Philemon'. The society was highly influenced by Pietistic views, and Nerreter continued in touch with Philipp Jakob Spener, one of the key figures of German Pietism, from the early 1680s.

Nerreter was ordained a Lutheran pastor in 1674, and from 1677 worked first as *Hofkaplan*, then *Diakon* and *Konsistorialrat* in Oettingen, from 1694 as deacon and preacher in Nuremberg, and finally as parish priest in Wöhrd, a suburb of Nuremberg. He wrote edifying and catechetical works and dedicated some of them to Spener, including *Catechetische Firmung oder Glaubens-Stärckung eines erwachsenen That-Christen* (1686), and *Beweglicher kurtzer Begriff des Thätigen oder zeitlich- ewigwahrhafftig- seeligmachenden Christentums* and *Wegweiser zur zeitlichen und ewigen Glückseligkeit* (1688).

Nerreter was considered by his contemporaries as a pious theologian with poetic abilities. In his *Schauplatz der streitenden Kirche*, dedicated to King Friedrich I of Prussia (r. 1701-13), he argued for the unity of the Church. In consequence, the king nominated him *Generalsuperintendent* and later *Konsistorialrat* in Pomerania. His works on theological or church-related and history of religion-related themes come from his time in Wöhrd, where, though a parish priest (*Gemeindepfarrer*), he had few duties.

MAIN SOURCES OF INFORMATION

Primary

C.A. Baader, *Lexikon verstorbener Baierischer Schriftsteller des achtzehenten und neunzehenten Jahrhunderts*, vol. 2, M–Z, Augsburg, 1824, pp. 75-7

H. Döring, *Die gelehrten Theologen Deutschlands im achtzehnten und neunzehn-ten Jahrhundert*, vol. 3, N – Scho, Neustadt an der Orla, 1833, pp. 29-31

Secondary

D. Cyranka, *Mahomet. Repräsentationen des Propheten in deutschsprachiger Lite-ratur des 18. Jahrunderts*, Göttingen, 2018, pp. 124–46

H. Bobzin and P. Kleine (eds), *Glaubensbuch und Weltliteratur. Koranüberset-zungen in Deutschland von der Reformationszeit bis heute*, Arnsberg, 2007, p. 26

R. Jürgensen, *Melos conspirant singuli in unum. Repertorium bio-bibliographicum zur Geschichte des Pegnesischen Blumenordens in Nürnberg (1644-1744)*, Wiesbaden, 2006, pp. 379-86

W. Wießner, 'David Nerreter (1649-1726). Ein Lebensbild aus dem Zeitalter des beginnenden Pietismus', *Zeitschrift für Bayerische Kirchengeschichte* 2 (1954) 144-64

M.-O. Rehrmann, *Ehrenthron oder Teufelsbrut? Das Bild des Islams in der deutschen Aufklärung*, Zürich, 2001, pp. 59-70

H. Weigelt, *Geschichte des Pietismus in Bayern. Anfänge – Entwicklung – Bedeutung*, Göttingen, 2001, pp. 66-7

WORKS ON CHRISTIAN-MUSLIM RELATIONS

David Nerreters Neu eröffnete Mahometanische Moschea
'David Nerreter's newly opened Muḥammadan mosque'

DATE   1703

ORIGINAL LANGUAGE   German

DESCRIPTION

David Nerreters Neu eröffnete Mahometanische Moschea was published in Nuremberg in 1703 (the title in full is *David Nerreters Neu eröffnete Mahometanische Moschea, worinn nach Anleitung der VI. Abtheilung von unterschiedlichen Gottes-Diensten der Welt, Alexander Rossens, Erstlich Der Mahometanischen Religion Anfang, Ausbreitung, Secten, Regierungen, mancherley Gebräuche, und vermuthlicher Untergang, Fürs andre der völlige Alkoran, Nach der besten Edition Ludovici Marraccii, verteutscht, und kürzlich widerlegt wird,* 'David Nerreter's newly opened Muḥammadan mosque, in which, following the sixth chapter of Alexander Ross' "On various religions of the world", first the beginning of the Mahometan religion, spread, sects, governments, various customs and probable fall, then the entire Qur'an according to the best edition by Ludovico Marracci is translated into German and briefly refuted') . The main body of the text, which is preceded by an introduction and dedication of 13 pages, is 1,222 pages long. Two indices (of the titles of suras and a general one, all together about 50 pages) come at the end of the volume.

Illustration 5. Frontispiece from David Nerreter, *Neu eröffnete Mahometanische Moschea.*
The book on the table reads 'La Allah, alla Allah, Mahumed Resul Allah'

The work consists of two main parts. For the first, Nerreter uses the text
of ch. 6 of Alexander Ross's *Pansebeia* (1653), and in the second he provides his own German translation of the Qur'an from Marracci's Latin
Alcorani textus universus, to which he adds his comments. Although in
the first part Nerreter retains the structure of Ross's chapter, his work
is not a simple translation. He alters the order of Ross's questions and
expands the information given there from other sources. He also at times
differs from Ross on certain issues. In effect, he treats Ross as a 'prompt'
(*Stichwortgeber*).

Pansebeia had been translated into German several times and published (Heidelberg, 1660 or 1667 (a problematic date), 1668, 1674) before
Nerreter made use of it. He took it as the starting point for three of his
works. First, he published the adopted and expanded material from its
first five chapters as *Der Wunderwürdige Juden- und Heiden-Tempel* (1701),
then from the sixth chapter in *David Nerreters Neueröffnete Mahometanische Moschea* (1703), and finally from the seventh in *David Nerreters
Schau-Platz Der Streitenden doch unüberwindlichen Christlichen Kyrchen*
(1707), the last dedicated to Frederick I of Prussia.

Nerreter follows Ross in stating that correct knowledge of God is the
happiness of human beings. However, it can be distorted by Satan because
of human sinfulness. People believe what they want, and Satan slips in
between the word of God and individuals. The reason for Muḥammad's
success was the lack of belief of many Christians, who paid little attention to God's word, or entered into heated disputes and followed the
desires of the flesh. In such ways, Christians themselves prepared the
ground for Muḥammad's success, though Muḥammad remains the 'arch-
deceiver', and Satan stands behind his success.

Nerreter contends that the judgement of God can be better perceived
when one gets to know for oneself the 'Mahometan teachings' as they
are presented in the 'Alkoran' and compares them with the 'bright light
of the Gospel'. For this reason, he includes his German translation of
Marracci's Latin translation of the Qur'an in the second part, together
with his own commentary. He also includes explanations of the historical context and adds his theological opinions. In order to give full information about Muḥammad and the Qur'an, and about Islamic religious
practice, he uses the German translation of Humphrey Prideaux's *Das
Leben Mahomets* (1699).

To the first answer from Alexander Ross's list of 12 questions, Nerreter adds explanations concerning Muḥammad's birth and life, and his

Companions. This additional information comes in answers to 20 new questions put by Nerreter himself. He draws the material for these from Marracci's *Alcorani textus universus* and from Hottinger's *Historia Orientalis*. In his presentation of Muḥammad's 'teachings', he repeats well-known traditional polemical stories, calling the elements of Muḥammad's teaching 'bizarre things'. In his description of the character and physical appearance of Muḥammad, Nerreter uses Marracci and other sources. He produces a picture without negative features, though it includes contradictions because he has clearly not digested this material.

He deals differently with the Qur'an (ch. 16). He relates the story of Muḥammad's contacts with a Christian monk, who is called Sergius, Bohairam and Bahiram, and with a Jewish friend called Abdalla, from whom Muḥammad learnt about the New Testament and the 'Talmudic fables'. On the basis of these two sources and of his knowledge about the pagan Arabs (from among whom he himself came), Muḥammad made a fourth religion, a blend between 'the flesh' and 'the world'.

When it comes to the 'disorderly' contents of the Qur'an, Nerreter presents them in three parts: stories, teachings and refutations of other religions. He also glances at other themes. He is certain that the Qur'an contains absurd and sacrilegious details, and refers to differences from the Bible, such as the roles of Isaac and Ishmael, the golden calf, and Mary as the sister of Moses and Aaron, to different spellings of names and contradictions in the text, and he also mentions the exceptions made from its general teachings for Muḥammad (that he had Q 33 and Q 66 issued for himself).

He points out that, while Christianity rejects the Qur'an as 'very absurd and basically corrupt' (p. 60), it nevertheless contains correct teachings about Christ and the Virgin Mary, though with the purpose of mocking them and denying the divine Sonship of Jesus, the crucifixion and the Trinity.

On the issue whether Muḥammad is the Great Antichrist, Nerreter takes a different stance from Ross, who argued against this identification (Muḥammad was an Arab and not someone from the tribe of Dan). Nerreter refers to the Book of Daniel 11:36-12:13, and comes to the conclusion that Muḥammad believed in a different god from that of the Bible (as stated in Daniel 11:37-8). Thus, for Nerreter, Muḥammad and his followers are indeed the Antichrist.

Nerreter also comments on the end of the Ottoman Empire, again taking a different position from Ross. For the latter, Islam was a sect that appeared as God's punishment, though Nerreter sees Muḥammad and the Turks as the Antichrist, and on the basis of a numerical argument he anticipates that their power will wane from 1701 until probably 1773 or 1776. Hence, since their final destruction was approaching it was imperative to evangelise among them and refute the Qur'an in their presence. This would be difficult in Turkey, but it should be carried out by merchants in all the places where the Qur'an is known. Above all, the good conduct of Christians will provide the most important example.

The last question in the first part of the book leads Nerreter to present the gist of Pope Pius II's (r. 1458-64) letter to Sultan Mehmet II, the Conqueror (r. 1444-81).

In the second part, Nerreter presents his own translation of the Qur'an from Marracci's Latin translation, which he intends as a help for missionary work. In his foreword, he refers to the Latin edition published by Theodor Bibliander and examines the translations of Robert of Ketton, Hermann Dalmata, André du Ryer, Salomon Schweigger and Andreas Arrivabene, judging all of them as 'deceptions' because they contain mistakes, while he himself aspires to provide the most accurate translation. He ends his introduction with the statement that, when Christians read the Qur'an, they will see its faults and their belief in Christ will get stronger. Thus, his translation is a means to conversion.

Nerreter highlights faults in the stories with biblical parallels, and often indicates that the qur'anic versions use the Talmud as their source. His comments on the text of the Qur'an are harsh and always directed against Muḥammad.

Although he is dependent on Ross in his arguments against Muḥammad, Nerreter goes far beyond what Ross and others had previously written. The tone of his arguments is, perhaps, closest to Prideaux, especially in his comments on the Qur'an, though in comparison with Prideaux, Nerreter's arguments are more grounded in biblical exegesis. But his intention was different from Ross's and his argumentation against atheism, and from that of Prideaux, who was part of the deistic debate on religions and deception. His focus was on the endtime, of which a sign would be the conversion of the Jews, 'Mahometans', and pagans. Refutation of the message of the Qur'an and criticism of Muḥammad served as a means for that conversion. His conversion programme had significant meaning in Pietist circles, as is shown by the establishment of the *Institutum Iudaicum et Muhammedicum* in Halle from 1728 to 1792.

SIGNIFICANCE

Nerreter's publications found their reception within the 18ᵗʰ century itself. Excerpts from *Neu eröffnete Mahometanische Moschea* were published in 1800 under the new title *Ueber muhamedanische Religion* (Elberfeld, 1800). Although the editor of this work said that he had drawn his material from d'Herbelot's work, it can be shown that in fact the book contains quotations from *Neu eröffnete Mahometanische Moschea*: a new edition of the whole 1,200-page work was probably not possible.

Nerreter's translation of the Qur'an, being 'second-hand', was not widely used and could neither compete with the later German translation of Sale's work, nor with the direct translations from Arabic into German made by Megerlin (1772) and above all Boysen (1773-5).

PUBLICATIONS

> David Nerreter, *Neu eröffnete Mahometanische Moschea, worinn nach Anleitung der VI. Abtheilung von unterschiedlichen Gottes-Diensten der Welt, Alexander Rossens, Erstlich Der Mahometanischen Religion Anfang, Ausbreitung, Secten, Regierungen, mancherley Gebräuche, und vermuthlicher Untergang, Fürs andre der völlige Alkoran, Nach der besten Edition Ludovici Marraccii, verteutscht, und kürzlich widerlegt wird*, Nürnberg, 1703; Jud 399 (digitised version available through *MDZ*)

> Anonymous, *Ueber muhamedanische Religion, deren Sekten, Gebräuche, Feste, geistliche Orden etc. Ein Beitrag zur Religionsgeschichte, allen Theologen und Liebhabern der Geschichte gewidmet von C..l R..e. Omne tulit punctum,/ qui miscuit utile dulci;/ lectorem delectando, pariterque monendo!*, Elberfeld, 1800

STUDIES

> Cyranka, *Mahomet. Repräsentationen des Propheten*, pp. 124-46
> Bobzin and Kleine, *Glaubensbuch und Weltliteratur*, p. 26
> Jürgensen, *Melos conspirant singuli in unum*, pp. 379-86
> Wießner, 'David Nerreter'
> Rehrmann, *Ehrenthron oder Teufelsbrut?*, pp. 59-70
> Weigelt, *Geschichte des Pietismus in Bayern*, pp. 66-7

Daniel Cyranka

Engelbert Kaempfer

DATE OF BIRTH   16 September 1651
PLACE OF BIRTH   Lemgo, Germany
DATE OF DEATH   2 November 1716
PLACE OF DEATH   Lemgo, Germany

BIOGRAPHY

Engelbert Kaempfer was the son of Johannes Kemper, the Lutheran pastor at St Nicholas' Church in Lemgo (Germany). He studied at the universities of Hamelin, Lüneburg, Hamburg, Lübeck and Danzig, during which time he changed his name to Kaempfer (meaning combatant or warrior). After graduating from the University of Krakow, he continued studying medicine, natural science, law and languages at the University of Königsberg (present-day Kaliningrad) in what was then Prussia, and at a number of universities in Poland. In 1681, he travelled to Uppsala (Sweden), where he was appointed secretary to the Swedish ambassadorial party that was sent to Persia during the reign of Charles XI (r. 1660-97). The two-year journey took in Moscow, Kazan and Astrakhan and, after crossing the Caspian Sea, the party reached Nizabad. From Shemakha, Kaempfer embarked on a number of research trips to Baku before finally reaching the Persian capital Isfahan, where he stayed for some 20 months between March 1684 and November 1685.

Kaempfer was fascinated by Safavid culture, was involved in numerous expeditions to important sites (including Persepolis and Naqs-e Rostam), and eagerly made use of the knowledge of the local population as well as soldiers and travellers in the region. He also consulted the superior of the Capuchins, Father Raphaël du Mans, who had been living in Isfahan since 1647 and who was widely regarded at the time as an authority on contemporary Persian society and as having an informed understanding of Safavid culture. There can be little doubt that Kaempfer's image of Persia was partially influenced by du Mans' descriptions (both written and oral).

Kaempfer is remembered not only for his written reports but also for the numerous detailed sketches he created to accompany them. As the Swedish ambassadorial party was set to return home after just one year, Kaempfer took up a position as surgeon-in-chief with the Dutch East

India Company's fleet. Despite falling seriously ill with fever in Bandar-Abbas, he remained in the port for some two and half years after his recovery. From there, his travels took him to Arabia, India and eventually to Siam, Japan and Java.

After almost 12 years abroad, Kaempfer returned to Europe in 1693 where he received a medical degree from the Dutch University of Leiden. He settled in his home town of Lemgo, where he assumed the role of court doctor to Friedrich Adolph, Count of Lippe-Detmold, and where he died in 1716.

Although Kaempfer is probably best known for his writings on Japanese society (an almost unknown phenomenon for Europeans at the time) and for his studies of Japanese fauna (on which the celebrated Swedish botanist Carl Linnaeus drew), he was at the same time a passionate commentator on the exotic cultures of which he had first-hand experience as a result of his extensive travels.

MAIN SOURCES OF INFORMATION

Primary

Englebert Kaempfer, *Amoenitatum exoticarum politico-physico-medicarum fasciculi v, quibus continentur variae relationes, observationes & descriptiones rerum Persicarum & ulterioris Asiae, multa attentione, in peregrinationibus per universum Orientum, collecta, ab auctore Engelberto Kaempfero*, Lemgoviae, 1712

J.B. Haccius, *Die beste Reise eines Christlichen Kämpffers nach dem himmlichen Orient*, Lemgo, 1716 (text of the eulogy at Kaempfer's funeral); https://www.ncbi.nlm.nih.gov/pubmed/8088564

J.G. Scheuchner, 'The life of the author', in E. Kaempfer, *The history of Japan, giving an account of the ancient and present state and government of that empire*, trans. J.G. Scheuchner, London, 1727, v-xv (first biography of Kaempfer)

Secondary

A life of Kaempfer and a full bibliography are given at: http://wolfgangmichel.web.fc2.com/serv/ek/index.html

D. Haberland (ed.), *Engelbert Kaempfer (1651-1716). Ein Gelehrtenleben zwischen Tradition und Innovation*, Wiesbaden, 2004

S. Klocke-Daffa, J. Scheffler and G. Wilbert (eds), *Engelbert Kaempfer und die kulturelle Begegnung zwischen Europa und Asien*, Lemgo, 2003

K. Meyer-Lemgo, *Die Reisetagebücher Engelbert Kaempfers*, Wiesbaden, 1968

K. Meyer-Lemgo, *Engelbert Kaempfer erforscht das seltsame Asien*, Hamburg, 1960

WORKS ON CHRISTIAN-MUSLIM RELATIONS

Amoenitates exoticae
'Exotic pleasures'

DATE   1712

ORIGINAL LANGUAGE   Latin

DESCRIPTION

Kaempfer's travel writings and scientific studies are written partly in
German and partly in Latin, and include the 'Report on Persia, 1648-85',
which was retrospectively published in 1712 in the Principality of Lippe
(complete with numerous engravings) by the court publisher Heinrich
Wilhelm Meyer. The work consists of approximately 900 (folio) pages
and is divided into five books. The first contains Kaempfer's 16 essays
on the state of Persia (pp. 1-250); the second contains some 14 essays on
topics relating to history and nature (including one on the ruins of Persepolis together with transcriptions of cuneiform writings). The third is a
compendium of observations on unusual physical and medical phenomena and other Oriental curiosities, while the fourth consists of a botanical study of the date palm considered in its agrarian and sociological
context. The final book contains a ground-breaking study of Japanese
fauna.

It was only posthumously that Kaempfer's work received due attention in the academic world. After Kaempfer's death, his nephew sold off
a large part of his archive to Sir John Sloane, the founder of the British
Museum; as a result many of Kaempfer's manuscripts, together with the
objects he collected, are to be found in the British Library.

The first book (pp. 1-250) of the *Amoenitates exoticae* (in full, *Amoenitatum exoticarum politico-physico-medicarum fasciculi v, quibus continentur variae relationes, observationes & descriptiones rerum Persicarum
& ulterioris Asiae, multa attentione, in peregrinationibus per universum
Orientum, collecta, ab auctore Engelberto Kaempfero*) is primarily concerned with the Safavid court and its administration, and offers a comprehensive academic account not only of the ruling dynasty and its
institutions, but also of Isfahan itself. What is particularly striking about
Kaempfer's work – and especially the sections in which he offers an
account of religious practices in Persia – is the neutral, objective tone of
his writing. There is no hint of any sense of European superiority in the
face of a foreign religion, or any trace of Christian missionary zeal. On

Illustration 6. From Engelbert Kaempfer, *Amoenitatum exoticarum*, facing p. 35, showing the coronation of Shah Sulayman

the contrary, his analysis is based on an extraordinarily detailed knowledge of Islam and its off-shoots, and demonstrates an understanding of
the different belief-systems embraced by Sunnī and Shīʿī Muslims. For
instance, he comments on the origins of the Shīʿī branch of Islam, their
pilgrimages to Mashhad and Karbalāʾ, their belief in 12 divinely ordained
leaders known as the Twelve Imams, Dervish culture, and Shīʿī law (see
Relatio 8 'Antistites spirituales. Aedificia sacra', Lemgo, 1712, pp. 98-119).
He also demonstrates a thorough understanding of the Qurʾan and correctly identifies those passages where there is a contradiction between
verses regarding attitudes towards Christians and contemporary Shīʿī
practices. By way of example, Kaempfer refers to the custom of certain
Shīʿī groups who follow a strict code of purity whereby they avoid eating
with Christians and having physical contact with them.

SIGNIFICANCE

There is nothing in Kaempfer's study that could be described as anti-
Islamic polemic. His (successful) attempt to grasp the character of an
alien non-Christian world in a way that is both scientifically objective
and free from the distortions of ideology is singular, and, given the context of his background, this should by no means be taken for granted.
Kaempfer was the product of a pre-Enlightenment society that was often
characterised by a lack of religious tolerance. During the 17th century,
his home town of Lemgo was a centre of witch-hunting, an activity that
his father as a member of the clergy, could hardly ignore. Accordingly,
Kaempfer's ability to arrive at an independent and objective account of
Islamic religion and culture is both remarkable and, in some ways, ahead
of its time. For all of these reasons Kaempfer, whose account of Safavid
culture and religion in Persia is striking in its impartiality (for example,
he is extremely critical of those Armenian Christians who converted to
the Shīʿa religion merely to profit from the then complex laws on inheritance), should be seen not only as a scholar of the Orient, but as one
of the most important precursors of the German Enlightenment and its
doctrine of religious tolerance.

PUBLICATIONS

> Engelbert Kaempfer, *Amoenitatum exoticarum politico-physico-medi-
> carum fasciculi v, quibus continentur variae relationes, observationes
> & descriptiones rerum Persicarum & ulterioris Asiae, multa atten-
> tione, in peregrinationibus per universum Orientum, collecta, ab auc-
> tore Engelberto Kaempfero*, Lemgo, 1712; CB758 (digitised version
> available through Hathi Trust Digital Library)

Engelbert Kaempfer, *Amoenitatum exoticarum politico-physico-medi-carum fasciculi v, quibus continentur variae relationes, observationes & descriptiones rerum Persicarum & ulterioris Asiae, multa atten-tione, in peregrinationibus per universum Orientum, collecta, ab auc-tore Engelberto Kaempfero*, Lemgo, 1752

Engelbert Kaempfer: Exotic attractions in Persia, 1684-1688: Travels and observations, trans. W. Floor and C. Ouahes, Washington DC, 2016 (English trans. of the 'Report on Persia')

STUDIES

M. Gronke, 'Am Hof von Isfahan. Engelbert Kaempfer und das safawi-dische Persien', in D. Haberland (ed.), *Engelbert Kaempfer*, 189-98

Birgit Röder

Heinrich Myrike

Heinrich Mirike; Hendricus Myrike; Hendrik Mierckens;
Henricus Mircken

DATE OF BIRTH   About 1639
PLACE OF BIRTH   Wesel, Germany
DATE OF DEATH   1710
PLACE OF DEATH   Edirne, the Ottoman Empire

BIOGRAPHY

The Reverend Heinrich Myrike was born in Wesel, in modern-day Germany close to the Dutch border, in 1639. He studied in Duisburg, presumably theology, matriculating on 17 May 1664. He then worked as an army chaplain before being appointed pastor to the Dutch embassy in Istanbul on 8 September 1678. He arrived there after a stop-over in Izmir (Smyrna) on 18 June 1679, filling a vacancy that had existed for almost three years, his predecessor having been suspended by the ambassador on account of personal differences. The Dutch community in Istanbul, which consisted of Protestants from various European countries, had maintained communal prayer and reading the scripture together, and children had even been baptised despite the absence of a proper pastor.

Since few members of the Dutch community actually spoke any Dutch, Myrike quickly acquired some Italian, the lingua franca of international trade and communication in most Levantine ports. In 1684, he made his pilgrimage to Palestine. Although it seems unlikely that he travelled alone, no companions are mentioned in his account. In 1686, Myrike sent several letters to the church authorities in Amsterdam about the position of French Huguenots in Istanbul, who had been enjoined by the new French ambassador to embrace Roman Catholicism or be deported back to France. Myrike's efforts were aimed at securing a welcome for these Huguenots in the Dutch Republic, but in the end the French ambassador did not act on his threats.

On 24 December 1699, Myrike was given permission to retire, at the age of 60, with a pension from the Dutch directors of the Levant Trade on account of his frail health. He did not return to Europe, however, but appears to have settled at Edirne, for it is there that he died in 1710.

MAIN SOURCES OF INFORMATION

Primary

Album Studiosorum Universitatis Duisburgensis (Online), section 9, 1663-1664, p. 70, entry 22

Secondary

O. Schutte, *Repertorium der Nederlandse vertegenwoordigers, residerende in het buitenland, 1584-1810*, The Hague, 1976, p. 316

J.W. Samberg, *De Hollandsche Gereformeerde Gemeente te Smirna. De geschiedenis eener handelskerk*, Leiden, 1928, pp. 80-1

Bulletin de la Commission pour l'histoire des églises Wallonnes. Tome quatrième, The Hague, 1890, pp. 259, 290-1

WORKS ON CHRISTIAN-MUSLIM RELATIONS

Reyse nach Jerusalem und dem Land Canaan
'Journey to Jerusalem and the land of Canaan'

DATE 1714

ORIGINAL LANGUAGE German

DESCRIPTION

In 1684, Myrike made a journey to 'the promised land of Canaan' from Istanbul, leaving the Ottoman capital on 15 January. On 6 March, he completed the final leg from Rama to Jerusalem, and by 2.00 pm he had reached the Damascus Gate, where new arrivals invariably had to wait several hours for the dragoman of the Franciscan monastery, which hosted most pilgrims. Myrike stayed in Jerusalem for four weeks. On his way back, he reached Crete by 2 May 1684, proceeding to Chios and Izmir, and returning to Istanbul overland. The exact date of his return is not mentioned in his published journal.

The original travelogue may have consisted of loose notes and observations which Myrike had sent to his relatives and friends in Wesel. It was there that the famous Pietist Johann Heinrich Reitz (d. 1720) gathered and critically collated the various fragments together. Reitz, who had published a new German translation of the New Testament in 1703, spent the last years of his life in Wesel, where he led a private school.

The first edition of Myrike's journal was published in 1714 in Osnabrück by Michael Andreas Fuhrmann under the title *Reyse nach Jerusalem und dem Land Canaan*, with extensive footnotes as well as appendices. This edition included an index which was not reproduced in any later edition.

The *Reyse* was reprinted in Itzstein in 1720 and again, in both Augsburg and Itzstein, in 1789 (see also below).

Myrike's travelogue was translated into Dutch by the editor's son, Wilhelm Otto Reitz, and published in Rotterdam in 1725. The Dutch translation remains very close to the German original, though Wilhelm Otto Reitz did add a fanciful title plate which includes an emblem with the words *Iudea capta*. He also inserted two illustrations (p. 39) of the 'chapel of the Holy Sepulchre within the great church' (although represented against a background of open sky) and of the Holy Sepulchre itself (showing a rectangular tomb in an unadorned cave), and two depictions (p. 69) of unidentified Ottoman mosques. Reitz the elder had deliberately left in Myrike's original comparisons between places in Canaan and contemporary Wesel, which Reitz junior substituted with comparisons to Dutch cities (e.g. Rotterdam and Utrecht) in the translation. These and other additions by the translator were placed between square brackets. The Dutch translation also includes an extensive index.

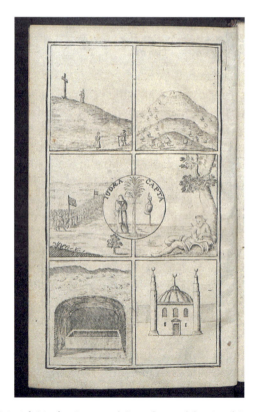

Illustration 7. Heinrich Myrike, *Reyse nach Jerusalem und dem Land Canaan,* frontispiece

Originally, Reitz the elder had justified the publication of Myrike's travelogue by stating that few earlier travellers had compared ancient Canaan with 'its present state', but this is not convincing because Myrike's observations about the 17th-century state of that part of Palestine tend to be superficial and are seldom explicitly comparative. It seems more likely that the original account by Myrike was little more than a pretext for Reitz to display his own (admittedly considerable) erudition. He does so in extensive footnotes, which often take up most (sometimes all) of the page, and which occasionally have only a tenuous connection with the main narrative (e.g. digressions about classical figures, an etymological disgression on the word 'Arab' with proverbs, etc.). Reitz also adds lengthy *Zugabe* on Islam and the Turks, including comments on their government, religiosity and superstitions, hospitality, etc., and on the conquest of Jerusalem by the 'Saracens'. These additional texts contain numerous references to Ogier Ghiselin de Busbecq's *Turkish letters* and the works of the Dutch scholar Adriaan Reland, the French traveller 'Monsieur Du Mont', and the Englishman Paul Rycaut.

For the German edition of 1789, some of these *Zugabe* were updated, perhaps by Reitz the younger, with events up to 1788 (e.g. pp. 181-5). In an Appendix, the Augsburg edition of 1789 also offers an account of the pilgrimage to the Holy Land undertaken in 1523 by Peter Fuessli (1482-1548), a bell-founder from Zurich who became a prominent leader of the local civil militia.

SIGNIFICANCE

The fact that Myrike's account was published in at least three German editions and was translated into Dutch suggests that it was distributed widely in (northern) Germany and the Low Countries. Ralf Elger has recently argued that Myrike's *Reyse* was a 'milestone' in the development of what he calls 'born-again Orientalism'. Nevertheless, no modern studies of Myrike's work appear to have been published.

For modern historians, the text offers various valuable observations that shed light on Christian pilgrimage to the Holy Places in the 17th century. For example, on the Mount of Olives Myrike visited the ruins of the Chapel of the Ascension, which houses a rock believed to bear a footprint 'which the Lord Jesus is believed to have made there, as if in wax, at his ascension, for eternal memory'. Myrike observed the detrimental effect of the pilgrimage on sites such as this and the ways the Muslim authorities profited from the Christian pilgrimage: 'This spot receives a great deal of attention, people kissing this footstep and carrying with them small pieces of rock broken off as the greatest relics. The Turks have forbidden this, lest they be robbed of the great benefit they reap from these visits and this kissing by Christians' (German, pp. 91-2; Dutch, p. 68).

PUBLICATIONS

> Henrich Myrike, *Reyse nach Jerusalem und dem Land Canaan*, ed. Joh. Henrich Reitz, Osnabrück: Michael Andreas Fuhrmann, 1714; It.sing. 1481 f (digitised version available through *MDZ*)
>
> Henrich Myrike, *Reyse nach Jerusalem und dem Land Canaan*, ed. Joh. Henrich Reitz, Itzstein: Johann Jakob Haug, 1720
>
> [Hendrik Myrike,] *Daghregister gehouden door den Heere Hendrik Myrike, in zijn Ed. Leven Gereformeert Predikant te Konstantinopelen op zijne reis naar en door 't beloofde Lant Kanaan. Met aanmerkingen verrykt*, trans. W.O. Reitz, Rotterdam: Philippus Losel, 1725 (Dutch trans.); BIB.HER.002322 (digitised version available through Universiteits Bibliotheek Gent)
>
> Heinrich Mirike, *Reize von Konstantinopel nach Jerusalem und dem Lande Kanaan. Mit vielen Anmerkungen von Palästina etc. von Johann heinrich Reiz. Nebst einem Fragment der von Herrn Peter Füeßlin aus Zürich, im J. 1523 gethanen Pilgerreize nach dem gelobten Lande*, ed. Joh. Henrich Reitz, Augsburg: Christoph Friedrich Bürglen, 1789

STUDIES

> R. Elger, 'Blessing and curse in the "Promised Land". Jonas Korte's *Travels in the Ottoman Empire, 1737-1739*', in M. Kemper and R. Elger (eds), *The piety of learning. Islamic Studies in honor of Stefan Reichmuth*, Leiden, 2017, 227-49

Maurits van den Boogert

Neu-eröffnetes Amphitheatrum

'Newly-opened amphitheatre'

DATE 1723-8
ORIGINAL LANGUAGE German

DESCRIPTION

Neu-eröffnetes Amphitheatrum (in full, *Neu-eröffnetes Amphitheatrum, worinnen nach dem uns bekanten gantzen Welt-Creiß, alle Nationen nach ihrem Habit, in saubern Figuren repräsentiret, Anbey die Länder nach ihrer Situation, Climate, Fruchtbarkeit, Inclination und Beschaffenheit der Einwohner, Religion, vornehmste Städte, Ertz-Bistümer, Universitäten, Häfen, Vestungen, Commercien, Macht, Statts-Interesse, Regierungs-Form, Raritäten und Müntzen Praetensionibus, vornehmsten Ritter-Orden und Wappen aufgeführet sind, und welches, mit Zuziehung der Land-Charten, zu vieler Belustigung, vornehmlich aber der studierenden Jugend, als ein sehr nützliches und anmuthiges Compendium Geographicum, Genea-logicum, Heraldicum, Curiosum, Numismaticum, kan gebrauchet werden,* 'Newly opened amphitheatre, in which all the known world is presented, i.e. all the nations in their costumes in clear pictures, the countries according to their situation, climate, fertility, attitudes and character of the inhabitants, religion, most important cities, archbishoprics, universi-ties, ports, fortresses, businesses, powers, state interests, forms of gov-ernment, curiosities and coins, aspirations (claims), the most important orders of knights and coats of arms. And which, with addition of maps, can be used for more amusement, especially for young students, as a very useful and encouraging *compendium geographicum, genealogicum, heraldicum, curiosum, numismaticum*') is a series of books in German by anonymous authors and edited by Johann Michael Funcke in Erfurt. Its intention was to provide young readers with a compendium of informa-tion about the world. It was published in folio format with a number of half-page woodcuts showing the inhabitants of the lands described. The full general title of the series indicates the topics addressed in vari-ous volumes: the situation of the country, climate, fertility, attitudes and character of the inhabitants, religion, most important cities, archbishop-rics, universities, ports, fortresses, businesses, etc. These are described in numbered chapters divided into subsections, with issues pertaining to religious matters appearing under section V in each chapter.

Apparently, only four volumes were published: Europe (1723; 96 pp.), Africa (1723; 96 pp.), America (1723; 124 pp.) and South Asia (1728; 142 pp.). A further volume, entitled *Neu-eröffnetes Amphitheatrum Turcicum*, was published in 1724, again with Johann Michael Funcke named as editor, though, despite its very similar title and layout, this volume seems to be at odds with the series. Daniel Cyranka (*Mahomet*, pp. 188-9) points out that the 1728 volume on South Asia does not refer to it, and its treatment of Muḥammad and Islam is surprisingly different from that in the others. The five-year gap between the third and fourth volumes – though puzzling – is in a way explained in the preface to the second volume (on Africa, pp. 1r-1v). Though Asia would have been a natural choice of the topic for the second volume because of its ties with Europe, the anonymous author decided to wait until the complicated situation there, arising from wars involving the Ottomans, Persians and Russians, had become clearer. Meanwhile, he turned his attention to Africa.

This entry gives an overview of the contents of vols 1 and 4 concerning Islam, and of the extraordinary 1724 volume. Further research should provide fuller clarification about the reason for this volume and its contents.

In vol. 1, on Europe, Islam is described in ch. 36, subsection V, which covers the Turks who lived in Europe. The description of their Islamic beliefs and practices is a mere 250 words, compressed into 13 points, and matter-of-fact in approach. The author allows himself a touch of sarcasm in only two instances, on the sensual Muslim paradise and their abstinence from wine.

The description of Islamic teachings (*die Türckische Theologie*) in vol. 4, on South Asia, occurs between items of geographical and cultural information. After a general description of Asia in ch. 1, there comes a section on the Asian Turks (chs 2-7, pp. 5-24). First, the fundamentals of the 'Turkish religion' are outlined (pp. 6-7; quoted in Cyranka, *Mahomet*, p. 190), and then each item is briefly described in subsection V of the following chapters. Continuity of description is sometimes interrupted by information on other religions, e.g. in chs 8-9 on Judaism.

This description of the 'Turkish religion' in vol. 4 is in accord with what has already appeared in vol. 1, and does not correspond with the contents of *Neu-eröffnetes Amphitheatrum Turcicum*. The first part enumerates the Five Pillars of the faith that are crucial in 'Turkish theology' (statement of belief, ritual prayer, alms, fasting, pilgrimage to Mecca).

Then, the author names the two areas within which Muslims operate, issues concerning belief and issues concerning practice, indicating that both are closely bound together. Attention is also given to 'Mahomed' and 'Alcoran'.

This information about 'Turkish theology' is given without any apologetic or polemical comments, and interestingly enough the question of truth is not raised. Two passages (vol. 4, ch. 5, pp. 16-17, quoted by Cyranka, *Mahomet*, pp. 191-2) state clearly the Muslim beliefs that not only the Qur'an but all the sacred books are to be believed in all their details, and that all the prophets brought God's revelation, being free from error, preserved from grave sins, believing the same religion, which was *Machometanische*. There is no mention of the qur'anic criticism of the Jewish and Christian scriptures, and it is emphasised that whoever doubts the message of the prophets and their books counts as an unbeliever. There are no authorial or editorial comments about these points, and they give young readers no reason to criticise 'Turkish theology'.

This approach is contrary to what is found in the separate volume, *Neu-eröffnetes Amphitheatrum Turcicum* of 1724. This is 172 pages long, of which four pages are devoted to 'the core of Turkish history' (pp. 5-8, quoted almost *in extenso* in Cyranka, *Mahomet*, pp. 515-20). The rest contains descriptions of the endeavours of the Ottoman sultans.

The author explains that the work serves both a theological purpose, to show the Turks as a divine scourge, and a political purpose, to relate their history. He notes the speed with which the Turks developed their state and also the extent of their conquests, underlining that one cannot really understand the history of many European states without understanding the history of the Ottomans. Although the author does not include the history of the Arabs ('Saracens'), the close relationship between them and the Turks requires him to give a brief account of Muḥammad, the founder of the 'Turkish unbelief' (*die Türckische Unglauben*): he was a prophet of the devil, a master of black magic and a lustful crook (*Betrüger*). The author mentions Johan Andreae (Juan Andrés, fl. c. 1500) as the source of his information.

This very polemically-minded presentation of Muḥammad is followed by a much more neutral description of the history of the Sublime Porte, given under the names of the sultans. According to Cyranka (*Mahomet*, p. 187), the author was much more focused on integrating the history of the Ottomans into European history than on developing an apparently theological understanding of them. Reports on battles (including the fall of Constantinople) are almost devoid of any religious or theological content.

The Ottomans are presented as implacably hostile but not as a 'religious enemy', despite descriptions of bloody wars and inhuman atrocities.

SIGNIFICANCE

The book series was meant to provide young readers with basic knowledge about the world. Given current knowledge about it, any impact it had is difficult to assess, though it seems that there were no further editions. The reason for the discrepancy between the approach to Islam in *Neu-eröffnetes Amphitheatrum Turcicum* (1724) and in the volumes on Europe and Asia has not been fully explained, not to mention the very existence of this volume outside the series.

The contents of the scattered material on Islam in vol. 4 in the series, on Asia, require fuller analysis, as instances such as the following occur: 'The Moghuls or Mahometans are those who follow the false belief of Mahomed' (vol. 4, p. 109). In a volume where polemic is absent, such condemnations jar.

PUBLICATIONS

> *Neu-eröffnetes Amphitheatrum, Worinnen Nach dem uns bekanten gantzen Welt-Creiß, Alle Nationen Nach ihrem Habit, in saubern Figuren repräsentiret, Anbey die Länder nach ihrer Situation, Climate, Fruchtbarkeit, Inclination und Beschaffenheit der Einwohner, Religion, vornehmste Städte, Ertz-Bistümer, Universitäten, Häfen, Vestungen, Commercien, Macht, Statts-Interesse, Regierungs-Form, Raritäten und Müntzen Praetensionibus, vornehmsten Ritter-Orden und Wappen aufgeführet sind, Und welches, mit Zuziehung der Land-Charten, zu vieler Belustigung, vornehmlich aber der studierenden Jugend, als ein sehr nützliches und anmuthiges Compendium Geographicum, Genealogicum, Heraldicum, Curiosum, Numismaticum, kan gebrauchet werden*, vol. 1. *Europa*, Erfurt, 1723; E 2-IX-8 (digitised version available through Biblioteca de Catalunya)
>
> *Neu-eröffnetes Amphitheatrum Turcicum, Worinnen Der Kern Türckischer Geschichten, Von Grundsetzung ihrer Religion und Reiches, ihrem Propheten Mahomed, seinen Nachfolgern oder Caliphen, Türckischen Käysern, irhen, wie auch einiger ihrer vornehmen Ministers seltsamen Fatis, geführten blutigen Kriegen, erstaunlichen Conquesten, Vertilgung der Christlichen Käyserthümer und derer Monarchen, ab- und Zunehmen ihres Staats, blutigen Belag- und Eroberungen, grausamen Schlachten, unmenschlicher Grausamkeit, Hochmut, Kriegs-Listen, wie auch von den Christlichen Victorien wider dieselben etc. etc. Kurtz, doch hinlänglich, mit Historischer*

Feder biß auf die allerneueste und gegenwärtige Zeiten beschrieben,
mit vielen Figuren und deren Beschreibung ausgeschmückt, darzu
mit dem nöthigen Register versehen wird, Erfurt, 1724 (repr. 2018);
2BZ159592402 (digitised version available through Österreichisches
Nationalbibliothek)

Neu-eröffnetes Amphitheatrum, Worinnen Aus dem Südlichen Asia Die
meisten Nationen nach ihrem Habit, in saubern Figuren repräsen-
tiret, Anbey die Länder nach ihrer Situation Climate, Fruchtbarkeit,
Inclination und Beschaffenheit der Einwohner, Religion, vornehmste
Städte, Ertz-Bisthümer, Universitäten, Häfen, Vestungen, Commer-
cien, Macht, Staats-Interesse, Regierungs-Form, Raritäten und Münt-
zen beschrieben sind. Und welches mit Zuziehung der Land-Charten,
zu vieler Belustigung, vornehmlich aber der studirenden Jugend, als
ein sehr nützliches und anmuthiges Compendium Geographicum,
Genealogicum, Heraldicum, Curiosum Numismaticum, kan gebraucht
werden, vol. 4, *Asia,* Erfurt, 1728; 2BZ159592505 (digitised version
available through Österreichisches Nationalbibliothek)

STUDIES

D.   Cyranka, *Mahomet. Repräsentationen des Propheten in*
deutschsprachiger Literatur des 18. Jahrhunderts, Göttingen, 2018,
pp. 182-93, 515-20

Stanisław Grodź

Johann Heinrich Callenberg

DATE OF BIRTH   12 January 1694
PLACE OF BIRTH   Molschleben, near Gotha, Germany
DATE OF DEATH   16 July 1760
PLACE OF DEATH   Halle

BIOGRAPHY

Johann Heinrich Callenberg was born into a peasant family in Molschleben, near Gotha. He attended school in Gotha and then studied Protestant theology and philology at Halle from 1715 to 1719. He was influenced in Gotha by the Pietist preacher Johann Müller (1649-1727), the author of *Das Licht am Abend* ('Light at evening') (1736), and in Halle by August Hermann Francke (1663-1727). As well as guiding him towards Pietism, they stirred his interest in mission to Muslims and Jews. As a student, he was taught Arabic by Salomon Negri (1665-1728) and later Theocharis Dadichi (1693-1734). He also studied Hebrew and Yiddish. He remained in Halle until his death in 1760, being appointed lecturer at the University of Halle in 1727, then Professor of Eastern Languages in 1735 and Extraordinary Professor of Theology in 1739 (Bautz, 'Callenberg', p. 863). He taught Arabic, Yiddish and Jewish studies, and was also librarian and archivist at the Francke Institute (*Hallesches Waisenhaus*).

In 1728, Callenburg established the *Institutum Judaicum et Orientale* in Halle, to aid missionary work and promote the conversion of Jews and Muslims in the Middle East (Bautz, 'Callenberg', p. 863). Through the Institute, he established a printing house for Oriental languages and published material in Arabic, Turkish, Persian and Hebrew (Bochinger, 'Abenteuer Islam zur Wahrnehmung', pp. 306-32). In addition, the Institute also sent out around 20 missionaries to various European and Middle Eastern countries.

With the decline of Pietism and, from 1740, the rise of rationalism in the Protestant theological faculties in Prussia, funding for the Institute fell steadily. It was finally closed by royal decree in 1792 (Clark, *Politics of conversion*, pp. 78-81).

Callenberg's students included Friedrich Eberhard Boysen (1720-1800), whose *Der Koran* (1773) was the second German translation of the Qur'an, and Johann Salomo Semler (1725-91), who became a professor of theology at Halle and was renowned for his ideas concerning Hermeticism.

Semler wrote that he was unimpressed by Callenberg, whose classes he found tedious and who availed himself of the proximity of his rooms to the university to lecture in his dressing gown (Hamilton, "'To rescue the honour of the Germans'", p. 193).

Callenberg's followers included Johann Jacob Reiske (1716-74) and Oluf Gerhard Tychsen (1734-1815) (Raup, 'Callenberg', p. 181).

MAIN SOURCES OF INFORMATION

Primary

J.H. Callenberg, *Programma qvo post brevem dissertationem de Christiano profes-soris philosophiae officio habendas a se praelectiones indicat M. Io. Henr. Callenberg Philos. Prof. Pvbl. Extraord*, Halle, 1727

J.H. Callenberg, *Spicilegium Instituti Muhammedici monumentis subserviens*, Halle, 1743

Secondary

D. Haas, 'Johann Heinrich Callenbergs Institutum Judaicum et Muhammedicum und die "alte orientalische Christenheit" mit besonderer Berücksichtigung des Wirkens des reisenden Mitarbeiters Stephan Schultz', Halle, 2016 (MA Diss. Martin Luther Universität Halle-Wittenberg)

A. Hamilton, "'To rescue the honour of the Germans". Qur'an translations by eighteenth- and early nineteenth-century German Protestants', *Journal of the Warburg and Courtauld Institutes* 77 (2014) 173-209

W. Raup, art. 'Callenberg, Johann Heinrich (1694-1760)', in H.F. Klemme and M. Kuehn (eds), *The dictionary of eighteenth-century German philosophers*, vol. 1, London, 2010, 180-1

RGG, art. 'Callenberg, Johann Heinrich', in R. Vierhaus (ed.), *Deutsche Biogra-phische Enzyklopädie*, vol. 2, Munich, 2005, 265-6

C. Rymatzki, *Hallischer Pietismus und Judenmission. Johann Heinrich Callenbergs Institutum Judaicum und dessen Freundeskreis (1728-1736)*, Halle, 2004

C. Bochinger, 'Pietistische Identität zwischen persönlicher Frömmigkeit und Gruppenprozessen', in W. Beltz (ed.), *Biographie und Religion. Zur Per-sonalität der Mitarbeiter des Institutum judaicum et muhammedicum J.H. Callensbergs*, Halle, 1997, 33-44

H. Bobzin, 'Vom Sinn des Arabischstudiums in Sprachkanon der Philologia Sacra', in W. Beltz (ed.), *Biographie und Religion. Zur Personalität der Mitarbeiter des Institutum judaicum et muhammedicum J.H. Callensbergs*, Halle, 1997, 21-32

C. Bochinger, 'Abenteuer Islam zur Wahrnehmung fremder Religion im Hal-lenser Pietismus des 18. Jahrhunderts', Munich, 1996 (Diss. Ludwig-Max-imilian University)

C. Clark, *The politics of conversion. Missionary Protestantism and the Jews in Prus-sia, 1728-1941*, Oxford, 1995

F.W. Bautz, art. 'Callenberg, Johann Heinrich, Orientalist und Theologe', *Biogra-phisch-Bibliographisches Kirchenlexikon*, vol. 1, Herzberg, 1990, cols 863-4
F. Lau, art. 'Callenberg, Johann Heinrich', in *Neue Deutsche Biographie*, vol. 3, Berlin, 1957, 96

WORKS ON CHRISTIAN-MUSLIM RELATIONS

Islam in the writings of Johann Heinrich Callenberg

DATE   1729-43
ORIGINAL LANGUAGE   German, Arabic and Latin

DESCRIPTION

Callenberg's interest in Islam was primarily motivated by his concern to find ways to evangelise Muslims. He published many short works, including grammatical and linguistic studies, as well as works on historical, theological and evangelistic topics.

Below is presented a preliminary survey of Callenberg's writings about Islam, as little has been done on this aspect of his work. The publications discussed were mainly written in Latin, often including some Arabic, though he also published articles in German in the local newspaper, *Wöchentlichen Hallischen Anzeigen*. They are presented in order of publication.

His earliest publications were based on translations that he himself made with the help of Salomon Negri (Sulaymān ibn Ya'qūb al-Shāmī l-Ṣāliḥānī): *Catechismus Lutheri minor arabice quem olim sub ductu B. Sal. Negri Damasceni in hanc linguam transtulit et vulgavit J. Henr. Callenberg* (1729) and *Colloquia arabica idiomatis vulgaris sub ductu B. Sal. Negri Damasceni olim composuit iamque in usum scholae suae vulgavit* (1729). Negri had taught Callenberg as a student, and together they translated these two texts, which were published following Negri's death in 1727 (Ghobrial, 'Life and hard times', pp. 326-7).

The *Catechismus Lutheri minor arabice* (*Al-ta'līm al-Masīḥī*) was originally produced at the suggestion of A.H. Francke; it is 48 pages long with a four-page preface in Latin that explains its origin as an exercise in translation and its purpose as to enable Muslims to read the Catechism in Arabic in order that they may understand and convert to Christianity. This is followed by the text of the *Shorter Catechism* in Arabic (41 pages), then a biblical passage headed in Latin, *Particula concionis montanae a Iesu Christo habitae* (Matthew 5:1-7, 28; four pages).

Colloquia arabica idiomatis vulgaris was prepared as a reader, with short selected Bible passages to help missionaries to communicate in Arabic. These passages include 1 Peter 2:11-25, Matthew 5:1-7, 28, parts of John's Gospel, and his letters. It was expanded and republished in 1740.

Juris circa Christianos muhammedici particulae (1729) is Callenberg's doctoral dissertation. It is a study of the legal status of Christians under Islamic rule, based on the legal compendium of the Ḥanafī jurist Abū l-Layth al-Samarqandī (d. 983), which Callenberg developed under Dadichi's guidance (Bochinger, 'Abenteuer Islam zur Wahrnehmung', pp. 107-8). It is 24 pages long and is divided into 8 numbered sections, which vary from one to four pages in length. It concludes with a *corollaria* giving six points that summarise Callenberg's understanding of Muslim law in relation to Christians. 'That conditions for Christians living under the Turks is miserable, but that Christians are suffering more in other places as well. [...] It is important to gain a greater understanding of Islamic law. [...] A greater understanding of Arabic is important in order to be able to understand the story of the Eastern people' (pp. 19-20). The local newspaper reported on the doctoral defence and its subject as follows:

> In this dissertation, in the words of the Muḥammadan jurists, the laws in use in Turkey, Persia and in other Muḥammadan kingdoms concerning Christians living in these countries are recalled and explained, especially from Arab Codicis Mscti [*sic*], whose author, Abulleithus, is one of the most celebrated of his fellow-believers, using the texts in the Arabic language, but whose translations are included in the text, and it is hoped that this will be very useful in order to be thoroughly informed of the state of the Oriental Church under the yoke of the Muḥammadan rulers which are more considerable than are generally desired, especially since so far no one has raised this matter from such authentic documents. (*Wöchentlichen Hallischen Anzeigen* for 5 September 1729, pp. 86-7)

Subsequently, due to the interest shown, Callenberg published *Loci codicum Arabicorum de iure circa Christianos muhammedico* (1741-2) in three parts, with a description of the manuscript sources he had used in his dissertation and other manuscripts he had discovered (Bochinger, 'Abenteuer Islam zur Wahrnehmung', p. 107).

Dritte Fortsetzung seines Berichts von einem Versuch das arme jüdische Volck zur Erkäntniß der christlichen Wahrheit anzuleiten [...] *Nebst einer Continuation der Nachricht von einer Bemühung auch den Muhammedanern mit einem heilsamen Unterricht zu dienen* (Halle, 1732, 1734²) sets out the purposes of *Institutum Judaicum et Orientale* in Halle, relating its achievements in publishing and missionary work up to 1730. It is 48 pages long, divided into 12 chapters. Chs 2-10 detail the production of material for work among the Jews, after which ch. 11 (pp. 44-8), entitled 'Of an essay to promote the salvation of the Mahometans', begins by explaining that following the 'late Persian war the Russians had brought many Mahometan prisoners to a certain place, where Protestant clergy had an opportunity to speak to them' (p. 44), which had led to Callenberg being asked to provide material suitable for use with these Muslims, as well as others in Persia. Having obtained Arabic type, he then published material that was also useful for work among the Jews: 'The errours of the Mahometans in many points having a near affinity with [the Jews], and the same language being understood by many of them, to shew them the true Way to their eternal salvation' (p. 45).

In this chapter the works in Arabic published by the Institute are first listed (pp. 45-7), followed by a list of the places where they have been distributed, including by Danish missionaries among the Moguls (India), in Batavia (Indonesia), Istanbul, the Levant, North Africa and various European ports (pp. 47-8). The final paragraph reports that the Tatars on the Persian borders willingly accepted the material (p. 48).

Symbolum muhammedicum ex Alcorano concinnatum (1733) is four pages long. In it Callenberg uses verses of the Qur'an to present a Muslim creed. It comprises three statements 'Divinitus ilustratus credo [...]' (pp. 1-2), 'Iesum, Dei filium' (p. 3) and 'Credo, Spiritum sanctum nullum alium esse' (pp. 3-4), summarising what the Qur'an says about God, Jesus and the Holy Spirit, accompanied by short comments with footnotes giving references to passages from the Qur'an to support the argument. Christoph Bochinger explains that:

> the treatise does not aim to depict Islam from its own theological-historical centre, but rather to compare qur'anic teachings with central statements of the Apostles' Creed, which serves as a structural principle. This leads to a formal inconsistency, which is deliberately accepted for the sake of the didactic-apologetic purpose. So the second article begins with the negative statement: *Iesum, Dei filium, dominumque nostrum esse, non credo* ['I do not believe that Jesus is Son of God and our Lord']. Callenberg's systematised 'tutoring' in the formulation of a creed aims not for a factual representation of Islam, but rather for a pointed apologetic. It stylises Islam as a uniform opposite, in order to better argue with it. ('Abenteuer Islam zur Wahrnehmung', p. 168)

Callenberg identifies the Holy Spirit in Islam as the angel Gabriel: *Credo Spiritum Sanctum nullum alium esse quam Gabrielem, angelum* ['I believe that the Holy Spirit is none other than the angel Gabriel']. He does not explicitly mention the *shahāda*, but states that in Islam God is 'infinite, eternal, omnipotent, omniscient, good and merciful', and that 'God is a single, not a triune God, the Creator of all things, even the angels'. The story of the fall of Iblis and thus the Islamic explanation of evil (Q 2:30-8) and the expulsion of the first humans from paradise are also briefly described.

The third section contains statements about believers – according to the Qur'an, Muslims form the community of those who worship God:

> By nature, in their view, all people belonged to this community, but their character was corrupt. Therefore, different prophets have brought laws to the people at different times, the last being Muḥammad, who invited them to the true religion (*veram religionem*). The people who followed him would be spared by God on the Day of Judgement. Muḥammad told them to perform ablutions, to pray, to fast, to do good to the poor, and to perform a religious pilgrimage. Those who live according to these rules would be forgiven their sins, live in paradise and be allowed to satisfy there all pleasures and desires. On the other hand, those who deny God are condemned to the eternal punishment of hell. (*Symbolum Muhammedicum*, pp. 3-4)

Here, as in other places in the work, Callenberg is using passages from the Qur'an to point out possible connections and points of difference for use in Christian-Muslim apologetics (Bochinger, 'Abenteuer Islam zur Wahrnehmung', p. 171).

In *Dissertatiuncula de conuersione Muhammedanorum ad Christum expetita, tentataque* (1733), a short 12-page tract, Callenberg records earlier attempts to conduct mission to Muslims from Western Europe. In a series of short statements, he describes these efforts, starting with Ramon Llull, Johann Potkens of Cologne, Erasmus and Nicolaus Clenardus and his visit to Africa; post-Reformation figures include Martin Crusius, Peter Kirsten, Hugo Grotius, Gisbert Voetius, Pietro Della Valle and Ruthger Spey; then from the 17th century Johannes Fabricius, Georg Calixt, Jacob Golius, Johann Heinrich Hottinger, Levinus Warner, Gottfried Arnold, Johann Heinrich May, Ludovico Marracci and Cotton Mather. The tract ends with an excerpt from Abraham Hinckelmann's foreword to his 1694 edition of the Qur'an, which discusses the need for a thorough knowledge of the Islamic scripture (Bochinger, 'Abenteuer Islam zur Wahrnehmung', pp. 113-14).

Scriptores de religione muhammedica (1734) is four pages long and contains a similar list to *Dissertatiuncula* of Christian works on Islam, adding Thomas Aquinas, Nicetas Choniates, Henricus Bullinger, Filippo Guadagnoli, Michel Baudier, Johann Zechendorff, Humphrey Prideaux, André du Ryer and Alexander Ross. The final section refers to those writing in Callenberg's own time, including David Nerreter, Adrianus Relandus and Johann David Michaelis.

Specimen indicis rerum ad litteraturam arabicam pertinentium (1735) is an eight-page sample for a dictionary in Latin of Islam and Christianity. It includes entries on: *Africanus*, *Leo* and his role as a teacher in Rome; *Alcoranus*, a longer entry with reference to various versions and to Hinckelmann's preface; *Bedwellus* (William Bedwell, 1563-1627), the British Arabist; *Biblia*, referring to the existence of an Arabic version of the Bible (pp. 2-3); *Sunna* (p. 8) does not discuss this term, but only refers to Johann Hottinger's *Historia orientalis* (1651).

Historia Adami muhammedica (1735), eight pages long, and *Historia Iesu Christi muhammedica* (1736), 24 pages long, both use various keywords and passages from the Qur'an to present the Muslim understanding of Adam and Jesus Christ. The former is in nine sections and follows the story of Adam through the Fall and the birth of his sons, very much in accordance with the account in Genesis 1-5 but giving references from the Qur'an. Likewise, the latter relates the life of Jesus in three chapters: ch. 1, *Muhammedica de Christi nativitate narratio* (pp. 1-8), gives the Muslim account of the birth of Jesus; ch. 2, *quomodo Christus legati munere functus sit* (pp. 8-16), considers how Jesus functioned as Christ; ch. 3, *fabulae de exitu vita Christi* (pp. 16-22), relates the results of Christ's work. The work ends with a two-page Appendix containing a list of references to the way Muslims portray the history of the Church, using the Qur'an, Johann Heinrich Hottinger and Ludovico Marracci.

Specimen bibliothecae arabicae qua libri arabici editi recensentur (1736), 16 pages long, is another sample. It contains short reviews of various Arabic grammars, text editions and translations, including Guillaume Postel, Theodor Bibliander, Thomas Erpenius and Johann Zechendorff. Bochinger sees it as 'clarifying Callenberg's knowledge of Arabic' (Abenteuer Islam zur Wahrnehmung', p. 113).

'Anmerckungen von dem Muhammedanischen Reiche', published in *Wöchentlichen Hallischen Anzeigen* for 20 October 1736, pp. 681-5, a newspaper article containing a systematic summary of the history of Islam from its beginnings, conveys a clear sense of Callenberg's attitude towards Islam. It describes Muḥammad as 'a malicious, domineering and voluptuous man, [...] who started a new religion [...] and attacked the use of images in Christianity, the remnant of the heresy of Christ's divine majesty' (p. 681), and sums up Islam as an erroneous religion, with teachings borrowed from Christianity and Judaism, that prescribes an outward form of worship. Its main precepts are the unity of God, the recitation of certain prayers, almsgiving, the month of Ramaḍān and pilgrimage to Mecca. Muslims have circumcision in common with the Jews, as well as other ceremonies. They recognise the Old and New Testaments as the Word of God, although they do not want to know anything of the salvation brought through the Messiah. They call their religion Islam, which means total surrender to God (p. 682). The Qur'an is the foremost book of the religion, with 114 suras, which Muḥammad recited in short sections recorded by his scribe or remembered by his listeners. These were stored in no special order, and Abū Bakr then compiled them into the Alcoran, but not in order of composition, explaining that contradictions that were disclosed later abrogated earlier verses (pp. 683-4). Finally, the article explains Muslim dealings with Christians and other non-Muslims: 'The Christians, Jews, and heathens, are called by them unbelievers, and those who associate with God. [...] They regard the Christians as better than the Jews and Heathen' (p. 683). The article concludes by discussing how the behaviour of Muslims towards infidels changed over time. Beginning with Muḥammad's declaration that 'no one should be forced into this religion', and quoting Q 2:256, Callenberg then cites Q 9 (pp. 684-5) to demonstrate that the earlier open teaching had changed so that unbelievers were to be regarded as enemies until they either accepted Islam or agreed to pay a tribute.

Summula historiae sacrae arabica. A Societate Anglicana publicatam in usum Muhammedanorum recudendam curavit Jo Henri Callenberg (1737), 28 pages long, in Arabic with the title page and a single-page preface in Latin, is a reprint of church histories, originally published by Society for the Promotion of Christian Knowledge in London, that Callenberg adapted for use amongst Muslims. Bochinger regards the text as a document of inter-confessional border crossing as it had been prepared by a Syrian Christian, Salomon Negri, and approved by an Anglican, William Wake, Archbishop of Canterbury (r. 1716-37), before being used by a Lutheran, Callenberg ('Abenteuer Islam zur Wahrnehmung', p. 107).

Repertorium muhammedicum (1738-42), in 11 parts, is a compilation of the results of Callenberg's research; in effect, it is a concordance of people and places found in the Qur'an, with additional explanations and references. The contents overlap with earlier publications.

'Nicolai Clenardi Bemühung, die Arabische Sprache in hohe Schulen einzüfuren', in *Wöchentlichen Hallischen Anzeigen* (1741), published in Latin as *Nicolai Clenardi circa Muhammedanorum ad Christum conversionem conatus* (1742), is 52 pages long. In it, Callenberg tells the story of the Belgian Nicolaes Cleynaerts (1495-1542) and his desire to master Arabic. Callenberg reveals something of his own intention when he writes of Cleynaerts' reasons:

> that he should understand Hebrew more fully from this language [Arabic], and to give others a guide to the reading of Arabic writers, but he never even thought of the refutation of the Muḥammadan errors. [...] He had initially objected to the call to write a Latin apology against Muḥammad: 'One must first read the Alcoran, and afterwards the Sunna, for it is foolish to refute what one did not fully understand.' (pp. 26-8)

Sylloge variorum scriptorum locos de Muhammedanorum ad Christum conversione expetita sperata tentataque exhibens (1743), 24 pages long, comprises a collection of 'excerpts' from mission works. The longest (pp. 1-16) is an extract from Guillaume Postel's *De orbis terrae concordia* (1544). This is followed by shorter extracts from a biography of Nicolaes Cleynaerts by Aubertus Miraeus, an alleged Turkish translation of Thomas à Kempis' *De imitatione Christi*, an extract from the preface of the Arabic grammar by Gabriel Sionita and Johannes Hesronita (1616), and finally an extract from the preface to Johannes Zechendorff's *Specimen suratarum* (1638). This compilation was intended to provide material for mission to Muslims.

The body of work produced by Callenberg is among the earliest Protestant Christian missionary material. His collaborative work with the British Society for Promoting Christian Knowledge, and with the Danish Mission to Tranquebar, predates the work of the religious tracts societies that began in the late 18th century.

SIGNIFICANCE

Callenberg's writings reveal his zeal to fulfil the missionary imperative of Matthew 28 'to go and tell'. In particular, his focus was to work among Jews and Muslims, seeking to prepare relevant material for missionaries as well as potential converts. The range of material produced reveals his facility for identifying sources and adapting them for his purposes. The various works reveal Callenberg's awareness of relevant literature and also his easy access to a printing press in order to print off speculative examples, possibly hoping for a patron to sponsor the publication of a full version.

Callenberg was a Pietist who adhered to conservative Protestant theology and upheld the truth of Christianity. Bochinger is of the opinion that Callenberg recognised the plurality of religions and, to a certain extent, their claims to truth (Bochinger, 'Abenteuer Islam zur Wahrnehmung', p. 171).

Even before his death, interest in Callenberg's approach to Islam had waned.

PUBLICATIONS

S. Negri and J.H. Callenberg, *Catechismus Lutheri minor arabice quem olim sub ductu B. Sal. Negri Damasceni in hanc linguam transtulit et vulgavit J. Henr. Callenberg*, Halle, 1729; A.or. 1355 (digitised version available through *MDZ*)

S. Negri and J.H. Callenberg, *Colloquia arabica idiomatic vulgaris sub ductu B. Sal. Negri Damasceni olim composuit iamque in usum scholae suae vulgavit*, Halle, 1729

J.H. Callenberg, *Juris circa Christianos muhammedici particulae*, Halle, 1729; 4 Diss. 32#Beibd.27 (digitised version available through *MDZ*)

J.H. Callenberg, *Dritte Fortsetzung seines Berichts von einem Versuch das arme Jüdische Volck zur Erkäntniß der christlichen Wahrheit anzuleiten [...] Nebst einer Continuation der Nachricht von einer Bemühung auch den Muhammedanern mit einem heilsamen Unterricht zu dienen*, Halle, 1732

J.H. Callenberg, *Dissertatiuncula de conuersione Muhammedanorum ad Christum expetita, tentataque*, Halle, 1733; VD18 10748989 (digitised version available through Universitäts- und Landesbibliothek Sachsen-Anhalt)

J.H. Callenberg, *Symbolum muhammedicum ex Alcorano concinnatum*, Halle, 1733; VD18 10316221 (digitised version available through Universitäts- und Landesbibliothek Sachsen-Anhalt)

J.H. Callenberg, *Dritte Fortsetzung seines Berichts von einem Versuch das arme Jüdische Volck zur Erkäntniß der christlichen Wahrheit anzuleiten [...] Nebst einer Continuation der Nachricht von einer Bemühung auch den Muhammedanern mit einem heilsamen Unterricht zu dienen*, Halle, 1734; De 4015-1/6 (digitised version available through Staatsbibliothek zu Berlin)

J.H. Callenberg, *Scriptores de religione muhammedica*, Halle, 1734; AC09754460 (digitised version available through Österreichisches Nationalbibliothek)

J.H. Callenberg, *Specimen indicis rerum ad litteraturam arabicam pertinentium*, Halle, 1735; AC09754462 (digitised version available through Österreichisches Nationalbibliothek)

J.H. Callenberg, *Historia Adami muhammedica*, Halle, 1735; VD18 10749004 (digitised version available through Universitäts- und Landesbibliothek Sachsen-Anhalt)

J.H. Callenberg, *Historia Iesu Christi muhammedica*, Halle, 1736; VD18 10749306 (digitised version available through Universitäts- und Landesbibliothek Sachsen-Anhalt)

J.H. Callenberg, *Specimen bibliothecae arabicae qua libri arabici editi recensentur*, Halle, 1736; VD18 10749454 (digitised version available through Universitäts- und Landesbibliothek Sachsen-Anhalt)

J.H. Callenberg, 'Anmerckungen von dem Muhammedanischen Reiche', *Wöchentlichen Hallischen Anzeigen*, 20 October 1736, 681-5

J.H. Callenberg, *Summula historiae sacrae arabica. A Societate Anglicana publicatam in usum Muhammedanorum recudendam curavit Jo Henri Callenberg*, Halle, 1737; H-11721 (digitised version available through BNF)

J.H. Callenberg, *Repertorium muhammedicum*, Halle, 1738-42, 11 parts; AC09754459 (digitised version available through Österreichisches Nationalbibliothek)

J.H. Callenberg, *Colloquia arabica idiomatis vulgaris sub ductu B. Sal. Negri Damasceni olim composuit iamque in usum scholae suae vulgavit*, Halle, 1740

J.H. Callenberg, 'Nicolai Clenardi Bemühung, die Arabische Sprache in hohe Schulen einzüfuren', *Wöchentlichen Hallischen Anzeigen*, Halle, 1741

J.H. Callenberg, *Loci codicum arabicorum de iure circa Christianos muhammedico*, Halle, 1741-2 (in 3 parts)

J.H. Callenberg, *Nicolai Clenardi circa Muhammedanorum ad Christum conversionem conatus*, Halle, 1742

J.H. Callenberg, *Sylloge variorum scriptorum locos de Muhammedanorum ad Christum conversione expetita sperata tentataque exhibens*, Halle, 1743

J.H. Callenberg, *Short account of an essay to bring the Jewish nation to the knowledge and practice of the truth of the Gospel and his endeavour to promote the conversion of the Mohammadans to Christianity [...] done into English*, Halle, 1751 (English trans. of the 1732 edition, made in 1734; Theol.Jud.300 (digitised version available through Sächsische Landesbibliothek – Staats- und Universitätsbibliothek)

STUDIES

J.-P.A. Ghobrial, 'The life and hard times of Solomon Negri. An Arabic teacher in early modern Europe', in J. Loop, A. Hamilton and C. Burnett (eds), *The teaching and learning of Arabic in early modern Europe*, Leiden, 2017, 310-31

Haas, 'Johann Heinrich Callenbergs Institutum Judaicum et Muhammedicum'

Hamilton, '"To rescue the honour of the Germans"'

Rymatzki, *Hallischer Pietismus und Judenmission*

Bochinger, 'Abenteuer Islam'

John Chesworth

Johann Leonhard Fröreisen

DATE OF BIRTH   9 May 1694
PLACE OF BIRTH   Breuwickersheim, near Strasbourg
DATE OF DEATH   13 January 1761
PLACE OF DEATH   Strasbourg

BIOGRAPHY

Born in 1694, Johann Leonhard Fröreisen was brought up in Francke's Foundation in Halle. He studied theology in Strasbourg, Giessen and Jena (where he also studied law), taught at Wilhelmsgymnasium in Strasbourg, and then was appointed professor of theology at Strasbourg University (1724). He became the president of the Kirchenkonvent in 1731. Fröreisen took part in theological disputes of his time, e.g. criticising theologians who posed as the highest arbiters of orthodoxy. During the heyday of Pietism in Strasbourg, he was active as a vehement defender of Lutheran orthodoxy. He directed the main force of his criticism against Count Nicolaus Ludwig von Zinzendorf (1700-60) and the Moravian Church (*Herrnhuter Brüdergemeinde*).

His publications mostly contain speeches he made on various occasions. In *De misero ecclesiae Augustanae Confessionis permultis in locis statu* (1743), his most famous text, he strongly deplores the condition of the Lutheran Church and argues for a stronger leadership that would restrain the proliferation of 'private circles of believers'. He expressed his criticism so strongly that some of his co-religionists believed the rumour that he would join the Roman Catholic Church. The text was confiscated by the Lutheran authorities but gained such a popularity among Roman Catholics that they published it in Latin, German and French.

From 1741, Fröreisen published a series of short writings against Count Zinzendorf, in which he was as authoritarian as the theologians he had criticised earlier.

MAIN SOURCES OF INFORMATION

Primary

J.J. Moser, *Beytrag zu einem Lexico der jeztlebenden Lutherisch- und Reformirten Theologen in und um Teutschland welche entweder die Theologie öffentlich lehren, oder sich durch theologische Schriften bekannt gemacht haben*, Züllichau, 1740, pp. 215-18

J.Ch. Strodtmann and E.L. Rathlef (eds), *Geschichte jeztlebender Gelehrten*, vol. 11, Celle, 1746, pp. 124-54

Secondary

Art. 'Fröreisen, Johann Leonhard', in W. Killy (ed.), *Deutsche Biographische Enzyklopädie*, vol. 3, Munich, 1996, 506

M. Schmidt, art. 'Fröreisen, Johann Leonhard', in *Neue Deutsche Biographie*, vol. 5, Berlin, 1961, 654

WORKS ON CHRISTIAN-MUSLIM RELATIONS

Vergleichung des Graf Zinzendorfs mit dem Mahomet
'Comparison of Count Zinzendorf with Muḥammad'

DATE 1748
ORIGINAL LANGUAGE German

DESCRIPTION

Vergleichung des Graf Zinzendorfs mit dem Mahomet, welcher die Bedencken der theol. Facultäten zu Altdorf, Giesen u. der evangel. Ministerien zu Augsbug, Hamburg von dem Gräuel der zinzendorfischen Lehren Auszugs-weise, nebst einigen andern dahin gehörigen Schriften des Verf. beygefüget sind ('Comparison of Count Zinzendorf with Muḥammad, to which extracts from the qualms of the theological faculties from Altdorf, Giesen, Göttingen, Halle, Jena, Wittenberg and of the Lutheran ministries in Augsburg, Hamburg, Lübeck, Nuremberg, Regensburg and Ulm about the abomination of the Zinzendorfian teaching and enterprises, with some other works of the author on that issue are added') is a polemical publication in an intra-Christian row between Fröreisen, who sees himself as a defender of Lutheran orthodoxy, and Count Nicolaus Ludwig von Zinzendorf (1700-60), the representative of the Moravian Church (*Herrnhuter Brüdergemeinde*).

The booklet contains four texts that Fröreisen had published earlier, together with a new preface, re-edited in a new attempt to instigate action on the part of the Lutheran Church authorities against Count Zinzendorf and his community.

The booklet consists of the preface (pp. 3-16), 'Description of Muḥammad and Zinzendorf as his contemporary ape' (pp. 3-20; the page count in the book begins anew after the preface), 'Confirmation of the

description of Muḥammad and Zinzendorf[...]' (pp. 23-34), 'Most necessary and well-intentioned warning against the contemporary rampant
Zinzendorfian soul-plague' (pp. 37-68), and a letter addressed to Count
Zinzendorf dated 23 January 1741 (pp. 71-8). The collection ends with a
series of excerpts from statements made by various German universities
(pp. 81-95), as announced in the title of the book (with the text in Latin,
then its German translation).

Fröreisen begins this re-edition of the texts in *Vergleichung* with the
booklet that makes his point most forcefully, changing the chronological
order of the texts' original appearance in print. He had actually started
his public attack on the count with the 1741 letter. Then, he expressed
his wish that the Lutheran Church authorities would take still stronger
measures to stop the proliferation of the 'Zinzendorfian plague' (*Höchst-
nöthige und Wohl-gemeine Warnung vor der heut zu Tag grassirenden
Zizendorffischen Seelen-Pest*, Strasbourg, 1742). A booklet in Latin followed, called *Brevis delineatio duorum impostorum magnorum Muhammedis et Zinzendorffii Muhammedis simiae* (Strasbourg, 1747), which was
translated into German and French. Then came the *Confirmatio brevis
delineationis*[...] in which he stated that Zinzendorf was in fact much
worse than he had depicted him.

Fröreisen reinstates the accusation that Zinzendorf was actually much
worse than Muḥammad in the preface to *Vergleichung*. He explains that
he intends to write about the two biggest impostors (*Betrüger*) because
'the actual state of *Muhammedaner* or Turkish superstition' (p. 4) is not
well known and many are unaware of Zinzendorf's deceit, which has
brought destruction to the whole world. One of the impostors lived
more than a thousand years ago but the second, 'the unscrupulous and
treacherous Herostratus of our times [...] earns the honour to be called
Muḥammad's ape' (*verdient die Ehre, des Muhammeds Affe genennet zu
werden*, p. 4; Herostratus was an ancient Greek, who, in a gesture to gain
fame set fire to the temple of Artemis in Ephesus). Fröreisen presents
both his targets as Antichrists.

Fröreisen outlines a depiction of Muḥammad (pp. 6-9; Cyranka,
Mahomet, pp. 339-40 quotes the text *in extenso*) that contains a number
of already well-known clichés. This is not, however, a scholarly comparison of two people but rather polemic in which Zinzendorf is compared
unfavourably with Muḥammad so that the latter is presented as only the
second worse impostor in the world – after Zinzendorf.

The summary of Fröreisen's attack on Zinzendorf is given in *Acta
historico-ecclesiastica. Oder gesammlete Nachrichten von den neusten*

Kirchen-Geschichten. Zwey und siebenzigster Theil. Mit Kön. Poln. und Churfürst. Sächs. allergn. Privilegio und unter Censur des Fürstl. Sachs. Weimar. Oberconsistorii (Weimar, 1748, pp. 1043-4; quoted in Cyranka, *Mahomet*, pp. 347-8).

SIGNIFICANCE

According to Cyranka (*Mahomet*, pp. 344-8), the image of Muḥammad presented by Fröreisen is a caricature formed for the polemical purpose of showing that Zinzendorf was a still more dangerous enemy of the Christian religion than Muḥammad. Fröreisen's work is an example of using elements of Muḥammad's biography as a weapon to mount strong criticism against a Christian opponent of another persuasion.

PUBLICATIONS

Johann Leonhard Fröreisen, *Höchst-nöthige und Wohl-gemeinte Warnung vor der heut zu Tag grassirenden Zizendorffischen Seelen-Pest*, Strasbourg, 1742 (included in *Vergleichung* as ch. 3, pp. 37-68)

Johann Leonhard Fröreisen, *Abschilderung des Mahomets und des Zinzendorfs alls seines heutigen Affens*, Strasbourg, 1747 (also in *Erlangischen gelehrten Zeitung*, 1747, pp. 221-6, 229-34)

Johann Leonhard Fröreisen, *Vergleichung des Graf Zinzendorfs mit dem Mahomet, welcher die Bedencken der theol. Facultäten zu Altdorf, Giesen u. der evangel. Ministerien zu Augsbug, Hamburg von dem Gräuel der zinzendorfischen Lehren Auszugs-weise, nebst einigen andern dahin gehörigen Schriften des Verf. beygefüget sind*, Frankfurt, 1748; Polem. 1075 (digitised version available through *MDZ*)

Johann Leonhard Fröreisen, *Vergleichung des Graf Zinzendorfs mit dem Mahomet, welcher die Bedencken der theol. Facultäten zu Altdorf, Giesen u. der evangel. Ministerien zu Augsbug, Hamburg von dem Gräuel der zinzendorfischen Lehren Auszugs-weise, nebst einigen andern dahin gehörigen Schriften des Verf. beygefüget sind*, Leipzig, 1749; H.ref. 270 d#Beibd.5 (digitised version available through *MDZ*)

STUDIES

D. Cyranka, *Mahomet. Repräsentationen des Propheten in deutschsprachigen Texten des 18. Jahrhunderts*, Göttingen, 2018, pp. 334-48

Stanisław Grodź

Johann Jakob Brucker

DATE OF BIRTH   21 January 1696
PLACE OF BIRTH   Augsburg
DATE OF DEATH   26 November 1770
PLACE OF DEATH   Augsburg

BIOGRAPHY

Johann Jakob Brucker was born into a tailor's family in Augsburg, where he attended St Anna's Grammar School. In 1715, he went to university in Jena, where he studied under Johann Franz Buddeus and Johann Andreas Danz, who taught him Oriental languages (Hamilton, "'To rescue the honour'", pp. 188-9). He returned to Augsburg in 1720, and in 1723 became the Lutheran pastor for Dreifaltigkeitskirche in Kaufbeuren and head of the Latin School. In 1724, he married Dorothea Rosina, the eldest daughter of Phillip Crophius, the rector, but she died in 1731. In 1732, he married Anna Bayer, the daughter of a Kaufbeuren merchant (Lüdke, "'Ich bitte mir Euer Hochedelgebohren Gedancken aus!'", p. 52).

In 1731, he was elected to the Prussian Academy of Sciences and, in 1736, to the German Society of Leipzig (Bautz, 'Brucker', p. 761).

Whilst in Kaufberen, Brucker corresponded widely with major figures of the Enlightenment, including Johann Lorenz Mosheim, Johann Christoph Gottsched, Johann Georg Zimmermann, Christoph August Heumann, Mathurin Veyssière de La Croze, Ludovico Muratori and Giovanni Lami (Lüdke, "'Ich bitte mir Euer Hochedelgebohren Gedancken aus!'", pp. 103-61).

It was during his time in Kaufberen that he wrote his five-volume *Historia critica philosophiae* (1742-4), in which he assessed philosophical systems in their relationship to Christianity (Bautz, 'Brucker', p. 761) and for which he is known as the founder of the study of the history of philosophy.

He resisted academic appointments, and in 1744 was recalled to Augsburg where he served as pastor of St Ulrich's Church until his death in 1770.

In addition to *Historia critica philosophiae*, for which he is remembered, other works include *Otium Vindelicum* (1731), *Kurze Fragen aus der philosophischen Historie* (1731-6) and *Miscellanea historiae philosophicae litterariae criticae olim sparsim edita* (1748).

MAIN SOURCES OF INFORMATION

Primary

Johann Jakob Brucker, *Historia critica philosophiae: a mundi incunabulis ad nostram usque aetatem deducta*, 5 vols, Augsburg, 1742-4

Secondary

A. Hamilton, 'Lutheran Islamophiles in eighteenth-century Germany', in A. Blair and A.-S. Goeing (eds), *For the sake of learning. Essays in honor of Anthony Grafton*, Leiden, 2016, vol. 1, pp. 327-43

A. Hamilton, '"To rescue the honour of the Germans". Qur'an translations by eighteenth- and early nineteenth-century German Protestants', *Journal of the Warburg and Courtauld Institutes* 77 (2014) 173-209

M. Longo, 'A "critical" history of philosophy and the early Enlightenment. Johann Jacob Brucker', in G. Piaia and G. Santinello (eds), *Models of the history of philosophy*, vol. 2. *From the Cartesian Age to Brucker*, Dordrecht, 2011, 477-578

CB [C. Blackwell], art., 'Brucker, Johann Jacob (1696-1770)', in H.F. Klemme and M. Kuehn (eds), *Dictionary of 18th century German Philosophers*, vol. 1. A-G, London, 2010, 152-60

C. Lüdke, '"Ich bitte mir Euer Hochedelgebohren Gedancken aus!" Beiträge zur Erschließung und Analyse von Jakob Bruckers Korrespondenz', Augsburg, 2008 (PhD Diss. Universität Augsburg), (biographical details, pp. 103-61; details of archival holdings of Brucker's correspondence, pp. 301-7)

W. Schmidt-Biggemann and T. Stammen (eds), *Jacob Brucker (1696-1770). Philosoph und Historiker der europäischen Aufklärung*, Berlin, 1998

E. François, 'Bruckers Stellung in der Augsburger Konfessionsgeschichte', in W. Schmidt-Biggemann and T. Stammen, (eds), *Jacob Brucker (1696-1770). Philosoph und Historiker der europäischen Aufklärung*, Berlin, 1998, 99-109

F.W. Bautz, art. 'Brucker, Johann Jakob, der erste deutsche Philosophiehistoriker, Theologe', *Biographisch-Bibliographisches Kirchenlexikon*, vol. 1, Herzberg, 1990, 761

WORKS ON CHRISTIAN-MUSLIM RELATIONS

Historia critica philosophiae
'The history of philosophy'

DATE   1742-4
ORIGINAL LANGUAGE   Latin

DESCRIPTION

Brucker's *Historia critica philosophiae: a mundi incunabulis ad nostram usque aetatem deducta* was first published in 1742-4 in five volumes, each around 1,000 pages in length, with a second expanded edition in six volumes published in 1766-7.

The work is set out chronologically, assessing various philosophical systems in their relationship to Christianity. Brucker also prepared an abbreviated version in Latin, *Institutiones historiae philosophicae* (1747; 884 pages), and a version in German, *Erste Anfangsgründe der philosophischen Geschichte* (1751; 554 pages). This was subsequently translated into Dutch (1778) and into Russian twice (1785 and 1788). William Enfield (1741-97), a British Unitarian minister, produced a two-volume work in English based on *Historia critica philosophiae* (1791), which became very influential in the English-speaking world.

The part of *Historia critica philosophiae* that deals with Islamic philosophers is vol. 3, which starts with *De philosophia saracenorum*, and is divided into two chapters, *De origine et progressu philosophiae inter Saracenos sive Arabes* (pp. 3-123), and *De natura et indole philosophiae saracenicae* (pp. 123-240).

The various abridged versions and translations follow the same pattern, whilst greatly reducing the length of the sections. Thus, in *Institutiones historiae philosophicae* (1747), section 3 runs from p. 353 to p. 369; in *Erste Anfangsgründe der philosophischen Geschichte* (1751), section 3 runs from p. 283 to p. 300; and in *The history of philosophy* (1791), vol. 2, the relevant pages are pp. 225-65; this section was not expanded in the second edition.

Brucker was conservative in his theology, following orthodox Lutheran teaching (François, 'Bruckers Stellung in der Augsburger Konfessionsgeschichte', pp. 101-5), and had an aversion to Muḥammad and the Qur'an. In Enfield's translation, the work says of Muḥammad: 'This imposter thought it necessary to keep his followers as ignorant as himself' (*History of philosophy*, vol. 2, p. 226), and of the Qur'an: 'This book, which was chiefly a compilation, sufficiently injudicious and incoherent, of the Nestorian Christians and of the Jews then resident in Arabia and from the ancient superstitions of the Arabians, long continued the only object of study amongst Mahometans' (*History of philosophy*, vol. 2, p. 227). In spite of this attitude, Brucker produced a reassessment of Arab philosophy and science (Israel, *Enlightenment contested*, p. 616).

Brucker states that 'Divine providence', acting in the person of the 'Abbasid caliphs, encouraged Muslim and Christian translations of Greek philosophy into Syriac and Arabic (*Historia critica philosophiae* [1742], pp. 134-5; the references that follow are to this edition, unless otherwise stated). He also praises Islamic philosophy, mathematics, astronomy and medicine (pp. 39-45, 121-2).

Brucker provides a reappraisal of the Arab philosophers and scientists (pp. 5-8), drawing on Pococke as well as on sources such as Leo Africanus, Golius, Pietro Della Valle, Hottinger, Reland, Boulainvilliers, and Thomas Erpenius's edition of *Historia Saracenica* (1625), a translation of the 13th-century Arab Christian historian al-Makīn Jirjis ibn al-'Amīd's *Al-majmū' al-mubārak* (Hamilton, 'Lutheran Islamophiles', p. 331).

He also notes that there were learned Jewish scholars living and writing among the Muslims – e.g. Isaac Ben Ezra (p. 122). He lists Muslim philosophers: Alkindi (Abū Yūsuf Ya'qūb ibn Isḥāq al-Kindī, c. 800-c. 873; pp. 63-9), noting that Pierre Bayle's entry on him is inaccurate; Alfarabi (Abū Naṣr al-Fārābī, 872-951; pp. 71-4), Avicenna (Ibn Sīnā, 980-1037; pp. 80-8), Al Gazel (al-Ghazālī, 1058-1111; pp. 93-5) and Averroes (Ibn Rushd, 1126-98; pp. 97-109). Brucker criticises them for not knowing Greek, and objects to one doctrine of philosophy in particular, Averroes' belief in the unity of the intellect (p. 158), and he disagrees with Bayle, claiming that Averroes never denied the immortality of the soul (Blackwell, 'Brucker', p. 157; Hamilton, 'Lutheran Islamophiles', p. 331).

Brucker strongly disapproved of the use of philosophical techniques for theological argument. Yet he did not completely condemn all scholastic philosophers, and quotes Erasmus's comment on Thomas Aquinas: 'He was a writer of the schools who was completely sane and the least inept'. For Brucker, Aquinas' major contribution to philosophy was his 'attack' on Averroes' 'heresy', this heresy being that humankind participated in the unity of the world intellect (Blackwell, 'Brucker', p. 158).

According to Hamilton, Brucker argued that the rise of Arab philosophy:

happened in spite of the Prophet Muhammad and the Koran. Philosophy, altogether unknown to the early Arabs or to the Prophet and his followers, was introduced by the Christians and came into its own in Islamic circles only under the Abassids in Baghdad. This was at a time when the rise of numerous Islamic sects stimulated a philosophical approach to the Koranic precepts that enabled them to differentiate themselves from one another. The result was a veritable flowering of philosophy and theology. The Christians could justly admire it, and many of the ideas produced were fully compatible with Christianity. (Hamilton, 'Lutheran Islamophiles', p. 331)

The section on Islamic philosophy in *Historia critica philosophiae* ends with an extensive list of Arab proverbs and sayings (pp. 217-39), drawn in part from the *Paroles remarquables, les bons mots, et les maximes des orientaux* published by Antoine Galland in 1694. Brucker even adds that 'the Muslims knew a morality that surpassed in its sobriety and beauty much that had been produced by the scholastic philosophers of the West' (p. 240; Hamilton, 'Lutheran Islamophiles', p. 332).

SIGNIFICANCE

One reason that Brucker wrote his *Historia critica philosophiae* was 'to "capture" the scholarly market for his Lutheran Protestant viewpoint', as this had 'become part of the education of future clergy and jurists, and its interpretation could not be left to the Catholics' (Laursen, 'Enfield's Brucker', p. 157).

Today, Brucker is only remembered for this work and its abridgements. In its day it was a best-seller, and was regarded as 'a universal encyclopaedia for philosophers and their advanced students' (Blackwell, 'Brucker', p. 155). There was a copy of *Historia critica philosophiae* in the French Royal Library, where Denis Diderot borrowed it for sources for his *Encyclopédie* (1751); Pope Benedict XIV (r. 1740-58) owned a copy (Lüdke, '"Ich bitte mir Euer Hochedelgebohren Gedancken aus!", p. 48); Hegel (1770-1831) quoted Brucker *verbatim*. In *Histoire abrégée de la philosophie* (1760), Jean Henri Formey summarised the *Historia* and visualised a history of philosophy, printed in both Latin and French, for classroom use (Blackwell, 'Brucker', p. 159).

The English translation and abridgement by William Enfield had a great influence on English-speaking writers, with Joseph Priestley (1733-1804) drawing heavily on it, and both John Adams (1735-1826) and Thomas Jefferson (1743-1826) still writing about it many years later. J.C. Laursen contends that, in his translation and abridgement, Enfield distorted Brucker's original for his own polemical purposes as a Unitarian, defending Unitarianism and attacking Trinitarian beliefs ('Enfield's Brucker and Christian anti-scepticism', p. 155).

Historia critica philosophiae served an important role in demonstrating the importance of Islamic philosophy as an essential bridge between ancient Greek philosophy and medieval scholastic Christian philosophy (Blackwell, 'Brucker', p. 157).

PUBLICATIONS

J.J. Brucker, *Historia critica philosophiae: a mundi incunabulis ad nostram usque aetatem deducta*, 5 vols, Leipzig, 1742-4, vol. 3. *De philosophia saracenorum*, pp. 3-240; 4 Ph.u. 12-1 - 4 Ph.u. 12-4,2 (digitised version available through *MDZ*)

J.J. Brucker, *Institutiones historiae philosophicae*, Leipzig, 1747 (Brucker's own abridgement); Ph.u. 64 t (digitised version available through MDZ)

J.J. Brucker, *Institutiones historiae philosophicae*, Leipzig, 1756[2]

J.J. Brucker, *Erste Anfangsgründe der philosophischen Geschichte*, Ulm, 1751 (German trans.); Ph.u. 64 (digitised version available through *MDZ*)

J.J. Brucker, *Historia critica philosophiae: a mundi incunabulis ad nostram usque aetatem deducta*, 6 vols, Leipzig, 1766-72; 4 H 104 -1 - 4 H 104 -6 (digitised version available through *MDZ*)

J.J. Brucker, *Eerste beginselen van de historie der filozofie*, 8 vols, Utrecht, 1778 (Dutch trans. of *Erste Anfangsgründe der philosophischen Geschichte*); OTM: O 60-3421 (digitised version available through Koninklijke Bibliotheek)

J.J. Brucker, *Sokrashchennaia istoriĭa filosofii ot nachala mĭra do nynieshnikh vremen*, Moscow, 1785 (abridged Russian trans.)

J.J. Brucker, *Kriticheskaia istoriĭa filosofii, sluzhashchaia rukovodstvom k priamomu poznaniĭu uchenoĭ istorii*, Moscow, 1788 (abridged Russian trans.)

J.J. Brucker, *Institutiones historiae philosophicae*, Leipzig, 1790[3]

J.J. Brucker, *The history of philosophy, from the earliest times to the beginning of the present century*, trans. W. Enfield, 2 vols, London, 1791 (English trans.); ESTC T113390 (digitised version available through *ECCO*)

J.J. Brucker, *The history of philosophy, from the earliest times to the beginning of the present century*, trans. W. Enfield, 2 vols, Dublin, 1791 (English trans.); ESTC T109659 (digitised version available through *ECCO*)

J.J. Brucker, *The history of philosophy, from the earliest times to the beginning of the present century*, trans. W. Enfield, 2 vols, London, 1819 (English trans.); 011543921 (digitised version available through Hathi Trust Digital Library)

J.J. Brucker, *The history of philosophy, from the earliest times to the beginning of the present century*, trans. W. Enfield, London, 1837 (English trans.)

J.J. Brucker, *The history of philosophy, from the earliest times to the beginning of the present century*, trans. W. Enfield, London, 1840 (English trans.)

J.J. Brucker, *Historia critica philosophiae*, 5 vols, Hildesheim, 1975 (repr. of first edition)

J.J. Brucker, *The history of philosophy, from the earliest times to the beginning of the present century*, trans. W. Enfield, Bristol, 2001 (English trans.; repr. of 1837 edition with Introduction by K. Haakonssen)

STUDIES

J.C. Laursen, 'Enfield's Brucker and Christian anti-scepticism in Enlightenment historiography of philosophy', in S. Charles and P.J. Smith (eds), *Scepticism in the eighteenth century. Enlightenment, Lumières, Aufklärung*, Dordrecht, 2013, 155-69

Longo, '"Critical" history of philosophy and the early Enlightenment' CB [Blackwell], 'Brucker'

J.I. Israel, *Enlightenment contested. Philosophy, modernity, and the emancipation of man, 1670-1752*, Oxford, 2006

François, 'Bruckers Stellung in der Augsburger Konfessionsgeschichte'

C. Blackwell, 'Jacob Brucker's theory of knowledge and the history of natural philosophy', in W. Schmidt-Biggemann and T. Stammen (eds), *Jacob Brucker (1696-1770). Philosoph und Historiker der europäischen Aufklärung*, Berlin, 1998, 198-217

H. Zäh, 'Verzeichnis der schriften Jacob Bruckers', in W. Schmidt-Biggemann and T. Stammen (eds), *Jacob Brucker (1696-1770). Philosoph und Historiker der europäischen Aufklärung*, Berlin, 1998, 259-351 (bibliography of Brucker's works)

John Chesworth

Jonas Korte

DATE OF BIRTH   1683
PLACE OF BIRTH   Laass, Saxony
DATE OF DEATH   1747
PLACE OF DEATH   Altona, near Hamburg

BIOGRAPHY

Jonas Korte (1683-1747) was a 'born-again' Christian author of one publication, his Oriental travelogue. His father, Christoph Korte, had 11 children, of whom Jonas was the second oldest. His father worked as a teacher, and Jonas also followed this profession for a while. In his autobiographical account in the travelogue, he says that, in 1703, while teaching children, he came across the words of Deuteronomy 29:22: 'Strangers from distant countries would come and see what the Lord did to his disobedient people and land.' These words impressed him so much that he decided to see for himself the land 'that God chose in order to reveal the greatness of his grace and his seriousness', though much time passed before he could go there.

Instead of choosing a quiet life in Saxony as a teacher, he went to Hamburg and Lübeck, though for what purpose is not known, as many parts of his biography are rather unclear. In 1709, he worked in the service of a gentleman who fought in Brabant during the War of the Spanish Succession (1701-14). Korte was wounded and lay ill in Rotterdam for 14 weeks. In this time, he experienced a 'rebirth' as a Christian.

In 1709 or 1710, he travelled to England, but he does not say what he did there. In 1713, he left England for the Orient and went to Constantinople via France and Italy. He decided not to continue to Jerusalem because he felt spiritually unfit for such an endeavour and returned to London via Smyrna. From there, he moved to Altona, a city near Hamburg, then under Danish rule, after which there is a period for which we have no information. Between 1720 and 1723, he suffered from an attack of what he calls *atheismo sceptico*. He does not give the reason for this but only that he was cured by a treatise that proved, he says, 'that Jesus was the true Messiah'. He continues: 'I wish that this proof could impress all mockers of religion as it did myself, after I lay ill for three years with sceptical atheism, but then began to recover from it' (Korte, *Reise*, 3rd edition 1751, pp. 101-3).

The subject of atheism continued to intrigue Korte, and also figures prominently in his travelogue. In 1725, he established a book shop and publishing house ('Jonas Korte') in Altona, which under liberal Danish rule was a vibrant intellectual milieu of religion and politics. Some 'Jonas Korte' publications appeared outside Altona, in Hamburg, Leipzig and elsewhere.

Korte had contacts with several 'pietist' groups. Especially dear to him was August Hermann Francke (1663-1727), the founder of *Franckesche Stiftungen* ('Francke's foundations') in Halle/Saale. Several letters, now in the archive of the *Stiftungen*, attest to their friendship. Korte was also close to the Moravians in Herrnhut, where he met Friedrich Christoph Oetinger (1702-82), later a major figure in Swabian Pietism, and urged him to come with him to the Orient. Oetinger declined and became a minister in Hirsau near Calw in 1738. While Korte was returning from his journey in 1739, the council of the Moravians considered sending him on a diplomatic mission to Istanbul, though this never transpired.

Jonas also had contacts with radical Enlightenment figures and atheists such as Johann Christoph Gottsched (1700-66) in Leipzig and Theodor Ludwig Lau (1670-1740) in Altona. It is unclear whether he was in contact with the chiliast Johann Wilhelm Petersen (1649–1727), as one of the contemporary biographies claims, and that he had chiliast leanings himself. Korte is silent about this matter. In 1737, the year he left on his Oriental journey, he handed his publishing house over to his younger brother Johann Georg Korte, and from then it was called 'Gebrüder Korte'. Starting from Altona, Korte travelled first to Venice, then to Alexandria, Rosetta, Cairo, Damietta, Joppa (Jaffa), Ramla, Jerusalem, Acre (Akkon), Tyre, Sidon, Tripoli, Laodicaea (Latakia), Aleppo, the Euphrates and Mesopotamia. He returned to Aleppo, continued to Antioch (Antakya), Scanderone (Iskenderun) and Cyprus, and came back to Altona via Venice in 1739.

Korte travelled alone, he writes, not as a pilgrim or a missionary but simply in order to discover proof of God's curse. He certainly had enough money to cover the cost of the journey but, since he did not know any Oriental languages, he was forced to rely on the help of Europeans living in the Orient, among them consuls, merchants and the Franciscans in Jerusalem. His most notable contact was the British Orientalist Richard Pococke (1704-65), who was travelling in the region between 1737 and 1742.

For Korte, all the Oriental places he visited belonged to the 'Promised Land' because, as he says, 'God promised the land from Egypt to Syria to the offspring of Abraham', though in their social and economic deterioration they showed the effects of God's curse. In his travelogue, Korte sees Islam as having been sent to the disobedient Christians and Jews as a part of the curse. He clearly continued to think and read about the Orient until his death.

After his return, Korte visited his hometown of Laass a number of times. In 1740, he donated a church clock and presented a copy of his travelogue to every household. He died in 1747 in Altona.

MAIN SOURCES OF INFORMATION

Primary

Jonas Korte, *Reise nach dem weiland gelobten, nun aber seit siebenzehn hundert Jahren unter dem Fluche liegenden Lande, wie auch nach Ägypten, dem Berg Libanon, Syrien und Mesopotamien*, Halle, 1751[3]

Anon., 'Obituary for Jonas Korte', in *Hamburgische Berichte von den neuesten Gelehrten Sachen Siebzehender Tomus auf das Jahr 1748*, 1748, 121-4 (dated 23 February 1748)

Anon., 'Jonas Korte, einer der bekanntesten Altonaischen Schriftsteller des vorigen Jahrhunderts', *Hamburg und Altona. Ein Journal zur Geschichte der Zeit, der Sitten und des Geschmaks* 3/7 (1804) 282-92 (anonymous biography)

Secondary

D. Cyranka, *Mahomet. Repräsentationen des Propheten in deutschsprachigen Texten des 18. Jahrhunderts*, Gottingen, 2018, pp. 258-88

R. Elger, 'Blessing and curse in the "Promised Land". Jonas Korte's travels in the Ottoman Empire, 1737-1739', in M. Kemper and R. Elger (eds), *The piety of learning. Islamic studies in honor of Stefan Reichmuth*, Leiden, 2017, 227-49

D. Cyranka, 'Studien zum deutschen Mohammed-Bild im 18. Jahrhundert', Halle, 2010 (Diss. Halle University)

WORKS ON CHRISTIAN-MUSLIM RELATIONS

Reise nach dem weiland gelobten [...] Lande
'Journey to the Promised Land'

DATE 1741, 1743, 1751
ORIGINAL LANGUAGE German

DESCRIPTION

Korte's only work, his Oriental travelogue (its full title is *Reise nach dem weiland gelobten, nun aber seit siebenzehn hundert Jahren unter dem Fluche liegenden Lande, wie auch nach Ägypten, dem Berg Libanon, Syrien und Mesopotamien*, 'Journey to the land that once was the promised land, but that over the last seventeen hundred years has been afflicted by the curse, and also to Egypt, Mount Lebanon, Syria and Mesopotamia'), appeared in three editions, the first in Altona in 1741, the second, with supplements in Halle and Grunert in 1743, and the third with changes at Grunert posthumously in 1751. The 1751 edition is 712 pages long (plus supplements amounting to 286 pages), and is used here.

Korte refers to Islam in a number of short passages and also includes a 30-page section on the character of Muḥammad. He employs works such as George Sale's (1697-1736) English translation of the *Koran* (1734) with its long introduction to Islam, and Adriaan Reland's (1676-1718) *De religione Mohammedica libri duo* (German trans., *Zwey Bücher von der Türkischen oder Mohammedischen Religion*, Hannover, 1716, 1717). In the supplement to the third edition he discusses *Das Leben des Mahomeds mit historischen Anmerkungen über die Mahomedanische Religion und die Gewohnheiten der Muselmänner* (Lemgo, 1747), the German translation of Henri de Boulainvilliers' (1658-1722) *La Vie de Mahomed* (1730). Other works are also mentioned, though there are no Arabic or other Eastern sources among them.

The aim of the work is to show European Christians, especially those 'born again', that the story of God's curse is correct. To do this, Korte presents a historical narrative, spread over several passages, that can be summarised as follows: Christianity in both the East and the West was in decline when Islam appeared; God cursed Christians and sent Muḥammad and Islam; God created Muḥammad as an individual who could see the shortcomings of Christianity and developed a counter-ideology, a kind of 'natural' religion that he spread throughout the East.

Korte enumerates ten reasons for the success of Islam: 1. Muḥammad prohibited the evil of alcohol; 2. he countered the widespread practice of sodomy by allowing men to marry more than one wife; 3. he preached charity; 4. he forbade *Disputiersucht* (addiction to dispute) among the Christians, especially theologians; 5. he granted religious freedom; 6. the version of paradise he preached was metaphorical; 7. he prohibited the use of church bells because Christians used them for magical purposes (*abergläubische Praktiken*); 8. he believed that his life was guided by God; 9. he forbade images in places of worship; 10. for worship in mosques he did not allow services such as the mass. Korte applauds these measures and says that Muḥammad was able to introduce them because 'God lent

His hand to it' (*Gott hatte seine Hand im Spiel*). Thus, Muḥammad partly acted as a natural human being, and partly as an instrument of God.

In some respects Muḥammad was characterised by human aberrations, such as his appetite for sex and polygamy. But he was not the source of some other shortcomings of Islam, such as the pilgrimage to Mecca and Medina, which was not ordered by Muḥammad but was introduced later. Here, Korte reveals his true intention in the work, which is to exonerate Muḥammad from all religious practices that Korte himself thought distasteful and to show that they were later innovations.

Korte argues that misguided Christians could not see the true nature of Muḥammad and Islam, and misrepresented them, and he warns against 'drinking of the foul water' of Catholic anti-Islamic polemics. He compares attacks on Islam to attacks on born-again Christians, and advocates that both these forms of belief must be looked on without prejudice. The earlier misrepresentation of Muḥammad as an imposter was dangerous because the same attack could be, and indeed was, directed against Moses and Jesus. Among the many misrepresentations of Catholic anti-Islamic polemic, he singles out the words of Pope Pius II (r. 1458-64), that Muslims believed in a corporeal God.

While Muḥammad was not a liar or an imposter, neither was he an immaculate hero, as Enlightenment authors such as Boullainvilliers claimed. For Korte, only true Christians, that is born-again Christians, were able to understand Islam correctly, and he urges his readers to learn Arabic and travel to the East in order to acquire a better image of Islam.

SIGNIFICANCE

Korte's book had some success. This is not only attested by the fact that it saw three editions and a translation into Dutch, but also by quotations in later travel writings. The 'Pietist' missionary Stephan Schultz (1714-76), who worked in the *Institutum Judaicum et Muhammedicum* that existed in Halle from 1728 to 1792, was clearly impressed by Korte, and emulated his style of writing to a certain extent in his own Oriental travelogue, *Die Leitungen des Höchsten nach seinem Rath auf den Reisen durch Europa, Asia und Africa* (5 vols, Halle, 1771-5).

Korte's thesis of the curse on Christians was repeated in a travelogue by Charles William Meredith van de Velde (1818-98), *Reis door Syrie en Palestina in 1851 en 1852*, Utrecht, 1854 (German translation, *Reise durch Syrien und Palästina in den Jahren 1851 und 1852, Aus d. Niederdt. übers. von K. Göbel*, Leipzig, 1855-6).

PUBLICATIONS

Jonas Korte, *Reise nach dem weiland gelobten, nun aber seit siebenzehn hundert Jahren unter dem Fluche liegenden Lande, wie auch nach Ägypten, dem Berg Libanon, Syrien und Mesopotamien*, Altona: Gebrüder Korte, 1741

Jonas Korte, *Reise nach dem weiland gelobten, nun aber seit siebenzehn hundert Jahren unter dem Fluche liegenden Lande, wie auch nach Ägypten, dem Berg Libanon, Syrien und Mesopotamien*, Halle, 1743[2]; 000697194 (digitised version available through Hathi Trust Digital Library)

Jonas Korte, *Reise nach dem weiland gelobten, nun aber seit siebenzehn hundert Jahren unter dem Fluche liegenden Lande, wie auch nach Ägypten, dem Berg Libanon, Syrien und Mesopotamien*, Halle, 1746

Jonas Korte, *Reise nach dem weiland gelobten, nun aber seit siebenzehn hundert Jahren unter dem Fluche liegenden Lande, wie auch nach Ägypten, dem Berg Libanon, Syrien und Mesopotamien*, Halle, 1751[3]; VD18 12236195-001 (digitised version available through *MDZ*)

Jonas Korte, *Reize van Jonas Korte, naar Palestina, Egypte, Phenicie, Syrie, Mesopotamie en Cyprus. Naar den derden druk uit het Hoogduitsch vertaald. Eerste Deel. Met platen*, trans. E.W. Cramerus, Haarlem, 1776 (Dutch trans.)

Jonas Korte, *Reize van Jonas Korte, naar Palestina, Egypte, Phenicie, Syrie, Mesopotamie en Cyprus. Naar den derden druk uit het Hoogduitsch vertaald. Eerste Deel. Met platen*, trans. E.W. Cramerus, Amsterdam, 1781 (Dutch trans.); KW 225 N 16[-17] (digitised version available through Koninklijke Bibliotheek)

Jonas Korte, 'Sammlung der merkwürdigsten Reisen in den Orient', in H.E.G. Paulus (ed.), *Übersetzungen und Auszügen mit ausgewählten Kupfern und Charten, auch mit den nöthigen Einleitungen, Anmerkungen und kollectiven Registern*, Jena, 1792, vol. 2, pp. vii-xv and pp. 27-240 (excerpt)

STUDIES

Cyranka, *Mahomet. Repräsentationen des Propheten*, pp. 258-88
Elger, 'Blessing and curse in the "Promised Land"'

Ralf Elger

Jakub Římař

Jacobus Ržimarž a Cremsirio; Giacomo da Cremsirio

DATE OF BIRTH   1682
PLACE OF BIRTH   Kroměříž, Margraviate of Moravia
    (Czech Republic)
DATE OF DEATH   5 June 1755
PLACE OF DEATH   Brno, Margraviate of Moravia

BIOGRAPHY

Jakub Římař's life before 1701, when he joined the Franciscan Order, remains largely unknown. From later ecclesiastical records, we learn that he was born in Kroměříž (German: Kremsier) in 1682, into a mixed Moravian Czech and German family. His parents, Jakub (Jacobus) Braxatoris and Anna, gave him the baptismal name Václav (Wenceslas). His name is sometimes given as Josef, but this is not attested in any primary sources and it was probably made up by a later biographer (Procházka, *Čeští františkáni v Habeši*).

Římař entered the Franciscan Order in his home town of Kroměříž on 27 January 1701. In February 1711, he left for Rome, where he was subsequently admitted to the Franciscan missionary college at San Pietro in Montorio.

After finishing his ten-month missionary course, Římař was appointed a Catholic missionary in Ethiopia and was dispatched to Egypt, where he arrived in July 1712. As his deployment was delayed, he visited the Holy Land before finally departing for Ethiopia in the autumn of 1715. But on landing at Mocha on the Red Sea coast of Yemen on 8 April 1716, he learnt about the recent martyrdom of his superiors in Ethiopia and he had to return to Europe, where he and his colleague arrived in April 1721.

Římař was almost immediately despatched back to Egypt, where he remained from April 1722 to June 1728. Following this second deployment, he returned to his home province, where he was appointed confessor to a community of nuns in Znojmo (German: Znaim) in August 1732, serving three consecutive one-year terms there.

In the autumn of 1737, Římař returned to Egypt, this time as prefect, or director, of the Franciscan mission. During his two consecutive terms in this office (1737-44, 1744-51), he was appointed vicar general (*in lieu* of a bishop) for the whole of Egypt. Before finally leaving Cairo in February 1753, he dispatched a missionary expedition to Ethiopia that was headed by his younger countryman Remedius Prutký (1713-70).

Via Livorno and Rome, Římař travelled to Brno (German: Brünn), where he spent the last days of his life. He died on 5 June 1755 aged 73.

In addition to his better-known *Itinerarium*, Římař authored one other major work, the *Diurnalia*, which is kept in the Strahov Library, Prague. Complemented by an unbound quire of 11 pages, which is kept in the National Archives in Prague, these two autobiographical volumes cover a period of 38 years, chronicling Římař's activities and observations during the years 1711-16 and 1721-52.

MAIN SOURCES OF INFORMATION

Primary

MS Prague, Library of the Czech and Moravian St Wenceslaus Province of the Reformed Order of the Friars Minor, in the Convent of our Lady of the Snows, Prague – Re 13, *Itinerarium missionum apostolicarum orientalium Aegypti, Aethiopiae, seu Abyssiniae, aliarumque regionum adjacentium* (Římař's personal account of his missionary experience)

MS Prague, Strahov Library, The Royal Canonry of Premonstratensians at Strahov – DE IV 5, *R(everendi) P(atris) Jacobi Ržimarž a Cremsirio, Ord(inis) Minor(um) S(ancti) P(atris) Francisci Reform(atorum) provinciae Bohemiae alumni, regnorum Aegypti, Abyssiniae et provinciarum adjacentium missionariorum praefecti et vicarii apostolici etc., Diurnalia, ab anno 1725 usque ad a(nnum) 1752 inclusive; cum quibusdam itinerariis et visitationibus canonicis; nunc pro bibliotheca Neo-Pragensi conventus S(anctae) M(ariae) ad Nives Ord(inis) Minor(um) S(ancti) Francisci Reform(atorum)*(Římař's account of his missionary experience; moved at some point from the library of the Convent of our Lady of the Snows to the Strahov Library)

MS Prague, National Archives – collection 'Franciscan Order', box 64, inventory no. 2070 (original documents written by or concerning Římař)

MS Vatican, Archivio Storico De Propaganda Fide (repository of documents emanating from Propaganda Fide, including many concerning Římař)

G. Giamberardini (ed.), *Lettere dei prefetti apostolici dell'Alto Egitto nel secolo XVIII*, Cairo, 1960 (correspondence of the Franciscan missionary prefects in Cairo, the majority composed by or concerning Římař)

G. Giamberardini (ed.), *'Historia' della missione francescana in Alto Egitto-Fungi-Etiopia, 1686–1720, scritta dal P. Giacomo d'Albano*, Cairo, 1961

G. Giamberardini (ed.), *Cronaca della missione francescana dell'Alto Egitto, 1719-1739, scritta dal P. Ildefonso da Palermo*, Cairo, 1962

Secondary

M. Dospěl, 'Counting the souls. Coptic Catholics in the mid-18th century census records of Jakub Římař OFM (1682-1755)' [forthcoming]

M. Dospěl, 'The Wādī al-Naṭrūn monasteries and a reassessment of the manuscript *Itinerarium* (c. 1765) of Remedius Prutký OFM', *Orientalia Christiana Periodica* 82 (2016) 211-26 (analysis of Prutký's account of Wādī al-Naṭrūn, and a critical reassessment of his *Itinerarium*, including the crucial role of the manuscripts by Římař)

M. Dospěl, 'Vicar General P. Jakub Římař OFM and his attempts at the mission to Ethiopia', in P.R. Beneš, P. Hlaváček, and C.V. Pospíšil (eds), *Františkánství v kontaktech s jiným a cizím*, Prague, 2009, 229-43 (in Czech, with an abstract in Italian)

A. Colombo, *La nascita della Chiesa copto-cattolica nella prima metà del 1700*, Rome, 1996

M. Krása and J. Polišenský, 'Czech missionary's first hand account of the 18th century Ethiopia, Arabia and India', *Archiv Orientální* 61 (1993) 85-90

K. Petráček, 'Der angebliche Aufenthalt von J.J. Římař in Nordost-Afrika und der Verfasser von Descriptio Aethiopiae', *Annals of the Náprstek Museum* 1 (1962) 91-9

G. Manfredi, *La figura del 'Praefectus Missionum' nelle Prefetture d'Egitto-Etiopia e dell'Alto Egitto-Etiopia affidate ai Frati Minori (1630-1792)*, Cairo, 1958

K. Petráček, 'Jakub Římař aus Kroměříž. Descriptio Aethiopiae seu Abissiniae (Land und Leute),' *Archiv Orientální* 25 (1957) 334-83

A. Colombo, *Le origini della gerarchia della Chiesa copta cattolica nel secolo XVIII*, Rome, 1953

WORKS ON CHRISTIAN-MUSLIM RELATIONS

Itinerarium
'Itinerary'

DATE Between 1711 and 1755
ORIGINAL LANGUAGE Latin

DESCRIPTION

The only extant copy of Římař's *Itinerarium* (its title in full is *Itinerarium missionum apostolicarum orientalium Aegypti, Aethiopiae, seu Abyssiniae, aliarumque regionum adjacentium, manu propria conscriptum a R(everendo) P(atre) Jacobo Ržimarž de Cremsirio*, 'The travels undertaken on behalf of the Oriental apostolic missions in Egypt, Ethiopia or Abyssinia, and other neighbouring countries, written down by the Reverend Father Jakub Římař of Kroměříž') is the manuscript in the library of the Franciscan convent of Our Lady of the Snows in Prague (shelfmark Re 13). Apart from short notes by the amanuensis (a librarian of the Prague convent) and R. Prutký, who entered a limited number of notes or corrections here and there, this manuscript is Římař's autograph. As an artefact, however, the manuscript is a posthumous creation of the amanuensis, who bound the quires into one volume, and whose trimming of the final product resulted in the loss of text from the margins of several pages. In addition, there allegedly exists a transcript made from this original manuscript by Damaso Piovacari in the early 20th century for the Franciscan convent in Cairo, but its current whereabouts and condition are unknown.

The Prague manuscript is a quarto containing 393 folia (with several concurring paginations), which are inscribed on both sides. Its binding has been severely damaged, and the spine has almost completely disintegrated.

With the title page missing since before Krása and Polišenský ('First hand account', p. 85 n. 4), the title provided above is adapted from Petráček ('Handschriften,' pp. 96-7). The manuscript was most likely bound, and the title page fashioned, by the amanuensis sometime in the late 18th century, so the title recorded by Petráček may not represent the original (now lost?) or intended title of the work.

Rather than being a narrative of travels in distant lands – as the extant title claims – this work is really a diary (or a collection of diaries), as it consists for the most part of short daily logs that detail significant events – hence the date range provided above. Although apparently not recorded daily, the dated entries follow a strict chronological order. Only occasionally is this structure interrupted by a more elaborate account or a narrative concerning a place, an incident or an anthropological observation. Nine short discourses devoted to specific topics (e.g. Coptic Christianity, a trip to the Nile cataracts, a description of Cairo) are appended at the back of the manuscript; these bear separate paginations and seem to have been written at different times.

Owing to this design, Christian-Muslim encounters and Římař's views about Islam or the Muslims are dispersed throughout the work. The only extended treatment appears in two short sections recorded in the autumn of 1712: *De religione Turcarum* ('On the religion of the Turks') and *Puncta fidei et errores* ('Points of faith and errors'), with more notes on matters such as Muslim prayers, feasts, mosques, dervishes, and the *ḥajj* dispersed through the pages covering Římař's first few years in Egypt.

Since this voluminous work is still only available in manuscript form, and no studies have been published that address the related issues, it is still too early to say much about Římař's knowledge of and opinions about Muslims and Islam, except for the following observations.

Římař consistently refers to Muslims as 'Turks' and views Islam as an 'impious sect'. He seems to subscribe to the contemporary view of Muslims as addicted to basic bodily pleasures and appetites, suggesting that Christian monogamy is a serious obstacle to conversion for Muslim men. Despite his firm position as a Catholic priest, however, Římař does not seem to engage in forceful refutation or mocking of Islam. As in his other recorded encounters, Římař emerges as non-dogmatic and pragmatic. His references to Muslims are mostly limited to his encounters with the local authorities, on whose benevolence the Franciscan mission depended. For this reason, Římař often expresses his appreciation for individual 'Turkish' administrators, who allow Franciscans to stay and work in places like Cairo and Akhmim and are even curious about and friendly to the friars – to the point of displeasing the local Coptic hierarchy. From this vantage point, Římař – an administrator himself – seems to see (high-ranking) Muslims as potential enablers rather than foes. This attitude surely relates to the fact that the Franciscan missionary enterprise was directed at the Coptic Christian minority, not the Muslim majority.

Another aspect to consider with respect to Římař's seemingly restrained judgements about Islam is his intended audience: his manuscript was apparently not meant for publication or wide circulation. When a comprehensive study of Římař's views of Muslims and Islam is written, it will be interesting to observe how (if at all) his views changed over time, from his first recorded encounters in 1711 to his departure from Egypt in 1753.

The chronological scope of this manuscript (1711-16, 1721-26, plus later appendices) is supplemented by Římař's other major manuscript, *Diurnalia* (The Royal Canonry of Premonstratensians at Strahov, the Strahov Library – DE IV 5), which covers the years 1725-9 and 1737-52. The chronological gap of 1730-36, during which Římař was back in his home province, is cursorily covered in Římař's handwritten notes found in the National Archives in Prague. These notes derive from letters that Římař apparently was receiving from his colleagues in Egypt.

The work relates to the accounts of other Franciscan missionaries, Římař's colleagues: Giacomo d'Albano (see Giamberardini, *'Historia' della missione francescana*), Ildefonso da Palermo (see Giamberardini, *Cronaca della missione francescana*), and Remedius Prutký (see Dospěl, *Remedius Prutký*, Itinerarium II; and Dospěl, 'Wādī al-Naṭrūn monasteries').

SIGNIFICANCE

An open-minded observer with 25 years of first-hand experience in Egypt and adjacent parts of the Middle East and the southern Red Sea, Římař offers in his writings an informed and profound knowledge of the region and its peoples, also providing insights into the workings of the Franciscan missionary enterprise and the relationship between the Roman Church and the Copts. But since his account remains in manuscript, which has not circulated widely, its significance in Christian-Muslim discourse is very limited, and so also is its influence on later works, with one prominent exception – the *Itinerarium* of Remedius Prutký.

Prutký's superior in Egypt and a fellow countryman, Římař was well acquainted with Remedius Prutký and his ambitions to publish his own account of travels in Egypt and Ethiopia. Similarities between the two manuscripts were first noticed by Vilhum in 1946 (see Vilhum, *Čeští misionáři*, p. 45), and recently elaborated upon in Dospěl, 'Wādī al-Naṭrūn monasteries,' pp. 222-4. Indeed, Prutký exploited his colleague's manuscript in a remarkable way, borrowing entire pages of text without even citing the source (or the sources cited in Římař's original text). Prutký appears to have plagiarised from Římař a substantial portion of Part 1 of his voluminous manuscript. Interestingly, Římař's *Itinerarium* contains a discourse ('Descriptio Aethiopiae seu Abissiniae', in *Itinerarium*, fols 343r-362r) inspired by Prutký's account of the country, and his *Diurnalia* (fols 258r-271) even feature a separate section penned in Prutký's hand ('Brevis extractus regni Aethiopiae'). Whether this was intentional or accidental (a misstep of the amanuensis) remains to be explored.

PUBLICATIONS

MS Prague, Library of the Czech and Moravian St Wenceslaus Province of the Reformed Order of the Friars Minor, in the Convent of our Lady of the Snows, Prague – Re 13, fols 393 (late 18th century) *Itinerarium missionum apostolicarum orientalium Aegypti, Aethiopiae, seu Abyssiniae, aliarumque regionum adjacentium, manu propria conscriptum a R(everendo) P(atre) Jacobo Ržimarž de Cremsirio, Ord(inis) Minor(um) S(ancti) P(atris) Francisci Reform(atorum) provinciae Bohemiae S(ancti) Wenceslai, d(ucis) et m(artyris), alumno et patre aggregato, earundem missionum per 30 annos missionario Apostolico indefesso, linguarum orientalium professore, Dei et S(acrae) Congregationis de Propaganda Fide gratia in illis partibus Vicario Generali Apostolico, uti et Pronotario Apostolico, qui tandem laboribus et senio fractus ad provinciam rediit et in conventu nostro Brunensi s(ancta) professione et sacerdotio jubilarius a(nno) 1755 die 5 Junii piissime in D(omin)o obiit, aetatis suae physicae 73, religionis vero 55* (a personal account of Římař's missionary experience)

No edition of Římař's *Itinerarium* has been published to date. Only the following partial translations exist:

J. Procházka, *Čeští františkáni v Habeši*, Prague, 1937 (Belletrist account of the lives of Prutký and Římař, with lengthy excerpts from their MSS in Czech translation, including from Římař's *Itinerarium*)

Z. Kalista, *Cesty ve znamení kříže. Dopisy a zprávy českých misionářů 17. a 18. věku ze zámořských krajů*, Prague, 1941, pp. 176-82 and notes on pp. 245-6 (Czech trans. of Římař's journey from Cairo to Suez in September 1715, from *Itinerarium*, fols 148v-150v)

K. Petráček, 'Jakub Římař aus Kroměříž. Descriptio Aethiopiae seu Abissiniae (Land und Leute)', *Archiv Orientální* 25 (1957) 334-83, pp. 345-81 (German trans. and paraphrase, with occasional quotations of the original Latin text of 'Descriptio Aethiopiae seu Abissiniae,' from *Itinerarium*, fols 343r-351r)

STUDIES

M. Dospěl, 'Chronicling the Franciscan mission ad Coptos. Manuscript accounts of Jakub Římař (1682-1755)' [forthcoming]

Dospěl, 'Wādī al-Naṭrūn monasteries'

M. Dospěl, 'Franciscan missionary and pastoral work among Egyptian and Ethiopian Christians in the context of coeval book production', in P. Hlaváček et al. (eds), *Františkánský kontext teologického a filosofického myšlení*, Prague, 2012, 388-412 (in Czech, with English abstract)

J. Förster (ed.), *Remedius Prutký OFM, O Egyptě, Arábii, Palestině a Galileji* [On Egypt, Arabia, Palestine, and Galilee], vol. 1, Prague, 2009, pp. 105-6 (in Czech; discusses the relationship between Prutký's *Itinerarium* and Římař's *Itinerarium*)

M. Dospěl, 'Dva misionáři a stéla krále Achnatona aneb příběh z říše archeologie textu' [Two missionaries and King Akhenaten's Stela. A story from the realm of text archaeology], *Pražské Egyptologické Studie* 6 (2009) 27-32 (in Czech)

M. Dospěl (ed.), *Remedius Prutký, Itinerarium II. De Abyssinia et Indiis Orientalibus. Edidit et introductione commentariisque supplevit Marek Dospěl*, Prague, 2007

M. Dospěl, 'Františkáni Římař, Prutký a Schneider. Zdroje a možnosti interpretace jejich zpráv (nejen) o Egyptě 18. Století' [Franciscans Římař, Prutký, and Schneider. Sources and interpretative possibilities of their accounts on (not only) 18th-century Egypt], *Pražské Egyptologické Studie* 3 (2004) 25-37 (in Czech)

Krása and Polišenský, 'Czech missionary's first hand account'

R. Grulich, *Der Beitrag der böhmischen Länder zur Weltmission des 17. und 18. Jahrhunderts*, Königstein/Ts., 1981, pp. 134-8

Giamberardini, *Cronaca della missione francescana*

Giamberardini, *'Historia' della missione francescana*

Petráček, 'Jakub Římař aus Kroměříž'

K. Petráček, 'Handschriften zur Kenntnis Ägyptens und Abessiniens im 18. Jhdt. aus der Bibliotheca Pragensis in Conventu Fratrum S. Francisci Reformatorum S. Mariae ad Nives', *Archiv Orientální* 23 (1955) 90-8

F.X. Vilhum, *Čeští misionáři v Egyptě a Habeši*, Prague, 1946

Marek Dospěl

Johann Salomo Semler

DATE OF BIRTH   18 December 1725
PLACE OF BIRTH   Saalfeld, Thuringia
DATE OF DEATH   14 March 1791
PLACE OF DEATH   Halle

BIOGRAPHY

Johann Salomo Semler was a leading German theologian of the 18ᵗʰ century. He is regarded as the founder of biblical criticism and is sometimes called the father of German rationalism. He was born on 18 December 1725 in Saalfeld, Thuringia, the son of Matthias Nicolaus Semler, a Lutheran pastor, and Dorothea Elisabeth Kampferin, herself the daughter of a Lutheran pastor. His father had studied at Jena and served as chaplain to the troops from Gotha who were fighting the Dutch in Italy. He returned to Saalfeld in 1718 and eventually became Archdeacon of Saalfeld (Carlsson, 'Johann Salomo Semler', p. 61).

Semler went to school in Saalfeld, studying Greek, Hebrew and Latin. Pietism arrived in the town when he was a teenager. It was the 'radical' form, from the Herrnhuter group connected to the Moravian Church under the protection of Count Nikolaus Ludwig von Zinzendorf (1700-60). Semler was initially attracted to this form of Pietism with its emphasis on individual conversion and spiritual rebirth, but its anti-intellectualism later led him to develop a dislike of 'enthusiasm' (Carlsson, 'Johann Salomo Semler', pp. 71-9).

Semler studied theology and classical languages at the Royal Prussian Friedrichs-University in Halle from 1743 to 1750. His teachers included the Orientalist Johann David Michaelis, with whom he read Greek, Hebrew and Syriac, while he studied Hebrew and Arabic under Michaelis' father, the celebrated philologist Christian Benedikt Michaelis. Other teachers were Joachim Lange, Benedict Gottlob Clausewitz, Johann Heinrich Callenberg and Johann Georg Knapp. However, Semler was most influenced by Siegmund Jacob Baumgarten (1706-57), professor of theology, whose application of Christian Wolff's philosophical methods and abstract rationalism led to his being attacked by the 'pious' members of the faculty.

Baumgarten's interest in history resulted in his becoming editor of *Allgemeine Welthistorie*, a revised translation of George Sale's *An universal history from the earliest account of time to the present*. Semler, a member of

Baumgarten's theological seminar group, lived in his house and assisted in checking entries of *Allgemeine Welthistorie* (Carlsson, 'Johann Salomo Semler', pp. 89-93).

During his time as a student in Halle, Semler came to the conclusion that 'critical philological and historical scholarship needed to proceed without hindrance on dogmatic grounds' (Carlsson, 'Johann Salomo Semler', pp. 101). This conclusion laid the ground for his development of historical-criticism of the biblical text.

While still a student in Halle, Semler published a number of text-critical works, including *Specimen examinis critici operum, quae ita feruntur, Macarii, sub laetissimos festosque dies Christo ab inferis magnifice redeunti sacros boni ominis caussa* (1745); *Specimen animadversionum in aliquot opuscula graeca Macarii* (1746); *De lectionibus variantibus in epistola Iudae* (1748); and *Notitiam splendidissimae Hesychani Lexici editionis, quae inter Batavos prodire coepit cura S.R. viri Joannis Alberti et specimen animadversionum addit* (1749).

After gaining his *Magisterwürde* in 1750, Semler moved to Coburg, where he taught in a school and edited a newspaper before moving to the University of Altdorf as professor of history and poetry in 1751. Whilst there, he completed his doctoral thesis on exegetical problems in the second epistle of Timothy. He married Christina Magdalena Philippina Dobler in 1751 and, after her death in 1771, he married Susanna Beata Schwarz in 1772.

Baumgarten asked him to apply for the post of professor of theology in Halle, and he returned there in 1753 (Raup, 'Semler'; Carlsson, 'Johann Salomo Semler', pp. 115-19). In Halle, his lectures were popular, leading to jealousy among his Pietist colleagues, who suspected him of Socinianism and Arianism. On Baumgarten's death in 1757, Semler succeeded him as head of theology and as editor of *Allgemeine Welthistorie*. He remained at the university until his death in 1791.

His major work, *Abhandlung von freier Untersuchung des Canon* ('Treatise on a free examination of the canon') (4 vols, 1771-5), applied historical criticism to the biblical canon. This led to charges of impiety and naturalism being brought against him by the Pietists (Carlsson, 'Johann Salomo Semler', p. 60 n. 1). On these charges Alastair Hamilton writes:

> For all the suspicions that weighed against him, especially on account of his bold treatment of the Bible, Semler remained devoted to the tradition of Melanchthon; he had no time for deism and always retained his belief in revelation. Even if he is generally regarded as having deviated from orthodox Lutheranism in the 1760s and 1770s, well before his death in

1791 he reverted to an orthodoxy that became ever more rigid. ('Lutheran Islamophiles', p. 335)

This return to orthodoxy raised questions among his liberal supporters that he had compromised himself.

In response to his critics, Semler published a two-volume autobiography, *Lebensbeschreibung von ihm selbst abgefaßt* (1781-2). The first volume gives details about his life, while the second catalogues the books that shaped his thinking. Carlsson says that his autobiography 'aimed to vindicate Semler's integrity as a Christian teacher by recounting how his thought had evolved' ('Johann Salomo Semler', p. 60 n. 1).

MAIN SOURCES OF INFORMATION

Primary

J.S. Semler, *Lebensbeschreibung von ihm selbst abgefaßt*, 2 vols, Halle, 1781-2; Biogr. 1092 h-1/h-2 (digitised version available through *MDZ*)

Secondary

A. Hamilton, 'Lutheran Islamophiles in eighteenth-century Germany', in A. Blair and A.-S. Goeing (eds), *For the sake of learning. Essays in honor of Anthony Grafton*, Leiden, 2016, vol. 1, 327-43

A. Hamilton, '"To rescue the honour of the Germans". Qur'an translations by eighteenth- and early nineteenth-century German Protestants', *Journal of the Warburg and Courtauld Institutes* 77 (2014) 173-209

MK [M. Kegel], art., 'Semler, Johann Salomo (1725-91)', in H.F. Klemme and M. Kuehn (eds), *Dictionary of 18th century German philosophers*, vol. 3, London, 2010, 1084-6

D. Fleischer, art. 'Semler, Johann Salomo', in *Neue Deutsche Biographie*, vol. 24, Berlin, 2010, 236-7

P.H. Reill, 'Between Theosophy and orthodox Christianity. Johann Salomo Semler's hermetic religion', in O. Hammer (ed.), *Polemical encounters. Esoteric discourse and its others*, Leiden, 2007, 157-79

E.W. Carlsson, 'Johann Salomo Semler, the German Enlightenment, and Protestant theology's historical turn', Madison WI, 2006 (PhD Diss., University of Wisconsin; includes a biography of Semler's early life, pp. 60-119, and an extensive bibliography of his writings, pp. 408-14)

K. Nowak, art. 'Semler, Johann Salomo', in R. Vierhaus (ed.), *Deutsche Biographische Enzyklopädie*, Münich, vol. 9, 2005, 399

R. Bordoli, *L'Illuminismo di Dio: alle origini della mentalità liberale. Religione teologica filosofica e storia in Johann Salomo Semler (1725-1791). Contributo per lo studio delle fonti teologiche, cartesiane e spinoziane dell'Aufklärung*,

Florence, 2004, pp. 12-37 (survey of Semler's life and thought, with a discussion of his relationship with orthodox Lutheranism)

D. Sorkin, 'Reclaiming theology for the Enlightenment. The case of Siegmund Jacob Baumgarten (1706-1757)', *Central European History* 36 (2003) 503-30

D. Sorkin, '"A wise, enlightened and reliable piety". The religious Enlightenment in central and western Europe, 1689-1789' [Parkes Institute Pamphlet No. 1], Southampton, 2002

W. Raup, art. 'Semler, Johann Salomo, führender ev. Theologe des 18. Jahrhunderts', *Biographisch-Bibliographisches Kirchenlexikon*, vol. 14, Herzberg, 1998, 1444-73

G. Hornig, *Johann Salomo Semler. Studien zu Leben und Werk des Hallenser Aufklärungstheologen*, Tübingen, 1996 (detailed account of Semler's intellectual development)

H.E. Hess, 'Theologie und Religion bei Johann Salomo Semler. Ein Beitrag zur Theologiegeschichte des 18. Jahrhunderts', Berlin, 1974 (PhD Diss., Kirchliche Hochschule Berlin)

L. Zscharnack, *Lessing und Semler. Ein Beitrag zur Entstehungsgeschichte des Rationalismus und der kritischen Theologie*, Giessen, 1905

WORKS ON CHRISTIAN-MUSLIM RELATIONS

Semler's writings about Islam

DATE   1759-60

ORIGINAL LANGUAGE   German

DESCRIPTION

Although Semler is primarily known for his work on developing biblical criticism and rationalism, he also had an interest in Islam. This is particularly obvious in his preface to vol. 19 of *Allgemeine Welthistorie* (1759) and his preface to Friedrich Eberhard Boysen's *Kritische Erleuterungen des Grundtextes der heiligen Schriften Altes Testaments* (1760).

While he was still a student, Semler assisted Baumgarten with the preparation of the early volumes of *Allgemeine Welthistorie*, a translation of *An universal history from the earliest account of time to the present* (1736-68), with which George Sale had been associated towards the end of his life, participating in the planning of the first 20 volumes. In 1757, Semler succeeded Baumgarten as editor, and continued in this role until 1766, being responsible for vols 17-30.

Vol. 19, published in 1759, includes material on Muḥammad, Islam and Arab history. Semler wrote the preface to the volume (38 pages long), in which he criticises the general reliance among European historians on

Byzantine sources and welcomes the wider availability and use of Arabic sources (p. 7). He 'deplored the standard Western approach to Islam' (Hamilton, 'Lutheran Islamophiles', p. 332), asking 'What right had the Church of Rome to cast aspersions on the Prophet Muḥammad when it was itself so prone to fraudulence and fanaticism?' (pp. 8-9). The preface comments on the range of sources used by Sale, and also by himself in his revision; these include Simon Ockley, Pierre Bayle, Henri Boulainvilliers and Jean Gagnier. Semler makes detailed remarks on their use of Arabic sources (pp. 9-17).

In 1760, Semler wrote the preface to *Kritische Erleuterungen des Grundtextes der heiligen Schriften Altes Testaments* ('Critical explanations of the base text of the Old Testament scriptures'), which was published in ten parts (1760-4). In this, Boysen followed the ideas of his teacher Christian Benedikt Michaelis, and referred to Arabic in order to elucidate some of the more obscure Hebrew terms in the Old Testament. This was common among Orientalists at the time, though it was derided by scholars such as Johann Jacob Reiske (Hamilton, 'Lutheran Islamophiles', p. 333).

In the preface, which is 30 pages long (sigs. a8v–b7r), Semler expresses his full support for the idea of explaining Hebrew words in the Old Testament through equivalent terms in Arabic, arguing that the words had a common linguistic root, and that the system of comparison had been used to good effect by the rabbis (Hamilton, 'Lutheran Islamophiles', p. 334). He then turns to his own views on Islam, acknowledging that the Qur'an contains serious errors in its references to Christian and Jewish matters in the Bible. He regards these errors as 'evidence of the lack of an Arabic translation of the scriptures at the time' (sig. b2r–v). Even so, he is enthusiastic about the rise of Islam, which he regards as a providential gift of God to the Christians (Hamilton, 'Lutheran Islamophiles', p. 334). This was because it was owing to Arabic translations of the science and philosophy of the Greeks, together with the scientific works produced by the Arabs and Persians, that the world could emerge from a state of total darkness, the influence of the Church Fathers and the Vulgate could be combated, and the Bible could be appreciated for its moral message. By means of the translation of these Arabic works into Latin and their introduction into Europe, scholasticism could break away from the stranglehold of the Catholic Church (sigs. b4v–b6r).

Semler also praises the development in the freedom that Christians enjoyed in Islamic lands, where there was no threat of an inquisition or other forms of ecclesiastical oppression (Hamilton, '"To rescue the honour of the Germans"', p. 194).

SIGNIFICANCE

Semler's positive attitude towards Islam must, at least in part, be connected with his negative attitude towards the dogmatic stance of the Catholic Church. His view that Islam's intervention in 'saving' Greek writings was through 'Divine providence' reflects that expressed by Johann Jakob Brucker in his *Historia critica philosophiae* (1742; vol. 3, pp. 134-5). As 'father of rationalism', he would presumably have influenced his followers in his views about Islam, while confirming the Pietists' suspicions about his Deist preferences.

There is a need for further work on Semler's views about Islam as expressed in his autobiography, *Lebensbeschreibung von ihm selbst abgefaßt* (1781-2).

PUBLICATIONS

Johann Salomo Semler, 'Vorrede', in S.J. Baumgarten and J.S. Semler (eds), *Uebersetzung der Algemeinen Welthistorie der Neueren Zeiten die in England durch eine Gesellschaft von Gelehrten ausgefertiget worden*, vol. 19, Halle, 1759, 3-40; Bibl.Mont. 1567-19 (digitised version available through *MDZ*)

Johann Salomo Semler, 'Vorrede', in F.E. Boysen, *Kritische Erleuterungen des Grundtextes der heiligen Schriften Altes Testaments*, ed. J.S. Semler, vol. 1, Halle, 1760, sigs. a8v–b7r; Exeg. 128-1/3 (digitised version available through *MDZ*)

STUDIES

Hamilton, 'Lutheran Islamophiles'
Hamilton, '"To rescue the honour of the Germans"'
Bordoli, *L'Illuminismo di Dio*
Hornig, *Johann Salomo Semler*

John Chesworth

Josef Franz

DATE OF BIRTH 1703
PLACE OF BIRTH Unknown
DATE OF DEATH 1776
PLACE OF DEATH Vienna

BIOGRAPHY

François-Xavier de Feller (*Dictionnaire*, p. 393) attributes the play *Godefroi de Bouillon* to Josef Franz (1703-76), a member of the Society of Jesus and the first director of the Academy of Oriental Languages (*Orientalische Academie*) in Vienna from 1754. The *Dictionnaire* also describes Franz as professor of experimental physics at the Academy of Vienna. It states that he was highly esteemed for his abilities, honesty and moral values. He had won the Empress Maria Theresa's trust with his vast knowledge and expertise in diverse fields, and through his service as tutor to the future Emperor Joseph II (r. 1780-90). When he died in 1776, the emperor organised an expensive funeral for him, indicating his on-going respect for his teacher (Beales, *Enlightenment and reform*, p. 220). Fluent in the Turkish language, Josef Franz had also served as the secretary of Count Anton Ulefeldt (1699-1760), the nuncio in Istanbul for some time.

Josef Franz's known works are listed as *Dissertatio de natura electri* (Vienna, 1751) and *Jeu de carte géographique* (1759) (de Feller, *Dictionnaire*, p. 393).

Metin And, a pioneering researcher of Turkish theatre, has proposed that *Godefroi de Bouillon* may have been written by a student or teacher at the Oriental Academy (*Şair evlenmesi'nden önceki ilk Türkçe oyunlar*, p. 11). But it is quite plausible to attribute the play to Josef Franz himself, or at least to his directorship, considering that, with two assistants, he was leading the academy (see Sarikartal, 'Two Turkish-language plays', p. 146).

MAIN SOURCES OF INFORMATION

Primary
F.X. de Feller, *Dictionnaire historique ou biographie universelle*, Paris, 1836

Secondary

Ç. Sarıkartal, 'Two Turkish-language plays written by Europeans at the Academy
    of Oriental Languages in Vienna during the age of Haydn', in M. Hüttler
    and H.E. Weidinger (eds), *Ottoman Empire and European theatre*, vol. 2.
    The time of Joseph Haydn. From Sultan Mahmud I to Mahmud II (*r. 1730-
    1839*), Vienna, 2014, 143-53

D.E.D. Beales, *Enlightenment and reform in eighteenth-century Europe*, London,
    2005

M. And, *Şair evlenmesi'nden önceki ilk Türkçe oyunlar*, Istanbul, 1983

WORKS ON CHRISTIAN-MUSLIM RELATIONS

Godefroi de Bouillon

DATE   1761

ORIGINAL LANGUAGE   French and Ottoman Turkish

DESCRIPTION

Godefroi de Bouillon (*Godefroi de Bouillon: représenté par les eléves de
L'Académie des langues orientales devant leurs tres-augustes fondateurs*,
'Godefroi de Bouillon, presented by students of the Academy of Oriental Languages before their most august founders') is a tragedy in three
acts, written in Ottoman Turkish and French. The play was performed
in Vienna on 18 December 1757 and 28 January 1758, and printed there
in 1761. The printed text is 48 pages in length. Very significantly, Muslim
characters speak in Ottoman Turkish, and the Christian characters speak
in French, so the play is printed in French and Ottoman Turkish.

The play must have been written between the Academy's opening in
1754 and 1757, given that it was first performed at the end of that year in
order to present to the founders of the school the first achievements of
the students after three years of education. The author's preface (p. 6)
explains his intention to create an occasion for German actors to practise
their Turkish in public for the first time in accordance with the main goal
of the newly established Academy, and to reveal Turkish character and
customs by an accurate and harmonious imitation.

Godefroi de Bouillon is about events immediately after the conquest of
Jerusalem by the Christian hero Godefroi (c. 1060-1100) during the First
Crusade (1095-9). It is based on Torquato Tasso's (1544-95) epic poem
Gerusalemme liberata ('Jerusalem delivered', 1580), as is mentioned in the
play's preface (p. 6). The play relates that Godefroi, despite his great vic-
tory against the Muslim Turks, modestly and virtuously refused the title

8 ⚔ (o) ⚔

Godefroi, ce tiran, qui brifa votre trône,
Qui de ma tête ofa ravir une couronne,
Donne enfin dans un piége à fa grandeur fatal,
Pour retrouver la mort au lieu du rang roïal.

(*) *ALET. Oui*, *même avant que vous
euſſiés pris cette penſée*, *mon eſprit abbatu ne s'oc-
cupoit*, *qu'à chercher quelque möien pour tirer une
vengeance éclatante de ces infidelles. Jamais je n'euſſe
ſurvécu à la perte de mon röiaume ſi cette eſpérance
ne m'eût ſoutenu. Sans douter ſi je ſuivrai vos fide-
les conſeils, montrés moi le chemin à prendre pour aller à mon but; exposés moi la maniére, dont je puis
parvenir au comble de mes ſouhaits. Les périls qui
rendent l'exécution difficile, ne me rebutent pas; pourvû
que la ville ſouillée de leurs crimes ſoit à la fin puri-
fiée ou par leur ſang, ou par le zéle des confeſſeurs
de la vraie foi.*

OR-

ā̈lāeddin. we hættā ſen
bu fikre zābib olmaden bu
kiāfirden kabzÿ intikam
ſewdāſi benüm ſemīrī zæ-
mirüm we teſellāï dīli me-
lāletpezīrümdür. Bu ümīd
hæjātümi mümidd olmaſa
rubüm tſchoktan teslim it-
miſch olürdüm, we mem-
leketü ſeltænet elden gittü-
kten ſon-ra baky kalmazi-
düm. Bu merāme wuſūlün-
tærÿkyni

(*) علاءالدّين و حتّى
سن بو فكره ذاهب اولدن
بو كافردن قبض انتقام
سوداسي بنم سمير ضميرم و
تسلّاي دل ملالتپذيرمدر
بو اميد حياتمي ممد اولمسه
روحم چوقدن تسليم اتمش
اولوردم و مملكت و سلطنت
الدن كتدكدن صكره باقي
قالمزدم بو مرامه وصولك
طريغني

Illustration 8. *Godefroi de Bouillon, représenté par les eléves de l'Académie des langues
orientales*, p. 8, showing the text in French and Ottoman Turkish,
and also Ottoman Turkish in transliteration

king of Jerusalem, believing that it belonged to Christ himself. Godefroi pardons Muslim slaves as well as Christian rebels in order to establish peaceful rule in Jerusalem.

Interludes follow the first and the second acts. In the first of these, the secular customs and traditions of the Turks are represented in detail, including how they paid visits, ate and attended an audience and assembly, and in the second their religious ceremonies and traditions, such as ablution, prayer, use of prayer beads, and the whirling of dervishes, are represented. The last of these is described in full detail so that it can be performed: the Qur'an is recited from the pulpit and a sermon is preached; the dervishes first perform the ecstatic state reached by Muslims who are enchanted by the love of God; they whirl numerous times (*semah*) and then fall down exhausted; the shaykh prays, and his breath causes them to recover; they resume their whirling and fall down again; this is repeated, and then they come together and lean on one another, and finally they exit in deep reverence for God.

At first sight, it could be assumed that the play adopts a negative attitude towards relations between Christians and Muslims, because of its narrative of military conflict during the First Crusade and the capture of Jerusalem by Christian forces. Yet, a closer examination reveals that a very positive attitude is adopted in the play's dramaturgy.

The plot develops concepts and values such as virtue, loyalty, true faith, justice and honesty, rather than the themes of war and heroism. While it celebrates the establishment of Christian rule in Jerusalem, it nevertheless attempts to infuse humanist ideals into Christian values. Thus, it emphasises the idea that it is possible for Christian rule to be respected by Muslim populations.

Furthermore, the play does not describe all the Christian characters as good and Muslims as bad; on the contrary, Godefroi is betrayed by a commander in his own army and escapes with his life at the last moment, while Sultan Alaeddin, ruler of the Muslim Turks who are Godefroi's opponents, is described as honest and faithful. In the finale, Godefroi's great benevolence and forgiveness cause the Turks to express their repentance, and Sultan Alaeddin says that he is almost ready to follow this faith which has such great power over souls. Pierre the hermit, who represents Christian ideals and functions as an advisor and a faithful supporter of Godefroi, is fascinated by this extraordinary situation and starts to make predictions about a brilliant and glorious future.

As a conclusion, though it supports the superiority of Christianity, the plot also promotes the hope that an ideal Christian rule, represented by

Godefroi in whose character true faith is merged with human values, could unite people and establish peace.

Although not directly related to the story of the play, a significant effort can be observed in the prologue and the interludes to understand and somehow appreciate the living conditions and the religious practices of Muslim Turks.

SIGNIFICANCE

The play's great interest in and sympathetic approach to the customs and traditions of Muslim Turks, written as it was by a Christian European author, may be based on one or both of two reasons.

The first is rather pragmatic. As is stated in the printed edition, the first performance of the play was given in the presence of the Empress Maria Theresa, the founder of the Academy, and her entourage. It is quite understandable that, in a school that had been established to educate diplomats, it was necessary to provide the students with some knowledge of the Orient, which would be needed in their future tasks. Nevertheless, the keen interest of the play in Christian-Muslim rela- tions, and its emphasis on certain religious practices of Muslim Turks, needs further interpretation. It can plausibly be argued that Josef Franz, to whom the play is attributed, had some greater concerns than simple educational ones. These were related to the cultural and political milieu in which the play was written and performed.

Chancellor Wenzel Anton von Kaunitz (1711-94), who served as the grand ambassador to Paris (1750-3), was probably influenced by the example of L'École des jeunes de langues de Louis-le-Grand. Conse- quently, he recommended to the Empress that she establish a new acad- emy of Oriental languages in Vienna that would replace the Institute *Dil Oğlanları Mektebi* ('The children of language') in Istanbul. He argued that this school was not well controlled, and the students thus acquired Ori- ental ways and became alienated from their country. As a result of this advice, by order of the empress, students in Istanbul were called back home, and with the enrolment of some of them on 1 January 1754 the new Academy was opened under the directorship of the Jesuit Father Josef Franz, accompanied by two assistants. The first curriculum of the Academy mostly focused on language education, supported by a general education in universal culture, theology, Latin, history, geography and calligraphy. Along with Turkish, as well as Arabic and Persian (to sup- port Turkish), German, French and Italian were also taught. The students would also perform theatre plays in Turkish, French and Italian as well as in German (see de Testa and Gautier, *Drogmans et diplomates*, pp. 53-6; Tomenendal, *Das türkische Gesicht Wiens*, pp. 63-6).

Given the context of the great reform of education in Austria under the influence of the Enlightenment, one can suppose that Franz was in a critical situation from the very beginning of his directorship. The crisis in which he found himself was part of a larger one between religious orders and the general reform of the Austrian educational system in which the Society of Jesus, which had monopolised the running of Austrian universities prior to 1749, gradually lost power until its total suppression in 1774, as far as the education system, royal confessorship and representation on the censorship commission were concerned (Beales, *Enlightenment and reform*, p. 214). Yet, the Jesuit religious influence on education was not totally eliminated. Despite the change in the academic curriculum, the next three directors of the Academy, from 1770 to 1849, were also Jesuits (Johann Nekrep, 1770-85; Franz Hoeck, 1785-1832; Joseph Ottmar, 1832-49; see Testa and Gautier, *Drogmans et diplomates*, p. 57, n. 1). It should also be noted that members of the royal family were mostly educated by Jesuit tutors, including the Emperor Joseph II, who was well known for his reformist policies.

Under those conditions, Father Franz must have attempted to find a balance between scholastic and religious traditions and the reformist policies of the time. The play *Godefroi de Bouillon* can be considered the product of such a search to integrate religious values with Enlightenment ideals – something explicit in the tone of its preface, which sounds fully aware that the first fruits of the education offered at the Academy were being presented to members of the royal family and leading members of the government.

Second, it is arguable that Josef Franz was particularly interested in the Bektaşi and Mevlevi Sufi orders (*tarikat*), as can be observed in the detailed description of the whirling dervishes in the second interlude. First, it must be related to the fact that the Janissary corps, which constituted the main force of the Ottoman army of the period, was associated with the Bektaşi order. Providing future diplomats with some knowledge of the order might have helped them to make informed contacts with their counterparts and the royal milieu in Istanbul. The possible connection between the Janissary corps and the Bektaşi order was the subject of at least one more play written in the Oriental Academy (Thomas Chabert, *Hadgi Bektache ou la création des janissaires: drame en langue turque, en trois actes*, Vienna, 1810; *Hikayet-i ibda-ı yeniçeriyan ba bereket-i pir-i bektaşiyan Şeyh Hacı Bektaş Veli-i müsliman: 3 perde dram*, ed. Niyazi Akı, Erzurum, 1969). Second, Josef Franz might have found in the teachings of the Bektaşi and Mevlevi orders a certain parallelism with, or a kind of openness to, Enlightenment ideals. In fact, some aspects of the teachings of Jalāl al-Dīn Rūmī, the founder of the Mevlevi order, and Shaykh Hacı Bektaş Veli, the founder of the Bektaşi order, have been generally associated with humanist values. Thus, it might have seemed quite reasonable and fruitful for Josef Franz to imply and somehow propagate a possible cultural bridge between Christian and Muslim civilisations in reference to Enlightenment ideals in the context of the Austrian educational system at that time.

Further stage performances of the play are unknown.

PUBLICATIONS

[Attr. to Josef Franz], *Godefroi de Bouillon: représenté par les Eléves de l'Académie des langues orientales devant leurs tres-augustes fondateurs le 18. Décembre 1757. & le 28. Janvier 1758*, Vienna, 1761; 23744 (digitised version available through Heidelberg University Library)

STUDIES

Sarıkartal, 'Two Turkish-language plays written by Europeans at the Academy of Oriental Languages in Vienna during the age of Haydn'

Beales, *Enlightenment and reform*

M. de Testa and A. Gautier, *Drogmans et diplomates européens auprès de la Porte Ottomane*, Istanbul, 2003

K. Tomenendal, *Das türkische Gesicht Wiens. Auf den Spuren der Türken in Wien*, Vienna, 2000

And, *Şair evlenmesi'nden önceki ilk Türkçe oyunlar*

                                        Çetin Sarıkartal

Remedius Prutký

Remedius a/de Praga; Remedius a/de Boemia; Rimedio da Praga

DATE OF BIRTH   2 January 1713
PLACE OF BIRTH   Uncertain; probably Kopidlo, Kingdom of
    Bohemia (Czech Republic)
DATE OF DEATH   8 February 1770
PLACE OF DEATH   Florence

BIOGRAPHY

Remedius Prutký was born on 2 February 1713, probably in the small village of Kopidlo in the western part of the present Czech Republic. His baptismal name is sometimes given as Václav (Wenceslas) in scholarly studies, but this is not attested in any primary sources, Remedius being his religious name. Hardly anything specific about Prutký is known before his entering the Franciscan Order in Plzeň (Pilsen), in 1735.

Prutký's religious education was straightforward: he took solemn vows in Plzeň on 8 February 1735; he was ordained a lower cleric and a subdeacon in Wrocław (Breslau) on 21 September 1737; ordained a priest, he finished his theological studies in Kroměříž (Kremsier) in 1741, and was approved a confessor and preacher in both Czech and German, on 19 September 1741.

It is not known when and why Prutký decided to become a missionary, nor is it clear how he eventually ended up going to Egypt. Sometime in the summer of 1749, he was admitted to the Franciscan missionary college in Rome, San Pietro in Montorio. When he finished his missionary course in May 1750, he was immediately dispatched to Egypt, arriving in Alexandria on 13 July 1750. After spending several weeks in Cairo, he left for Girga in southern Egypt on 11 September 1750 and, in August 1751, he was appointed to lead a missionary expedition to Ethiopia.

After a failed attempt to convert King Iyasu II, Prutký was expelled from the Ethiopian royal court in Gondär. Sailing via India and around Africa, he arrived in Europe in May 1754. He returned to Egypt on 23 June 1755, spending most of the year in the Franciscan headquarters in Cairo until his departure from Egypt on 31 July 1756.

On his second return to Europe, Prutký served as an army chaplain for the Holy Roman Emperor Francis I's (r. 1745-65) Florentine troops during and after the Seven Years' War, before becoming a missionary prefect in St Petersburg in late 1765. He was expelled from Russia in the spring of 1769, and returned to Rome to give an account of his work. He died in Florence on 8 February 1770, on his way back to Bohemia, and was buried in the Franciscan convent church in Fiesole, where a stela in the left atrium commemorates his life and work.

MAIN SOURCES OF INFORMATION

Primary

MS Prague, Library of the Czech and Moravian St Wenceslaus Province of the Reformed Order of the Friars Minor – Re 14, *R(everendi) P(atris) Remedii Prutký, ord(inis) minor(um) S(ancti) P(atris) Francisci reform(atorum)* [...] *Itinerarium* (Prutký's manuscript account of his missionary experience)

MS Prague, National Archives – collection 'Franciscan Order', box 62, inv. no. 1992 (collected documents written by or relating to Prutký)

MS Vatican, Archivio Storico 'de Propaganda Fide' – (repository of documents emanating from Propaganda Fide, including Prutký's five official reports from his missions)

MS Vienna, Österreichisches Staatsarchiv – division 'Kriegsarchiv', collection 'Musterlisten und Standestabellen', box 11.322 (military records of the ranks and positions of the Toscana Infantry Regiment in 1760-3, which document Prutký as the regiment chaplain)

G. Giamberardini (ed.), *Lettere dei prefetti apostolici dell'Alto Egitto nel secolo XVIII*, Cairo, 1960 (correspondence of the Franciscan missionary prefects in Cairo, containing references to Prutký and his expedition to Ethiopia)

Secondary

M. Dospěl, 'The Wādī al-Naṭrūn monasteries and a reassessment of the manuscript *Itinerarium* (c. 1765) of Remedius Prutký OFM', *Orientalia Christiana Periodica* 82 (2016) 211-26 (analysis of Prutký's narrative of his alleged visit to Wādī al-Naṭrūn, and a critical reassessment of the originality of his *Itinerarium*)

M. Dospěl, 'After the scorching sunshine, relief eternal. The ultimate journey of an Egyptian missionary Remedius Prutký, ofm', *Pražské Egyptologické Studie* 8 (2011) 35-41 (study exploring the last months of Prutký's life, and identifying his place of burial; in Czech, English abstract)

J. Förster, 'De primo infideles adeundi animo. A sketch of Remedius Prutký's life prior to his departure for Ethiopia, in 1751', in J. Förster (ed.), *Remedius Prutký OFM, O Egyptě, Arábii, Palestině a Galileji* [On Egypt, Arabia,

Palestine, and Galilee], vol. 1, Prague, 2009, 14-106 (partial biography of Prutký; in Czech)

M. Dospěl, 'P. Remedius Prutký OFM – život a dílo', Prague, 2007 (MA Diss. Charles University in Prague)

M. Dospěl (ed.), *Remedius Prutký, Itinerarium II. De Abyssinia et Indiis Orientalibus. Edidit et introductione commentariisque supplevit Marek Dospěl*, Prague, 2007; acecs.cz/media/ dospel_prutky_itin_ii_sec.pdf (preliminary edition and Czech trans. of Part II of Prutký's *Itinerarium*, with an extensive introduction, in Czech)

J. Förster, 'De primo infideles adeundi animo. A life sketch of the missionary Remedius Prutký prior to his departure for Ethiopia, in 1751', *Listy Filologické* 129 (2006) 309-31

M. Krása and J. Polišenský, 'Czech missionary's first hand account of the 18th century Ethiopia, Arabia and India', *Archiv Orientální* 61 (1993) 85-90

J. Reinhold, 'Die St. Petersburger Missionspräfektur der Reformaten im 18. Jahrhundert', *Archivum Franciscanum Historicum* 54 (1961) 114-215, 329-402; 55 (1962) 193-251, 320-66; 56 (1963) 91-156

K. Petráček, 'Handschriften zur Kenntnis Ägyptens und Abessiniens im 18. Jhdt. aus der Bibliotheca Pragensis in Conventu Fratrum S. Francisci Reformatorum S. Mariae ad Nives', *Archiv Orientální* 23 (1955) 90-8

T. Somigli di S. Detole, 'L'*Itinerarium* del P. Remedio Prutky viaggiatore e missionario francescano (Alto Egitto) e il suo viaggio in Abyssinia 21 Febrario 1752-22 Aprile 1753', *Studi Francescani* 22 (1925) 425-60

WORKS ON CHRISTIAN-MUSLIM RELATIONS

Remedii Prutký, Itinerarium

'The travels of Remedius Prutký', 'Itinerary'

DATE   around 1765
ORIGINAL LANGUAGE   Latin

DESCRIPTION

The only complete copy of this work is the manuscript kept today in the Franciscan convent library in Prague, under the shelf number Re 14 (see Dospěl, *Remedius Prutký, Itinerarium II*, pp. cci-ccxxvii). Except for the title page, preface, the last few chapters, and the appendix, which were all written by an amanuensis, this is Prutký's autograph. In addition, there is a much-abridged version in the Strahov Library, Prague (shelf number DA III 36, fols 57r-112v). Written in Prague in 1789 by a Franciscan named Pavel Wolf, this manuscript was created at the request of a Premonstratensian named Josef Octavianus Prutký (1747-1814), who was Prutký's nephew (see Dospěl, *Remedius Prutký, Itinerarium II*, pp. lxiv, cciv).

Although not stated by the author himself, several hints in the work and the preface (by the amanuensis) confirm that the manuscript was finished in 1765 (possibly in the autumn), and that it had taken about one or two years. The title on the front page of the Prague manuscript is not in the author's own hand and may not represent the original (now lost?) or intended title of the work.

Prutký apparently made use of numerous sources, which he credits only rarely. Just how heavily he relied on information obtained at second hand remains to be mapped (see Dospěl, 'Wādī al-Naṭrūn monasteries'). His dependence on work by the following authors has so far been demonstrated: the French Jesuit missionary Claude Sicard (see Dospěl, 'Wādī al-Naṭrūn monasteries'; Dospěl, 'Dva misionáři'); the Portuguese Jesuit Nicolao Godinho (see Dospěl, 'Jaká je víra Etiopů'); the Jesuit polymath Athanasius Kircher; and the German scholar Hiob Ludolf. For Part I, Prutký also depended heavily on the manuscript *Itinerarium* by Jakub Římař.

Prutký most probably kept diaries or notes during his travels, and only sat down to compose his *Itinerarium* when he had the time and could consult other sources; this would have been sometime in 1764-5.

Manuscript Re 14, which contains 485 folios, comprises two main parts, one on Egypt and the other on Ethiopia, arranged into 85 and 82 chapters respectively .

In his attempt to offer an exhaustive account of Egypt and the adjacent regions of the Middle East, Prutký pays due attention to Islam, Muslims and their way of life. While he expresses his opinions of the Muslims and Islam throughout his work, the following chapters of Part I are specifically devoted to the subject: 54. *De secta Mahomethanorum* ('On the Muḥammadan sect'); 55. *De praecipuis hujus sectae punctis* ('On the principal teachings of this sect'); 56. *De vestitu mulierum* ('On women's dress'); 57. *De circumcisione Turcarum* ('On circumcision among the Turks'); 58. *De festis ac orationibus Turcarum* ('On Turkish feasts and prayers'); 59. *De jejunio, mosqvitis et lotionibus Turcarum* ('On Turkish fasting, mosques and ablutions'); 61. *Qvidnam sit nomen daruisch* ('The meaning of the word "Darwish"'); 62. *De caeremoniis mortuorum Turcarum* ('On Turkish funerary rites'); 63. *De justitia Turcarum* ('On Turkish justice'); and 64. *De aliqvibus adhuc Turcarum usibus* ('On some more Turkish customs').

Part II contains the following relevant chapters: 7. *De civitate Mecca et caravanis* ('On the city of Mecca and caravans'); 8. *Alia adhuc notabilia de domo Dei Mahomethanorum* ('Some more interesting facts about the Muḥammadan house of God'); 9. *Peregrinatio in Medine ad corpus Mahomethi* ('Pilgrimage to Muḥammad's tomb in Medina').

Despite Prutký's considerable dependence on the writings of others, it seems safe to assume that he agreed with whatever he has appropriated from them. Much of his factual reporting on Islam and Muslims appears to have been adopted from Jakub Římař's *Itinerarium*, especially fols 70v-104v.

His views and judgements of Islam are determined by his fundamental thesis that Islam is not based on God's revelation and is not even a true religion, but rather a sect. For him, Islam was not the product of a genuinely inspired revelation, but a forgery, made up from bits and pieces of existing religions and pagan cults with the aim of deceiving people. Consequently, Muslims are deplorable for blindly and devotedly following the precepts of the Qur'an (and its 'pig laws') and their leaders, starting with Muḥammad, 'the false prophet'. Although reliable translations of the Qur'an and fair-minded scholarship on Islam were available in several Western languages (including Italian and Latin) in his day, Prutký probably did not know the Qur'an at first hand, and in his work seems to be drawing on old stereotypes about Islam and Muslims.

Prutký uses several terms to refer to Muslims, probably because he used different sources for different parts of his work: Saracens, Mahometists, Mahumetists and Turks; the last term he also used to refer to the foreign ruling class in Egypt. Prutký also refers to the Muslims as 'infidels', and he rightly distinguishes the Arabs, i.e. the (semi)itinerant pastoralists of the desert, from the sedentary *fallahin*, who farm the land.

Occasionally, he writes appreciatively of Muslims, pointing to their piety, devotion and charity, but mostly he merely reproaches his intended Christian audience for their shortcomings in proper worship and Christian virtues.

SIGNIFICANCE

No known works appear to have been influenced by Prutký's *Itinerarium* in their portrayal of Islam or Muslims, and it is not likely there ever were any, given that, although Prutký apparently wanted to publish his work, it remained as a manuscript, which did not circulate widely.

PUBLICATIONS

MS Prague, Library of the Czech and Moravian St Wenceslaus Province of the Reformed Order of the Friars Minor – Re 14, *R(everendi) P(atris) Remedii Prutký, ord(inis) minor(um) S(ancti) P(atris) Francisci reform(atorum), provinciae Bohemiae S(ancti) Wenceslai, d(ucis) et m(artyris), alumni, per plures annos Aegypti, Abyssiniae seu Aethiopiae aliarumque regionum adjecentium, deinde etiam Magnae Russiae missionarii apostolici Itinerarium, in quo omnia imperia, regna et provinciae earumque principaliores civitates et oppida cum suis antiquitatibus, raritatibus et memorabilibus, montes et valles, maria et flumina, portus et promontoria, Scyllae et Charybdes, scopuli et vortices, volatilia et quadrupedia, pisces et ferae, auri-, argenti-, metalli fodinae ac diversa mineralia, gemmae et lapides pretiosi, arbores et fructus, herbae et radices, aromata et medicamenta, esculenta et potulenta, item populi et nationes earumque religio et ritus, mores et consuetudines, vita et conversatio, vitia et virtutes utriusque sexus etc. etc. fideliter et genuine describuntur. Quae omnia memoratus Pr. missionarius oculis vidit, auribus audivit, nec non personali praesentia per novennalem peregrinationem expertus est, deinde vero propria manu conscripsit et in duas partes divisit, cum adjunctis sedecim tabulis* (around 1765; Prutký's manuscript account of his missionary experience)

MS Prague, Strahov Library – DA III 36, fols 57r-112v, P. Wolf (ed.), *Itinerarium R. P. Remedii Prutký, ord(inis) minor(um) S. P. Francisci reformatorum, provinciae Bohemiae alumni, per plures annos Aegypti, Abyssiniae seu Aethyopiae aliarumque adjacentium regionum, deinde etiam Magnae Russiae missionarii apostolici* (Prague, 1789; an abridged version of MS Prague Re 14)

R. Ryšavý, 'Die Reformatenmission in Russland unter dem Missionspräfekten P. Remedius Prutký, O.F.M. (Mitte 1766 – 24. April 1769)', *Archivum Franciscanum Historicum* 27 (1934) 179-223 (with an edition of the Preface [fol. 6v] and much of the Appendix [fols 407-10] on pp. 220-3)

J. Procházka, *Čeští františkáni v Habeši*, Prague, 1937 (belletrist account of the lives of Prutký and Římař, with lengthy excerpts from their MSS in Czech trans., including Part II, ch. 71, on pp. 183-6, and Part II, chs 13-15, on pp. 142-62)

Z. Kalista, *Cesty ve znamení kříže. Dopisy a zprávy českých misionářů 17. a 18. věku ze zámořských krajů*, Prague, 1941, pp. 183-6, and notes on pp. 248-50 (Czech trans. of the Preface [*Animadversio*] and Part II, ch. 49 [*De reditu ex Aethyopia*])

Z. Kalista, *České baroko*, Prague, 1941, pp. 196-200, and notes on pp. 291-2 (Czech trans. of Part II, ch. 15 [*De adventu in civitatem regiam Gondar*])

M. Verner, 'Staroegyptské památky, jak je viděl v 18. stol. český cestovatel Václav Remedius Prutký', *Nový Orient* 22 (1967) 84 (Czech trans. of Part I, ch. 20 [*De Sphinge idolo*])

M. Verner, 'Ancient Egyptian monuments as seen by a Bohemian missionary V. R. Prutký in the 18th century', *Archiv Orientální* 36 (1968) 378 (English trans. of Part I, ch. 20 [*De Sphinge idolo*])

T. Pearson, [English trans. of Part II, ch. 43 (*De vermibus et eorum medicina*)], in R. Pankhurst and T. Pearson, 'Remedius Prutky's 18th century account of Ethiopian *taenicides* and other medical treatment', *Ethiopian Medical Journal* 10 (1972) 3-6

J.H. Arrowsmith-Brown (ed. and trans.), *Prutky's travels in Ethiopia and other countries*, notes by R. Pankhurst [and C. Beckingham], London, 1991 (English trans. of the whole of Part II; the introduction and translation raise problems)

M. Dospěl, 'Václav Remedius Prutký OFM – misionářem u pramenů Nilu', *Salve* 13 (2003) 67-75 (Czech trans. of Part II, ch. 71 [*Compendiosa relatio status missionis Aethyopiae Sacrae Congregationi Propagandae Fidei representata*])

M. Dospěl (ed.), *Remedius Prutký, Itinerarium II: De Abyssinia et Indiis Orientalibus. Edidit et introductione commentariisque supplevit Marek Dospěl*, Prague, 2007, pp. 1-376; http://www.acecs.cz/media/dospel_prutky_itin_ii_sec.pdf (edition and Czech trans. of the whole of Part II; preliminary version)

J. Förster, 'Václav (Remedius) Prutký OFM. Itinerarium Missionum Apostolicarum (úvodní studie, edice a překlad s komentářem části I. dílu)', Prague, 2007 (PhD Diss. Charles University in Prague; edition and Czech trans. of Part I, chs 3-32; unreliable)

J. Förster (ed.), *Remedius Prutký. O Egyptě, Arábii, Palestině a Galileji*, vol. 1, Prague, 2009, pp. 136-419 (edition and Czech trans. of Part I, chs 3-32; unreliable)

M. Dospěl, 'Jaká je víra Etiopů? Komentovaný překlad jedné kapitoly z Itineraria Remedia Prutkého OFM', *Parrésia. Revue pro Východní Křesťanství* 4 (2010) 275-95 (Czech trans. of Part II, ch. 34 [*Qvae sit Aethyopibus fides?*], pp. 284-94)

M. Dospěl, 'Etiopské křesťanství očima františkánského misionáře Remedia Prutkého (1713–1770)', *Clavibus Unitis* 1 (2012) 124-56 (edition and Czech trans. of Part II, ch. 71 [*Compendiosa relatio status missionis Aethyopiae Sacrae Congregationi Propagandae Fidei representata*], pp. 150-6, revised version; http://www.acecs.cz/media/cu_2012_01.pdf)

STUDIES

Dospěl, 'Wādī al-Naṭrūn monasteries'

M. Dospěl, 'Franciscan missionary and pastoral work among Egyptian and Ethiopian Christians in the context of coeval book production', in P. Hlaváček et al. (eds), *Františkánský kontext teologického a filosofického myšlení*, Prague, 2012, 388-412 (in Czech, with English abstract)

Dospěl, 'Etiopské křesťanství očima františkánského misionáře Remedia Prutkého'

Dospěl, 'After the scorching sunshine'

M. Dospěl, 'Dva misionáři a stéla krále Achnatona, aneb příběh z říše archeologie textu', *Pražské Egyptologické Studie* 6 (2009) 27-32 (in Czech)

J. Förster, 'De Aegypto, Arabia, Palaestina et Galilaea. A literary-critical study of Part I of Prutký's Itinerarium,' in Förster, *Remedius Prutký OFM. O Egyptě, Arábii, Palestině a Galileji*, vol. 1, pp. 67-106 (an introduction to the edition of Part I, chs 3-32; in Czech)

M. Dospěl, 'Fr Remedius Prutký OFM and the Holy Roman Emperor Francis I. Stephen', in J. Holaubek, H. Navrátilová and W.B. Oerter (eds), *Egypt and Austria III. The Danube monarchy and the Orient* (*Proceedings of the Prague Symposium, September 11th to 14th, 2006*), Prague, 2007, 51-63

Dospěl, 'P. Remedius Prutký OFM – život a dílo'

J. Förster, 'Itinerarium Václava (Remedia) Prutkého. Cestopis na rozhraní epoch (literárněvědná studie na základě rozpracované kritické edice díla)', *Auriga. ZJKF* 47 (2005) 43-53, 80-4

J. Förster, 'Sine experientia nihil sufficienter sciri potest. (Die Welt der Antike im Itinerarium von Remedius Prutký, 1713-1770)', *Listy Filologické* 128 (2005) 65-74

J. Förster, 'Sine experientia nihil sufficienter sciri potest (Svět antiky v Itinerariu Remedia Prutkého)', in P.R. Beneš and Petr Hlaváček (eds), *Historia franciscana*, vol. 2. *Sborník textů*, Kostelní Vydří, 2005, 204-13

M. Dospěl, 'The eighteenth-century Franciscan missionaries of the Czech crown lands and their first-hand accounts of Levant, Egypt, and Ethiopia in the perspective of the so-called Orientalism', in

J. Holaubek and H. Navrátilová (eds), *Egypt and Austria, I. Proceedings of the Symposium (31/8 to 2/9 2004) at the Czech Institute of Egyptology*, Prague, 2005, 31-42

J. Förster, 'Václav (Remedius) Prutký (1713-1770): Itinerarium', in E. Frimmová and E. Klecker (eds), *Itineraria Posoniensia. Zborník z medzinárodnej konferencie Cestopisy v novoveku, ktorá sa konala v dňoch 3.-5. novembra 2003 v Bratislave*, Bratislava, 2005, 152-8

M. Dospěl, 'Františkáni Římař, Prutký a Schneider. Zdroje a možnosti interpretace jejich zpráv (nejen) o Egyptě 18. Století', *Pražské Egyptologické Studie* 3 (2004) 25-37

M. Dospěl, 'Církevně-náboženské poměry v Habeši a jejich obraz v latinském Itinerariu českého františkánského misionáře Václava Remedia Prutkého (1713-1770)', České Budějovice, 2001 (MA Diss. Jihočeská univerzita v Českých Budějovicích)

Krása and Polišenský, 'Czech missionary's first hand account'

J. Pávová, 'Rukopisné památky české provenience k poznání zemí severovýchodní Afriky v 18. a 19. století', Praha, 1984 (MA Diss. Charles University in Prague)

R. Grulich, *Der Beitrag der böhmischen Länder zur Weltmission des 17. und 18. Jahrhunderts*, Königstein/Ts., 1981, pp. 139-44

O. Raineri, 'Le relazioni fra chiesa etiopica e chiesa romana (Lettere di Remedio missionario in Etiopia nel 1752-1753)', *Nicolaus* 8 (1980) 351-64

Pankhurst and Pearson, 'Remedius Prutký's 18th century account'

Verner, 'Ancient Egyptian monuments'

Verner, 'Staroegyptské památky'

Reinhold, 'Die St. Petersburger Missionspräfektur'

K. Petráček, 'Český přínos k poznání Ethiopů a jejich země', *Československá Etnografie* 6 (1958) 55-68

K. Petráček, 'Jakub Římař aus Kroměříž. Descriptio Aethiopiae seu Abissiniae (Land und Leute)', *Archiv Orientální* 25 (1957) 334-83

Petráček, 'Handschriften zur Kenntnis Ägyptens und Abessiniens'

F.X. Vilhum, *Čeští misionáři v Egyptě a Habeši*, Prague, 1946

Ryšavý, Die Reformatenmission in Russland'

Detole, 'L'*Itinerarium* del P. Remedio Prutcky'

T. Somigli di S. Detole, 'La francescana spedizione in Etiopia del 1751-1754 e la sua relazione del P. Remedio Prutky di Boemia O.F.M.', *Archivum Franciscanum Historicum* 6 (1913) 129-43

Marek Dospěl

David Friedrich Megerlin

DATE OF BIRTH   Around 1698
PLACE OF BIRTH   Königsbronn
DATE OF DEATH   1778
PLACE OF DEATH   Frankfurt am Main

BIOGRAPHY

There is some uncertainty about the date and place of David Friedrich Megerlin's birth. It is generally thought that he was born to a Lutheran family in Württemberg between 1698 and 1700, although the place is sometimes given as Königsbronn and sometimes Stuttgart. When he matriculated at the University of Tübingen in 1716, Megerlin described himself as 'Brackenheimensis'. This could mean either that he was in fact born in Brackenheim or that he had simply been to the Latin school there before proceeding to university. At Tübingen, where he was probably taught by the professor of Oriental languages Johann Christian Klemm, he became a good Hebraist and must have learnt the rudiments of Arabic. In 1718, he received his master's degree in theology, and from 1725 to 1729 he was a *Repetent* or tutor at the clerical training college closely connected with the university, the Tübinger Stift.

In 1729, Megerlin published plans for a college of Oriental languages, the *Tractatus de scriptis et collegiis orientalibus*, which recalled the designs of Christian Ravius and Matthias Wasmuth, and the ideals of Andreas Acoluthus, as well as the project of the great Pietist reformer August Hermann Francke at the University of Halle, in whose presence Megerlin claimed to have made a speech in Arabic. Megerlin himself was clearly sympathetic to Pietism, and his tract appeared with a preface by another distinguished Pietist reformer, Christian Matthäus Pfaff. In an appendix, Megerlin stressed the importance of studying Hebrew and Aramaic and of publishing an introduction to the Qur'an, which should include a synopsis of Arabic grammar and a Hebrew harmony, the text of a dozen suras (which could also be used as linguistic exercises) together with confutations, some notes on the use of Arabic in the Bible, and an essay on the present state of learning in Turkey. He suggested that such questions should be asked as whether the Prophet Muḥammad was Antichrist, to which figures in the Bible he might correspond, and when the Turks could be expected to convert to Christianity.

On leaving Tübingen in 1729, Megerlin was appointed rector of the
Latin school and second Lutheran pastor of the German church in Montbéliard, the enclave in the Franche-Comté that belonged to Württemberg. From there, in 1731 he travelled briefly to Basel, where he called on
the Swiss Orientalist and theologian Johann Ludwig Frey and discussed
with him the existing translations of the Qur'an. Frey was planning to
translate it himself, and the two men agreed in their criticisms of earlier
efforts to do so. In 1734, when Montbéliard was occupied by the French,
Megerlin was appointed second preacher in Maulbronn, and in 1736
he was promoted to first preacher. He seems to have been invited to
St Petersburg but he declined. In 1748, he was made dean of the nearby
village of Güglingen. In the following year, however, he was accused of
embezzlement and placed under house arrest, but managed to flee to
Heilbronn. Arrested again, he was taken back to Güglingen and relieved
of his ecclesiastical duties.

Megerlin then retired to Laubach. There, in 1766, he described himself as minister and rector. Both in Laubach and in Frankfurt, to where
he subsequently moved, he gave French lessons and tuition in Arabic.
A constant champion of the conversion of the Jews to Christianity and
with a sustained interest in Jewish thought, he published in 1751 a translation from Rabbinical Hebrew, which also included a Latin version, of
the last two chapters of Maimonides' *Mishneh Torah* and, in 1766, an edition in Hebrew of a work by the Jewish doctor Aser Anselmus Wormsius
maintaining the antiquity of the Masoretic text of the Bible. In 1755, he
also confirmed his commitment to the defence of Protestantism against
Catholicism with his *Vertheidigung der Protestantischen Religion, gegen
die allerneueste Angriffe der Römisch-Catholischen Clerisey*, dedicated to
the landgrave Wilhelm VIII von Hessen-Kassel.

In the meantime, Megerlin continued to work on his German translation of the Qur'an. He had issued a small sample of his rendering of the
Qur'an in Latin in 1750. In 1755, he compared the 12th-century version
of Robert of Ketton, published by Theodor Bibliander in 1543, with two
Arabic manuscripts – one was his own and the other had belonged to the
great Ethiopicist and Orientalist Hiob Ludolf – and he planned to produce an edition of Sura 61 in Arabic accompanied by various translations.
He was unable to do so, however, for lack of Arabic types. He completed
his own translation of the whole Qur'an in 1771 and had it published
in the following year, *Die türkische Bibel, oder des Korans allererste
teutsche Uebersetzung aus der Arabischen Urschrift*. He died in Frankfurt
in 1778.

MAIN SOURCES OF INFORMATION

Primary

David Friedrich Megerlin, *Tractatus de scriptis et collegiis orientalibus*, Tübingen, 1729

David Friedrich Megerlin, *Die türkische Bibel, oder des Korans allererste teutsche Uebersetzung aus der Arabischen Urschrift*, Frankfurt, 1772

A. Bürk and W. Wille (eds), *Die Matrikeln der Universität Tübingen*, Tübingen, 1953

Secondary

A. Hamilton, '"To rescue the honour of the Germans". Qur'an translations by eighteenth- and early nineteenth-century German Protestants', *Journal of the Warburg and Courtauld Institutes* 77 (2014) 173-209

M. Wolfes, art. 'Megerlin, David Freidrich', in *Biographische-Bibliographisches Kirchenlexikon*, Hamm, 1999, vol. 16, cols 1043-7

WORKS ON CHRISTIAN-MUSLIM RELATIONS

Die türkische Bibel
'The Turkish Bible'

DATE   1772
ORIGINAL LANGUAGE   German

DESCRIPTION

Die türkische Bibel (in full, *Die türkische Bibel, oder des Korans allererste teutsche Uebersetzung aus der Arabischen Urschrift selbst verfertiget: welcher Nothwendigkeit und Nutzbarkeit in einer besondern Ankündigung hier erwiesen von M. David Friedrich Megerlin, Professor,* 'The Turkish Bible or the very first German translation of the Qur'an made from the Arabic original itself, the necessity and use of which is demonstrated in a special announcement by M. David Megerlin, Professor') was published in Frankfurt am Main in 1772 by Johann Gottlieb Garbe. An octavo volume of 876 pages, it is dedicated to the directors and assessors of the Württemberg consistory. Both the Dedication and the 30-page Foreword are dated 29 September 1771. They are followed by a German prose translation in which the verses are clearly numbered.

Megerlin's translation was the first published German translation of the complete text to be made directly from the Arabic. In his Foreword, he says that one of his intentions is 'to rescue the honour of the Germans', who had hitherto had to read the Qur'an either in other languages or in German translations of translations. He lists his predecessors and is particularly critical of André du Ryer, the French translator who, as Megerlin points out, had failed to number the verses and had, on occasion, been unduly free in his rendering. Megerlin does, however, express great respect for Ludovico Marracci, whose bilingual Arabic-Latin edition of the Qur'an had appeared in 1698, even if he follows Andreas Acoluthus in saying that Marracci's version contained mistakes and omissions. He also bestows high praise on the English translator George Sale, who had himself used Marracci's translation to good effect and had produced what Megerlin calls *ein gelehrtes Meisterstück* ('a learned masterpiece') with his English Qur'an of 1734. Megerlin had read it in the German translation by Theodor Arnold, which came out in 1746.

When it comes to judging the Qur'an itself, Megerlin regards it primarily as the blasphemous work of an impostor, although he admits that it is not entirely without qualities. Why then should it be translated? Megerlin expresses his satisfaction that the Qur'an and the Talmud are no longer being burnt by the popes in Rome and he lauds the progress of Arabic studies. He agrees with Theodor Bibliander, the editor of Robert of Ketton's translation published in 1543, that a reading of the Qur'an would necessarily strengthen the readers' faith in Christianity and lead them to pray for the destruction of Islam and the conversion of the Muslims. This, he believes, will soon come about. One sign of it was the Russian conquest of Islamic territory, which might, he hoped, be a first step towards a united crusade against the Turks.

SIGNIFICANCE

Megerlin's translation was largely dependent on Marracci and Sale, but it does not read well. It is in an awkward, wooden prose, and makes no attempt to capture the poetic qualities of the original. Its reception varied. It was reviewed by Johann Friedrich Hirt, professor of theology at the University of Jena, in the second volume of his *Orientalische und exegetische Bibliothek*. Hirt was probably flattered by Megerlin's placing him at the head of a list of illustrious German Arabists, and he consequently described Megerlin's version as a 'fine new German translation of the Qur'an' which was better than the previous German translations (of translations) and, on the whole, accurate, even if it was not entirely free of mistakes. Other critics were less benevolent. Johann Bernhard Köhler, a pupil of Johann Jacob Reiske and professor of Oriental languages at Göttingen, was clearly irritated by the anti-Islamic tone of Megerlin's Foreword and had no good word for the translation. It was, he said, *von Herzen schlecht gerathen* ('thoroughly bad'), the work of a man who 'understands neither enough Arabic nor enough German, and German still less' – one of the very worst, in short, of the existing German versions. Köhler was in full agreement with the 23-year-old Johann Wolfgang von Goethe. Writing in the *Frankfurter gelehrte Anzeigen,* Goethe dismissed Megerlin's translation as *diese elende Produktion* ('this miserable product').

Köhler and Goethe were not alone in their annoyance about the hatred for Islam that pervaded Megerlin's Foreword. By the early 1770s, there was a strong tendency in German intellectual circles to admire Arab culture and to appreciate Islam, just as there was a growing interest in Eastern poetry and a feeling that the Qur'an was above all a poetic work. Although it was generally admitted that Marracci had produced a reliable translation from a linguistic point of view, it was also acknowledged that he had never captured its poetic qualities. Megerlin had done so even less. It was now time for a translator to appear who was capable of doing so. Even if Friedrich Eberhard Boysen's translation, which appeared in 1773, was still short of the mark, it was regarded as far better than Megerlin's, and *Die türkische Bibel* fell into permanent neglect.

PUBLICATIONS

David Friedrich Megerlin, *Die türkische Bibel, oder des Korans allererste teutsche Uebersetzung aus der Arabischen Urschrift,* Frankfurt, 1772; A.or. 6530 e (digitised version available through *MDZ*)

STUDIES

Hamilton, '"To rescue the honour of the Germans"'

J.H. Hirt, 'Die Türkische Bibel[...]', in J.H Hirt (ed.), *Orientalische und exegetische Bibliothek,* Jena, 1772, vol. 2, pp. 433-59

J.B Köhler, 'Der türkische Bibel[...]', *Allgemeine Deutsche Bibliothek* 17 (1772) 426-37

J.W. von Goethe, 'review of *Die Türkische Bibel*', *Frankfurter gelehrte Anzeigen,* 22 December 1772, p. 811

Alastair Hamilton

Johann Jacob Reiske

DATE OF BIRTH   25 December 1716
PLACE OF BIRTH   Zörbig
DATE OF DEATH   14 August 1774
PLACE OF DEATH   Leipzig

BIOGRAPHY

The best source for Johann Jacob Reiske's life is his autobiography, *Von ihm selbst aufgesetzte Lebensbeschreibung*, covering events up to January 1770, with an appendix by his wife, Ernestine Christine (1735-98). However, as Detlef Döring has shown in an insightful essay, Reiske's self-portrayal throughout the text as an unrecognised genius and a 'martyr to Arabic scholarship' should be treated with caution. Useful information can also be found in Johann Fück's chapter on Reiske in his *Die Arabischen Studien in Europa bis in den Anfang des 20. Jahrhunderts*, Richard Förster's entry on him in *Allgemeine Deutsche Biographie*, vol. 28, pp. 129-43, and Förster's 1897 edition of Reiske's letters. In addition to his pioneering work as an Arabist, Reiske was also an eminent scholar of Greek literature. His contributions in this field are acknowledged by, among others, Conrad Bursian (*Geschichte der classischen Philologie*) and, most recently, Asaph Ben-Tov ('Hellenism').

This and the following paragraphs are by no means exhaustive descriptions of Reiske's life and work. A book length study of this great German scholar is still a desideratum.

Reiske was born on 25 December 1716, at Zörbig, near Leipzig and Halle. Between 1729 and 1732, he was schooled at the Pietist orphanage of the Franckesche Stiftung at Halle, where Johann David Michaelis (1717-91) was one of his fellow students. All his life, Reiske suffered from a weak physical constitution and severe depression, chronic migraines, insomnia and other mental afflictions (see the short biography by the physician Christian Gottfried Gruner, in Reiske and Faber, *Opuscula medica*, and the report of an autopsy carried out by the Leipzig Professor of medicine, Johann Christoph Pohl; Reiske and Faber, *Opuscula medica*, pp. xviii-xix). These conditions seem to have been aggravated by quackish treatments in his childhood and severe and abusive discipline at the church school. In 1733, he enrolled at Leipzig University, where he studied for five years, most of which he later considered a waste of time. During these years, he became 'obsessed' with the idea of learning Arabic: 'A certain, ineffable and unstoppable desire, of which I don't know the origin, to learn Arabic took hold of my soul' (*Lebensbeschreibung*, p. 9). However, he also gives more specific motives for studying Arabic: an encounter with Johann Heinrich Hottinger's pioneering bibliography of Arabic literature in the *Bibliotheca Orientalis* and the desire to become famous and to 'distinguish himself in an uncommon manner' (Reiske, 'Gedanken', p. 155), seem to have been decisive factors.

In 1738, without graduating at Leipzig, Reiske decided to travel to Leiden, attracted by the unique collection of Arabic manuscripts and the fame of their keeper, Albert Schultens (1686-1750). By that time, Schultens had already gained international attention with an attractive programme of study that promised an infallible way to unlock the mysteries of the Old Testament: the use of Arabic as an etymological archive of biblical Hebrew (see Loop, 'Language of Paradise'). He also produced a pioneering edition of the first three *maqāmāt* by the Arab poet and grammarian al-Ḥarīrī (1054-1122), which he started in 1731 with the publication of *Haririi eloquentiae Arabicae principis tres priores consessus*. Early modern Orientalists praised al-Ḥarīrī's difficult work not only as an ideal text with which to practise and teach Arabic, but also as a testimony to the quality of the Arabic rhetorical and literary tradition, which some of them likened to the Graeco-Roman tradition. Among them was the Hamburg pastor Abraham Hinckelmann (1652-95), who, in the preface to his edition of the Qur'an at the end of the 17th century, had enthusiastically called for an edition of the work of the 'Arabic Cicero', al-Ḥarīrī (A. Hinckelmann, *Al-Coranus s[eu] Lex Islamitica Muhammedis, Filii Abdallae pseudoprophetae, ad optimorum codicum fidem edita ex museo Abrahami Hinckelmanni*, Hamburg, 1694, preface sig. [j]). Hinckelmann had been in possession of a manuscript of the *Maqāmāt*, which was handed down to Johann Christoph Wolf, who later gave it to Reiske (J.C. Wolf, *Bibliotheca Hebraea*, Hamburg, 1723, vol. 4, p. 776; and C. Brockelmann, *Katalog der orientalischen Handschriften der Stadtbibliothek zu Hamburg*, part 1, Hamburg, 1908, pp. 46-7, no. 97). Probably as an 'admission ticket' to the circles of Albert Schultens, the 20-year-old Reiske transcribed and translated the greater part of it. Later in life, however, he regretted the premature publication – *eine elende Schülerprobe, deren ich mich jetzt schäme* – and was glad that the work was only printed in a few copies (*Lebensbeschreibung*, p. 14; see also Förster, *Briefe*, pp. 5-17).

Reiske arrived in Leiden in June 1738 and was warmly welcomed by Schultens, who seems to have recognised the talent of this student and supported him both financially and academically. He let him borrow Arabic manuscripts from the library, which Reiske copied, and also gave him – probably for free – daily private Arabic lessons, together with his son Jan Jacob Schultens (1716-78), although Reiske did not think much of these *collegia* (Reiske, 'Gedanken', pp. 159). He also encouraged Reiske to focus his attention on classical Arabic poetry, in which, Schultens was convinced, the original and pure Arabic language was preserved. This language, according to Schultens, was closely related to Old Testament Hebrew and would be the best source for understanding its true meaning. According to Reiske's autobiography, he spent most of his first years in Leiden transcribing and translating Arabic poetry: *mehr dem alten Schultens zu Liebe, als aus eigenem Triebe* (Reiske, *Lebensbeschreibung*, p. 26). Ernestine Christine, in the catalogue of her husband's papers, listed all the manuscripts that he transcribed during his time in Leiden, among which are a great number of poems, ranging from the *Maqṣūra* of Ibn Durayd to the *dīwān* of the early Islamic poet Jarīr and the collections of Abū Tammām and al-Buḥturī (Reiske, *Lebensbeschreibung*, pp. 152-67). In his editions of Arabic texts, he would often refer to examples from these works in order to elucidate the meaning of rare words and difficult passages – a completely different methodological approach from Schultens. It was an approach he described as 'philological' and which equally guided his work on Greek and Arabic texts. He summarised this principle in the prologue to the edition of Ṭarafa's *Muʿallaqa* from 1740:

> I have made an effort in my comments and annotations to shed clear light on the author's [intended] meaning, and the quality of the poetical style, the refined choice of words, and the charm. Descending to [grammatical] analysis of words would have been beneath the dignity of this poem and a waste of paper, of which we do not have enough anyway. (Reiske, *Tharaphae Moallakah*, prologus, p. xii)

This was an implicit criticism of Albert Schultens' grammatical and etymological approach. The edition of Ṭarafa's *Muʿallaqa*, Reiske later wrote, marked the beginning of the bitter discord between the two men (Reiske, *Lebensbeschreibung*, p. 23). What seems to have angered Schultens most was that Reiske, in spite of Schultens' demands, did not abstain from printing a verbal attack on a Leipzig professor (see Fück, *Die arabischen Studien*, p. 111).

The dispute burst into the open in 1748, two years after Reiske had left Leiden. Before his departure, and with Schultens' support, Reiske had obtained a PhD in medicine in May 1746, apparently in spite of the resistance of some members of the faculty (Reiske, *Lebensbeschreibung*, p. 32). He left Leiden in June of the same year and arrived back in Leipzig in July 1746. As he did not feel qualified or able to work as a physician, he had to earn a living with poorly paid scholarly work, such as writing reviews for the *Nova acta eruditorum*, the *Zuverlässige Nachrichten von dem gegenwärtigen Zustande, Veränderung und Wachstum der Wissenschaften* (*Deutsche Acta Eruditorum*) and the *Brittische Bibliothek*. The reviews for the last two are listed in his *Lebensbeschreibung* (pp. 53-7). Reiske was outspoken, dogmatic and stubborn, and he used his reviews in a critical and forthright way, which was rather uncommon at a time when reviews were usually neutral summaries of content (Döring, 'Leben in Leipzig', p. 120). This was not conducive to the advancement of his career and his standing in the Republic of Letters, as he later regretted:

> I confess that my bluntness, which I use indiscriminately against everybody, has damaged me much and still does; and I acknowledge lack of prudence. But I prefer to be seen as someone who understands the things he writes about, judicious and dutiful, rather than prudent or nice, or, more precisely, a mealy-mouthed eulogist. ('Letter to J.St. Bernard, 1 February 1749, in Förster, *Briefe*, p. 327; see also Döring, 'Leben in Leipzig', p. 121)

In particular, a number of scathing book reviews of works published by Schultens and two of his students in the *Nova acta eruditorum* caused a complete breakdown in Reiske's relationship with Schultens (*Nova acta eruditorum*, 1747, pp. 535-40). Schultens responded with two open letters, which circulated widely in the academic community, and which put Reiske in a very negative light (*Epistola prima* [*et secunda*]; see Loop, 'Kontroverse Bemühungen').

By this time, however, Reiske had already been awarded an extraordinary (i.e. unpaid) professorship in Arabic at Leipzig university and an annual stipend of 100 thaler. The position had been vacant since its former holder, the Orientalist Johann Christian Clodius, had died on 23 January 1745 (b. 1676). Döring has shown that, contrary to the commonly accepted narrative, this appointment was widely supported by Reiske's colleagues at the university. It seems that the reason for many of the difficulties with his appointment to a chair had to do with the fact that he had not graduated from Leipzig University (Döring, 'Leben in Leipzig', p. 127). It appears that the stipend was not paid regularly after

1755 and the outbreak of the Seven Years' War in 1756, and that Reiske found it very difficult to make ends meet. According to his own account, influential adversaries – he explicitly mentions Johann August Ernesti (1707-81), professor of theology in Leipzig – actively tried to undermine his advancement, but here again, other voices disagreed. Michaelis, in his public response to Reiske's *Lebensbeschreibung*, defended Ernesti repeatedly against Reiske's allegations and claimed 'that this benefactor, on whom Reiske in his biography pours so much black suspicion, was much better disposed towards him than he thought' (Michaelis, review of Reiske's *Lebensbeschreibung*, p. 145).

Reiske's material situation improved somewhat with his appointment as principal ('Rector') of the Nicolai School on 1 July 1758, which position he occupied until his death on 14 August 1774. He was survived by his wife, Ernestine Christine, née Müller, whom he had married on 23 July 1764. An author and scholar in her own right, she collaborated with her husband during his lifetime, and after his death edited numerous works that he left. Her life and work are the subject of Bennholdt-Thomsen and Alfredo Guzzoni's, *Gelehrsamkeit und Leidenschaft*.

Reiske's appointment as principal of the Nicolai School put an end to most of his Arabist projects and so numerous works remained unprinted and still await historical appraisal. Reiske's archive is preserved in the Royal library in Copenhagen (uncatalogued; I have not studied Reiske's papers; see Rasmussen, *De orientalske samlinger*, p. 421-3, where 28 of Reiske's manuscripts are described).

*I would like to thank Asaph Ben-Tov, Alastair Hamilton, Robert Jones and Clemens Müller for suggestions and corrections.

MAIN SOURCES OF INFORMATION

Primary
Johann Jacob Reiske, *Tharaphae Moallakah cum Scholiis Nahas e. mss. Leidensi-bus Arabice edidit*, Leiden, 1742
Johann Jacob Reiske, reviews in *Nova acta eruditorum*, 1747, pp. 535-40 (review of G. Kuypers, 'Ali Ben Abi Taleb'); pp. 679-701 (review of G.J. Lette, *Caab ben Zoheir*); 1748, pp. 689-704 (review of. Schultens' new edition of Erpenius's Grammar), *Nova acta eruditorum*, 1749, pp. 5-20 (review of Schultens' *Proverbia Salomonis*)
A. Schultens, *Epistola prima (et secunda) ad Ampl. et. excell. virum F.O. Menkenium perscripta*, Leiden, 1749

Johann Jacob Reiske, 'Gedanken, wie man der arabischen Literatur aufhelfen könne, und solle', in *Geschichte der königlichen Akademie der schönen Wissenschaften zu Paris, darinnen verschiedene Zusätze und Verbesserungen, nebst einem ausführlichen Register über alle zehn Theile enthalten sind...*, vol. 11, Leipzig, 1757, 148-200

Johann Jacob Reiske and J.E. Faber, *Opuscula medica ex monumentis Arabum et Ebraeorum*, Halle, 1776

Johann Jacob Reiske, *Von ihm selbst aufgesetzte Lebensbeschreibung*, ed. E.C. Reiske, Leipzig, 1783

J.D. Michaelis, review of Reiske's *Lebensbeschreibung*, in *Neue Orientalische und exegetische Bibliothek* 1 (1786) 131-60

R. Förster (ed.), *Johann Jacob Reiskes Briefe*, Leipzig, 1897

Secondary

J. Loop, 'Language of Paradise. Protestant Oriental scholarship and the discovery of Arabic poetry', in N. Hardy and D. Levitin (eds), *Confessionalisation and erudition in early modern Europe. An episode in the history of the humanities*, Oxford, 2019, 395-415

A. Ben-Tov, 'Hellenism in the context of Oriental Studies. The case of Johann Gottfried Lakemacher (1695-1736)', *International Journal of the Classical Tradition* 25 (2018) 197-314

S.T. Rasmussen, *De orientalske samlinger. En guide – The oriental collection. A guide*, Copenhagen, 2016

A. Bennholdt-Thomsen and A. Guzzoni, *Gelehrsamkeit und Leidenschaft. Das Leben der Ernestine Christine Reiske 1735-1798*, Munich, 1992

H.G. Ebert and T. Hanstein (eds), *Johann Jacob Reiske. Leben und Wirkung. Ein Leipziger Byzantinist und Begründer der Orientalistik im 18. Jahrhundert*, Leipzig, 2005

J. Loop, 'Kontroverse Bemühungen um den Orient. Johann Jacob Reiske und die deutsche Orientalistik seiner Zeit', in Ebert and Hanstein (eds), *Johann Jacob Reiske*, 54-63

D. Döring, 'Johann Jacob Reiskes Verbindungen zum wissenschaftlichen und literarischen Leben in Leipzig', in Ebert and Hanstein (eds), *Johann Jacob Reiske*, 117-140

J. Fück, *Die arabischen Studien in Europa bis in den Anfang des 20. Jahrhunderts*, Leipzig, 1955

R. Förster, art. 'Reiske, Johann Jacob', in *Allgemeine Deutsche Biographie*, vol. 28, Leipzig, 1889, 129-43

C. Bursian, *Geschichte der classischen Philologie in Deutschland von den Anfängen bis zur Gegenwart*, Munich, 1883

WORKS ON CHRISTIAN-MUSLIM RELATIONS

Reiske's contribution to the study of Arabic-Islamic literature

DATE   1742-73
ORIGINAL LANGUAGE   Latin, Arabic and German

DESCRIPTION

It may not seem immediately obvious why there should be an entry for Johann Jacob Reiske in a series dedicated to Christian-Muslim relations. Religion plays hardly any role in the work of the greatest German Arabist of the 18th century, or in his personal life. According to his autobiography, there was a time in his childhood, during the years he spent at the orphanage at Francke's Pietist Foundation in Halle between 1728 and 1732, when he prayed devotedly for hours: *Ich ward ein Betnarr* ('I became a prayer fool'). However, the 'heat' of his naive piety soon 'evaporated' and he became a 'naturalist' (Reiske, *Lebensbeschreibung*, p. 8). He probably did not entertain a systematic deistic or even atheistic world view, but according to his wife was more interested in the practical and moral aspects of religion than in theological subtleties (*Lebensbeschreibung*, p. 150).

The fact that Reiske did not approach Arabic studies with a religious mindset is, however, extremely significant. In contrast to most of his European predecessors and contemporaries, his interest in Arab language, literature and culture was not driven by theological, missionary or exegetical objectives. He was extremely critical of the use of Arabic as a linguistic key to the Hebrew Bible, as it was practised and promoted by the leading Orientalists of his day, and he was not interested in apologetic comparisons between Islam and Christianity, which had for centuries been made by Christian polemicists and were still advocated by his famous contemporary Johann David Michaelis (see Loop, 'Kontroverse Bemühungen'). Reiske, on the contrary, insisted that the study of Arabic and Arab history, literature and culture should be free of theological objectives and follow purely scholarly principles. In numerous publications, he argued that Arabic and Islamic literature and culture were as worthy of independent study as the European Christian tradition.

His approach was based on the assumption that Oriental texts should be treated in exactly the same way as texts of Greek and Roman Antiquity (*Ein jedes altes Buch, es sey in welcher Sprache es wolle, muß man so, wie einen alten griechischen oder lateinischen Autoren behandeln*; Reiske,

'Gedanken', p. 190). Hence, the fact that Reiske was an outstanding scholar of both Greek and Arabic texts is of significance. His Orient was a classical Orient, and so he was decidedly concerned with texts of the (classical) past. Contemporary Arab culture, and questions of religious competition or even practical missionary, political or diplomatic uses of Arabic scholarship, were of no interest to him.

Although Reiske was arguing against the academic mainstream of his time, he was not without predecessors. He followed an intellectual tradition that he himself acknowledged and which went back to the 17th-century pioneers of Arabic studies, Thomas Erpenius, Jacobus Golius, Edward Pococke and the tradition of humanist philology. Furthermore, classical scholars before Reiske had also desacralised the (biblical) Orient by interpreting it within the context of religiously neutral Greek antiquity (see Ben-Tov, 'Hellenism in the context of Oriental Studies').

Reiske repeatedly argued that editing and printing Arabic books was the only way to advance Arabic learning in Europe (Reiske, 'Gedanken', p. 162). Serious Arabic studies and an adequate understanding of Arabic literature could only be achieved through 'extensive and diligent reading of poets and other writers'. This was the only way to become fully acquainted with 'the oriental manner of thinking, writing, poetising, joking etc.' (Reiske, 'Gedanken', p. 150), and to understand the 'meaning, vigour and full scope' of words and texts.

Reiske himself edited and translated a number of texts, many for the first time. Among them were poetical and literary works, such as the editions of a *maqāma* by al-Ḥarīrī in 1737 and of Ṭarafa's *Muʿallaqa* in 1742, already mentioned above. In 1755, he edited in Arabic with a Latin translation the *Risāla l-hazliyya* by the Andalusī poet Ibn Zaydūn. He had excerpted the famous letter from the commentary on it by Ibn Nubāta, which he had found among Levinus Warner's papers in Leiden (Leiden UB, MS Or. 705; the transcription and partial translation of the commentary is among Reiske's papers (see Reiske, *Lebensbeschreibung*, p. 158) and was published by J.F. Hirt in his *Institutiones*, pp. 516-36). In the preface, he describes the letter as being 'woven from allusions to Arab histories, proverbs, and sayings of the poets', and compares it to the 64th oration by the famous first-century Greek orator Dio Chrysostom. His commentary was intended to elaborate on those historical events to which Ibn Zaydūn only alludes, and thus give philological and historical guidance to a correct understanding of the work (Reiske, *Abi'l Walidi*, p. vi). In the following year, Reiske published the first German translation of the most popular Arabic poem in Europe – al-Ṭughrā'ī's *Lāmiyyat al-ʿajam* (*Thograi's sogenanntes Lammisches Gedicht*, pp. 8-25). This too was only issued in a small print run of some 100 copies. The fact that Reiske translated this and many other Arabic and Greek works into German (rather than Latin) is remarkable, and a testimony to his efforts to promote the German language (on this see Döring, 'Leben in Leipzig', pp. 128-30). The translation was prefaced by a 'Short sketch of Arabic poetry' (Reiske, 'Ein kurtzer Entwurf der arabischen Dichterey'), by far the best European account before William Jones, in which Reiske recommends Robert Lowth's lectures on biblical Hebrew poetry and suggests that 'many of his principles can also be applied to Arabic poetry' (Reiske had earlier reviewed Lowth's *De sacra poesi Hebraeorum*; see Reiske, 'Review of Robert Lowth').

In 1758, he published a 'Collection of Arabic proverbs on sticks and staffs' (*Sammlung einiger arabischer Sprüchwörter, die von Stecken oder Stäben hergenommen sind*), taken from the collection of proverbs by the 12th-century Persian linguist Aḥmad ibn Muḥammad al-Maydānī (see Vrolijk, '"Entirely free"').

Ten years later, in 1765, he was the first to print a number of verses by the great 10th-century Kūfan poet al-Mutanabbī in *Proben der arabischen Dichtkunst in verliebten und traurigen Gedichten, aus dem Motanabbi* (1765). There are earlier samples of a few verses by al-Mutanabbī in one of Erpenius's outstanding contributions to oriental scholarship, his edition of al-Makīn's *Tārīkh al-Muslimīn*, the *Historia saracenica* (Leiden, 1625), and some additional verses were also published by Jacobus Golius (see Loop, 'Arabic poetry', p. 233). The occasion of Reiske's edition was the 30th birthday of his wife, whom he had married the year before. The publication and some of the admittedly rather awkward passages in the introduction provoked a sarcastic review in the *Göttingische Anzeigen von gelehrten Sachen* (1765, pp. 465-71), possibly penned by Michaelis. The edition was based on Reiske's transcription and translation of al-Mutanabbī's *dīwān* from a Leiden manuscript. The introduction, addressed to a non-specialist readership, conveyed a sense of the cultural difference between Arabs and Europeans not only in the composition of their poetry, but also in the expression of their affections: the samples could give an impression, Reiske thought, 'of how the Arabs caress their beauties' (*wie die Araber ihre Schönen liebkosen*; Reiske, *Proben*, p. 5).

Although he was hailed by Silvestre de Sacy as its greatest expert, Reiske was a reluctant student of Arabic poetry (de Sacy, *De l'utilité*, p. 7). He repeatedly expressed his aversion to 'the pompous, foolish, furious fancies of Arab poetry' (*die schwülstigen, närrischen, rasenden Einfälle der Arabischen Dichterey*; Reiske, *Thograi's sogenanntes Lammisches Gedicht*, p. 8) and he made it clear that his true intellectual passion was elsewhere: 'My heart was always strongly attracted to historical studies' (*animus mihi semper ad historica studia gestiit*; Reiske, *Taraphae Moallakah*, p. iv). But here too, his passion only bore fragmentary fruits. During his time at Leiden, he copied a number of historical and geographical works, most importantly the *Kitāb al-mukhtaṣar fī akhbār al-bashar* ('A short history of humankind') and the *Taqwīm al-buldān* ('Survey of the countries') by the Ayyūbid prince Abū l-Fidā' (1273-1333). Despite being a work of outstanding learning, his (partial) Latin translation of *Kitāb al-mukhtaṣar* (1754) only sold 30 copies (see Michaelis, review of Reiske's *Lebensbeschreibung*, p. 159; Michaelis blames Reiske's mismanagement and self-publishing).

As with Arab poets, Reiske was unrestrained in his critical notes on Arab historians. He regarded Abū l-Fidā', particularly at the beginning of his world-history, as very sketchy and unoriginal. Closer to Abū l-Fidā''s own time, however, the text was fuller and became a great source of empirical information, which you 'seek elsewhere in vain', Reiske commented (*Abilfedae annales*, p. xviii). Western historians had failed to preserve many historical events in the inner provinces of the Orient, often because they did not do justice to Islamic history, which 'they ought to have presented better, more grandly and splendidly' (*Abilfedae annales*; see Bevilacqua, *Republic of Arabic letters*, p. 160). Reiske publicly promoted the scholarly value of Islamic history in his remarkable introduction to Islamic history ('Prodidagmata'), written in August 1747, but not published until 1766. The main thoughts within it were echoed a year later in his inaugural lecture, on 21 August 1748, the occasion of his appointment as extraordinary professor of Arabic at the University of Leipzig ('Oratio'), published after his death by his wife, together with his *Coniecturae in Iobum et Proverbia Salomonis* (see Fück, *Die arabischen Studien*, pp. 113-15). The central idea of both texts is that Islamic history is as rich, useful and worthy of study as the history of Christianity and of classical Antiquity. For the historian who wants to know the reasons behind events rather than just dates and the sound of names, Islamic history can provide ample material: it can teach as much about political wisdom, divine providence or the blind paths of fortune, and about the characters and thoughts of men, as Christian history does ('Oratio', p. 282; see Loop, 'Kontroverse Bemühungen').

He promoted a similar idea in his 'Dissertation on Muḥammadan princes who were renowned for their erudition or for their love of letters and of lettered men' (*Dissertatio de principibus Muhammedanis*; see Bevilacqua, *Republic of Arabic letters*, pp. 149-51). The book is a survey of Muslim leaders, among them 'Alī, Muḥammad's cousin and the legendary author of numerous collections of sayings, the 'Abbasid Caliph al-Ma'mūn, the great patron of the *falāsifa*, and Abū l-Fidā', the learned Ayyūbid prince. The dissertation, celebrating the patronage and erudition of great Muslim leaders, was a fitting gift for the crown prince of the Electorate of Saxony, Friedrich Christian, whose support Reiske hoped to win. Islamic history, such was Reiske's message to the Saxon prince, 'is very worthy of the study of an honest mind, and does not deserve any less than European history to be taught publicly in universities' (Reiske, *Dissertatio*, p. ix, and Bevilacqua's translation in *Republic of Arabic letters*, p. 149).

Reiske's unpublished papers, preserved at the Royal Library in Copenhagen, are voluminous and await thorough study. Ernestine Christine, his widow, had given many of his manuscripts to Gotthold Ephraim Lessing (1729-81), with whom she and her husband had been acquainted and who had planned to write a scholarly biography of Reiske. They were acquired in 1777 by the Danish collector Peter Frederik Suhm, who later sold his book collection, including Reiske's manuscripts, to the Danish state. Some of the works that Reiske had copied during his stay at Leiden entered the annotations and comments on his published work, and some were later edited by successors. Reiske's full transcription and Latin translation of Abū l-Fidā''s world history were edited by Jacob Georg Christian Adler, who also included the philological annotations in which Reiske had explained old and rare words and difficult expressions 'with the help of his great thesaurus of Arabic learning', and had illustrated them with quotations from other authors in his collection, Ibn Durayd, al-Maydānī's proverbs, al-Ḥarīrī's *Maqāmāt*, the *Ḥamāsa* and the *dīwān* of the Banū Hudhayl etc. (Reiske, *Abulfedae annales*, ed. Adler, vol. 1, p. iv).

Reiske's transcriptions and translations of other Arab historians, notably Ibn Qutayba's historical handbook, the *Kitāb al-maʿārif* (MS Leiden UL, Or. 782), were printed in Jens L. Rassmussen (*Additamenta*), and later by Johann Gottfried Eichhorn (*Monumenta*; see also Wüstenfeld, *Ibn Coteiba's Handbuch*, p. v). Eichhorn was also responsible for the publication of Reiske's 14 *Briefe über das arabische Münzwesen* ('Letters on Arabic numismatics') in his *Repertorium für Biblische und Morgenländische Litteratur* in 1781 and 1782. These essays are important contributions to the development of Islamic numismatics as a scholarly discipline in the 18th century (see Heidemann, 'Die Entwicklung').

Reiske himself used Ibn Qutayba's work, together with Ibn Durayd's etymological dictionary *Kitāb al-ishtiqāq* and Ḥamza l-Iṣfahānī's chronology of pre-Islamic and Islamic dynasties (*Taʾrīkh sinī mulūk al-arḍ wa-l-anbiyāʾ*) (MS Leiden UL, Or. 767), to write a sketch of pre-Islamic history – which the eminent Arabist Ferdinand Wüstenfeld deemed worthy to be edited 100 years later, in 1747 (Reiske, *Primae lineae*). Reiske also annotated the chapter on 'The history of Muḥammad, the Arabs and the caliphs' in the German edition of William Guthrie's *General history of the world* (Heyne, *Allgemeine Weltgeschichte*). Reiske's archive also includes a heavily annotated copy of d'Herbelot's 1697 edition of the *Bibliothèque orientale: ou dictionnaire universel, contenant tout ce qui fait connoître les peuples de l'Orient*. The copious annotations add new entries or correct and expand on existing ones, creating new cross-references as well as external references to manuscripts held in European collections (see Bevilacqua, 'How to organise the Orient'). Some of Reiske's annotations were included in vol. 4 of the edition prepared in The Hague between 1777 and 1779.

SIGNIFICANCE

Reiske complained repeatedly that a hostile and unsupportive academic environment had hampered his work on Arabic and limited the significance and impact it could have had. While this seems to be true, Reiske's own personal shortcomings appear to have played a certain role in this as well. Even his adversaries admired him and recognised him as the most accomplished Arabic scholar that Germany had ever seen (see e.g. Michaelis, review of Reiske's *Lebensbeschreibung*, p. 155). But to the same extent, his 'taste' and aesthetic judgement, as well as his stylistic talent were questioned across the board. A mixture of stubbornness and general mistrust made him publish most of his books himself – to the detriment of himself and of his readers, as Michaelis rather pointedly illustrates: 'If a scholar who wants one of his books first has to correspond about it several times, needs to ask for the price, send the money in advance, pay postal charges for everything, provide packaging material or risk damage through rain, the peculiar fact [that Reiske sold hardly any of his books] can be explained at least partly' (Michaelis, review of Reiske's *Lebensbeschreibung*, p. 160).

In modern historical accounts, Reiske has been lionised as the first scholar to free Arabic studies from the shackles of theology and to call for the study of the Arabs' language, literature and culture in their own right. But while he was indeed a lone voice in the community of northern European Protestant Orientalists in the mid-18ᵗʰ century, Reiske owed more to this tradition than his personal testimonies imply. The works of Thomas Erpenius, Jacobus Golius, Levinus Warner, Johann Heinrich Hottinger, Edward Pococke and many others were deeply anchored in the Christian faith and drew inspiration from biblical studies, Church history and missionary endeavours. They all prepared the ground for Reiske's scholarship, and some of them epitomised his ideal of a scholarly Arabist almost perfectly and would probably have shared many of his ideas.

Reiske's efforts to promote Arabic literature were inspired by an attempt to 'humanise' and 'normalise' the Arabs and to integrate their literature into the remit of the *Studia humanitatis*. *Arabes homines sunt nobis similes* ('The Arabs are human beings similar to us') he writes in one of his reviews in the *Nova acta eruditorum* (1747, p. 691). He repeatedly compared Arab cultural, political and literary achievements to those of the Greeks and Romans, and made the case that contemporary Muslims belonged to the same classical tradition as their Christian counterparts. It was, he argued, their inheritance from Antiquity, rather than their adherence to Islam, that shaped their 'principles of behaviour and of civil organization' (Bevilacqua, *Republic of Arabic letters*, p. 142). He therefore contended that Arab culture and history should be recognised as part of the history of mankind: 'Arab history is a necessary complement to the history of the human mind. [...] Also from this angle the philosopher wants to know man' (Reiske, *Thograi's sogenanntes Lammisches Gedicht*, p. 9). Arab history, he stated, would provide ample material for the philosophical historian to reflect upon the hidden drivers of history, the manners and minds of men and the marvellous fortunes of empires (Reiske, 'Oratio', p. 282). From this perspective, Reiske argues, it would be irrelevant whether the products of the Arab mind, be it poetry, literature or historical texts, conform to our taste and our sense of decorum. They should be judged according to the place and time in which they were produced, and the character, the genius and the manners of the people for whom they were composed (Reiske, *Taraphae Moallakah*, preface).

This relativistic approach is linked to the philological and hermeneutical rules discussed above. The correct translation and interpretation of Arabic texts, Reiske writes, needs to be based on a wide knowledge of Arabic literature and cannot be achieved with the use of a grammar and a lexicon alone.

They write commentaries on Arabic poets, which they do not understand and they think it sufficient quickly to copy and defile the Golius [lexicon] in a few days. The true and hidden sense of the poets, the histories to which they refer, the better versions (*puriores lectiones*) which only an understanding critic of language can assess and distinguish, and the fate of the poems, and of the poets and of all the Arab people, without which they can never be understood, they fail to investigate, be it out of contempt, as something they consider to be useless or of no importance, or be it because they are too lazy to investigate properly, since such commentaries cannot be brought out as quickly as the offspring of rabbits. (*Nova acta eruditorum*, 1748, p. 694)

Poor understanding of the Arabic language naturally also leads to poor, unintelligible translations: 'There are not a few translators of Arabic, who, as they show them speaking in such an unhuman way, give you the impression of hearing people fallen from the moon' (Reiske, 'Oratio', p. 224). In one of his reviews in the *Nova acta eruditorum*, he accuses the translator of an Arabic poem, Johann Gerhard Lette, a student of Albert Schultens, of having produced a translation that would 'confirm all those in their opinion who think that the Arabs have lost their minds and that they blurt out whatever comes into their mouths'. But Reiske reminds his readers that 'the Arabs speak very much like human beings', although 'the ignorance of this translator makes them bray like asses and moo like cows' (*Nova acta eruditorum*, 1747, p. 691).

Reiske's philological and hermeneutical rules also inform his discussion of the requirements that a new edition and translation of the Qur'an would need to fulfil (Reiske, 'Gedanken', pp. 190-7; see Loop, 'Kontroverse Bemühungen'). This disquisition in his 'Thoughts on how we can and should encourage the study of Arabic literature' is probably Reiske's most important contribution to Christian-Muslim relations.

Like any other book, he writes, the Qur'an should be critically edited, translated and philologically interpreted. For a proper understanding of Islamic history, it was important that an edition of the Qur'an should contain the variant readings: 'In Muḥammadan Church history and the history of heresies (if I may call it so), the variant readings of the Qur'an, as the basis of interpretation, are of great importance' (*In der muhammedanischen Kirchen- und Ketzergeschichte, (wenn ich so sagen darf), kömmt auf die verschiedenen Lesarten des Alkorans, als auf den Auslegungsgrund, viel an,* 'Gedanken', pp. 191-2). An editor of the Qur'an would need to base such an edition on the vast body of textual criticism of the qur'anic text that exists in the Islamic tradition. Reiske compares the achievements of this 'Arabic Masorah' to the pinnacles of New Testament criticism in the works of Johann Jakob Wettstein (1693-1754) Ludolph Küster (1670-1716), and John Mill (1644/5-1707) (Reiske, 'Gedanken', p. 191). The implicit message here is that, in the field of textual criticism, Islamic scholars had as much or even more to offer than Christians and Jews.

A new translation and interpretation of the Qur'an, Reiske argues, would need to be based on extensive knowledge of Islamic theology and history, and particularly on Islamic qur'anic studies and *tafsīr* literature. What meaning certain instances could have was irrelevant, but we should ask what meaning Muslims themselves find in it:

> What would we say to a Muḥammadan, who would, without knowing our theology in its full extent, make a translation of the New Testament and pour his philosophical broth over it? That would be a Muḥammadan New Testament, and not a Christian one. If we do the same with the Qur'an, we will have a Christian Qur'an, which is no longer a Muḥammadan one. ('Gedanken', pp. 192-3)

Applying the rules of classical philology to Arabic literature, and his attempt to 'humanise' and 'normalise' Muslims and their culture and history, are probably the most significant aspects of Reiske's work. All the other principles that guided him result from the conviction that the Arabs are 'human beings, very similar to us'. Approached with this conviction, Islamic literature, culture and history deserve to be studied with the same diligence, independence and philological precision with which the ancient literary heritage has been studied since the early modern period.

PUBLICATIONS

MS Copenhagen, Det Kgl. Bibliotek – Reiske's unpublished papers and annotations (1730s-1774)

Reiske, *Tharaphae Moallakah, cum scholiis Nahas*

Johann Jacob Reiske, *Dissertatio de principibus Muhammedanis qui aut eruditione aut ab amore literarum et literatorum claruerunt*, Leipzig, 1747; 4 Diss. 3473,5 (digitised version available through *MDZ*)

Johann Jacob Reiske, *Abilfedae annales Moslemici*, Leipzig, 1754; 4 A.or. 327 m (digitised version available through *MDZ*)

Johann Jacob Reiske, 'Review of Robert Lowth *De sacra poesi Hebraeorum*', *Zuverläßige Nachrichten* 169 (1754) 631-53, 832-58;

PPN556032098 (digitised version available through Göttinger Digitalisierungszentrum)

Johann Jacob Reiske, *Abi'l Walidi ibn Zeiduni Risalet seu Epistolium*, Leipzig, 1755; 4 A.or. 327 m#Beibd.1 (digitised version available through *MDZ*)

Johann Jacob Reiske, *Thograi's sogenanntes Lammisches Gedicht aus dem Arabischen übersetzt nebst einem kurtzen Entwurf der Arabischen Dichterey*, Friedrichstadt, 1756, pp. 8-25; 69761 (digitised version available through Sächsische Landesbibliothek; Staats- und Universitätsbibliothek Dresden (SLUB))

Reiske, 'Gedanken', pp. 148-200; bsb10534914 (digitised version available through *MDZ*)

Johann Jacob Reiske, *Sammlung einiger arabischer Sprüchwörter, die von Stecken oder Stäben hergenommen sind*, Dresden, 1758; 4 A.or. 1416 (digitised version available through *MDZ*)

Johann Jacob Reiske, *Proben der arabischen Dichtkunst in verliebten und traurigen Gedichten, aus dem Motanabbi*, Leipzig, 1765; 4 A.or. 1306 (digitised version available through *MDZ*)

Johann Jacob Reiske, 'Prodidagmata ad Hagji Chalifae librum', in *Abulfedae Tabula Syriae cum excerpto geographico ex Ibnol Wardii*, ed. J. Bernhard Köhler, Leipzig, 1766, 215-40; 4 A.or. 320 (digitised version available through *MDZ*)

C.G. Heyne (ed. and trans.), *Allgemeine Weltgeschichte von der Schöpfung an bis auf gegenwärtige Zeit : [...] angefertigt von Wilhelm Guthrie, Johann Gray*, vol. 6/1, 'Die Geschichte der Araber', Leipzig, 1768; H.un. 236-5,1 (digitised version available through *MDZ*)

J.F. Hirt, *Institutiones arabicae linguae*, Jena, 1770; L.as. 14 (digitised version available through *MDZ*)

J.G. Eichhorn, *Monumenta antiquissimae historiae Arabum*, Jena, 1775; BIB.HIST.003769 (digitised version available through Universiteitsbibliotheek Gent)

Johann Jacob Reiske, 'Oratio studium Arabicae linguae commendans', in Johann Jacob Reiske, *Conjecturae in Jobum et Proverbia Salomonis cum eiusdem orationes de studio Arabicae Linguae*, Leipzig, 1779, 219-92; 81055 (digitised version available through BL)

Johann Jacob Reiske, 'Briefe über das arabische Münzwesen von Johann Jacob Reiske mit Anmerkungen und Zusätzen von Johann Gottfried Eichhorn', *Repertorium für Biblische und Morgenländische Litteratur* 9 (1781) 199-268; 10 (1782) 165-240; 11 (1782) 1-44; Exeg.

291-7/9 (vol. 9); Exeg. 291-10/12 (vol. 11) (digitised version available through *MDZ*)

Johann Jacob Reiske, 'Prodidagmata ad Hagji Chalifae librum', in *Abulfedae Tabula Syriae cum excerpto geographico ex Ibn ol Wardii*, ed. J. Bernhard Köhler, Leipzig, 1786; 4 A.or. 320 (digitised version available through *MDZ*)

Johann Jacob Reiske, *Abulfedae annales Muslemici Arabice et Latine*, ed. J.G.C. Adler, 5 vols, Copenhagen, 1789-94; 4-O2G-73 (1-5) (digitised version available through BNF)

J.L. Rassmussen, *Additamenta ad historiam Arabum ante Islamum excerpta ex Ibn Nabatah, Nuveirio, atque Ibn Koteibah*, Copenhagen, 1821; 4 A.or. 1389 (digitised version available through *MDZ*)

A. Silvestre de Sacy, *De l'utilité de l'étude de la poésie Arabe*, Paris, 1826

Johann Jacob Reiske, *Primae lineae regnorum Arabicorum et rerum ab Arabibus medio inter Christum et Muhammedem tempore gestarum*, ed. F. Wüstenfeld, Göttingen, 1847; H.ant. 319 q (digitised version available through *MDZ*)

STUDIES

A. Bevilacqua, *The republic of Arabic letters. Islam and the European Enlightenment*, Cambridge MA, 2018

Ben-Tov, 'Hellenism in the context of Oriental Studies', 197-314

A. Bevilacqua, 'How to organise the Orient. D'Herbelot and the *Bibliothèque orientale*', *Journal of the Warburg and Courtauld Institutes* 79 (2016) 213-61

A. Hamilton, '"To rescue the honour of the Germans". Qur'an translations by eighteenth- and early nineteenth-century German Protestants', *Journal of the Warburg and Courtauld Institutes* 77 (2014) 173-209

J. Loop, 'Arabic poetry as teaching material in early modern grammars and textbooks', in J. Loop, A. Hamilton and C. Burnett (eds), *The learning and teaching of Arabic in early modern Europe*, Leiden, 2017, 230-51

A. Vrolijk, '"Entirely free from the urge to publish". H.A. Schultens, J.J. Reiske, E. Scheidius and the 18th-century attempts at an edition of the Arabic proverbs of al-Maydānī', in S. Brinkmann and B. Weismüller (eds), *From codicology to technology. Islamic manuscripts and their place*, Berlin, 2012, 59-80

S. Heidemann, 'Die Entwicklung der Methoden in der Islamischen Numismatik im 18. Jahrhundert. War Johann Jacob Reiske ihr

Begründer?', in Ebert and Hanstein (eds), *Johann Jacob Reiske*, 147-202

Loop, 'Kontroverse Bemühungen', 54-63

Döring, 'Johann Jacob Reiskes Verbindungen'

Fück, *Die arabischen Studien*

F. Wüstenfeld, *Ibn Coteiba's Handbuch der Geschichte*, Göttingen, 1850

Michaelis, review of Reiske's *Lebensbeschreibung*

Jan Loop

Friedrich Eberhard Boysen

DATE OF BIRTH   1720
PLACE OF BIRTH   Halberstadt
DATE OF DEATH   1800
PLACE OF DEATH   Quedlinburg

BIOGRAPHY

Friedrich Eberhard Boysen was born in 1720 to a Lutheran family in Halberstadt in Sachsen-Anhalt, which had been part of the kingdom of Prussia since 1701. He learnt the rudiments of Hebrew at the Märtenschule in Halberstadt, and then, at the cathedral school he started Syriac and Aramaic. He continued to study these languages at the gymnasium in Magdeburg and received some tuition in Hebrew from Johann Gottfried Lakemacher, professor of Greek and Oriental languages at Helmstedt. On 2 May 1737, Boysen matriculated at the theological faculty of the University of Halle. There, he lodged with the professor of theology, Christian Benedikt Michaelis, and first met Michaelis's son, Johann David. At Halle, he studied Ethiopic and Arabic under the elder Michaelis and progressed in Hebrew, Syriac and Aramaic. At the same time, he developed his interest in the Qur'an, reading it not only with Michaelis but also with the professor of theology Johann Heinrich Callenberg and the professor of antiquity Johann Heinrich Schulze, and using the Arabic grammars of Lakemacher and Johann Christian Clodius, professor of Arabic at Leipzig. On 4 July 1739, he defended a thesis dictated by Michaelis on those passages in the Qur'an that illustrate Jewish rituals described in the Old Testament. It seems to have been at Halle that he became a friend of Johann Wilhelm Ludwig Gleim, a distinguished poet who was in touch with some of the greatest exponents of the German Enlightenment such as Friedrich Gottlieb Klopstock, Johann Gottfried Herder, Johann Uz, Heinrich Voss and Christoph Martin Wieland.

After completing his studies at Halle, Boysen worked as a tutor in Osterburg before being appointed rector of the town school in Seehausen, from where he told Gleim of his desire to teach his students Arabic as well as Hebrew. In 1742, he moved to Magdeburg, where he was appointed preacher. Within three years, he was immersed in the study of the Qur'an and, as he studied it, so his admiration for it increased.

But he had few sources. Unable to obtain a copy of Ludovico Marracci's bilingual version, which had appeared in Rome in 1698, he had to rely on Abraham Hinckelmann's edition of the Arabic and Christian Reineccius's edition of Marracci's Latin. He also questioned some Turkish prisoners of war in Magdeburg about the meaning of certain words.

Boysen remained in Magdeburg until 1760 and published two works on biblical criticism, one on the Syriac New Testament and the other on the text of the Old Testament, in which he followed Christian Benedikt Michaelis's technique of explaining Hebrew words with the help of Arabic words. The work had a preface by Johann Salomo Semler, one of the fathers of modern biblical criticism who, at the time, was drifting away from orthodox Lutheranism and was himself expressing a deep admiration for Islam. He regarded the philosophical and scientific writings of the Persians and the Arabs as a bulwark against the cultural decline to which he believed the medieval Church would otherwise have led. Although Boysen seems to have held a conservative position within the Lutheran Church and was strongly opposed to many features of the Enlightenment, he was always open to amicable discussions with Muslims, members of the Jewish communities, and men who held more liberal views.

In 1760, Boysen moved to Quedlinburg where he was appointed first court preacher to the princess-abbess of Quedlinburg Abbey, Sophia Albertina of Sweden, inspector of grammar schools and *Konsistorialrat*. He remained in Quedlinburg for the rest of his life and there published his German translation of the Qur'an, the first edition in 1773 and the second in 1775. Boysen was drawn by the prospect of producing a verse translation, but, as he told Gleim, he felt unable to do so. After the publication of the second edition he seems to have abandoned qur'anic studies. In 1795, he published his autobiography and five years later, in 1800, he died in Quedlinburg.

MAIN SOURCES OF INFORMATION

Primary
Briefe vom Herrn Boysen an Herrn Gleim, 2 vols, Frankfurt, 1772
Friedrich Eberhard Boysen, *Der Koran, oder Das Gesetz für die Muselmänne, durch Mohammed den Sohn Abdall*, Halle, 1773
Friedrich Eberhard Boysen, *Der Koran, oder Das Gesetz für die Moslemer durch Muhammed den Sohn Abdall*, Halle, 1775
Friedrich Eberhard Boysen, *Eigene Lebensbeschreibung*, 2 vols, Quedlinburg, 1795

Secondary

A. Hamilton, 'Lutheran Islamophiles in eighteenth-century Germany', in A. Blair
     and A.-S. Goeing (eds), *For the sake of learning. Essays in honor of Anthony
     Grafton*, Leiden, 2016, vol. 1, 327-43
A. Hamilton, '"To rescue the honour of the Germans". Qur'an translations by
     eighteenth- and early nineteenth-century German Protestants', *Journal of
     the Warburg and Courtauld Institutes* 77 (2014) 173-209

WORKS ON CHRISTIAN-MUSLIM RELATIONS

Der Koran
'The Qur'an'

DATE   1773, 2nd edition 1775
ORIGINAL LANGUAGE   German

DESCRIPTION

The two editions of Friedrich Eberhard Boysen's *Der Koran* (in full *Der
Koran, oder das Gesetz für die Muselmänner, durch Muhammed des Sohn
Abdall. Nebst einigen feyerlichen koranischen Gebeten, unmittelbar aus
dem Arabischen übersetzt*, 'The Qur'an or the Law given to the Muslims
by Muhammad the Son of Abdul. Together with some solemn qur'anic
prayers, translated directly from the Arabic') were published in an octavo
format by the firm of Gebauer in Halle in 1773 and 1775. They are dedicated to Crown Prince Karl Wilhelm Ferdinand of Braunschweig and
Lüneburg. In the first edition, the dedication is followed by a brief preface (sigs a5r.-a7v.), in which Boysen thanks his teachers at the University of Halle and gives a short list of the manuscripts and editions of the
Arabic text he has used. He also dwells on the beauty of the text and
the persuasive powers of the Prophet. There follows an index of suras
(sigs a8r-v.) and then the translation, which ends with 12 Muslim prayers
taken from *Bi-smi illahi. Muhammedanus precans* published by Hennin-
gius Henning in 1666, and a subject index, all amounting to 680 pages.
The verses of the suras are not numbered. The second edition, in which
the translation, the prayers and the subject index come to 678 pages, has
a far longer Introduction (pp. 9-40), which differs considerably from the
first. It contains a survey of the genealogy of the Prophet and is written
with a still more marked sympathy for Islam.

   Boysen's translation of the Qur'an was the second published German translation to have been made directly from the Arabic. The first,
David Friedrich Megerlin's version, which had come out in 1772, had

been heavily criticised, especially by a younger generation of scholars and poets influenced by the Enlightenment and resentful of the anti-Islamic prejudice in Megerlin's Foreword. Boysen did better. In the Foreword to the first edition he praised the poetic qualities of the Qur'an and the Prophet's 'fiery wit' and 'sharpness of mind', and lamented his own inability to convey 'the lofty and fiery drive' or the 'melodic' tone of the original which, in a letter to Gleim, he had described as *ein Gedichte* ('a poem'). In the second edition, he went further still. He attacked many of his predecessors – Ludovico Marracci, Humphrey Prideaux, Jean Gagnier – who had distorted Muḥammad's words and message, and he even dismissed Henri de Boulainvilliers, author of a laudatory biography as 'more a eulogist than a biographer'. Boysen presented the Prophet as a hero in terms resembling those used by Gibbon in the last volume of his *Decline and fall of the Roman Empire*, and as a thinker who took all the points he believed to be best in Judaism and Christianity and introduced 'a philosophical religion'.

Boysen's friendship with Gleim, himself close to so many thinkers of the Enlightenment, had also exerted an influence on his translation. Not only had Gleim helped Boysen correct the proofs, but the two men had long debated whether the translation should be in prose or in verse. Gleim's *Halladat oder das Rothe Buch* was a long orientalising poem that was partly intended to give an idea of what the Qur'an might be like were it translated into German verse, and Boysen quoted the tenth stanza in his preface to the first edition of his translation. He decided, however, to leave the text in prose.

Boysen, albeit less than Megerlin, depended to a certain extent on the versions by Marracci and George Sale. Nearly all his citations of the Muslim commentaries, the *tafsīr*, can be found in Marracci or, in a couple of cases, in Sale. But Boysen also used a *tafsīr* that was unknown to Marracci – the work of a 12th-century Persian scholar, Abū Muḥammad al-Ḥusayn ibn Masʿūd al-Farrāʾ al-Baghawī. In his actual translation, on the other hand, Boysen proved more independent – too independent according to certain critics, who pointed out that he made mistakes that Marracci and Sale had avoided.

SIGNIFICANCE

The new translation was greeted with more approval than Megerlin's. The most enthusiastic review was by J.F. Hirt in the sixth number of his *Orientalische und exegetische Bibliothek* of 1774. Boysen's translation, wrote Hirt, 'brings honour to its author in Germany'. He was less happy, however, about Boysen's high opinion of Islam, the all too favourable image he presented of the Prophet, and Boysen's dismissal of Humphrey Prideaux. Johann David Michaelis, the son of Boysen's professor at Halle and a friend of many years' standing, now a professor at Göttingen who was recognised as one of the greatest Orientalists in Germany, reviewed Boysen's translation in the eighth volume of his own *Orientalische und exegetische Bibliothek* of 1775. He agreed that Boysen's version was far better than Megerlin's, but, like Hirt, he was unable to share Boysen's enthusiastic endorsement of Islam and he pronounced himself against excessive reliance on *tafsīr*. He also corrected certain errors in Boysen's translation. In Q 4:24, for example, on the punishment for female slaves caught in adultery, Boysen gives the same punishment as that for free and married women, but in fact the Qur'an says that slaves should receive *half* the punishment of free women. Michaelis was dissatisfied, too, by the almost complete lack of explanatory notes and by the absence of verse numbers. Johann Bernhard Köhler, writing in the *Allgemeine Deutsche Bibliothek* in 1777, was hardly better pleased by Boysen's translation than he had been by Megerlin's. Boysen, he said, was not sufficiently acquainted with the original text and had entirely failed to convey its poetic quality.

Despite such reservations, Boysen's Qur'an was remarkably successful. It went through two editions in his lifetime and, in 1828, it was thoroughly revised by Samuel Friedrich Günther Wahl, professor of Oriental languages at Halle. He corrected Boysen's mistakes, added a certain amount of new information to the footnotes, removed Boysen's prefaces and replaced them by an attack on Islam so violent that it was reminiscent of the anti-Islamic tracts of far earlier periods. In his hands, Boysen's rendering was no longer the fruit of the philo-Islamic German Enlightenment that it had once been.

It was not until 1840 that Boysen's translation found a rival. This was the new version by Ludwig Ullmann. But in the following year Heinrich Leberecht Fleischer, one of the best Arabists of his generation, who had studied under Sylvestre de Sacy in Paris and was revolutionising the study of Arabic in Germany, published a review of earlier Qur'an translations in which he only had praise for Marracci and Sale. Since then, he wrote, translations of the Qur'an had gone from bad to worse. He regarded Ullmann's version, which was excessively dependent on Boysen and Wahl, as worthless, and maintained that Wahl had made Boysen's translation even worse than it was in the original. But by then approaches to the translation of the Qur'an had changed. By the late 18th century, increasing efforts were being made in the German-speaking world and elsewhere in Europe to translate it into verse. 'We are', as Ziad Elmarsafy has written, 'dealing with a new generation of Qur'anic translation; one where sound and form matter as much as, if not more than, content.'

PUBLICATIONS

Friedrich Eberhard Boysen, *Der Koran, oder Das Gesetz für die Muselmänne, durch Mohammed den Sohn Abdall*, Halle, 1773; A.or. 575 (digitised version available through *MDZ*)

Friedrich Eberhard Boysen, *Der Koran, oder Das Gesetz für die Moslemer durch Muhammed den Sohn Abdall*, Halle, 1775; A.or. 576 (digitised version available through *MDZ*)

Samuel Friedrich Günther Wahl, *Der Koran, oder Das Gesetz der Moslemen durch Muhammed den Sohn Abdallahs. Auf den Grund der vormaligen Verdeutschung F. E. Boysen's von neuem aus dem Arabischen übersetzt, durchaus mit erläuternden Anmerkungen, mit einer historischen Einleitung und einem vollständigen Register versehen*, Halle, 1828; A.or. 577 (digitised version available through *MDZ*)

STUDIES

A. Hamilton, 'After Marracci. The reception of Ludovico Marracci's edition of the Qur'an in northern Europe from the late seventeenth to the early nineteenth centuries', *Journal of Qur'anic Studies* 3 (2018) 175-92

Hamilton, 'Lutheran Islamophiles'

Hamilton, '"To rescue the honour of the Germans"'

Z. Elmarsafy, *The Enlightenment Qur'an. The politics of translation and the construction of Islam*, Oxford, 2009

H.L. Fleischer, 'Orientalische Literatur', *Allgemeine Literatur-Zeitung* 53 (1841) cols. 417-22; 54 (1841) cols. 430-2

J.B. Köhler, 'Der Koran[...]', *Allgemeine Deutsche Bibliothek* 24 (1777) 830-47

J.D. Michaelis, 'Der Koran[...]', in J.D. Michaelis (ed.), *Orientalische und exegetische Bibliothek*, vol. 8, Frankfurt am Main, 1775, 30-98

J.F. Hirt, 'Der Koran[...]', in J.F. Hirt (ed.), *Orientalische und exegetische Bibliothek*, vol. 6, Jena, 1774, 341-53

Alastair Hamilton

Gotthold Ephraim Lessing

DATE OF BIRTH   22 January 1729
PLACE OF BIRTH   Kamenz, Upper Lusatia, Saxony
DATE OF DEATH   15 February 1781
PLACE OF DEATH   Braunschweig (Brunswick)

BIOGRAPHY

Gotthold Ephraim Lessing was a highly regarded German playwright, critic and writer on aesthetics and philosophy. From a staunchly Lutheran family, he was the third son among 12 children. From 1741, he studied at an elite school and acquired a deep knowledge of classical languages and literature. Though he registered to study theology at Leipzig University in 1746, his interest lay in literature, philosophy and the arts. His comedy *The young scholar* was successfully staged in 1748, when he was only 19.

Financial problems led to Lessing leaving his studies and moving to Berlin, where he engaged in translation and literary criticism (in 1751 alone, he wrote more than 100 reviews). He also undertook Oriental studies; he translated Augier de Marigny's *History of the Arabs* and acquired a profound knowledge of the Qur'an, among other matters to do with the Arab world. In 1749, he wrote a comedy, *The Jews*, the first sign of his commitment to tolerance at a time when the Jews were forced to live in ghettos. From his time in Berlin, he maintained his friendship with the philosopher Moses Mendelssohn and the publisher C.F. Nicolai.

In 1751-2, he obtained a degree in medicine at Wittenberg, though on his return to Berlin he engaged in literature and drama. As early as 1753-5, he published a six-volume edition of his own works, part of it consisting of translations and reviews. He studied Orientalist themes, which provided him with a good understanding of Islam.

In 1760, Lessing became the secretary to General Tauentzien in Breslau – a post that left him sufficient time and money for extensive study, but also for his passion for gaming. He worked on his major treatise *Laokoon, or On the limits of painting and poetry* (1766). After returning to Berlin, he became a celebrated and successful playwright and critic. In his comedy *Minna von Barnhelm* (1767), the characters are ordinary people who nevertheless express the Enlightenment ideals of Lessing's concept of humanity.

In 1770, he accepted a post as librarian at Wolfenbüttel, the final stage of his career and one in which he experienced many hardships, though it was rich in achievements. He entered into a fierce controversy after publishing extracts from the works of the late biblical scholar Herman Samuel Reimarus, which contained extremely radical and critical ideas on biblical texts, not necessarily in line with Lessing's own conviction but as a proposal for discussion. Because of this involvement, he was banned from publishing and had to submit to censorship. However, he continued his controversy against the Hamburg chief pastor J.M. Goeze, and insisted on his own conviction that the search for truth is superior to a thoughtless acceptance of any orthodox doctrine.

In 1772, his tragedy *Emilia Galotti* was staged, and in 1779, two years before his death, he published his dramatic poem *Nathan the wise*, though he did not live to see it performed. He also wrote philosophical and literary treatises (notably *The education of the human race*, 1780), but these years were a time of tribulation and loneliness. He died in poverty and was buried in a pauper's grave.

During his own lifetime, Lessing was looked on as a symbol of the spirit of Enlightenment. He was praised for the breadth of his knowledge and his acute critical talent, but more so for his singular thrust in argument and reasoning.

MAIN SOURCES OF INFORMATION

Primary

K.G. Lessing, *Gotthold Ephraim Lessings Leben*, ed. Otto F. Lachmann, Leipzig, 1887 (first edition 1793-5)

Secondary

C. Wiedemann, art. 'Lessing, Gotthold Ephraim', in W. Kühlmann (ed.), *Killy Literaturlexikon. Autoren und Werke des deutschsprachigen Kulturraumes*, 2. *vollständig überarbeitete Auflage*, vol. 7, Darmstadt, 2016, 360-70 (extensive bibliography pp. 368-70)

J. Müller, art. 'Lessing, Gotthold Ephraim', in *Encyclopaedia Britannica*, vol. 7, London, 1998, 299-300

D. Hildebrandt, *Lessing. Biographie einer Emanzipation*, Munich, 1979

WORKS ON CHRISTIAN-MUSLIM RELATIONS

Nathan der Weise. Ein Dramatisches Gedicht, in fünf Aufzügen
'Nathan the wise. A dramatic poem in five acts'

DATE   1779
ORIGINAL LANGUAGE   German

DESCRIPTION

Lessing wrote *Nathan* in 1778-9. The reason behind it and its date are quite precise: he had engaged in a controversy on reason and revelation through the publication of radical extracts from Herman Samuel Reimarus's papers. Because of this conflict with the orthodox theology of his time, represented by Goeze, the senior pastor of Hamburg, the Braunschweig Ministry withdrew his licence to publish on 13 July 1778. This made Lessing return to his 'old pulpit': 'I must try whether they will let me preach at my old pulpit, at least in the theatre' (in a letter dated 6 September 1778).

In mid-August 1778, he wrote to his brother about the 'crazy idea' for a play he had dreamt of, returning to a draft he had developed from a story in Boccaccio's *Il Decamerone* (third tale on the first day: 'How the Jew Melchizedek avoided a great danger placed on him by Saladin, through a story of three rings'). He evidently worked with dedication, because he started to compose the verses for Act 5 as early as 7 March 1779 and had finished by May 1779 (Jung, *Lessing*, pp. 84-6; Kuschel, *Jud, Christ und Muselmann*, pp. 44-7; Kuschel, *Im Ringen*, pp. 50-3).

Already on 8 August 1778, Lessing had issued an invitation to subscribe to the play, in order to ascertain his rights in face of the widespread practice of pirating texts. Indeed, there were at least four pirated editions in 1779 alone (see the postscript to Bremer and Hantzsche, *Gotthold Ephraim Lessing, Nathan*, pp. 222-3; invitation to subscribe, pp. 170-1). The play was first performed in Berlin on 14 April 1783 at Theater in der Behrenstraße, two years after Lessing's death.

Lessing published his *Nathan* in 1779 in three authorised versions. The first was printed for the subscribers, under considerable pressure, as it was to be distributed during the Leipzig Easter Fair in May 1779. This led to repeated interventions during its typesetting (Lessing was still finishing some of the verses while the text was being set), and this version understandably contains many errors. Some of his corrections of the galley proofs could not be introduced and so the subscription edition is not really the definitive first text.

Lessing himself authorised two further reprints in 1779. Kai Bremer and Valerie Hantzsche in their study edition (2013) argue in favour of the second printing of *Nathan* and use this version in their edition of the play (see their comment and post-script in *Gotthold Ephraim Lessing, Nathan*, pp. 208-28).

The entire text is composed of 3,850 lines, in five acts.

The action takes place in Jerusalem during the Third Crusade (1189-92). Saladin took the city in 1187 and the Christian troops under Richard I of England and Philip II of France could not recover it. During the ensuing armistice, Saladin, who is advised by his sister Sittah, needs money for his troops. There is also Nathan, a wealthy Jew, who has lost his entire family in a massacre in Gath several years earlier. He has an adopted daughter, Recha, who has lost her parents, a Muslim father and a Christian mother. The Christian patriarch considers that, living in a Jew's household, this Christian girl is in danger of being converted and is inclined to eliminate Nathan in order to save Recha. There is also a Templar who has been pardoned by Saladin because he looks astonishingly like the sultan's dead brother. On Sittah's advice, Saladin plans to get his hands on Nathan's money. In a meeting, he poses Nathan a tricky question to test his wisdom: 'Which faith appears to you the better?' (Lessing, *Nathan*, Act 3, scene 5, lines 1,838-45). Nathan understands the trap Saladin has laid out for him and tells the sultan a 'little story' about three rings – the famous 'ring parable':

There was a king in the East who had received a precious ring. The bearer of this ring was loved and appreciated by God and people, and was always intending to hand over the ring to his favourite son, who, as the new bearer, would become king. The king who had received the ring had three sons whom he loved equally and he promised each of them that he would give him the ring. In order to keep his promise, he ordered two identical copies of the ring to be made by a skilful jeweller, who completed his job so well that even the king could not tell which was the original. On his deathbed, he gave each of his sons a ring, and when they discovered that there were suddenly three rings instead of the one, they tried to find out which was the original. They could not, and they ended up before a judge, who could only give them this advice: Your father loved you all and did not like to make any of you better than the others ('By favouring one to be of two the oppressor'), so 'Let each feel honoured by this free affection'. Since the ring has the power to make the bearer beloved by God and people, 'let each endeavour to vie with both his brothers in displaying the virtue of his ring'. After many thousand years someone greater than this judge would make the final decision as to which was the true, original ring. (Lessing, *Nathan*, Act 3, scene 7, lines 1,911-2,054)

Saladin is surprised by this story, and he comes to see that neither force nor power can prove the truth of religion. He offers Nathan his friendship, and in turn Nathan is pleased to help Saladin by offering his money.

Meanwhile, the Templar falls in love with Recha at first sight and asks for her in marriage. Through a friar, who incidentally had handed over an orphan girl to Nathan 18 years earlier, they learn that Recha is the Templar's sister and that the Templar is Saladin's nephew – they all discover that they are actually members of the same family.

The play ends in silence with shared embraces, and the curtain falls.

SIGNIFICANCE

The novelty of this 'dramatic poem' lies in making the representatives of the three religions relatives of one another. Nathan the Jew is marginalised despite his wealth and he is threatened by the powerful (the patriarch and Saladin). The Christians are represented negatively through a corrupt and fanatical patriarch who despises the Jews and fights against the Muslims; he stands for merciless orthodoxy. But there is also another Christian, the Templar, a warrior 'for his God', who finds himself finally in close relationship with the others: a Muslim (his father), another Muslim, as he owes his life to Saladin, and a 'Jewess' Recha, with whom he is in love and who, alas, turns out to be his sister. It is the Templar who undergoes the most dramatic 'conversion' in the drama.

In the location of Jerusalem, a holy place for all three religions, conflict is expected to be the 'natural' relationship between them. However, Lessing constructs a setting in which each religion can present its options for conflict and reconciliation. Through the story, or even fairy tale, the three parties come to realise that they are one family, clearly a utopian suggestion. As Lessing wrote his *Nathan* in the context of censorship and the suppression of his discussion around orthodoxy, the real conflict and violence does not rest with Muslims and/or Jews and the criticism focuses on intolerant Christianity and its claim to the only revealed truth.

Against the *Zeitgeist* of his time, Lessing presents his Muslim and Jewish characters in a positive manner from the outset. He himself states in the Preface to *Nathan*: 'I shall want to draw your attention to the fact that Jews and Muslims at that time [of the Crusades] were the only learned people' (see Kuschel, *Im Ringen*, p. 21). This attitude towards others is characteristic of him. His first drama, *The Jews* (1749), criticised the prejudiced view that Jews were liars and crooks. Earlier, in the course of his Oriental studies, Lessing had analysed the philosophical position of the Italian mathematician, philosopher and physician Hieronymus Cardanus (1501/6-76), who presented the arguments of Muslims and Jews as weaker than those of Christians (Lessing, *Salvation of Hieronymus Cardanus*, 1754). Thus, in his own version of the arguments in *Nathan*, he went far beyond the public image of Islam in his times and also transcended the idea of tolerance. His interest was not just in giving a fair presentation of the other religions but also in allowing them to have their own voice in public discourse (see Kuschel, *Im Ringen*, pp. 42-50).

In Lessing's rendering, Nathan does not match the stereotypical image of Jews. Despite losing his seven sons through the actions of Christian soldiers, he adopts the Christian girl Recha – thus appearing to be a 'better Christian' (*Nathan*, Act 4, scene 7). Similarly, Saladin is portrayed as a deeply human person. The Templar, and particularly the patriarch, are at various stages the villains, showing mercilessness and fanaticism.

Against the non-religious humanist conception and demand for 'humanity beyond religions' Lessing takes up

> a more complex perspective, which is dialectical: Humanity should be realised through being a Jew (Christian, Muslim), and vice versa. Nathan's affirmation is precisely not: Christians and Jews should become nothing else than humans (i.e. forget their faiths all together). His question, 'Are Christian and Jew rather Christian and Jew than human?' does not place exclusivity on the human, but [gives] priority over the religious in such a manner that the religious identity is put into practice as humanity and humanity is grounded in the religious. (Kuschel, *Im Ringen*, p. 91)

Thus, humanity can be achieved in any religion or culture (see *Nathan*, Act 2, scene 5).

The important twist in solving the relationship between the religions lies in Lessing's suggestion that there is no point in trying objectively to identify 'the true religion'. Nobody is able to identify the original ring – not even the father (line 1,951). However, his intention in making two copies is not to cheat his three sons, but to show his love for each of them. Therefore, in his verdict the judge gives this advice: 'Let each endeavour to vie [...] in displaying the virtue of his ring' (line 2,043), which renders the owner 'of God and man beloved' (lines 1,915-16). The point of presenting religious differences lies in overcoming them through human/humanist behaviour, as the purpose of any religion lies in making the person a better human being. This can be achieved if each follower of his own religion lives as though his were the authentic ring and behaves as if his religion were the true one in living 'of God and man beloved'.

One of the central motifs in the play is 'submission to God'. In several places, the various characters confess their admiration for such a submission: Recha is the first to mention it (Act 3, scene 1). Lessing was quite aware that this 'submission' and 'resignation to God's will' (*Gottergebenheit*) is the German term for 'Islam' (see Kuschel, *Im Ringen*, pp. 180-92; Overath, Kermani and Schindel, *Toleranz*, pp. 33-4). Such submission has real and practical implications for life and is understood as the opposite of mere theoretical discourse about God – the central purpose of theology and the conflictive backdrop for the composition of Nathan.

Lessing was a celebrated playwright in his time. In the 60 years after his comedy *Minna von Barnhelm* (completed in 1765, staged in 1767), as many as 260 plays may have been directly influenced by his work (Jung, *Lessing*, p. 77).

Lessing expanded on his ideas about humanism in several treatises, particularly his essay on *The education of the human race* (1780), where he states his belief in the perfectibility of humankind. In his view, the history of religions shows the development of moral consciousness, which will eventually arrive at a universal brotherhood and moral freedom beyond dogmas and doctrines.

Similarly, a dialogue between two freemasons in *Falk and Ernest. Conversations for Freemasons* (1778) deals with topics of religion, revelation and reason (see Jung, *Lessing*, pp. 84-98).

Lessing is considered one of the fathers of German drama and has a definitive place in German-language theatre. His *Nathan* and *Minna von Barmhelm* in particular are basic reading in secondary schools. Kuschel states that, in the aftermath of 9/11, there were at least 24 productions of *Nathan* in German-speaking theatres, many of them heavily disputed because of their interpretation and/or approach to the drama and to religious conflict and identity (see Kuschel, *'Jud, Christ und Muselmann vereinigt'*, pp. 9-32; Overath, Kermani and Schindel, *Toleranz*).

The 'parable of the rings' has become a central conceptualisation for the understanding of the relationship between religions, at least in German speaking contexts. However, its interpretation is disputed. Authors such as the Catholic theologian Karl-Josef Kuschel and the Islamicist

Navid Kermani contest simplistic interpretations of relativism or tolerance without convictions (see Kuschel, *Im Ringen*, and *'Jud, Christ und Muselmann vereinigt'*; Overath, Kermani and Schindel, *Toleranz*; Tück and Langthaler, *Es strebe*).

As Lessing became a 'classic' even in his own time, *Nathan* was one of the first literary works to undergo a historical-critical edition according to philological and Germanic criteria.

PUBLICATIONS

Selected editions and translations are given below; for a full list, see S. Seifert, *Lessing-Bibliographie*, Berlin, 1973 (a comprehensive bibliography of Lessing's works).

Gotthold Ephraim Lessing, *Nathan der Weise. Ein Dramatisches Gedicht, in fünf Aufzügen*, Berlin, 1779 (three editions); Rar. 1470, Rar. 877, P.o.germ. 2045 x (digitised versions of the three different editions are available through *MDZ*)

Gotthold Ephraim Lessing, *Nathan the Wise. A philosophical drama*, trans. R.E. Raspe, London, 1781 (English trans.); ESTC T061094 (digitised version available through *ECCO*)

Gotthold Ephraim Lessing, *Nathan der Weise. Ein Dramatisches Gedicht, in fünf Aufzügen*, Berlin, 1791

Gotthold Ephraim Lessing, *Nathan the Wise. A dramatic poem, written originally in German, etc.*, trans. W. Taylor, Norwich, 1791, repr. London, 1803, 1805 (English trans.)

Gotthold Ephraim Lessing, *Nathan der Weise. Ein Dramatisches Gedicht, in fünf Aufzügen*, Vienna, 1819; Augsburg, Staats- und Stadtbibliothek – LD 4300 (digitised version available through *MDZ*)

Gotthold Ephraim Lessing, *Nathan der Weise. Ein Dramatisches Gedicht, in fünf Aufzügen*, Gotha, 1827; P.o.germ. 1988 m-1/5 (digitised version available through *MDZ*)

Gotthold Ephraim Lessing, *Nathan the Wise*, trans. W. Taylor, London, 1865 (English trans); see http://www.fullbooks.com/Nathan-the-Wise.html.

Gotthold Ephraim Lessing, *Nàtan heḥakham*, trans. A.B. Gottlober, Vienna, 1874 (Hebrew trans.)

Gotthold Ephraim Lessing, *Noson he-ḥokhem. Ayne dramaṭishe unṭerhandlung iber emune un religion*, trans. I.J. Linietsḳi, Odessa, 1884 (Yiddish trans.)

Gotthold Ephraim Lessing, *Natán el sabio*, trans. A.A. Rodrigo, Madrid, 1985, Barcelona, 2008 (Spanish trans.)

Gotthold Ephraim Lessing, *Nathan the Wise. With related documents*, trans. R. Schechter, Boston MA, 2004 (English trans.)

K. Bremer and V. Hantzsche (eds), *Gotthold Ephraim Lessing, Nathan der Weise. Ein Dramatisches Gedicht, in fünf Aufzügen. Studienausgabe*, Stuttgart, 2013

STUDIES

J.-H. Tück and R. Langthaler (eds), *'Es strebe von euch jeder um die Wette'. Lessings Ringparabel – ein Paradigma für die Verständigung der Religionen heute?*, Vienna, 2016

K.-J. Kuschel, *Im Ringen um den wahren Ring. Lessings 'Nathan der Weise' – eine Herausforderung der Religionen*, Ostfildern, 2011

K.-J. Kuschel, *'Jud, Christ und Muselmann vereinigt'? Lessings 'Nathan der Weise'*, Düsseldorf, 2004

A. Overath, N. Kermani and R. Schindel, *Toleranz. Drei Lesarten zu Lessings Märchen vom Ring im Jahre 2003*, Göttingen, 2003

W. Jung, *Lessing zur Einführung*, Hamburg, 2001

D. Neiteler and W. Woesler, 'Zur Wahl der Textgrundlage einer Neuedition von Lessings Nathan der Weise', *Lessing Yearbook* 31 (1999) 39-64

Christian Tauchner

Johann Christoph Döderlein

DATE OF BIRTH   20 January 1746
PLACE OF BIRTH   Windsheim, Franconia
DATE OF DEATH   2 December 1792
PLACE OF DEATH   Jena

BIOGRAPHY

Johann Christoph Döderlein was educated in his hometown and then, in 1764, went to study in Altdorf, near Nuremberg. He worked as a private teacher before becoming a deacon in Windsheim (1768). His book *Curae criticae et exegeticae* (Altdorf, 1770) made him known. He obtained his master's degree in Altdorf and became professor of theology there in 1772. Two years later, he earned his doctorate. He became a professor of theology (dogmatics and biblical exegesis) in Jena in 1782. He served several times as dean and rector in Altdorf and Jena.

Döderlein married twice, first Rosina Maria Merklein in 1771, then, after her death, Rosina Christina Eleonora von Eckardt in 1790, and had four children. He was a good scholar but apparently not very popular with his colleagues because of his irritable nature.

He was a proponent of neology, a moderate Enlightenment theology based on the reception of German Enlightenment ideas into Lutheran thought. His main work, *Institutio theologi Christiani in capitibus religionis theoreticis nostris temporibus accommodate*, 2 vols (Nuremberg, 1782-3), saw two more editions in 1787 and 1797.

MAIN SOURCES OF INFORMATION

Primary

G.E. Waldau, *Diptycha continuata ecclesiarum in oppidis et pagis Norimbergensibus, oder Verzeichniße und Lebensbeschreibungen aller Herren Geistlichen in dem zu Nürnberg gehörigen Landstädten und Dörfern von 1756 biß zu Ende des Jahres 1779*, Nuremberg, 1780, p. 20

G.A. Will and Ch.C. Nopitsch, *Nürnbergisches Gelehrten-Lexicon oder Beschreibung aller Nürnbergischen Gelehrten beyderley Geschlechts nach Ihrem Leben, Verdiensten und Schriften, zur Erweiterung der gelehrten Geschichtskunde und Verbesserung vieler darinnen vorgefallenen Fehler aus den besten Quellen in alphabetischer Ordnung fortgesetzt*, Altdorf, vol. 5, 1802, pp. 235-42

Art. 'Döderlein', in J.-G. Meusel (ed.), *Lexikon der vom Jahr 1750 bis 1800 verstor-benen teutschen Schriftsteller*, Leipzig, 1803, 388-93

H. Döring, *Die deutschen Kanzelredner des achtzehnten und neunzehnten Jahr-hunderts*, Neustadt an der Orla, 1830, p. 36

H. Döring, art. 'Döderlein', in J.G. Ersch and J.G. Gruber (eds), *Allgemeine Ency-clopädie der Wissenschaften und Künste, Dir-Dom*, Section 1, vol. 26, Leipzig, 1835, 251-5

Art. 'Döderlein', in J.J. Herzog (ed.), *Realenzyklopädie für protestantische Theolo-gie und Kirche, Stuttgart und Hamburg*, vol. 3, 1855, 432-3

G. Frank, art. 'Döderlein, Johann Christoph', in *Allgemeine Deutsche Biographie*, vol. 5, Leipzig, 1877, 280-1

Secondary

A. Beutel, art. 'Döderlein, Johann Christoph', in H.D. Betz et al. (eds), *Religion past and present*, vol. 4, Leiden, 2008

F.W. Bautz, art. 'Döderlein, Johann Christoph', in *Biographisch-Bibliographisches Kirchenlexikon*, vol. 1, Hamm, 1975, col. 1341

K. Leder, *Universität Altdorf, zur Theologie der Aufklärung in Franken, die theologische Fakultät in Altdorf 1750-1809*, Nuremberg, 1965, pp. 161-242

WORKS ON CHRISTIAN-MUSLIM RELATIONS

Fragmente und Antifragmente
'Fragments and antifragments'

DATE   1779

ORIGINAL LANGUAGE   German

DESCRIPTION

Fragmente und Antifragmente appeared in two volumes, of which only the second (in full, *Fragmente und Antifragmente. Einige von Herrn Les-sing herausgegebene Fragmente abgedruckt mit Betrachtungen darüber*, 'Fragments and antifragments. Some fragments edited by Mr Lessing, reprinted and commented upon' – see both full titles in 'Publications') contains references to Islam. The work is not primarily devoted to Chris-tian-Muslim relations, but is part of a general debate on religious beliefs conducted among German Christian theologians. Only a brief summary of the issues concerning Christian-Muslim relations is presented here. The quite nuanced discussions and the arguments it contains deserve a full and profound examination.

The work contains Döderlein's reaction to the contents of *Fragmente eines Ungenannten* ('Anonymous fragments'), published by Gotthold

Ephraim Lessing in 1774-8. These were seven fragments of *Apologie oder Schutzschrift für die vernünftigen Vereher Gottes* by Hermann Samuel Reimarus (1694-1768), published posthumously and anonymously out of anxiety over possible reactions to their critical views about some Christian beliefs (revelation, the miracles and resurrection of Christ, and so on). The publication ignited the so-called *Fragments* controversy, in which many scholars engaged. Döderlein was one of these, and was very critical of Reimarus's arguments, though he considered the publication itself of the *Fragments* as positive.

The first volume of *Fragmente und Antifragmente*, 268 pages (1778), with Döderlein's comments on two *Fragments* texts (on the crossing of the Red Sea by the Israelites and on the account of Jesus' resurrection) was published anonymously. The second volume, 248 pages (1779), signed by Döderlein (no name on the title page but he signed the preface, dated 29 March 1779), contains his argument against the *Fragment* called *Unmöglichkeit einer Offenbarung, die alle Menschen auf eine gegründete Art glauben könnten* ('Impossibility of a revelation that all people could believe on a solid basis'). The same volume contains the reprinted text of the *Fragment* (pp. 3-120 in the 1779 edition, which is the edition cited in the references that follow) and Döderlein's response (pp. 121-248), omitting the comments that Lessing had made in his publication.

The forms *Muhamed, Muhammed, Muhamedaner, Mahomedaner, Alkoran, Alcoran* are used randomly throughout the text.

Reimarus questions whether Christianity could be seen as a universal revelation that would be recognised and accepted by all people, because every human group has followed and cherished its own religion, which it has inherited from its forebears, and will have no desire to learn about other religions. Political power also comes into play, as in the Ottoman state, and will prevent the spread of new religions. The Turks are obedient to their faith, and are so convinced about the divine origin of *Muhamed*'s prophethood, the truth of his miracles and the divine origin of *Alkoran* that they cannot be diverted from these beliefs. Besides, they have learned from *Alkoran* such a deep hatred for Christianity as a form of polytheism and superstition that they need no coercion to reject it and keep to their own beliefs. Thus, he argues, it is impossible that a Turk in Turkey would become a Christian.

In his response to this, Döderlein sets rationality in religion, rather than universality of appeal, as the benchmark. He argues that, before Christ, monotheism was the natural religion, though it was often forgotten by 'natural people', even the wise ones. That is why the Jewish religion emphasised monotheism so strongly, and why the Apostle Paul preached the truth of monotheism to the heathens, and it is why *Muhamedanismus* with its strongly monotheistic emphasis that draws people mainly of pagan origin can be regarded as a preparation for Christianity (p. 158; this interpretation of Islam was sometimes used by Christians living in the early Islamic Empire). He continues that not every human society is at the same level of understanding the world and so they have received different revelations, explaining what he means through an imaginary dialogue between a father and a son: the loving father has given him and his brother different books according to their different levels of perception. He maintains that, on the basis of love for people and for truth, Christianity is the religion that should be spread, because it has brought such a clear understanding, calmness of heart and so much good in people's lives. However, Döderlein pleads for a rational (enlightened) Christianity, which takes the highest place in his schema of the history of religions.

Döderlein defends the feasibility of missionary activity, which is questioned by Reimarus. He argues that missionaries among the pagans should begin with the message about the Creator, though he admits that they often preach about the Saviour, which brings misunderstandings because the pagans operate within a very different worldview from that of Christianity. He indicates that God deals with different people as a doctor who applies a variety of medicines in order to restore health. There are also people who do not need any medicine because 'Nature itself helps them' (p. 163).

He insists that it is possible to recognise and choose a better religion than one's own: 'When a polytheist becomes a *Mahomedaner* before he gets to know Christianity, it is equally laudable as when a *Muhamedaner* becomes a Christian' (p. 172). Döderlein appreciates *Muhamedanismus* for its monotheism but tempers his appreciation by indicating problematic issues, e.g. its spread through the use of arms, its acceptance of polygamy, and its prohibition of wine.

Döderlein counters Reimarus's view that missionary effort in places like the Ottoman Empire is futile. Reimarus states that, as long as a *Muhamedaner* adheres to his religion, he will not become a Christian, but Döderlein wonders whether it would not be possible to bring a nation or its learned ones to an enlightenment by which they would see

> the folly of *Muhamed*, his deceitfulness and the ungodliness of his religion? Would it not be possible to subdue the preference for the religion of the fathers and to remove hatred of Christendom (in which I deeply

doubt)? This is the question. It is known that the *Muhamedaner* readily read the New Testament; that *Muhamed* spoke respectfully of Jesus and did not deny or question his divine mission; that *Alcoran* contains many more statements against which the human mind rebels than any Christian system, however laden with mysteries; that the teaching about One God is the basic teaching for Christians as well as for the *Muhamedaner*; and would it also be so difficult to explain to the Turks that the Christian teaching about the Trinity is not idolatry? (pp. 236-7)

To Reimarus's observation that the Ottoman state hinders the spread of any other religion than Islam, Döderlein responds:

Is a revolution not possible by which the Turkish state would fall into Christian hands? Any enlightenment that would lead to expunging the burden of superstition and of the priests? (p. 237) [...]

The rationality of the Christian revelation in relation to *Muhamedanismus* is made immediately clear as soon as the statements from both [religions] are rightly known and proved in a proper comparison. In the latter [*Muhamedanismus*], there always remains a remnant of Christianity, the core but covered with superstition, though perhaps so long hidden until the peel decays while it [the core] prepares itself gradually for a new development. So great is the damage that *Muhamed* has done to Christianity, so light is it to think that *Muhamedanismus* could be accepted without damage when it is considered as a preparation for Christianity. Many heathen peoples have got to know the true God through it, acquired reverence for Jesus, for whom – by a more accurate learning of his teaching – reverence will grow and that for *Muhamed* will diminish through recognising his character and his deception. Who knows how long the linchpins of the *Muhamedan* religion, the worldly power and dominion that already now look clearly weaker and gradually declining, will still stand? How soon will a change come in the ethnic system (*Völkersystem*) and the prevailing religious system in the Turkish state? However, I am far from uttering any prophecies. (pp. 245-6)

SIGNIFICANCE

In this argument about the universality and rationality of divine revelation, Döderlein includes Muḥammad in the history of religion not as an opponent who must be resisted, but as a full participant, admittedly with flaws but the proponent of a somehow rational religion. While Islam is inferior to Christianity, it represents a preparatory stage towards full rational faith.

Such works as this acted as breakthrough points that contributed to creating new perspectives of understanding the religious history of humankind, and Islam as an integral element within it that served the positive purpose of introducing humankind to truth.

PUBLICATIONS

[Johann Christoph Döderlein], *Fragmente und Antifragmente; zwey Fragemente eines Ungenannten, aus Hrn. Lessing's Beyträgen zur Litteratur abgedruckt, mit Betrachtungen darüber; nebst einigen Landkarten*, Nuremberg, 1778

Johann Christoph Döderlein, *Fragmente und Antifragmente. Einige von Herrn Lessing herausgegebene Fragmente abgedruckt mit Betrachtungen darüber. Zweiter Theil*, Nuremberg, 1779; nyp.33433068243561 vols 1 and 2 (digitised version available through Hathi Trust Digital Library)

Johann Christoph Döderlein, *Fragmente und Antifragmente*, Nuremberg, vol. 1, 1780; vol. 2, 1781 (second improved edition); Dogm. 359-1/2 (digitised version available through *MDZ*)

Johann Christoph Döderlein, *Fragmente und Antifragmente*, vol. 1³, Nuremberg, 1788

STUDIES

D. Cyranka, *Mahomet. Repräsentationen des Propheten in deutschsprachigen Texten des 18. Jahrhunderts*, Göttingen, 2018, pp. 452-65

Leder, *Universität Altdorf*, pp. 194-225

Stanisław Grodź

Johann David Michaelis

DATE OF BIRTH   27 February 1717
PLACE OF BIRTH   Halle
DATE OF DEATH   22 August 1791
PLACE OF DEATH   Göttingen

BIOGRAPHY

Johann David was born to the theologian and Orientalist Christian Benedikt Michaelis and his wife Dorothea Hedwig. He obtained his master's degree in philosophy and arts at Halle University in 1739, then qualified as a university lecturer. Thanks to contacts with F.M. Ziegenhagen, a German court preacher in London, he went to England in 1741. On the way, he made acquaintance with the Dutch Orientalist Heinrich Albert Schultens, whose views proved influential in Michaelis's later scholarly career. In Oxford, he was influenced by R. Lowth, a poetry professor and later a bishop.

After his return to Halle, Michaelis became a promotor of English culture and biblical scholarship. Between 1742 and 1745, he taught at Halle as *Privatdozent*, also having duties as a preacher. In 1745, he accepted an invitation to teach at the University of Göttingen, where he was promoted to the status of *professor ordinarius* in the Faculty of Philosophy in 1750. He served as the secretary to the *Göttinger Gesellschaft der Wissenschaften* (1751-6) and then its director (1761-70). He was the editor of *Göttinger Gelehrten Anzeigen* (1753-70) and then edited his own *Orientalische und Exegetische Bibliothek* from 1771 till his death in 1791.

Although he was an expert in Oriental languages, he was best known for his writings on Christian theological themes and on the study of the Bible. Oriental studies were for him a sub-discipline of biblical studies (non-Hebrew languages and literatures, 'antiquities' of the Orient). He is credited with initiating the preparations for the Danish Arabia Expedition led by Carsten Niebuhr and Peter Forsskål (1761-7).

MAIN SOURCES OF INFORMATION

Primary

Anonymous, 'Betrachtungen eines Laien über die Sensation, welche der Tod des Ritter Joh. David Michaelis hat', *Journal von und für Deutschland* 8/11 (1791) 947-52

J.D. Michaelis, *Lebensbeschreibung von ihm selbst abgefaßt, mit Anmerkungen von Hassencamp Nebst Bemerkungen über dessen litterarischen Character von Eichhorn, Schulz und dem Elogium von Heyne*, Rinteln, 1793

Anonymous, Review of *Lebensbeschreibung von ihm selbst abgefaßt, Göttingische Anzeigen von gelehrten Sachen* 40 (1793) 907-8

Anonymous, 'Der Ritter Michaelis', *Der neue teutsche Merkur* 2 (1799) 284-8

Secondary

M. Rauchstein, *Fremde Vergangenheit. Zur Orientalistik des Göttinger Gelehrten Johann David Michaelis (1717-1791)*, Bielefeld, 2017, esp. pp. 15-44

Ch. Bultmann, art. 'Michaelis, Johann David', in *Neue Deutsche Biographie*, vol. 17, Berlin, 1994, pp. 427-9

K. Gründer, 'Johann David Michaelis und Moses Mendelssohn', in J. Katz and K. Gründer (eds), *Begegnung von Deutschen und Juden in der Geistesgeschichte des 18. Jahrhunderts*, Tübingen, 1994, 25-50

K.-G. Wesseling, art. 'Michaelis, Johann David', in F.W. Bautz and T. Bautz (eds), *Biographisch-bibliographisches Kirchenlexikon*, vol. 5, Herzberg, 1993, 1473-9

A.R. Löwenbrück, 'Johann David Michaelis' Verdienst um die philologische-historische Bibelkritik', in H. Graf Reventlow et al. (eds), *Historische Kritik und biblischer Kanon in der deutschen Aufklärung*, Wiesbaden, 1988, 157-70

F. Schaffstein, *Johann David Michaelis als Kriminalpolitiker. Ein Orientalist am Rande der Strafrechtswissenschaft*, Göttingen, 1988

R. Smend, 'Johann David Michaelis und Johann Gottfried Eichhorn. Zwei Orientalisten am Rande der Theologie', in B. Moeller (ed.), *Theologie in Göttingen. Eine Vorlesungsreihe*, Göttingen, 1987, 58-81

J. Ringleben, 'Göttinger Aufklärungstheologie – von Königsberg her gesehen', in B. Moeller (ed.), *Theologie in Göttingen*, Göttingen, 1987, 82-110

WORKS ON CHRISTIAN-MUSLIM RELATIONS

Reviews of German Qur'an translations

DATE   1752-84
ORIGINAL LANGUAGE   German

DESCRIPTION

Michaelis expressed views about Muḥammad and the Qur'an from both literary and theological points of view. Although the contributions he made did not belong to the mainstream of his scholarly interests, they had an impact as soon as they were published and later.

Michaelis first addressed Islamic themes in his preface to a book of poems by Johann Friedrich Löwen, *Poetische Nebenstunden in Hamburg. Mit einer Vorrede des Herrn Prof. Johann David Michaelis, von dem Geschmack der morgenländischen Dichtkunst* (Leipzig, 1752, pp. ix-xlvii). Here, he approached the Qur'an as a work of Arabic poetry, claiming that Arab poetical tastes were not very different from European tastes. He argued that the Qur'an was originally seen as part of the ancient tradition of Arabic poetry, though in later generations it lost its appeal as a poetic masterpiece and was taken only as revealed scripture. This aside, he maintained that Islam as a religion was false (*falsche*) and fraudulent (*lügenhafte*).

In 1771, Michaelis published a reworked version of Erpenius's *Grammatica Arabica* (1613) and wrote an introduction, *Abhandlung vom Arabischen Geschmack*, that drew on his earlier introduction to Löwen's book. This later essay shows that he was sensitive to the change in public attitudes (*kulturelle Klima*). The growing interest in the Qur'an, with two new German translations from Arabic appearing at the beginning of the 1770s, provoked a strong reaction in Christian conservative circles. So, in his 1771 work, Michaelis underlines more clearly the idea that Christianity was a more complete and worthy religion than Islam (p. XII). In 1751, he had called Muḥammad the 'poet of Arabia' (*Dichter Arabiens*) who drew people to his teachings through the beauty of his poems. But in 1771, he writes that Muḥammad was not a poet by nature and was too uneducated to be a good writer. He judges that, despite some eloquent lines, the style of the Qur'an is too weak even to be considered good prose, and that Muḥammad declared it a sign of God's revelation because he liked his writing style so much (pp. XLII-XLV). The Turks were adherents of a 'superstitious sect' who did disservice to the reasonableness of the Qur'an with their interpretations of the text. They destroyed the 'good [literary-poetic] taste' (*gute Geschmack*) of the Arabs. Michaelis's readjustment of his perspective did not go unnoticed, as is evident from the comments of a reviewer in *Allgemeine Deutsche Bibliothek* 16 (1772) 166-7 (see Croitoru, *Der Deutschen und der Orient*, pp. 157-8).

Michaelis engaged with the Qur'an again a few years later, when he published a review of Boysen's German translation (which had been published in Halle in 1773) in *Orientalische und Exegetische Bibliothek*. Here he was more concerned with giving his own personal opinion about the contents of the Qur'an than with a critical assessment of the translation. He stresses that the Qur'an deserves extensive consideration from a philosophical point of view because, apart from the religion that can be learnt from the Bible, there is no other as reasonable as the *Muhammedanische* (pp. 31-3). Islam retains almost all the contents of 'natural religion', particularly in its teachings about the one and only, almighty and infinite God, the future life in which one will be either rewarded or punished, and the worship of the true God replacing other cults. Apart from the Christian and Jewish religions, Islam also provides the best possibility for 'improvement of the hearts'. Furthermore, political changes introduced by Islam should also awaken a desire to discover the driving force that stands behind them.

Michaelis assesses Muḥammad under four categories, first as a *Moralist – für Araber ziemlich gut* (quite good for the Arabs), second as a *Gesetzgeber* (law-giver) – *viel schlechter* (much worse), third as a *Logicus und Disputator – sehr schlecht* (very bad), and fourth as a *Historicus – womöglich noch schlechter* (possibly still worse) (Rauchstein, *Fremde Vergangenheit*, p. 221).

The high point comes with his assessment of Muḥammad's apparent historical incompetence: he confused biblical stories. Muḥammad knew that his teachings could not withstand any serious scholarly investigation, so he forbade the study of the Qur'an and of his religion, and laid a claim for the unattainability and miraculousness of the Qur'an as the word of God.

Michaelis saw the elements of 'natural religion' present in the Qur'an. They were not an effect of Muḥammad's deep philosophical study but were rooted in 'a philosophical sect of Arabia'. Had Muḥammad preached only this 'natural religion', he would have deserved only praise. Instead, he became a fraudulent prophetic claimant, shown by the many mistakes he made. In Michaelis's view, Islam was not a credible religion, because historical study of the Qur'an was not allowed, and scholarly studies were eventually suppressed in the lands of the Muslims. Assessing the damaging effects of *Muhammedanische Religion* on the state, Michaelis judges that: 'Such an ignorant religion full of enthusiasm will always bring a lot of unhappiness and could make states resemble tumultuous seas' (pp. 34-5).

Still another engagement with the Qur'an appeared in Michaelis's *Dogmatik. Zweite umgearbeitete Ausgabe* (Göttingen, 1784). In the first article, 'Von der Göttlichkeit der den Juden und Christen gegebenen Offenbarung', he sets out to verify the authenticity of revelations. Unlike in his review of Boysen's translation of the Qur'an, he states that he will present the results of an objective examination and not of his subjective perception. Setting the 'signs' that will help to distinguish between true and false revelation, he gives priority to what he calls 'negative signs' that demonstrate fallacy or error, and thus prove that a revelation is objectionable or false. God makes no mistakes, so a revelation that contains errors cannot come from God. There are five types of errors: contradictions against sound reason and true philosophy; historical errors; self-contradictions; logical errors; false prophecies. Comparing the Bible and the Qur'an, Michaelis states that no book in the world has withstood so thorough a critical study as the Bible. The Bible also withstands critical examination according to the 'negative signs'. He therefore concludes that either God was so cruel that he left humankind without any revelation, or the Bible is the only true divine revelation.

SIGNIFICANCE

Michaelis opened the way for later generations of scholars to read the Qur'an in a new way, as a piece of poetic art. Earlier, his contemporaries (not only theologians) had looked at it exclusively within a theological framework and saw it as the book of a false religion. His view of the Qur'an led the way to such literary attempts as Johann Wilhelm Ludwig Gleim's *Halladat oder Das rothe Buch* (Hamburg, 1774), a lengthy poem inspired by verses of the Qur'an.

PUBLICATIONS

Johann D. Michaelis, *Von dem Geschmack der morgenländischen Dichtkunst*, Leipzig, 1752, pp. ix-xlvii (preface to Friedrich Löwen, *Poetische Nebenstunden in Hamburg*); BLL01017135180 (digitised version available through BL)

Johann D. Michaelis, 'Abhandlung vom Arabischen Geschmack' ('Vorrede zur ersten Ausgabe, in der vom Arabischen Geschmack gehandelt wird'), in J.D. Michaelis, *Erpenii Arabische Grammatik, abgekürzt, vollständiger und leichter gemach, nebst den Anfang einer Arabischen Chrestomathie, aus Schultens Anhang zur Erpenischen Grammatik*, Göttingen, 1771, pp. iii-cxii; L.as. 4 (digitised version available through *MDZ*)

Johann D. Michaelis, 'Der Koran übersetzt durch Fridr. Eberhard Boysen', *Orientalische und Exegetische Bibliothek* 8 (1775) 30-98; A 25 BS (7-8) (digitised version available through Bodleian Library)

Johann D. Michaelis, *Arabische Grammatik, nebst einer Arabischen Chrestomathie, und Abhandlung vom Arabischen Geschmack, sonderlich in der poetischen und historischen Schreibart. Zweite, umgearbeitete und vermehrte Ausgabe*, Göttingen, 1781, 1812 (repr. Berlin, 2011); L.as. 18 b (digitised version available through *MDZ*)

Johann D. Michaelis, *Dogmatik. Zweite umgearbeitete Ausgabe*, Göttingen, 1784, pp. 14-20; Dogm. 691 (digitised version available through *MDZ*)

STUDIES

J. Croitoru, *Der Deutschen und der Orient. Faszination, Verachtung und die Widersprüche der Anfklärung*, Munich, 2018, pp. 126-36, 156-60, 176-9, 182-6, 192-5

Rauchstein, *Fremde Vergangenheit*, esp. pp. 212-32

A. Hamilton, '"To rescue the honour of the Germans": Qur'an translations by eighteenth- and early nineteenth-century German Protestants', *Journal of the Warburg and Courtauld Institutes* 77 (2014) 179-203, pp. 181-2, 189, 197, 201-2

M.C. Legaspi, *The death of scripture and the rise of biblical studies*, New York, 2010, pp. 105-28

J. Loop, 'Divine poetry? Early Modern European Orientalists on the beauty of the Koran', *Church History and Religious Culture* 89 (2009) 455-88, pp. 474-5

A. Polaschegg, *Der andere Orientalismus. Regeln deutsch-morgenländischer Imagination im 19. Jahrhundert*, Berlin, 2005, pp. 163-6

Stanisław Grodź

Gottfried Less

DATE OF BIRTH   31 January 1736
PLACE OF BIRTH   Konitz, Pommerellen, West Prussia
(now Chojnice, northern Poland)
DATE OF DEATH   28 August 1797
PLACE OF DEATH   Hannover

BIOGRAPHY

Gottfried Less was born in what was then Konitz, West Prussia, in 1736. After his education at Collegium Fridericianum in Königsberg (1750-2), he studied theology in Jena and Halle. He then lived in Danzig (Gdańsk) between 1758 and 1763 and taught theology in the Akademisches Gymnasium there from 1761. In 1763, he made a study visit to England and on his return moved to Göttingen, taking up a teaching position and becoming a university preacher. He became professor ordinarius (1765) and primarius (1784). He served as the court preacher, *Konsistorialrat* and superintendent in Hannover from 1791, and in the last years of his life was the head of the Hof-Töchter und Söhne-Schule in Hannover.

As a representative of enlightened Lutheran theology, Less wrote many works, including *Handbuch der Christlichen Religionstheorie für Aufgeklärtere. Oder Versuch einer Praktischen Dogmatik* (1789³).

MAIN SOURCES OF INFORMATION

Primary

[J.C.A. Holscher], *Gottfried Leß. Ein biografisches Fragment*, Hannover, 1797

J.G. Meusel, *Lexikon der vom Jahr 1750 bis 1800 verstorbenen teutschen Schriftsteller*, vol. 8, Leipzig, 1808, pp. 165-71

Secondary

A. Beutel, *Kirchengeschichte im Zeitalter der Aufklärung, ein Kompendium*, Göttingen, 2009, p. 145

Art. 'Less, Gottfried', in W. Killy and R. Vierhaus (eds), *Deutsche Biographische Enzyklopädie*, vol. 6, Munich, 1997, 342-3

S. Siebert, art. 'Less, Gottfried', in F.W. Bautz and T. Bautz (eds), *Biographisch-Bibliographisches Kirchenlexikon*, Herzberg, vol. 4, 1992, cols 1543-5

E. Berneburg, art. 'Less, Gottfried', in *Neue Deutsche Biographie*, vol. 14, 1985, 334-5

O. Fambach, *Die Mitarbeiter der Göttingischen Gelehrten Anzeigen, 1769-1836*, Tübingen, 1976, pp. 474-5

WORKS ON CHRISTIAN-MUSLIM RELATIONS

Beweis der Wahrheit der Christlichen Religion
Ueber die Religion
'Proof of the truth of the Christian religion',

DATE   1768-85
ORIGINAL LANGUAGE   German

DESCRIPTION

In these works on Christian apologetics, Less reacts against various opinions (often attacks) on Christianity and argues in favour of its primacy over other religions. At various points he devotes some attention to *Muhammed* – as he calls him – and his religion.

Beweis der Wahrheit der christlichen Religion ('Proof of the truth of the Christian religion') was first published in Göttingen and Bremen in 1768; it is 648 pages long. Expanded editions appeared in 1773, 1774 and 1776 (Cyranka, *Mahomet*, p. 466, n. 3).

After engaging in the controversy on *Fragmente eines Ungenannten* published by G.E. Lessing (1774-8), Less came up with a new book called *Geschichte der Religion* (Göttingen, 1784). This was intended as the first part of a trilogy under the title *Ueber die Religion. Ihre Geschichte, Wahl, und Bestätigung in Dreien Theilen* ('On religion. Its history, selection, and endorsement in three parts'). The second volume, called *Ueber die Religion. Ihre Geschichte, Wahl und Bestätigung. Der Zweite Band, oder Beweis der Wahrheit der christlichen Religion* ('On religion. Its history, selection, and endorsement. The second volume, or Proof of the truth of the Christian religion'; Göttingen, 1785) contained a reworked version of *Beweis der Wahrheit* (the volume has the second title page, *Wahrheit der christlichen Religion*). Apparently, the third volume never appeared. Vols 1 and 2 were republished in 1786.

The passages concerning Muḥammad and his religion appear in *Beweis der Wahrheit der christlichen Religion* (1768) on pp. 627-8 (quoted in Cyranka, *Mahomet*, pp. 467-8), in *Geschichte der Religion* (*Ueber die Religion*, vol. 1, 1784) on pp. 437-67 as § 26, entitled 'Vom Koran der Muhammeder' (excerpts quoted in Cyranka, *Mahomet*, pp. 475, 477-9), and in *Wahrheit der christlichen Religion* (*Ueber die Religion*, vol. 2, 1785) on pp. 633-4 (quoted in Cyranka, *Mahomet*, pp. 470-1).

Defending the Christian religion against its critics from within the western European milieu, Less writes that its accusers praise other religious traditions as better, e.g. J.J. Rousseau on Judaism, Voltaire on Chinese religion, others on Islam. He remarks:

> This is true: Koran, the purported divine book, in which Muḥammad included the precepts of his religion, contains many true teachings about the oneness of God, about life after death, and many beautiful moral [rules]. However, all these right, salutary teachings had been already included in the Christian revelation hundreds of years before him. And the Arab prophet, who collated his religion from the teachings of the Jews, Pagans and Christians, doubtless borrowed them. (*Beweis*, p. 627; Cyranka, *Mahomet*, p. 468)

As the Qur'an was not an original book but a collection compiled from various sources, so Muḥammad was not a true prophet but an alleged messenger of God with no proof of his being sent, who compelled people to believe by force. No particular education is required to see that the Qur'an is full of fallacies (*Irrtümen*). Muḥammad foolishly believed the tale about the seven sleepers (Q 18), repeated fables about Alexander the Great (Q 4), ordered war against unbelievers (Q 9), and encouraged polygyny and arbitrary divorce; 'similar fallacies, harmful, improper to God's tenets and other obvious nonsense can be found in that religion of Muḥammad about which many Naturalists tender such favourable opinions' (*Beweis*, p. 628, Cyranka, *Mahomet*, p. 468).

Cyranka remarks that in Less's first discussion, in *Beweis der Wahrheit der christlichen Religion* (1768), Muḥammad appears as someone who brings compulsiveness/instinctiveness [*Triebhaftigkeit*], violence, and irrationality.

After the *Fragments* controversy, Less applied the concept of rational religion to Christianity more thoroughly. For him, the religion that arose from the New Testament took the highest position as the utterly rational religion (*ganz Reine Vernunft-Religion*) (*Geschichte*, p. 468).

Less reworked the text of *Beweis* and published it as the second volume of the intended trilogy *Ueber der Religion* (1785), entitled *Beweis der Wahrheit der christlichen Religion*. He referred to sources he had not considered earlier, but again rebuked all those who were ready to support any religion only in order to undermine Christianity, and he pointed out that the *muhammedanische* religion found a leading panegyrist in the person of the Count de Boulainvilliers (1658-1722), who claimed that it proposed even better moral precepts than Christianity, though his praises were shallow. The same passage as in *Beweis* ('This is true', *Wahr ist es, der Koran*[...]) comes at the end, with the following summary:

> Briefly, the entire religion – according to its precepts – consists of fasts, recitation of so-called prayers, giving alms and other bodily or merely mechanical actions, which leave the licentious passions in utter calm. This is the religion which some set as parallel to Christianity or even want to give it preference. (*Wahrheit*, p. 634; Cyranka, pp. 470-1)

The final critical judgement passed on Muḥammad's religion did not prevent Less from admitting earlier that the religion of the Arabs and Turks 'teaches many pure and sublime concepts about one true God and God's nature, and morality. It has been accepted by the larger part of the Earth for many centuries' (*Beweis*, pp. 441-2). However, this acknowledgement is made only in the course of affirming the fact that many of these noble elements were taken over from the Old and New Testaments.

He begins paragraph § 26 of *Geschichte der Religion* with praise for the Arab people, who were known for their wit and poetic talents, which are proved by many Arab poets, philosophers and historians (and later the Turks who took over from them). He then describes the religious situation in Arabia at the time of Muḥammad, with Christian groups of different persuasions preparing ground for his coming. He also appreciates some of Muḥammad's followers among the Arabs and Turks as people of great heart, integrity and fidelity, simplicity, humanity and magnanimity (in contrast, the Crusaders attract criticism as a band of fanatics, robbers and murderers who invaded the land to which they had no rights; *Geschichte*, p. 422).

As part of the description of the early life of Muḥammad, Less asks whether the new religion was introduced according to a premeditated plan, or appeared by accident (*Geschichte*, p. 446). Would that be a case of fanaticism (*Schwärmerei*) or deceit (*Bertüg*)? He states that the large amount and variety of information available means that one cannot easily answer these questions. Less is only ready to indicate that Muḥammad had known Christians (particularly a Syrian monk called Bohira [*sic*]) for a long time (a reference to Edward Pococke is given in the text). Muḥammad announced his wish to re-establish the religion of Adam, Noah, Abraham and Jesus (reference to Johann Heinrich Hottinger and to Q 2), and to improve the religion of his compatriots. For that reason, he claimed that he saw apparitions of the angel Gabriel and pretended to receive divine revelations, like some people of old times such as Numa Pompilius, king of ancient Rome. Knowing that Moses and Christ had presented themselves as God's messengers, he did the same, 'perhaps with a good intention, perhaps from a thirst for glory, perhaps from both reasons' (*Geschichte*, p. 448). Less further asserts that there is no reason to consider Muḥammad as a fanatical visionary or a deceiver: Muḥammad sincerely believed – like many of his honest predecessors – that such an invention would be best for his people. 'So, he was erring (*Irrender*) but not a deceiver (*Betrüger*)' (*Geschichte*, p. 449). The same reason that led him to invent revelation caused him to resort to arms to spread his religion. His strong desire to improve the religion of his compatriots was bound up with his wish to rule over them.

> At least at the beginning, his intentions were irreproachable and partly laudable. Whether subsequently power turned him into a cheat and spoiled his character – history does not even now give us enough information to assess this. He saw every atrocity and assassination perhaps not as such but as a harshness for the sake of self-preservation and the common good. (*Geschichte*, pp. 449-50)

The sentence about the lack of information is marked with a footnote in which Less states that many of the most acclaimed authors – D'Herbelot, Marracci, Gagnier, Prideaux, Guthrie – are unjust in perceiving Muḥammad as a fanatical visionary (*Schwärmer*) or deceiver (*Betrüger*).

> If Muḥammad invented his divine revelations – then [the fact] that he did not believe them guarantees to us his good wit and his sober reflection – so he did not do anything different from Numa [Pompilius], Pythagoras and almost all the great noble lawmakers and philosophers of the Greeks and Romans, people whom no impartial observer [*kein Unpartheiischer*] would consider as deceivers, and whom we Christians, according to the precepts of our noble virtues, take rather as erring ones [*Irrende*] and also for honest, virtuous men because of their good intentions and the prevailing integrity of their behaviour. (*Geschichte*, pp. 450-1, Cyranka, *Mahomet*, p. 478)

Less underlines the fact that Muḥammad ended the worship of false gods, introduced the teaching about one true God [*die Lehre von den Einigen Wahren Gott*], and mostly spoke correctly about God's attributes (*Eigenschaften*) and God's providence, and taught good ethical and moral precepts. All this, however, belonged neither to him nor to the Qur'an, but rather he took it from the Bible (pp. 456-7). Further on, Less states that out of 1.1 billion people who live on the earth almost 600 million 'know the one true God and many other virtuous truths of the *Natur-Religion* through the religion of Muḥammad' (*Geschichte*, p. 465). However, Less's assessment of the Qur'an as a book with a claim to contain God's revelation is definitely negative, as he said in a longer passage a few pages earlier: 'Such a book that contains no single truth that has not been known earlier [...] cannot be God's revelation' (*Geschichte*, pp. 462-4).

For Less, the Qur'an contains anti-Trinitarian traits that were introduced by Sabellian, Nestorian or Arian Christians, who passed on their ideas to Muḥammad. Some of them had a clear understanding of religion, but some nurtured fallacies. However, because Muḥammad was an uncultured and lustful man, he preferred the gross, childish and carnal fables of the rabbis.

> And this is *Muhammedanismus*, the religion about which the Qur'an teaches and which is now known to most of the people of the world. What is good and sublime in it, in addition to all the true merits that have been given to Arabia and to a large part of the world, belongs truly not to Muḥammad but to the Bible and especially to Christianity. (*Geschichte*, pp. 466-7)

SIGNIFICANCE

Less mentions Muḥammad and Islam only as examples in his argument in favour of the rationality of Christianity. He admitted that he could give *Muhammedanismus* a reserved positive assessment only because he perceived it as a religion derived from the Old and New Testaments. A very critical assessment of Muḥammad and his religion appears in reaction to those critics of Christianity who attempted to diminish or dismiss it, and pointed to what in their opinion was superior in Islam and other religions.

The number of editions of the three works indicates that they must have had a wide readership. It seems that they were attracting less interest by the end of the 18th century, which was perhaps linked to Less's loss of influence in German academic circles.

Given the time and the context in which they appeared, Less's opinions on Muḥammad and Islam are intriguing. The current entry does them only partial justice, and a more substantial contribution on Less's views is required.

PUBLICATIONS

Gottfried Less, *Beweis der Wahrheit der christlichen Religion*, Göttingen, 1768; H 1336 (digitised version available through *MDZ*)

Gottfried Less, *Bewys der waarheid van den christelyken godsdienst*, trans. J.W. van Haar, The Hague, 1771 (Dutch trans.); OTM: O 06-6872 (digitised version available through Koninklijke Bibliotheek)

Gottfried Less, *Beweis der Wahrheit der christlichen Religion*, Göttingen, 1773², Dogm. 608 (digitised version available through *MDZ*)

Gottfried Less, *Beweis der Wahrheit der christlichen Religion*, Göttingen, 1774[3]

Gottfried Less, *Beweis der Wahrheit der christlichen Religion*, Göttingen, 1776[4]; Dogm. 609 (digitised version available through *MDZ*)

Gottfried Less, *Bewys der waarheid van den christelyken godsdienst*, trans. J.W. van Haar, The Hague, 1778 (Dutch trans.); KW 2212 A 5 (digitised version available through Koninklijke Bibliotheek)

Gottfried Less, *Ueber die Religion, ihre Geschichte, Wahl und Bestätigung*, vol. 1. *Geschichte der Religion*, Göttingen, 1784; Dogm. 606-1 (digitised version available through *MDZ*)

Gottfried Less, *Ueber die Religion, ihre Geschichte, Wahl und Bestätigung*, vol. 2. *Wahrheit der christlichen Religion*, Göttingen, 1785; Dogm. 606-2 (digitised version available through *MDZ*)

Gottfried Less, *Ueber die Religion, ihre Geschichte, Wahl und Bestätigung*, vol. 1. *Geschichte der Religion*, Göttingen, 1786; Dogm. 607-1 (digitised version available through *MDZ*)

Gottfried Less, *Ueber die Religion, ihre Geschichte, Wahl und Bestätigung*, vol. 2. *Wahrheit der christlichen Religion*, Göttingen, 1786; Dogm. 607-2 (digitised version available through *MDZ*)

STUDIES

D. Cyranka, *Mahomet. Repräsentationen des Propheten in deutschsprachigen Texten des 18. Jahrhunderts*, Göttingen, 2018, pp. 466-85

Stanisław Grodź

Johann Traugott Plant

DATE OF BIRTH   9 December 1756
PLACE OF BIRTH   Dresden
DATE OF DEATH   26 October 1794
PLACE OF DEATH   Gera, Thuringia

BIOGRAPHY

Johann Traugott Plant was a poet and novelist, and wrote books about German literature, politics, geography and Islam. Only a few things about his life are known. He was born in Dresden, and studied there and in Leipzig. In Stettin, working as *königl. preussischer Referendar* (royal Prussian official in a law court or administration), he published his first poems, and between 1782 and 1783, he prepared a study on medieval *Minnesänger* literature. Around 1789, he worked in Hamburg, and after 1791 lived as an independent scholar first in Leipzig, and then, from 1793 until his death, in Gera. Eighteenth-century reviewers often attacked him because, for example, he published a work twice with different titles. One of his books was called 'mediocre', another was criticised for its 'tasteless wittiness' (*abgeschmackter Witz*). An especially malicious commentary by an anonymous author in the periodical *Allgemeine deutsche Bibliothek* (1793, p. 184) says that if Plant's books were really well received by the public, as was sometimes said, then the taste of the century must be even lower than the reviewer had thought in the first place. Are these critical judgements just? Yes, and the worst point was not even mentioned: Plant plagiarized and lied, especially in his works about Islam.

Throughout his career, Plant published belles-lettres works. His novel in the form of letters, *Karl und Julie* (1782), reminds one of Goethe's *Werther* (1774). The novel about the Persian hero *Hiran* (1794) is modelled after Montesquieu's *Lettres persanes* (first German trans. 1759) and Voltaire's *Candide* (translated into German in 1776). His 1782 volume about German medieval *Minnesänger* poets is also imitative, relying on recently published works about the *Manessische Liederhandschrift*, a manuscript of mediaeval songs, by Johann Jacob Bodmer and Johann Jakob Breitinger (*Proben der alten schwäbischen Poesie*, 1784) and others.

Through the years 1787-92, Plant offered a series of works on politics, history and Islam. Most notable for the field of Christian-Muslim relations is, first, *Unpartheiische Charakteristik* ('Impartial characteristic'), published with the variant title *Freimüthige Briefe* ('Outspoken letters'). The second is *Birghilu risale*, also published with two variant titles: *Ist die muhammedanische Religion an sich böse und verwerflicht?* ('Is the Muḥammadan religion evil and dangerous as such?') and *Türkischer Catechismus* ('Turkish catechism'). Both works copy without acknowledgement from Christian Daniel Beck's (1757-1832) *Allgemeine schilderung des ottomanischen Reichs* (vol. 1, Leipzig, 1788), which is a partial translation of Ignatius Mouradgea d'Ohsson's (1740-1807) *Tableau général de l'Empire othoman* (2 vols, Paris, 1788). Plant says that the *Birghilu risale* was translated by a certain C.H. Ziegler in Istanbul, which is a plain lie.

In his geographical work about Polynesia from 1793, which in fact covers Southeast Asia in a broad sense, Plant claims that he relied on two friends, traders in the region, who supplied him with information, but he does not say who they were or what he learned from them. He does not generally name his sources, but he certainly knew, for example, William Marsden's *The history of Sumatra* (London, 1783). Though an important religion in this area, Islam is rarely mentioned by Plant, the most notable reference being on p. 403, where he says that in some places 'Muslims live who are lazy to an extent that disgusts the European'.

The hero of the 1794 novel *Hiran* is a Persian whose high moral standards prevent him from ever lying. For his honesty he is punished by the ruling shah of Persia and leaves the country in a westerly direction, via Turkey and Damascus to Europe, where most of the novel's action takes place. His critical view of Europe is a reminder of *Candide*, but more interesting here is his description of Oriental Muslim characters: a scholar and mufti whom he meets in Diyarbakir is a deeply dishonest person; the people of Damascus are ignorant in the extreme and honour those who falsely boast of knowledge, so that they regard an idiot as a philosopher.

Plant probably thought that, by using familiar topoi on Islam and offering common positive and negative judgements, he could attract the reading public and sell his books. Given his treatment of Islam with all its plagiarising, Plant does not play an independent role in the history of Christian-Muslim relations.

MAIN SOURCES OF INFORMATION

Primary
Johann Traugott Plant, *Launenhafte, zärtliche und moralische Gedichte*, Stettin, 1782

Johann Traugott Plant, *Chronologischer, biographischer und kritischer Entwurf einer Geschichte der deutschen Dichtkunst und Dichter von den ältesten Zeiten bis aufs Jahr 1782*, Stettin, 1782 (in some volumes the two works are combined)

Johann Traugott Plant, *Karl und Julie. Eine Geschichte in Briefen*, Frankfurt, 1782

Johann Traugott Plant, *Die Akademische Liebe oder Röschens und Fritzchens Geschichte*, Stettin, 1783

Johann Traugott Plant, *Publizistische Übersicht aller Regierungsarten sämtlicher Staaten und Völkerschaften auf der Welt*, Berlin, 1788

Johann Traugott Plant, *Türkisches Staats-Lexicon, oder vollständige und wahre Erklärungen aller türkischen Staats- und Hofbedienungen im Militair- Civil und geistlichen Stande, und richtige Vergleichung derselben mit unsern Bedienungen von gleichem Range: nebst andern den Hof und Sultan, die Politik, [...] betreffenden Dingen, und einer Geschichte des Propheten Muhammeds, des Korans und des jetzigen Kaisers Abd-ul-Hamids*, Hamburg, 1789

Johann Traugott Plant, *Abhandlung und Raisonnements über die teutsche Reichsregierung und Wahlfolge des Oesterreichischen Hauses in der römisch-teutschen Kaiserwürde*, Germanien, 1790

Johann Traugott Plant, *Schon wieder ein Kaiser aus dem Oesterreichischen Hause? [...] oder freim üthige Aufklärung über die Kaiserwahl Leopolds II.*, [s.l.], 1790 (same text as *Abhandlung*)

Johann Traugott Plant, *Unpartheiische Charakteristik der Türkischen Reichs-Verfassung und des Verhältnisses seiner Macht gegen andere Staaten Europens und Asiens im jezigen Zeitraum*, Berlin, 1790

Johann Traugott Plant, *Freimüthige Briefe über gegenwärtige Verfassung und Regierungsform, Stärke und Schwäche der europäischen Staaten*, Otahiti, 1790 (same text as *Unpartheiische Charakteristik*)

Johann Traugott Plant, *Birghilu risale oder Elementarbuch der muhammedanischen Glaubenslehre / nach dem Arabischen des Nedschmuddin Omar Nessefy. Nebst Komm. u. erklärenden Zusätzen von Johann Traugott Plant*, Ißlambul-Genf [Leipzig], 1790

Johann Traugott Plant, *Ist die muhammedanische Religion an sich böse und verwerflich? Hat sie Aehnlichkeiten mit der christlichen? Verdient sie nach der christlichen den ersten Rang?*, Ratiopolis, 1790

Johann Traugott Plant, *Türkischer Catechismus der Muhammedanischen Religion / Nach dem arabischen Original übersetzt von C. H. Ziegler mit erklärenden Zusätzen vermehrt*, Hamburg, 1792 (this and the two preceding are identical texts)

Anonymous reviewer, 'Plant, J.T. Romantische Erzählungen und Gedichte', *Neue allgemeine deutsche Bibliothek* 3 (1793) 183-6

Johann Traugott Plant, *Erato und Euterpe, oder zärtliche scherzhafte und komische Lieder zur Unterhaltung beym Clavier*, Hamburg, 1790

Johann Traugott Plant, *Warum sprechen die Menschen in ihren gesellschaftlichen Unterhaltungen so wenig von Gott?*, Leipzig, 1791

Johann Traugott Plant, *Kupido's Mobiliar-Verloosung*, [s.l.], 1791

Johann Traugott Plant, *Vorrede zu Taube, F. A. Consuls in Constantinopel, comfpectus iuris scientiae turcicae, oder Uebersicht der türkischen Rechtswissenschaft*, Leipzig, 1792

Johann Traugott Plant, *Schriften über das türkische Reich und die Muhamedanische Religion*, Leipzig, 1792 (three earlier works in one volume)

Johann Traugott Plant, *Romantische Erzählungen und Gedichte komischen und zärtlichen Inhalts*, Leipzig, 1793

Johann Traugott Plant, *Handbuch einer vollständigen Erdbeschreibung und Geschichte Polynesiens oder des fünften Erdtheils*, vol. 1, Leipzig, 1793

Johann Traugott Plant, *Hirans komische Abenteuer und Wanderungen auf dem Welttheater: Ein Kumpan des Faustins, Erasmus Schleichers, Paul Ysops und Johann Bunckels*, Gera, 1794

G.S. Rötger (ed.), *Nekrolog für Freunde deutscher Litteratur*, Helmstädt, 1799, pp. 152-4

J.G. Meusel, *Lexikon der vom Jahr 1750 bis 1800 verstorbenen Teutschen Schriftsteller*, vol. 10. *N-Qu*, Leipzig, 1810, pp. 445-8

Secondary

A. Aurnhammer, art. 'Plant, Johann Traugott', in *Killy Literaturlexikon*, vol. 9, Berlin, 2010, 255

K. Kreiser, 'Einleitung', in Johann Traugott Plant, *Türkisches Staats-Lexicon oder vollständige und wahre Erklärungen aller türkischen Staats- und Hofbedienungen*[...], ed. K. Kreiser, Melle, 2005, v-xix

WORKS ON CHRISTIAN-MUSLIM RELATIONS

Türkisches Staats-Lexicon
'Lexicon of the Turkish state'

DATE 1789
ORIGINAL LANGUAGE German

DESCRIPTION

Plant says that he wrote the *Staatslexikon* (in full, *Türkisches Staats-Lexicon, oder vollständige und wahre Erklärungen aller türkischen Staats- und Hofbedienungen im Militair-, Civil- und geistlichen Stande, und richtige Vergleichung derselben mit unsern Bedienungen von gleichem Range, nebst andern den Hof und Sultan, die Politik, Regierung, das Kriegswesen, die*

Finanzen, die Münzen, Gesetze, Religion, Moral, Künste, Wissenschaften, Industrie, Handlung, Sprache, Sitten, Zeitvertreibe, Galanterien und das gemeine Leben der Türken. Betreffenden Dingen, und einer Geschichte des Propheten Muhammeds, des Korans und des jetzigen Kaisers Abd-ul-Hamids, aus den sichersten Quellen für Zeitungsleser und Freunde der Staaten- und Völkerkunde, in alphabetischer Ordnung abgefaßt) because he perceived a lack of information about the Ottoman Empire among the German public. It is 194 pages long in the 1789 Hamburg edition. Plant also wanted to correct prejudices and improve negative images of Ottomans.

He mostly treats the Ottoman Empire's administration and military, and only a few specifically Islamic terms occur, such as 'Charadsch' (originally from the Arabic *kharāj*, a form of tax in Islamic law, pp. 39-40 in the 1789 edition) and 'Derwische' (dervish, a Muslim ascetic pp. 47-50). His articles about the 'Koran' (pp. 110-15) and 'Muhammed' (pp. 129-34), five pages each, give both factual information and critical assessments. The Qur'an, he says, is an unorganised book containing absurd stories, though it also contains some wisdom. Muḥammad fabricated miracles *durch einige Kenntnisse in der Experimental-Physik* ('using his knowledge in experimental physics', p. 131), and was 'a damned imposter', though not evil . He should be considered a major figure of his time, who propagated some *edle Tugendlehren* ('noble moral teachings', p. 134) that were successful *durch ihre unleugbaren Vorzüge vor dem Heidenthum und schändlichen Götzendienst* ('because of their undeniable advantages over the heathens and the shameful cult of idols', p. 133). Plant poses as an *Aufklärer* (representative of Enlightenment thought) against superstition in religion in general, and in Islam in particular. He claims objectivity, and states that he only attacks Muḥammad for what deserves criticism.

SIGNIFICANCE

Klaus Kreiser, in the only modern research on the *Staatslexikon*, praises the book for its 'fair treatment' of the Ottomans and Islam. That being said, it reproduces topoi that were current in Plant's time. It was obviously not regarded by its readers as an independent contribution, and it left no significant trace in Orientalist literature.

PUBLICATIONS

Johann Traugott Plant, *Türkisches Staats-Lexicon, oder vollständige und wahre Erklärungen aller türkischen Staats- und Hofbedienungen im Militair- Civil und geistlichen Stande, und richtige Vergleichung derselben mit unsern Bedienungen von gleichem Range: nebst andern den Hof und Sultan, die Politik, [...] betreffenden Dingen, und einer Geschichte des Propheten Muhammeds, des Korans und des jetzigen Kaisers Abd-ul-Hamids,* Hamburg, 1789; Turc. 107 a (digitised version available through *MDZ*)

Johann Traugott Plant, *Türkisches Staats-Lexicon, für Zeitungsleser und Freunde der Staaten- und Völkerkunde,* Weissenfels, 1793²

Johann Traugott Plant, *Türkisches Staats-Lexicon oder vollst ändige und wahre Erklärungen aller türkischen Staats- und Hofbedienungen*[...], ed. K. Kreiser, Melle, 2005

STUDIES

Kreiser, 'Einleitung'

Unpartheiische Charakteristik
'Impartial characteristic'

DATE 1790

ORIGINAL LANGUAGE German

DESCRIPTION

The text, published twice under two different titles, *Unpartheiische Charakteristik* (in full, *Unpartheiische Charakteristik der Türkischen Reichs-Verfassung und des Verhältnisses seiner Macht gegen andere Staaten Europens und Asiens im jezigen Zeitraum*) and *Freimüthige Briefe über gegenwärtige Verfassung und Regierungsform, Stärke und Schwäche der europäischen Staaten,* consists of 22 fictional letters written to a person addressed as *theuerster freund* ('dearest friend'). In the publication entitled *Freimüthige Briefe* it is 104 pages long.

What Plant has to say about the Ottoman Empire and Islam is mostly copied from Christian Daniel Beck's *Allgemeine Schilderung des ottomanischen Reichs,* which was translated from d'Ohsson's *Tableau général de l'Empire othoman.* From this source comes the information that the Ottoman Empire rested on two normative realms, the dogmatic and the juridical. The dogmatic side is represented by the *Profession of faith* of Najm al-Dīn ʿUmar al-Nasafī (1067-1142), the juridical side by *Multaqā l-abḥur* ('The confluence of the seas') by Ibrāhīm al-Ḥalabī (d. 1549). D'Ohsson translated both into French, and Beck translated them from the French into German. Plant plagiarised from this translation in his fictional letters, concentrating on the juridical basis of the empire that was represented in the *Multaqā*, a work that was an important legal manual in the Ottoman Empire, not only in al-Ḥalabī's own time but until at least the 18th century.

In Beck's book, Plant found a summary of al-Ḥalabī's work and a translation of its first chapters, starting with the subject of ablutions, then prayer and so on until the chapters on 'mosques' and 'endowments'. Plant comments on this, posing as a specialist in Islamic law, although most of what he says is copied from Beck. Only rarely do sentences of his own occur, such as 'Islamic law is similar to Roman law', a statement for which he gives no evidence.

SIGNIFICANCE

Before d'Ohsson's translation of the *Multaqā*, information about Islamic law in the Ottoman Empire came mostly from European reports rather than original sources. His translation is one of the oldest, or maybe the oldest, of a Muslim Arabic juridical text into a western European language. Neither he nor Plant knew that they were part of a very early phase of research about Muslim law.

Yet Plant was neither researcher nor translator, but a plagiariser. His role in the history of Orientalist research was later forgotten. The Austrian Orientalist Joseph Freiherr von Hammer-Purgstall (1774-1856), who treats the *Multaqā* following d'Ohsson (*Des osmanischen Reichs Staatsverfassung und Staatsverwaltung: dargestellt aus den Quellen seiner Grundgesetze*, Vienna, 1815) does not mention Plant's work.

PUBLICATIONS

Johann Traugott Plant, *Unpartheiische Charakteristik der Türkischen Reichs-Verfassung und des Verhältnisses seiner Macht gegen andere Staaten Europens und Asiens im jezigen Zeitraum*, Berlin, 1790; VD18 11862858 (digitised version available through Thüringer Universitäts- und Landesbibliothek Jena)

Johann Traugott Plant, *Freimüthige Briefe über gegenwärtige Verfassung und Regierungsform, Stärke und Schwäche der europäischen Staaten*, Otahiti [Leipzig], 1790; J.publ.e. 65 f (digitised version available through *MDZ*)

Birghilu risale
'The treatise written by Birghilu'

DATE 1790
ORIGINAL LANGUAGE German

DESCRIPTION

Birghilu risale (in full, *Birghilu risale oder Elementarbuch der Muhammedanischen Glaubenslehren. Nach dem Arabischen des Nedschmuddin Omar Nessefy nebst Kommentar und erklärenden Zusätzen von Johann Traugott Plant*) is described by Plant in *Türkisches Staats-Lexicon* as *eine Art Katechismus, oder kurzer Inhalt der Vorschriften der Religion und Gebete der Türken* ('a sort of catechism or short overview of the Turkish rules of religion and prayers'). The work was published under three different titles (the other two being *Ist die muhammedanische Religion an sich böse und verwerflich? Hat sie Aehnlichkeiten mit der christlichen? Verdient sie nach der christlichen den ersten Rang?* and *Türkischer Catechismus der Muhammedanischen Religion*) with identical text, in 1790 and 1792; it is 172 pages in length.

Plant's text was not a catechism but a creed composed by the Arab author Najm al-Dīn al-Nasafī (1067-1142), which was often read together with the commentary by Saʿd al-Dīn al-Taftāzānī (1322-90). The creed and commentary were well-known in Ottoman intellectual circles, and were typical Muslim statements of faith with nothing exceptional in their contents. They had recently been translated into French by the Swede of Armenian descent, Ignatius Mouradgea d'Ohsson (1740-1807) in his *Tableau général de l'Empire othomane* (vol. 1, Paris, 1788, pp. 57-9), which was translated into German by Christian Daniel Beck (1757-1837) in *Allgemeine Schilderung des ottomanischen Reichs* (vol. 1, Leipzig, 1788, pp. 41-4). Plant copied this, rearranging the structure and making a few changes. For example, where Beck (p. 55) translates 'Qur'an' as *das Lesen (oder gelesenes Buch)* ('reading, or a book that is read'), Plant (*Birghilu risale*, p. 37) says that it means *nothwendige Lektüre* ('necessary reading'). He also compares the Muslim creed with German catechisms and says it is better arranged. Later (p. 134) he refers to the Muslim ban on fortune-telling as *kluges Gesetz Muhammeds* ('a wise law of Muḥammad') but concedes that fortune-telling still existed in Islam. He also refers to the *fanatisch sinnlicher Geschmack der moslemischen Völker* ('the fanatical voluptuous taste of the Muslim peoples') (p. 160).

SIGNIFICANCE

The Christian d'Ohsson was the first European Orientalist to translate the creed of al-Nasafī. An edition of the Arabic text, *Pillar of the creed of the Sunnites* (London, 1843), was prepared by William Cureton (1808-64). An English translation by E.E. Elder followed, *A commentary on the creed of Islam* (London, 1950). The fact that none of these authors mentions Plant is an eloquent attestation to its lack of influence.

PUBLICATIONS

Johann Traugott Plant, *Birghilu risale oder Elementarbuch der muhammedanischen Glaubenslehre / nach dem Arabischen des Nedschmuddin Omar Nessefy. Nebst Komm. u. erklärenden Zusätzen von Johann Traugott Plant*, Ißlambul-Genf [Leipzig], 1790

Johann Traugott Plant, *Ist die muhammedanische Religion an sich böse und verwerflich? Hat sie Aehnlichkeiten mit der christlichen? Verdient sie nach der christlichen den ersten Rang?*, Ratiopolis, 1790

Johann Traugott Plant, *Türkischer Catechismus der Muhammedanischen Religion / Nach dem arabischen Original übersetzt von C. H. Ziegler mit erklärenden Zusätzen vermehrt*, Hamburg, 1792

STUDIES

Anonymous reviewer, 'Plant, J.T. Romantische Erzählungen und Gedichte', *Neue allgemeine deutsche Bibliothek* 3 (1793) 183-6

Ralf Elger

South-Eastern Europe

Pavao Ritter Vitezović

DATE OF BIRTH   7 January 1652
PLACE OF BIRTH   Senj, Croatia
DATE OF DEATH   20 January 1713
PLACE OF DEATH   Vienna

BIOGRAPHY

Pavao Ritter Vitezović, from Senj on the Croatian coast, was a writer and historian. His father, originally from Alsace, was an officer serving on the Habsburg military border, and his mother was Croatian. He was educated in the Jesuit gymnasium in Zagreb and later acquired further knowledge in history and geography in informal ways. After visiting Rome, and then staying with the Slovenian humanist Johann Weichard von Valvasor between 1676 and 1677 at his castle at Wagensberg (Bogenšperk in Carniola), where he produced a number of engravings of castles and towns in Carniola and Croatia, he returned to his hometown of Senj in 1678.

In the war against the Ottomans in 1683, Vitezović fought in battles along the Drava River, and also in the vicinity of Siget. But his military career was short and he entered politics. He was chosen as representative of his home town in the Hungarian diet, and in the years 1684-7 he represented the Croatian *ban* (viceroy) and diet in Vienna. In 1690, he moved to Zagreb. Four years later, the Croatian diet entrusted him with the establishment of a printing shop, but the success of this enterprise was limited: Vitezović produced only four books, all of which he himself wrote.

The end of the Viennese War in 1699 allowed him to resume his political activities. As representative of the Croatian diet, he participated in the commission to define the new borders with the Ottoman Empire and the Republic of Venice. On his return to Zagreb in 1701, he could find no paid position, and in 1706 his house was destroyed in a fire that also damaged his printing shop. Because of a legal dispute over an estate near Zagreb, he moved to Vienna, where he spent his last years in poverty. His only possessions at the time of his death were his manuscripts.

Vitezović wrote in both Croatian and Latin. He was the author of a Latin-Croatian dictionary, and his orthography and vocabulary influenced Croatian language reforms in the early 19th century. He also wrote a large amount of poetry and a number of historical works.

MAIN SOURCES OF INFORMATION

Secondary

V. Budišćak, 'Treće Vitezovićevo izdanje *Odiljenja sigetskog* (1695)' [The third
    edition of Vitezović's Odiljenje sigetsko (1695)], *Kaj* 49/5-6 (2016) 82-104

V. Budišćak, 'Poganska sila. Slika Turaka u Vitezovićevu *Odiljenju sigetskom*' [The
    pagan force. The picture of the Turks in Vitezović's *Odiljenje sigetsko*],
    Senjski Zbornik 40 (2013) 343-62

D. Dukić, *Sultanova djeca. Predodžbe Turaka u hrvatskoj književnosti ranog
    novovjekovlja* [The Sultan's children. Images of Turks in early modern
    Croatian literature], Zadar, 2004, pp. 155-8

Z. Blažević, *Vitezovićeva Hrvatska između stvarnosti i utopije* [Vitezović's Croatia
    between reality and utopia], Zagreb, 2002

C.A. Simpson, 'Pavao Ritter Vitezović, defining national identity in the Baroque
    age,' London, 1991 (PhD Diss. University of London)

J. Vončina, 'Pavao Ritter Vitezović', in J. Vončina (ed.), *Zrinski – Frankopan
    – Vitezović, Izabrana djela* [Selected writings]. *Pet stoljeća hrvatske
    književnosti* [Five centuries of Croatian literature], Zagreb, vol. 17, 1976,
    337-56

V. Klaić, *Život i djela Pavla Rittera Vitezovića* [The life and works of Pavao Ritter
    Vitezović], Zagreb, 1914

WORKS ON CHRISTIAN-MUSLIM RELATIONS

Odiljenje Sigetsko
'Siget's farewell'

DATE   1684
ORIGINAL LANGUAGE   Croatian

DESCRIPTION

Odiljenje sigetsko ('Siget's farewell', meaning that the fortress of Siget bids
farewell to the widows of the men who were killed defending it) is a
poem about the siege of Siget in southern Hungary in 1566. It was first
published in Linz in 1684. It begins with a Latin dedication to Count
Adam Zrinski, followed by a short introduction written in prose together
with 16 verses of poetry, and then the poem itself in four parts consisting of 2,314 verses. The siege was famous for two reasons: first, almost all
the defenders, including their commander, the Croatian *ban* (viceroy)
Nikola Zrinski, perished rather than surrender to the Ottomans; and second, the great losses suffered among the Ottoman soldiers, together with

the death of Sultan Süleyman, prevented the Ottomans from advancing towards Vienna. In Croatia, it was believed that the majority of the 2,300 or so defenders were Croats, and Nikola Zrinski acquired mythical status among his countrymen almost immediately after his death.

Vitezović's poem was not the first literary account of the siege of Siget, and for a long time it was considered by literary historians as a work with little, if any, artistic value. Only recently, since the 1990s, have critics recognised the originality of the poem because of its form, its intention and the way in which Vitezović managed to reach both educated readers (mostly noble officers and clergy, who could recognise the poem's various metric forms) and the less educated (who could enjoy sequences written in a more popular style). Unlike earlier and later authors, Vitezović starts his poem by describing not the beginning of the siege, but rather its end. This is because *Odiljenje* was conceived as a continuation of or a reference to another epic, the *Opsida Sigecka* ('The siege of Siget'), written by Petar Zrinski, the great-grandson of Nikola, and published in Venice in 1660 as part of his *Adrianskoga mora sirena* ('The mermaid of the Adriatic Sea').

The poem is composed of four very different parts. Vitezović claimed that it remained unfinished and that he was planning to write another three parts, but it is more likely that he had some reason not to present it as a completed work. In the first part, after addressing the reader, he gives his voice to the fortress of Siget itself, a poetic innovation. The fortress speaks to the women of Croatia about the bravery of their husbands, sons and brothers, who all fell defending it. Then Nikola Zrinski speaks to his son and vice versa.

This form of 'conversation' continues throughout the second part, in which Nikola addresses the king, the country, Siget, and his soldiers, receiving answers from all of them. In the same way, Siget talks to its defenders, the king and the Roman Church, with a reply coming from the king. The fortress ponders about itself, and it is praised by the Croatian fairy. This part ends with a conversation between an imaginary lady, Sophia, and an eagle that belongs to Zrinski.

The third part is a conversation between a traveller arriving at Siget at a later time and asking about the battle and the fate of the fortress after it fell to the Ottomans, and an echo that gives him brief answers (a typical baroque figure).

The final part consists of 38 epitaphs written in different metric forms, starting with four for Sultan Süleyman, followed by two for Nikola Zrinski. A further 30 are dedicated to various Christian and Ottoman heroes who fell in the battle and are mentioned in *Opsida sigecka*. Finally, two are for Siget itself.

The attitude towards the Ottomans, or the 'Turks' as Vitezović calls them, is similar to that in *Kronika*. There is no sign of contempt or disregard. On the contrary, Vitezović often praises their bravery, and their display of some sort of knightly ethical code: the combatants are brave men fighting each other. That does not mean, however, that he has no negative feelings towards the pagans, as he sometimes calls them, who worship the moon and are bloodthirsty. He blames them for the deaths of many Christians and the sad state of Siget.

Of course, the central theme is the heroism of the defenders of Siget, who willingly sacrified their lives for their homeland and the Christian faith. These two – homeland and Christianity – often appear together in Vitezović's verses, sometimes accompanied by reference to the king. The defence of Siget is compared to the defence of Troy, and the lady Sophia equates Turks with Greeks.

It seems that the reason for the composition of the poem was not animosity towards Muslims, but, as Vitezović himself explains in the foreword to the second edition (Vienna, 1685), his desire to preserve the Croatian language and nation. Another component of this patriotic programme was the praise of Zrinski and his family. Hence his dedication of the work to the young Adam Zrinski, who for many was a last symbol of the independence that the country had earlier enjoyed. It seems that this dedication provoked criticism, because Vitezović withdrew almost the whole edition (though some claim it was sold out) and presented a second edition with a different dedication. Finally, in 1695, Vitezović printed a new edition in Zagreb, this time dedicated to the commander who expelled the Ottomans from Siget, Colonel Ivan Andrija Makar.

SIGNIFICANCE

In a literary sense, it seems that *Odiljenje* had no influence on later Croatian writers. However, Vitezović can be considered one of the first authors to express Croatian nationalism, so that his writings, including *Odiljenje*, influenced the ideology of the movement to construct the Croatian nation in the first half of the 19th century. This is also evidenced by the printing of another edition of *Odiljenje* in Zagreb in 1836.

PUBLICATIONS

Pavao Ritter Vitezović, *Oddilyenje sigetsko, tuliko razlicsitom kuliko necsujenom dosle Hërvatske risme lipotom spravlyeno po Plemenitom i Hrabrenomu Gospodinu Pavlu Vitezovichu aliti Ritter, Hërvatskomu i Senyskomu vlastelinu, slavnog Vojvostva Ricardijanskoga*

Capitanu, U Lincu [Linz]: kalupom Gaspara Frajsmidovicha, Letta
Gospod, 1684

Pavao Ritter Vitezović, *Oddilyenje sigetsko,* Zagreb, 1695

Pavao Ritter Vitezović, *Oddiljenja Sigetskoga čentiri děla. S uvodom
životu Nikole kneza Zrinjskoga,* Zagreb, 1836

Pavao Ritter Vitezović, *Oddilyenje sigetsko,* Zagreb, 1971

Odiljenje sigetsko, in *Zrinski – Frankopan – Vitezović. Izabrana djela*
[Selected writings], ed. J. Vončina, *Pet stoljeća hrvatske književnosti*
[Five centuries of Croatian literature], vol. 17, Zagreb, 1976,
357-431

STUDIES

P. Pavličić, *Epika granice* [The border epics], Zagreb, 2007, pp. 253-84

Z. Kravar, *Das Barock in der kroatischen Literatur,* Cologne, 1991,
pp 236-43

Vončina, 'Pavao Ritter Vitezović'

Klaić, *Život i djela Pavla Rittera Vitezovića,* pp. 61-2

Kronika aliti spomen vsega svijeta vikov
'Chronicle, or the remembrance of ages of the entire world'

DATE 1696

ORIGINAL LANGUAGE Croatian

DESCRIPTION

Kronika aliti spomen vsega svijeta vikov ('Chronicle, or the remembrance
of ages of the entire world') was published in Zagreb in 1696. It has eight
introductory pages and 222 pages of text. Vitezović points out that he
has relied on his predecessor, Antun Vramec, who composed his *Short
chronicle* in Croatian in 1578, though he makes additions and corrects
many mistakes. For the Middle Ages and the major part of the 16th century, he relies on a number of Croatian authors, but it is not clear which
sources he uses for the period after 1578. His work follows the traditional
form of histories of this kind, starting with God's creation of the world,
though he does not divide the period before the birth of Christ into eras
but presents it as a continuum up to the year 3961, followed by the new
age from the year 1 to 1690.

Vitezović wrote the chronicle in Croatian because he wanted to reach
a broader and less educated audience than would be able to access a
Latin text, and, since his work should be considered as an expression of

the political ideas and attitudes of the Croatian estates after their successes in the wars against the Ottoman Empire and the liberation of large parts of Slavonia, it is not surprising that he should cover both Croatian and Slavonian history in an attempt to construct both the past and the territorial extent of a nascent Croatian nation. What the reader would maybe not expect is his attitude towards the 'Turks'.

Despite the fact that the Croats had been fighting against the Ottomans for more than two centuries (Vitezović describes this in another work, *Plorantis Croatiae saecula duo carmine descripta*, Zagreb, 1703), he makes few negative remarks about the traditional enemy. His descriptions of battles, regardless of whether they were won or lost by the Christian side, are usually neutral, mentioning only facts without any evaluation. Only rarely does he use terms such as 'unfaithful pagans', as when he describes the fall of Gyula in 1566 to the Ottomans, who promised the defenders free passage but then slaughtered all who surrendered, and only once does he mention that Christian churches were destroyed by the conquerors, after the fall of Chios in 1566. On the contrary, for Vitezović the 'Turks' are brave and virtuous knights, like those who fell in 1593 at the battle of Sisak, the first important Christian victory, or in the triumph of Petar Zrinski in 1654 at the battle of Jurjeve Stijene. Even when he describes the events of the war in which he himself took part, he recognises Turkish heroism in the defence of Udbina in 1689.

His attitude towards Islam appears to be similarly neutral. He does not mention Muḥammad and refers to 'Saracens' for the first time under the year 640 and the conquest of Persia and some Roman provinces. He makes no use of the words 'Muslim' or 'Islam' and it is mostly because he describes 'our' side as Christian that it can be inferred that the other side are Muslims. Reporting on the situation after the Christian seizure of Udbina, Vitezović claims that most of the 'Turks' had their heads baptised but in their hearts they remained Turkish, thus revealing that, for him, 'Turk' and 'Muslim' are synonyms.

Vitezović does not give an explanation for this largely positive image of the 'Turks' in his *Kronika*. We might imagine that it was because he was influenced by the memory of Muslim families in Bosnia who remembered their Christian origins and even maintained contacts with relatives on the other side of the military border. On the other hand, his idea of a large Croatian nation spreading from the Holy Roman Empire to Bulgaria might have prevented him from demonising Bosnian Muslims, who were potential members of this imagined possibility.

SIGNIFICANCE

With his concepts of Croatian history and the idea of a Croatian nation living in the territories of Croatia proper, Dalmatia and Slavonia, Vitezović laid the foundations for the creation of a Croatian national ideology. His influence on Croatian intellectuals in the 18th century and the ideologues of the Croatian national movement in the first half of the 19th century can hardly be overestimated. His *Kronika* was published twice in the 18th century, in 1744 and 1762, both times supplemented with descriptions of events up to the year of publication.

PUBLICATIONS

Pavao Ritter Vitezović, *Kronika aliti szpomen vszega szvieta vikov u dva dela razredyen; koterih pervi, dershi od pocsetka szvieta, do Kristusevoga porojenja, druggi, od Kristusevoga porojenja do izpunyenja letta 1690 szloshen i na svitlo dan po Pavlu Vitezovichu zlatnomu vitezu*, Zagreb, 1696; RIID-8-163 (digitised version available through NSK Zagreb)

Pavao Ritter Vitezović, *Kronika aliti szpomen vszega szvieta vikov u dva dela razredyen*, Zagreb, 1744

Pavao Ritter Vitezović, *Kronika aliti szpomen vszega szvieta vikov u dva dela razredyen*, Zagreb, 1762

Pavao Ritter Vitezović, *Kronika aliti spomen vsega svieta vikov*, ed. Alojz Jembrih, Zagreb, 2015

STUDIES

S. Antoljak, *Hrvatska historiografija do 1918* [Croatian historiography up to 1918], vol. 1, Zagreb, 1992, pp. 206-8

Klaić, *Život i djela Pavla Rittera Vitezovića*, pp. 105-12

F. Šišić, *Priručnik izvora hrvatske historije* [A handbook of sources for Croatian history], Zagreb, 1914, pp. 62-3

Neven Budak

Dositheos of Jerusalem

DATE OF BIRTH   31 May 1641
PLACE OF BIRTH   Arachoba, Northern Peloponnese
(present-day Exochi)
DATE OF DEATH   7 February 1707
PLACE OF DEATH   Constantinople

BIOGRAPHY

The future patriarch Dositheos II of Jerusalem was born on 31 May 1641, son of Nikolaos Skarpetēs and his wife Anna, in the village of Arachoba in the Northern Peloponnese (present-day Exochi). His baptismal name is unknown.

In August 1657, Patriarch Païsios of Jerusalem (r. 1645-60) admitted Dositheos, deacon since 1652, into his service. On 6 April 1661, Patriarch Nektarios of Jerusalem (r. 1661-9) appointed Dositheos archdeacon, and on 23 October 1666, Dositheos was ordained metropolitan of Kaisareia in Palestine, though on 13 January 1669, at the request of Patriarch Nektarios, the patriarchal synod in Constantinople transferred him to the patriarchate of Jerusalem as Patriarch Dositheos II (r. 1669-1707). In March 1672, Dositheos assembled a synod of the episcopate and the clergy of his patriarchate, first in Bethlehem and then in Jerusalem. In the first part of the Acts of this synod is a refutation of the pro-Calvinistic Confession of Faith of Patriarch Kyrillos Loukarēs of Constantinople (r. 1620-38), while the second part consists of a detailed Confession of Faith, composed by Dositheos himself and therefore called *Confessio Dosithei*, divided into 18 articles and four questions. In rejection of Calvinistic tendencies, Dositheos emphasises the importance of the episcopal office and of the seven sacraments.

In 1674, a conflict arose between Dositheos and the Franciscan friars in Jerusalem, who with the support of the French ambassador in Constantinople were trying to gain complete control over the Church of the Holy Sepulchre and other holy places in the city. In the 30 years between 1677 and his death in 1707, Dositheos travelled to or stayed in Constantinople and in the Romanian principalities of Moldavia and Wallachia. In Wallachia, he acquired the monastery of the Holy Apostles in Bucharest and other monasteries, and in Moldavia the monasteries of Bistriţa, Caşin, Hlincea, Mărgineni, and Probota.

In 1680, he purchased a printing press, which was set up first in Iaşi and later in the monastery of Cetăţuia. This enabled him to publish a refutation of papal primacy in 1682, written by his predecessor Nektarios (*Peri tēs archēs tou papa antirrēsis*). In 1690 followed the refutation of the pro-Calvinistic Confession of Faith of Kyrillos Loukarēs, written by the monk and priest Meletios Syrigos (1585-1664), together with a revised version of his own Confession of Faith. Over the next two decades, he compiled three voluminous collections of texts of Byzantine and post-Byzantine Greek theological authors to defend the doctrine of the Orthodox Church against Roman Catholic critics (in 1694 the *Tomos katallagēs*, in 1698 the *Tomos agapēs* and in 1705 the *Tomos charas*).

In 1685, Dositheos II returned to Jerusalem for the last time. In April 1689, the French ambassador was successful in enforcing the transfer of the Church of the Holy Sepulchre and the other holy places in Jerusalem to the Franciscan friars. In vain, Dositheos II sent his nephew Chrysanthos Notaras to Moscow to mobilise Russian diplomatic support against the French and the Franciscan friars, first in autumn 1692 and then again in autumn 1701. Likewise, his efforts to attain the deposition of Stephen Javorskij (1658-1722), the Latinophile *locum tenens* of the patriarchal throne in Moscow, by Tsar Peter the Great (r. 1682/1696-1725) proved unsuccessful.

In April 1702, Dositheos ordained his nephew Chrysanthos Notaras as metropolitan of Kaisareia, and named him as his successor. On 7 February 1707, he died in the *metochion* of the Church of the Holy Sepulchre in Constantinople.

MAIN SOURCES OF INFORMATION

Primary

Dositheos II of Jerusalem, *Historia peri tōn en Hierosolymois patriarcheusantōn, diērēmenē en dōdeka biblois* [...], Bucharest, 1715, pp. 1196-1240 (Book 12, ch. 2, § 7-ch. 13)

N.F. Kapterev, *Snosheniia ierusalimskogo patriarkha Dosifeiias russkim praviteln'stvom (1669-1707 gg.)*, Moscow, 1891

'Dositheou patriarchou Hierosolymōn praxeis kai grammata', in A. Papadopoulos-Kerameus (ed.), *Analekta Hierosolymitikēs Stachyologias ē Syllogē anekdotōn kai spaniōn hellēnikōn syngraphōn peri tōn kata tēn Heōan orthodoxōn ekklēsiōn kai malista tēs tōn Palaistinōn*, Brussels, 1963 (reprint of the St Petersburg, 1894 edition), vol. 2, pp. 285-309

K. Delikanēs (ed.), *Ta en tois kōdixi tou patriarchikou archeiophylakeiou sōzomena episēma ekklēsiastika engrapha ta aphorōnta eis tas scheseis tou oikoumenikou patriarcheiou pros tas ekklēsias Alexandreias, Antiocheias, Hierosolymōn kai Kyprou (1574-1863)*, Constantinople, 1904, pp. 374-467

D.G. Apostolopoulos and P.D. Michaelarēs, *Hē Nomikē Synagōgē tou Dositheou. Mia pēgē kai ena tekmērio*, Athens, 1987, vol. 1

D.A. Yalamas, 'Ierusalimskij Patriarkh Dosifeĭ i Rossija. 1700-1706 gg. Po materialam Gosudarstvennogo Arkhiva Drevnikh Aktov. Chast 2 (1701 g.)', *Rossija i Christianskij Vostok* 2-3 (2004) 472-92

D.A. Yalamas, 'Ierusalimskij Patriarkh Dosifeĭ i Rossija. 1700-1706 gg. Po materialam Gosudarstvennogo Arkhiva Drevnikh Aktov. Chast 1 (1700 g.)', *Rossija i Christianskij Vostok* 4-5 (2015) 593-647

Secondary

V. Kontouma, 'La *Confession de Foi* de Dosithée de Jérusalem. Les versions de 1672 et de 1690', in M.-H. Blanchet and F. Gabriel (eds), *L'Union à l'épreuve du formulaire. Professions de foi entre Églises d'Orient et d'Occident (XIIIe- XVIIIe s.)*, Leuven, 2016, 341-72

N. Miladinova, *The 'Panoplia Dogmatike' by Euthymios Zygadenos. A study on the first edition published in Greek in 1710*, Leiden, 2014, pp. 36-56, 112-27

K. Sarrēs, 'Ena "ethnos akakon" gia ton Dositheo Hierosolymōn. Hē Rōsikē Ekklēsia anamesa apo tis grammes tēs Dōdekavivlou', in E. Hatzēkyriakydēs and K. Geōrganopoulos (eds), *Hellēnōn dromoi. Meletes aphierōmenes stēn Artemē Xanthopoulou-Kyriakou*, Thessaloniki, 2014, 9-40

N. Russell, 'From the *Shield of Orthodoxy* to the *Tome of joy*. The anti-Western stance of Dositheos II of Jerusalem (1641-1707)', in G. Demacopoulos and A. Papanikolaou (eds), *Orthodox constructions of the West*, New York, 2013, 71-82

O. Olar, '*Point indignes d'occuper une place dans la Bibliothèque du Roi*. La diffusion et l'écho des livres grecs publiés dans les Pays Roumains aux soins de Dosithée de Jérusalem († 1707)', *Transylvanian Review* 21 (2012) (Supplement 1) 169-82

O. Olar, '"A time to speak". The printing activity of Dositheos Notaras, Patriarch of Jerusalem († 1707)', *Annales Universitatis Apulensis. Series Historica* 15/2 (2011) 35-45

M. Săsăujan, 'Die Instruktion des Patriarchen Dositheos für Athanasie' / 'Instrucțiunea patriarhului Dositei pentru Atanasie', in J. Marte et al. (eds), *Die Union der Rumänen Siebenbürgens mit der Kirche von Rom / Unirea românilor transilvăneni cu Biserica Romei*, Bucharest, 2010, vol. 1, 196-214

O.M. Popescu, 'Din însemnările lui Dosithei Notara despre călătoria sa și a patriarhului Paisie al Ierusalimului în jurul Mării Negre', *Studii și Materiale de Istorie Medie* 28 (2010) 231-46

K.-P. Todt, 'Dositheos von Jerusalem', in C.G. Conticello and V. Conticello (eds), *La théologie byzantine et sa tradition*, Turnhout, 2002, vol. 2, 659-720 (with comprehensive bibliography)

G. Podskalsky, *Griechische Theologie in der Zeit der Türkenherrschaft (1453-1821).* *Die Orthodoxie im Spannungsfeld der nachreformatorischen Konfessionen des Westens*, Munich, 1988, pp. 79, 282-95

E.C. Suttner, 'Die Erneuerung eines orthodoxen Schulwesens in den Metochien des hl. Grabes im letzten Drittel des 17. Jahrhunderts', *Ostkirchliche Studien* 34 (1985) 281-99

I.V. Dură, 'Ho Dositheos Hierosolymōn kai hē prosphora autou eis tas Roumanikas chōras kai tēn ekklēsian autōn', Athens, 1977 (PhD Diss. University of Athens)

G.A. Maloney, *A history of Orthodox theology since 1453*, Belmont MA, 1976, pp. 151-7

H.M. Biedermann, 'Die Confessio des Dositheos von Jerusalem (1672)', in T. Kramer and A. Wendehorst (eds), *Aus Reformation und Gegenreformation. Festschrift für Theobald Freudenberger*, Würzburg, 1974, 403-15

T.A. Gritsopoulos, 'Patris kai monē metanoias Dositheou Hierosolymōn (Christianika mnēmeia Phelloēs Kalabrytōn)', *Theologia* 41 (1970) 137-51, 283-320

S. Runciman, *The Great Church in captivity. A study of the Patriarchate of Constantinople from the eve of the Turkish conquest to the Greek War of Independence*, Cambridge, 1968, pp. 217, 218, 234, 308, 316, 318, 347-52, 369

B.L. Fonkich, 'Ierusalimskiĭ patriarkh Dosifeĭ i ego rukopisi v Moskve', *Vizantijskiĭ Vremennik* 29 (1968) 275-99

I. Karmirēs, 'Hē en Bēthleem kai Hierosolymois synodos tou 1672 hypo ton patriarchēn Dositheon', *Nea Siōn* 50 (1955) 25-56

E. Turdeanu, 'Le livre grec en Russie. L'apport des presses de Moldavie et de Valachie (1682-1725)', *Revue des Études Slaves* 26 (1950) 69-87 (repr. E. Turdeanu, *Études de littérature roumaine et d'écrits slaves et grecs des Principautés roumaines*, Leiden, 1985)

N. Chiţescu, 'O dispută dogmatică din veacul al XVII-lea, la care au luat parte Dosithei al Ierusalimului, Constantin Brâncoveanu şi Antim Ivreanu', *Biserica Ortodoxă Română* 63 (1945) 319-52

I. Karmirēs, 'Hē homologia tēs orthodoxou pisteōs tou patriarchou Hierosolymōn Dositheou', *Theologia* 19 (1941-8) 695-707; 20 (1949) 99-119, 245-79, 457-94, 657-703

C.R.A. Georgi, *Die Confessio Dosithei (Jerusalem 1672)*, Munich, 1940

A. Kallistos, 'Ho patriarchēs Dositheos (1669-1707) kai hoi agōnes autou kai tēs adelphotētos hyper tōn hagiōn topōn', *Nea Siōn* 23 (1928) 733-48; 24 (1929) 33-48, 98-114, 162-71, 234-43

É. Legrand, *Bibliographie hellénique ou description raisonnée des ouvrages publiés par des Grecs au dix-huitième siècle*, Paris, 1918, vol. 1, pp. 43-5 (no. 37)

C.A. Papadopoulos, *Historia tēs ekklēsias Hierosolymōn*, Jerusalem, 1910, pp. 535-605

A. Palmieri, *Dositeo, Patriarca greco di Gerusalemme (1641-1707). Contributo alla storia della teologia greco-ortodossa nec secolo XVII*, Florence, 1909

É. Legrand, *Bibliographie hellénique ou description raisonnée des ouvrages publiés par des Grecs au dix-septième siècle*, vol. 2, Paris, 1894, pp. 202 (no. 474), 336-7 (no. 536), 401-7 (no. 568), 458-73 (no. 632); vol. 3, Paris, 1895, pp. 28-9 (no. 658), 30-7 (no. 661), 54-69 (no. 681), 61-75 (no. 684); vol. 5, Paris, 1903, pp. 115-16 (no. 170)

WORKS ON CHRISTIAN-MUSLIM RELATIONS

Historia peri tōn en Hierosolymois patriarcheusantōn, diērimenē men en dōdeka bibliois
'History of those who acted as patriarchs in Jerusalem, divided into 12 books'

DATE   Between 1691/1692 and 1705
ORIGINAL LANGUAGE   Greek

DESCRIPTION

The two editions of the *Historia peri tōn en Hierosolymois patriarcheusantōn* (Bucharest 1715/1723, one volume comprising 1,240 pages, and Thessalonikē 1982/1983, divided into six volumes ranging between 300 and 800 pages each) do not represent Dositheos's original text as handed down in the extant manuscripts. The editor, Patriarch Chrysanthos Notaras of Jerusalem (r. 1707-31), Dositheos's nephew, heir and successor, not only subdivided his uncle's text into books, chapters and paragraphs, but also replaced the vernacular Greek of the original text with a more classicising form of language (thus, an edition of the original text of the history would be a great benefit). Chrysanthos also removed all parts of the text that might eventually prove too offensive to the Ottomans or Muslims in general (these were not published until 1891, by Athanasios Papadopoulos-Kerameus). Moreover, the work was not published in 1715, as the title page reads, but most probably only in 1723. This can be shown by the correspondence between Chrysanthos and the priest and monk Mētrophanēs Grēgoras in the years 1720-1. Chrysanthos had appointed Grēgoras to prepare the printed edition.

    The full title of the book is *Historia peri tōn en Hierosolymois patriarcheusantōn, diērimenē men en dōdeka bibliois, archomenē de apo Iakōbou tou Adelphotheou kai prōtou Hierarchou tōn Hierosolymōn heōs tou parontos etous. Periechousa tas te theias syneleuseis tōn Hagiōn Apostolōn,*

kai tas ana pasan tēn Oikoumenēn synathroistheisas epiphanesteras Syno-
dous, orthodoxous kai kakodoxous, Oikoumenikas te kai Topikas, kai pan
dogma tēs katholikēs tou Christou hagias kai apostolikēs Ekklēsias [...]
kai tous en autō Patriarchas, kai heterōn pollōn axiomnēmoneutōn
hypotheseōn. Syngrapheisa men para tou en makaria tē lēxei genom-
enou hagiōtatou kai aoidimou Patriarchou tōn Hierosolymōn kyriou
kyriou DOSITHEOU, Kosmētheisa de, kai en taxei aristē tetheisa para tou
makariōtatou Patriarchou tōn Hierosolymōn kyriou kyriou CHRYSANTHOU
('History of those who acted as patriarchs in Jerusalem, divided into
twelve books, beginning from Jacob [James], the brother of the Lord
and first hierarch of Jerusalem, until the present year, comprising the
divine meetings of the Apostles and the more notable synods assembled
all over the inhabited world, the orthodox and the ill-reputed, the general and the local, and every doctrine of the catholic, holy and apostolic
Church of Christ [...] and the patriarchs in it [the Holy Sepulchre], and of
a multitude of other things worthy of mention, written by the most holy
and glorious patriarch of Jerusalem, Lord Dositheos, deceased, adorned
and arranged in best order by the most blessed patriarch of Jerusalem,
Lord Chrysanthos'). But this title is misleading, because Dositheos deals
not only with the history of the Greek Orthodox patriarchs of Jerusalem,
but with that of the whole Greek Orthodox Church. Moreover, a good
number of pages are filled with refutations of papal primacy and of the
arguments of Roman Catholic theologians, such as cardinals Bessarion
(1403-72) and Bellarmine (1542-1621), who defended the papacy or the
other 'errors' of the Latin Church. In Book 10, Dositheos strongly criticises
the decisions of the Council of Ferrara and Florence (1438/9), fighting
not only against the Latin Church but also against the Armenians, with
whom the Greeks were permanently in conflict in Jerusalem (see Book
12, ch. 7 and ch. 8, § 1).

By comparison with the polemics directed against the Latin Church,
Islam is a subject of only minor importance. Muslims (*Sarakēnoi*) are
mentioned for the first time in Book 6, ch. 4, § 9, though only incidentally, in the context of the controversy over Monotheletism. Only in Book
6, chs 18 and 19, does Dositheos give a more detailed account of the
Arab conquests in the Near East and North Africa, which were brought
to an end with the victory of Charles Martell in the battle near Tours
and Poitiers in 732, and the second siege of Constantinople in 717/18.
Dositheos adopts the view from the Byzantine chronicle of Theophanes
that the Saracens' successes were made possible by divisions within
Christendom, especially the Monothelete controversy. The Syrian Bersēs,

an adviser to the Emperor Leo III (r. 717-41), introduced the iconoclasm of the Muslims to Byzantium and so instigated Byzantine iconoclasm. From this point, Dositheos gradually narrates the information he had gleaned from Theophanes about the history of the patriarchs of Alexandria, Antioch and Jerusalem in the 8th century.

In Book 8, ch. 22, Dositheos gives a summary of the history of the patriarchs from the time of Zacharias (r. 609-c. 628/31) down to his own lifetime. This is based partly on a translation of the Arabic chronicle of Eutychius of Alexandria (r. 933-40), translated into vernacular Greek by Christodoulos of Gaza. It is only at this point that Dositheos mentions twice the Arab conquest of Jerusalem by the Caliph ʿUmar (r. 634-44) in 638. For the printed editions of the patriarchal history, this chapter was revised by Chrysanthos. Another example of the latter's editing work is that, while in the original version Dositheos reported on the destruction of the Church of the Holy Sepulchre by the order of the Fāṭimid Caliph Azizios (al-Ḥākim, r. 996-1021) in 1009, this information is suppressed by Chrysanthos.

In Book 8, covering the period from the mid-11th century until the Sicilian Vespers in 1282, he mentions the Ayyūbid Sultan Ṣalāḥ al-Dīn (r. 1169/71-1193), and his victories over the crusaders and conquest of Jerusalem in October 1187 (Book 8, ch. 11, §2-5). In the original version of Book 8, ch. 9, Dositheos reports on the controversy between the Byzantine Emperor Manuel I Comnenus (r. 1143-80) and the patriarchal synod of Constantinople concerning the anathema against the god of Muḥammad in the Book of Catechism. This chapter, too, was suppressed by Chrysanthos in the printed edition.

In Book 9, ch. 4, Dositheos tells of Osman, the founder of the Ottoman dynasty, and the beginnings of the Ottoman Empire. In Book 11, ch. 1, he rejects the assertion by the Latin Church that God permitted the conquest of Constantinople by the Ottomans in 1453 because the Orthodox Church had rejected the Union of Florence with the papal church (1439), thus refusing obedience to the pope. As he saw it, the Ottoman sultans, such as Selim I (r. 1512-20), who conquered Syria and Egypt in 1516-17, granted numerous favours and privileges to the Monastery of Soumela in the Pontos and to the Patriarchate of Jerusalem, as well as to other Orthodox Christians (Book 11, ch. 4). Dositheos denounces the expulsion of the Muslims and the Jews from Spain with particular harshness (Book 11, ch. 6).

In Book 12, Dositheos's narrative becomes autobiographical. Ch. 2 relates the arrest, imprisonment and torture of Patriarch Païsios of

Jerusalem (r. 1645-60) by Ottoman officials, on the charge that he had ordered that a precious crown be made and given as a present to the tsar of Moscow. Only when it became evident before the tribunal of the grand vizier and the mufti that this crown was part of the liturgical dress of the patriarch, was Païsios released and granted permission by the sultan to wear it for liturgical services. During the stay of Patriarch Païsios in Georgia, the Ottoman governor of Jerusalem encroached upon the rights and liberties of the Christians and the Holy Sepulchre. The Armenians managed to take possession of the Church of St James by bribing high Ottoman officials and with the support of the Grand Drago-man Panagiōtēs Nikousios, who was an enemy of Patriarch Païsios (Book 12, ch. 2, § 16-17). The patriarch appealed to the grand vizier in Edirne to have the church returned, but in vain. On 2 December 1660, while he was returning to Jerusalem Païsios died on the lonely island of Castellorizo in the arms of Dositheos (Book 12, ch. 2, § 19). According to Dositheos, one of the most remarkable achievements of this patriarch was his success in retrieving half of the Church of St George in Lydda, which the Muslims had seized (Book 12, ch. 2, § 21).

The true precariousness of the patriarchate's position under Otto-man rule became evident in 1672, when Dositheos resumed the rebuild-ing of the Church of the Nativity in Bethlehem. As this contravened the restrictions imposed by Islamic law, the grand vizier sent a fact-finding commission to report on the restoration work. In November 1672, the patriarch, with the support of the grand dragoman Panagiōtēs Nikousios, travelled to Edirne for an audience with the vizier to try to prevent him from ordering the restoration work to be reversed (Book 12, ch. 5, § 6).

In Book 11, ch. 11, § 7, Dositheos refers to Païsios Ligaridēs (1609/10-1678), who had written a history (*historikon*) of the patriarchs of Jerusa-lem preceding him. Dositheos himself states that he used Ligaridēs as a source for his own historical work, even though Ligaridēs was a supporter of the Latin Church (*latinophrōn*), for which he had been condemned as a heretic by the patriarchs Methodios III of Constantinople (r. 1668-71) and Nektarios of Jerusalem (r. 1661-9).

SIGNIFICANCE

The focus of attention in the *Historia peri tōn en Hierosolymois patriarcheusantōn* is the controversy with the papacy and the Latin Church. Nonetheless, the work provides rich and valuable informa-tion about the periodically difficult situation experienced by the Greek Orthodox Church and its leading representatives in the Ottoman Empire, especially in the autobiographical sections in Book 12. Where Dositheos mentions Muslims, e.g. in Books 1-11, he mainly does so through citations from the works of Byzantine chroniclers and historians, such as Theophanes, George Kedrēnos/John Scylitzes, Anna Komnēnē and Nikētas Chōniatēs. This maybe points to his acute awareness that he risked repercussions by making direct references to the Ottoman authorities or anything to do with Muslim religion or manners.

PUBLICATIONS

MS Athens (National Library), formerly Metochion of the Holy Sepulcre in Constantinople – 230 (end of the 17th century, with Dositheos's own annotations and corrections)

MS Athens (National Library), formerly Metochion of the Holy Sepulcre in Constantinople – 621 (before March 1692)

MS Athens (National Library), formerly Metochion of the Holy Sepulcre in Constantinople – 242 (1703, with Dositheos's own annotations and corrections)

MS Jerusalem (Patriarcal Library), formerly Monastery of the Holy Cross – 11, fols 1-962 (18th century)

MS Jerusalem (Patriarcal Library), formerly Monastery of the Holy Cross – 21 (October 1858)

Dositheos, *Historia peri tōn en Hierosolymois patriarcheusantōn, diērimenē men en dōdeka bibliois*, Bucharest, 1715

'Dositheou Notara, patriarchou Hierosolymōn, paraleipomena ek tēs historias peri tōn en Hierosolymois patriarchēsantōn', in Ath. Papadopoulos-Kerameus (ed.), *Analekta Hierosolymitikēs Stachyologias*, St Petersburg, 1891 (repr. Brussels, 1963), vol. 1, pp. 231-307

Dositheou, patriarchou Hierosolymōn, *Historia peri tōn en Hierosolymois patriarcheusantōn, diērēmenē en dōdeka bibliois, allōs kaloumenē Dōdekabiblos Dositheou. Eisagōgē Archimandritou Eirēnaiou Delēdēmou*, Thessaloniki, 1982-3, 6 vols

STUDIES

K. Sarrēs, 'Diapragmateuomenos ena amphilegomenko zētēma stēn augē tou 18ou aiōna: Hē othōmanikē kataktēsē stis ekklēsiastikes histories tou Dositheou Hierosolymōn kai tou Meletiou Athēnōn', *Egnatia* 15 (2011) 117-25

K. Sarrēs, 'Hierē Historia. Oi apoklinouses diadromes enos eidous metaxy Dysēs kai Anatolēs. Apo tē *Dōdekavivlo* tou Dositheou

Hierosolymōn stēn *Ekklēsiastikē Historia* tou Meletiou Athēnōn', Thessaloniki, 2010 (PhD Diss. Aristotle University of Thessaloniki)

K. Sarrēs, 'Ho Chrysanthos Notaras kai hē ekdosē tou *Dōdekavivlo* tou Dositheou Hierosolymōn: mia periptōsi analēthous chronologias ekdosēs (1715/c. 1722)', *Mnēmōn* 27 (2005) 27-53

Todt, 'Dositheos von Jerusalem', pp. 679-80 and 682-3

Podskalsky, *Griechische Theologie*, pp. 77-8, 293-4

G.P. Kournoutos, 'Hē dōdekabiblos tu Dositheou eis tēn typographian tou Boukourestiou', *Theologia* 24 (1953) 250-73 (very important)

Legrand, *Bibliographie hellénique* [...] *dix-huitième siècle*, vol. 1, pp. 120-2, no. 97

Klaus-Peter Todt

Meletios of Athens

Michaēl Mētros the Priest

DATE OF BIRTH   1661
PLACE OF BIRTH   Ioannina
DATE OF DEATH   1714
PLACE OF DEATH   Istanbul

BIOGRAPHY

Michaēl Mētros – the secular name of Meletios of Athens (other names by which he is known include Meletios Athēnōn, Meletios ho geōgraphos, Meletios Mitrou, Meletio) – was born in 1661 in Ottoman Ioannina. He pursued his higher education with the illustrious scholar Vēssariōn Makrēs at the Giou(n)ma School in his home town, presumably between 1677 and 1680. He was then ordained priest and in 1681 he arrived in Venice. Although his anonymous biographer does not provide information about any studies he may have pursued in Venice, his erudition and language skills, as well as the quality of his writings, indicate that he became acquainted with modern European thought during his time there. From his time in Venice, 'Michaēl Mētros the priest' appears as redactor and reviser of at least nine books published by Greek printing houses (1685-7). In addition, he was preaching at the Greek Orthodox church of San Giorgio dei Greci and teaching at the school of the Greek Confraternity of Venice (c. March 1686 to June 1687). In the summer of 1687, he returned to Ioannina and continued teaching at the Epiphaneios School until the summer of 1692. By the end of that year, he had been ordained metropolitan of both Venetian Naupaktos (Lepanto) and Ottoman Arta under the name Meletios.

The culmination of the Venetian-Ottoman war of 1684-99 had serious repercussions for Meletios's diocese. In August 1696, a Venetian militia plundered Ottoman Arta, and Meletios was accused of plotting and collaborating with the Venetians. As a consequence, in February 1697 the Patriarch of Constantinople deposed him. Six years later, in October 1703, Meletios succeeded in being elected metropolitan of Athens. Over the following years, he faced many ecclesiastical, financial and social problems in his new see. Finally, in autumn 1714, he left Athens to assume his appointment in the recently vacated bishopric of Ioannina but died in December 1714 in Istanbul.

None of Meletios's major writings were published during his lifetime, despite attempts on his part. Among identified extant manuscripts of his works there are two versions of a theoretical geography (astronomy), a miscellaneous work on medicine and paradoxes, a small treatise regarding the plague, as well as some introductions to books and a few letters. Meletios of Athens was better known to posterity than to his contemporaries due to two of his works that were published many years after his death. The posthumous editions of his *Geōgraphia palaia kai nea* ('Geography ancient and modern') and *Ekklēsiastikē historia* ('Ecclesiastical history') were particularly influential in the development of geographical and historiographical knowledge during the Modern Greek Enlightenment in the second half of the 18th century.

MAIN SOURCES OF INFORMATION

Primary

D. Prokopiou, 'Epitetmēmenē eparithmēsis, tōn kata ton parelthonta aiōna logiōn Graikōn, kai peri tinōn en tō nyn aiōni anthountōn, succincta Eruditorum Graecorum superioris et praesentis saeculi recensio', in J.A. Fabricius (ed.), *Bibliothecae graecae*, vol. 11, Hamburg, 1722, 768-808, p. 784

Meletios of Athens, *Meletiou Geōgraphia palaia kai nea syllechtheisa ek diaforōn syngrapheōn palaiōnte kai neōn, kai ek diaphorōn epigraphōn, tōn en lithois, kai eis koinēn dialekton eketetheisa charin tōn pollōn tou hēmeterou genous. Prosphōnētheisa de tō entimotatō kai eugenestatō kyriō kyriō Panagiotē Saraphē tanyn prōton ekdotheisa typois, kai met' epimeleias diorthōtheisa,* Venice, 1728, (short biography in fol. 4, without pagination)

Meletios of Athens, *Ekklēsiastikē historia Meletiou mētropolitou Athēnōn*, vol. 1, Vienna, 1783, pp. k-ka = pp. 20-1 (short biography by G. Ventotēs)

N.M. Vaporis, *Codex gamma of the Ecumenical Patriarchate of Constantinople*, Brookline MA, 1974, pp. 50-1, no. 21 (February 1697, Meletios of Naupaktos and Arta is deposed, unfrocked, and anathematised)

Secondary

K. Sarrēs, 'Hierē historia. Oi apoklinouses diadromes enos eidous metaxy Dysēs kai Anatolēs: apo tē Dōdekavivlo tou Dositheou Hierosolymōn stēn Ekklēsiastikē historia tou Meletiou Athēnōn', Thessaloniki, 2010 (PhD Diss. Aristotle University of Thessaloniki), pp. 56-66

K.Th. Kyriakopoulos, *Meletios (Mētros) Athēnōn, ho geōgraphos (1661-1714), symvolē stē meletē tou viou kai tou ergou tou kai genikotera tēs epochēs tou prōimou Diaphōtismou*, Athens, 1990, vol. 1, pp. 45-163

Sp.G. Makrēs, art. 'Meletios. Ho ex Iōanninōn, mētropolitēs Athēnōn (1703-1714)', in *Thrēskeutikē kai Ēthikē Enkyklopaideia*, Athens, 1966, vol. 8, cols 956-8 (with bibliography of early works on Meletios)

St.N. Bettēs, 'Meletios ho geōgraphos, ē to prōto ēpeirōtiko panepistēmio 1661-
    1714. Hē zōē kai to ergo tou', *Ēpeirōtikē Estia* 13 (1964) 522-44 (repr. Athens,
    2007)
B. Knös, *L'histoire de la littérature néo-grecque. La période jusqu'en 1821*, Stock-
    holm, 1962, p. 476

WORKS ON CHRISTIAN-MUSLIM RELATIONS

Meletiou Geōgraphia palaia kai nea
'Geography of Meletios ancient and modern'

DATE   Between 1696/7 and 1706/7
ORIGINAL LANGUAGE   Greek (vernacular)

DESCRIPTION

Meletios's *Geōgraphia* figures prominently among the most influential
18th-century Greek geographical works. According to the testimony of
Meletios himself and his biographer, it was composed between about
1696/7 and 1706/7, with Meletios writing the main parts during his stay
in Naupaktos, and adding further detail after he became metropolitan of
Athens. In 1707, Meletios did not manage to get the work published in
Venice, and two further attempts by Chrysanthos Notaras immediately
after Meletios's death in 1714, and Neophytos Mauromatēs between 1721
and 1726, were also unsuccessful. Eventually, it was published in 1728 in
Venice by the Greek printing house of Nikolaos Glykys, in an edition that
came to 620 pages in folio, along with 10 pages of introductory texts and
51 pages of index. Its full title is *Meletiou Geōgraphia palaia kai nea syllechtheisa ek diaphorōn syngrapheōn palaiōnte kai neōn, kai ek diaphorōn
epigraphōn, tōn en lithois, kai eis koinēn dialekton ektetheisa charin tōn
pollōn tou hēmeterou genous* ('Geography of Meletios ancient and modern compiled from various authors both ancient and modern, and by
several epigraphs carved on stones, and displayed in vernacular dialect
for the sake of the many of our people').

According to Kyriakopoulos (*Meletios Athēnōn*, vol. 1, p. 519), Meletios
consciously wrote a '"composite", "historical", global, general, comparative *Geography*, voluminous, systematic and methodical [...] an unprec-
edented work' within the Greek literature of the Ottoman period. The
work begins with a comprehensive introduction to theoretical geography (pp. 1-41; all references are to the 1728 edition) and proceeds with a
description of the four known continents divided into separate 'Books'.

These differ in length: the first, on Europe, takes up the bulk of the *Geōgraphia* (pp. 42-441), including an extensive description of 'Greece' (pp. 304-412), whereas the others get progressively shorter (pp. 442-571 on Asia; pp. 572-608 on Africa, and only pp. 609-20 on America). The typical structure is to present first aspects of natural geography, and then political and historical geography – a system of presentation and description similar to that found in early modern European geographical works. Kyriakopoulos (*Meletios Athēnōn*, vol. 1, pp. 583-607) notes Meletios's dependence on books by contemporary geographers, such as Philippe Briet and Philippe Cluver.

As Meletios states in his Introduction, the primary division of *Geōgraphia* is political, i.e. by state, while the moral division of the inhabitants, referring primarily to their religious beliefs, comes after. Therefore, Meletios divides the world of his time into Christianity, 'Mōametismos where the teaching of Muḥammad is being preached', 'Judaism [...] Atheism [...] Idōlomania, Skythism, Hellenism, and Barbarism' (p. 37). The description of the Muslim states covers 177 pages, and a further 109 pages are devoted to a detailed description of Ottoman Greece. There are only a few occasional references to Christian-Muslim relations.

Although the first Muslim state to be mentioned is European Tatary in Crimea (pp. 221-7), the *Tourkos* (Turk/Ottoman) represents the dominant Muslim other of the *Geōgraphia*. According to Meletios, 'there are three religions in Europe [...] of Christ, of Muḥammad, of Moses. That is Christians, Hebrews and Turks' (p. 41). Just as the description of Greece and Asia Minor contains occasional references to Ottoman conquest (pp. 385, 400-2, 421, 439, 449, 478, 486-7, 492), the geographical account of central and south-eastern Europe contains numerous, albeit brief, mentions of the long-standing confrontations between the Ottoman and Christian states (pp. 210, 229-31, 233-5, 413-14, 416). Meletios records many individual confrontations (e.g. pp. 408-10), and generally portrays them in religious terms: the generic term 'Turks' is used for Muslims, while 'Christians' is regularly used to refer to ethnic or political denominations, such as Hungarians, Habsburgs, Venetians and so forth. Even when Meletios draws on European geographical sources, his own prejudice against the 'Turks' is evident from the vocabulary he uses (pp. 158, 324, 328): while they 'conquer', 'subdue' or 'enslave', the Christians – in particular Venetians – 'liberate' (pp. 233, 236-7, 239, 359, 371, 377-8, 380).

The very first mention of Islam itself is found in the middle of the Book on Asia, which contains a description of Arabia. Writing about Mecca and Medina, Meletios provides some unbiased information about the life of Muḥammad and the *hijra*, indicating the holiness of the two cities in Islam (p. 518). Surprisingly, at the beginning of the section on Persia, a few pages later, the details he provides about Shīʿism are more comprehensive; he attributes both the revival of the Persian kingdom and the emergence of Iranian Shīʿism to Shah Ismāʿil I (r. 1501-24) and reproduces a sort of spiritual and family genealogy for him, recording members of the Safavid dynasty up to ʿAbbās II (r. 1642-66, pp. 531-2). The remaining pages that concentrate on Asia include a few sporadic mentions of the Muslim culture of central Asia (e.g. p. 569), with very occasional allusions to the Mughal Empire (p. 537) and the Muslim presence in India and South-East Asia (pp. 544, 550, 554). Finally, while it contains a comprehensive account of North Africa, the *Geōgraphia* provides mainly political information about Egypt and the other Islamic states of North and North-West Africa (pp. 575, 584, 586-9, 592).

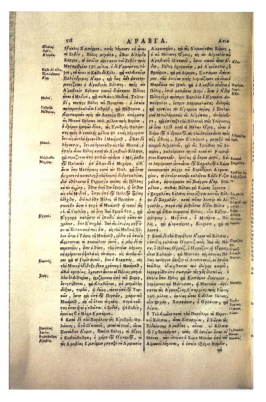

Illustration 9. Meletios of Athens, *Geōgraphia palaia kai nea syllechtheisa ek diaphorōn syngrapheōn palaiōnte kai neōn*, p. 518, where Islam is mentioned for the first time

Meletios's *Geōgraphia* does not provide any comprehensive account of Islam *per se*. Although it contains a short passage about Muḥammad, there is no mention of any aspect of his teachings (p. 518). In reference to the difference between Sunnī and Shīʿa Islam, it merely notes that they originate from different Companions of Muḥammad and that 'the teaching of Umar (ʿUmar ibn al-Khaṭṭāb) [...] was considered more pure and better' (p. 531). While Meletios appears to be critical of Alī (ʿAlī ibn Abī Ṭālib) and his 'doctrines which were not spread as much' (p. 531), and in particular Persian Shīʿism, described as a 'new Heresy [...] in the teaching of Muḥammad' (p. 532), it seems that here he is merely drawing – probably indirectly – from the source he cites at the end of this chapter, namely Pietro Bizzarri's *Persicarum rerum historia in XII. libros descripta* (Antwerp, 1583[1]).

The *Geōgraphia*'s description of Ottoman Greek lands provides some original insights into the convoluted perception of a Greek-speaking author rather than presenting the actual complexity of the coexistence of Christians and Muslims. Typically, Meletios describes Constantinople and other cities as 'enslaved' by the 'Turks' (pp. 293, 319), just as other Christian cities in the Near East were by the 'Saracens' (p. 499). Moreover, numerous cities in Asia Minor, where 'Christianity had shone [...] were devastated by the Turks [...] turned from the past glory and nobility into a barbarous valley of sorrows' (p. 444). The Peloponnesians similarly 'had started getting worse in such a way that, during the Empire of the Turks, ah, that light of the World was completely faded by a long-lasting night of the dark, and the Rage of the barbarous Dog defeated the forces of the powerful Lion' (p. 356).

However, Meletios does sometimes display more complex views. Introducing the section on 'Greece', while praising its 'great and illustrious name in the ancient times' and deploring its 'insignificant and miserable [one] nowadays', he nonetheless does not directly blame its most recent conquerors, the 'Turks', but rather the endless warfare due to which 'alas for the deplorable condition, the previously most illustrious [Greece] has been almost entirely blemished and barbarised' (pp. 304-5). Characteristically, the representation of the 'Turk' is completely reversed in the chapter on Constantinople/Istanbul, the capital of the two empires – Byzantine and Ottoman – and the two religions – Christianity and Islam. Constantinople/Istanbul, 'since it was conquered by the Turks, came in great growth, became very wealthy [...] it is the greatest and the most beautiful among the cities of Europe [...] and [there are] many other and significant results of those Turks' (p. 437). It is the coexistence of these contrasting attitudes in Meletios's writing that adds to their fascination.

While complex, Meletios's remarks about the 'Turks' contain important elements for the understanding of his perception of Muslims as a whole. Specifically, the locus of 'barbarism', referring to Greece, recurs in the description of North Africa where it is further explained: 'Barbary, or speaking more barbarously Berberia, was named by the Europeans, since the time its inhabitants had left the Roman laws and cringed under the yoke of Tyranny, abandoned the Greek dialect and accepted the Arab one, ignored the faith of Christ and embraced the religion of Muḥammad. And therefore, the once praised [...] have been barbarised regarding both their mind and their morals' (p. 583). In this passage, Meletios establishes three antithetical conceptual pairs relating to politics (Roman law v. tyranny), culture (Greek v. Arab) and religion (Christ v. Muḥammad), where the latter in each case is considered a constituent element of 'barbarism'. Thus, Islam and Arab culture are identified with large-scale human regression as, according to Meletios, 'barbarism' formed the first era in human history, from Adam until the Flood (p. 37, see also pp. 221-2). While this is the only concrete attack on the Muslims and their religion found in Meletios's *Geōgraphia*, it is fairly explicit.

The descriptive terms used for Muslims tend to vary, depending on the various geographical regions. In general, Meletios does not use purely religious definitions, instead showing a preference for political terms associated with Islam. Thus, when describing Europe and Asia Minor, the Muslim other falls under the umbrella term of the 'Turk' (e.g. p. 41), while the term 'Saracen' is preferred over 'Arabian' (pp. 523-4) for predominently representing the Muslim population of the Near East and North Africa (e.g. p. 50). Meletios regards the 'Saracens' as one of the prominent nations of Arabia, 'who were once named Agarēnoi, later Ismaēlitai by Sōzomenos, derived from Agar, the Young girl of Abraham, and from Ismaēl, her son, and lastly Sarakēnoi, from the Province of Saraca' (p. 517). In addition, there are occasional references to the 'Persai' of Iran (p. 531) and the 'Mauroi' (Moors) of the Iberian Peninsula and Morocco (pp. 50, 596). However, despite their sharing a common Muslim faith, Meletios discerns the non-religious, political differences among these various groups (e.g. pp. 50, 443, 523-4). It is worth noting, however, that on just two occasions in *Geōgraphia* he uses the religious definitions 'Mōamethanoi' (Mohammedans) and 'Mousoulmanoi' (Muslims): first, in reference to the 'Ta(r)taroi' (Tatars), so as to distinguish them from the Tatars who practise Shamanism (pp. 222, 569), and second, in descriptions of India and south-east Asia, in order to distinguish the Muslims there from the 'Eidōlolatrai' (idolaters), 'Ethnikoi' (heathens) or 'Paganikoi' (pagans) (pp. 550-4).

In summary, Meletios of Athens in his *Geōgraphia* presents a complex, rather than a vague attitude towards Islam. While possibly avoiding explicit expression of his negative stance when writing about the Ottoman Empire, in his description of North Africa he does not hesitate to equate Islam and the Arabs with 'barbarism'. For Meletios, the very coexistence of Christians and Muslims under Ottoman rule at the beginning of the 18th century underlies his ambiguous perception – or indeed, strategy – vis-à-vis Islam, as he himself is an Ottoman subject. Nonetheless, there are some unusual passages describing religious coexistence between Christians and Muslims in the *Geōgraphia*. In Muslim Barbary, ironically, Meletios describes a temple on a small desolate island, where both Christians and Muslims perform their worship with due respect for the other. This island belonging both to no one and everyone 'is called Lōpadousa, namely Lampadousa in vernacular' (pp. 591-2), present-day Italian Lampedusa.

SIGNIFICANCE

Although it was very costly to publish a work as voluminous as the *Geōgraphia*, and excerpts from it were rarely found in manuscripts, it soon became a well-known geographical book among Greek-speaking scholars. In 1807, Anthimos Gazēs republished the work (Venice, 4 vols, in octavo), adding supplements and silent 'corrections' (Kyriakopoulos, *Meletios Athēnōn*, vol. 1, pp. 407-31), but reproducing faithfully the passages relevant to Christian-Muslim relations. In addition, a school compendium was edited by Stephanos Kommētas (in his series *Paidagōgika mathēmata* ['Pedagogical courses'], Pest, 1828), who settled on a rearrangement of the purely geographical information, without any specific mention of Islam.

PUBLICATIONS

MS Athens, Dependency of the Holy Sepulchre – 241, 566 fols (1716, ordered by Anastasios Papavasilopoulos, Meletios' nephew, by Chrysanthos Notaras, Patriarch of Jerusalem)

Meletios of Athens, *Meletiou geōgraphia palaia kai nea syllechtheisa ek diaphorōn syngrapheōn palaiōnte kai neōn, kai ek diaphorōn epigraphōn, tōn en lithois, kai eis koinēn dialekton ektetheisa charin tōn pollōn tou hēmeterou genous. Prosphōnētheisa de tō entimotatō kai eugenestatō kyriō kyriō Panagiotē Saraphē tanyn prōton ekdotheisa typois, kai met' epimeleias diorthōtheisa*, Venice: Nikolaos Glykys, 1728[1]; BLLo1017392587 (digitised version available through the British Library)

Meletios of Athens, *Meletiou geōgraphia palaia kai nea syllechtheisa ek diaphorōn syngrapheōn palaiōn te kai neōn, kai ek diaphorōn epigraphōn tōn en lithois, kai eis koinēn dialekton ektetheisa, charin tōn pollōn tou hēmeterou genous. Pleistois de sēmeiōmasin epauxētheisa meta kai tinōn parartēmatōn kai pente geōgraphikon pirakōn, kai epidiorthōtheisa, exedothē ēdē to deuteron hypo Anthimou Gazē tou Mēliōtou*, Venice: Panos Theodosiou, 1807[2], 4 vols (with supplements and 'corrections'); 3 3433 00066134 2 (digitised version available through Hathi Trust Digital Library)

Stephanos Kommētas, *Paidagōgika mathēmata, synthenta para Stephanou Kommēta tou ek Phthias, ek chōrarchias men Kokosiou, kōmēs de Kōphōn. Geōgraphia palaia, periechousa tas onomasias tōn topōn, kai poleōn, kai diaphorōn merōn tēs gēs; hoion, epikrateiōn, eparchiōn, potamōn, thalassōn, kai tōn toioutōn, kathōs ta ōnomazon hoi palaioi*, Pest: Matthias Trattner, 1828 (school compendium); APB 3123 (digitised version available through the Digital Library of Modern Greek Studies 'Anemi')

STUDIES

P.M. Kitromilidēs, *Enlightenment and revolution. The making of modern Greece*, Cambridge MA, 2013, pp. 91-4, 99

N.M. [N. Matsopoulos], art. 'Geographia - Astronomia', in G. Karas (ed.), *Historia kai philosophia tōn epistēmōn ston hellēniko chōro (17os-19os ai.)*, Athens, 2003, 431-76, pp. 437-8

G. Tolias, art. 'Hieros, kosmikos kai ethnikos chōros stēn hellēnikē geōgraphikē grammateia kata ton 18o aiōna', in *Hē epistēmonikē skepsē ston hellēniko chōro 18os-19os ai.*, Athens, 1998, 147-72, pp. 155-8

Kyriakopoulos, *Meletios Athēnōn*, vol. 1, pp. 360-644; vol. 2, pp. 657-907

Bettēs, 'Meletios ho geōgraphos'

C.Th. Dimaras, *A history of modern Greek literature*, New York, 1972, pp. 125, 136

Knös, *Litterature néo-grecque*, p. 476

K.Th. Dēmaras, *Historia tēs neohellēnikēs logotechnias. Apo tis prōtes rizes hōs tēn epochē mas*, Athens, 1949 (2000[9]), p. 173

Ekklēsiastikē historia Meletiou mētropolitou Athēnōn
'Ecclesiastical history by Meletios Metropolitan of Athens'

DATE   Between 1707 and 1713
ORIGINAL LANGUAGE   Greek (vernacular)

DESCRIPTION

The *Ekklēsiastikē historia* is a monumental book. It was composed in two distinct phases during Meletios's period as bishop of Athens. Composition of the first and shorter version, recounting the period 1580-1700, began sometime after 1707 and appears to have been at an advanced stage by late 1710. It is highly likely that Meletios then modified his plans and decided to expand the project to cover the entire period from the 1st century AD to 1700. In summer 1713, the work seems to have been almost complete (Kyriakopoulos, *Meletios Athēnōn*, vol. 1, pp. 163-71), but Meletios died the following year without having published it. Manuscripts of the *Ekklēsiastikē historia* had a wide circulation among the Greek-speaking readership until 1783-4, when a prominent publisher of the Modern Greek Enlightenment, Polyzōēs Lampanitziōtēs, decided to print it in Vienna in three volumes. Many years later, the previous editor of the book, Geōrgios Ventotēs, wrote his own *Supplement*, which was issued as a fourth volume (Vienna, 1795) (Kyriakopoulos, *Meletios Athēnōn*, vol. 1, pp. 143-7). In the three-volume edition (Vienna, 1783-4), the *Ekklēsiastikē historia* comes to 1,319 pages in quarto, in addition to 171 pages with editorial introductions, contents and indexes.

Though mentions of Muslims can be found on approximately 110 pages, comprehensive accounts do not exceed 40 pages. This is not surprising when we consider that the cohesive elements of *Ekklēsiastikē historia* are as explicit as its historiographical genre is unambiguous. The title, as well as the lengthy Introduction, leave no room for doubt; Meletios was fully aware that this work belonged to the historiographical genre of church history. The history of the Church occupies the central position in the narrative, while apologetics (either within or outside the Christian Church) functions complementarily and is always dependent on history. Thus, the text presents a solid structure, moving systematically through time, as conceived by church historians. In this respect, it is already telling that the work is divided into books, each covering a particular century.

The first volume of the 1783-4 edition (all the references that follow are to this edition) begins with a general Introduction on church history and continues with four books concerning the history of the Christian Church up to the 4th century. The second volume contains Books 5-11, covering their respective centuries, while the third volume contains the remaining centuries up until 1700. In general, each book/century is made up of specific clusters of chapters of different sizes. Each cluster begins with a chapter on the reign of a Roman emperor (either occidental or oriental), a Muscovite tsar or, later, an Ottoman sultan, that presents both the episcopal succession and the most important events in church history during that reign. The following chapters refer, *ad hoc*, to the synods, theological debates, heresies, schisms and ecclesiastical or intellectual personalities of the period. Although there are exceptions in this scheme, the focus always remains on church history.

Within this narrative structure, mentions of Muslims are, by and large, regular but fairly brief, beginning with the first account in the 7th book/century, which is associated with the advance of the Arab conquest. In the chapters covering the Byzantine emperors and the state of the Eastern Church, there are short descriptions of the wars against the *Sarakēnoi* in the Middle East and Asia Minor (vol. 2, pp. 157-8, 172-3, 182, 215, 299). On the other hand, in the chapters dealing with the Western Church, there are references to the long-standing struggles between Christian rulers and the 'Saracens' or *Mauroi* (Moors) in southern Italy and France, but mainly in the Iberian Peninsula (vol. 2, pp. 216-17, 230, 267, 283, 328, 375, 384, 398; vol. 3, p. 107). Relatively longer accounts cover the Crusades (vol. 2, pp. 429, 432-4; vol. 3, pp. 90, 177-8), but even more comprehensive are the passages referring to 'the Ottoman Empire, namely of the Turks' (vol. 3, p. 178). The 'Turkish' threat is present in each chapter that deals with the Byzantine Empire and Church (vol. 3, pp. 178-9, 201-2, 206-8, 218, 237, 241-4, 265-6, 268-71, 289, 296, 299), while the 'Ottoman emperor' and the political history of the Ottoman Empire replace those of the Byzantines after the fall of Constantinople in 1453 (vol. 3, pp. 321-2, 329-30, 337-9, 367-9, 372, 400-1, 411, 428-9, 445, 464, 476, 481-3).

Some aspects of Christian-Muslim relations that go beyond the merely military can be detected. In his very first mention of Muḥammad's beliefs, Meletios characterises them as 'impious doctrines' (vol. 2, p. 150). An entire chapter entitled 'About the false-prophet Muḥammad and his heresy' appears further along (vol. 2, pp. 154-8). This contains a critical biography of Muḥammad, depicting him as a magician, demoniac and deceiver, whose teachings were a 'monstrous chaos' made up of Jewish and Christian heresies, a spiritual 'poison' and a 'superstition'. 'But', as Meletios points out, 'it is not surprising that Muḥammad managed to delude a crowd of vulgars with his teaching, since it is both pleasing through its warped word and agreeable for those who have succumbed to the pleasures' (vol. 2, p. 156). In order to prove this, he provides a selective brief summary of the Qur'an, covering theology, Christology, Muḥammad, the provenance of the Qur'an, the Muslim heaven, alimentary restrictions, Ramaḍān, polygamy and its prohibitions, the punishment for sexual crimes and crimes against property, and the banning of usury (vol. 2, pp. 156-7). Meletios's list ends with the pilgrimage of Muslims to Mecca and Medina, where the tomb of the 'loathsome' 'scallywag' Muḥammad is situated.

Throughout the *Ekklēsiastikē historia*, hostility to Islam and Muslims is explicit. Recounting a theological debate during the reign of the Emperor Manuel I Komnēnos (r. 1143-80) about 'the anathema of the God of Muḥammad', Meletios reproduces its argument against the *holosfyros* god (i.e. 'one-faced', unlike the Trinitarian Christian God) as an 'invention of [Muḥammad's] evil mind' (vol. 3, pp. 28-9). Similar is the attitude displayed towards emerging Safavid Shī'ism. In particular, it is expressed in two extensive excerpts about the 'Persian heresy' (vol. 3, pp. 219, 336-7). The first deals with the teaching of the forerunner, Shaykh Safi al-Din from Ardabil (Ṣafī al-Dīn Isḥāq Ardabīlī, 1252-1334), while the other recounts the deeds of the founder of the Safavid dynasty, Ismāʿīl I (r. 1501-24), and his contribution to the spreading of 'Muḥammad's religion according to ʿAlī's heresy' (vol. 3, p. 336). Finally, the Muslim religious orders of the Ottoman Empire do not escape Meletios's disapproval. Drawing a parallel between the mendicant orders of the Western Church and the Turkish dervishes, Meletios gives a description of the latter as well as of the ʿulamāʾ, concluding that 'the way of living and the mores of them all are ridiculous and abominable' (vol. 3, p. 353).

It is hardly surprising that the 'Turk' would be the central representative of the Muslim in a Greek-speaking church history of the 18th century. In the chapter against Muḥammad, Meletios adds after a description of the caliphs' rule that 'a little later there came into being the Ottoman Empire of the Turks, which proved fearful' (vol. 2, p. 157). He becomes more specific when he writes about the successor to the founder of the Ottoman dynasty, Orhan (r. 1326-62), that 'it is obvious to everyone the size and the abjection of the devastation and the annihilation he caused to the Christian religion' (vol. 3, pp. 178-9). Moreover, there are several points where the 'Turks' or an 'Ottoman emperor' are characterised as 'barbarians' (vol. 2, pp. 411-12, 416; vol. 3, pp. 206-7, 242, 299), or even as 'the most warlike foes of the Christian Church' (vol. 3, p. 314). There is only one exception: Sultan Selim I (r. 1512-20), who was 'meek to the Christians' and showed the Church much beneficence and favours (vol. 3, pp. 338-9).

In fact, the position of the Eastern Church within the Ottoman order represents an important aspect of the relationship between Christians and Muslims depicted in the *Ekklēsiastikē historia*. Meletios focuses primarily on the so-called 'privileges' granted by Mehmed II (r. 1451-81) to Gennadios Scholarios, the first Greek Orthodox patriarch after the Ottoman capture of Constantinople in 1453. Moreover, regarding the implication of these 'privileges', Meletios comments that they reinforced further patriarchal power over the dioceses as compared to the Byzantine period (vol. 3, p. 330). However, in the passages concerning the close relationship between the Ottoman authorities and the Patriarchate of Constantinople, a completely different picture is painted. The *Ekklēsiastikē historia* recounts in detail numerous Ottoman interventions in the internal affairs of the Great Church (vol. 3, pp. 339-40, 368, 401-2, 429-30, 446-7, 483), but few incidents provoke the open disaffection of Meletios (vol. 3, pp. 338, 369). In contrast to his earlier fervent polemics against Muḥammad and the Muslim religion, he is remarkably detached in recording the profitable interferences of the Ottoman Porte in the competition for the patriarchal see of the Greek Orthodox Christians.

This contradiction in Meletios's approach to Islam reveals some interesting layers in the complexity of the Christian understanding of Islam, especially among those living within the Ottoman Empire in the early 18th century. For one thing, Meletios's open attack on Islam is rare in Greek books from this period (with the exception of apocalyptic literature, preserved in manuscripts). One explanation could be that the *Ekklēsiastikē historia* was only published many decades after it was written, and far away from the Ottoman Empire. But however rational this explanation might be, it does not explain the internal contradiction.

One approach to interpreting – but not refuting – this contradictory attitude towards Islam and the Ottomans may lie in examining the sources used by Meletios. In particular, it has been assumed that the *Ekklēsiastikē historia* was based on one, if not more, of the Latin church histories written in France in the 17th century (Sarrēs, 'Hierē historia', pp. 539-50). Meletios's reliance on Western sources is apparent in the chapter on the origins of Islam, where he draws on the old medieval tradition of Christian polemical biographies of Muḥammad. Meletios cites, in particular, the anti-Muslim treatises written by the Byzantine Emperor Ioannēs Kantakouzēnos (14th century), Nicholas of Cusa and Marsilio Ficino (15th century), Juan Luis Vives (16th century) and Hugo Grotius (17th century), among others (vol. 2, p. 157; vol. 3, p. 216). Moreover, it is unlikely that Meletios had any personal views on Persian Shīʿism, or on the Western authors he quotes. His main source here is likely to have been Adam Olearius and his *Beschreibung der muscowitischen und persischen Reise* (Schleswig, 1647, afterwards republished in several enlarged editions and translations). On the other hand, the main supplementary sources for the Greek Orthodox Christians of the Ottoman period were a manuscript collection of patriarchal documents located in Constantinople (Sarrēs, 'Hierē historia', pp. 451-5, 699-710) and some Greek chronicles published by Martin Crusius in his *Turco-Graecia* (Basel, 1584). Thus, the perception of Christian-Muslim relations in the *Ekklēsiastikē historia* originates from two literary traditions characterised by different intellectual starting points and functioning within different political and religious contexts.

Augustine's dual concept of the Christian Church as expressed in *De civitate Dei*, which is analysed by Meletios in his Introduction (vol. 1, pp. 2-3), helps explain the reconciliation of these different traditions. According to Meletios, the Church (i.e. the 'City of God') is separate from the 'Worldly City' and 'has to service only true piety towards God' (vol. 1, p. 2). This explains the use of Latin controversial treatises against the 'false-god' of Muḥammad, regardless of whether in reference to Sunnī or Shīʿa Islam (vol. 3, p. 337). On the other hand, 'these two cities [...] are interconnected in this present World' (vol. 1, p. 3), a statement with multiple implications for the Eastern Church under Ottoman rule. Following his Greek Orthodox sources, Meletios emphasises the question of the 'privileges' granted to the patriarchs by the Ottoman sultans; these formed a crucial constitutional element in the ideological armoury of the Great Church in its complicated interactions with the Muslim authorities. The difficulties of negotiating with the Muslim other in the *Ekklēsiastikē historia* reflect the difficulties faced by Meletios himself in establishing a personal *modus vivendi* with the Ottomans, as well as with the Great Church.

The *Ekklēsiastikē historia* covers many centuries, and many different names are used to describe the Muslims. In the chapter on the teachings of Muḥammad, Meletios uses the terms *Mōamethdanoi* and *Ismaēlitai*, in contrast to the tribal definitions *Araves* (Arabs) and *Sarakēnoi* (Saracens). Nevertheless, the generic term used thereafter to refer to the Muslims is 'Saracens', derived rather from the Latin sources of the *Ekklēsiastikē historia*, as well as the very occasional use of the term *Mauroi* for the Iberian Moors. From the 11th book/century onwards, the term 'Saracens' is gradually replaced by *Tourkoi* (Turks). Meletios regularly uses the term 'Turks' with its dual ethnic and religious designations, in distinction from the *Tataroi* (used to refer to both Tatars from the Black Sea and Egyptian Mamlūks) and the 'Saracens'. Meanwhile, the initially ethnic definition *Persai* (Persians) acquires its Shī'ite connotation through the Safavids of Iran, unlike the 'Turks'. Once or twice, the terms *Agarēnoi* (descendants of Agar), *ethnikoi* (heathens) and the Shī'ite *Hasanitai* (descendants of al-Ḥasan, son of 'Alī) appear. Finally, there are two alternative verbs describing the act of converting to Islam: *tourkeuō* ('converting to the religion of Turks', vol. 3, p. 269) and *mōametizomai* ('converting to the religion of Muḥammad', vol. 3, p. 471).

SIGNIFICANCE

Excerpts from the *Ekklēsiastikē historia* can be found in numerous manuscripts of the 18th and early 19th centuries, since abridged versions were used in the classroom. Though many contemporary Greek-speaking scholars praised Meletios's work, it was in fact never republished, apart from an incomplete attempt by Nikolaos Adamidēs (who published the first volume alone, in 1853). However, it was both abridged and translated. There are two Romanian translations: the first by Metropolitan Veniamin Costache of Moldavia (Iaşi, 1841-2), and the second by the Wallachian scholar Naum Râmniceanu (see the list below). Furthermore, in 1855 the government printing house in Belgrade issued an abbreviated and supplemented Bulgarian translation edited by Averky Petrović and Grigor Goga.

The widespread use of the *Ekklēsiastikē historia* for educational purposes was sealed by the publication of a school compendium by Stephanos Kommētas (in his series of *Pedagogical courses*, Pest, 1827, with three reprints: Constantinople, 1841; Zakynthos, 1861; and Smyrna, 1862). Kommētas' work was also translated into Romanian by Alexandru Geanoglu Lesviodax and published in 1845. It is noteworthy that, although Kommētas' compendium contains the chapter on the life of Muḥammad and his teachings, it does not reproduce any of the polemics against Islam found in the original (pp. 87-9).

It appears that the enormous authority granted to the *Ekklēsiastikē historia* was due to the simple fact that it was the only Greek Orthodox general church history in existence, at least up until the mid-19th century. Considering the very moderate depiction of Muḥammad provided by Kommētas in 1827, it could be assumed that Meletios's contradictory treatment of Islam and the Muslims throughout the *Ekklēsiastikē historia* had come to prove meaningless and outdated in Greek-speaking educational circles of the second quarter of the 19th century.

PUBLICATIONS

MS Chios, 'Koraēs' Library – 154, 540 fols (18th century)

MS Sinai, Holy Monastery of St Catherine – 1769, 581 fols (18th century)

MS Alexandria, Patriarchate of Alexandria – 47-8, 342 + 386 fols (18th century)

MS Athens, Hellenic Parliament – 144, 573 fols (18th century)

MS Patmos, Monastery of St John the Theologian – 397-400, 623 fols (18th century)

MS Athens, Dependency of the Holy Sepulchre – 225, 593 fols (18th century, ordered by Chrysanthos Notaras, Patriarch of Jerusalem)

MS Kraków, Jagiellonian University – gr. 71-2, 180 + 196 fols (truncated, post 1766)

Meletios of Athens, *Ekklēsiastikē historia Meletiou mētropolitou Athēnōn. Metenechtheisa ek tēs hellēnikēs eis tēn hēmeteran haploellēnikēn phrasin, eis tomous treis diairetheisa; kai ploutistheisa me pollas chrēsimous, kai anankaias hyposēmeiōseis, kai akriveis pinakas; para Geōrgiou Vendotē ek Zakynthou, kai par' autou diorthōtheisa. Nyn prōton typois ekdotheisa di' epistasias, kai akribous epimeleias Polyzōē Lampanitziōtē tou ex Iōanninōn. Kai par' autou prosphōnētheisa tō hypsēlotatō, eusevestatō, kai galēnotatō authentē, kai hēgemoni Oungrovlachias kyriō kyriō, Iōannē Nikolaō Karantza*, Vienna: Joseph Baumeister, 3 vols, 1783-4; APB 2942 (digitised version available through the Digital Library of Modern Greek Studies, 'Anemi')

Stephanos Kommētas, *Paidagōgika mathēmata, syntethenta para Stephanou Kommēta tou ek Phthias, ek chōrarchias men Kokosiou, kōmēs de Kōphōn. Ekklēsiastikē historia, periechousa, ta anankaiotata symvevēkota eis tēn hieran ekklēsian; hoion; to kērygma tēs pisteōs, tous diōgmous, tas haireseis, tas synodous, kai tl.*, Pest: Matthias Trattner, 1827 (school compendium; repr. Constantinople, 1841; Zakynthos, 1861; Smyrna, 1862); APB 3126 (digitised version available through the Digital Library of Modern Greek Studies, 'Anemi')

Meletios of Athens, *Besericeasca istorie a lui Meletie mitropolitului Athinelor. Tălmăcită din Ellineasca limbă în cea proastă Ellinească, şi îmbogăţită, cu multe trevnice şi de nevoe supt-însemnări, şi cu scumpătăţite tabule, de Gheorghie Vendoti din Zachinth. Iar acum tălmăcită în limba românească de smeritul Veniamin Costachi mitropolitul Moldaviei*, Iaşi, 1841-2 (4 tomes in 8 vols; Romanian trans.); R3775 (digitised version available through Hathi Trust Digital Library)

Al. Geanoglu Lesviodax, *Istoria bisericească pre scurt*, Bucharest, 1845 (Romanian trans. following the abridged edition by S. Kommētas, Pest, 1827)

Meletios of Athens, *Ekklēsiastikē historia Meletiou Athēnōn mētropolitou, syngrapheisa men hellēnisti, meta de tēn teleutēn tou syngrapheōs ekdotheisa chydaisti to prōton eis treis tomous, epauxētheisa de kai tetartō hypo G. Vendotou, ēdē to deuteron diaskeuastheisa epi to katharōteron hyphos, kai tisin anankaiais epistasiais kai diorthōsesi ploutistheisa hypo K. Euthyvoulou. Kathēgētou tēs Philosophias en tē M. tou Genous Scholē, ekdidotai diērēmenē hōsautōs eis tessaras tomous hypo N. Adamidou tē enkrisei tēs Megalēs tou Christou Ekklēsias. Tomos prōtos*, Constantinople: Nikolaos Adamidēs, 1853 (archaising Greek trans.); APB 3348 (digitised version available through the Digital Library of Modern Greek Studies, 'Anemi')

Meletios of Athens, *Tserkovna istoria s naĭ-nuzhdnite sluchai v sviatata tsŭrkva, t.e. s propovedaneto na viarata, goneniĭata, eresite, soborite i prochaia. Prigledana tochno i dopŭlnena s raspis na patriarsite, papite, sultanite i zapadnite samoderzhtsi, a pechatana dvapŭti ot" G.V.M. s udobreniĭeto na tserkovnoto patriarshesko nadziratelstvo. Prevedena ot" grecheskiĭ na slavianobŭlgarskiĭ iazyk ot" Averkiia Petrovicha i Grigoriia Goga, diakoni*, Belgrade, 1855 (abbreviated and supplemented Bulgarian trans.)

STUDIES

K. Sarrēs, art. 'Composing and publishing a non-confessional history in the age of Greek Orthodox confessions. The *Ecclesiastical History* by Meletios of Athens', in T. Anastassiadis et al. (eds), *Livres et confessions chrétiennes orientales. Histoire connectée entre Empire ottoman, monde slave et Occident (XVIe-XVIIIe siècles). Actes du colloque de Rome, 15-16 décembre 2016*, Paris, 2020 (forthcoming)

V.Ē. Panagiōtopoulos, 'Diaphōtismos kai historia. Hē hellēnoglōssē historiographia tou 18ou aiōna', Athens, 2014 (PhD Diss. National and Kapodistrian University of Athens), pp. 174, 177, 182-3, 187, 192-4, 223-8, 239, 251-2

I.Ē. Kyriakantōnakēs, 'Historikos logos tēs Megalēs Ekklēsias kata tēn prōimē neōterikotēta', Athens, 2011 (PhD Diss. National and Kapodistrian University of Athens), pp. 71-2, 78-9, 147-9, 329-30

Sarrēs, 'Hierē historia'

Kyriakopoulos, *Meletios Athēnōn*, vol. 1, pp. 219-33

C.G. Patrinelēs, *Prōimē neohellēnikē historiographia (1453-1821)*, Thessaloniki, 1990, p. 88

G. Ştrempel (ed.), *Bibliografia românească modernă (1831-1918)*, Bucharest, 1989, vol. 3, pp. 89-90 (no. 32664), 288-9 (no. 36019) (description of the Romanian editions)

G. Ştrempel, *Catalogul manuscriselor româneşti*, Bucharest, 1983, vol. 2, pp. 114-15 (nos 1948-50), 152 (no. 152) (description of Romanian manuscript trans.)

G. Ştrempel, *Catalogul manuscriselor româneşti*, Bucharest, 1978, vol. 1, pp. 130-1 (nos 509-10), 192-3 (nos 913-15), 369-9 (no. 1561) (description of Romanian manuscript trans.)

D.A. Zakythēnos, 'Metavyzantinē kai neōtera hellēnikē historiographia', *Praktika tēs Akadēmias Athēnōn* 49 (1974) 57-103, pp. 64-5 (repr. in D.A. Zakythēnos, *Metavyzantina kai Nea Hellēnika*, Athens, 1978)

C. Erbiceanu, *Viaţaşi activitatea Protosinghelului Naum Râmniceanu* (Academia Română. Discursuri de recepţie 22), Bucharest, 1900, pp. 79-80 (the manuscript of Naum Râmniceanu's trans.)

Kostas Sarris

Krsto Pejkić

Christophorus Peichich Bulgarus

DATE OF BIRTH   14 September 1666
PLACE OF BIRTH   Probably Chiprovtsi, present-day Bulgaria
DATE OF DEATH   1730 or shortly after
PLACE OF DEATH   Vienna

BIOGRAPHY

There are at least two views concerning Krsto Pejkić's place of birth. According to Church historians Paul Aigl (*Historia brevis*) and Joseph Brüsztle (*Recensio*) he was born in Thessaloniki, although the sources they may each have used have not been traced. In contrast, Pejkić himself says that he was born on 14 September 1666 in Chiprovats (Kiprovats, present-day Chiprovtsi) in north-west Bulgaria, which at the time fell within the borders of the Ottoman Empire. This latter is generally considered more probable as it was never challenged by members of the Chiprovats refugee community in Transylvania, which Pejkić served as parish priest for some years.

In the second half of the 17th century, Chiprovats was the centre of Bulgarian Catholicism, and the archbishop of Sofia had his seat in the Observant Franciscan monastery there in preference to the city of Sofia. During the 17th century, the Catholic community of Chiprovats, despite representing a minority within the traditionally Greek-Orthodox Bulgarian population, enjoyed a period of economic and cultural growth. However, the rise of Catholicism in Chiprovats came to an abrupt end in 1688, when a regional revolt against the Ottoman Empire failed, resulting in the destruction of the town and the flight of over 2,000 refugees, who sought protection in various places throughout Wallachia and Transylvania.

In 1689, a year after the failure of the Chiprovats uprising, Krsto Pejkić was accepted as a student at Urban College, the college of the Propaganda Fide in Rome. He studied there for almost nine years, until 1698, when he left the college (without having obtained a degree) to become an apostolic missionary among his compatriots exiled in Transylvania.

In various phases of his life, Pejkić worked as a missionary, parish priest and canon in various locations in Hungary, Transylvania, Wallachia and Croatia. For a period of four years (1705-9), he was the prior of the Pia Casa dei Catecumeni (Holy House of the Catechumens) in Venice. With this sole exception, Pejkić's entire missionary activity was carried out in Central Europe, in the so-called 'new acquisition' territories of the Habsburg Empire. These territories had been annexed to the empire after the treatises of Karlowitz (1699) and Passarowitz (1718), and in Pejkić's time they were undergoing a process of Catholic confessionalisation. There are documents testifying that in 1728 Pejkić was appointed as the first canon of Belgrade cathedral, although they reveal that in 1730 he was not yet in residence there. The date and circumstances surrounding his death are not known, although the letters he wrote during the last years of his life were all composed in Vienna, and information contained in them suggests that he died there in 1730.

Pejkić was the author of five works of interconfessional polemics. Written in *lingua illirica* (a generic denotation for various South Slavic dialects), *Zarcalo istine* (Venice, 1716) was Pejkić's first publication. *Speculum veritatis* (Venice, 1725) was an extended Latin version of the *Zarcalo*. These two works deal with the schism between the Churches of Constantinople and Rome. *Concordia orthodoxorum Patrum orientalium et occidentalium* (Trnava, 1730) examined one aspect of the same issue in more detail. The *Additamentum* was an appendix to *Speculum veritatis. Mahometanus dogmatice et catechetice in Lege Christi instructus*, published in Latin in 1717, was Pejkić's only work dealing with anti-Muslim polemics.

MAIN SOURCES OF INFORMATION

Primary

MS Vatican City, Archivio Storico della Sacra Congregazione de Propaganda Fide – Acta Sacrae Congregationis: vol. 59 (1689), fol. 251; vol. 68 (1698), fol. 253; vol. 75 (1705), fol. 180

MS Vatican City, Archivio Storico della Sacra Congregazione de Propaganda Fide – Scritture originali riferite nelle Congregazioni generali: vol. 505, fols 58r and 59r; vol. 550, fols 371r-2v and 373r; vol. 566, fol. 333r-v; vol. 567, fol. 328r; vol. 612, fol. 122r-v; vol. 615, fols 174r-5v; vol. 624, fols 69r-70r; vol. 628, fol. 345r-v; vol. 649, fols 411r-4v; vol. 661, fols 272r-3v; vol. 666, fol. 83r-v; vol. 668, fols 191r-2v

MS Vatican City, Archivium Collegii de Propaganda Fide – Iuramentum, 145; Registro I, 177

MS Venice, Archivio delle Istituzioni di Ricovero e di Educazione [henceforth AIRE] – CAT G 3: Serie de' Priori del Pio Luogo de' Catecumeni (21 June 1558-15 April 1788)

MS Venice, AIRE – CAT B 16 (6 March 1703-28 February 1707): Terminazioni, fol. 66r (16 March 1705)

MS Venice, AIRE – CAT B 17 (6 March 1708-September 1711): Terminazioni, fol. 34v (9 April 1709)

MS Vienna, Austrian State Archives – Finanz- und Hofkammerarchiv (1170-1918), Alte Hofkammer (c. 1527-1762), Hoffinanz Ungarn (1544-1762), Vermischte ungarische Gegenstände (c. 1500-1762) 31: Protokolle der neoaquistischen Subdelegation (1719-45) 663-8, 736-7

Karsto Peikič, *Zarcalo istine med Carkve Istočne i Zapadnje*, Venice: Nikola Peccano, 1716

Christophorus Peichich, *Mahometanus dogmatice, et catechetice in lege Christi, Alcorano suffragante, instructus*, Trnava: Fridericus Gall, 1717

Christophorus Peichich, *Speculum veritatis inter Orientalem et Occidentalem Ecclesias refulgens*, Venice: Societas Albrizianae, 1725

Christophorus Peichich, *Additamentum ad Speculum veritatis*, Trnava (?), 1727 (?)

Christophorus Peichich, *Concordia orthodoxorum Patrum orientalium et occidentalium in eadem veritate, de Spiritus Sancti processione ab utroque, adamussim convenientium: ex commentariis Gennadii Patriarchae Constantinopolitani excerpta* [...], Trnava: Fridericus Gall, 1730

Secondary

I. Manova, 'An eighteenth-century project for the conversion of Southern Slavs to Catholicism. Krastyo Peykich's *Zarcalo istine* (1716)', in S. Zavarský, L.R. Nicholas and A. Riedl (eds), *Themes of polemical theology across early modern literary genres*, Cambridge, 2016, 143-60, pp. 144-8

I. Manova, 'The cultural project of Krastyo Peykich (1666-1730). A "spiritual weapon" for the Catholic undertaking in eighteenth-century East Central Europe', Padua, 2012 (PhD Diss. University of Padua), pp. 32-62; http://paduaresearch.cab.unipd.it/5153/1/Tesi_Manova_PDF-A.pdf

P.I. Zorattini, *I nomi degli altri. Conversioni a Venezia e nel Friuli Veneto in età moderna*, Florence, 2008, pp. 110, 135, 137

I.G. Tóth, *Bŭlgarskoto uchastie v katolicheski misii iz Ungariia i Transilvaniia prez XVII–XVIII v. Dokumenti ot Arkhiva na Svetata kongregatsiia za razprostranenie na viiarata, Vatikana 1637-1716 g.*, Sofia, 2008, pp. 432-3

K. Stanchev, art. 'Krüstiu Pejkich', in D. Petkanova (ed.), *Starobŭlgarska literatura. Entsiklopedichen rechnik*, Veliko Türnovo, 2003[2], 271-2

E. Sgambati, 'Cultura e azione europea di un missionario patriota bulgaro. Karsto Pejkič', in *Atti dell'VIII Congresso Internationale di Studi sull'Alto Medioevo*, Spoleto, 1983, 281-301

K. Telbizov, 'Küm biografiiata na Khristofor Pejkich (1665-1730)', *Vekove* 9 (1980) 26-35

J. Turčinović, *Misionar Podunavlja Krsto Pejkić (1665-1731)*, Zagreb, 1973

B. Pejchev, 'Krüstiu Pejkich (1665-1731)', in M. Büchvarov (ed.), *Antologiia na bŭlgarskata filosofska misŭl*, vol. 1, Sofia, 1973, 143-5

B. Pejchev, 'Katolicheskiat skholastitsizüm v istoriata na bülgarskata filosofska misül – XVIII vek', Sofia, 1972 (PhD Diss. Bulgarian Academy of Sciences, Institute of Philosophy)

B. Pejchev, 'Filosofskite e politicheskite vüzgledi na Krüstiu Pejkich (1665-1730)', in M. Büchvarov and K. Andreev (eds), *Istoria na filosofskata misül v Bŭlgaria*, vol. 1, Sofia, 1970, 121-32

B. Pejchev, 'Bogoslovsko-filosofskite i politicheskite vüzgledi na Krüstiu Pejkich', *BAN. Izvestiia na Instituta po Filosofia* 17 (1969) 217-38

E. Angyal, 'Krstju Pejkic, ein bulgarischer Schriftsteller der Barockziet', *Annales Instituti Philologiae Slavicae Universitatis Debrecensis, Slavica* 7 (1967) 129-35

N. Žic, 'Novi bio-bibliografski prilozi za Krstu Pejkića', *Napredak. Glasilo Hrvatskog Kulturnog Društva* 8 (1933) 68

M. Kostić, 'Biobibliografski prilozi za Krstu Pejkića', *Prilozi za Kniževnost, Jezik, Istoriju i Folklor* 12 (1932) 84-5

I. Moga, 'Ştiri despre Bulgarii din Ardeal', *Anuarul Institutului de Istorie Naţională* [Cluj] 5 (1928-30) 513-9

E. Fermendžin, *Acta Bulgariae ecclesiastica ab a. 1565 usque ad a. 1799*, Zagreb, 1887, pp. 325-7

J. Brüsztle, *Recensio universi cleri dioecesis Quinque-Ecclesiensis*, Quinque-Ecclesiis, 1876, pp. 420-1

P. Aigl, *Historia brevis venerabilis capituli cathedralis ecclesiae Quinque-Ecclesiensis a prima eiusdem origine usque finem anni 1838*, Quinque-Ecclesiis, 1838, p. 89

WORKS ON CHRISTIAN-MUSLIM RELATIONS

Mahometanus dogmatice et catechetice in lege Christi, Alcorano suffragante, instructus
'The Muslim educated dogmatically and catechetically in the law of Christ, with the support of the Qur'an'

DATE 1717
ORIGINAL LANGUAGE Latin

DESCRIPTION

The *Mahometanus*, as the work is known, is intended as a handbook for Catholic missionaries working among Muslims. Pejkić presents it as a 'spiritual weapon', to be taken up in the struggle against the Ottoman Turks, the 'greatest foe' of the Habsburgs and of the whole of Christianity.

At the same time, he also recommends it as a useful guide for preaching Catholicism to 'schismatics' and 'heretics', thereby placing it within the wider perspective of the Habsburgs' policy of consolidating the Catholic faith as the 'state religion' in the borderlands of their empire. The book was printed in Trnava in 1717, and its publication was directly associated with the Austro-Turkish war of 1716-18, though it was probably composed several years earlier during Pejkić's stay in Venice.

The book consists of a letter of dedication to the Holy Roman Emperor Charles VI (r. 1711-40), a preface to the reader, ten chapters, a corollary in which Christian and Muslim laws are compared, and a conclusion. The first six chapters may be described as forming the apologetic/polemical

MAHOMETANUS
DOGMATICE,
ET
CATECHETICE
IN LEGE
CHRISTI,
ALCORANO
SUFFRAGANTE,
Conventus INSTRUCTUS, *Viennensis*
Augustinianum ER *Excalceatoris*
CHRISTOPHORUM
PEICHICH BULGARUM
Chiprovatienſem Miſſionaꝛium
Apoſtolicum, & Cathedralis Eccleſiæ
Quinque Eccleſienſis Canonicum.

TYRNAVIÆ,
Typis Academicis per Fridericum Gall, Anno 1717.

Illustration 10. Krsto Pejkić /Christophorus Peichich, *Mahometanus dogmatice*, title page

section of the work. Here, Pejkić aims to confirm that all the dogmas of the Catholic Church were received through revelation, and to confute some of the 'classical' accusations that Muslim theologians have directed at Christians (for example, the idea that Christians have falsified the Bible to bring it into accord with their religion). The remaining chapters, 7-10, form the doctrinal and instructive part of the *Mahometanus*. They take up 160 of the 195 pages, in quarto, of the book, and constitute its main body. They offer discussions of the three theological virtues (faith, hope and charity), the symbol of the cross, the Trinity, the Incarnation, the Lord's Prayer, the Decalogue, the Catholic Creed, the sacraments and the sacramentals. Although this main part of the *Mahometanus* is devoted to expounding Catholic doctrine, it is frequently interrupted by polemical passages in which Pejkić criticises Muslim opinions and practices. For example, when he is expounding the doctrine of eternal life, he comments on the Muslim paradise as narrated in the Qur'an, examines the sacrament of baptism alongside the ceremony of circumcision, and introduces the first Commandment, together with a defence of the custom of the veneration of icons.

In his line of argument, Pejkić assigns a central place to refuting the Islamic teaching on matrimony, divorce and polygamy. He states that divorce is against natural law, that it harms the correct upbringing and education of children and that the marriage contract, by which each spouse concedes his or her own body to the other, cannot be infringed or terminated. Like divorce, polygamy is contrary to both natural and divine law, and has a harmful effect on the education of children and an objectionable, intensifying effect on the libido. Pejkić dedicates a great deal of space to these discussions, for he is convinced that there can be no better arguments than those connected to divorce and polygamy to expose the falsity of the Qur'an and its teachings. At the same time, he probably judged that combating the Islamic views on these issues had considerable practical importance.

Pejkić's acquaintance with the Qur'an and with Islamic teachings comes almost exclusively from a single source, Ludovico Maracci's refutation, *Prodromus ad refutationem Alcorani*, published in Rome in 1691. The exposition of the Catholic doctrine is based on the *Roman catechism* conceived by the Council of Trent. Pejkić follows it so closely that his book might justly be described as a compendium of the *Roman catechism* adapted to the needs of missionaries operating among Muslim converts to Catholicism.

SIGNIFICANCE

In the 'Preface to the reader', Pejkić states that the innovative aspect of his book consists in the attempt to defeat Muslims with their own weapons, borrowing from their own commonly held teachings. However, despite his insistence to the contrary, this approach, designed to demonstrate 'the falsity of Qur'an through the Qur'an itself', was fairly traditional. He could have found it, for example, in the *Manuductio ad conversionem mahumetanorum* ('Handbook for the conversion of Muslims', 1687) by Tirso González de Santalla (1624-1705), a book he claims to have received as a personal gift from the author, and regards as 'indispensable' in his missionary work (*Mahometanus*, p. 193). Compared to similar writings, the main distinctive feature of the *Mahometanus* is, in fact, that the anti-Muslim polemics it contains are merely an external shell enclosing an essentially catechistic work. From this perspective, it turns out to be not so much a handbook for the *conversion* of Muslims as a genuine handbook for the religious *education* of Muslim converts to Catholicism.

According to Pejkić's own testimony, offered in the Preface, all the 'refutations of accusations' and 'persuasive arguments' it comprises had been tested in practice during his work as a missionary in Transylvania in 1700-3, and when he was prior of the Pia Casa dei Catecumeni in Venice in 1705-9. And indeed, as prior of that institution Pejkić's main duty was to conduct the proselytisation and catechisation of converts, more than half of whom, according to the registers, came from Islam. In light of this, the *Mahometanus* may appropriately be read as a clue to the form and content of the religious education carried out at the Pia Casa.

PUBLICATIONS

Christophorus Peichich, *Mahometanus dogmatice, et catechetice in lege Christi, Alcorano suffragante, instructus*, Trnava: Fridericus Gall, 1717; 4 Polem. 2316 (digitised version available through *MDZ*)

STUDIES

I. Manova, 'An adaptation of the *Roman catechism* for the religious education of Muslim converts to Catholicism. Krastyo Peykich's *The Mohammedan educated in the law of Christ* (1717)', in A. Prosperi and M. Catto (eds), *Trent and beyond. The Council, other powers, other cultures*, Turnhout, 2017, 583-98

I. Manova, 'L'*ars convincendi Mahometanos*. Krastyo Peykich e la Casa dei Catecumeni nella Venezia di inizio Settecento', *Atti dell'Istituto Veneto di Scienze, Lettere ed Arti. Classe di Scienze Morali, Lettere ed Arti* 174 (2015-16) 127-45

I. Manova, 'Krüstiu Pejkich (1666-1730) i negoviat *Mohamedanin, obu-chen v süglasie s Korana spored Hristovia zakon* (1717)', *Arkhiv za Srednovekovna Filosofiia i Kultura. Archiv für Mittelalterliche Philosophie und Kultur* 18 (2012) 193-235

Turčinović, *Misionar Podunavlja*, pp. 97-101

Pejchev, 'Katoličeskiiat skholastitsizüm'

Pejchev, 'Filosofskite e politicheskite vüzgledi'

Pejchev, 'Bogoslovsko-filosofskite i politicheskite vüzgledi'

Iva Manova

Anastasios Gordios

DATE OF BIRTH   1654/5
PLACE OF BIRTH   Vraniana, Eurytania, central Greece
DATE OF DEATH   7 June 1729
PLACE OF DEATH   Vraniana

BIOGRAPHY

The Greek hieromonk Anastasios Gordios counts as one of the most prominent 'tutors of the nation' (*didaskaloi tou genous*), who sought to preserve Greek culture in Greece under Ottoman rule (16th-19th centuries). He received his elementary education in Vraniana (Eurytania), and then until 1676 in Karpenisi and Vraniana. In order to access higher education in philosophy and theology, he enrolled under the hieromonk Eugenios Yannoulis, whose philosophy was based on the neo-Aristotelian commentaries of Theophilos Korydalleus. He then continued his studies in philosophy with hieromonk Nikodemos Mazarrakis in Athens, and Arta and Ioaninna in Epirus (around 1676/8). He succeeded Yannoulis as a teacher in the school of Vraniana/Agrapha, and in the years following Yannoulis' death in 1682 he continued to teach in Vraniana. Between 1687 and 1689 he appears to have been an auditor at the school of the *Artisti* in Padua, and, after his return to Greece and a short sojourn in Zakynthos (Zante) between 1690 and 1710, he taught at the school of Aetolicon, close to Messolonghi in Aetolia. In summer 1710, he returned to his birthplace, Vraniana, where he worked mainly as a private teacher until his death on 7 June 1729.

A scholar with a broad education, Anastasios Gordios was active as both a teacher and a writer. As well as his roles as priest and monk, he is also recognised as an important ecclesiastical personality and was deeply involved in the political, economic and religious situation in the Agrapha region, supporting his close relatives, students, hometown and suffering villagers. Apart from the *Vita* of his teacher, Eugenios Yannoulis, he wrote about 30 philological, didactic, theological and hagiographical treatises, and about 700 letters. His most important work is the treatise *Peri Mōameth kai kata Lateinōn syngramma* ('On Muḥammad and against the Latins'). He is acknowledged as one of the most important ecclesiastical scholars from the period 1680-1730 within Greece, and his

national and theological thought deeply influenced subsequent generations of Greek Orthodox believers.

MAIN SOURCES OF INFORMATION

Primary

Anastasios Gordios, *Allēlographia* (*1675-1728*), vols 1-2, ed. Ch. Karanasios and I. Kolia, Athens, 2011

Secondary

O. Olar, 'Prophecy and history. Matthew of Myra († 1626), Paisios Ligaridis († 1678), and Chrysanthos Notaras († 1731)', in R.G. Păun (ed.), *Histoire, mémoire et dévotion. Regards croisés sur la construction des identités dans le monde orthodoxe aux époques byzantine et post-byzantine*, Seyssel, 2016, 364-88

A. Argyriou, 'Hē allēlographia Anastasiou tou Gordiou. Mia prosektikē anagnōsē', *Epirotiko Hēmerologio* 32 (2013) 189-226

I. Kolia, 'Athanasios hieromonachos ho ex Agraphōn († 1719). Hē epistolographia tou', *Mesaiōnika kai Nea Hellēnika* 3 (1990) 215-54; 4 (1992) 81-159

G. Podskalsky, *Die griechische Theologie in der Zeit der Türkenherrschaft* (*1453-1821*), Munich, 1988, pp. 305-8

P. Vasileiou, *Ho megalos didaskalos tou Genous Eugenios Giannoulēs ho Aitolos kai hoi spoudaioteroi mathētes tōn Scholōn tōn Agraphōn*, Athens, 1985²

Anastasios Gordios, *Sur Mahomet et contre les Latins*, ed. A. Argyriou, Athens, 1983, pp. 285-93

P. Vasileiou, 'Ho Anastasios Gordios kai to ergo tou (1654-1729)', *Thessalika Chronika* 10 (1971) 129-56

WORKS ON CHRISTIAN-MUSLIM RELATIONS

Peri Mōameth kai kata Lateinōn syngramma
'On Muḥammad and against the Latins'

DATE Approximately 1717-21
ORIGINAL LANGUAGE Greek (modern)

DESCRIPTION

This treatise is Gordios's most remarkable theological work, demonstrating his theological and ideological attitude towards the religious and
historical developments of his time. It is extant in a large number of
manuscripts; in the critical edition it is around 90 pages long.

In the Preface (chs 1-4), Gordios mentions verses in the Book of Revelation that he claims refer to Muḥammad. Developing these, in Part I (chs 5-17) he traces the history of the Church through the first three seals (Revelation 6:1-6), which for him symbolise the spread of the Gospel (the white horse), the establishment of the Church through the preaching of the Apostles and the blood of the martyrs (the bright red horse), and the emergence of monasticism and the teaching of the great Fathers of the Church (the black horse). These three periods, which formed the prime era of divine grace, lasted 600 years. During this time the devil suffered three overwhelming defeats: by Jesus and his disciples, by the martyrs, and by the Fathers of the Church and the monastic orders.

Part II (chs 18-58) is devoted to the Antichrist as portrayed in Revelation. The defeat of the dragon by Michael and his angels (12:7-8) represents the fullness of the Church during the period of grace. The fall of the dragon (12:9) denotes the appearance of the Antichrist in the figures of Muḥammad and the pope, and the beast rising out of the sea (13:1-10) is a symbol of Muḥammad, who was born in the year 600 and lived 66 years (corresponding to 666, the number of the beast in Revelation 13:18). Muḥammad is the incarnation of the Antichrist, diverting people from the true faith, while the reign of the Turks ensured unbelief in the countries of the Orthodox East. The woman pursued into the wilderness (Revelation 12:13-17) represents the Orthodox patriarchates under Ottoman rule. They fled to the desert, or Russia, which adopted Christianity at a time when Islam imposed its domination over the Orthodox East. Russia will play the role of the protector and the defender of the Orthodox faith for 1,260 days (42 months, as in 13:5), for the entire reign of the Antichrist, until the end of the world.

The second beast, 'rising out of the sea' (13:11-18), is the pope, the other personification of the Antichrist. His title *Lateinos* corresponds to the number 666, which is also the number of the beast and the number of a person, and the two horns of the beast represent the pope's political and ecclesiastical authority. The phrase 'it spoke as a dragon' (13:11) reflects the pride that led the bishop of Rome to name himself 'the one and only vicar of Christ on earth, Pontifex Maximus and head of the whole Church, earthly king and God'. The pope separated himself from God and the Christian emperor, betraying the Orthodox Church and the Eastern Empire, 'so that he takes his seat in the temple of God, declaring himself to be God' (2 Thessalonians 2:4).

Clearly, the pope is portrayed as a bitter enemy of the Orthodox East, engaged, like Muḥammad, in an attempt to eradicate the Orthodox faith and worship. Muḥammad and the pope are two personifications of the Antichrist, and their kingdom is that of the Antichrist. Those who have embraced the Latin doctrine have accepted the mark of the beast on their forehead, while Muslims have received this mark on their right hand.

Part III (chs 59-89) consists of a doctrinal essay aimed against the Latin Church, and in Part IV (chs 90-7), which is in the form of a lament, Gordios argues that the end of the world 'is near' (Revelation 22:10) and that humankind is living in the reign of the Antichrist. This is the world inhabited by Orthodox Christians, who are impoverished, weak, helpless and tormented, facing the daily risk of falling into the mouth of either the first or the second beast.

Gordios wrote this treatise to provide relief and strength for Orthodox believers who were suffering under Ottoman rule, to help them stand firm in their Orthodox convictions, and to strengthen them against succumbing to the deception of either Antichrist.

SIGNIFICANCE

The importance of *Syngramma* lies in its interpretation of contemporary historical and political realities through the Book of Revelation in order to strengthen Greek national and religious identity under Ottoman rule. Its defining characteristic is that there will be no imminent end to the current state of affairs, and that the glories of the Byzantine past will not suddenly be reinstated. This is not what scripture teaches, though the course of history has already been mapped out.

Despite a certain lack of coherence and historical accuracy, Gordios's clear opinions in the work profoundly affected the thought and attitudes of oppressed Orthodox Greeks for at least a century. They were also to form the basis for all subsequent Greek interpretations of the Book of Revelation up to 1922.

The work is counted among the most influential and daring Greek texts of the period of Turkish rule. To understand it properly, it should be regarded as an expression of an ideological strand that had Orthodoxy at its core.

PUBLICATIONS

MSS Athens, Ethnikē Vivliothēkē tēs Hellados – 1257 (around 1787); 1256 (around 1790); 411 (18th century); 443 (18th century); 2138 (18th century); 2327 (18th century); 444 (19th century)

MS Athens, Ethnikē Vivliothēkē tēs Hellados, Metochion tou Panagiou Tafou – 120 (18th century)

MS Athens, Benaki Museum – 194 (TA 39, 18th century)

MS Xenophontos – 65 (18th century)

MS Koutloumousiou – 197 (18th century)

MS Kavsocalyvion – 4 (18th century)

MS Iviron – 604 (18th century)

MSS Panteleemonos – 639 (18th century); 674 (18th century)

MSS Meg. Lavra – Θ 109 (17th century?); Θ 128 (around 1763); Λ 16 (around 1755)

MS Dochiareiou – 94 (18th century)

MSS Vatopediou – 526 (before 1806); 646 (around 1748); 683 (18th century)

MS Iosaphaion – 118 (18th century)

MSS Bucharest, Biblioteca Academiei Romậne – gr. 1029 (around 1788); gr. 1197 (18th century)

MS Kykkos – 6 (date unknown)

MS Dimitsana, Dēmosia Vivliothēkē – (around 1798)

MS Istanbul, Theological School of Chalki – 87 (date unknown)

MS Istanbul, Monastery of Panaghia Kamariotissa – 161 (date unknown)

MS Izmir (Smyrna), Evangelical School – 39 (around 1756); 50 (18th century)

MS Jerusalem, Patriarchikē Vivliothikē – gr. 153 (around 1790); gr. 269 (18th century); gr. 302 (18th century)

MS Larisa, Dēmosia Vivliothēkē – 5 (around 1787)

MS Leros, Dēmosia Vivliothēkē – 27 (18th century)

MS Meteora – Varlaam 20 (around 1760)

MS Patmos – gr. 303 (around 1741)

MS Prousos – 5 (18th century)

MS Sofia, Ivan Dujcev Centre – gr. 3 (18th century)

MS Venice, Instituto Ellenico – cod. 17 (date unknown)

MS Vienna, Österreichische Nationalbibliothek – Suppl. gr. 112 (17th century ?)

MSS Zagora/Magnesia, Dēmosia Vivliothēkē – 87 (18th century); 88 (18th century)

MS George Zaviras (Private Library) – 900 (around 1770)

See also A. Argyriou, *Les exégèses grecques de l'Apocalypse à l'époque turque (1453-1821). Esquisse d'une histoire des courants idéologiques au sein du peuple grec asservi*, Thessaloniki, 1982, p. 311-15

Anastasios Gordios, *Sur Mahomet et contre les Latins*, ed. A. Argyriou, Athens, 1983 (pp. 1-27, comments; pp. 28-120, critical edition)

STUDIES

A. Argyriou, 'Diamorphōsē mias hellēnorthodoxēs syneidēsēs mesō tōn hermēneiōn stēn Apokalypsē kata tous chronous tēs Tourkokratias', in Chr. Oikonomou et al. (eds), *Hagia graphē kai synchronos kosmos. Timētikos tomos ston kathēgētē Iōannē D. Karavidopoulo*, Thessaloniki, 2006, pp. 57-74

Argyriou, *Les exégèses grecques*, pp. 306-54

A. Argyriou, 'Anastassios Gordios et la polémique anti-islamique postbyzantine', *Revue des Sciences Religieuses* 43 (1969) 58-87

Asterios Argyriou and Chariton Karanasios

Dimitrie Cantemir

Demetrius Cantemir, Dimitrios Kantemiris, Demetrius Kantemir,
Dmitrii Kantemir, Kantemiroğlu, Küçük Kantemiroğlu

DATE OF BIRTH   26 October 1673, 1674 or 1675
PLACE OF BIRTH   Unknown; probably Moldavia
DATE OF DEATH   21 August 1723
PLACE OF DEATH   Dmitrovsk, Orlovsk oblast, Russia

BIOGRAPHY

Dimitrie Cantemir was the son of the Moldavian prince Constantin Cantemir (d. 1693) and his third wife, Ana (Anița) Bantăș (d. 1677). His paternal forefathers were freeholders from Silișteni, a village on the Elan river (Fălciu). He was well aware of his descent, as is shown by the genealogy he gives in the self-interested Latin biography he wrote of his father between 1698 and 1705, *Vita Constantini Cantemyrii, cognomento Senis, Moldaviæ Principis* ('Life of Constantin Cantemir, called "the Old", Prince of Moldavia'). However, he repeatedly claimed a more prestigious affiliation, sometimes even referring back to the 14th-century Mongolian warlord Tamerlane.

His date of birth is disputed – variously given as 26 October 1673, 26 October 1674, and 26 October 1675 – as is his place of birth. He was sent to Constantinople as a guarantee for his father's loyalty, and there learnt Latin and Turkish. He returned to Moldavia in 1691 and became a pupil of the learned hieromonk Ieremias Kakavelas of Crete. After his father's death in March-April 1693, he ruled for three weeks, but failed to secure confirmation from the Ottomans. He returned to the Porte as an aristocratic hostage and then served as diplomatic representative on behalf of the Porte to his brother, who had been appointed prince of Moldavia. He returned to Constantinople in 1700, and remained there until 1710.

Cantemir wrote a number of works during this time, though he published only one, the bilingual Romanian-Greek *Divanul sau Gâlceava înțeleptului cu lumea sau Giudețul sufletului cu trupul* ('Divan or the wise man's dispute with the world, or the litigation between soul and body', Iași, 1698).

In November 1710, Cantemir was appointed prince of Moldavia. Soon after, he signed a treaty of alliance with Tsar Peter the Great (r. 1682-1725) and joined forces with the Russian army in its 1711 anti-Ottoman campaign. The army was thoroughly defeated by the Ottomans, and this marked the end of Cantemir's political dreams. He was forced to take refuge in Russia, and one year later became a senator and secret advisor to the tsar. In 1722, he joined Peter the Great on his Persian campaign, producing along the way descriptions of the route to the Caspian and of the 'Caucasian wall' that ran between the Caspian and the Black Sea.

In spite of all the setbacks he experienced, the Russian period proved highly productive for Cantemir as an author, but the only work he published was *Kniga sistima ili Sostoianie muhammedanskiia religii* ('The system or structure of the Mohammedan religion'), on the Qur'an. He died on 21 August 1723.

MAIN SOURCES OF INFORMATION

Primary

For references to primary sources on Cantemir, see A. Eşanu (ed.), *Neamul Cantemireştilor. Bibliografie*, Chişinău, 2010, pp. 23-308.

See also:

Dimitrie Cantemir, *Opere complete*, vol. 4. *Istoria ieroglifică*, ed. S. Toma and N. Stoicescu, Bucharest, 1973

Dimitrie Cantemir, *Opere complete*, vol. 6/1. *Vita Constantini Cantemyrii, cognomento Senis, Moldaviæ principis*, ed. D. Sluşanschi, I. Câmpeanu and A. Pippidi, Bucharest, 1996

Dimitrie Cantemir, *Opere complete*, vol. 6/2. *Scurtă povestire despre stârpirea familiilor lui Brâncoveanu şi a Cantacuzinilor. Memorii către Petru cel Mare (1717 şi 1718)*, ed. P. Cernovodeanu et al., Bucharest, 1996

Demetrii principis Cantemirii Incrementorum et decrementorum avlæ othman[n]icæ sive aliothman[n]icæ historiæ a prima gentis origine ad nostra vsqve tempora dedvctæ libri tres, ed. D. Sluşanschi, Timişoara, 2001

I. Neculce, *Opere. Letopiseţul Ţării Moldove şi O samă de cuvinte*, ed. G. Ştrempel, Bucharest, 1982

V. Cândea, 'La vie du prince Dimitrie Cantemir écrite par son fils Antioh. Texte intégral d'après le manuscrit original de la Houghton Library', *Revue des Études Sud-Est Européennes* 23 (1985) 203-21

V. Ţvircun, *Epistoliarnoe nasledie Dmitriia Kantemira. Jizni i sud'ba v pis'mah i bumagah*, Chişinău, 2008

V. Ţvircun, *Dimitrii Cantemir. Stranitsy jizni v pis'mah i dokumentah*, St Petersburg, 2010

S.A. Frantsouzoff, 'Le fonds de Dimitrie Cantemir dans les archives de l'Institut des manuscrits orientaux de l'Académie des sciences de Russie', *Revue des Études Sud-Est Européennes* 49 (2011) 123-37

M. Maxim, *O istorie a relaţiilor româno-otomane cu documente noi din arhivele turceşti*. II. *De la Mihai Viteazul la fanarioţi (1601-1711/1716)*, Brăila, 2013, pp. 218-33

Secondary

For references to modern sources on Cantemir, see Eşanu, *Neamul Cantemireştilor. Bibliografie*, pp. 23-308.

See also:

Ş.S. Gorovei, 'Cantemireştii. Contribuţii genealogice şi heraldice', *Cercetări Istorice* 37 (2018) 123-40

N. Pissis, 'Dimitrie Cantemir, the *monarchia borealis* and the Petrine instauration', *Sonderforschungsbereich 980 Episteme in Bewegung. Working Paper* 4, Berlin, 2015

V. Ţvircun, *Viaţa şi destinul lui Dimitrie Cantemir*, Bucharest, 2015

I. Feodorov, art. 'Dimitrie Cantemir', in *EI3*

B. Creţu, *Inorogul la porţile Orientului. Bestiarul lui Dimitrie Cantemir*, 2 vols, Iaşi, 2012-13

M. Leezenberg, 'The Oriental origins of Orientalism. The case of Dimitrie Cantemir', in R. Bod, J. Maat and T. Weststeijn (eds), *The making of the humanities*, vol. 2. *From early modern to modern disciplines*, Amsterdam, 2012, 243-63

B. Creţu (ed.), *Dimitrie Cantemir. Perspective interdisciplinare*, Iaşi, 2012 (especially M.M. Székely, 'Moldova lui Dimitrie Cantemir şi *Descrierea* ei', pp. 145-76)

V. Pelin, 'Manuscrisele operelor lui Dimitrie Cantemir în arhivele şi bibliotecile Rusiei', in A. Eşanu, C. Iordan (ed), *Cultură şi politică în Sud-Estul Europei (sec. XV-XX)*, Chişinău, 2011, 16-45

M. Timuş, 'Monuments et inscriptions. Le voyage du Prince Démètre Cantemir vers la Perse par le Caucase (1722-1723)', *Res Orientales* 20 (2011) 147-64

S. Lemny, *Les Cantemir. L'aventure européenne d'une famille princière au XVIIIe siècle*, Paris, 2009 [Romanian version: *Cantemireştii. Aventura europeană a unei familii princiare din secolul al XVIII-lea*, Iaşi, 2010]

A. Eşanu (ed.), *Dinastia Cantemireştilor (secolele XVII-XVIII)*, Chişinău, 2008

A. Pippidi, 'Cantemir. Portret intelectual', in A. Pippidi, *Despre statui şi morminte. Pentru o teorie a istoriei simbolice*, Iaşi, 2000, 119-34

O. Wright, *Demetrius Cantemir. The collection of notations*, London, 2 vols, 1992-2000

E. Ţarălungă, *Dimitrie Cantemir. Contribuţii documentare la un portret*, Bucharest, 1989

G. Cioranesco, 'L'activité de Démètre Cantemir pendant la campagne russe en Perse (1722)', *Cahiers du Monde Russe et Sovietique* 29 (1988) 257-71

A. Brezianu, 'Swift and the Cantemirs. An eighteenth-century case in literary contingency', *Revue des Études Sud-Est Européennes* 23 (1985) 223-31

P. Cernovodeanu, 'Démètre Cantemir vu par ses contemporains (le monde savant et les milieux diplomatiques européens)', *Revue des Études Sud-Est Européennes* 11 (1973) 637-56

V. Cosma, 'Le musicien Démètre Cantemir dans la littérature européenne du XVIIIe siècle', *Revue des Études Sud-Est Européennes* 11 (1973) 657-76

P.P. Panaitescu, *Dimitrie Cantemir. Viaţa şi opera*, Bucharest, 1958

P. Panaitescu, 'Le prince Démètre Cantemir et le mouvement intellectuel russe sous Pierre le Grand', *Revue des Études Slaves* 6 (1926) 245-62

Şt. Ciobanu, 'Dimitrie Cantemir în Rusia', *Analele Academiei Române. Memoriile Secţiunii Literare*, 3rd series 2 (1925) 381-543 [Bucharest, 2000²]

WORKS ON CHRISTIAN-MUSLIM RELATIONS

Incrementa atque decrementa
'Growth and decay'

DATE   first version 1706-10; final version possibly 1714-19
ORIGINAL LANGUAGE   Greek

DESCRIPTION

In 1714, in a letter to a member of the Berlin Academy, Dimitrie Cantemir expressed his intention to write a trilogy on the Ottoman Empire. The first part, which Cantemir said in his letter was completed, was a 'summary of Turkish history' called *The growth of the Othman court*, while the second and the third parts were planned to address religious and institutional issues. But things did not go according to plan: the treatise on Ottoman organisation and government was never written, while the book on the Muḥammadan religion was published in Russian translation only. As for the historical part, it appeared posthumously, divided into three books, in English translation through the efforts of Dimitrie's son, Antioh (London, 1734-5). Known as *Incrementa atque decrementa*, its full title is *Demetrii principis Cantemirii Incrementorum et decrementorum Aulæ Othman[n]icæ sive Aliothman[n]icæ Historiæ a prima gentis origine ad nostra usque tempora deductæ libri tres* ('Prince Dimitrie Cantemir's history of the growth and decay of the Othman or Aliothman court drawn from the very beginnings of the people down to our times, in three books').

Cantemir's *Incrementa atque decrementa* is 1064 pages long in the Houghton manuscript, and 511 pages in the Latin edition by Dan Sluşanschi (Timişoara, 2001). It has two sections, each accompanied by

extensive annotations called *Annotationes*. The first, entitled *Incrementa*,
goes from 611 AH (1214 CE) to 1083 AH (1672 CE), the date of the Ottoman
expedition against the Polish-Lithuanian Commonwealth, which was, in
Cantemir's view, the last meaningful Ottoman victory. This part presents the lives and deeds of 19 sultans, from Süleyman the Magnificent
(r. 1520-66) to Mehmed IV (r. 1648-87), whose reigns are equated with
the 'growth' of the Ottoman Empire. The second section, called *Decrementa*, covers the latter years of Mehmed IV's reign and continues until
1122 AH (1711 CE), the year of the Ottoman victory against the Russians
at Stănileşti. The last pages are dedicated to the Russian Tsar Peter I 'the
Great'. The *Annotationes* provide detailed additional information on a
wide range of subjects tackled in the main work. For example, Cantemir
includes an eyewitness account of the Ottoman defeat by the Habsburgs
at Zenta (1697).

As Andrei Pippidi ('Ideea de "creştere şi decădere"') has argued, there
is a strong possibility that the *Incrementa atque decrementa* was composed in Greek, between 1706 and 1710; it was completed after 1714 in
Russia, where Cantemir had found sanctuary, and then translated into
Latin. However, the Greek version (if it indeed existed) is for the moment
lost. The *Annotationes* were composed in Russia, directly in Latin. In
Virgil Cândea's view ('Life story'), the Harvard manuscript represents
the original Latin text of the final version revised by Cantemir, though
according to V. Ţvircun ('Reperele') it represents a revision of the original Latin text, made by the German Orientalist Gottlieb Siegfried Bayer
(d. 1738), professor at the Imperial Academy in St Petersburg. Since a
Russian translation was ready by 1719, Cantemir must have finished his
text by then.

Cantemir starts the *Incrementa atque decrementa* by explaining the
hijrī calendar and how to convert the *hijrī* year to the Christian year. He
reflects on the name and origins of the Turks, and the founding of the
Ottoman dynasty, and then he narrates Ottoman history, explaining that
he is closely following Ottoman historiography. His sources were diverse.
He quotes several Byzantine historians, including Nicephorus Gregoras
(d. c. 1360), Laonicus Chalcocondyles (d. c. 1490), and the *Chronicon
maius* attributed to George Sphrantzes (d. c. 1478; in fact, as Cantemir
suspected, this was a 16th-century expanded version by Makarios Melis-
sinos, d. 1585). He is familiar with the works of Lonicerus, Leunclavius,
Rycaut and Sieur de La Croix, and is very critical of Mauro Orbini, author
of *Regno degli Slavi*, whom he considers to be an embarrassment to his
fellow historians. Among Ottoman authors, he refers to Sa'di Efendi of

Larissa (not identified; for a hypothesis, see Guboglu, 'Considérations', p. 157), author of a *Synopsis historiōn*, and Ali Efendi of Philippopolis (not identified; according to Guboglu, 'Considérations', p. 157-8, he was Muṣṭafā ʿAlī, d. 1600), author of a history of the Ottoman dynasty, *Tevārīh-i Āl-i ʿOsmān*. He mentions Johan Gaudier, perhaps referring to his translation of the *Annales sultanorum othmanidarum*, edited by Leunclavius and quite popular in late 16th-century Europe. The depiction of the fall of Constantinople in 1453 seems to be indebted, perhaps indirectly by means of a common source, to Hüseyin Hezarfenn (d. 1691).

Cantemir uses these sources to show that, like living organisms, the Ottoman Empire was prone to decay after a long period of growth. Thus, although the *Incrementa* and the *Decrementa* are concerned mostly with the physical dimensions of the state as the empire began to lose ground, they also acquire a philosophical dimension. In addition, towards the end of the narrative, he becomes increasingly keen to show that his decision to side with Peter the Great against the Ottomans was correct. He could no longer put his faith in the untrustworthy sultan and opted to join the tsar, who stood by his side even in defeat.

There is a significant difference between the history, with all its later 'Russian' additions, and the *Annotations*. While the former has a sober, chronicle-like tone, the latter are of a far more composite nature, as they combine erudite notes, personal memories and even gossip. They seem designed to explain terms such as *muftī* or *derviş* and to introduce characters such as Prince Ștefan of Moldavia (Ștefan 'the Great', r. 1457-1504) and İskender, the Albanian hero Gjergj Kastriot Skanderbeg (d. 1468). In fact, they are a highly effective rhetorical device. Writing about the Phanar district of Istanbul, for example, Cantemir describes at length the Patriarchal Academy and its professors, many of whom were also his teachers. The entry on Daltaban Mustafa Paşa presents Cantemir's own version of the 1703 Edirne rebellion and the fall of Feyzullah Efendi, the powerful Şeyhülislâm. The entry on the French ambassador Charles de Ferriol gives Cantemir an opportunity to depict the close connection between Ferriol and the Ottoman Grand Dragoman Alexandros Mavrokordatos (1641-1709). Unlike the *Incrementa atque decrementa*, the *Annotations* include anecdotes, such as that describing a meeting between the Mongol warlord Tamerlane and Nasreddīn Ḥoca.

Cantemir had obtained from Levni Çelebi a series of miniatures of the sultans, which he intended to include in his work, while quotations from Ottoman sources, in Turkish written in Arabic and Latin letters, as well as a detailed *Plan of Constantinople* were to add to its value. Unfortunately, only the *Plan* was published during Cantemir's lifetime and only in Russian translation (St Petersburg, 1720), while none of the posthumous editions, no matter how useful, succeeded in doing justice to Cantemir's *magnum opus*. Nevertheless, the interplay between the *Incrementa* and the *Annotations*, the changes that were made while Cantemir was still alive, their impact on his writing strategies, the different audiences he wanted to address – all these and more make study of the history rewarding.

The *Incrementa atque decrementa* attempts to establish correspondences between Ottoman and European history. The focus on *hijrī*/ Christian chronological conversion is telling in this respect, as is the systematic rendering of Ottoman proper names. In addition, Cantemir tries to correct as many as possible of the errors made by Christian historians with regard to the Ottomans, whether about the first sultans, or about the conquest of Constantinople. It was not always easy to do this – the legal and ecclesiastical systems of the two civilisations were not compatible; yet in spite of the differences, the Ottoman state is depicted as part of Europe.

According to Cantemir, there was an indestructible link between the Ottoman State and Islam. The sultans would constantly strive to prove their faith and spread it everywhere, mostly by means of war, while the grand mufti's interpretation of the law would provide proper guidance. Nevertheless, forced conversions were prohibited, and unless they were raising arms against the Ottomans, as the Albanian warlord Skanderbeg had done, non-Muslims could keep their faith in exchange for a tribute, as had been instituted by Muḥammad himself.

As Cantemir believed that a part of Constantinople had surrendered rather than been conquered, the history depicts (mostly) a contractual relationship between the Ottoman rulers and their Constantinopolitan Christian subjects. Although sultans such as Selim I (r. 1512-20) wished to turn all stone churches but one into mosques, and although some viziers wanted to force Christian subjects to wear particular forms of dress, Christians were respected imperial subjects. Among the Ottoman functionaries, there were many converts who still respected their original faith, and personalities such as the grand interpreters Panagiōtēs Nikousios (d. 1673) and Alexandros Mavrokordatos (d. 1709) served as protectors of their co-religionists thanks to their elevated social status. In recounting such matters, Cantemir reveals an attitude that is more nuanced than those of many earlier European scholars in the field.

SIGNIFICANCE

A Russian translation of the *Incrementa atque decrementa*, commissioned by Peter the Great, was finished in 1719, though no copy is known at present. Between 1735 and 1738, Cantemir's son, Antioh, prepared a partial Italian translation with the help of Abbot Ottaviano di Guasco. Entitled *Dell'Accrescimento e decadenza dell'Impero Othomano osia Epitome dell'Istoria Turca*, this version was also never published. Fortunately, during his stay in London as Russian ambassador, Antioh managed to publish an English translation of his father's history. The edition included 22 portraits of sultans engraved by Claude du Bosc (the models had been provided to Antioh's father by Levni), and a folding map of the Ottoman capital, translated from Russian. As shown by Hugh Trevor-Roper ('Dimitrie Cantemir's *Ottoman history*'), the book was received with indifference. However, Antioh took advantage of his new appointment as Russian ambassador in Paris and arranged a French translation in 1743. Made by de Joncquières, it was based on Tindal's translation.

After it was published in English, and as other translations followed, Cantemir's history gradually became the standard work on the Ottoman Empire. The *Acta Eruditorum* of Leipzig reviewed it very positively, and Edward Gibbon, while he thought that Cantemir was 'guilty of strange blunders in oriental history', thought that 'he was conversant with the language, the annals, and the institutions of the Turks', which made his work highly valuable (*The History of the Decline and Fall of the Roman Empire*, vol. 11, London, 1788, p. 312, n. 41).

In 1824, Joseph von Hammer-Purgstall delivered a devastating critique of the history, saying that few books had ever enjoyed longer-lasting but less-deserved academic fame ('Sur l'histoire ottomane', p. 32). Today, the discovery by Virgil Cândea of the Latin manuscript in the Houghton Library, the edition provided by Dan Sluşanschi, and the researches carried on in the Russian archives offer the opportunity of a re-evaluation of the book.

PUBLICATIONS

MS Harvard, Houghton Library of Harvard University – Lat. 224, 1064 pages (before 1723; the only complete witness of the final Latin version, which includes the *Annotations*. *Creșterile și descreșterile Imperiului otoman. Textul original latin în forma finală revizuită de autor. Facsimil al manuscrisului Lat-124 de la Biblioteca Houghton, Harvard University, Cambridge, Mass.*, ed. V. Cândea, Bucharest, 1999 (facsimile); *Incrementorum et decrementorum Aulæ Othmannicæ. Manuscris facsimil inedit*, ed. C. Barbu, s.l., s.a. [Craiova, 2013] (facsimile))

MS Moscow, Rossiïskiï gosudarstvennyï arkhiv drevnikh aktov (RGADA) – fond 181 (inv. 15), 1362, 251 fols (first half of the 18th century; first part of the history)

MS Moscow, Rossiïskiï gosudarstvennyï arkhiv drevnikh aktov (RGADA) – fond 181 (inv. 15), 1363, pp. 1-185, 253-406 (1735-8; partial Italian trans. by Antioh Cantemir and Abbot Ottaviano di Guasco, *Dell'Accrescimento e decadenza dell'Impero Othomano osia Epitome dell'Istoria Turca*)

MS Moscow, Rossiïskiï gosudarstvennyï arkhiv drevnikh aktov (RGADA) – fond 181 (inv. 15), 1366, 193 fols (c. 1738; Italian trans. of the first part of the *Annotations*. *Epitome dell'Istoria Turca A. Dell'Accrescimento e decadenza dell'Impero Othomano osia Epitome dell'Istoria Turca B. Annotazioni. Manuscris facsimil inedit*, ed. C. Barbu, s.l, s.a [Craiova, 2013])

MS St Petersburg, Institut Vostochnykh rukopisi Rossiïskoi Akademii nauk – fond 25 (Dmitrii Kantemir), 1-4, 292 fols, 309 fols, 295 fols and 224 fols, respectively (after 1726, before 1738; almost complete version of the history and the *Annotations*, possibly made by Gottlieb Siegfried Bayer)

MS St Petersburg, Institut Vostochnykh rukopisi Rossiïskoi Akademii nauk – fond 25 (Dmitrii Kantemir) – 5-6, 133 fols and 52 fols, respectively (between 1726 and 1738; incomplete version of the *Annotations* probably made by Bayer)

MS Bucharest, Biblioteca Academiei Române – Lat. 74 and 75 (1878, copy of the St Petersburg MS brought to Romania by Gr.G. Tocilescu from a research trip to Russia)

On the MSS, see:

V. Pelin, *Manuscrisele românești din secolele XIII-XIX în colecții străine (Rusia, Ucraina, Bielorusia). Catalog*, ed. A. Eșanu, V. Eșanu and V. Cosovan, Chișinău, 2017, pp. 273-6, nos 257-60

V. Țvircun, 'Reperele cantemirologiei. Prezent și perspective', *Plural* (Chișinău) 4 (2016) 127-43

Pelin, 'Manuscrisele operelor lui Dimitrie Cantemir'

Frantsouzoff, 'Le fonds de Dimitrie Cantemir'

V. Cândea, 'Life story of a manuscript. Dimitrie Cantemir's *History of the Ottoman Empire*', *Revue des Études Sud-Est Européennes* 23 (1985) 297-312

Dimitrie Cantemir, *The history of the growth and decay of the Othman Empire*[...], trans. Nicolas Tindal, 2 vols, London, 1734-5 (English trans.); 001239477 (digitised version available through Hathi Trust Digital Library)

Dimitrie Cantemir, *Histoire de l'Empire othoman, où se voyent les causes de son aggrandissement et de sa décadence. Avec des notes très-instructives*, trans. M. de Joncquières, 2 vols, Paris, 1743 (French trans. of the 1734-5 English trans.); 4 Turc. 39-2 (digitised version available through *MDZ*)

Dimitrie Cantemir, *Geschichte des osmanischen Reichs nach seinem Anwachse und Abnehmen* [...], trans. Christian Herold, Hamburg, 1745 (German trans. of the English trans.); 4 H 318 (digitised version available through *MDZ*)

Dimitrie Cantemir, *The history of the growth and decay of the Othman Empire*[...], trans. N. Tindal, 2 vols, London, 1756[2] (English trans.); ESTC T135847 (digitised version available through *ECCO*)

Dimitrie Cantemir, *The history of the growth and decay of the Othman Empire*[...], trans. N. Tindal, 2 vols, London, 1766[3] (English trans.)

Dimitrie Cantemir, *The history of the growth and decay of the Othman Empire*[...], trans. N. Tindal, 2 vols, London, 1784-5[4] (English trans.)

Dimitrie Cantemir, *Istoriia Turetskogo gosudarstva ot samogo osnovaniia onogo do poveishih vremen*, 2 vols, Moscow, 1828 (Russian trans. of the German trans.)

Dimitrie Cantemir, *Istoria Imperiului ottomanu. Crescerea şi scăderea lui cu note fórte instructive de Demetriu Cantemiru principe de Moldavia*, trans. I. Hodoşiu, 2 vols, Bucharest, 1876-8 (Romanian trans. of the 1828 German version)

Dimitrie Cantemir, *Historian of South East European and Oriental civilizations. Extracts from The history of the Ottoman Empire*, ed. A. Duţu and P. Cernovodeanu, Bucharest, 1973 (selections from the 1734-5 English trans.)

Dimitrie Cantemir, *Osmanlı İmparatorluğu'nun Yükseliş ve Çöküş Tarihi*, trans. Ö. Çobanoğlu, 2 vols, Ankara, 1979 (Istanbul, 1998-9[2]; 2001[3]; 2002[4]; 2006[5]) (Turkish trans.)

Dimitrie Cantemir, *Demetrii principis Cantemirii Incrementorum et decrementorum avlæ othman[n]icæ sive aliothman[n]icæ historiæ a prima gentis origine ad nostra vsqve tempora dedvctæ libri tres*, ed. D. Sluşanschi, Timişoara, 2001 (the first critical edition of the Latin text, following the Harvard MS)

Dimitrie Cantemir, *Demetrius Cantimir princeps Moldaviæ. Istoria creşterilor şi a descreşterilor Curţii Othman[n]ice. Historia Incrementorum atque Decrementorum aulae Othomanicae. Versiune românească în ediţie princeps*, ed. and trans. D. Sluşanschi, Bucharest, 2012 (Romanian trans. of the 2001 Latin edition)

Dimitrie Cantemir, *Istoria măririi şi decăderii Curţii othmane*, ed. O. Gordon, F. Nicolae and M. Vasileanu, trans. I. Costa, 2 vols, Bucharest, 2015 (Romanian trans., revised version of D. Sluşanschi's edition)

STUDIES

For a comprehensive bibliography, see Eşanu, *Neamul Cantemireştilor*, pp. 175-81 (editions), pp. 181-7 (studies). The following list includes only fundamental works and the most significant titles published since Eşanu's 2010 work.

I. Costa, 'Cantemir, auctor şi persona (*Historia Othmanica*)', *Quaestiones Romanicae* 3 (2015) 20-5

I. Costa, 'Historia Othmanica. Sources and personal memories', in F. Nicolae and N. Stanca (eds), *International Journal of Cross-Cultural Studies and Environmental Communication. Special issue: Constantin Brancoveanu's Legacy from Cross-Cultural Perspectives*, Constanţa, 2015, 55-60

I. Costa, 'Incrementa vs Decrementa. Bibliography and recollection', in I. Boldea (ed.), *Globalization and intercultural dialogue. Multidisciplinary perspectives*, Târgu-Mureş, 2014, 613-18

I. Costa, 'Lector oculatus (Dimitrie Cantemir, "Incrementa et decrementa Aulæ Othmanicæ")', *Revista de Istorie şi Teorie Literară* 7 (2013) 143-9

K. Petrovszky, '*Observers of Ottoman decline*? Osmanische Reichsgeschichte als Gegenstand orthodoxer Geschichtsschreibung (16.-18. Jahrhundert)', in A. Helmedach, M. Koller, K.P. and S. Rohdewald (eds), *Das osmanische Europa. Methoden und Perspektiven der Frühneuzeitforschung zu Südosteuropa*, Leipzig, 2013, 433-61

I. Costa, 'Dimitrie Cantemir's *Annotationes* in *The growth and decay of the Othoman Empire*', *Synthesis* 39 (2012) 13-17

Leezenberg, 'Oriental origins of Orientalism'

C. Kovácsházy, 'Cantemir, Zrínyi, Mehmet Aga et l'Europe orientale. Constructions baroques du modèle classique de l'Orient', in A. Duprat and H. Khadhar (eds), *Orient baroque / Orient classique. Variations du motif oriental dans les littératures d'Europe* (*XVIe-XVIIe siècle*), Paris, 2010, 243-55

Lemny, *Les Cantemir*, pp. 136-41

Eşanu, *Dinastia Cantemireştilor*, pp. 292-7

Şt. Lemny, 'Burke et une lecture de l'*Histoire de l'Empire ottoman* de Démètrius Cantemir à Westminster Hall: 22 avril 1788', in Kl. Bochmann and V. Dumbravă (eds), *Dimitrie Cantemir. Fürst der Moldau, Gelehrter, Akteur der europäischen Kulturgeschichte*, Leipzig, 2008, 198-204

H.-Ch. Maner, 'Geschichtsschreibung im 18. Jahrhundert. Anmerkungen zum Werk des Fürsten Dimitrie Cantemir unter besonderer Berücksichtigung der Geschichte des osmanischen Reiches', in Bochmann and Dumbravă, *Dimitrie Cantemir*, 88-100

N.-A. Haleş, 'Dimitrie Cantemir şi izvoarele bizantine ale operelor sale', *Studia Universitas Babeş-Bolyai. Teologia Ortodoxa* 52 (2007) 263-75

M. Maxim, art. 'Dimitrie Cantemir', Chicago, 2006; https://ottoman-historians.uchicago.edu/en/historian/dimitrie-cantemir

E. Popescu-Judetz, *Beyond the glory of the sultans. Cantemir's view of the Turks*, Istanbul, 2007

C. Bîrsan, *Dimitrie Cantemir and the Islamic world*, Istanbul, 2004 (= *Dimitrie Cantemir şi lumea islamică*, Bucharest, 2005)

A. Pippidi, 'La décadence de l'Empire ottoman comme concept historique, de la Renaissance aux Lumières', *Revue des Études Sud-Est Européennes* 35 (1997) 5-19

P. Cernovodeanu, 'Démètre Cantemir et l'Orient musulman', *Revue des Études Sud-Est Européennes* 19 (1991) 87-91

P. Cernovodeanu, 'Le plan de Constantinople par Dimitrie Cantemir', *Revue des Études Sud-Est Européennes* 17 (1989) 35-47

H. Trevor-Roper, 'Dimitrie Cantemir's Ottoman history and its reception in England', *Revue Roumaine d'Histoire* 24 (1985) 51-66 [repr. in *History and the Enlightenment*, London, 2010, 54-70, 284-6]

A. Pippidi, 'Ideea de "creştere şi decădere" a Imperiului Otoman în istoriografia occidentală din secolele al XVI-lea – al XVIII-lea', Cluj-Napoca, 1981 (PhD Diss. University Babeş-Bolyai)

V. Cândea, 'Cantemir et la civilisation islamique', *Romano-Arabica* 2 (1977) 15-41

G. Cioranesco, 'La contribution de Démètre Cantemir aux études orientales', *Turcica* 7 (1975) 205-32

P. Cernovodeanu, 'Les œuvres de Démètre Cantemir présentées par "Acta Eruditorum" de Leipzig (1714-1738)', *Revue des Études Sud-Est Européennes* 12 (1974) 537-50

T. Gemil, 'Considérations concernant l'*Histoire ottomane* de Dimitrie Cantemir', *Dacoromania* 2 (1974) 155-66

M. Stoïanova, 'Au sujet des illustrations de l'Histoire ottomane de Cantemir', *Revue des Études Sud-Est Européennes* 12 (1974) 586-7

E. Werner, 'Bemerkungen zur Geschichte des osmanischen Reiches von Dimitrie Cantemir', in *Ein bedeutender Gelehrter an der Schwelle zur Frühaufklärung: Dimitrie Cantemir (1673-1723)*, Berlin, 1974, 43-51

M.-M. Alexandrescu-Dersca, 'Dimitrie Cantemir, istoric al Imperiului Otoman', *Studii. Revistă de Istorie* 26 (1973) 971-89

Al. Duțu, 'L'Abbé Prévost et les Roumains II. L'Abbé Prévost traducteur de l'*Histoire ottomane* de Cantemir', *Revue de Littérature Comparée* 45 (1971) 234-7

M. Guboglu, 'Dimitrie Cantemir – orientaliste', *Studia et Acta Orientalia* 3 (1961) 129-60

M. Guboglu, 'Dimitrie Cantemir și *Istoria Imperiului otoman*', *Studii și Articole de Istorie* 2 (1957) 179-208

F. Babinger, 'Izvoarele turcești ale lui Dimitrie Cantemir', *Arhiva Românească* 7 (1941) 111-21 (German version, 'Die türkischen Quellen Dimitrie Kantemirs', in *60. Doğum yīlī münasebetiyle Zeki Velidi Togan'a armağan. Symbolae in honorem Z.V. Togan*, Istanbul, 1951, 50-60; also, *Aufsätze und Abhandlungen zur Geschichte Südosteuropas und der Levante*, vol. 2, Munich, 1966, 142-50)

P.V. Haneș, 'Istorie literară în călătorii. Istoria Imperiului Otoman a lui Dimitrie Cantemir', *Convorbiri Literare* 66 (1933) 210-44

Gr.G. Tocilescu, *Raport asupra cercetărilor istorice făcute în bibliotecele din Russia*, Bucharest, 1878, pp. 2, 6, 12-13, 15

J. de Hammer, 'Sur l'Histoire ottomane du prince Cantemir', *Journal Asiatique* 4 (1824) 32-45

Kniga sistima ili Sostoianie muhammedanskiia religii
'The book [called] The system or structure of the Muḥammadan religion'
De Curani etymologico nomine
'On the etymology of the name Qur'an'

DATE   c. 1718-22
ORIGINAL LANGUAGE   Latin

DESCRIPTION

While his seminal *Incrementa atque decrementa* has excited the curiosity of many scholars, Dimitrie Cantemir's *Kniga sistima ili sostoianie muhammedanskiia religii* ('The book [called] The system or the structure of the Muḥammadan religion') has been (and still is) largely ignored by both scholars and general readers. Written in Latin, but printed in Russian at St Petersburg (22 December 1722, 404 pages), probably as a companion to a Russian translation of the Qur'an from French now generally agreed to have been made by Pyotr Postnikov (on whom see later in this volume), it has never made an impact, even though it can be considered a major cultural product of its time.

The study on the Qur'an, entitled *Curanus*, and the enlarged version of this, *De Curani etymologico nomine*, were to be part of Cantemir's Ottoman trilogy (the title is curious, because only the first few pages are devoted to the Qur'an). The project was already mentioned in his correspondence with the Berlin Academy in 1714, which points to a long period of preparation because he only actually wrote *Curanus* between 1718 and 1719. At the request of Peter the Great, a revised version of *De Curani etymologico nomine* was translated into Russian by Ivan Il'inskiĭ, Cantemir's secretary and, despite opposition from the Synod of the Russian Orthodox Church, was published in 1722 as *Kniga sistima ili sostoianie muhammedanskiia religii*. This was to be a companion to the 1716 anonymous Russian translation of the Qur'an.

The sources used by Cantemir are difficult to identify, as it is not easy to reconstruct his Russian library or to identify passages he quotes from memory. He names his main guide, the highly popular 15th-century poem *Risāle-i Muhammediye* by Yazıcıoğlu Mehmed, and also a few other works, such as the 16th-century *Vasiyetnāme* ('Book of wills') by Mehmed

Birgivi, and the anonymous *Cevahir ül-Islām* ('Jewels of faith'). As Virgil Cândea has shown ('Studiu introductiv'), it is highly probable that he also consulted Ludovico Marracci's *Refutatio Alcorani* (1698), as well as the 1672 Italian translation of Paul Rycaut's *The present state of the Ottoman Empire* (1667). According to Florentina Nicolae (*Curanus*, p. xiv), he also used Theodor Bibliander's publication of Robert of Ketton's Latin translation of the Qur'an, *Machumetis Saracenorum principis, eiusque successorum vitae, ac doctrina, ipseque Alcoran* (Basel, 1543, 1550²).

The initial work *Curanus* deals only with the Qur'an itself, the life of the 'false Prophet', and briefly with some aspects of Islamic theology, such as God, hell and paradise. However, the enlarged version and Russian translation are more complex in structure. *Kniga sistima ili sostoianie muhammedanskiia religii* has six parts: on the false Prophet Muḥammad; on the Qur'an; on the Muḥammadan Apocalypse; on Muḥammadan theology; on the Muḥammadan religion; on other Muḥammadan teachings, which includes a description of the Sufi brotherhoods.

The 1722 edition of *Kniga sistima* has at the beginning an engraving depicting Osman's founding dream: the tree representing the rise of the Ottoman Empire springs forth and covers Asia, Africa and Europe, but its branches are poisonous snakes. The Foreword equally suggests a very polemical approach; it treats 'the law of Muḥammad' as an animalistic 'law for pigs' and states that the aim of the book is to fortify the Christian faith by exposing the errors of Islam – indeed, Cantemir's perspective is that of a Christian convinced by the absolute truth of his own faith.

Cantemir's text is a comprehensive work on Islam, seen not only from a theological point of view but also from a social and historical perspective. The focus is on the Ottomans, but not exclusively, and there are moments when he praises Muslims, whether Arabs, Turks or Persians. His personal observations and the discussions he had with learned Muslims, such as Es'ad Efendi, make reading the work all the more interesting.

A 'funny story' attached to the excursus on the Islamic pilgrimage (Cantemir, *Kniga sistima*, pp. 195-9; Cantemir, *Sistemul*, 1987, pp. 318-25) provides an additional clue to the intended audience and purpose of the 1722 Russian edition, as opposed to the target audience of the Latin text. Politically incorrect yet highly amusing, the story deals with the efforts made by Cornelis Haga (1578-1654), a Dutch diplomat in Istanbul, to visit the Islamic holy sites in Jerusalem. Why would Cantemir place such an irreverent story at the end of a scholarly account? A possible answer is revealed by a comparison of the published (Russian) version of the story with the unpublished (Latin) one. As the Latin version is not irreverent, but rather sympathetic to Muslims, it follows that Cantemir made changes in order to adapt the story to a different audience. Following a suggestion made by Virgil Cândea ('Studiu introductiv'), this audience can be identified as the All-Mad, All-Jesting, Most-Comical and All-Drunken Council that assembled regularly at Peter the Great's favourite retreat. According to Ivan Il'inskiĭ's journal (Ţvircun, *Epistoliarnoe nasledie*, pp. 288-316; Ţvircun, *Dimitrii Cantemir*, pp. 334-68), Cantemir took part in the 'monastic masquerades' that so delighted the tsar. If this interpretation is correct, *Sistima ili Sostoianie muhammedanskiia religii* appears in a new light. On the one hand, this book, commissioned by Tsar Peter himself, had a didactic purpose to inform its audience about Islamic beliefs. On the other, Cantemir sought to inculcate the idea that the mighty Ottoman Empire had its flaws, which showed that it was far from invincible and helped readers see that it could be defeated. Laugh at the devil and he will flee from you.

The work departs in certain ways from earlier European scholarship on Islam. For example, unlike Adriaan Reland in his *De religione Mohammedica* (Utrecht, 1705), Cantemir planned to provide a description of Islam, not a refutation. Of course, for him Muḥammad was still a false prophet and the Qur'an was still a false scripture containing many 'ridiculous' statements (he believed it was written by Abū Bakr, Muḥammad's father-in-law and the first caliph), but *Sistima* follows, often closely, its original Islamic sources, and sometimes Cantemir considers it necessary to warn his readers that some of the stories included were for 'simple', uneducated people, and must thus be handled carefully (*Sistemul*, 1987, p. 70). Furthermore, Cantemir goes as far as to state that Christian depictions of Islam are valid only for Christians, operating as they do within the framework of the Bible. Muslims would definitely not share this perspective, as they function within a completely different paradigm. My aim is not to judge the other according to my own set of values, explains Cantemir; my purpose is to describe as accurately as possible what the other himself actually believes in (pp. 46, 48). The way Cantemir uses Rycaut's *Present state of the Ottoman Empire* is telling to this respect. The section on 'heresies', for example, follows Rycaut's text but adds or omits data as Cantemir thought appropriate. In addition, the analogy drawn between Christian apophatic theology and Islamic thought shows remarkable perspicacity.

SIGNIFICANCE

Unlike *Incrementa atque decrementa*, *Kniga sistima* rapidly fell into obscurity. Soon after its publication in 1722 parts were translated into German, but a complete German edition was never published. Bishop Sofroniï Vrachanski translated part of it into Bulgarian in 1805, but this version did not name Cantemir as its author. It was translated into Romanian in 1977, and in 1987 the original was published with this Romanian translation, though neither had the impact the work deserves.

Unlike Joseph von Hammer-Purgstall ('Sur l'histoire ottomane', p. 32), Franz Babinger ('Izvoarele turcești') postponed any judgement on Cantemir's merits as a historian of the Ottoman Empire until the publication of the Latin original of both *Incrementa atque decrementa* and *Sistima*. One can only share this prudent attitude: the joint edition of *Curanus* and *De Curani etymologico nomine* has been published, but research is still to be carried out on it. There are indications that detailed study of *Sistima* will help to understand better not only its author, but also early Orientalism (as defined by Ivan Kalmar, *Early Orientalism. Imagined Islam and the notion of sublime power*, New York, 2012) and Russian Orientalism (as defined by David Schimmelpenninck van der Oye, *Russian Orientalism. Asia in the Russian mind from Peter the Great to the emigration*, New Haven CT, 2010, pp. 38-43, 49).

PUBLICATIONS

MSS of Kniga sistima ili Sostoianie muhammedanskiia religii

MS Berlin, Deutschen Akademie der Wissenschaften zu Berlin – In fol. I-V-Bd. 3, fols 38r-41r (after 1722; *Continuatio*. Extractus auss dem russischen Buch des Fr. Cantemiri von der türkische Religion; German trans. of several passages)

MS St Petersburg, Rossiïskaia Natsionalnaia Biblioteka – Fonds M.P. Pogodin 1204, fols 179-340 (1805, partial Bulgarian trans. by Bishop Sofroniï Vrachanski)

On these MSS, see D. Cantemir, *Opere complete*, vol. 8/2. *Sistemul sau Întocmirea religiei muhammedane*, ed. and trans. V. Cândea and A.I. Ionescu, Bucharest, 1987 (*Opere complete* 8/2)

MSS of Curanus. De Curani etymologico nomine

MS Moscow, Rossiïskiï gosudarstvennyï arkhiv drevnikh aktov (RGADA) – Fonds 181, 1325, fols 2-43v (*Curanus*), 44-128v (*De Curani etymologico nomine*) (1717-18; *Curanus. De Curani etymologico nomine. Manuscris facsimil inedit. Prefață de Virgil Cândea*, ed. C. Barbu, s.l., s.a. [Craiova, 2013], facsimile edition)

MS Bucharest, Biblioteca Academiei Române – lat. 76, fols 41-100v (partial copy of the Moscow MS, brought to Romania by Gr.G. Tocilescu from a research trip to Russia in 1878)

Useful bibliography of publications of these works is provided in Eşanu, *Neamul Cantemireştilor*, p. 188 (editions), pp. 188-9 (studies). The following list includes only fundamental works and the most significant titles published after 2010.

Kniga sistima ili Sostoianie muhammedanskiia religii
Dimitrie Kantemir, *Kniga sistima ili Sostoianie muhammedanskiia religii*, St Petersburg, 1722 (Russian trans., probably by Ivan Il'inskiĭ)
Dimitrie Cantemir, *Sistemul sau Întocmirea religiei muhammedane*, ed. and trans. V. Cândea, Bucharest, 1977 (Romanian trans.)
Dimitrie Cantemir, *Sistemul sau Întocmirea religiei muhammedane*, ed. and trans. V. Cândea and A.I. Ionescu, Bucharest, 1987 (biligual Russian-Romanian edition)
Dimitrie Cantemir, *Sistema şi religia mohamedană. Cartea celor trei religii, partea a treia. Transcriere dupa manuscrisul bulgar de Sofronie Vraceanski*, ed. and trans. A.I. Ionescu, Bucharest, 2000 (Bulgarian-Romanian-Russian edition and trans. of Sofroniĭ Vrachanski's 1805 Bulgarian partial trans.)

Curanus and *De Curani etymologico nomine*
I. Georgescu, 'Dimitrie Principele Cantemir, Despre Coran. După copia latinească de la Academia Română, acum mai întâiu tălmacit şi tipărit în românește', *Analele Dobrogei* 7 (1927) 67-121 (Romanian trans. based on an incomplete MS copy made by Gr.G. Tocilescu)
D. Cantemir, *Curanus. Collectanea Orientalia. De muro Caucaseo*, ed. F. Nicolae, trans. I. Costa, Bucharest, 2018 (first edition of the Latin text of *Curanus*, following the 2013 facsimile edition, and Romanian trans.)

STUDIES
I. Costa, '*Curanus* în *Historia Othmanici Imperii*', in A. Vlădescu and C. Lupu (eds), *Études sur le XVIIIᵉ siècle*, Bucharest, 2016, 23-34
P.V. Gusterin, *Pervyĭ rossiĭskiĭ vostokoved Dmitriĭ Kantemir / First Russian Orientalist Dmitry Kantemir*, Moscow, 2008
Bîrsan, *Dimitrie Cantemir*
E.A. Rezvan, *Koran i ego mir*, St Petersburg, 2001, pp. 383-455; http://www.kunstkamera.ru/lib/rubrikator/02/978-5-85803-183-3/

E.A. Rezvan, 'The Qur'ān and its world, VIII/2. *West-Östlichen Divans* (the Qur'ān in Russia)', *Manuscripta Orientalia* 5 (1999) 32-62

C. Bîrsan, 'Teologia islamică în scrierile cantemiriene', *Revista de Istorie și Teorie Literară* 45 (1997) 21-30

V. Cândea, 'Studiu introductiv', in D. Cantemir, *Sistemul sau Întocmirea religiei muhammedane*, Bucharest, 1987, pp. v-xxxix (fundamental)

A.I. Ionescu, 'Considérations sur la traduction du *Livre sur le système de la religion des Musulmans* de Cantemir par Sofronie Vračanski', *Revue des Études Sud-Est Européennes* 15 (1977) 101-12

Y. Goldenberg, 'Notes en marge de quelques écrits roumains sur le Coran et l'Islam', *Analele Universității din București. Limbi clasice și orientale* 21 (1972) 121-7

Tocilescu, *Raport asupra cercetărilor istorice făcute în bibliotecele din Russia*, pp. 2, 5

Ovidiu-Victor Olar

Vasilios Vatatzes

Vasileios Vatatzēs, Vasileios Vatatzis, Basile Vatatzès,
Basile Vatace, Vatazzi

DATE OF BIRTH 1694
PLACE OF BIRTH Therapeia (suburb of Constantinople)
DATE OF DEATH After 1748
PLACE OF DEATH Unknown; possibly Russia

BIOGRAPHY

Vasilios Vatatzes was born in Therapeia, a suburb of Constantinople, in 1694. He was the son of an Orthodox priest, who at some point held an official title (*megas oikonomos*) of the Ecumenical Patriarchate in Constantinople. Émile Legrand (in Vatatzès, 'Voyages', p. 185) hypothesises that the young Vasileios initially studied with his father, and then pursued his studies in Constantinople until he was 14, when he left the city for Russia to become a merchant. Vatatzes' literary efforts, although criticised by some modern scholars, reflect a good classical education. It is reasonable to assume that the foundations for this were set in Constantinople, as it would have been very difficult to acquire the necessary knowledge elsewhere during his travels as a merchant.

Everything known about Vatatzes' biography comes from his three written works, *Persika*, the *Periēgetikon* (a poem about his travels), and the map of Central Asia he published in London in 1732. There are no other known contemporary sources about his life but, given the semi-official status he once had in diplomatic relations between Russia and Persia, it is likely that such sources exist in Russian archives.

Vatatzes travelled to Isfahan, the Caucasus, Khiva, Bukhara, Astrakhan and Afghanistan. Nāder Shah, ruler of Persia (r. 1736-47), appointed him to deliver a diplomatic message to the Russian General Vasili Levasov. After spending some time in Western Europe, Vatatzes returned to Russia, later setting off on further travels in Central Asia. He describes his journeys in a long poem, the *Periēgetikon*. It is possible that he wrote his *Persika* during his time in Central Asia, as the anti-Ottoman aspects of the work make it difficult to imagine that it was composed in Constantinople. It is not clear whether he ever returned to Russia, and there is no known information about him in the sources after 1748, the year he finished *Persika*.

In October 1732, Vatatzes published in London a map of Central Asia including the Caspian Sea and the Aral Sea, with rich explanations in both Greek and Latin concerning the geography and people of the region. The publisher was the well-known map dealer and cartographer John Senex. The map provides a wealth of information and, although it has been the object of some studies, it deserves to be republished in a new edition.

MAIN SOURCES OF INFORMATION

Primary

Basilio Batazi, *Charta, in qua eruditis spectanda exhibetur pars Asiae* [...] *nunc primum typorum ope publici juris*, London: John Senex, 1732 (map with Greek and Latin text)

Basile Vatatzès, 'Voyages de Basile Vatace en Europe et en Asie', trans. and ed. É. Legrand, in *Nouveaux mélanges orientaux*, Paris, 1886, 183-295 (Greek text and French commentary of *Periēgetikon*)

Basile Vatatzès, *Persica. Histoire de Chah-Nadir*, ed. N. Iorga, Bucharest, 1939

Secondary

M. Sariyannis, 'An eighteenth-century Ottoman Greek's travel account in Central Asia', in İ. Şahin, B. İsakov and C. Buyar (eds), *CIÉPO Interim Symposium. The Central Asiatic roots of Ottoman culture*, Istanbul, 2014, 47-60

E. Venetis, art. 'Vatatzes, Vasilios. Greek scholar, merchant, traveler, pioneer explorer, and diplomat', in *EIr*

M. Sarigiannēs, 'Hoi Phanariōtes kai hē othōmanikē paradosē. Epidraseis kai stegana, 170s-180s aiōnes', in G. Salakidēs (ed.), *Tourkologika. Timētikos tomos gia ton Anastasio K. Iordanoglou*, Athens, 2012, 305-22, pp. 309-10

Ch.A. Mēnaoglou, 'Hellēnes periēgētes stēn Eurōpē tou Diaphotismou', in K.A. Dēmadēs (ed.), *Ho hellenikos kosmos anamesa stēn epochē tou Diaphotismou kai ston eikosto aiōna*, Athens, 2007, vol. 1, pp. 269-78

M. Axworthy, *Sword of Persia. Nader Shah, from tribal warrior to conquering tyrant*, New York, 2006

M. Peranthēs, *Historia tēs neoellēnikēs logotechnias kai zōēs apo tis prōtes rizes ōs tēn epanastasē (1000-1821)*, Athens, 2006, vol. 2, pp. 138-9

S. Gorshenina, *Explorateurs en Asie centrale. Voyageurs et aventuriers de Marco Polo à Ella Maillart*, Geneva, 2003, p. 147

Ch.A. Mēnaoglou, 'Hoi periēgēseis tou Basileiou Batatzē', *Parnassos* 44 (2002) 233-46

H. Angelomatē-Tsoungarakē, 'Hellēnika periēgētika keimena (16os-19os ai.)', *Mesaiōnika kai Nea Hellēnika* 6 (2000) 155-80

B. Knös, *L'histoire de la literature néo-grecque. La période jusqu'en 1821*, Stockholm, 1962, pp. 479-80

Sp.P. Lampros, 'Kananos Laskaris kai Basileios Batatzēs. Dyo Hellēnes perigētai tou dekatou pemptou kai tou dekatou ogdōou aiōnos', in Sp.P. Lampros, *Miktai selides*, Athens, 1905, 579-99, pp. 590-9 (with some new information added to the 1881 article)

Sp.P. Lampros, 'Autographon tou Basileiou Batatzē', *Neos Hellenomnēmōn* 2 (1905) 238-9 (with a reproduction of an autograph note by Vatatzes)

A.M. Idrōmenos, 'Symplērōtika peri Basileiou Batatzē', *Parnassos* 5 (1881) 801-4

Sp.P. Lampros, 'Kananos Laskaris kai Basileios Batatzēs. Dyo Hellēnes perigētai tou IE kai IĒ aiōnos', *Parnassos* 5 (1881) 705-19, pp. 713-19

K. Sathas, *Neoellēnikē philologia*, Athens, 1868, p. 618

WORKS ON CHRISTIAN-MUSLIM RELATIONS

Vatatzou Persika
'Vatatzes' Persika'

DATE 1748
ORIGINAL LANGUAGE Greek (modern)

DESCRIPTION

Vatatzes' *Persika*, completed in 1748, remained in manuscript until 1939, enjoying only a very limited circulation. However, at least two early 19th-century Greek scholars, Daniel Demetrios Philippides and Iakovakis Rizos-Neroulos, were aware of the existence of the manuscripts and Philippides studied them. The Romanian historian Nicolae Iorga published an edition of *Persika* in 1939, but it was not widely known despite a review by Louis Bréhier published in 1941. The war and the situation in post-war Romania made it highly unlikely that more than a few copies of Iorga's edition left the country in the decades following its publication. It is illustrative, for example, that when MS Athens was catalogued in 1996, they were unaware of the 1939 edition of the work.

Persika describes the history of the Persian Empire from 1694 to 1747 in 12 books, each book containing a different number of chapters. In Iorga's edition, the work consists of 304 pages in octavo. The full title of the work is *Vatatzou Persika. Ta en Persidi, hosa en etesi trisi kai pentēkonta, ek te tou 1694 kai mechri te tou 1747, en vivliois t'eisin ētoi tmēmasin dyo te kai deka, en hois ki'ē apasa tou sachē Nadiri kath'holou historia, peri hēs kai ho tou xyngraphenta ho holos skopos. Syntethenta men kai xyngraphenta par'aytoy Vasileiou tou Vatatzē, tou kai to poly tōn en toutois periexomenōn, prosōpōn te kai ethnōn kai poleōn kai gaiōn kai thalattōn te kai potamōn, autoptoy kai periēgētou* ('Vatatzes' Persika. The events in Persia through 53 years, from 1694 to 1747, and they are [described] in 12 books, i.e. parts, in which there is also the whole history of Nadir Shah, which [was] the entire objective of the writer. [These were] put together and written by the same Vasileios Vatatzēs, who was an eyewitness and travelled to many [of the things] in these [books], people, nations, cities, lands, seas and rivers').

Strictly-speaking, *Persika* is not historical writing in the modern sense, but rather follows the model of ancient 'histories', such as those of Herodotus, with the author considering himself a *periegetēs* (traveller) in the style of the Ancients. The aim of the work is to describe the life and deeds of Nāder Shah (r. 1736-47), an 18th-century Persian ruler of Turkmen origin, who distinguished himself through his military exploits. Vatatzes had the opportunity to meet and converse with his hero on two or three occasions, which probably did not add objectivity to his writing, as he does not hesitate to compare Nāder to Alexander the Great.

The language used by Vatatzes is archaising, a feature not uncommon among some works by Greek intellectuals of the 18th century. Some scholars, following Legrand's observations on *Persika* and the author's own statements about his literary abilities, have noted the weaker points in his works.

Vatatzes displays a good knowledge of classical Greek language and literature. He often mentions the classical writers and makes reference to mythology. Some 'barbarisms' or odd forms of words might be attributed to linguistic choice rather than to a poor knowledge of classical Greek. After all, the 18th century was a period of linguistic experimentation in Greek literature. Moreover, Vatatzes was not a full-time author or philologist. He was a travelling merchant and his main activity was commerce. He also had an interest in other European and Oriental languages (he often cites words and phrases in Persian).

Vatatzes was a devout Orthodox Christian and he affirms his faith throughout his writings, including *Persika*, and appears as a perceptive and attentive observer of the religious realities he encountered during his travels. When describing Kiev and Moscow, for instance, he praises the churches and the freedom to practise Christianity, a situation that stands in striking contrast to what he had been accustomed to in the

Ottoman Empire. In Moscow, he compares the splendour of the Russian cult with that of the Byzantines. Even more interestingly, Vatatzes provides a short description of the religion of Tibet, even though he had never been there and his information was gleaned from others. Vatatzes is among the first authors in Modern Greek literature to mention the Dalai Lama and the structure of Tibetan society. Although his aim was not to write a treatise on religion, information on religious matters is scattered throughout the book. In describing religious facts he often uses and adapts classical Greek words, but he does not hesitate to use foreign words or names when necessary, a practice avoided by some other archaising writers.

Vatatzes is particularly critical of the Ottomans, whom he describes as a 'beast' or a 'hydra', thus *Persika* could also be considered anti-Ottoman writing. On the other hand, he also criticises the European powers that, at various points in history, allowed Ottoman expansion. In fact, one reason for the choice of the life of Nāder Shah as subject matter may have been Nāder's struggle against the Ottomans. Vatatzes also mentions the Christian (mainly Armenian) troops in the Persian army.

Vatatzes seems to have a fairly good knowledge of Islam and Islamic religious practices, acquired either during his early years in the Ottoman Empire or during his travels in the Orient. In *Persika*, although he focuses on historical and often geographical accounts, he frequently mentions religious beliefs and practices. Sometimes such descriptions are more extensive, as in the case of the mosque and the shrine in Mashhad (he renders this in Greek as 'Meset'), which he admires for its beauty and opulence. He also presents in some detail the personality of the Shīʿī Imam Rezā ('Alī ibn Mūsā al-Riḍā, 765-818), revered by many in Persia.

He is aware of the differences between Sunnī and Shīʿa Islam, and describes them in some detail. Likewise, he writes about Mirwais (spelled 'Murveiz'), a 'zealot of the Sunni faith', who attempted to organise an uprising against Persian rule in Afghanistan, using religious differences to convince his followers and assure them they would have the support of the Ottoman Empire. Vatatzes describes how Ṭahmāsp Kuli Khan (the future Nāder Shah), on entering the city of Mashhad, visited the mosque and the tomb of Imam Rezā. However, he notes, 'the man was far from religion' and revered the tomb of the Imam as a parade of piety, with 'fake tears'.

Vatatzes' account of the history of Imam Rezā offers him the opportunity to present a sketch of the differences between the Sunnīs and the

Shīʻa. He explains the meaning of the term 'imam' as *grammateis* (clerks) and *nomikoi* (judges) in Greek. He says that the Persians revered Imam Rezā because he wrote against the 'enemies' of ʻAlī, mainly against ʻUmar and Abū Bakr (the two first successors of Muḥammad as leaders of the Muslim community), and Imam Rezā was responsible for the diffusion of Shīʻa Islam in Persia. Those who make the pilgrimage to the Imam's tomb in Mashhad are called 'meseti', an equivalent of the Turkish 'hadjis' (*Persika*, ed. Iorga, pp. 105-6). A detailed description of Imam Rezā's mosque and shrine brings the digression to a conclusion (*Persika*, pp. 106-7).

At the end of *Persika*, Vatatzes includes several short poems that are associated in some way with the contents of the book. Among them is one containing the sayings of a Persian dervish ('gymnosophist') on humility, further proof that his knowledge of religious life in Persia was more than superficial. In the main body of *Persika*, Vatatzes mentions a dialogue he had with one of these 'gymnosophists'.

The *Periēgetikon*, a poem based on his travels, was the first work by Vatatzes to be published in a proper edition. The nature of the poem means that the information provided is mainly geographical and concise in character. Nevertheless, the poem constitutes an important source for the historical geography of Persia and Central Asia. The fact that he mentions his work *Persika* in the poem indicates that he may have written it after 1748, though it is also possible that *Persika* took some time to complete, and in the meantime Vatatzes also worked on his poem. Common themes run through both *Persika* and the *Periēgetikon*, such as references to Nāder Shah and descriptions of certain places.

Members of the Vatatzes family are attested in the 18th century in the principalities of Wallachia and Moldavia. Both existing manuscripts of his *Persika* (and possibly a third, potentially different one, mentioned by Iakovakis Rizos-Neroulos) come from collections in Moldavia. It is possible that the Greek scholar Daniel Demetrios Philippides read Vatatzes' *Persika* in Moldavia, and published a short account of the work in his *Historia tēs Roumounias* ('History of Romania').

SIGNIFICANCE

The importance of Vatatzes' work lies in his choice of subject and his direct knowledge of the oriental world. In fact, his works are among the first in Modern Greek literature that deal with topics related to Central Asia. An earlier example is the account by Nikolaos Spatharios (1636-1708; also known as 'Milescu' in Romanian historiography), who travelled overland to China, starting, as Vatatzes did, from Russia.

As a travel account, including many direct observations and first-hand information about the facts and events the author describes, *Persika* remains a valuable source, written by a direct witness, for the life and deeds of Nāder Shah of Persia. Even if Vatatzes used other sources (oral and possibly written) alongside his own observations, this does not diminish the value of his work. In the context of the history of Greek literature, the work is of even greater value, and its overall concept as well as some of Vatatzes' linguistic choices, might have influenced Philippidēs' 1816 work, *Historia tēs Roumounias* ('History of Romania').

PUBLICATIONS

MS Bucharest, Biblioteca Academiei Române – gr. 1320 (18th century, after 1748; see M. Carataşu, *Catalogul manuscriselor greceşti BAR 1067-1350*, ed. E. Popescu-Mihuţ and T. Teoteoi, Bucharest, 2004, vol. 3, p. 352)

MS Athens, Ethnikē Vivliothēkē tēs Hellados – no 1861 (2061) (18th century, after 1748; see P.G. Nikolopoulos, *Perigraphē cheirographōn kōdikōn tēs Ethnikēs Bibliothēkēs tēs Hellados arith. 3122-3369*, Athens, 1996, pp. 3-4)

D. Philippidēs, *Geōgraphikon tēs Roumounias*, Leipzig, 1816, pp. 3-22 (second epilogue at the end of the main text, with separate page numbering, an abstract of *Persika* by Philippidēs)

Basile Vatatzès, *Persica. Histoire de Chah-Nadir*, ed. N. Iorga, Bucharest, 1939 (based on the Bucharest MS)

STUDIES

Sariyannis, 'Eighteenth-century Ottoman Greek's travel account'

Venetis, 'Vatatzes, Vasilios'

Mēnaoglou, 'Hellēnes periēgētes'

Ch.A. Minaoglou, 'Greek travellers and travel literature from the fifteenth to the eighteenth century', in E. Close, M. Tsianikas and G. Couvalis (eds), *Greek research in Australia. Proceedings of the sixth biennial international conference of Greek Studies*, Adelaide, 2007, 305-12, p. 308

M. Axworthy, 'The army of Nader Shah', *Iranian Studies* 40 (2007) 635-46

Axworthy, *Sword of Persia*

M. Axworthy, 'Basile Vatatzes and his history of Nader Shah', *Oriente Moderno* 86 (2006) 331-43

Gorshenina, *Explorateurs en Asie centrale*

Angelomatē-Tsoungarakē, 'Hellēnika periēgētika keimena'

L. Bréhier, 'Basile Vatatzès. Persica. Histoire de Chah-Nadir', *Journal des Savants* (Jan.-Mar. 1941) 46 (book review)

I. Rizo-Néroulos, *Cours de littérature grecque moderne donné à Genève*, Geneva-Paris, 1828, pp. 142-3

Philippidēs, *Geōgraphikon tēs Roumounias*, pp. 3-22 (first mention of *Persika* in a printed book)

Mihai Ţipău

Nikola Lašvanin

Nicolaus à Lasva; Nicolaus Marcsincussich

DATE OF BIRTH   Approximately 1703
PLACE OF BIRTH   Lašva
DATE OF DEATH   2 September 1750
PLACE OF DEATH   Jajce

BIOGRAPHY

Nikola Lašvanin was born in the Catholic parish of Lašva near Travnik in central Bosnia, probably around 1703. Even though he is better known by his toponymic surname à Lasva or Lašvanin, his real surname was Marcsincussich (Marčinkušić). In 1719, he entered the Franciscan order at the monastery in Fojnica. Nothing is known of his further education, though it is probable that he studied in Italy, like other prominent Bosnian Franciscans of his time. He visited Italy in his early twenties during September 1726, stopping at some of the important academic centres of the time, such as Padua, Ferrara, Bologna, Cesena, Macerata and Rome. His Bosnian/Croatian writing reveals the strong influence of Italian vocabulary and syntax. Between 1730 and 1735 he served as the teacher of the Franciscan novices in the monastery of Fojnica.

In 1740, Lašvanin is mentioned as the head (*guardian*) of another Franciscan monastery in central Bosnia, Kreševo. Later, back in the monastery at Fojnica, being a senior member of his community, he was involved as Franciscan representative in several legal disputes before the Ottoman authorities, during one of which he was imprisoned by the authorities in Travnik for five days.

In 1745, Lašvanin was elected custodian of the Franciscan Province of Bosna Srebrena (Bosna Argentina), becoming the *de facto* head of Franciscans in Ottoman Bosnia, since the provincial resided in Habsburg-ruled Slavonia. In this capacity, accompanied by the former provincial Filip Lastrić, he travelled to the Habsburg court in Vienna to ask for the support of the Empress Maria Theresa (r. 1740-80). The mission was partially successful. Lašvanin died on 2 September 1750 during a visit to relatives in Jajce in western Bosnia. He was buried in the Church of St John in Podmilačje.

MAIN SOURCES OF INFORMATION

Primary

MS Livno, Library of the Franciscan Monastery Ss Peter and Paul, Gorica – Kut. 35, Rijet. 1 (Nikola Lašvanin, *Kronika*, 1750; modern edition in Croatian: N. Lašvanin, *Ljetopis*, ed. and trans. I. Gavran, Sarajevo, 1981, 2003[2])

Philippo ab Occhievia, *Epitome vetustatum bosnensis provinciae seu brevissimum compendium historico-chronologicum*, Ancona, 1776, p. 20 (modern bilingual Croatian-Latin edition: F. Lastrić, *Pregled starina Bosanske provincije*, ed. A. Zirdum, trans. I. Gavran and Š. Šimić, Sarajevo, 1977, p. 78; 2003[2], pp. 81-2)

MS Sarajevo, Archive of the Province Bosna Srebrena – *Liber Inductionis Clericorum pro Conventu Fojnicensi Jussu Adm. Rndi Patris Gregorii a Varess Minri Provlis Provisus*, fol. 4 (1784)

MS Kraljeva Sutjeska, Library of the Franciscan Monastery of St John the Baptist – Pok. 14 (Bosnian Franciscan chronicle of the monastery of Kraljeva Sutjeska written by Bonaventura Benić under the title *Protocollum conventus Suttiscae*, 1785; modern edition in Croatian: B. Benić, *Ljetopis sutješkog samostana*, ed. and trans. I. Gavran, Sarajevo, 1979, pp. 61-4, 141; 2003[2], pp. 67-9, 161)

J. Jelenić, 'Necrologium Bosnae Argentinae', *Glasnik Zemaljskog Muzeja u Bosni i Hercegovini* 28 (1916) 337-57, p. 347

J. Jelenić (ed.), *Spomenici kulturnog rada franjevaca Bosne Srebreničke*, Mostar, 1924, pp. 22, 24-6, 67-9

J. Matasović (ed.), 'Fojnička regesta', *Spomenik Srpske kraljevske akademije*, 67, drugi razred 53, Belgrade, 1930, 61-431, p. 198

I. Stražemanac, *Povijest franjevačke provincije Bosne Srebrene*, Zagreb, 1993, pp. 206-7; Osijek, 2010[2], p. 69 (a modern edition of the chronicle in Latin entitled *Paraphrastica et topographica expositio totius almae provinciae Bosnae Argentinae fratrum minorum de opservantia*, written between 1730 and 1757; today preserved in three MSS in Požega and Slavonski Brod)

B.S. Pandžić, *Acta Franciscana Hercegovinae*, Mostar, 2003, vol. 2, pp. 185-9

Secondary

P. Ćošković, art. 'Lašvanin, Nikola', in *Hrvatski biografski leksikon*, Zagreb, 2013; http://hbl.lzmk.hr/clanak.aspx?id=11292

M. Karamatić, *Franjevačka književnost u Bosni u XVIII. stoljeću*, Zagreb, 2011, pp. 44-5

A.S. Kovačić, *Hrvatski franjevački biografski leksikon*, Zagreb, 2010, pp. 331-2

V. Kursar, 'Nikola Lašvanin', in C. Kafadar, H. Karateke and C. Fleischer (eds), *Historians of the Ottoman Empire*, 2006, http://web.archive.org/web/20080624224611/http://www.ottomanhistorians.com/database/html/lasvanin_en.html

I. Gavran, 'Uvod', in N. Lašvanin, *Ljetopis*, ed. and trans. I. Gavran, Sarajevo, 2003², 5-32

M. Marjanović, *Leksikon hrvatskih književnika Bosne i Hercegovine od najstarijih vremena do danas*, Sarajevo, 2001, p. 145

A.S. Kovačić, *Biobibliografija franjevaca Bosne Srebrene. Prilog povijesti hrvatske književnosti i kulture*, Sarajevo, 1991, pp. 210-11

M. Džaja, 'Pravo prezime fra Nikole Lašvanina i fra Filipa Laštrića-Oćevca', *Dobri Pastir* 11-12 (1962) 288-92

WORKS ON CHRISTIAN-MUSLIM RELATIONS

Ljetopis
Kronika
'Chronicle'

DATE   Between 1726 and 1750
ORIGINAL LANGUAGE   Croatian

DESCRIPTION

Lašvanin's *Ljetopis* or *Kronika*, as it is called in critical editions and scholarly works, is actually a compendium of a number of texts: a world chronicle and two local Bosnian Franciscan chronicles, a story of the fall of Bosnia to the Ottomans, a list of Bosnian bishops, copies of historical documents, and smaller trivial texts, including an ink formula, folk songs and a list of Turkish proverbs and sayings with translation. The autograph, preserved in the archive of the Monastery of Ss Peter and Paul in Gorica, Livno, consists of 181 numbered and two unnumbered pages written predominantly in the Bosnian Cyrillic alphabet. Twelve-and-a-half pages of the text are written in Latin and are a copy of a pamphlet, *Bosna captiva* ('Bosnia captive'), written by the Croatian author Pavao Ritter Vitezović (Trnava, 1712), concerning the last days of the Bosnian kingdom and its conquest by the Ottomans. The first and longest text is a slightly revised copy of the chronicle written by Pavao Ritter Vitezović, entitled *Kronika aliti szpomen vsega szvieta vikov* ('Chronicle, or the remembrance of all centuries of the world') (Zagreb, 1696; modern critical edition by A. Jembrih, Zagreb, 2015). It covers the period from the creation of the world to 1690.

Despite being a history of Christian Europe, with Central Europe and Croatia its main focus, this chronicle includes topics from general world history and Islamic history, such as the birth of Muḥammad and the emergence of Islam, and Islamic conquests in Asia and Africa. In descriptions of Muslim-Christian relations, typically the emphasis is on wars and conflicts. In this respect, the Ottoman conquest of the Balkans is represented as a continuation of the early Islamic Arab conquests. While Vitezović in his chronicle differentiated between Muslim groups such as Turks, Saracens and Persians, Lašvanin in his version equates all Muslims with Turks, disregarding their particular ethnic, cultural, geographical or historical origins and contexts. In addition, he leaves out certain dates and entries that he does not consider relevant for the purpose of his work as a whole. In this way, his adaptation of Vitezović's chronicle becomes an introduction that contextualises the remaining major part of the work, which he designed to be a local, Franciscan chronicle. Vitezović's chronicle in Lašvanin's interpretation differs from the original not only in language (Lašvanin substitutes the original's north Croatian *kajkavskie kavski* dialect with the predominantly *štokavski ikavski* idiom of central Bosnia) and style, but also in its focus on main events, thus becoming less central and west European, and more south-east European and Balkan. Lašvanin's own original contribution, which covers the period of Bosnian history between 1731 and 1750, and is based on his first-hand experience and personal observations, represents the most valuable part of the text.

The other two Bosnian chronicles included in *Ljetopis* are not mere copies. The first, written by the Franciscan Stipan Margitić and covering the period 1682-1750, would have been lost had it not been preserved in Lašvanin's copy. Although it is not certain whether or to what extent it was modified by Lašvanin, it can be presumed that Lašvanin did make additions and modifications, as is the case with other texts he copied and adapted. The second is an anonymous 17th-century chronicle of Lašvanin's own monastery, covering the period between 1300 and 1696 and known as the 'Chronicle of Fojnica'. Its original is today preserved in the archive of the Monastery of the Holy Spirit in Fojnica (for a modern edition, see Ć. Truhelka [ed.], 'Fojnička kronika', *Glasnik Zemaljskog Muzeja u Sarajevu* 21 (1909) 443–59 + 15 fascimiles). Comparison of the two texts shows that while Lašvanin followed the original's main stream of narration and string of events, he did in fact make additions, modifications and interpretations that significantly enriched it. His additions and modifications were based, according to his own words, on 'various old texts' (*Ljetopis*, p. 193), as well, presumably, as historical documents he consulted.

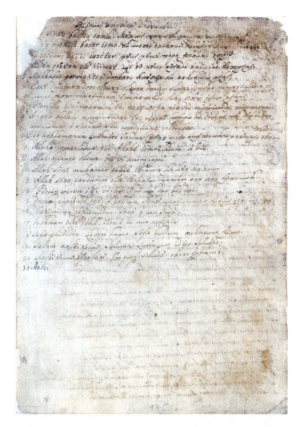

Illustration 11. MS page from Nikola Lašvanin, *Kronika*

Lašvanin follows the classical division between Muslims and Christians as Turks v. us, when, for example, he describes conflicts between Ottoman and Habsburg armies. On the other hand, he refers to the sultan as *car* ('tsar'), while the Ottoman capital is always called *Carigrad* ('the town of the Tsar') following the south Slav tradition, not Constantinople or Istanbul. Perhaps more surprisingly, in the description of fighting between the Habsburg and Ottoman forces in northern Bosnia in 1717, Lašvanin refers to the Christian side, which was eventually defeated, as *kauri* (from vulgar Ottoman *gāvur*, derived from Ottoman and Arabic *kāfir*), i.e. infidels, giaours, thereby adopting Muslim terminology (*Ljetopis*, p. 203). In general, terms and words of Ottoman origin are unexpectedly numerous in the text, even when a suitable form exists in Lašvanin's mother tongue.

Although Lašvanin includes a paragraph entitled *Aliquot turcica proverbia* ('Several Turkish proverbs') that contains 20 proverbs and phrases in Ottoman Turkish and Arabic transliterated into roman script, including some that invoke Allāh (*Ljetopis*, p. 297), thus indicating his interest in the language of the 'Turks', his general tone towards Islam and Muslims is negative. Ottoman rule is described as unjust and violent, while repression of Christians and the Church is explained as motivated by Muslim hatred for everything Christian, accompanied by greed and inherent lack of moral qualities. Thus, the history of Catholicism in Bosnia is represented as the chronicle of suffering for the faith illustrated by numerous martyrs and destroyed churches and monasteries. The remaining monasteries are falling into ruin due to restrictions on renovation, the church is impoverished by the extortion of high taxes and fees, monks are being imprisoned, threatened and tortured on suspicion of treason, espionage and converting Muslims to Christianity. As a senior member of the Franciscan order, Lašvanin was personally involved in several legal disputes concerning accusations of illegal renovation of a church or erection of a cross on the grave of a Franciscan. In 1743, he was even imprisoned for several days on suspicion of rebuilding the monastery of Fojnica higher and larger than was permitted (*Ljetopis*, pp. 219-21), so his personal experience may have influenced his writing. The general situation in the border province of Bosnia in Lašvanin's time was aggravated by the misdeeds of unruly Muslim militia (so-called local Janissaries, or *başa*s), rebellion by local dignitaries (*aʿyān*), upheavals among the Muslim peasantry, general brigandage, wars with the Habsburgs, and rebellions by Montenegrins. As a minority, the Catholics, and, in particular, the Franciscans as their representatives, were more exposed and sensitive to instabilities than other confessional communities (Muslim and Orthodox Christian). All these factors may have contributed to Lašvanin's more critical stance regarding Muslim-Christian relations.

Nevertheless, Lašvanin was ready to recognise the positive sides of some Turks. Following the death of the pasha of Bosnia, Muḥsinzāde ʿAbdullah Pasha, Lašvanin praises him as a proper and just man. On several occasions, Lašvanin describes how his Muslim neighbours, *džemat* (from Ottoman *cemāʿat*), helped the Franciscans' case by testifying on their behalf against fellow Muslims before the authorities.

Lašvanin also provides examples of joint devotions by Muslims and Christians. He repeats a story from Vitezović about a 'holy body' buried near Udbina in Croatia that was held in high esteem by both Muslims and Christians, the Muslims believing they were the remains of a Muslim saint and the Christians convinced they were of a Christian (*Ljetopis*, p. 191). A similar practice is noted close to Travnik in Bosnia, where Muslims venerated the tomb (*turbe*) of a martyr (*šehit* from Ottoman *şehīd*), 'a holy body, as we would say', because they believed the saint possessed miraculous healing powers, while local Christians maintained that the martyr was actually a Christian, 'a great servant of God', though they could not remember his name. A large poplar tree nearby and a well called *kanli bunar* or 'the bloody water' were also venerated by pilgrims (*Ljetopis*, p. 200).

On other occasions, Lašvanin is ready to dismiss popular Muslim beliefs and magical practices concerning the plague as useless, because 'there is no other cure than the holy mass, prayer and fasting' (*Ljetopis*, p. 197). In a word, his rare relatively positive remarks about individual Muslims or their popular practices do not challenge his generally negative polemical tone.

SIGNIFICANCE

Lašvanin's chronicle is the first of the major Bosnian Franciscan chronicles written in the 18th century. Despite the critical and somewhat deprecatory attitude of some modern scholars to Lašvanin as being too close to the medieval tradition and leaving a less personal imprint on the text than later Franciscan chroniclers in Bosnia, *Ljetopis* was used as a main source of information and inspiration by many of his successors. Indeed, Bono Benić (c. 1708-85), the chronicler of the monastery of Kraljeva Sutjeska, who is praised as the greatest Franciscan chronicler of the 18th century, used the work as a model and source for a significant part of his chronicle.

The general lines of the Franciscan attitude towards Muslims and Ottomans are firmly formed in the chronicle. For this reason, as well as the fact that the works of other authors were preserved and revived in a new guise for later generations by being copied into his work, Nikola Lašvanin should be appreciated as not only the first but perhaps also the most influential of the 18th-century Franciscan chroniclers of Bosnia.

PUBLICATIONS

MS Livno, Library of Ss Peter and Paul Monastery, Gorica – Kut. 35, Rijet. 1 (Nikola Lašvanin, *Kronika*, 1750)

Ć. Truhelka, 'Izvadak iz ljetopisa fra Nikole Lašvanina', *Glasnik Zemaljskog Muzeja Bosne i Hercegovine* 1 (1889) 77-80, 127-34; 2 (1890) 220-5, 304-5 (extracts)

J. Jelenić, 'Ljetopis fra Nikole Lašvanina', *Glasnik Zemaljskog Muzeja Bosne i Hercegovine* 26 (1914) 335-67, 555-83; 27 (1915) 1-35, 269-312 (omits some passages of minor importance)

J. Jelenić (ed.), *Ljetopis fra Nikole Lašvanina*, Sarajevo, 1916 (collects together passages published separately in the journal cited immediately above) (collects together passages published separately in the journal cited immediately above)

N. Lašvanin, *Ljetopis*, ed. and trans. I. Gavran, Sarajevo, 1981, 2003[2]

STUDIES

V. Kursar, 'Ambiguous subjects and uneasy neighbors. Bosnian Franciscans' attitudes toward the Ottoman State, "Turks", and Vlachs', in H.T. Karateke, H.E. Çıpa, and H. Anetshofer (eds), *Disliking others. Loathing, hostility, and distrust in pre-modern Ottoman lands*, Boston MA, 2018, 148-86, pp. 156-60, 163, 165-6, 168-75, 178

V. Kursar, 'Živjeti krstjanski pod turskim gospodstvom. Osmansko Carstvo u djelima bosanskih franjevaca', in D. Grmača, M. Horvat and M. Karamatić (eds), *Zbornik radova sa znanstvenog skupa Matija Divković i kultura pisane riječi II*, Zagreb, 2017, 449-75, pp. 457-9, 464-5

Ćošković, 'Lašvanin, Nikola'

Karamatić, *Franjevačka književnost*, pp. 44-5

A.S. Kovačić, art. 'Lašvanin, Nikola (Marčinkušić)', in *Hrvatski franjevački biografski leksikon*, Zagreb, 2010, 331-2

Kursar, 'Nikola Lašvanin'

A. Barun, *Svjedoci i učitelji. Povijest franjevaca Bosne Srebrene*, Sarajevo, 2003, p. 454

Gavran, 'Uvod'

Marjanović, *Leksikon hrvatskih književnika Bosne i Hercegovine*, p. 145

I. Pranjković, *Hrvatski jezik i franjevci Bosne Srebrene*, Zagreb, 2000, pp. 23-46

Leksikografski zavod Miroslav Krleža, art. 'Lašvanin, Nikola', in *Hrvatski leksikon*, Zagreb, 1997, vol. 2/8

V. Koroman, *Hrvatska proza Bosne i Hercegovine od Matije Divkovića do danas*, Mostar, 1995, pp. 41-5

M. Karamatić (ed.), *Bosanski franjevci*, Zagreb, 1994, pp. 43-7

Kovačić, *Biobibliografija franjevaca Bosne Srebrene*, pp. 210-11

Kovačić, art. 'Lašvanin-Marčinkušić Nikola', in Leksikon pisaca Jugoslavije, Belgrade, 1987, vol. 3, 590

I. Alilović, *Biobibliografija hrvatskih pisaca Bosne i Hercegovine do god. 1918*, Zagreb, 1986, pp. 42-3

A. Zirdum, 'Franjevački ljetopisi u Bosni i Hercegovini', *Croatica Christiana Periodica* 9/15 (1985) 43-64, pp. 50-1

A. Zirdum, 'Banjalučki rat u franjevačkim kronikama (izvješća fra N.L. i fra Bone Benića)', *Jukić* 3 (1973) 99-106

Jugoslavenski leksikografski zavod, art. 'Lašvanin, Nikola,' *Enciklopedija Jugoslavije*, vol. 5, Zagreb, 1962, 475

M. Džaja, 'Pravo prezime fra Nikole Lašvanina i fra Filipa Laštrića-Oćevca', *Dobri Pastir* 11-12 (1962), 288-92

A. Mladenović, 'O jeziku ljetopisa fra Nikole Lašvanina', *Građa Naučnog društva Bosne i Hercegovine*, vol. 10, Sarajevo, 1961, 53-123

J. Jelenić, 'Izvori "Ljetopisa fra Nikole Lašvanina"', *Naša Misao* 30 (1916) 61-2

Vjeran Kursar

Theoklytos Polyïdis

DATE OF BIRTH   End of the 17th century
PLACE OF BIRTH   Adrianople (Edirne)
DATE OF DEATH   Around 1760
PLACE OF DEATH   Unknown

BIOGRAPHY

Although identified as the author of the pseudo-prophetic work on the restoration of the Byzantine Empire, *Agathangelos*, which enjoyed widespread popularity long after his death, little is known about the biography of Theoklytos Polyïdis. He was the son of a wealthy merchant of Adrianople (present-day Edirne), in the Ottoman Empire. After his schooling, he became a monk at the Athonite monastery of Iviron, where he was ordained deacon in 1713 and priest in 1719. After a period spent as priest to the Greek community in Habsburg Hungary, he was given the rank of archimandrite in 1725. He undertook a trip to Germany two years later, with the primary goal of obtaining political and financial support for the Ecumenical Patriarchate. He spent some time in Württemberg and Hesse and several years in Leipzig, where he founded an Orthodox church for the Greek merchants of the city in 1743. He also travelled to Berlin, where he met the archimandrite Athanasios Dorostamos. The last documented evidence of his stay in Germany refers to his participation in a ceremony at the University of Halle in 1746.

During his time in Germany, in 1736 Polyïdis published a book on the doctrine of the Orthodox Church (*Sacra tuba fidei*), in both Latin (Stockholm) and German translation (Neubrandenburg). The work was intended as a polemical tool to be used against Catholics and Protestants. After a presumed trip to Russia, it is likely that Polyïdis returned to Mount Athos. He died sometime around 1760. During the final decade of his life, in about 1750, he composed the work that made him famous, *Agathangelos*, an apocalyptic prophecy claiming the liberation of Greeks from Ottoman rule and the restoration of Byzantium with the help of Russia.

MAIN SOURCES OF INFORMATION

Primary

MS Iviron Monastery, Mount Athos – 613/4733 Lampros: *Leukōma Theoklētou Polyeidous* (18th century)

Secondary

G. Podskalsky, *Griechische Theologie in der Zeit der Türkenherrschaft* (*1453-1821*), Munich, 1988, pp. 335-7

E.K. Lavriotis, *Theoklētos ho Polyeidēs kai to leukōma autou en Germania* (*ex anekdotou kōdikos*). *Ho philellēnismos tōn Germanōn*, Athens, 1935

WORKS ON CHRISTIAN-MUSLIM RELATIONS

Chrēsmos ētoi Prophēteia tou makariou
hieromonachou Agathangelou
'Oracle, namely Prophecy of the blessed hieromonk
Agathangelos'
Optasia tou makariou Hierōnymou Agathangelou
'Vision of Agathangelos'

DATE   Around 1750
ORIGINAL LANGUAGE   Greek (modern)

DESCRIPTION

Agathangelos or the 'Vision of Agathangelos' (45 pages in its first edition) is a pseudo-prophetic Greek work, conventionally attributed since the late 19th century to Theoklytos Polyïdis, its purported translator. Divided into ten chapters, it relates the political oracles of a Byzantine monk from Sicily, Hieronymos Agathangelos, that were supposedly written in 1279, translated into Italian and printed in Milan in 1555, and retranslated into Greek (from Italian or French) by Polyïdis himself in 1751. Its main framework is shaped by the topic common to post-Byzantine apocalyptic literature, the inevitable fall of the Ottoman Empire and the recovery of Byzantium at the end of times by Russia, the 'Third Rome', which is predestined to liberate Constantinople and restore the Byzantine Empire. This event is fixed for 1853, four centuries after the conquest of Constantinople by the Turks. The bulk of the work consists of *ex eventu* prophecies (a typical element in prophetic and apocalyptic literature), mostly related to European political figures and events from the first half of the 18th century. These include the Russo-Turkish War of 1735-9, the dynastic crisis of the Habsburgs after the death of Charles VI in 1740, and the Romanov dynasty from Peter the Great (r. 1682-1725), who is depicted as a new Alexander, to Elisabeth Petrovna (r. 1741-62).

The narrative begins with a prophecy about the fall of the Byzantine Empire, depicted as a punishment inflicted by God for its sins, a common topic in post-Byzantine political theology. The Turks are recognised as the instrument of God's providence, and their rule, compared to the Babylonian captivity of Israel, is predicted to last four centuries. Then Polyïdis sets out a number of political oracles related to historical events prior to the mid-18th century, starting with the rise of Luther and the Protestant Reformation, the main purpose of which is to validate the general prophetic framework relating to the restoration of Byzantium, the collapse of the Ottoman Empire and the final triumph of Orthodoxy. These apocalyptic events will be brought about by a messianic emperor named Peter V, identified with an imaginary successor of Peter the Great, who will 'spread Christ's victorious sign over Byzantium, and will destroy the power of the Ishmaelites' (Ch. 5). Under the influence of the successful Russian military campaigns in the Russian-Turkish war (1735-9), Polyïdis sees the Russian tsar as an instrument of divine providence and identifies him with the 'Last Emperor' who was supposed to liberate Constantinople, another common theme of the Byzantine apocalyptic tradition. A striking element of this apocalyptic scenario is the role that Polyïdis ascribes to Protestant Germany, which would have converted to Orthodoxy, in the revival of the Byzantine Empire after its restoration.

SIGNIFICANCE

Agathangelos is without doubt the most famous piece of 18th-century prophetic writing that foresaw the impending recovery of Byzantium and the liberation of the Greeks from the Ottoman Empire. It was not, however, the only work of this kind. A similar work is the *Optasia tou kyr Daniēl pany ōphelimos* ('Vision of kyr Daniel'), an anonymous Greek prophetic work on the restoration of Orthodoxy in Constantinople, composed in about 1770, that circulated widely not only in Greece but also in Wallachia and Moldavia in the late 18th century and first half of the 19th century. Part of the Byzantine apocalyptic tradition that shaped the composition of *Agathangelos* are the *Apocalypse of Pseudo-Methodius* and the various oracles ascribed to Stephanos of Alexandria, Patriarch Tarasios and Leo the Wise. Not by coincidence, these works were frequently copied in manuscripts together with Polyïdis' work. Moreover, the *Apocalypse of Pseudo-Methodius* and the *Oracles of Leo the Wise* are repeatedly alluded to in a thorough 1859 commentary on the prophecies of Agathangelos, preserved in a single Romanian manuscript that defers the recovery of Constantinople to 1866. This kind of intertextuality and mutual validation is one of the elements that ensured Polyïdis' work remarkable and lasting success.

If Polyïdis predicts the recovery of Constantinople and the downfall of the Ottoman Empire for 1853, similar apocalyptic calculations are also attested in the second half of the 18th and early 19th centuries, some of them inspired by *Agathangelos*. In his exegesis of the Revelation of John, Pantazēs of Larissa (d. 1795), who taught at the Princely Academy in Bucharest from 1780 to 1795, quotes Polyïdis' works and establishes the recovery of Constantinople by the Russian tsar in 1803. According to Cyril Lavriotis' (1741/4-1829) commentary on the Revelation of John, completed in Bucharest in 1821, the final defeat of the Turks was expected to take place in 1845. Moreover, the image of the messianic emperor who would come riding on a white horse in the reconquered Constantinople in the prophecy of *Agathangelos* (Ch. 9), inspired by Revelation 6:2, appears in a similar context both in Pantazēs's commentary on Revelation, and in the combined exegesis of the Old and New Testament by Theodoret of Ioannina (c. 1740-1823), composed in 1817, where the messianic emperor is explicitly identified with the Russian Tsar Alexander I (r. 1801-25), to whom the work is dedicated.

The first edition of *Agathangelos*, without mention of date or place, was discovered in the second half of the 20th century in the Folklore Archive of the University of Thessaloniki. It was presumably printed in Vienna in about 1790, and was tentatively attributed to Rhigas Velestinlis (around 1757-98), who would have adapted it to his editorial and political agenda, though the only evidence of his involvement appears in a later edition of *Agathangelos* in the 1830s. The work was very popular in the first half of the 19th century, during the Greek War of Independence and its aftermath. New editions were published at Missolonghi in 1824 during the siege, and in Athens in 1837 and 1838, the latter on the initiative of Constantine Oikonomos (1780-1857), a clergyman and theologian, in the context of the rise of the Russian Party in Greece. A new Athenian edition was published in 1849 by the Orthodox militant Kosmas Flamiatos (1786-1852), who was also the author of an extensive commentary. It was also printed in the Aegean island of Syros and in Bucharest in 1838, and again in Athens in 1853, a revival of interest in the prophecies of Agathangelos being well attested during the Crimean War (1854-6). It also knew wide circulation in manuscript form from the time of its first appearance and remained popular in the 20th century, especially during the First and Second World Wars.

Shortly after its first edition, *Agathangelos* was twice translated into Romanian. The first translation, preserved in a single manuscript from 1835, was undertaken in Wallachia in 1806, when it was under Russian occupation. The second was carried out in Moldavia and printed in Iași, at the Metropolitan Printing House, in 1818, with the approval of Metropolitan Veniamin Costache (r. 1803-46), who published religious books that showed a philo-Russian attitude. The second translation enjoyed wide popularity. It was reprinted in the 19th century at least seven times, especially in Bucharest and Iași, mostly at key points of modern Romanian history (1848, 1859, 1877), an indication of the strong political urge for the Romanian struggle for union and independence. The first edition was also extensively spread through manuscript copies, both in Wallachia and Moldavia. The interest of both Greeks and Romanians in the prophecies of Agathangelos in the 19th century is associated with the hopes of Balkan Orthodox Christians for imminent liberation from Ottoman rule. In Greece, it was strongly connected with the Megali Idea and philo-Russian political ideology. Its enormous success was also due to its literary style, imitating biblical prophecy, especially the Revelation of John, in conformity with the Byzantine apocalyptic tradition, particularly the *Apocalypse of Pseudo-Methodius*.

Agathangelos was popular not only among the uneducated, but was read, interpreted and used by such prominent figures as Pantazēs of Larissa, Rhigas Velestinlis, Constantine Oikonomos and the Wallachian writer and politician Ion Heliade Rădulescu (1802-72), under the patronage of whom an edition of *Agathangelos* was published in 1838. The work expresses the political and religious aspirations of Orthodox Greeks under Ottoman rule, but was also a stimulating factor for political action during the Russian-Turkish wars and the struggle for the independence of the Balkan peoples. In the 20th century, it continued to shape the attitudes of the Orthodox Greeks toward European politics, especially towards the roles played in it by the Russians, the Germans, and Turks.

PUBLICATIONS

For the Greek MSS, see:

Lavriotis, *Theoklētos ho Polyeidēs*, pp. 214-18

D. Doikos, 'Ho Agathangelos hōs prophētikon apokalyptikon ergo kai to mēnyma tou', in *Mnēmē 1821. Aphierōma eis tēn Ethnikēn Palingenesian epi tē 150 epeteiō*, Thessaloniki, 1971, 95-126, p. 96 n. 3

A. Timotin, *Profeții bizantine și postbizantine în Țările Române (secolele al XVII-lea - al XIX-lea)*, Bucharest, 2015, pp. 65, n. 5, 72

For the Romanian MSS, see Timotin, *Profeţii*, pp. 66-78, in particular p. 66 (on MS Bucharest, Biblioteca Academiei Române – rom. 1698, including the first Romanian translation) and pp. 75-8 (on MS Bucharest, Biblioteca Academiei Române – rom. 1434, 166 fols (1859), containing an unpublished exegesis of *Agathangelos*)

Chrēsmos ētoi Prophēteia tou makariou hieromonachou Agathangelou tēs monadikēs politeias tou Megalou Vasileiou, [s.l.], [s.a.] (probably Vienna, around 1790) (repr. in A. Politis, 'Hē prosgraphomenē ston Rēga prōtē ekdosē tou Agathangelou. To mono gnōsto antitypo', *Ho Eranistēs* 42 [1969] 173-92)

Hrismos, adecă prorocie a fericitului ieromonah Agathanghel, Iaşi, 1818 (Romanian trans.)

Chrēsmoi tou Agathangelou, Athens, 1837, 1878, 1895 (repr. Edessa, 1994)

Optasia tou makariou Hierōnymou Agathangelou, Athens, 1838, 1865

Chrēsmoi ētoi Prophēteia tou makariou hieromonachou Agathangelou, Bucharest, 1838

Eusebous tinos syntaktou, kata charin men tou Iēsou, tou Dontos tois dysi martysin autou to Pneuma tēs Prophēteias, kat' Apostolikon de tou Paulou Zēlon, tonde ton tropon elachistou Zēloprophētou, Syntagma pneumatikon, dichē diērēmenon, eis theōrētikon te, kai praktikon, Ermoupoli, 1838

Syllogē diaphorōn prorrēseōn, ekdotheisa de para tou iatrou P.L. Stephanitzē Leukadiou, Athens, 1838

Hrismos, adecă prorociia fericitului Ieromonah Agatanghel, Bucharest, 1838 (Romanian trans.)

Agathangelos hē Gnēsia prophēt. Hierōn. Agathangelou, Athens, 1848

Hrismos, adecă prorociia fericitului Ieromonah Agatanghel, Bucharest, 1848 (Romanian trans.)

K. Flamiatos, *Hermēneia tōn chrēsmōn tou Agathangelou*, Athens, 1849 (repr. in K. Flamiatos, *Apanta ētoi Phōne Orthodoxos peri tōn mellontōn kathōs kai Epistolē pros tous en tō Agiō Orei Pateras*, Athens, 1976; exegesis of *Agathangelos*)

Hrismos, adecă prorocie a fericitului ieromonah Agathanghel, Iaşi, 1850 (Romanian trans.)

Chrēsmoi Agathangelou, Athens, 1853

Hrismos, adecă prorociia fericitului Ieromonah Agatanghel, Bucharest, 1859 (2 editions, Romanian trans.)

Ho Palaios kai ho Neos Agathangelos, ētoi Prorrēseis peri tēs ptōseōs tou mōamethanikou kratous, Athens, 1860

Prophēteiai Agathangelou, Ermoupoli, 1876

Optasia tou makaritou kai Hierōnymou Agathangelou ētoi Syllogē diaphorōn prorrēseōn dapanē N. Staikovits kai G. Kampasē, Athens, 1877

Hrismos, adecă prorociia fericitului Ieromonah Agatanghel, Bucharest, 1877 (Romanian trans.)

Optasia tou Makariou Hierōnymou Agathangelou tou ek tēs monadikēs politeias tou Megalou Basileiou. Eranisteisa [...] ek dodeka palaiōn cheirographōn. Ekdidetai dapanē Geōrgiou A. Michalakea, Kalamata, 1890

Chrēsmos Agathangelou kai to telos tēs Othōmanikēs Autokratorias apo ta 1895 mechri 1899, Athens, 1895

Ai prophēteiai tou Agathangelou kai hē katastrophē tēs Tourkias, Athens, 1897

Ho Agathangelos ētoi Biblion periergotaton peri tou mellontos tōn ethnōn, ekdosis neōtatē epimeleia Iōannou Triantaphyllou, Athens, 1897

Hrismos, adecă prorociia fericitului Ieromonah Agatanghel, Bucharest, 1914 (Romanian trans.)

Ai apokalypseis tou Neou Agathangelou peri tou telous tēs Tourkias kai tou mellontos tēs Kōnstantinoupoleōs, Athens, 1915

Timotin, *Profeţii*, pp. 144-65 (critical edition of the Romanian print edition of 1818)

STUDIES

M. Hatzopoulos, 'Prophetic structures of the Ottoman-ruled Orthodox community in comparative perspective. Some preliminary observations', in P.M. Kitromilides and S. Matthaiou (eds), *Greek-Serbian relations in the age of nation-building*, Athens, 2016, 121-47

Timotin, *Profeţii*, pp. 64-79

A. Timotin, 'Agathangelos dans les pays Roumains au XIXe siècle. Lectures et lecteurs', *Studia Universitatis Babeş-Bolyai. Series Historia* 59 (2014) 34-44

A. Argyriou, 'Eschatologikoi prosanatolismoi kai hermēneies stēn Apokalypsē stis paramones tou Krimaikou polemou (Ho Kōd. arith. 639 tēs I.M. Panteleēmonos)', *Theologia* 85 (2014) 263-302

N. Pissis, 'Apokalyptik und Zeitwahrnehmung in griechischen Texten der osmanischen Zeit', in A. Helmedach et al. (eds), *Das osmanische Europa. Methoden und Perspektiven der Frühneuzeitforschung zu Südosteuropa*, Leipzig, 2014, 463-86

M. Hatzopoulos, 'Oracular prophecy and the politics of toppling Ottoman rule in south-eastern Europe', *The Historical Review / La Revue Historique* 8 (2011) 95-116

D. Karamberopoulos, *Ētan telika ho Rēgas ekdotēs tou 'Agathangelou'?*, Athens, 2009

Ph. Iliou and P. Polemi, 'Greek bibliography of the 19th century', *Electronic Catalogue*; http://oldwww.benaki.gr/bibliology/en/19.htm (information about the 19th-century Greek editions)

J. Nicolopoulos, 'From Agathangelos to the Megale Idea. Russia and the emergence of modern Greek nationalism', *Balkan Studies* 26 (1985) 41-56

A. Argyriou, *Les exégèses grecques de l'Apocalypse à l'époque turque (1453-1821)*, Thessaloniki, 1982, p. 110

Doikos, *Ho Agathangelos*, pp. 95-126

Politis, 'Hē prosgraphomenē ston Rēga'

Lavriotis, *Theoklētos ho Polyeidēs*, pp. 198-233

Andrei Timotin

Parteniĭ Pavlović

Partenij Pavlović; Parteniĭ Pavlovič;
Partenij Pavlovič; Partenij Pavlovich

DATE OF BIRTH   About 1695
PLACE OF BIRTH   Silistra, present-day Bulgaria
DATE OF DEATH   1760
PLACE OF DEATH   Sremski Karlovci, present-day Serbia

BIOGRAPHY

Parteniĭ Pavlović was born around 1695 in Silistra, an Ottoman administrative centre and an Orthodox metropolitan see (the Silistra metropolitans in his lifetime were scholars, and supported local education). He studied at a Greek monastery school and took a course with a teacher from Constantinople.

His biography is a vivid illustration of the peripatetic lifestyle of Balkan intellectuals. In 1714, he continued his schooling in Bucharest, at the Greek Academy of St Sava, which was financially supported by the Phanariot princes and attracted some of the best Greek-speaking scholars of the time. There, he studied Aristotelian philosophy and contemporary rational ideas. The Academy was under the influence of the Patriarchate of Jerusalem and promoted a zealous Orthodox spirit, with a particular emphasis on anti-Catholic intolerance. The Wallachian prince then sent him to Italy, together with other students, to continue his education. Because of his Orthodox fervour he could not continue his education there, but he did manage to visit many cities: Venice, Bologna, Florence, Padua, Rome, and Naples, where he engaged in theological debates about the Great Schism (1054) and the issue of papal infallibility.

After leaving Italy, Parteniĭ travelled in present-day Albania, Greece and Macedonia. In Kastoria, he studied mathematics, geometry, logic and Cartesian philosophy. Around 1718, he was a teacher in the Dalmatian town of Risan. He was tonsured as a monk in 1720 at the Serbian monastery of St Sava in Boka Kotorska (Dalmatia, in present-day Montenegro) and dedicated his 40-years service to the Serbian Orthodox Church, including both the Peć Patriarchate, located in the Ottoman

Empire, and the Metropolitanate in Sremski Karlovci, which served the Orthodox Serbs in the Habsburg Empire.

Parteniĭ rose from deacon-monk to hieromonk, coajutor, archimandrite and then bishop. Enjoying the trust of Patriarch Arsenije IV of Peć (Archbishop of Peć and Serbian Patriarch, 1725-37; head of the Serbian Orthodox Church in the Habsburg Empire, 1737-48), he was charged with various religious and political missions. In all likelihood, he became involved in securing local support for the Habsburgs in the impending Austro-Ottoman war. He travelled to monasteries and towns in both the Ottoman and Habsburg Empires. In 1733-5, he stayed at Rila Monastery (in present-day Bulgaria), where he read manuscripts and wrote marginal notes.

In 1737, during the Austro-Ottoman War (1737-9), Parteniĭ joined a wave of migrants leaving the Ottoman Empire and wrote a vivid description of this traumatic experience. From 1737 until his death, he lived and worked among the Serbs in the Habsburg Empire, mostly in Sremski Karlovci, Belgrade, Peć and Vienna. In 1741-4, he was a priest of the Orthodox chapel of St George in Vienna and often served as a translator for Serbian prelates visiting high officials, including the Empress Maria Theresa (r. 1740-80). In 1744-6, the Wallachian boyars (nobles) Radu and Constantin Cantacuzino organised a political plot against the Habsburgs involving the Romanian Orthodox population in Transylvania. Although the plan failed, Parteniĭ was arrested and imprisoned for 16 months. After his release, he received financial compensation from the authorities.

In 1751, Parteniĭ was promoted to metropolitan *in partibus* (without an eparchy) and was a close aide to the Karlovci Metropolitan Pavel Nenadović (r. 1749-68), serving as his vicar. He expressed his support for the Russian involvement in the Balkans in two letters: to the Russian Empress Elisabeth Petrovna (r. 1741-62), and to the Russian Synod.

Parteniĭ was a polyglot. He wrote four types of works, most of which were not published: liturgical books, reports and letters, autobiographical marginal notes (between 1720 and 1760) and the autobiographical work *Avtobiografija*, and two poems.

He died on 29 April 1760 at Sremski Karlovci.

MAIN SOURCES OF INFORMATION

Primary

MS Belgrade, Arhiv Srpska Akademija Nauka i Umetnosti – number unknown; Partenij Pavlovič, *Avtobiografija* (1757)

Secondary

R. Detrez, 'Partenij Pavlovič. The "wandering monk" as a networker', *Slavia Meridionalis* 17 (2017) 1-19; https://doi.org/10.11649/sm.1311

R. Detrez, 'De Wereld Volgens Partenij Pavlovic', in P. Boulogne et al. (eds), *"Ik Hou Van Jou, Peters Creatie". Festschrift voor Emmanuel Waegemans*, Amsterdam, 2016, 511-30

R. Detrez, 'Parteniĭ Pavlovich revisited', *Literaturna Misl'* 49 (2016) 35-50

V. Maragos, 'The nation of faith. Partenij Pavlović and aspects of the Orthodox Commonwealth', in P.M. Kitromilides and A. Tabaki (eds), *Greek-Bulgarian relations in the age of national identity formation*, Athens, 2010, 83-107

P. Boiadzhiev, *Parteniĭ Pavlovich*, Sofia, 1988

P. Boiadjiev, 'Chronologie de la vie et de l'*Autobiographie* de Partenij Pavlovič', *Bulletin de l'Association Internationale d'Études du Sud-Est Européen* 13-14 (1976) 73-92

B. Angelov, *Sŭvremennitsi na Paisiĭ*, vol. 2, Sofia, 1964, pp. 5-59

WORKS ON CHRISTIAN-MUSLIM RELATIONS

Avtobiografija
'Autobiography'

DATE   1757
ORIGINAL LANGUAGE   Church Slavonic

DESCRIPTION

Parteniĭ's *Avtobiografija* remained in manuscript until 1905, when it was published by the Serbian scholar Dimitrije Ruvarac (1842-1931). It consists of 140 pages, and presents a fragmentary narration of some of Parteniĭ's experiences as an adult rather than a linear account of his life. It has a didactic character, though many people assume he did not intend to publish it.

Some scholars think that the work was influenced by pilgrimage literature. As a polyglot and seasoned traveller, Parteniĭ's language is full of foreign words, especially administrative and political terms, as well as certain neologisms. On the one hand, the text has a secular dimension in its depiction of both political events and daily personal experiences, though on the other, its tone, contents, interpretive stance and vocabulary reveal his pious outlook. References to events are based mostly on religious chronology.

A theme that runs through the text concerns Parteniĭ's visits to various monasteries, and the saints in the Balkan region whose relics he venerated. This part of the manuscript, devoted to historical saints, concludes with details about a contemporary Christian martyr who had not yet been canonised, the tone suggesting that Christians at that time continued to face martyrdom. *Avtobiografija* ends with two homilies, the first a glorification of the Habsburg and Russian imperial families, and the second on a dogmatic dispute with Catholicism.

Parteniĭ seems to have been a fervent Orthodox believer and more anti-Catholic than anti-Muslim, but he provides examples of Muslim religious fanaticism, the conversion of many churches into mosques, and the prohibition on the use of church bells and clappers. He says he was beaten in Ohrid (northern Macedonia) by the 'Hagarenes' because he used a clapper to call for a service in a mosque that had formerly been a church. Yet, despite Muslim fanaticism he was saved by the local pasha.

Parteniĭ's interpretation of Ottoman rule over Christians is the traditional explanation that it was punishment for Christian sins. Islam for him is 'Mohamedan unbelief' that consists of 'superstitious deceitful Turkish prayers', and Muslims are 'Hagarenes', the term (usually interpreted as meaning 'descendants of Hagar') used by Christians in the early centuries of Islam. His choice of adjectives to describe them is predictable: 'ill-fated', godless, 'conceited and infidel' and 'unbelieving and harsh'.

Old and new Christian martyrs are repeatedly referred to in the *Avtobiografija*. Their relics maintain the faith and put to shame the 'impious Hagarenes and malevolent heretics, such as Latins, Armenians, Nestorians and other apostates'. Interestingly, Parteniĭ groups together unbelievers and heretics, though, since he thinks that every faith comes from God, he does not use disparaging words about the sultan.

It seems that Parteniĭ does not acknowledge that Islam is one of the Abrahamic faiths, and he emphasises the superstition Muslims express in both ritual and daily practice. While he is reluctant to engage in religious disputes with Muslims (which could be explained by the fact that he was living mostly in Habsburg territory, where the main 'enemies' were the Catholics), by presenting Muslims as superstitious and unbelieving, he clearly implies that Christianity is superior. This is confirmed in a marginal note on the chrysobull (decree) issued by the medieval Bulgarian ruler Ivan Šišman (r. 1371-95) for the monastery of Rila, about which he writes: the 'unbelieving and cruel Hagarenes [...] are doomed to eternal torment together with their teacher, devil, and the false prophet Mohamed'.

SIGNIFICANCE

Avtobiografija is considered the pioneering text of the autobiographical genre among the South Slavs. It had an impact on both Serbian (Dositej Obradović, c. 1739-1811) and Bulgarian (Sofroniĭ Vračanski, 1739-1813) literature. It highlights personal experiences and combines praise for Orthodox piety with the disparagement of Islam, which was known not in accurate detail but mostly through daily contacts and recycled clichés.

All Parteniĭ's works are written from a devout Orthodox and Slav perspective. Thus, he is considered to be part of the last generation that shared Christian and Slavic identity before the explosion of nationalisms in the Balkans. In this respect, it is telling that Parteniĭ looks forward to Peter the Great liberating Balkan Orthodox Christians from the Muslim yoke, seeing the Russian monarch as a tool in the hands of God to fight unbelievers (Muslim Ottomans) and heretics (Swedes and others) (Detrez, 'Parteniĭ Pavlovich revisited'). His ambition of maintaining the Christian Slavic commonwealth may also explain his generic portrayal of Muslims as Hagarenes, a term used in early Syriac and Greek sources, in the Psalms, and in various Byzantine texts.

PUBLICATIONS

MS Belgrade, Arhiv Srpska Akademija Nauka i Umetnosti – number unknown (1757)

D. Ruvarac, 'Avtobiografija Partenija Pavlovića', *Srpski Sion* 15 (1905) kn. [issue] 14, 396-9; kn. 15, 430-2; kn. 17, 493-5; kn. 18, 526-8, kn. 19, 553-6
Angelov, *Săvremennitsi*, pp. 197-210

STUDIES

Detrez, 'Parteniĭ Pavlovich revisited'
Detrez, 'De Wereld Volgens'
S. Plachkova, 'Izledvanijata na bŭlgarski ezik vŭrkhu Parteniĭ Pavlovich i negovata "Avtobiografija" (Vtora chast)', *Proglas. Filologichesko Spisanie* 24 (2015) 85-102
S. Plachkova, 'Izledvanijata na bŭlgarski ezik vŭrkhu Parteniĭ Pavlovich i negovata "Avtobiografija" (Pŭrva chast)', *Proglas. Filologichesko Spisanie* 23 (2014) 48-67
Maragos, 'The nation of faith'
W. Bracewell, 'The limits of Europe in East European travel writing', in W. Bracewell and A. Drace-Francis (eds), *Under eastern eyes. A*

comparative introduction to East European travel writing on Europe, Budapest, 2008, 61-120, pp. 88-9

Boiadzhiev, *Parteniĭ Pavlovich*

Boiadjiev, 'Chronologie'

Angelov, *Sŭvremennitsi*, pp. 5-59

V. Kiselkov, *Prouki i ocherti po starobŭlgarska literatura*, Sofia, 1956, pp. 384-98

I. Ivanov, *Starobŭlgarski razkazi. Tekstove, novobŭlgarski prevodi i belezhki*, Sofia, 1935, pp. 82-6

Evguenia Davidova

Vision of kyr Daniel

'Vision of kyr Daniel, very useful'

DATE   Around 1770
ORIGINAL LANGUAGE   Greek (modern)

DESCRIPTION

Optasia tou kyr Daniēl is a short anonymous Greek pseudo-prophetic work (covering around 10 pages in a modern edition), written down in about 1770 as an extension of the hagiography of a Greek neo-martyr, Anastasios (d. 1750). It is also attested as an isolated text. The work relates the vision of a Muslim convert to Orthodox Christianity who was tonsured as a monk and given the name Daniel. The vision is of the recovery of Constantinople by the Greeks, and its Byzantine religious topography. The text adapts several common themes of post-Byzantine apocalyptic literature, such as the restoration of Byzantium, the 'sleeping emperor' (Constantine XI Palaiologos [r. 1448-53], the last Byzantine emperor), who was expected to liberate the city and restore the empire, and the interrupted divine liturgy in Hagia Sophia on 29 May 1453, which was expected to continue on the day of the liberation of the city. Although the text is anonymous, its moral author can be regarded as Sophronius V, Patriarch of Jerusalem (r. 1771-4), who became Ecumenical Patriarch Sophronius II (r. 1774-80). He was still holding the archbishopric of Ptolemais when Daniel was advised to visit him to tell him what he had seen in his vision.

The text, unpublished until the end of the 19th century, circulated in manuscript copies in the monasteries of Mount Athos and in the secular milieu, both in Greece and in the Romanian Principalities. Shortly after its production in Greek, *Optasia tou kyr Daniēl* was translated into Romanian, where it circulated in two versions. One of them enjoyed a fairly wide manuscript transmission from the last decade of the 18th century, though its spread was limited to the monastic environment.

In *The life of St Neomartyr Anastasios*, an Epirote peasant describes the context of Anastios's martyrdom and the influence he had on the future monk Daniel, who was the son of his persecutor, the local governor Ahmed Pasha. This son, Musa, secretly embarks on a boat to Venice, where he is baptised in the Church of San Giorgio dei Greci, although his father, after learning of his baptism, believes it took place in Wallachia.

After spending some time in Venice, he joins pilgrims travelling to the tomb of St Spyridon in Corfu, where he becomes a monk. After a while, wishing to receive martyrdom, Daniel goes to the Peloponnese, where some Christians prevent him from fulfilling his desire as they fear the Muslims will take revenge. Going then to Constantinople, he meets Archbishop Sophronius of Ptolemais (the future patriarch of Jerusalem), who advises him to fast and pray in order to know God's will, and Daniel consequently gives up his wish and returns to a monastery in Corfu, where he spends the rest of his life.

Optasia tou kyr Daniēl summarises this story from the moment when Daniel reaches Constantinople to receive martyrdom, and depicts the vision he has after fasting and praying as advised by his confessor, who some versions identify as Archbishop Sophronius. On 18 November (the date of the martyrdom of St Anastasios) 1763 or 1764, Anastasios appears to Daniel in a vision and leads him through the imperial city, a journey during which the old Byzantine churches (All Saints, Holy Apostles, St George *tou Deuterou*, Hagia Sophia and one of the churches of St Constantine), which had disappeared or been transformed into mosques, are revived and the Turks are chased out of the city by St Constantine and the Virgin, the traditional protectors of Constantinople. The main stopping place on this journey is Hagia Sophia, where Daniel attends the divine liturgy celebrated by Christ himself surrounded by all the saints and the Virgin. There, an old man is sitting asleep on a throne, an allusion to the legend of the 'sleeping emperor'. When the liturgy ends, the Virgin intercedes with Christ to liberate the Christians who were being punished for their sins, a common topic in post-Byzantine political theology. Christ's reply reveals his wish to liberate them during the reign of Sultan Mahmud I (r. 1730-54), an allusion to the recent Russo-Turkish war (1735-9).

In Hagia Sophia, the Virgin receives the news of the execution by the sultan of three bishops and two Christian dignitaries. These dignitaries may have been the chief dragoman Nicholas Soutzos and the Moldavian prince Gregory Kallimachis (r. 1761-4 and 1767-9), both executed in Constantinople on 9 September (Old Style: 29 August) 1769. If so, *Optasia tou kyr Daniēl* was written down after September 1769 and in any case before 1771, when Sophronius became patriarch of Jerusalem. The news displeases the Virgin who goes to the Topkapı Palace and confronts Sultan Mustafa III (r. 1757-74), revealing to him the innocence of his victims and the support she has given to his enemies, first among them Catherine the Great of Russia (r. 1762-96). Daniel's vision ends with the expulsion of Muslims from the Church of St Constantine, which had been transformed into a mosque, and with the reiterated prophecy about the impending restoration of Constantinople.

SIGNIFICANCE

Optasia tou kyr Daniēl and the related *Life of St Neomartyr Anastasios* provide a unique and vivid account of the biography, travels and religious life of an educated 18th-century Muslim convert to Christianity, in particular of his martyrdom-oriented piety. The narrative of the journey Daniel undertakes in his vision also supplies a remarkable, albeit biased, description of the religious topography in Ottoman Constantinople.

The work includes a prophecy about the imminent recovery of Constantinople by the Greeks, a post-Byzantine theme that stimulated Greek rebel movements before and during the Greek War of Independence. Written down around 1770, the text was very probably meant to support Greek hopes of an impending liberation during the Russo-Turkish War of 1768-74. A similar role was played by other writings, in which the Byzantine apocalyptic tradition was intertwined with Russian politics in the Balkans in the second half of the 18th century. An example of such a text can be found in the commentary of Nicholas Zerzoulis (1710-73), a pupil of Eugenios Voulgaris and professor at the Princely Academy of Iași, on the *Oracle* attributed to Stephanos of Alexandria (1768), where the recovery of Constantinople is predicted for 1774. The *Vision of Agathangelos* (c. 1750), the most famous 18th-century prophecy on the restoration of Byzantium, is a work with which the *Optasia tou kyr Daniēl* shares more than one theme, including the legend of the icon from Hagia Sophia that is supposed to perform miracles on the day Constantinople is won back by the Christians.

PUBLICATIONS

> For details of the Greek and Romanian MSS, see A. Timotin and E. Timotin, *Scrieri eshatologice postbizantine. Vedenia Sofianei, Vedenia lui chir Daniil*, Bucharest, 2002, pp. 89-91 (Greek MSS), 66-88 (Romanian MSS)

> *Ho neōphōtistos Othōmanos kai hē peri tēs hellēnikēs ethnegersias optasia autou. Diēgēsis*[...] *syngrapheisa men hypo tou idiou ekdotheisa de ēdē kata to en tē hagia Monē tēs Myrtiōtissēs euriskomenon prōtotypon*, Athens, 1865
> *Othōmanos ho neōphōtistos kai hē peri hellēnikēs ethnegersias optasia autou*, (s.l.), 1873
> *Ho neōphōtistos Othōmanos kai hē peri tēs hellēnikēs ethnegersias optasia autou. Diēgēsis psychōphelestatē kai thaumasia*, ed. A. Kōnstantinides, Athens, 1878

P.V. Paschos, 'Islam kai neomartyres. Ho ek Paramythias neomartys Anastasios kai ho ismaēlitēs (Mousa) Daniēl ho omologētēs', *Epistēmonikē Epetēris tēs Theologikēs Scholēs* 30 (1995) 413-74, pp. 432-51 (edition of two Greek versions, preserved in MS Skete S. Anna – 85-4, fols 703-11v [19th century], and in MS Kozani, Dēmosia Vivliothēkē – 34, fols 1091-102 [late 18th century])

Timotin and Timotin, *Scrieri eshatologice*, pp. 155-68 (critical edition of the first Romanian version based on MS Bucharest, Biblioteca Academiei Române – rom. 1994, fols 279r-90r [from 1793])

A. Timotin, *Profeții bizantine și postbizantine în Țările Române (secolele al XVII-lea – al XIX-lea)*, Bucharest, 2015, pp. 126-43 (edition of two Romanian versions, preserved in MS Bucharest, Biblioteca Academiei Române – rom. 1994, fols 279r-90r [from 1793], and in MS Bucharest, Biblioteca Academiei Române – rom. 2509, fols 295v-306r [c. 1825-8])

STUDIES

Timotin, *Profeții bizantine*, pp. 50-63

A. Timotin, 'La vision de kyr Daniel. Liturgie, prophétie et politique au XVIIIe siècle', in K.A. Dimadis (ed.), *O ellīnikós kósmos anámesa stīn epochī tou Diafōtismoú kai ston eikostó aiṓna / The Greek world between the age of Enlightenment and the twentieth century*, Athens, 2007, vol. 1, pp. 127-34

A. Argyriou, 'Hē megalē idea stēn poiēsē tou Aristotelē Valaōritē', *Revue des Études Néo-Helléniques*, new series 1 (2005) 85-132, pp. 103-5

A. Timotin, 'Eschatologie post-byzantine et courants idéologiques dans les Balkans. La traduction roumaine de la Vision de kyr Daniel', in E. Siupiur et al. (eds), *Peuples, états et nations dans le sud-est de l'Europe*, Bucharest, 2004, 123-32

Timotin and Timotin, *Scrieri eshatologice*, pp. 24-9 and 66-124

A. Timotin, 'La *vision de kir Daniil*. Les manuscrits de la Bibliothèque de l'Académie Roumaine. Édition critique', *Archæus. Études d'Histoire des Religions* 4 (2000) 187-212

Paschos, 'Islam kai neomartyres', pp. 413-9, 471-4

A. Argyriou, *Les exégèses grecques de l'Apocalypse à l'époque turque (1453-1821)*, Thessaloniki, 1982, p. 103 n. 2

Andrei Timotin

Josip Ruđer Bošković

Roger Joseph Boscovich; Ruggiero Giuseppe Boscovich

DATE OF BIRTH   18 May 1711
PLACE OF BIRTH   Ragusa
DATE OF DEATH   13 February 1787
PLACE OF DEATH   Milan

BIOGRAPHY

Josip Ruđer Bošković was born in Ragusa (Dubrovnik) on 18 May 1711 to Nikola Bošković and his wife Pavica. His education began at the age of eight at the Jesuit College in Ragusa. In 1725, he entered the novitiate of the Society of Jesus in Rome, and in 1727 he enrolled for literary and philosophical studies at the Collegium Romanum. As soon as he had completed the course of ordinary studies, he was appointed a full professor of mathematical science in the Collegium. From 1734 to 1735, he was a lecturer at the Jesuit College in Fermo (Italy) and, from 1740 to 1759, he held a chair in mathematics at the Collegium Romanum.

In this period, Bošković wrote and published numerous dissertations in Latin on various mathematical, astronomical, geodetical and physical problems. Besides scientific work, Bošković also dealt with practical problems as the advisor to the papal government on important technical questions (e.g. the reconstruction of the great dome of St Peter's, irrigation of the Pontine marshes, and a geographical survey and map of the Papal States). What is more, he excelled in writing Latin texts in verse, which is convincingly proved by his numerous epigrams, eclogues, elegies and didactic dialogues.

In 1757, Bošković was sent by the city of Lucca to the Court of Vienna to urge the damming of the lakes that were threatening the city. In recognition of his diplomatic achievements, he was made an honorary citizen of Lucca and given generous assistance on his scientific journeys in Italy, France and England. As a reward for drawing the attention of British scientists to the impending transit of Venus over the sun, he was elected a member of the Royal Society on 15 January 1761.

In September 1761, Bošković sailed to Constantinople with the Venetian ambassador, Pietro Correr, in order to make geographical and archaeological studies of the maritime part of the Ottoman Empire. To avoid the dangers caused by the Seven Years' War, Bošković made his way back to Europe through Wallachia, Moldavia and Poland in the company of the British ambassador, Sir James Porter, and his family. The arduous journey, which took him from 24 May to 15 July 1762, was meticulously described in his *Giornale di un viaggio da Constantinopoli in Polonia con una sua relazione sulle rovine di Troja*, published in Bassano in 1784.

In 1765, Bošković established the observatory in Brera (Italy), which he ran until 1772. After the suppression of the Society of Jesus in 1773, he went to Paris, where Louis XV (r. 1715-74) granted him the new office of Director of Optics for the Marine. He retained this position until 1782, when he returned to Bassano to supervise the printing of his collected works, which were published in five volumes in 1785. He went to Milan with a plan to finish his philosophical works, but death overtook him at the age of 76. He was buried in the Church of Santa Maria Podone.

The complete works and letters of Bošković are currently being edited within the framework of a joint international project run by Accademia nazionale delle scienze detta dei XL, Hrvatska Akademija znanosti i umjetnosti, INAF – Osservatorio astronomico di Brera and Pontificia università gregoriana (http://www.edizionenazionaleboscovich.it/).

MAIN SOURCES OF INFORMATION

Primary

A. Fabroni, 'Elogio dell'abate Ruggero Boscovich', *Memorie di matematica e fisica della Societa italiana* 4 (1788) vii-xlv

J. Bajamonti, *Elogio del Padre Ruggero Giuseppe Boscovich*, Ragusa, 1789

A. Ricca, *Elogio storico dell'abate Ruggiero Giuseppe Boscovich*, Milan, 1789

A. Meneghelli (ed.), *Lettere del P. Boscovich, pubblicate per le nozze Olivieri-Balbi*, Venice, 1811

D. Vaccolini, 'Della vita e degli studi di R. Boscovich', *Giornale Arcadico di Roma* 92 (1842) 174-87

B. Šulek, *Memoria Rogerii Josephi Bošković*, Zagreb, 1867

C. Cantu, *Italiani illustri*, Milan, 1887, pp. 435-47

C. Sommervogel, *Bibliothéque de la Compagnie de Jésus*, Brussels, 1890-1909, vol. 1, pp. 1828-50

Secondary

A. Bogutovac (ed.), *Leksikon Rudera Boškovića*, Zagreb, 2011

S. Kutleša, *Ruđer Josip Bošković*, Zagreb, 2011

D. Cerqueiro, *Boscovich, el viajero del tiempo*, Buenos Aires, 2008

R. Dimitrić, *Ruđer Bošković*, Pittsburgh PA, 2006

L. Agnes, *Ruggero Giuseppe Boscovich. Un professore gesuita all'Università di Pavia, 1764-1768*, Milan, 2006

G.K. Cverava, *Rudžer Iosip Boškovič*, St Petersburg, 1997

Ž. Dadić, art. 'Bošković, Josip Ruđer', *Hrvatski biografski Leksikon*, 1989; http://hbl.lzmk.hr/clanak.aspx?id=2533

R.J. Boscovich, *Vita e attivita scientifica/His life and scientific work*, ed. P. Bursill-Hall, Rome, 1993

Ž. Dadić, *Ruđer Bošković*, Zagreb, 1987

L.L. White (ed.), *Roger Joseph Boscovich. Studies of his life and work*, London, 1961

WORKS ON CHRISTIAN-MUSLIM RELATIONS

Giornale di un viaggio da Costantinopoli in Polonia
'Diary of a journey from Constantinople to Poland'

DATE   1784
ORIGINAL LANGUAGE   Italian

DESCRIPTION

The *Giornale* (in full, *Giornale di un viaggio da Costantinopoli in Polonia dell'Abate Ruggiero Giuseppe Boscovich, con una sua Relazione sulle rovine di Troja*) was written during Bošković's journey in 1762. It was translated into French from Bošković's Italian autograph and published in 1772 without his permission. Seven years later followed a German edition (Leipzig, 1779) translated from French but again without Bošković's approval. A revised and approved Italian original was published in 1784 in Bassano, using the manuscript that Bošković had left in Warsaw at the end of his trip and the comments and corrections made by Pierre La Roche, the French secretary of the Moldavian Prince Grigore Callimachi (r. 1761-4). This edition comprises 162 pages in octavo and it is written in the form of a diary.

The narrative sequences are ordered by date, from 24 May to 15 July 1762. The published text consists of an introductory dedication to Count Ch. G. de Vergennes, the French ambassador in Constantinople, and the author's preface. There, Bošković claims that the main aim of the work is to depict his journey in the company of the British ambassador, Sir James Porter, his family and entourage 'through these barbaric regions with diverse customs and habits' (Bošković, *Giornale*, 1784, p. XVII; all the references that follow are to this edition, unless otherwise stated). Bošković's journey started in Constantinople, went through Bulgaria, Wallachia and Moldavia and ended in Kamianets-Podilskyi at the Polish frontier, with longer stops at Silivri, Kırklareli, Karnobat, Galaţi, Vaslui and Iaşi.

Bošković's narrative style is simple, concise and informative. There are no poetic digressions, stylistic ornamentations or private reflections, which points to the fact that his discourse reveals the outlook and world-view that is emblematic of the enlightened natural scientist. Accordingly, the overall narrative and ideological representation of Christian-Muslim relations is structured around two main opposing positions: freedom v. despotism, and culture v. barbarism.

In a manner typical of European Enlightenment discourse on the Other, Bošković is mostly concerned with the political deterioration, eco-nomic inefficacy and moral corruption of Ottoman rule. He meticulously describes and critically comments on the arrogance, crudeness and avarice of the Ottoman military and civil officials he meets during his journey. They are contrasted with educated, polite and civilised Europe-ans, irrespective of their confessional allegiance. As far as the Orthodox Christians in the Ottoman Empire are concerned, Bošković estimates that they are not much better than Muslims as a result of the centu-ries of cultural and civilisational neglect they have experienced under Ottoman rule. This is especially evident in Bošković's description of the political and administrative system in Moldavia, which is 'dreadfully tyrannised' by the Greek elite (p. 110). His general opinion of Christian-Muslim relations within the Ottoman Empire is most clearly expressed in the statement 'Turks treat Christians much worse than we treat our Jews in ghettos' (p. 137).

The economic devastation of the lands along Bošković's route is rep-resented through the contrast between their natural beauty and abun-dance and their agricultural and infrastructural decline. Consequently, the greatest drawbacks to Bošković and his entourage during the whole journey were dilapidated roads, poor food supply and inadequate lodg-ing as omnipresent features of 'uncultivated barbarity' (p. 157). This is corroborated by frequent examples of uncleanness and pestilence, which also signalled the pervasive moral corruption of Ottoman soci-ety. In conformity with his enlightened scientific worldview, religious differences between Christians and Muslims are rarely thematised and Bošković adduces the opinion of Janissaries among his escort that Turks are mostly indifferent to religion (p. 76).

The *Giornale* is a unique work within Bošković's opus. To a certain extent it might be compared in structure to the first part of his *De lit-teraria expeditione per pontificiam ditionem* ('Scientific expedition across the Papal States' [Rome, 1755]), in which Bošković minutely describes the journey made for the astronomical and geographical measurement of territories under papal jurisdiction (Bošković, *De litteraria expeditione*, pp. 1-120). Numerous references on Greek and Roman Antiquity indicate that the diary strongly draws upon earlier, humanist travel literature, while his erudite and detached point of view connects his work with contemporary French and Habsburg travelogues.

SIGNIFICANCE

Bošković's representation of the Muslim other mostly exemplifies the entrenched conventions of the travel literature of his time. He is far more interested in describing the 'scientific' features of the Muslim world, such as topographical and archaeological heritage from Antiquity, civil and military institutions, urban settings, and ethnic, demographical, economic and climatological data, than in sharing his own impressions of common people, their appearance, everyday life practices, customs and beliefs. The rare exceptions are his mention of girls fishing in Moldavia (p. 83) and a detailed description of a see-saw in Bulgaria (p. 55). An interesting specificity of Bošković's representation of the natural environment is his frequent mention of the Muslim *lieux de mémoire*, i.e. artificial hills built in memory of Ottoman battles. Although Bošković's discourse on the Muslim other, by reflecting the intellectual and cultural superiority of enlightened Europe, might be called hegemonic, the Italian transliteration of 'untranslatable' Turkish words for Ottoman administrative functions reveals the discursive presence of the silenced other.

The fact that Bošković's drafts of the diary were translated and published in French 12 years before the appearance of the authorised Italian version attests to the great interest in Bošković's work within French intellectual circles. Due to the author's indisputable intellectual and scientific reputation, Bošković's diary has certainly made an important contribution both to enlightened knowledge of the Muslim other and to the eighteenth-century discourse on Ottoman despotism.

PUBLICATIONS

> R.P. Joseph Boscowich, *Journal d'un voyage de Costantinople en Pologne fait à la suite de son Excellence Mr. Jacq. Porter, ambassadeur d'Angleterre par le R.P. Joseph Boscowich de la Comp. de Jésus en MDCCLXII*, Lausanne: Chez Franç. Grasset et Comp., 1772 (French trans., published without author's approval); 13634151(digitised version available through e-rara.ch)
>
> R.G. Boscowich, *Des Abt Joseph Boscowich Reise von Constantinopel durch Romanien, Bulgarien und die Moldau nach Lemberg in Pohlen*

aus dem Französischen übersetzt und mid einigen Zusätzen beglei-tet nebst einer Karte, Leipzig: Johann Gottlob Immanuel Breitkopf, 1779, repr. 1789 (German trans., without the author's permis-sion); Geogr.C.956 (digitised version available through Sächsische Landesbibliothek – Staats- und Universitätsbibliothek Dresden (SLUB))

R.G. Boscovich, *Giornale di un viaggio da Costantinopoli in Polonia dell'Abate Ruggiero Giuseppe Boscovich, con una sua Relazione sulle rovine di Troja*, Bassano, 1784 (published with the author's approval); RIIF-8°-647 (digitised version available through Nacio-nalna i sveučilišna knjižnica u Zagrebu)

J.R. Bošković, *Dnevnik putovanja iz Carigrada u Poljsku*, trans. M. Katalinić, Zagreb, 1951 (Croatian trans.)

R.G. Boscovich, *Giornale di un viaggio da Costantinopoli in Polonia dell'abate Ruggiero Giuseppe Boscovich, con una sua realazione delle rovine di Troia*, foreword by D. O'Connell and Fr Zagar, Milan, 1966

Rudzher Josip Boshkovich, *Dnevnik na edno pŭtuvane*, ed. M. Todorova, Sofia 1975 (Bulgarian trans.)

R.G. Boscovich, 'Ruggiero Giuseppe Boscovich (1711-1787), *Jurnalul călătoriei de la Constantinopol în Polonia*', in M. Holban, M.M. Alex-andrescu-Dersca Bulgaru and P. Cernovodeanu (eds), *Călători străini despre țările române*, vol. 9, Bucharest, 1997, 454-89 (partial Romanian trans., with useful notes and comments)

J.R. Bošković, *Dnevnik putovanja iz Carigrada u Poljsku*, trans. M. Katalinić and M. Manin, Zagreb, 2006 (Croatian trans.)

R.G. Boscovich, *Giornale di un viaggio da Costantinopoli in Polonia dell'abate Ruggiero Giuseppe Boscovich: con una relazione delle rovine di Troia ed infine il prospetto delle Opere nuove matematiche contenute in cinque tomi*, ed. E. Proverbio, Milan, 2008

STUDIES

I. Pederin, *Hrvatski putopis*, Rijeka, 2007

N. Iorga, 'Rogeriu Iosif Boscovich și Moldova', *Analele Academiei Române. Memoriile Secțiunii Istorice* 19 (1936) 153-65

N. Iorga, *Istoria românilor prin călători*, vol. 2, Bucharest, 1928², 177-86

Zrinka Blažević

Ianache Văcărescu

Ienăchiță Văcărescu

DATE OF BIRTH   Unknown, maybe 1738/40
PLACE OF BIRTH   Unknown, probably Bucharest
DATE OF DEATH   11 July 1797
PLACE OF DEATH   Bucharest

BIOGRAPHY

Ianache (Ienăchiță) Văcărescu came from an old Wallachian aristocratic family, his father being the high dignitary Ştefan Văcărescu (d. 1763) and his mother the Moldavian noblewoman Ecaterina (Catinca) Done, a niece of the Moldavian chronicler Ion Neculce (1672-1745). Several members of his family are famous for their cultural and literary works.

Văcărescu's date of birth is not known, but may have been between 1738 and 1740. Little is known about his education, but it is likely that he was instructed by private teachers, as was the custom among aristocratic families. Some scholars have stated that he studied at the Greek princely Academy in Bucharest (Camariano-Cioran, *Académies*, pp. 299, 431), though this is not certain. It is known that one of his teachers was the famous Greek scholar Neophytos Kausokalyvitēs (1689-1784). Văcărescu acquired a good knowledge of several languages (Greek, Ottoman Turkish, Italian) and was familiar with Greek and Western literatures, but it is not certain that he knew Arabic or Persian, as some of his biographers claim.

Văcărescu married three times: first in 1762 to Elena Rizò (Rhangabè) (d. 1780), with whom he had three children (Ecaterina, Maria and Alecu, who became a poet), second to Elena Karatzas (d. 1783), daughter of Georgios (Iordachi) Karatzas, the former grand dragoman of the Porte, and last in 1783 to Caterina (d. 1808), daughter of Nikolaos Karatzas, the former grand dragoman of the Porte, 1777-82, and then Prince of Wallachia, 1782-3, with whom he had three more children (Constantin, Mihai and Nicolae, who was also a poet). All these marriages enhanced Văcărescu's social and political position: through the first he became brother-in-law to Prince Alexandru Grigore Ghica (r. 1764-1777 with interruptions, in both Wallachia and Moldavia); the second brought him

close to the Karatzas family and their allies, who held important positions in Constantinople.

Văcărescu's political career started around 1760 and continued bril-
liantly until his death. It allowed him to accumulate a significant fortune,
as is proved by the disputes between his heirs. Besides the high offices he
held within the Wallachian state apparatus, he was granted the honorary title of *dikaiophylax* of the Ecumenical Patriarchate. However, important achievements alternated with periods of persecution and exile, as
Văcărescu proved to be quite an embarrassing character for many of the
Phanariot princes who ruled the country.

His troubles began when he was in his early 20s: in 1763, he had to flee
to Constantinople after the violent death of his father, assassinated at
the instigation of the ruling prince Constantin Racoviţă. In the imperial
capital, he improved his knowledge of Ottoman Turkish with the scribe
Khalil Hamid, who was later to become grand vizier. Văcărescu returned
to Wallachia in 1767, but only two years later the first Russian-Ottoman
war broke out, forcing many of the Wallachian noble families to choose
exile in Transylvania. Văcărescu left the country in 1772 and settled in
Braşov (Kronstadt), where he spent almost two years. It was in this context that he composed a short petition addressed to the Ottoman government, in which he presents the main lines of the political organisation
of his country and of the status of Wallachia with respect to the Porte
(Georgescu, *Mémoires*, vol. 1, pp. 38-41).

When he returned to Wallachia in 1774, Văcărescu had very good relations with Prince Alexandros Hypsilantēs (r. 1774-82), with whom he coop-
erated in composing an important juridical treatise, *Pravilinceasca condică*
(1780). He also undertook several diplomatic missions and often served
as the prince's interpreter. In 1781, Hypsilantēs sent Văcărescu to Vienna
as part of the mission to persuade the Habsburg authorities to send back
his sons, who had fled the country. On that occasion, he met the imperial
chancellor Wensel Anton von Kaunitz (1711-94) and Emperor Joseph II
(r. 1780-90).

Văcărescu maintained his prominent position under the next two
princes, Nikolaos Karatzas (r. 1782-3) and Michaël Soutzos (r. 1783-6).
Things changed radically under Prince Nikolaos Mavrogenēs (r. 1786-
90), with whom Văcărescu's relations were so bad that the prince even
planned to kill him. A long and extremely critical petition (most probably composed by Văcărescu himself in Italian) was addressed to the Russians, in which the opponents of Mavrogenēs' policy depict the dramatic

Illustration 12. Anton Chladek, portrait of Ienachiță Văcărescu

situation in the country (September 1786). However, Văcărescu was not at all marginalised, as one might expect. He continued to hold high offices in the state apparatus, which attracted the criticism of the opposition. Fully aware of Văcărescu's qualities and reputation, Mavrogenēs entrusted him with the selection of future students in the Turkish language school he intended to create in Constantinople (Urechia, *Istoria şcoalelor*, vol. 1, pp. 63-4; Camariano-Cioran, *Académies*, p. 52 n. 103).

In the years that followed, Văcărescu spent long months in exile: first in 1788 by order of Mavrogenēs and again in 1791, forced out by the Austrians who had occupied the country. Văcărescu's influence on Wallachian political life continued during his later years, when he was involved in major decisions taken by Princes Michaēl Soutzos (r. 1791-2) and Alexandros Muruzis (r. 1792-6). As a prominent figure on the Wallachian scene, Văcărescu met foreign travellers who recorded information about him, among them Franz-Josef Sulzer (*Geschichte des transalpinischen Daciens*, Vienna, 1781), Stephan Ignaz Raicevich (*Osservazioni storiche, naturali et politiche intorno la Valachia e la Moldavia*, Naples, 1788), Charles-Marie de Salaberry (*Voyage à Constantinople, en Italie et aux Îles de l'Archipel, par l'Allemagne et la Hongrie*, Paris, 1791) (see Holban et al. (eds), *Călători străini*, vol. 10/1, pp. 472, 510-18; vol. 10/2, p. 1011).

Ienăchiţă Văcărescu died on 11 July 1797, and some sources state this was the direct consequence of a harsh discussion with the ruling prince Alexandros Muruzis (Corfus, *Însemnările Androneştilor*, p. 40).

Besides the *History of the almighty Ottoman emperors*, Ienăchiţă Văcărescu composed a large number of Romanian and Greek poems, and the first published treatise on Romanian grammar, *Observaţii sau băgări de seamă asupra regulilor şi orânduielilor gramaticii româneşti* ('Observations or reckonings on the rules and dispositions of Romanian grammar') (Râmnic and Vienna 1787), in which he followed the model of the *Greek grammar* by Antonios Katiphoros (Venice, 1734). His interest in languages is also proved by the important material he collected for various dictionaries: Romanian-German and German-Romanian (MS Bucharest, Biblioteca Academiei Române – rom. 1392), Romanian-Turkish and Turkish-Romanian (MS Bucharest, Biblioteca Academiei Române – rom. 1393; I. Matei, 'Contribution', p. 110). An edition of a Romanian-Slavonic dictionary was also prepared under his guidance but it was never published (MS Bucharest, Biblioteca Academiei Române – rom. 2252, *Lexicon, adecă Cuvinternicul sau vistieria limbii sloveneşti şi a ceii româneşti*).

Văcărescu was also the author of some translations of Ottoman official documents: at least two orders delivered by the sultans Abdul Hamid I (1774) and Selim III (1791) to the Wallachian princes (Bianu, Hodoş, *Bibliografia*, vol. 2, pp. 206 (no. 386), 341-2 (no. 545); Dima, 'Contribuţii', pp. 84-101). He also translated some fragments from the Greek treatise of logic by Vikentios Damodos, published in Venice in 1759 (MS Bucharest, Biblioteca Academiei Române – rom. 4768; N.A. Ursu, 'Un fragment'). Historians also attribute to him the realisation of a map of Bulgaria and Thrace printed in 1791, and the initiative behind a detailed map of Wallachia printed in Vienna (1796) by the famous Rhigas Valestinlis (c. 1757-98) (Pippidi, 'Activitatea cartografică').

MAIN SOURCES OF INFORMATION

Primary
MS Bucharest, Biblioteca Academiei Române – CM XXXI B/157 f. 6
MS Bucharest, Biblioteca Academiei Române – Hm 1145 = C XXXVII-25
MS Bucharest, Biblioteca Academiei Române – rom. 2905 (*Istoria prea puternicilor înpăraţi othomani*)
Documente privitoare la Istoria Românilor culese de Eudoxiu de Hurmuzaki, vol. 7, Bucharest, 1876, pp. 343-4
V.A. Urechia, *Istoria şcoalelor de la 1800 la 1864*, vol. 1, Bucharest, 1892, pp. 63-4
V.A. Urechia, *Istoria românilor*, vol. 7, Bucharest, 1894, pp. 10-11, 83-4, 191, 348-57, 386
N. Iorga, *Acteş i fragmente cu privire la istoria românilor*, vol. 2, Bucharest, 1896, pp. 326-7
N. Iorga, 'Documente şi regeste pentru viaţa lui Ienachi Văcărescu', in N. Iorga, *Studii şi documente cu privire la istoria romînilor*, vol. 3, Bucharest, 1901, 76-90
I. Bianu and N. Hodoş, *Bibliografia românească veche, 1508-1830*, vol. 2, Bucharest, 1910, pp. 206, 318-22, 341-2
I.I. Nistor (ed.), *Documente privitoare la Istoria Românilor culese de Eudoxiu de Hurmuzaki*, vol. 19, Bucharest, 1922, pp. 23-4, 28, 41-2, 118-20, 279-80, 332-3, 377-8, 807-8
N. Iorga, 'Originea moldoveană a lui Ienăchiţă Văcărescu', *Academia Română. Memoriile Secţiunii Istorice* (3rd series) 10 (1929) 345-51
N. Iorga, 'De unde a învăţat italieneşte Ienăchiţă Văcărescu', in *Omagiu lui Ramiro Ortiz cu prilejul a douzeci de ani de învăţământ în România*, Bucharest, 1929, 106-58
M. Holban et al. (eds), *Călători străini despre Ţările Române*, vol. 10/1, Bucharest, 2002, pp. 472, 510-18

M. Holban et al. (eds), *Călători străini despre Ţările Române*, vol. 10/2, Bucharest, 2001, p. 1011

Secondary

E. Dima, 'Contribuţii privitoare la viaţa şi activitatea lui Ienăchiţă Văcărescu', *Revista de Istorie şi Teorie Literară* 7 (2013) 79-106

G.E. Dima, '"Cântecul lui Ienăchiţă" redactat în neogreacă. Izvoare şi răspândire', *Revista de Istorie şi Teorie Literară* 7 (2013) 117-27

Al. Elian, 'Ienăchiţă Văcărescu la Viena', in Al. Elian, *Bizanţul, Biserica şi cultura românească. Studii şi articole de istorie*, ed. V.V. Muntean, Iaşi, 2003, 277-86

N.A. Ursu, 'Un fragment de logică tradus de poetul Ienăchiţă Văcărescu', in N.A. Ursu, *Contribuţii la istoria culturii româneşti. Studii şi note filologice*, Iaşi, 2002, 238-42

G. Ştrempel, 'Introducere', in I. Văcărescu, *Istoria Othomanicească*, ed. G. Ştrempel, Bucharest, 2001, v-lxxv, pp. ix-xxxiii

A. Pippidi, 'Activitatea cartografică a lui Ienăchiţă Văcărescu', *Sud-Estul şi contextul european. Buletin* 1 (1994) 141-52 (repr. in M. Coman et al. [eds], *Andrei Pippidi mai puţin cunoscut. Studii adunate de foştii săi elevi cu prilejul împlinirii vârstei de 70 de ani*, Iaşi, 2018, 361-71)

A. Pippidi, 'Despre Ienăchiţă Văcărescu', *Revista de Istorie şi Teorie Literară* 35 (1987) 297-309 (repr. in Coman et al. [eds], *Andrei Pippidi mai puţin cunoscut.*, 344-60)

I. Matei, 'Contribution aux débuts des études de turcologie en Roumanie, XVIe-XVIIIe siècles', *Revue des Études Sud-est Européennes* 26 (1988) 99-112

Poeţii Văcăreşti, *Opere*, ed. C. Cîrstoiu, Bucharest, 1982, pp. 7-23

G. Potra, *Documente privitoare la istoria oraşului Bucureşti (1634-1800)*, Bucharest, 1982, p. 254

Al. Teodorescu, 'Văcărescu, Ienăchiţă', in *Dicţionarul literaturii române până la 1900*, Bucharest, 1979, pp. 893-5 (with rich bibliography)

M. Carataşu, *Documentele Văcăreştilor*, Bucharest, 1975, pp. 58-61

A. Camariano-Cioran, *Les Académies princières de Bucarest et de Jassy et leurs professeurs*, Thessaloniki, 1974, pp. 52, 299, 431

C. Cîrstoiu, *Ianache Văcărescu. Viaţa şi opera*, Bucharest, 1974, pp. 47-138, 120-8, 217-50

Kl. Steinke, 'Problema modelelor gramaticii lui Ienăchiţă Văcărescu', *Anuar de Lingvistică şi Istorie Literară* 24 (1973) 17-35

D. Popovici, *Studii literare*, vol. 1. *Literatura română în epoca 'Luminilor'*, Bucharest, 1972, pp. 382-7

Th. Rădulescu, 'Sfatul domnesc şi alţi mari dregători ai Ţării Româneşti din secolul al XVIII-lea. Liste cronologice şi cursus honorum', *Revista Arhivelor* 34 (1972) 673-90, p. 688

Vl. Georgescu, *Mémoires et projets de réforme dans les Principautés roumaines,
1769-1830*, Bucharest, 1970, pp. 38-41

A. Nestorescu, 'Dicţionarele lui Ienăchiţă Văcărescu şi limba română literară la
sfârşitul secolului al XVIII-lea', *Studii de Limbă Literară şi Filologie* 1 (1969)
51-63

V. Cândea, C.C. Giurescu and M. Maliţa, *Pagini din trecutul diplomaţiei româneşti*,
Bucharest, 1966, pp. 200-7

A. Camariano-Cioran, 'Influenţa poeziei lirice neogreceşti asupra celei româneşti.
Ienăchiţă, Alecu, Iancu Văcărescu, Anton Pann şi modelele lor greceşti',
Bucharest, 1935 (repr. in L. Rados [ed.], *Relaţii româno-elene. Studii istorice
şi filologice [secolele XIV-XIX]*, Bucharest, 2008, 51-75)

Al. Odobescu, 'Poeţii Văcăreşti', *Revista Română Pentru Ştiinţă, Litere şi Arte* 1
(1861) 481-532 (repr. in Al. Odobescu, *Opere*, vol. 2, ed. M. Anineanu and
V. Cândea, Bucharest, 1967, pp. 42-83 [editors' comments, pp. 472-512])

D. Simonescu (ed.), *Cronici şi povestiri româneşti versificate (sec. XVII-XVIII)*,
Bucharest, 1967, pp. 138, 238

A. Oţetea (ed.), *Documente privind istoria României. Colecţia Eudoxiu de Hurmuzaki. Serie nouă. Rapoarte consulare ruse, 1770-1796*, vol. 1, Bucharest, 1962,
pp. 32, 353-4, 366, 396-8, 428, 450, 457

G. Potra, *Documente privitoare la istoria oraşului Bucureşti (1694-1821)*, Bucharest,
1961, pp. 488-9

I. Corfus, *Însemnările Androneştilor*, Bucharest, 1947, p. 40

D. Popovici, 'Ienăchiţă Văcărescu şi cronica mondenă a timpului', *Studii Literare*
1 (1942) 229-31

WORKS ON CHRISTIAN-MUSLIM RELATIONS

Istoria prea puternicilor înpăraţi othomani
Istoria Othomanicească
'History of the almighty Ottoman emperors'

DATE   1791
ORIGINAL LANGUAGE   Romanian

DESCRIPTION
The complete title of Văcărescu's work is *Istoria prea puternicilor înpăraţi
othomani adunată şi alcătuită pă scurt dă dumnealui Ianache Văcărescul,
dicheofilax a Bisericii cei mari a Răsăritului şi spatar al Valahiei, începându-
se în vremea prea puternicului înpârat, sultan Abdul Hamid I, la văleatu
hâgiret 1202 şi mântuitoriu 1788, la Nicopoli a Bulgariei şi s-a săvârşât în
zilele prea puternicului înpărat sultan Selim III, la văleatul 1794 şi 1208 în
luna lui şevali* ('History of the almighty Ottoman emperors, collected

and composed in abridged form by Ianache Văcărescu, *dikaiophylax* of the Great Church of the Orient and spatharius of Wallachia, begun in the times of the almighty emperor Sultan Abdul Hamid I, the year of Hijra 1202 and of the Salvation 1788, in Nicopolis, in Bulgaria, and accomplished during the days of the almighty emperor Sultan Selim III, in the year 1794 and 1208 month of Shawwāl'). It was intended to cover Ottoman history from the beginning of the dynasty up to the reign of Sultan Selim III (1789-1807), though it was left unfinished in the year 1791.

Istoria prea puternicilor înpărați othomani was conceived in two parts, and each is preserved in a unique manuscript. The first part is 91 leaves long, while the second contains 50 leaves. Neither is in the author's own hand, but since the text is accompanied by many marginal notes written by Văcărescu himself, one may infer that the manuscripts were written under his guidance. The *History* was not published until 1863, by Alexandru Papiu-Ilarian. Gabriel Ştrempel's 2001 edition is the latest and best, though it is not a true critical edition; historical notes and explanations are minimal and sometimes misleading. In Ştrempel's edition, which is used here, the *History* contains 172 pages.

Văcărescu wrote his work in Romanian, in order to acquaint Romanian readers with Ottoman history, although for a present-day reader the text appears very difficult, as it is full of Turkish and Greek words in Romanian phonetic transcription, as well as neologisms taken mainly from Italian.

Văcărescu says that he started to write his *History* in exile in Nicopolis, where people repeatedly asked him about the history of the Ottoman conquest of Bulgaria, so that he became aware that ordinary individuals did not know much about Ottoman history. As he did not have much time, he decided to write a short and easily understandable history of the Ottoman state, in which he intended to set out the foundations and political rise of Ottoman power. It seems that Văcărescu had this work in mind long before he started to write it, as it is very unlikely that he had the means to transport all the books he mentions to Nicopolis, his place of exile.

The *History of the almighty Ottoman emperors* follows chronologically the reigns of the sultans, from Osman I to Selim III; each chapter ends with a short portrait of the sultan in verse. The earlier part of Ottoman history is generally dealt with concisely, and the stories of some sultans, such as Mehmed III, Ahmed I, Mustafa I, Osman II, do not exceed a few lines. From 1688 onwards, the chapters become more detailed, while the last part of the work, which corresponds to

Văcărescu's own lifetime, is full of stories and information drawn on his personal experience. Chronological mistakes are not rare (for example, Văcărescu states that Moldavia came under the Porte's suzerainty under Prince Bogdan the One-Eyed in 1529, though the latter died in 1517, p. 45) and some episodes are invented (the face-to-face discussion between Bogdan and Süleyman the Magnificent in Philippopolis, p. 45).

Văcărescu's *History* was neither the first nor the only history of the Ottomans that was in circulation in Wallachia and Moldavia at the time. As well as a large number of chronological lists of the Ottoman sultans, some more elaborate histories of the Ottoman Empire are known in both Romanian and Greek, and it is likely that Văcărescu had seen at least some of them. Among them is the so-called *Caşin chronicle*, written by a Moldavian monk Andronic in August 1673, which is a history of the Ottoman sultans from Osman I to 1656, the eighth year of Mehmed IV's reign (Iorga, 'Încă două povestiri', pp. 185-9 [commentaries]; pp. 190-207 [text] Iorga attributes the work to Nicolae Spatharius, known as 'Milescu' [1636-1708]). A similar work, entitled *Chipurile împăraţilor turceşti dimpreună cu istoriile lor* ('Portraits of the Ottoman emperors together with the history of their reigns'), is enriched by portraits of the sultans from Osman I to Ahmed III (r. 1703-30), and narrates events down to 1710 (it is kept in L'vivs'ka Natsional'na Naukova Biblioteka Ukraïni imeni Vasilia Stefanika, as Manuscripta Instituti Ossoliniani 5835/III; see Duzinchievici, 'O necunoscută istorie'; Papacostea, 'O istorie'; Balmuş, 'Chipurile').

Among Greek historical writings, it is worth mentioning *Historikon tōn ex archēs vasileōn tourkōn, metaphrasthen eis graikōn dialekton, apo tourkikon* ('A history from the beginning of the Ottoman emperors, translated from Turkish into Greek language') (Camariano, *Catalogul*, pp. 70-1; Matei, 'Contribution', pp. 104-5), produced in August 1704 for the Wallachian prince Constantin Brâncoveanu (r. 1688-1714). First written in Ottoman Turkish by the prince's secretary for Ottoman language, it was then translated into Greek by Matthaios of Chios and revised by the well-known scholar Matthaios Vyzantios. It deals with events from the time of Süleyman the Magnificent to Mehmed IV (r. 1648-87). A similar text (from the 18th century) covers the history from Bayezid II (r. 1481-1512) to the first years of Ahmed III (Camariano, *Catalogul*, p. 71; Matei 'Contribution', p. 107). MS Bucharest, Biblioteca Academiei Române – gr. 1234 (end of the 18th century) probably falls into the same category (if it is not a copy of a Greek chronograph), as it contains a Byzantine-Ottoman chronicle from the time of Christ to 1692 (Carataşu, *Catalogul*, pp. 239-40; Matei, 'Contribution', pp. 104-5). To these should be added

Eugenios Voulgaris' *Katalogos genealogikos tōn Soultanōn tōn Otmanidōn,* from Osman I to Mustafa III (r. 1757-74) (MS Bucharest, Biblioteca Academiei Române – gr. 1247; Carataşu, *Catalogul,* pp. 251-2), published in J.-N. Duponcet, *Epitomē tēs historias Geōrgiou tou Kastriōtou tou eponomasthentos Skentermpey, Vasileōs tēs Alvanias,* translated from French by Voulgaris himself (Moscow, 1812, pp. 293-348; see V. Makrides, 'Eighteenth-century Greek Orthodox contacts with Russia', in this volume of *CMR*). The hypothesis that Văcărescu also had knowledge of the *Historia tōn symvantōn epi tēs vasileias tou soultan Mechmetē, epitropeuontos tou Kiproulē gerontos Mehmet pasa, mechri tēs vasileias tou soultan Achmetē hyiou tou autou soultan Mechmetē, epitropeuontos tēnikauta tou Damat Hasan pasa* ('History of the events that occurred during the reign of Sultan Mehmed, when Mehmed Köprülü Pasha the Elder was grand vizier, to the reign of Sultan Ahmed, the son of the same Sultan Mehmed, when Damad Hasan Pasha was grand vizier') should not be completely ruled out. This *History,* for a long time attributed to Kōnstantinos (Kaisarios) Dapontes (1713/4-84), was in fact composed by Dēmētrios Ramadanēs, a high dignitary in Wallachia between 1717 and 1737 (Païzē-Apostolopoulou, 'Dēmētrios Ramadanēs'; Païzē-Apostolopoulou, 'To cheirographo'). Both copyists of the manuscripts known so far, Dapontes himself and Nikolaos Karatzas, a relative of Văcărescu (both died between 1786 and 1789), had contacts with Wallachia similar to Văcărescu's with the Constantinopolitan milieu.

Two later works also deserve to be named here in order to complete the picture. The first, *Hronologhia împăraţilor turceşti* ('Chronology of the Turkish emperors') (1803), is a Romanian compilation made by the Transylvanian scholars Samuil Micu-Klein (1745-1806) and Ioan Piuariu-Molnar (1749-1815) (Câmpianu, 'O lucrare'). The second, which is unfinished, is attributed to the well-known historiographer, poet and musician Dionysios Phōteinos (1777-1821), *Hē genikē epitomē Othōmanikēs historias apo Othmanos tou prōtou mechri tou nyn vasileuontos Soultan Machmoud* ('Abridged treatise of Ottoman history from Osman I to the now reigning Sultan Mahmud') (see Papacostea, 'O istorie', '*Vieţile Sultanilor*', which reveals some connections between Phōteinos' text and the Ossolineum manuscript mentioned above).

Until a proper critical edition of *Istoria prea puternicilor înpăraţi othomani* is prepared, it will be hard to know for sure which histories Văcărescu read and used, if any, and identification of his sources must rely solely on the references he himself makes in the text. He mentions 'Nichifor', 'Zonara' and 'Laonic' among Byzantine historians. It has been suggested that 'Nichifor' might be either Patriarch Nicephorus I (c. 758-828), the author of the popular *Chronographikon syntomon*, or Nicephorus Bryennius (1062-1137), who wrote *Hylē historias* ('Material for a history') (Ştrempel, 'Introducere', p. xxxvii n. 80). However, the period covered by these two works is completely omitted from Văcărescu's *History*, so Nicephorus Grēgoras (c. 1295-1360), whose *Rhomaikē historia*, covering the years 1259-1359, was widely read after its first (partial) publication by Hieronymus Wolf in 1562, and in Italian translation by Lodovico Dolce in 1564, seems to be the only plausible identification. It was the same Wolf who was the first to edit the *Epitomē historiōn* by Iōannēs Zonaras in 1557 (it was re-edited by Charles du Fresne du Cange as *Chronikon. annales*, Paris, 1686-7). The *History* of 'Laonic', Laonicus Chalcocondyles, was first published by Conrad Clauser (*De origine et rebus gestis Turcorum*, Basel, 1556) and re-edited several times. It is likely that Văcărescu used a later Greek edition, presumably that by Charles Annibal Fabrot (Paris, 1650, Venice, 1729). 'Leungravie' clearly refers to Johannes Leunclavius (Johannes Löwenklau, 1541-94), the author of *Annales sultanorum othmanidarum* (Basel, 1569) and *Historiae musulmanae turcorum* (Frankfurt, 1591). All these works were in circulation in Wallachia and Moldavia, as is shown by the inventories of various libraries. It is also reasonably certain that Văcărescu used one or several copies of the famous *Chronographos* attributed to Dōrotheos of Monemvasia (on whose historicity, see *CMR* 10, pp. 174-84), probably in Romanian translation, as is suggested by a manuscript that used to be part of his library (MS Bucharest, Biblioteca Academiei Române – rom. 1921, dated 1718; see Cernovodeanu, 'Filiaţia', p. 118).

Among modern historians, Văcărescu mentions Cantemir, 'Ladvocat', 'Volter', 'Buşing' and 'Beringheru' or 'Bering'. It is very unlikely that Văcărescu could have used the English translation of Dimitrie Cantemir's *Incrementorum et decrementorum aulae othomannicae* by Nicholas Tindal, which appeared in *The history of growth and decay of the Ottoman Empire* (London, 1734-5), because he did not know English. Instead, he would have used either the French edition by Monsieur de Joncquières (*Histoire de l'Empire ottoman, où se voyent les causes de son agrandissement et de sa décadence, avec des notes très instructives*, Paris, 1743) or the German edition by Johann Lothar Schmidt (*Geschichte des osmanisches Reiches, nach seinem Anwachse und Abnehmen*, Hamburg, 1745), both based on Tindal's book. It is also probable that he found some information in Cantemir's *Descriptio Moldaviae*, published in German translation, first in Anton Friedrich Büsching's *Magazin für die Neue Historie und Geographie* (vols 3-4, 1769-70) and then as *Demetrii Kantemirii, ehemaligen Fürsten in der Moldau, historisch-geographish- und politische Bescheibung der Moldau, nebst dem Leben des Verfassers und einer Landkarte* (Frankfurt-Leipzig, 1771). *Sistema de religione et statu Imperii Turcici* may not have been available to our author, as it had only been published in Russian up to that time ('Kniga Sistima, ili Sostoianie mukhammedanskiia religii', St Petersburg, 1722).

'Ladvocat' is Jean-Baptiste Ladvocat (1709-65), librarian of the Sorbonne and author of, among others, *Dictionnaire géographique portatif ou Description de tous les royaumes, provinces, villes* [...] *des quatre parties du monde* (Paris, 1747; re-edited several times) and of an abridged version of Louis Moreri's *Grand dictionnaire historique* (Lyon, 1674), published under the title *Dictionnaire historique et bibliographique portatif* [...] (several volumes, first published in Paris, 1752; translations into Italian [Milan, 1757] and German [Ulm, 1761]). *Volter, istoriia de obşte* ('Voltaire, general history') means either Voltaire's *Abrégé de l'Histoire universelle depuis Charlemagne jusques à Charles Quint* (The Hague, 1753) or *Essai sur l'histoire générale et sur les moeurs* (Dresden, 1754-8) or both, as these works were in circulation within the Romanian Principalities.

'Buşing' is obviously Anton Friedrich Büsching (1724-93), who composed the famous *Neue Erdbeschreibung* (Hamburg, 1754-92). The last editor of the *History* maintains that Văcărescu did not use this work itself, but the *Magazin für die Neue Historie und Geographie* (1767-93) (Ştrempel, 'Introducere', p. xxxvii n. 87). However, Văcărescu explicitly refers to 'Beringheru', who should be identified as Mr Bérenger, who translated into French Büsching's *Neue Erdbeschreibung* as *Géographie de Busching abrégée dans les objets les moins intéressants, augmentée dans ceux qui ont paru l'être, retouchée partout & ornée d'un Précis de l'histoire de chaque état* (Lausanne, 1776; the first nine of the 12 volumes are a translation of the German original, while the last three were compiled by Bérenger himself). Elsewhere in the text, Văcărescu gives an even more precise indication when he mentions 'Bering la gheografia lui Buşing' ('Bérenger in Büshing's *Geography*') (p. 54, referring to the reign and personality of Murad IV). This means that he did use the French version of the *Neue Erdbeschreibung*, more precisely vol. 8 (Lausanne, 1780), which deals with the Ottoman Empire, Arabia and Persia.

Văcărescu also mentions 'Meletie', who is, without any doubt, the Greek ecclesiastical historian and geographer Meletios, known as Meletios of Athens or of Ioannina (Mētros), author of *Geōgraphia palaia kai nea* (Venice, 1728) and of *Ekklēsiastikē historia* (see the entry 'Meletios of Athens, *Ekklēsiastikē historia*', in this volume, pp. 281-9). It is certain that Văcărescu made extensive use of this work in its printed form (Vienna, 1783-4) and not in manuscript (as is stated by Ştrempel, 'Introducere', p. xxxviii n. 88, who believes that Meletios's *History* was not published until 1798).

In addition, Văcărescu's knowledge of Ottoman Turkish allowed him to access Ottoman historiography. Of the four Ottoman historians he refers to, 'Naima', 'Raşid', 'Subhî' and 'Eiveri', the first three have long been identified: Muṣṭafā Naʿīmā (1655-1716), whose *Rawḍat al-Ḥusayn fī khulāṣat akhbār al-khāfiqayn*, better known as *Taʾrīkh-i Naʿīmā*, covers the years 1591-1659; Rashīd Meḥmed (d. 1735), Naʿīmā's successor, who wrote *Taʾrīkh-i Rashīd*, dealing with the period between 1660 and 1721 (published in three volumes in İbrahim Müteferrika's printshop, in 1741), and Ṣubḥī Meḥmed Efendi (d. 1769), whose chronicle, covering the years 1739 to 1743, was published in Constantinople in 1784, together with the work of Sāmī and Shākir, under the title *Taʾrīkh-i Sāmī we Shākir we Ṣubḥī*. It is likely that Văcărescu used the printed version of the chronicle, also giving him access to Muṣṭafā Sāmī and Ḥusayn Shākir's works, which both deal with the years 1730 (Babinger, *Die Geschichtsschreiber,* pp. 270-1, 277-8). For instance, he cites Ṣubḥī as a source for the 1730 revolt of Patrona Khalil (p. 85), but as this episode does not exist in Ṣubḥī's chronicle, which deals with later events, he is in fact referring to the printed edition as a whole. The fourth Ottoman author, 'Eiveri', is depicted in the *Istoria* as the official historiographer of the Porte at the time when Văcărescu was writing. He should be then identified with Enwerī Hājjī Saʿd Allāh Efendi (c. 1733-94) from Trebizond, who began his career in 1769 and was close to several grand viziers and other high Ottoman dignitaries. He composed five chronicles in three volumes known as *Taʾrīkh-i Enwerī*, which cover the period from 1769 up to the Russian-Ottoman peace of Iaşi in 1792 (Babinger, *Die Geschichtsschreiber,* pp. 320-2; Karahan, 'Enwerī Hādjdjī Saʿd Allāh Efendi'). It must be noted that Enwerī accompanied the grand vizier in the Wallachian and Moldavian theatres of war from 1788 to 1792, a perfect opportunity to meet Văcărescu, who was himself involved in these events.

In addition to these narrative sources, the historian Dionysios Phōteinos states that during his stays in Constantinople Văcărescu had copied official Ottoman documents pertaining to Romanian history (*Historia tēs palai Dakias*, p. 372). And Văcărescu surely had oral sources too.

While in Constantinople and during his exile in Nicopolis and Rhodes, he had opportunities for discussion with several Ottoman dignitaries, such as the Grand Vizier Khalil Hamid Pasha (1736-85; in charge 1782-5), who was his former teacher of Ottoman Turkish, Selim Pasha of Nicopolis, and various Orthodox Christians who held official positions in the Ottoman administrative apparatus, such as Athanasios Komnēnos Hypsilantēs (1711-after 1789), the historiographer of the Ecumenical Patriarchate and author of an important historical compilation in Greek.

In *Istoria prea puternicilor înpărați othomani* religious matters are presented as a kind of introduction to Ottoman history (pp. 4-11), and Văcărescu does not return to them later in the book – with a single exception: he associates the creation of the Janissary corps during the reign of Murad I (r. 1362-89) with Hadji Bektash, who he says organised the Betktashi dervishes into four orders: *bectaşii* (Bektashis), *mevlevi* (Mevlevis), *cadri* (Kadiris) and *seiah* (Saadiyeh?). However, while the relationship between the Bektashis and the Janissary corps is documented, it is also known that the order was not founded by Hadji Bektash (Hājjī Bektāsh Walī, 13ᵗʰ century), as Văcărescu says, but was only named after him.

Văcărescu's presentation of Islam is very schematic and simple, even simplistic, in line with the purpose of his work: to make clear to his Romanian readership the basic principles of Islam, without entering into much detail. However, the text, which is full of Turkish words and expressions, would surely have been very difficult for his Romanian contemporaries. He discusses the names assigned to Muslims by various authors: 'Ishmaelites', which supposedly comes from Ishmael; 'Hagarians', which comes from Hagar, Ishmael's mother; and 'Saracens', from Sarah, Hagar's owner. He concludes that these etymologies are not appropriate, as Sarah and Ishmael did not have anything in common (p. 4). He lists what he considers to be the main features of Islam, and religious practices such as prayers, ritual washing, food customs and fasting, marriage and polygamy, prohibition of images and beliefs about the afterlife. On this last point, he relates a discussion he had with the Ottoman governor in Nicopolis about heaven and hell, and the fact that in Islam all the faithful are destined for heaven, regardless of the sins they commit in their earthly life, in contrast to the equivalent Christian doctrine (p. 8-10). He also emphasises the relations between the Qur'an and the Bible, saying that Muslims respect Christian books, as they are the basis of the Qur'an. He asserts that Muslims took their religious songs from the Psalter, and found the idea of the second coming of the Prophet in the Gospels (p. 8). He also says that they hold some Christian prophets (beginning with Jesus Christ himself) and saints in high esteem, but without celebrating their feastdays, and illustrates some of the religious principles he presents in the book with practices he knows in the Ottoman world. He adds that, according to Muslim teachings, it was Ishmael who was to be sacrificed by his father and not Isaac, the incident that inspired the Ottoman Kurban Bayramı ('*Īd al-aḍḥā*), when every Muslim, starting with the sultan, had to slaughter a lamb following Abraham's example (p. 8).

Văcărescu refrains from any criticism and polemics when he deals with Islam, which was very rare in his time. For instance, while in both Meletios's *Ekklēsiastikē historia* (vol. 2, pp. 156-7) and Ladvocat's *Dictionnaire historique et bibliographique portatif* (vol. 2, pp. 146-7), on which he relies heavily, Muḥammad is constantly called the 'false prophet', in Văcărescu's *History* he is designated only as a 'prophet'. Likewise, he does not mention that the Prophet suffered from epilepsy – a widespread topos in the biographies of Muḥammad by non-Muslim authors – and never calls Islam a 'heresy' or 'impious doctrine' (as both Meletios and Ladvocat do). He even composes a quatrain in Muḥammad's honour, in which he praises his qualities: from a simple servant Muḥammad was able to become the founder of a new religion and a famous ruler. He says nothing about Ottoman persecutions or Islamisation policies, two topics frequently referred to by non-Muslim historians of the Ottoman Empire.

SIGNIFICANCE

Văcărescu's *Istoria* was not published till 1863, and as far as is known it did not circulate very much in manuscript form, so it was not widely consulted. However, its importance cannot be denied. Besides composing the most complete history of the Ottomans in Romanian up to his own time, Văcărescu committed himself to achieving an educational goal. He asserted that one fifth of the people on three continents were Muslims. Romanian readers should thus know how such a thing could become possible. 'In this history I am writing here in Romanian', he states. 'I have considered it useful to give people an idea about Muḥammad and the Muḥammedan law [religion], in order for anyone to acquire some knowledge of the ethics of rulership and of faith which is proper to the power whose history I am narrating [in this work]' (p. 11). In his view, these ethics were fundamental for an understanding of both the rise of Ottoman political power and the Ottoman system of rule, which should directly interest Romanians as they were living under the empire's dominion.

In this respect, Văcărescu maintained that Ottoman power was intimately related to the Islamic religion, 'namely to Muḥammad, who was a ruler or an emperor, a prophet and a lawgiver' (p. 6). Thus, the Ottoman law code (*şeri şerif*) was established on the basis of the Qur'an, and not only contains fatwas concerning 'the ethics of human behaviour' (p. 15), but was also meant to provide Ottoman politicians with guidance in political matters. Law and religion were therefore one and the same: in the Ottoman Empire nothing was done without a fatwa and without consultation with, and the decision issued by, the religious authority, the Grand Mufti or Şeyhülislam.

PUBLICATIONS

MS Bucharest, Biblioteca Academiei Române – rom. 2905, 92 fols (end of the 18th century?)

MS Bucharest, Biblioteca Academiei Române – rom. 2906, 50 fols (end of the 18th century)

Details of these two manuscripts are given in G. Ştrempel, *Catalogul manuscriselor româneşti*, vol. 2, Bucharest, 1982, p. 400 (here it is stated that both manuscripts are from the beginning of the 19th century, but this cannot be possible if it is accepted that the text was annotated by Văcărescu himself).

Ianache Văcărescu, 'Istorie a prea puternicilor înpăraţi otomani adunată şi alcătuită pă scurtu dă dumnealui Iannache Văcărescul, dicheiofilax a bisericii cei mari a Răsăritului şi spatar al Valahiei', ed. Al. Papiu-Ilarian in *Tesauru de monumente istorice pentru România*, vol. 2, Bucharest, 1863, 238-302; Rom 5070.15 (2) (digitised version available through Hathi Trust Digital Library)

Ianache Văcărescu, 'Istorie a prea puternicilor înpăraţi othomani adunată şi alcătuită pă scurtu dă dumnealui Iannache Văcărescul, dicheofilax a bisericii cei mari a Răsăritului şi spatar al Valahiei. Începându-se în vremea prea puternicului înpăratu sultan Abdul Hamid I, la văleatu Hijretu 1202 şi mîntuitoriu 1788, la Nicopoli a Bulgariei şi s-a săvârşitu în zilele prea puternicului înpăratu sultan Selim III, la văleatul 1794 şi 1208 în luna lui şevalu', in Poeţii Văcăreşti, *Opere*, ed. C. Cîrstoiu, Bucharest, 1974, 181-310

Ianache Văcărescu, 'Istoria prea puternicilor înpăraţi othomani adunată şi alcătuită pă scurt dă dumnealui Ianache Văcărescul, dicheofilax a Bisericii cei mari a Răsăritului şi spatar al Valahiei, începându-se în vremea prea puternicului înpârat, sultan Abdul Hamid I, la văleatu hâgiret 1202 şi mântuitoriu 1788, la Nicopoli a Bulgariei şi s-a săvârşât în zilele prea puternicului înpărat sultan Selim III, la văleatul 1794 şi 1208 în luna lui şevali', in Ianache Văcărescu, *Istoria Othomanicească*, ed. G. Ştrempel, Bucharest, 2001, 1-172 (text), 173-214 (notes and bibliography)

STUDIES

K. Petrovszky, *Geschichte schreiben im osmanischen Südosteuropa. Eine Kulturgeschichte orthodoxer Historiographie des 16. und 17. Jahrhunderts*, Wiesbaden, 2014, pp. 167-70

C. Felezeu, 'Între fanariotism şi mişcarea de emancipare naţională. Modelul cantemirian de abordare a imaginii Imperiului Otoman în cultura românească scrisă', *Tabor* 6 (2012) 47-61

P. Balmuş, 'Chipurile împăraţilor turceşti', in *Texte uitate – texte regăsite*, vol. 4, Bucharest, 2005, 7-12 (comments), 17-29 (edition)

M. Carataşu, *Catalogul manuscriselor greceşti din Biblioteca Academiei Române*, vol. 3, ed. E. Popescu-Mihuţ and T. Teoteoi, Bucharest, 2005, pp. 239-40, 251-2

M. Païzē-Apostolopoulou, 'To cheirographo tou "Chronographou tou Daponte" kai hē lysē enos ainigmatos. To chph. Kyriazē tēs Gennadeiou', *Ho Eranistēs* 24 (2003) 85-94

Ştrempel, 'Introducere', pp. xxxiv-lxxv

M. Païzē-Apostolopoulou, 'Dēmētrios Ramadanēs. 'Enas historiographos tou 18ou aiōna se aphaneia', *Ho Eranistēs* 20 (1995) 20-35

A. Karahan, art. 'Enwerī Ḥādjdjī Sa'd Allāh Efendi', in *EI*2

Matei, 'Contribution'

P. Cernovodeanu, 'Filiaţia cronografelor româneşti de tip Danovici (II)', *Biserica Ortodoxă Română* 106 (1988) 116-29

Poeţii Văcăreşti, *Opere*, pp. 33-43

Cîrstoiu, *Ianache Văcărescu*, pp. 177-216

Popovici, *Studii literare*, vol. 1, pp. 165-8

P. Cernovodeanu, 'Préoccupations d'histoire universelle dans l'historiographie roumaine des XVIIᵉ et XVIIIᵉ siècles' (III), *Revue Roumaine d'Histoire* 10 (1971) 705-28, p. 717

C. Câmpianu, 'O lucrare necunoscută a lui Samuil Micu: *Hronologhia împăraţilor turceşti*', *Studii şi Cercetări de Istorie* 8 (1957) 213-31

N. Camariano, *Catalogul manuscriselor greceşti*, vol. 2, Bucharest, 1940, pp. 70-1

V. Papacostea, 'O istorie a tucilor în româneşte', *Revista Istorică Română* 5-6 (1935-6) 393-9

Gh. Duzinchievici, 'O necunoscută istorie a Imperiului turcesc în manuscris românesc', *Revista Istorică Română* 4 (1934) 289-91

V. Papacostea, '*Vieţile Sultanilor*. Scriere inedită a lui Dionisie Fotino', *Revista Istorică Română* 4 (1934) 175-214 (repr. in C. Papacostea-Danielopolu and N.-Ş. Tanaşoca (eds), *Civilizaţie românească şi civilizaţie balcanică. Studii istorice*, Bucharest, 1983, pp. 431-62)

F. Babinger, *Die Geschichtsschreiber des Osmanen und ihre Werke*, Leipzig, 1927, pp. 268-71, 277-8, 320-2

N. Iorga, 'Încă două povestiri istorice româneşti', in N. Iorga, *Studii şi documente cu privire la istoria românilor*, vol. 9, Bucharest, 1905, 185-207

Historia tēs palai Dakias, ta tēs Transilvanias, Vlachias kai Moldavias. Ek diaphorōn palaiōn neōterōn syngrapheōn syneranistheisa para Dionysiou Phōteinou serdarou, vol. 3, Vienna, 1819, p. 372

Radu G. Păun

Eighteenth-century Greek prophetic literature

DESCRIPTION

Medieval and early modern Greek prophetic literature was literature with a purpose. It aimed at restoring hope and dignity to the community of Orthodox Christians during times of threat, anxiety and change by offering divine assurances that the present, sad state of affairs tormenting the community of the faithful would not last. The long period of Byzantine decline, from the 13ᵗʰ to the 15ᵗʰ century, had refined the meaning of two ideas that played a critical role for Greek prophetic literature and lore after the fall of Constantinople (1453): first, that the sacralised centre of the Eastern Roman Empire could be taken back after a period of loss – a prospect experienced historically in 1261, when the Byzantines recaptured Constantinople from the Latins; second, that the Prophet Muḥammad was a personification of the Antichrist, and thus the rule of his followers and believers was the rule of the Antichrist.

In the *longue durée* of Ottoman rule, Greek prophetic literature developed two strands of interpretation corresponding to these two ideas: messianic and eschatological. The first was primarily concerned with space and focused on the prospect of restoring the empire and its sacred centre, Constantinople, to Christian hands. The second was mainly focused on time and reckoned that the ultimate event signalling the definitive victory of good over evil, of Christianity over Islam, was near: the end of times. Messianic and eschatological interpretative strands spanned the Ottoman centuries, either overlapping or conflicting with each other – in the 18ᵗʰ century they tended more to overlap than to clash. Both strands preached the impermanence of Ottoman rule, treating Muslims in a strict and rather myopic manner, as chastisers of the Church and persecutors of Christ's flock. Both claimed that *hē hēmera Kyriou* ('the day of the Lord'), the day of deliverance, would soon arrive. The major difference lay in the way each strand conceptualised the way deliverance was expected to be brought about.

Messianists fostered belief in the coming of a deliverer, a saviour Christian king of this world who would crush Muslim military might and restore lost space and sovereignty to Christians. The questions they posed were 'who' and 'when': who would be the chosen one to restore the Byzantine Empire and recover the sacred space lost (meaning primarily but not exclusively Constantinople and the holy temple of Hagia Sophia), and when would this happen? Though this development was usually expected to take place before the Last Days, messianic thinking was based more on mundane politics and less on eschatology. If anything, what the king-deliverer was expected to do was to revive a past phase of human history, whose stage had been the earth: the Byzantine Empire in all its glory. The agent and the time of deliverance had to be decoded from the hermetic utterances of the prophetic text.

Messianists used biblical prophecy instrumentally so that specific parts of the scripture (chapters, paragraphs and even sentences) could be employed to advance their own views. The texts they would use first and foremost, however, had a name of their own in medieval and early modern Greek literature: they were called *chrēsmoi* ('oracles') and the genre as a whole *chrēsmologia* ('oracular literature'). It is worth noting that the Greek noun *chrēsmos* (pl. *chrēsmoi*) was deliberately recalled from the pagan past, instead of the alternative term *prophēteia* ('prophecy'), which is used in theological contexts, to set oracular literature apart from canonical prophecy. By employing oral and visual forms, oracular predictions could overcome the need for literacy (Hatzopoulos, 'Oracular prophecy', pp. 112-13). Oracular literature might use scholarly or vulgar language, shift from prose to verse and appear in the form of long compositions, short tracts, poems or adages. The texts were obscure enough for their meaning to be changed according to the course of events through suitable interpretations or interpolations. Besides the chosen king-deliverer, for instance, a people-deliverer would regularly appear on stage. The key myth of the oracular tradition, that of the advent of a messianic agent who would wrest power and space from Muslim hands and restore it to Christians, resonated in the hearts and minds of Christians and Muslims alike, thereby becoming a shared cultural pattern. Messianists had no qualms about appealing to any Christian king of this world who, irrespective of denomination, could be deemed capable of threatening the territorial integrity of the Ottoman state. In the course of the 18th century, however, more and more were eager to identify the expected king-deliverer with the tsar of Russia.

Eschatologists had another view about the shape of things to come. They too felt unsatisfied with viewing the historical experience of Ottoman subjection simply as God's punishment for Christian sins. They too expected the end of the present order and the inauguration of a new order of justice and happiness. But, unlike messianists, they based their predictions on the Bible, and especially on Daniel and the Revelation of John and theological commentary on them. It was in these terms that, from 1453 up to the 1790s, the Orthodox Church would see the production of about 20 commentaries on the book of Revelation by what Asterios Argyriou has called the 'Greek exegetical movement' (Argyriou, *Les exégèses*).

Eschatologists were mostly theologians and clerics trying to answer how the fall of the Eastern Christian Empire and the advance of Muslims and Catholics at the expense of the only 'true' Church, the Orthodox, could fit into the cosmic countdown to Salvation. Seeing the Eastern Christian flock in the Balkans spectacularly diminishing because of Islamisation and Catholic proselytism, they could not but reflect on the 'great tribulation' that was supposed to precede the Kingdom to come. In this line of interpretation, the subjugation of God's people by the ungodly Turkish Muslims was nothing but the long-awaited 'beginning of sorrows' foretold by the Book of Revelation. The reign of the sultan was thus identified with the reign of the Antichrist – and from the 17th century onwards, under Protestant influence, the pope would also come to be identified with the Antichrist, more specifically with the apocalyptic two-horned beast from out of the earth (Revelation 13:11). Eschatological literature emphasised that only the Kingdom would inaugurate the era of rejoicing for the Ottoman-ruled Orthodox. Only faith and repentance could bring this about.

Initially, eschatologists tended to reject 'unholy' alliances with Western Christians – a prospect that messianists treated with sympathy – and dismiss oracular literature as man-made and unhallowed. However, towards the end of the 18th century, when Russian power and military prowess had become manifest, the two strands of Greek prophetic interpretation converged, favouring, one way or another, the rise of quasi-supernatural Russophilia within the Greek exegetical movement.

Peri Mōameth kai kata Lateinōn

The first 18th-century work that belongs to the eschatological strand is *Peri Mōameth kai kata Lateinōn* ('About Muḥammad and against the Latins'), written by Anastasios Gordios (1654-1729) around 1717-18, shortly after the Ottoman reconquest of the Peloponnese in 1715. Known as a physician, monk, teacher and preacher, Gordios was also believed to have the charisma of being able to foresee the future. The problem that motivated him is overtly stated in the preface: if the Bible contains everything about the past and the future of humankind, it must also refer to the rise of Islam, explaining the great power it wields in the present and predicting its future demise. The interpreter's duty, therefore, would be to find out which part or parts of scripture describe the present state of things and decode what is foretold about the future.

Although himself preoccupied about the future of the Orthodox people, Gordios does not fail to underline that 'the oracles' about the advent of a Christian king are uncertain and false because they lack a real foundation in scripture. Only God's intervention, as prophesied in the Bible and *par excellence* in the Revelation of John, tells the truth: Islam will only fall at Christ's second coming, but the faithful do not have to wait long; it is coming soon (See A. Argyriou and C. Karanasios, 'Athanasios Gordios', in *CMR* 14, 298-303).

Vivliarion kaloumenon Pistis

If Christian losses to Islamisation were only one of Gordios's concerns, they were the major causes of apprehension for the author of *Pistis*, Nektarios Terpos (or Terpou; latter part of the 17th century - 1740/1). Terpos was a monk who was an itinerant preacher for a decade or so (1720s) and then went on to Venice and had his teachings published as a book, whose full title is *Vivliarion kaloumenon Pistis, anankaion eis kathe aploun anthrōpon, vevaiōmenon apo prophētas, euangelion, apostolous, kai allous sophous didaskalous* ('A booklet called Faith, necessary to every simple man, confirmed by prophets, the Gospel[s], Apostles, and other wise teachers'). From the time it first came out in 1732, *Pistis* proved a commercial success by the publishing standards of the time, seeing 12 editions in 86 years.

Little is known about Terpos's life other than what is contained in (or can be inferred from) his own book. He was born in Moscopole (Voskopojë), once the commercial hub of the Aromanians, near Korçë in present-day Albania. It was a prosperous city that had become a leading centre of Greek culture with a higher educational institution, where Terpos probably studied, and possibly taught after a sojourn on Mount Athos. Terpos apparently covered an extensive area with his preaching, from his native town up in the eastern highlands to the Ardenica monastery near the Adriatic in the west, and from there south into present-day Greek Epirus. The area was at the time experiencing mass, and often unprompted, conversions to Islam. *Pistis* is not in fact a booklet, as the title suggests, but a comprehensive preacher's compendium whose purpose, according to the author, is to aid priests in the task of catechism. The content covers a wide range of religious subjects drawing on biblical and patristic teachings peppered with popularised ancient Greek wisdom. The implicit, if clear, aim of the author is to reverse people's decision to leave Christianity, and to help them stay the course. Therefore, Terpos popularises a great deal of theology and church practice, and when it comes to Islam he employs eschatology and apocalypticism to sustain anti-Islamic arguments. Eschatology is employed when Terpos contrasts heaven and hell. Time and again, he paints a vivid picture of the unfading light of God, the shining of the angels and the rejoicing that awaits the faithful in heaven. He then contrasts these with the darkness of hell and the torments of eternal damnation that await the infidels, thereby making clear what a Muslim should expect in the afterlife. Apocalypticism is employed when Terpos explicitly identifies the Antichrist with Muḥammad, thereby suggesting that conversion to Islam is more than just a matter of choice: it is an unconditional surrender of one's self to the forces of evil.

In the first edition of *Pistis*, Terpos devotes a separate chapter to this argument, entitled *Enkomion alētheinon eis ton laoplanon Mōameth kai Alēn* ('True praise for the people-deceiver Muḥammad and 'Alī'), while in the second edition (1733) he adds a brand new chapter on the same subject. In the book's contents this new chapter bears the title *Symvoulion tōn ponērōn pneumatōn* ('Council of evil spirits'), while inside the book the title changes to *Methodos, ēgoun technē panourgikē tou diavolou* ('Method, that is to say the vile art of the devil'). In both chapters, Terpos draws on Revelation, trying to prove that the identification of Antichrist with Muḥammad, and with the Ottomans, has a firm foundation in scripture. First, he states that the numerical values of the Greek letters in the word *Otmanes* ('Ottomans') when added together make up the number of the beast. Second, he freely interprets scattered lines from Revelation 13 to underpin the conclusion that the Turk is the very embodiment of the Antichrist (see Revelation 13:3: 'and all the world wandered after the beast'; 13:7-8: 'and power was given him over all kindreds, and tongues, and nations. And all that dwell upon the earth shall worship him'). Had not the Ottoman Empire managed to defeat every nation? In order to illustrate his moral and spiritual lesson, Terpos uses a parable: the evil spirits allegedly convene in hell to debate how to tempt Christians, and they come up with the idea to 'plant [on earth] a disciple, a forerunner like Christ's John the Baptist' (Garitses, *Ho Nektarios Terpos*, p. 446) and they use Muḥammad for the task. Terpos takes the opportunity here to concede that the easy life and material prosperity enjoyed by most Muslims are the devil's tricks to tempt Christians to

change their faith. The very essence, however, of 'the vile art of the devil'
does not stem from religious oppression, as one might expect, but from
a stick and carrot trick that the Ottoman masters deliberately employ to
drive Christians slowly into despair: tolerance of the Christian religion
in conjunction with heavy and often unbearable taxation. The evil spirits advise Muḥammad: 'Let them have their churches, have patriarchs,
metropolitans, abbots and primates, [let them] chant the way they like.
But do as I tell you to do. From month to month, and from year to year,
tax them as hard [as you can] and increase their debts. First they [...]
will give away their cash, then they will sell their silverware, then their
brass, then their land and in the end, with nothing left to give, they will
stay poor and desolate. And then, whether they like it or not, they will
refuse Christ through their own will, becoming Turks in religion and [in
this way] our own servants' (Garitsēs, *Ho Nektarios Terpos*, p. 447). It is
worth noting here that, in contrast to other interpreters of Greek prophetic literature, Terpos does not comfort his reader with the prospect
of an imminent change in the fate of Christians. Toppling the Antichrist's
rule on earth is the responsibility not of man but of God. 'See, the day
of the Lord is coming', he proclaims citing Isaiah 13:9, but the time of
his arrival is unknown to man (Terpos, *Vivliarion kaloumenon Pistis*,
p. 60). The duty of the faithful, therefore, is to repent, withstand the pain
inflicted by the Muslim yoke, and ultimately use their own free will to
choose their fate in the afterlife.

The preaching and teaching of Kosmas of Aitolia

Kosmas of Aitolia (1714-79) was very similar to Terpos in all but three
points: he came roughly one generation later, left no written record and
was canonised by the Orthodox Church. Kosmas was a monk who tire-
lessly toured the Greek and Albanian lands between 1759 and 1779. His
preaching left a deep imprint on the collective memory of not only Christian but also Muslim communities in the places he visited. His was a
mission approved by Patriarch Seraphim II of Constantinople (1757-61)
to inspire local Christians and reverse a persistant trend of conversion
to Islam. His action involved four major tours whose exact dates remain
uncertain; the first two apparently took place before the Russo-Turkish
war of 1768-74 and the other two in the aftermath. To preach the Gospel, Kosmas would normally choose an open village space, set up a big
wooden cross and start preaching from a stool before it, and before long
he would succeed in attracting crowds. Unfortunately, a great deal of
what he said has been handed down only in oral tradition. His sermons

before 1768, when the Russo-Turkish war broke out, were apparently religious in content and quietist in outlook. Kosmas would usually take up various biblical episodes, elaborating on the teaching of Church Fathers and drawing on the lives of saints. He would also urge the faithful to obey the sultan or the doge of Venice, depending on the region, and to pay their taxes. However, after the end of the war and the failure of the great Christian uprising of 1770, which spread from Crete up to the Albanian lands, triggering harsh reprisals by the Porte, Kosmas's sermons became 'acutely political' according to contemporary evidence (Mertzios, 'To en Venetia kratikon archeion', p. 8). Kosmas committed himself to the spread of Greek education and schooling among the illiterate peasant masses and also got involved in prognostications about the shape of things-to-come, most famously about the end of Ottoman rule. Venetian intelligence reports dated to the year 1779 note clear eschatological references in his sermons (Mertzios, 'To en Venetia kratikon archeion', pp. 11-12).

Kosmas was executed by the Ottoman authorities in the same year, 1779 but, interestingly, the oral tradition after his death is replete with prophetic maxims attributed to him, which contain references to the resurrection of the Byzantine Empire dubbed [to] Romeiko, or the end of the Ottoman power codenamed [to] pothoumeno ('this we are longing for'). In any event, Kosmas must have been well versed in oracular and apocalyptic prophecy. During his restless life, he repeatedly found rest on Mount Athos, whose monasteries were never short of scrutinisers of Greek prophetic literature. It is very likely that he knew personally the author of Agathangelos, Theoklytos Polyïdis. It is worth noting that the simple folk who formed his audiences were not only Christians but also Muslims – and sometimes they were not simple folk at all, because they included local notables and regional officials. Though it is not improbable that Kosmas was eventually put to death as a popular agitator (ehl-i fesad) (Kotzageorgis, '"Messiahs" and neomartyrs', pp. 228-9), threatening public order in the province rather than the security of the empire, his predictions did not perish with him because they were perceived as the revelation of God's will to a holy and ascetic man. Kosmas's fame as a saint and prophet survived his death as much for the Christians of south-east Albania and Epirus as for the Muslims.

The Vision of Agathangelos

The Vision of Agathangelos, a long oracular composition with strong apocalyptic overtones, was much celebrated by the readers and interpreters of 18th-century Greek prophetic literature and beyond. According to the preface, the work was written in Greek by a monk named Agathangelos in 1279, then turned into Italian in 1555, and finally translated back into Greek by Theoklytos Polyïdis in 1751. Since the late 19th century, however, research has established that *Agathangelos* was actually conceived and composed by Polyïdis himself, around 1750. (See the entry 'Theoklytos Polyïdis, *Chrēsmos ētoi Prophēteia tou makariou hieromonachou Agath-angelou*', in this volume, pp. 341-7).

Optasia tou kyr Daniēl

Optasia tou kyr Daniēl, pany ōphelimos ('Vision of Kyr Daniel, [a text] very useful') is an oracular tract written probably in or around 1764. In its original manuscript form, it is sometimes found attached to the hagiographical account of Anastasios the neomartyr. According to recent research (Karydēs, 'Ho neomartyras Anastasios', pp. 26-7), it is very likely that its main character, the monk *Daniēl ex Hagarinōn* (Daniel from the Hagarenes), was a real person. Whether this Daniel actually authored the tract is unclear because all oracular works were of alleged authorship. What is clear, however, is that the work had been conceived before and probably during the run up to the Russo-Turkish war of the late 1760s and the Christian uprising of 1770. Although the text openly states that the collapse of Ottoman power reflects the will of God, it also suggests that toppling the Ottomans is an undertaking that would require human action as well as divine guidance (Paschos, 'Islam kai neomartyres', p. 446). Those who will annihilate the sultan and his people are none other than the elites of the subjected Christians, Orthodox prelates, and primates in particular. It is in these terms that insurrection against Ottoman rule would bring into being on earth the will of heaven. (See the entry *Vision of kyr Daniel* in this volume, pp. 354-7).

Oracular interpretations by early Greek supporters of the Enlightenment

As the Ottoman Empire started to decline during the 18th century, a new great power with vested interests in South-Eastern Europe appeared on the international political stage. Soon, the increase in Russian military prowess, coupled with the universalistic claims that the tsars were promoting, created the collective impression on the Ottoman-ruled Orthodox that the Russian monarch was assuming responsibility for their protection. Those among them who sympathised with messianic views were for the first time free to envisage liberation by a fellow Orthodox nation. Inevitably, these developments increased the resonance of messianism and diversified its social constituencies (see V. Makrides, 'Eighteenth-century Greek Orthodox contacts with Russia', in this volume, pp. 403-34).

The course of the 18th century also witnessed the emergence of a prosperous Greek merchant class. Living in highly dispersed communities far beyond Ottoman borders, these merchants were often keen to finance scholarship and learning deep within Ottoman domains. Local schools multiplied and higher institutions of Greek learning were established in the empire's major centres. The Western-educated teachers who came to staff them were in contact with the ideas of the Western Enlightenment, as most of this merchant class had also been, thus becoming conduits for an intellectual revival in South-Eastern Europe known as the 'Greek Enlightenment'. Indeed, messianism proved a source of political inspiration for the Greek Enlightenment's first generation: Eugenios Voulgarēs (1716-1806), Nikēphoros Theotokēs (1731-1800) and Nikolaos Zerzoulēs (1706-72/3). These three 'leading men of learning' were attracted by the so-called 'Russian expectation', namely the prospect of Greek political redemption through Russian intervention, in which the age-old messianic myth and tradition loomed large (Kitromilides, *Enlightenment and revolution*, pp. 120-33). Eugenios Voulgarēs, the most renowned of the three, who had expressed serious interest in oracular literature in his early life and career besides his long-standing interest in Western philosophy and science, set out to turn traditional thinking into a comprehensive programme of political action. He elaborated a theory of enlightened absolutism and drafted various geopolitical plans apparently intended to be received by Tsarina Catherine II (r. 1762-96) – plans ranging from the creation of an independent Greek principality to the emergence of a new empire in the form of a Graeco-Russian condominium over the Balkans.

Others, such as Nikolaos Zerzoulēs (in Latin, Nicolae Cercel) stuck with tradition. A Padua-educated natural scientist and mathematician who had succeeded Voulgarēs at the Athoniada learning institution on Mount Athos, and later directed the princely academy of Iași (Moldavia), Zerzoulēs, a Vlach from Metsovo, Greece, authored a short prophetic work called *Hermēneia eis ton chrēsmon Leontos tou Sophou peri anastaseōs tēs Kōnstantinoupoleōs* ('Interpretation of the oracle of Leo the Wise about the resurrection of Constantinople'). What had fascinated him was a passage in the late Byzantine prophetic collection attributed to the Emperor Leo VI (r. 886-912), known as *Tou sophōtatou vasileōs Leontos chrēsmos peri anastaseos tis Konstantinoupoleōs* (*Sapientissimi Imp[eratoris] Leonis*

Graecum de restitutio Constantinoupoleos; see Migne, *Patrologiae cursus completus*, vol. 107, cols 1149-50).

The passage refers to the coming of a *xanthon genos* ('fair-haired people'), who would burn Constantinople to ashes and destroy the empire at a calculable point in human history, after which the city would rise more glorious and powerful than before. Though it is unsure what the form of the Leonine oracles might have been before 1453, it is almost certain that, originally, the notion of *xanthon genos* identified the invader who would one day annihilate Byzantium, more specifically the Normans or other, usually blonde, threatening peoples from the north or the west. As the masters of Constantinople changed after 1453, so did the line of prophetic interpretation. Those threatened by the ferocity of the fair-haired invaders were now the Ottomans, and prophecy interpreters in the late 18th century, whether Muslim or Christian, tended to identify the fair-haired people with the Russians. It was in this context that Zerzoulēs 'foresaw' the demise of the Ottoman Empire and the conquest of Constantinople by the 'fair-haired' Russian troops accompanied by the rise of a new Eastern Roman Empire even more glorious than the last. According to Zerzoulēs' own calculations, this was destined to happen in 1774.

Zerzoulēs also became occupied with interpreting another piece of oracular literature, the *Oracle of Stephanos of Alexandria*, a prophecy with a similar frame of meaning that was believed to be as old as the Emperor Heraclius's reign (610-41), at the time when 'the name of Muḥammad begun to be heard'.

Zerzoulēs did not live to see whether his interpretations were correct – he died in 1772 – but Pantazēs the Larissean (d. 1795), another intellectual and a teacher at the princely Greek Academy of Bucharest, was already following on his path. Unfortunately, little is known about this paragon of the Greek Enlightenment apart from his distinguished occupation and his prophetic work, which survived not only in manuscripts but also appeared in print (1838). Pantazēs worked with more or less the same prophetic material as Zerzoulēs. He started his prophetic career as an interpreter with the oracle attributed to Stephanos on Constantinople's resurrection and he too came up with the date 1774, the year in which the Russo-Turkish war did in fact end with the Treaty of Küçük Kaynarca. In 1787, when a new Russo-Turkish war broke out, Pantazēs went on to interpret the oracle attributed to Patriarch Tarasios of Constantinople, as well as two chapters of the Book of Revelation. This time, he predicted that Byzantium's resurrection would come in 1798.

Pantazēs' last work was written in 1792, right after the Treaty of Iaşi concluded the last Russo-Turkish war of the 18th century. Although he could not hide a sense of disappointment in his interpretation of the *Oracle of Stephanos of Alexandria*, he still argued for the messianic mission of Russia, viewing the treaty as just another milestone towards the Ottomans' decisive and final defeat, which this time he put in 1803, some 350 years after the fall of Constantinople (for the original text, see Stephanitzēs, *Syllogē*, pp. 57-67).

Exegetical treatises on the Book of Revelation in the *1790s*

Greek hopes cultivated by the repeated Russo-Turkish wars, the intellectual and political challenges posed by the Enlightenment, and the ferment of political radicalisation inspired by the French Revolution spurred the authoring of four sophisticated exegetical treatises on Revelation within a single decade, a development that marked the last phase of the Greek exegetical movement.

Metropolitan Iōannēs Lindios of Myra (in Lycia, Asia Minor) (c. 1710-90), Patriarch Anthimos of Jerusalem (1717-1808) and the monks Theodōritos of Ioannina (c. 1740-1823) and Kyrillos Lauriotēs from Patras (1741/4-1826) viewed the subjection of the Orthodox Church and the prospect of its eventual triumph through the lens of the turmoil that Europe was experiencing at the time. Employing a combined anti-Islamic and anti-Enlightenment perspective, while at the same time drawing on the old exegetical tradition, these four authors identified the two beasts that chastised the Church in Revelation 13 as Islam and the pope. In doing so, however, they introduced some interesting innovations. They did not suggest that 'the throes' would cease with the Second Coming, maintaining instead that they would end with the advent of Russian power. For the Greek prophetic tradition, this was a major shift in favour of messianism.

Only Anthimos of Jerusalem presents an exception with his *Interpretation on the Apocalypse* (1794-5), a theological treatise distanced from the worldly agonies of the time and closer to traditional Orthodox eschatology (Argyriou, *Les exégèses*, pp. 646-82). The *Hermēneia eis tēn Apokalypsin* ('Interpretation of the Apocalypse') by Iōannēs Lindios (1791; see Argyriou, Les exégèses, pp. 390-442), the *Interpretation* of Theodōritos of Ioannina (1793-9; see Argyriou, *Les exégèses*, pp. 443-525), and that of Kyrillos Lauriotēs (written between 1792 and 1821; see Argyriou, *Les exégèses*, pp. 587-645) predict a Russian-led Eastern Orthodox restoration over which the millenarian idea of world supremacy looms large.

Their stance towards Islam is at times extremely harsh, no less so than that which they reserve for their fellow Christians in the West. Lindios paints the image of Orthodox 'captivity' in black, Theodōritos refers with aversion to the 'dodgy, malevolent, carnal and beastly teaching of Muḥammad [standing] on a par with the corrupt and vile conduct of the pope' (Argyriou, *To ideologiko periechomeno*, p. 170), while Lauriotēs traces the beginning of the rule of the Antichrist back to the day on which the Muslim religion appeared and the Catholics broke from the Church. What the late 18th-century Greek exegetes of Revelation did in their treatises was to substitute the idea of the Kingdom-to-come with post-Byzantine messianism, the prophetic expectations of which were fed on Russian power and glory. Thus, as the 18th century was waning, the literary contribution of Lindios, Theodōritos and Lauriotēs came to resolve the age-old tension within the Greek prophetic tradition: messianism had finally won over traditional eschatological thinking.

SIGNIFICANCE

The fact that Greek exegetes of the 1790s were hard-line Russophile clerics who yearned for something of a Russian global monarchy does not necessarily mean that Greek prophetic literature was a mere manifestation of Russian propaganda. Nor does it make this literature the product of religious fervour or apocalyptic madness. Within the ranks of adherents, exponents and interpreters of Greek prophetic literature not everyone was a cleric, let alone mad: apart from monks and preachers, Western-educated teachers of the Greek Enlightenment were also involved – and the picture becomes even more diverse if one goes back in time. Besides, as the case of Gordios, Voulgarēs, Theotokēs and others shows, one could be a cleric or monk and at the same time be an 'enlightened' educator-intellectual. Not every prophecy interpreter was Russophile either, as is clear from the cases of Nektarios Terpos and of the anonymous author of *Kyr Daniēl*. As far as other 18th-century Greek prophetic writings are concerned, research has pinpointed that the Russophile excerpts in *Agath-angelos* are later interpolations (Politēs, 'Agathangelos', p. 39) and that the Russophilia of Gordios is not fully intentional, while that of Pantazēs is not consistent (Argyriou, 'To ideologiko periechomeno', p. 166). Moreover, despite the virulent anti-Catholicism of the majority of interpreters, Terpos takes the opposite stance by explicitly favouring the union of the two Churches, while *Kyr Daniēl*'s author remains judiciously silent on the issue. In terms of social vocation, the adherents, exponents and interpreters of Greek prophetic literature had always been a diverse bunch of people, and they continued to be so throughout the 18th century. What had brought them all together was the objective of seeing their community restored to its former glory.

This objective had anti-Islamic underpinnings. In the eyes of the Greek prophecy interpreters and/or authors, Islam represented an existential threat to Christianity. It was actually the force that had subdued the once powerful Eastern Roman Empire and had brought the mighty Eastern Christian Church to its knees. The symbolic allusions in Revelation to one obscure diabolic beast that would be 'given power to wage war against God's holy people and to conquer them' (Revelation 13:7), or to a mysterious false prophet who would act on behalf of the beast (Revelation 19:20) offered a scriptural foundation for this view. Those who cherished the ideas of Greek prophetic literature sought to counter-balance the hardships of Christian subjection and the burden of being humbled before Muslim rulers through an agenda of more or less politicised metaphysics. To this end, they adopted two strands of prophetic interpretation and belief, each of which used biblical and extra-biblical prophecy in different proportions. For their adherents, messianism and eschatology were more than mere ideological currents. They were capable of furnishing a myth for the Ottoman-ruled Orthodox community that stemmed from shared memories and collective experiences: Ottoman power would eventually be defeated and Islam would collapse, either right here in this world through the military action of a messianic ruler, or under the cataclysmic conditions of a swiftly approaching Day of Judgement. The myth offered the faithful more than mere assurance that their political status was destined to be reversed. By invoking a common past with a view to serving current needs and future purposes (Smith, *Chosen peoples*, p. 170), the myth furnished an important bond for the Ottoman-ruled Orthodox community – at the very least for those individuals or groups who found it hard to accommodate themselves to Muslim rulership. As the 18th century witnessed the progressive rise of a fellow-Orthodox great power in international politics, the eschatological strand of Greek prophetic interpretation became increasingly 'messianised'. The last decade of the 18th century saw the composition of sophisticated exegetical treatises on the Book of Revelation whose orientation was entirely messianic, in contrast to the earlier tradition.

As far as Christian-Muslim relations are concerned, Greek prophetic literature is important for two reasons. First, this literature proved effective for a long time in galvanising anti-Ottoman and anti-Muslim sentiment on the political and religious level. When the age of revolution arrived, at the end of the 18th century, Greek prophetic literature became a validating charter for collective actions and political stances that would otherwise have appeared unacceptably revolutionary from a traditional point of view (Hatzopoulos, 'From resurrection to insurrection'). Second, the Muslim community, or at least sizeable parts of it, also accepted the validity of the key myths and their meanings, if not of Greek prophetic literature as a whole, then of its messianic strand in particular. The prophetic expectation of a Christian instrument of divine will who would wrest power and space from Muslim hands is itself a *topos* of the Islamic apocalyptic tradition (Şahin, 'Constantinople and the end time' pp. 324-5). And apart from this, the key myth of the Greek prophetic tradition could be received by Muslims too, especially if it was not read but heard from the lips of a saintly man, such as Kosmas, whom popular Islam also revered. For anyone eager to explain imperial decline in terms of human error and sin, irrespective of one's own religion, losing power to the enemy was merely a manifestation of theodicy. In this light, it could be said that a great deal of the legacy of the Greek prophetic tradition and literature evolved to become a shared cultural pattern for both Christians and Muslims ruled by the Sublime Porte.

PUBLICATIONS

Sources for each author are given before their publications.

Information on all the 19th-century Greek editions can be found in Ph.Ē. Ēliou and P. Polemē, *Greek bibliography of the 19th century. Electronic catalogue*; http://oldwww.benaki.gr/bibliology/en/19.htm

Nektarios Terpos (also referred to as Nektarios Terpou)

K. Garitsēs, *Ho Nektarios Terpos kai to ergo tou. Eisagōgē, scholia, kritikē ekdosē tou ergou tou 'Pistis'*, Thera, 2002, p. 165

Nektarios Terpos, *Vivliarion kaloumenon Pistis, anankaion eis kathe aploun anthrōpon, vevaiōmenon apo prophētas, euangelion, apostolous, kai allous sophous didaskalous*, Venice, 1732; PPK 122438 (digitised version available through Digital Library of Modern Greek Studies)

Nectarius Terpes, *Biblion kaloumenon pistis*, Venice, 1813; 26.Y.40 ALT PRUNK (digitised version available through Österreichische Nationalbibliothek

T.I. Papadopoulos, *Hellēnikē vivliographia (1466-1800). Tomos prōtos. Alphavētikē kai chronologikē anakatataxis*, Athens, 1984, no 5547.00

(1732), 5548.00 (1733), 1097 (1734), 5549.00 (1750), 5550.00 (1755), 5551.00 (1756), 5552.00 (1779), 5553.00 (1799)

Ph.Ē. Ēliou, *Hellēnikē Vivliographia tou 19ou aiōna. Vivlia – Phylladia, tomos 1, 1801-1818*, Athens, 1997, nos 1813.9 (1813), 1818.9 (1818)

D. Polemēs, 'Tria agnosta entypa tou IH aiōna', *Tetradia Ergasias* 10 (1988) 449-56 (an unknown edition from 1785)

K. Garitsēs, *Ho Nektarios Terpos kai to ergo tou. Eisagōgē, scholia, kritikē ekdosē tou ergou tou 'Pistis'*, Thera, 2002, p. 157 (an unknown edition from 1779)

Kosmas of Aitolia

I. Menounos, *Kosma tou Aitōlou didaches kai viographia*, Athens, 1979, p. 11

W. Krause, 'Kosmas der Ätoler und seine Prophezeiungen', *Mitteilungen des Österreichischen Staatsarchivs* 3 (1950) 404-25

K.S. Konstas, '72 prophēteies tou pater-Kosma', *Ēpeirōtikē Hestia* 51-3 (1956) 678-82

I. Menounos, *Kosma tou Aitōlou didaches kai viographia*, Athens, 1979

N.M. Vaporis, *Father Kosmas, the Apostle of the poor. The life of St Kosmas Aitolos together with an English translation of his teaching and letters*, Brookline MA, 1977

Nikolaos Zerzoulēs (also referred in Greek primary sources as Nikolaos Zertzoulēs or Tzartzoulēs or Tzertzelēs or Kyrkou)

A. Chatzēmichalē, 'Hoi en tō hellēnoscholeio tou Metsovou didaxantes kai didachthentes', *Ēpeirōtika Chronika* 15 (1940), 119-40

Pantazēs the Larissean

MS Bucharest, Biblioteca Academiei Române – gr. 560 (19th century; see C. Litzica, *Catalogul manuscriptelor greceşti*, vol. 1, Bucharest, 1909, pp. 504-5, no. 758)

A. Argyriou, *Les exégèses grecques de l'Apocalypse à l'époque turque (1453-1821). Esquisse d'une histoire des courants idéologiques au sein du peuple grec asservi*, Thessaloniki, 1982, pp. 358-60

P.D. Stephanitzēs, *Syllogē diaphorōn prorrēseōn*, Athens, 1838 (prophetic collection partly containing the prophetic work of Pantazēs the Larissean), pp. 8-44, 57-87, 90-132

Iōannēs Lindios

Argyriou, *Les exégèses*, pp. 397-8

Patriarch Anthimos of Jerusalem

A. Papadopoulos-Kerameus, *Hierosolymitikē vivliothēkē ētoi katalogos tōn en tais vivliothēkais tou hagiōtatou apostolikou te kai katholikou orthodoxou patriarchikou thronou tōn Hierosolymōn kai pasēs Palaistinēs apokeimenōn hellenikōn kōdikōn*, vol. 3, St Petersburg, 1897, pp. 120-1; vol. 5, St Petersburg, 1915, p. 233
Argyriou, *Les exégèses*, p. 650

Patriarch Anthimos of Jerusalem, *Hermēneia eis tēn Hieran Apokalypsin tou Hagiou Endoxou kai Paneuphimou Apostolou kai Euangelistou Iōannou tou Theologou. Syntetheisa hypo tou aoidimou Patriarchou Hierosolymōn Anthimou. Nyn prōton typois ekdidotai Keleusei tou Makariōtatou kai theiotatou Patriarchou tōn Hierosolymōn Kyriou Kyriou Kyrillou*, Jerusalem, 1856; 11855/1215 (digitised version available through Academy of Athens)

Theodoritos of Ioannina

MS Athos, Docheiariou 81 (1798); see Sp. P. Lampros, *Catalogue of the Greek manuscripts on Mount Athos*, vol. 1, Cambridge, 1895, p. 243, no. 2755)

Theodoritos of Ioannina, *Hermēneia eis tēn Hieran Apokalypsin Iōannou tou Theologou*, Leipzig, 1800; 8557 (digitised version available through Aristotle University of Thessaloniki)

See Papadopoulos, *Hellēnikē vivliographia (1466-1800)*, no. 0923. 00; Argyriou, *Les exégèses*, p. 459

Kyrillos Lauriotēs

On the unique manuscript of his work, see K. Duovouniōtēs, 'Hē Hermēneia tēs Apokalypseōs tou Kyrillou tou Patreōs', *Theologia* 22 (1951) 446-62
Argyriou, *Les exégèses*, pp. 594-7

K. Duovouniōtēs, 'Hē Hermēneia', *Theologia* 22 (1951) 446-62, 568-76; 'Hai en tē Hermēneia tēs Apokalypseōs tou Kyrillou tou Patreōs thrēskeutikai gnōmai kai kriseis autou peri diaphorōn prosōpōn', *Theologia* 24 (1953) 345-74, 504-19; 25 (1954) 47-57; 'Historikai eidēseis ek tēs Hermēneias tēs Apokalypseōs tou Kyrillou tou Patreōs', *Theologia* 26 (1955) 441-4, 541-7; 27 (1956) 22-31, 181-95, 357-66 (Lauriotēs' work has never appeared in print. Fragments are found in the articles listed here); see http://www.ecclesia.gr/greek/press/theologia/archive.asp?eti=19501959

STUDIES

K. Giakoumis, 'Textual visuality and visual textuality in texts corre-
lated with artworks. Nektarios Terpos' Pistis and Last Judgement
scenes from Myzeqe, central Albania', in E. Montafov and J. Erdel-
jan (eds), *Texts, inscriptions, images*, Sofia, 2017, 203-44

M. Hatzopoulos, 'Prophetic structures of the Ottoman-ruled Orthodox
community in comparative perspective. Some preliminary observations', in P.M. Kitromilides and S. Matthaiou (eds), *Greek-Serbian
relations in the age of nation-building*, Athens, 2016, 121-47

S. Karydēs 'Ho neomartyras Anastasios "ho ek Paramythias" kai ho
monachos Daniēl. Ta prosōpa kai hē geōgraphia tou martyriou',
in V. Gounaris (ed), *Praktika 34 Panellēniou Historikou Synedriou,
Thessalonikē 31 Maïou-2 Iouniou 2013*, Thessaloniki, 2016, 21-34

N. Pissēs, 'Chrēsmologia kai "rōssiki prosdokia"' [Oracular literature and the "Russian expectation"], in *Slavoi kai Hellēnikos kosmos. Praktika prōtēs epistimonikēs hēmeridas tmēmatos slavikōn
spoudōn*, Athens, 2015, 149-68

A.B. Glaros, 'Eschatologikes proektaseis sto vivliarion kaloumenon
Pistis tou Nektariou Terpou', *Altarul Banatului* 1-3 (2014) 106-14

P.M. Kitromilides, *Enlightenment and revolution. The making of modern Greece*, Cambridge MA, 2013

K. Garitsēs 'Kōnstantinos Resinos kai Nektarios Terpos. Hē periptōsē
mias ekdosēs', in *XII Syntantēsē vyzantinologōn Hellados kai Kyprou.
Paradosē kai ananeōsē sto Vyzantio*, Komotēnē, 2011, 313-15

M. Hatzopoulos, 'Oracular prophecy and the politics of toppling Ottoman rule in south-east Europe', *The Historical Review / La Revue
Historique* 8 (2011) 95-116

N. Pissēs, 'Apokalyptikos logos kai messianikē prosdokia. Chrēseis
kai leitourgies apo tē vyzantinē stēn othōmanikē periodo', in
S. Zoumboulakēs (ed.), *Hē messianikē idea kai hoi metamorphōseis
tēs. Apo tēn Palaia Diathikē ōs tous politikous messianismous tou
20ou aiōna*, Athens, 2011, 339-59

K. Şahin, 'Constantinople and the end time. The Ottoman conquest
as a portent of the last hour', *Journal of Early Modern History* 14
(2010) 317-54

A. Ziaka, *Metaxy polemikēs kai dialogou. To Islam stē vyzantinē,
metavyzantinē kai neoterē hellēnikē grammateia* [Between polemic
and dialogue. Islam in Byzantine, post-Byzantine and modern
Greek literature], Thessaloniki, 2010

M. Hatzopoulos, 'From resurrection to insurrection. "Sacred" myths, motifs, and symbols in the Greek war of independence", in R. Beaton and D. Ricks (eds), *The making of modern Greece. Nationalism, Romanticism and the uses of the past (1797-1896)*, London, 2009, 81-93

N. Pissēs, 'Tropes tēs "rōssikēs prosdokias" sta chronia tou M. Petrou', *Mnēmōn* 30 (2009) 37-60

N.B. Rotzōkos, *Ethnaphypnisē kai ethnogenesē. Orlofika kai hellēnikē historiographia* [National awakening and ethnogenesis. Greek historiography and the Orlov revolt], Athens, 2007

A. Argyriou, 'Diamorphōsē mias hellēnorthodoxēs syneidēsēs mesō tōn hermēneiōn stēn Apokalypsē kata tous chronous tēs Tourkokratias', in Chr. Oikonomou et al. (eds), *Hagia Graphē kai synchronos kosmos. Timētikos tomos ston kathēgētē Iōannē D. Karavidopoulo*, Thessaloniki, 2006, 57-74

N. Theotokas, 'Hē epanastasē tou ethnous kai to orthodoxo genos. Scholia gia tis ideologies sto eikosiena' [The revolution of the nation and the Orthodox *genos*. Comments on the ideologies in 1821], in N. Theotokas and N. Kotaridēs (eds), *Hē oikonomia tēs vias. Paradosiakes kai neōterikes exousies stēn Hellada tou 19 aiōna*, Athens, 2006, 11-57

Ph. Kotzageorgis, '"Messiahs" and neomartyrs in Ottoman Thessaly. Some thoughts on two entries in a *mühimme defteri*', *Archivum Ottomanicum* 23 (2005/6) 219-31

K. Garitsēs, 'Hoi xylographies tou entypou "Pistis" ypo Nektariou Terpou', *Epeirōtika Chronika* 39 (2005) 437-54

A. Timotin, 'La littérature eschatologique byzantine et post-byzantine dans les manuscrits roumains', *Revue des Études Sud-Est Européennes* 40 (2002) 151-66

A.D. Smith, *Chosen peoples. Sacred sources of national identity*, Oxford, 2003

K. Petsios, 'Nikolaos Zerzoulēs (ca. 1710-1773) kai Petrus van Musschenbroek (1692-1761). Nea stoicheia', *Ho Eranistēs* 23 (2001) 48-96

K.Th. Dimaras, *Historia tēs neoellinikēs logotechnias. Apo tis protes rizes ōs tin epohē mas*, Athens, 2000[9]

A. Kariōtoglou, *Orthodoxia kai Islam*, Athens, 2000[2]

A. Kariōtoglou, *Islam kai christianikē chrēsmologia. Apo ton mytho stēn pragmatikotēta*, Athens, 2000

A. Argyriou, 'To ideologiko periechomeno tōn hermēneiōn stēn apocalypsē kata tēn periodo tou neoellēnikou Diaphotēsmou', in

S. Agouridēs et al. (eds), *1900 Etēris tis Apokalypseōs tou Iōannou*, Athens, 1999, 163-81

St. Yerasimos, 'De l'arbre à la pomme. La généalogie d'un thème apocalyptique', in B. Lellouch and St. Yerasimos (eds), *Les traditions apocalyptiques au tournant de la chute de Constantinople*, Paris-Montreal, 1999, 153-92

R. Clogg, 'The Byzantine legacy in the modern Greek world. The *megali idea*', in R. Clogg, *Anatolica. Studies in the Greek East in the 18th and 19th centuries*, London, 1996, 253-81

P.B. Paschos, 'Islam kai neomartyres. O ek Paramythias neomartys Anastasios kai ho ismaēlitēs (Mousa) Daniēl ho homologētēs', *Epistēmonikē Epitheōrēsē Theologikēs Scholēs Panepistēmiou Athēnōn* 30 (1995) 413-74

K. Kyriakou, *Hoi historēmenoi chrēsmoi tou Leontos VI tou Sophou. Cheirographē paradosē kai ekdoseis kata tous 15-19 aiōnes*, Athens, 1995

A. Argyriou, 'Hē apeleutherōsē tōn Hellēnōn kai ho eschatologikos rolos tēs Rōsias kai tēs Gallias mesa sto hermēneutiko ergo tou Theodōritou Iōanninōn (per. 1740-1823)', in *Timētikos tomos ston homotimo kathēgētē Damiano Ath. Doïko*, Thessaloniki, 1995, 11-24

L. Benakēs, 'Nikolaos Zerzoulēs, metaphrastēs tōn mathēmatikōn ergōn tou Christian Wolff', *Ho Eranistēs* 20 (1995) 47-57

Ch. Karanasios, 'Ho kōdikas VI-9 (188) tēs kentrikēs panepistimiakēs vivliothēkēs "Mihai Eminescu" tou Iasiou (aneuresē lanthanontos ergou tou Nikolaos Zerzoulē)', *Hellēnika* 44 (1994) 182-7

E. Amoiridou, 'Nektarios Terpou kai to ergo tou. *Vivliarion kaloumenon Pistis*', in *Ellinikē Historikē Hetairea. 14th panellēnio historiko synedrio (28-30 Maiou 1993). Proceedings*, Thessaloniki, 1993, 251-66

P. Magdalino, 'The history of the future and its uses. Prophecy, policy and propaganda', in R. Beaton and Ch. Roueché (eds), *The making of Byzantine history*, London, 1993, 3-34

A. Argyriou, 'Hē ideologikē sēmasia tōn kriseōn tou Kyrillou Lauriōtē enantion tou Rēga', *Hypereia* 1 (1990) 407-15

J. Nicolopoulos, 'From Agathangelos to the megalē idea. Russia and the emergence of modern Greek nationalism', *Balkan Studies* 26 (1985) 41-56

C. Mango, 'The legend of Leo the Wise', *Zbornik Radova Vizantološkog Instituta* 65 (1960) 59-93 (repr. C. Mango, *Byzantium and its image*, London, 1984, 59-93)

A. Xanthopoulou-Kyriakou, *Ho Kosmas Aitōlos kai hoi Venetoi (1777-1779)*. *Ta teleutaia chronia tēs drasēs tou kai to provlēma tōn didachōn*, Thessaloniki, 1984

Argyriou, *Les exégèses*

A. Argyriou, 'L'attitude des Grecs face à la Russie orthodoxe et aux États occidentaux (1767-1821), telle qu'elle apparaît à travers les textes eschatologiques de l'époque', *Cahiers de l'Institut des Langues Vivantes* 30 (1982) 9-28

T.E. Sklavenitēs, 'Chrēsmologiko eikonographēmeno monophyllo tōn archōn tou 18ou aiōna', *Mnēmōn* 7 (1978) 46-59

L. Benakēs, 'Apo tēn historia tou metavyzantinou aristotelismou ston hellēniko chōro. Amphisvētēsē kai hyperaspisē tou Philosophou. Nikolaos Zerzoulēs kai Dōrotheos Lesvios', *Philosophia* 7 (1977) 416-54

Vaporis, *Father Kosmas*

L. Droulia, 'Ho lauriōtēs monachos Kyrillos apo tēn Patra kai hē vivliothēkē tou', *Ho Eranistēs* 11 (1974) 456-503

A. Camariano-Cioran, *Les académies princières de Bucarest et de Jassy et leurs professeurs*, Thessaloniki, 1974, pp. 407-13 (Kyrillos Lauriotēs), 431-2 (Pantazēs the Larissean), 599-604 (Nikolaos Zerzoulēs)

K. Sardelēs, *Analitikē vivliographia Kosma tou Aitōlou*, Athens, 1974

Ch. Tzogas, 'Nikolaos Zarzoulis o ek Metsovou', in I.E. Anastasiou and A.Gr. Geromichalos (eds), *Mnēmē 1821. Afierōma eis tēn ethnikēn palingennesian epi tē 150ē epeteiō*, Thessaloniki, 1971, 129-42

G. Valetas, *Armatōmenos logos. Hoi antistasiakes didaches tou N. Terpou vgalmenes sta 1730*, Athens, 1971

A. Kantiōtēs, *Kosmas ho Aitōlos (1714-1779)*, Athens, 1966[3]

W. Krause, 'Kosmas der Ätoler und seine Prophezeiungen', *Mitteilungen des Österreichischen Staatsarchivs* 3 (1950) 404-25

K.Th. Dimaras, 'Hoi chrēsmoi sti nea mas historia', *Eklogē* 3 (1947) 196-203

Chatzēmichalē, 'Hoi en tō hellēnoscholeio tou Metsovou', pp. 59-158

K.D. Mertzios, 'To en Venetia kratikon archeion', *Epeirōtika Chronika* 15 (1940) 5-12

N.A. Bees, 'Peri tou historēmenou chrēsmologiou tēs kratikēs vivliothēkēs tou Verolinou kai tou thrylou tou "marmarōmenou vasilia"', *Byzantinisch-Neugriechische Jahrbücher* 13 (1937) 203-44

K. Duovouniōtēs, 'Kyrillou Lauriotou anekdotos hermēneia eis tēn Apokalypsin', *Praktika tēs Akadēmias Athēnōn* 6 (1931) 36-53

N.G. Politēs, 'Agathangelos', *Hestia* 27 (January-June 1889) 38-40

J.-P. Migne (ed.), *Patrologiae cursus completus. Series Graeca posterior,* vol. 107, Paris, 1857, cols 1122-68

D. Kleopas, *Vios kai politeia tou en makaria tē lexei aeimnēstou patriarchou tōn Hierosolymōn Anthimou,* Jerusalem, 1856

Marios Hatzopoulos

Eighteenth-century Greek Orthodox contacts with Russia

DATE 18th century

ORIGINAL LANGUAGE Greek

DESCRIPTION

After the fall of Constantinople and the Byzantine Empire to the Otto-man Turks in 1453, a new era began for the Eastern Orthodox world, in which Russia – as a budding new Orthodox centre of power and influence – gradually acquired a multiple role and to a large extent filled the vacuum left by the demise of Byzantium. It became not only the most important Orthodox Christian power, claiming continuity with the Byzantine political, cultural and religious heritage, but also eventually a protector and defender of the rights of the Orthodox peoples, especially of the Greeks, under Ottoman rule in South-Eastern Europe. A rich and multi-faceted chapter opened in Graeco-Russian relations, which lasted for many centuries (see *Les relations gréco-russes*; Katsiardē-Hering et al., *Rōsia kai Mesogeios*). One aspect, among many others, was that a large number of Greeks left the Ottoman-ruled areas and settled temporarily or permanently in Russia.

In the 18th century, the issue of Graeco-Russian relations acquired additional importance because Russia was gradually becoming a signifi-cant player in European politics on an equal level with Western powers. This began in the reign of Peter I (r. 1682-1725), who initiated a moderni-sation process intended to bring the Russian Empire more closely into line with Western European standards and articulated its further designs on the Ottoman Empire. In 1700, Russia established official diplomatic representation in Constantinople for the first time (Hennings, *Russia*). Several years later, after his victory over the Swedes at Poltava (1709), Peter issued a Latin memorandum in which he clearly outlined Russia's protective policy towards the Orthodox Balkan communities under Otto-man rule (6 January 1711). The Ottoman victory at Stănileşti, on the River Pruth (July 1711), stopped Russian expansion towards the east and south for a while but did not put an end to Balkan Orthodox hopes for a Rus-sian triumph over the 'infidels'.

Indeed, despite this harsh defeat, Peter I was hailed in numerous ways as the protector of the Orthodox and a powerful new opponent to the

Ottomans (Vakalopoulos, 'Ho megas Petros'; Cernovodeanu, 'Pierre'). The Greek scholar Alexander Helladius (born 1686), who spent many years in Western Europe and met Peter I in 1712 in Karlsbad (Karlovy Vary, in the present-day Czech Republic), dedicated his book *Status praesens Ecclesiae Graecae* (1714) to the Russian emperor. In Helladius' view, Peter was 'Defender of the Oriental Orthodox Church and the Greeks', as he states in the long laudatory address he wrote in the latter's honour: *Serenissimo ac potentissimo Principi ac Domino PETRO ALEXIADI IMPERATORI ac Magno Duci Moscoviae nec non Totius Magnae Parvae et Albae Russiae Autocratori quin et Multarum Aliarum Orientalium Occidentalium ac Septentrionalium Provinciarum atque Regionum Antiquo Haeredi Regi atque Monarchae Invictissimo etc. etc. etc. Ecclesiae Orientalis Orthodoxae Graecorumque Defensori Hyperaspistē ac Patri Clementissimo Indulgentissimo Salutem Prosperitatem ac Omnigenam Felicitatem!*

Helladius' work illustrates a general state of mind, which was largely shared by his contemporaries, as is shown by the important corpus of eschatological-apocalyptic literature that circulated in the Balkan area and the Levant. Among other things, this literature predicted the end of Ottoman power through Russian intervention on behalf of the Orthodox Greeks, and in some cases the restoration of the Byzantine Empire. Several such texts mention the *xanthon genos*, the fair-haired people from the north (often identified with the Russians) who were expected to free the Orthodox from Ottoman rule.

This positive view of Russia was sometimes combined with anti-Catholic and anti-Islamic interpretations of the Book of Revelation in a strongly eschatological framework, as in the work of Anastasios Gordios (1654/5-1729) (see the entry 'Anastasios Gordios, *Peri Mōameth kai kata Lateinōn syngramma*', in this volume, pp. 299-303). Some of the authors of these texts had strong contacts with Russia and even travelled there, as did Archmandrite Theoklētos Polyeidēs (c. 1698-c. 1759), the supposed author of *Agathangelos*, maybe the most widely read Greek prophetic writing of that time (see the entry 'Theoklytos Polyïdis, *Chrēsmos ētoi Prophēteia tou makariou hieromonachou Agathangelou*' in this volume, pp. 341-7). Another important scholar of the period, Nikolaos Zerzoulēs (c. 1710-73), who had contacts with Russian officials (e.g. with Count P.A. Rumiantsev-Zadunaĭskiĭ, 1725-96), also had a lively interest in interpreting such prophecies. He is also reported to have composed four laudatory speeches in honour of Catherine II (r. 1762-96; Zaviras, *Nea Hellas*, p. 496; see Marios Hatzopoulos, 'Eighteenth-century Greek prophetic literature' in this volume, pp. 381-402).

These expectations were further strengthened in the second half of the 18th century, which more or less coincided with the reign of Catherine II, by her aggressive policy towards the Ottomans and by substantial changes within Ottoman society, such as the consolidation of the so-called 'Phanariote' aristocracy in the Danubian Principalities, with the growth of Bucharest and Jassy as important cultural, economic and political centres, the emergence of a strong merchant class and significant commercial urban centres (Smyrna, Ioannina, etc.), and the numerous Orthodox émigré merchants and students in Western Europe.

Russia was victorious in a series of Russo-Turkish wars, leading to its territorial expansion to the south and its gaining permanent access to the Black Sea. The 1768-74 war marked a turning point in the history of the two empires. The victories of the Russians (the naval battle of Çeşme, 1770) and their control of the Aegean archipelago were widely celebrated and commemorated (Bruess, 'The Chesme church'; Smilianskaia, Velizhev and Smilianskaia, *Rossiia*). The Russians also attempted to create a main base for the Russian fleet in the Mediterranean on the island of Paros, and a 'Greek state' consisting of the islands of the Aegean archipelago that took an oath of loyalty to Catherine II (late autumn 1770). They had to supply food and pay taxes to Russia, but received in return the protection of the Russian army. Thus, a related administration and capital were created in Paros together with other local administrations on such other islands (Smilianskaia, *Grecheskie*; "'Protection" or "'Possession'"). This was the first Russian attempt to create a Greek state under its immediate control, but it was very short-lived, as the war finally resulted in the Treaty of Küçük Kaynarca (July 1774).

This treaty was beneficial in many respects for the Orthodox subjects of the Ottoman Empire, although its background and context have been critically reassessed by modern scholarship (Davison, "'Russian skill'"). It provided, *inter alia*, an amnesty for those involved in the war and allowed them to sail freely and safely under the Russian flag, to enjoy immunity from Ottoman intervention, and to gain commercial benefits and compensation for war damages. Russia was also given the right to appoint consuls and vice-consuls in various cities of the Ottoman Empire. The Greeks were granted the right to trade freely through an additional commercial capitulation agreement in Constantinople (June 1783; Camariano-Cioran, 'La guerre russo-turque'; Smilianskaia, 'Catherine's liberation'), provided they became Russian subjects and their vessels flew the Russian flag. In addition, Catherine II promised particular benefits to foreigners who settled or did business in the Black Sea ports

(February 1784). The immediate result was that, in the following years, the Black Sea experienced a rapid rise in Greek commercial activity and the strengthening of their naval presence in the area (Pissis, 'Investments'). In addition to systematic Greek immigration into the northern littoral of the Black Sea, many of those who were nominated consuls by Russia were influential Greek residents in the Ottoman Empire and supported its interests in the area. All this greatly contributed to the formation of a strong pro-Russian orientation among the Greeks, with far-reaching repercussions (Mēnaoglou, *Historia*, pp. 107-33).

On the other hand, the Treaty of Küçük Kaynarca led to the notorious 'Greek project' or the 'Grand plan' (Hösch, 'Das sogenannte'; Ragsdale, 'Evaluating the traditions of Russian aggression'), a joint Russo-Austrian project directed against the Ottomans that involved Russia's further expansion to the south, the capture of Constantinople and the partition of the Ottoman Empire, the control of the Turkish Straits, and the liberation of the Greeks. Catherine II's second grandson, born in 1779, was given the symbolic name 'Constantine'. Following an appropriate education by Greek nurses and tutors, he was expected to become king of Greece in Constantinople as heir to the Byzantine emperors. Prince Grigoriĭ Alexandrovich Potëmkin (1739-91), governor of New South Russia (*Novorossiia*), played a central role in this project and supported the massive Greek settlement there after 1774 and especially after 1783, when Russia annexed the Crimean Khanate (Fisher, *The Russian annexation*). An organised battalion of Greek soldiers was also entrusted with the task of guarding the Crimean coast. All this led to the outbreak of another Russo-Turkish war (1787-92), which once more triggered Greek hopes for liberation. As a result, there were numerous expressions of gratitude from Greeks to Catherine II and Potëmkin (e.g. dedications of books), often accompanied by criticism of 'barbarian' Ottoman rule and expressions of a desire to be liberated (Makrides, 'Orthodoxie'). The same can be observed in the surviving correspondence between Greeks residing in Russia and those within the Ottoman Empire (Dēmaras, 'Neoellēnikē', pp. 94-8). But aside from these dreams, the entire political constellation of the era was against any realisation of the 'Greek project', which is why it was never attempted or implemented in concrete practical terms. Furthermore, Russian support for Orthodox coreligionists in the Ottoman Empire should not be overestimated, for it was rather an instrument and not the source of Russian foreign policy at that time (Taki, 'Limits').

The Treaty of Küçük Kaynarca also boosted Greek immigration to Russia. This involved various categories of people who moved there with a variety of objectives, such as seeking security and refuge from Ottoman persecution, engaging in commercial activities, studying, profiting from various opportunities on Russian soil or being employed in governmental, ecclesiastical, military, diplomatic and scientific positions. These migrants included: Orthodox clerics and monks (Papoulidis, 'Le patriarche'; Papoulidēs, *Anatolios*; Batalden, 'A further note'; Papoulidēs, *To politiko*); princes, members of noble families and related élites (Spathēs, 'Phanariōtikē'; Cazacu, 'Familles'); merchants and their families (Carras, *Emporio*); soldiers and mercenaries, as well as agents, envoys and diplomats in the Ottoman territories (Pappas, *Greeks*; Priakhin, *Greki*; Priakhin, *Lambros*; Priakhin, *Geroi*; Arsh, 'Rossiĭskie émissary'); scientists (mostly physicians) and numerous other scholars (Karathanassēs, *Ho hellēnikos kosmos*, pp. 255-393; Arsh, *Grecheskaia kul'tura*; Carras, *Emporio*, pp. 528-39); students, such as those in the 'Greek Gymnasium' in St Petersburg, founded in 1775 (Fedorova, 'Grecheskaia'); public servants and dignitaries in various administrative posts (Nicolopoulos, 'Resultats'; Papoulidēs, *Rōsoellēnika*, pp. 101-45); numerous settlers (c. 500,000) in the last quarter of the 18th century used to populate, colonise and fill the new territories acquired by Russia across the northern shore of the Black Sea (Arsh, 'Grecheskaia émigratsiia'; Karidis, 'The Mariupol'; Kardasēs, *Ho Hellēnismos*; Kardasis, *Diaspora merchants*; Sapozhnikov and Belousova, *Greki*; Ivanov, *Greki*, pp. 36-86; Chrēstou, *Hoi Hellēnes*; Sifnaiou and Harlaftē, *Oi Hellēnes*).

There were also others who just visited Russia for shorter periods of time in order, for example, to collect alms for various purposes, usually for the support of Orthodox Christians under Ottoman rule (Ialamas, 'Arkhimandritou'). All this led to the creation of significant Greek communities in cities such as St Petersburg (Papoulidēs, *Hoi Hellēnes*), Moscow (Alexandropoulou, 'Hē hellēnikē monē') and Odessa (Mazis, *The Greeks*). The next generations of those who remained permanently in Russia were often 'russified', albeit in most cases keeping their Greek connections and contacts intact. All in all, Russian interest in the Greeks within the Ottoman Empire was an important factor in establishing contacts between the two peoples, and went beyond the usual Philhellenic sentiments and actions found in central and Western Europe, as it was connected with specific Russian designs on the Ottoman Empire (Taki, *Tsar and sultan*, pp. 169-79).

Channels and agents

In the context of this long and multifarious Graeco-Russian interaction, there was also a transfer of knowledge and news from the Greek Orthodox world under Ottoman rule to Russia in various domains, notably in church and theological matters, and secondarily in scholarly and scientific domains. This took place through a variety of channels including, for example, the circulation of Greek manuscripts and books in Russia, the publication or translation of Greek books into Russian and correspondence between diverse actors, both official and private. Indeed, there was a wealth of Greek manuscripts in Russia (Fonkich, *Grecheskie dokumenty*; Fonkich, *Grecheskie rukopisi*), which had already at that time attracted the attention of various Western scholars, as the case of the the the German philologist Christian Friedrich Matthäi (1744-1811) shows (Tiurina, *Iz istorii*). The same applies to various religious objects, such as icons and prints, which circulated widely in Russia (Fonkich, *Grecheskie dokumenty*; Khromov and Ialamas, *Gravura*; Fonkitch, Popov and Evseeva, *Mount Athos*). Such contacts were often initiated by Russian higher institutions and individuals acting as patrons and protectors of the Greeks fleeing to Russia. But they also took place on a more informal level through, for example, the Greeks living at the Monastery of St Nicholas in Moscow, which was for a long time the focal point of Graeco-Russian interaction and the main book-selling market (Alexandropoulou, 'Hē hellēnikē monē'). In addition, the geographical dissemination of these contacts was uneven between the lands west of the Briansk-Belgorod frontier and 'Russia proper' on the northern and eastern side of this frontier that formed the core of Muscovy. The ease of movement for Greeks in the western regions (present-day Ukraine) was much greater for most of the 18th century, and so the level of Graeco-Russian interaction was higher here (Carras, 'Connecting').

All the above does not signify the absence of Russian influences (theological, cultural, artistic, etc.) on the Greeks; on the contrary, these influences proved to be important (Boycheva and Drandakē, *Thrēskeutikē*; Boycheva, *Routes*), and they witness to the existence of constant mutual interaction. Perhaps the most important person connecting the two worlds was Archbishop Eugenios Voulgaris (1716-1806), who will be dealt in more detail below. Another prominent figure in this Graeco-Russian exchange was Count Iōannēs Kapodistrias (1776-1831) from the island of Corfu, which (together with the other Ionian islands) never experienced Ottoman rule. Interestingly enough, in 1799 Russia and the Ottomans drove the French out of the Ionian islands and organised them as a

federation (the so-called 'Septinsular Republic'), an aristocratic constitutional, semi-independent state under the sovereignty of the Porte and
the direct protection of Russia (Saul, *Russia*; Stanislavskaia, *Rossiia*). Kapodistrias became one of its ministers until 1807, when the French recaptured the islands. Later, he joined the Russian diplomatic service and
rose to become Russian Foreign Minister (Zanou, 'Imperial nationalism').

Although issues pertaining to the Ottoman Turks and Islam were not
at the top of Graeco-Russian exchanges, we do find evidence of a transfer
of related knowledge, because the Turks and their religion, history and
culture interested the Greeks at this time, albeit mostly from a critical
and negative perspective (de Herdt, 'Greeks'). Yet it should be mentioned
that the Russians themselves also had other opportunities for acquiring
information about the Ottomans and Islam on topics that interested Russian politics and thought (Sverchevskaia and Cherman, *Bibliografiia Turtsii*; Taki, *Tsar and sultan*) through, for example, the Muslim populations
of Central Asia and the Muslim Tatars in Crimea (Khanate of Crimea),
which was a vassal state of the Ottoman Empire (Klein, *The Crimean
Khanate*); or through Russian travellers and pilgrims in the Ottoman
Empire and the Levant (see the entry on 'Russian travellers to Jerusalem
in the first half of the 18th century' in this volume, pp. 620-7). A case in
point is the wandering Ukrainian monk Vasiliĭ Grigorovich Barskiĭ (1701-
47), who undertook a long trip to various places in central Europe, and
especially in the Orthodox East between 1723 and 1747. Among other
places, he visited numerous Greek-populated areas under Ottoman rule
and also learnt Greek. His memoirs, published posthumously first in
1778 and in a better edition in 1885-7 (both in St Petersburg), include
rich information on the differences between the Orthodox Christian and
Islamic faiths, based on his first-hand observations (della Dora, 'Light').

In addition, during the Russo-Turkish War of 1768-74, the Russian
navy was able to make a first planned expedition to the Aegean archipelago to collect information on Ottoman subjects and to map the area
(Ialamas, *Atlas*). Other channels of information included Russian diplomatic services in Ottoman territories (*Rōsoi diplōmates*; Spiridonakis,
'Le consulat'; Dvoichenko-Markov, 'Russia') and the permanent Russian
representatives in Constantinople (Gosudareva, 'Russkaia'), as well as
Ottoman diplomatic missions to Russia (Itzkowitz and Mote, *Mubadele*;
Conermann, 'Das eigene'). The same holds true for Ottoman prisoners of war in Russia and for Russian slaves and fugitives in the Ottoman Empire, who were freed, given amnesty and allowed to settle in
the southern territories of New Russia (Smiley, 'Let whose people go?';

Smiley, 'Meanings'; Smiley, 'Burdens'; Smiley, 'After being'; Taki, *Tsar and sultan*, pp. 17-128). Finally, the Russians could learn a lot about the Ottomans from Western works. Worth mentioning here are the so-called *Kuranty*, Russian hand-written newspapers (replaced under Peter I with the first printed newspaper, the *Sankt-Peterburskie Vedomosti*, 1702). The *Kuranty* gathered news (though often outdated and unreliable) from the Western (mainly German and Dutch) press (Shamin, *Kuranty*; Maĭer and Shamin, 'Otbor'; Waugh, 'News'). Interestingly enough, they also included information about events in the Greek area under Ottoman rule and the Ottoman Empire in general (Shamin, 'Izvestiia grecheskikh'; Shamin, 'Izvestiia "grecheskoĭ"'; Shamin, 'Grecheskaia zemlia'; Shamin, 'Izvestiia o grekakh').

It was in this broader context that knowledge about Islam and the Ottoman Turks was transferred to Russia. This process started in the later decades of the 16th century and involved several categories of agents (Tchesnokova, *Khristianskiĭ Vostok*). Among them, were Greeks and Hellenophones from the Ottoman Empire and the Danubian Principalities who travelled to Russia, mostly as merchants. Their knowledge of the languages of the Ottoman Empire and of Ottoman political affairs made them uncommonly valuable to the Muscovite rulers, who often employed them as spies. Some of them decided to settle in Muscovy and officially entered the Muscovite diplomatic apparatus, such as the Moldavian-Greek scholar Nicolae Spatharius (Russian, Spafariĭ), better known as Nicolae Milescu (1636-1708), who was invested by Tsar Alekseĭ Mikhailovich (r. 1645-76) with a mission to explore the Central Asia regions. The results of his travels are presented in several works written in or translated into Russian, which circulated widely among Russian political and learned circles (Mihail, 'La diffusion'; Belobrova, 'O rukopisnoĭ traditsii'). A similar case is that of Vasilios Vatatzēs (1694-after 1748), a Constantinople-born scholar, merchant, traveller, explorer and diplomat, who emigrated to Russia at an early age. His poem *Persika* (1748), written in Greek, includes a lot of historical and ethnographic information based on his observations during his travels in Iran and Central Asia and during the diplomatic missions he conducted between Russia and Iran (see the entry 'Vasilios Vatatzēs, *Vatatzou Persika. Ta en Persidi, hosa en etesi trisi kai pentēkonta, ek te tou 1694 kai mechri te tou 1747*', in this volume, pp. 325-30).

Greek prelates dreaming of the final victory of Orthodox Russia over the 'infidel' Turks were involved in exchanges with Russia as early as the 16th century (von Scheliha, *Rußland*; Tchesnokova, *Khristianskiĭ*

Vostok; Tchentsova, 'Le clergé grec'). The learned Patriarch Dositheos II of Jerusalem (1641-1707), for instance, had very close contacts with Russia (Todt, 'Dositheos II'). In a letter he sent to Peter I (1 September 1701), following the beginning of Russian diplomatic relations with the Ottomans, he extols the achievements of Peter's reign and his care for the Orthodox peoples. He also refers to an incident involving the Russian ambassador to the Sublime Porte, who had asked for more titles for the Russian emperor to be added to an *ahdname* (the official agreement between the Ottoman Empire and European states), but to no avail. Dositheos explained that this was usual and understandable, given that the Ottomans could not refer to Christians with such titles because it would be considered an insult to their own religion. Dositheos also collected other such agreements to examine whether this was the case with other European states. In fact, it was true, and such characterisations of Christian rulers were always uttered by the Ottomans in an indirect and reserved way. Therefore, Dositheos suggested to Peter that he should follow the same policy and speak only indirectly about the Ottomans (as being the most important in the religion of Muḥammad, etc.) (Ialamas, 'Ierusalimskiĭ', pp. 480-1).

Dositheos II's learned nephew and successor Chrysanthos Notaras (c. 1663-1731) also had close relations with Russia, where he participated twice in official missions on behalf of his uncle and made useful contacts. He was the author of important theological and scientific writings including several works about Islam, such as on Mecca and Medina, on insurrections in the Ottoman Empire in the early 18th century and on Arab astronomy, which was also applied to religious matters (Stathē, *Chrysanthos*, pp. 192-3, 197-201). It is also known that several of Notaras' works were translated into Russian and disseminated accordingly (Ramazanova, 'Perevody').

Other Greeks were also involved in the dissemination of knowledge about Islam and the Ottoman Turks in Russia. Helladius's book mentioned above has a polemical character and criticises the Halle Pietists and other Western European scholars, but it contains a lot of information (not always reliable) about the Orthodox Church and the Greeks under Ottoman rule, and in some cases gives indirect information about the Ottomans and their religious culture. Helladius moved to Russia in 1715 to work as a physician. His book was circulated there as well and was read by an important advisor of Peter I in church matters, Archbishop Feofan Prokopovich of Novgorod (1681-1736), who had a copy of it in his personal library (Makridēs, 'Stoicheia').

Needless to say, many other Greek scholars at the time went to Petrine Russia or were invited to work there (Karathanassis, 'Pierre'). Among them, one may count the learned Anastasios Michaēl (c. 1675-1725) from Naousa in Macedonia (often called and known as 'Nausios' and 'Macedo'; see Mēnaoglou, *Ho Anastasios*; Mēnaoglou, *Historia*, pp. 15-51), who had travelled and studied extensively in Central and Western Europe (e.g. in Germany), where he established close contacts in many academic and political circles and published several works. Among other things, he extolled the role of Peter I as protector of the Orthodox peoples under Ottoman rule in a panegyric delivered in Moscow in 1709 and published in Russian and Greek a little later (Michaēl, *Teatr*). In 1715, Michaēl went to live permanently in Russia and held important administrative positions, becoming in 1722 one of the assessors of the Holy Synod of the Russian Church (Cracraft, *Church reform*, pp. 173-4, n. 7).

Michaēl was associated with the polymath and multilingual Moldavian Prince Dimitrie Cantemir (1673-1723), whom he served in various positions. After the Stănileşti defeat, in which he was personally involved as Peter the Great's ally, Cantemir spent the last years of his life in Russia. His works on the Ottoman Empire and Islam (*Incrementorum et Decrementorum Aulae Othomanicae*, *Sistema de religione et statu Imperii Turcici*, *Curanus*) became internationally acclaimed and he was considered a pioneer in Oriental studies. Some of his writings were translated into Russian and circulated among the high echelons of Russian society. *Sistema de religione et statu Imperii Turcici* was published in St Petersburg (as *Kniga Sistema, ili Sostoianie mukhammedanskiia religii*, 1722) by order of Peter the Great, to whom it is dedicated (see the entry 'Dimitrie Cantemir' by Ovidiu-Victor Olar, in this volume, pp. 317-21).

Cantemir spoke very positively of Michaēl and his skills. He also referred to the Greek Anastasius (renamed Athanasius after his ordination) Condoidi (1677-1737), who was the tutor to his sons (Cantemir, *History*, p. 100) and later played a significant role in Russian public life. Condoidi moved to Russia with Cantemir, and in 1721 he was also appointed assessor of the Holy Synod, before becoming Bishop of Vologda and later of Suzdal (Cracraft, *Church reform*, pp. 171-2; Karathanassis, 'Contribution', pp. 159-71).

All this shows the role of the intellectual, religious and political élite of the time as a channel of communication and exchange between Balkan Orthodox peoples living under Ottoman rule and Russia.

Eugenios Voulgaris and the anti-Ottoman literature of his time
A prominent figure in Graeco-Russian cultural relations was the church hierarch and polymath Eugenios Voulgaris, who studied in Italy, taught at various Greek schools in the Ottoman Empire, and published his works while pursuing his studies further in Germany. In 1771, he moved to Russia at the invitation of Catherine II, and lived there until the end of his long life, pursuing a distinguished career, from 1775 as archbishop of Slaviansk and Kherson in Novorossiia, the new strategic frontier of the Russian Empire. Voulgaris was a highly esteemed person in his time, and also had a place in Russian designs to expand to the south on the demise of the Ottoman Empire. He was thus a welcome and extremely useful addition to the 'Greek project' and Potëmkin's policies (Batalden, *Catherine II's Greek prelate*).

Concerning Islam, it is worthwhile mentioning here a booklet written by Voulgaris entitled *Stochasmoi eis tous parontas krisimous Kairous, tou Kratous tou Othōmanikou* ('Reflections on the current critical moments of the Ottoman state', no place or date, but probably printed in St Petersburg between 1771 and 1772 with no mention of the author; reedited in Corfu in 1851 and 1854, as well as later reprints). It was also translated into Russian by Aleksandr Kruglikov under the title *Razsuzhdenie na deistvitel'no kriticheskoe sostoianie Ottomanskoĭ Porty* and published in Moscow in 1780 (dedicated to Count Mikhail Petrovich Rumiantsev, 1751-1811) and again in 1788 during the Russo-Turkish War (Batalden, *Catherine II's Greek prelate*, p. 157). There was also a French translation of the booklet (Stiernon, 'Eugène', pp. 766-7), which shows that it was circulated and widely read in Russia, attracting significant attention (Bacmeister, *Russische Bibliothek*, pp. 418-24).

Voulgaris tries in this work to assess the political situation of the time in view of the Russo-Turkish War and to explore the potential for active European (especially Russian) intervention in Ottoman affairs. He also touches upon a topic that was amply discussed at the time, namely the progressing decay and expected demise of the Ottoman Empire, as well as its questionable potential for reform (Lewis, 'Some reflections'; Lewis, 'Ottoman observers'; Howard, 'Ottoman historiography'; Kafadar, 'Question'; Pippidi, 'Décadence'; Kaiser, 'Evil empire?'; Aksan, 'Breaking'). Voulgaris had intimate knowledge of socio-political conditions within the Ottoman Empire and was able to contextualise it within the wider European geopolitical and military coordinates of his era. He thought that, apart from France, which had considerable commercial interests in the Levant, all other European nations could easily undertake a common enterprise against the Ottomans. Otherwise, the Ottoman threat would lead to tragic and disastrous consequences for the preservation of the Christian identity of Europe. He also rejected various circulating hopes of a Muslim-Ottoman messianism concerning alleged divine support for the Ottoman Empire, which was expected to conquer the entire world in the wake of some radical internal reforms.

In his booklet, Voulgaris drew heavily on the work of the Hungarian-born Ottoman diplomat, polymath and convert to Islam İbrahim Müteferrika (1674-1745) entitled *Uṣūl al-ḥikam fī niẓām al-umam* ('Rational bases for the order of nations'; Constantinople/İstanbul, 1731 or 1732), which had been translated into French by the Austrian diplomat Karl Emmerich Alexander, Baron Reviczky von Revisnye (1737-93) under the title *Traité de la tactique ou méthode artificielle pour l'ordonnance des troupes* (Vienna, 1769). He also drew on Voltaire, Montesquieu and Dimitrie Cantemir. He remarks in his work that it is precisely the Turks' religion and religious ardour that do not allow them to accept their obvious decline, given that everything they believe in is based on the prophecies of Muḥammad about the magnificent future of Islam. Muslims believe that they are the most holy, God-pleasing and elect people on earth, chosen by God to conquer the entire world. The same arrogant attitude driven by their religious zeal applies to their reign, which – according to these convictions – will never be threatened with extinction and will not be shaken by the small and insignificant political powers of Europe. History is regarded as amply corroborating this strong belief, given that Islam still thrives despite Christian counter initiatives and attempts in the past (crusades, etc.), which in the end achieved nothing worthwhile. Hence, both the glorious faith and the reign of the Muslims depend strongly on each other and form a robust and durable unity, which it is believed will remain unchanged until the end of the world. In this respect, they are both basically out of this world – contrary to the reign and the faith of the Christians (Voulgaris, *Stochasmoi*, pp. 2-3). If there is a temporary decline or defeat of the Muslim army, this will take place in accordance with the will of God, who allows such things to happen in order to make Muslims better and more capable in the long run. Muslims believe that there are many reasons for such infelicities, ranging from transgressions against the divine law and the abolition of justice to insubordination, corruption and lack of tactics among the soldiers. Yet, all this by no means threatens the unshaken Muslim belief that Ottoman rule is basically indestructible and indissoluble. The whole story resembles for Voulgaris eclipses of the sun: these only last for a while, and the sun always shines again. It is thus strongly believed that if Muslims put their hopes in the righteousness, goodness and power of the eternal God and follow the precepts of the Prophet Muḥammad, their glorious victories are guaranteed and will inevitably continue in the future (Voulgaris, *Stochasmoi*, pp. 3-4).

Yet, according to Voulgaris, things seem to be different with regard to the Russo-Turkish confrontation in his time. This is because the Russians are posing for the first time a serious threat to the Ottomans, even if the latter are mostly reluctant to acknowledge it. For Voulgaris, it is an indisputable fact that the Ottomans are the cardinal and systemic enemies of Christendom, and this is something that will never change. War against Christians is clearly outlined in the chapter on war in the Qur'an. It is about the so-called jihad, holy war, which is engaged in solely for the glory of God and the true faith of Islam, not to obtain material things and mundane glory, as other states and religions usually try to do. This is why Muslims are ready to sacrifice their lives for their faith and to attain eternal happiness in heaven (Voulgaris, *Stochasmoi*, pp. 4-5). In a footnote, Voulgaris mentions a story he had heard during the Russo-Turkish War of 1768-74 about an incident involving an Ottoman prisoner who suddenly attacked his Russian guards. When he was arrested, he asked them to kill him so that he could receive the compensation promised by Muḥammad and enjoy milk, honey and virgins in Paradise (Voulgaris, *Stochasmoi*, pp. 15-6). For Voulgaris, there is little, if any, chance that Muslims, who are basically barbarians, uneducated, unthankful and malicious, will abandon their 'pseudo-religion' and humanise themselves by coming closer to Christian and civilised Europe and by reforming their own characters and their state. But even if this possibility is minimal, the long-term prospects for Christian Europe are still precarious because the Ottomans may improve themselves to such a degree that they will pose a greater danger in the future, which will be more difficult to deal with. Voulgaris goes back through history to recall the grave dangers posed by Muslims to Europe since the early 8th century, mentioning the fall of Constantinople in 1453 and the two unsuccessful sieges of Vienna in 1529 and 1683. During the 18th century, the Ottomans certainly did not achieve any major successes, but all this has more to do with the overall stagnation in their religion and nation, the pathologies of their socio-political system, and their weakening military power, complacency and mentality, as well as their overall way of life (Voulgaris, *Stochasmoi*, pp. 6-7).

Voulgaris further rejects a widespread argument of the time that the Ottomans were no longer as powerful as they had been in the past and that they had definitely lost momentum. On the contrary, he believes that they still share the military virtues and self-confidence that had rendered them very successful in the past. They also have a number of advantages in warfare, because they are resolutely driven by the fervour of their religion and their passion for the glory of their state. Their current problems have mostly to do with their arrogance and contempt for other nations and their neglect of development, including the improvement of their military training and operations, with the result that they lack a tactical army and other advantages that have been implemented by the European powers. Ottoman modernisation should thus not be allowed to take place, as the Ottoman danger will eventually become much greater, the more so because authors like Müteferrika himself, after learning about European progress, have started to think on this situation and have called for a thorough modernisation of the Ottoman army and political system along the European model. In order to be able to move the Ottomans away from their comfortable inertia, Müteferrika has also tried to counter Ottoman beliefs about fate and the deterministic view of history according to which the divinely ordained Ottoman nation will never succumb or be destroyed by 'infidels', because these have only restricted permission to inflict damage. However, apart from God's plans and providence for the Muslims, Müteferrika argues that they must modernise themselves in every respect in order to be able to remain successful (Voulgaris, *Stochasmoi*, pp. 4, 7-12).

Despite all this, Voulgaris adds, many still argue that various reasons and hindrances, including their religion and traditionalism, will ultimately prevent the Muslims from managing to learn and profit from other peoples and cultures. Voulgaris considers this argument completely wrong, given that numerous examples from history clearly show exactly the opposite. Apart from the deficits in their character, Muslims have various advantages, such as bravery, an ingenious spirit, magnanimity, ambition and impetuosity. They are thus ready to leave aside even things considered 'sacred' in order to make room for military progress and success. Accordingly, they have employed many foreigners in their service and learned from their expertise. They may dislike European mores and way of life, but they admire European science and technological progress. The very same Müteferrika has also contributed to this and has introduced for the first time a printing press in Constantinople and even published books using Arabic characters (Voulgaris, *Stochasmoi*, pp. 12-7).

Therefore, Muslim traditionalism no longer enjoys absolute value. The potential reactions of the ulemas and their concern to safeguard traditional Islam intact, even if real, do not possess eternal value, for their decisions can be revoked. Passages of the Qur'an can be interpreted in many ways, whereas in the end everything is possible if it relates to the protection and salvation of the Muslims and their victory. In some cases, Muslims have even been pioneers, and it was in fact from them that the Europeans learned various novel things (Voulgaris, *Stochasmoi*, pp. 17-20). The same holds true of their supposed resistance to learning, which can also be changed. Voulgaris mentions here as a comparison the pre-modern and modern level of the development of Russia under Peter I and Catherine II, in order to show that development and progress are possible for all peoples, including the Ottomans. In the same vein, he criticises those Christians who work in Ottoman service and help their masters to achieve progress in various domains. In addition, the Ottomans' lack of order and punctuality has, in his view, been much exaggerated, because these elements can be observed in their palaces, mosques and elsewhere. In fact, *firmans* and *fetvas* are means that are used to bring discipline and order and the same is true of their army, where lack of order and punctuality are unknown. There are also many ongoing internal discussions among the Ottomans on how to improve things and progress. Müteferrika himself acknowledges this, claiming that such changes have already been made in the Ottoman navy. He also takes the modernisation of Petrine Russia as a model for the Ottomans and gives them concrete advice on how to improve their army (Voulgaris, *Stochasmoi*, pp. 20-7). All this should alert Christian Europe and make it more vigilant. Ottoman progress will not be delayed much longer, as has already been shown by many events in the 18th century. In other words, the Ottomans are even ready to question their religious authorities in order to achieve a better goal for themselves, and this is bound to happen in the near future (Voulgaris, *Stochasmoi*, pp. 27-30).

Given the Ottomans' potential to develop and pose anew a real threat to Europe, Voulgaris finally proceeds to a discussion of the issue of the balance of power in Europe, especially in the eventuality of the dissolution of the Ottoman Empire, although some European states were categorically against such a plan. Among the weaknesses of the Ottoman Empire, Voulgaris includes the dissatisfaction and frustration of its non-Muslim subjects, especially the Greeks, who are discriminated against and tortured by the Ottomans in many ways. This 'Holocaust' is a sacrifice to the Ka'ba in Mecca and can no longer be tolerated by Christian Europe.

Ironically enough, the potential creation of a small free Greek state is considered by some to threaten the balance of power in Europe, although other much more significant changes in European political affairs are allowed to happen or have been accommodated without problems. Voulgaris criticises here the double standards of the Christian powers of Europe and accuses them of hypocrisy because they lack the Christian zeal to proceed to a more effective and decisive military assault against the Ottomans and the 'pseudo-religion of Muḥammad', one that could radically change the current map of Europe (Voulgaris, *Stochasmoi*, pp. 30-6). The counter-argument is that such a plan will automatically strengthen the Russian Empire and its expansionist policies, yet this is discarded by Voulgaris as totally unpersuasive. First, the threat from the Ottomans is much greater because of their religion and their inherent determination eventually to subject all Christian Europe, which the Russians by no means intend to do. Second, Russia has already expanded enough and appears to be completely self-sufficient as a country. What Russia needs is only people ready to populate its existing and newly-acquired territories. Third, the uncontrolled new territorial expansion of Russia would have various detrimental effects (in terms of organisation, administration, etc.), so it is currently unwelcome. Fourth, other European powers may also profit more than Russia from the end of Ottoman control over the European provinces in their Empire, which may allow the creation of a Greek sovereign state there. However, because of their commercial interests and relations with the Ottomans, three European powers, England, France and Holland, have traditionally supported the continuation of Ottoman control over these European provinces and have always portrayed this situation as beneficial for the whole of Europe. At that time, this position was strongly supported by France, which, for Voulgaris, was totally insane considering the huge damage historically inflicted by the Muslims and their religion on Christian Europe. Voulgaris particularly emphasises here the religious opposition between the two worlds and tries to avert the incoming 'Islamisation' of Europe. His is an appeal to Christian rulers in Europe and to Christians in Europe generally to overcome their differences and reach a compromise to combat their common Muslim enemy. In his opinion, the Ottoman Empire is in decline and, as the Russian victories over it have vividly shown, its fall does not lie in the remote future, so this is a unique opportunity for Christian Europe to defeat the Turks and enhance the security of Europe, or face disastrous consequences (Voulgaris, *Stochasmoi*, pp. 36-40).

Voulgaris's work for the Russians is a political manifesto and an assessment of the state of the Ottomans written from a Greek perspective with hopes for eventual liberation (Carras, "'Topos" and utopia', pp. 144-9). For him, the creation of an independent Greek state of moderate size through a partition of certain Ottoman provinces would not change the balance of power. Thus, his work fits well into a series of similar endeavours by various Western and Russian actors analysing the observed decline of the Ottoman Empire and reflecting on how to profit from it (Taki, *Tsar and sultan*, pp. 131-41). During the Russo-Turkish War between 1771 and 1772, Voulgaris and others wrote or translated a number of books and pamphlets into Greek (including some philhellenic and anti-Ottoman texts by Voltaire) in the context of the Russian expansionist policies against the Ottoman Empire and in support of the Greek dreams for liberation, praising Catherine II's patronage of Orthodox Christians in the Ottoman Empire and her just war against the Ottomans. These were published in St Petersburg and Moscow, and some were also later translated into Russian (Bacmeister, *Russische Bibliothek*, pp. 431-6, 468-71; Camariano, 'Hepta'; Stiernon, 'Eugène', pp. 767-8, 776-8; Zorin, *Kormia*, pp. 59-62).

It should also be mentioned that Voulgaris published in Greek a genealogical list of Ottoman sultans as an appendix to a book about Georgios Kastriotis/Skanderbeg (c. 1405-68), which he had translated from French, and was posthumously published in Moscow in 1812 (Voulgaris, 'Genealogikos'). There was also a Russian translation of this book, published in 1852 in Moscow (Batalden, *Catherine II's Greek prelate*, pp. 153-4; Stiernon, 'Eugène', p. 782). Given Voulgaris's general contacts with the highest echelons of Russian society at the time, the general admiration and recognition that he enjoyed, and his extensive network (e.g. with Platon Levshin, Metropolitan of Moscow, 1737-1812; see Carras, 'Understanding'), it is very probable that he was also instrumental in disseminating information about the Ottomans and their culture to a Russian audience. This was, of course, in line with Russia's position at that time against the Ottoman Empire.

There is also a lot of scattered information in these anti-Ottoman texts about the situation in the declining Ottoman Empire, Ottoman culture and the religion of Islam. This applies to a short work that was initially wrongly attributed to the Florentine philologist and philhellene Giovanni Maria del Turco (1739-1800), with a Greek translation also attributed to Voulgaris (*Iketēria tou genous tōn Graikōn pros pasan tēn Christianikēn Eurōpēn* ['A supplication of the Greek people to the whole of Christian Europe']; Stiernon, 'Eugène', pp. 767-8). Its original author was most probably a Greek from Naples named Antōnios Gkikas, who published it first in the Italian newspaper *Notizie del mondo* (issues 54 and 55 of 6 and 9 July 1771). A French translation (20 July 1771) in the *Courrier du Bas-Rhin* and a Russian translation in the *Sankt-Peterburskie Vedomosti* (issue 65, 8 August 1771) followed. The text was also translated into various other languages (Greek, Romanian) and enjoyed wide circulation, both in manuscript and in print. It was published anonymously separately as a pamphlet in Greek in St Petersburg in 1771 or 1772 (Kanellopoulos, 'Poios synegrapse'; Camariano, 'Hepta', pp. 5-7). Voulgaris had most probably something to do with the Greek version of the text and its publication in Russia, given that this Greek translation contains various ideas and even terms found in his own *Stochasmoi*, which appeared at the very same time in Russia.

This work was written from the perspective of the 'poor Greek genos' and it is clearly pro-Hellenic. It constitutes an appeal by the enslaved Greek nation to the European powers for help and support because it has been suffering for many centuries under the tyrannical and despotic Ottoman yoke. The Ottomans are basically driven by their 'Mohammedan religion', which functions as either a retarding or a destructive force. If they had followed their own interests based on their religion, the Ottomans would have eliminated all Greeks long ago because persecution of all other peoples on religious grounds is considered a distinguishing feature of the Ottomans. Nevertheless, the Greeks have managed to maintain their identity under extremely harsh conditions, and to develop intellectually, artistically, commercially and financially, from which even the barbaric reign of the Ottomans, which views learning as useless and potentially dangerous, has been able to profit (Gkikas, *Iketēria*, pp. 1-2). There is also a danger that thousands of Christian Greeks may freely or forcibly convert to Islam and support the Ottomans in their military operations against Christian Europe. This would certainly not only be an abominable act of betrayal of Christianity, but would also clearly go against the interests of Christian Europe. Such a danger is quite imminent for the Greeks, unless God supports them actively because of their infirmities. A joint Christian war against the Ottomans would primarily serve the purpose of liberating Christians and their religion from a harsh foreign yoke. It has been attempted by various Christian nations (Venetians, Austrians, etc.) in the past, and at this very time it is also being attempted by Catherine II. But any attempt that failed would result in the Ottomans taking brutal revenge against the local Christian population, as has already taken place in several places in the Ottoman Empire (Gkikas, *Iketēria*, pp. 3-6).

The author argues here for a united Christian Europe against the Ottomans and Islam, who are regarded as alien to European culture. In the eyes of the Ottomans, though, there is a closer alliance between Russians and Greeks because of their shared Orthodox faith. This makes the whole situation much more critical and dangerous, as the Ottomans would now try to exterminate any potential threat from this alliance by targeting and attacking the Orthodox Greeks, which makes the wider European Christian support of the Greek case an absolute imperative. In fact, it would have been much easier for the Greeks to convert to Islam and enjoy privileges in the Ottoman Empire instead of waiting for help from Christian Europe. However, despite their disappointment, they still prefer to follow the path of martyrdom and perseverance in extremely harsh conditions by firmly adhering to their Christian identity. Gkikas also claims that the number of Christians in the Ottoman Empire surpasses that of the Turks, so it would certainly be detrimental to the interests of the Christian powers if this huge number of Christians under Ottoman rule eventually converted to Islam. This was because these converted Christians would then be used against Christian Europe, as is demonstrated by the cases of the famous, merciless and most brave Janissary corps of the Ottoman army, the Turco-Albanians and the Bosnians, who are all 'Turkicised Christians'. It is thus crucial to keep the existing balance of power between Europe and the Ottomans under control. In addition, it is possible that the Ottomans could gradually learn and profit from the military power of Christian Europe, not least because they often use such military experts in their own cause and wars (Gkikas, *Iketēria*, pp. 6-8). Finally, Gkikas hopes that a political leader (a king) would arise in Western Europe, truly driven by Christian convictions, who, on the one hand would finally free the Greeks from the Ottomans, and on the other would liberate Christian Europe from the Ottoman fear once and for all. Such a person would act in accordance with Divine Providence and would be responsible before God for the souls of Orthodox Greeks (Gkikas, *Iketēria*, pp. 8-9).

Gkikas concludes that there is no possibility of peace or compromise between the Ottomans and other nations. This has primarily to do with the Ottomans' religion, which not only does not allow trust in people of other faiths, but also urges Muslims not to befriend other believers. By being non-Muslim, these people are basically deprived of any privileges in the eyes of the Ottomans according to their religion. Even if the Ottomans are repeatedly defeated, they will continue their military assaults against Christians precisely because of this fundamental and permanent element of their religion that urges them to destroy, to obstruct development or to enslave other nations, namely their fundamental sense of being stronger and superior. Thus, a new peace treaty with the Ottomans would be useless, and its initiators would bear the burden of all the evil that Christians have suffered at the hands of the Ottomans so far and in the future. The events of 1683, when the Ottomans were about to capture Vienna, show the imminent and constant danger they are able to pose. There is an absolute need to act towards the Ottomans with perseverance, braveness and determination, and certainly not with a compromising, soft and tame attitude. Because of their religion, the Ottomans are destined not to change and will always be characterised by uncontrollable violence and brutality against all other peoples. In contrast, the Christian powers of Europe (and at present Russia, being at war with the Ottomans) have a different point of departure when they fight against the Ottomans. Therefore, it is pointless to go on making inadequate and inoperable compromises with the Ottomans, as was often the case in the past, instead of exterminating once and for all this 'enemy of all humankind'. Gkikas makes clear at the end that the plea to the Christian powers of Europe was not to sacrifice their armies or their citizens for the Greek cause, but to protect and save the Greeks from massive extermination due to Ottoman retaliations and other revenge measures (Gkikas, *Iketēria*, pp. 9-10). This work reflects Greek fears in the wake of the later developments in the Russo-Turkish War of 1768-74, which did not lead to the liberation of Greece, as many Greeks expected and dreamed of at that time.

SIGNIFICANCE

The 18th century is certainly crucial in the long history of Graeco-Russian relations; it was a time when they intensified and made an essential contribution to the Greek national awakening and the outbreak of the Greek War of Independence in 1821. Because of Orthodox Christian ties between Greeks and Russians, these relations had a clear anti-Ottoman character, as both peoples were keenly interested in the demise of Ottoman rule in the Balkans. Although the two partners were not always intent on exactly the same goals, this Graeco-Russian collaboration aimed, among other things, at creating a free Greek Orthodox state or a new Christian

Empire, whether under direct Russian influence or not. In the context of such close relations and exchanges between Greeks and Russians in the 18ᵗʰ century, knowledge about the Muslim tradition of the Ottomans and Islam in general was also disseminated through numerous channels by various Greeks to Russia. It is understandable that in this frame of reference the initial Orthodox hostility to the Ottomans often turned into a broader opposition to Islam. Both the Orthodox Christian Graeco-Russian alliance and the broader European community were portrayed in Greek works as directed against the alien Muslim invader. The progressive weakening of the Ottoman Empire was presented as a unique opportunity for the formation of a wider Christian European coalition aimed at expelling the Ottomans from the Christian European continent. If this did not happen, it was thought certain that the European Christian powers would once more face a renewed and strong Ottoman Empire, whose expansion could put the Christian character of Europe in great jeopardy. In addition, the antithesis between Christianity and Islam was outlined in absolute terms, and emphasis was put on the tribulations of Christians under Ottoman rule. The religion of Islam was further presented as having had a great and wholesale formative impact upon the character of the Ottoman people, their socio-political structures, and their culture.

By portraying the entire socio-political and religious situation in this way, Greeks hoped to persuade both Russia and the other European powers to stop commercial and other exchanges with the Ottomans and to undertake a more systematic crusade against them in order to solve the problem of the Muslim presence in Europe once and for all. All these Greek attempts fitted well into the wider philhellenic spirit of the 18ᵗʰ century across Europe, which envisaged the liberation of modern Greeks, the worthy descendants of the glorious Hellenes of Antiquity, from Ottoman rule.

Certainly, disseminating information about Islam as a religion was not the central aspect of this Graeco-Russian exchange, because the relationship had a broader scope and was basically underscored by Russian political and military designs against the Ottomans. Nevertheless, it was one of the numerous channels through which information about the Ottomans and Islam reached Russian soil.

It should finally be noted that both Greek and Russian perceptions of the Ottomans and Islam at that time usually come under the heading 'Orientalism' (de Herdt, 'Greeks'; Taki, 'Orientalism'), although there were many forms of 'Orientalism' and the East European one was not identical with its West European counterpart (David-Fox, Holquist and Martin, *Orientalism*).

PUBLICATIONS

Anastasios Michaël, *Teatr ili Zercalo Monarkhov* [...] *Vasilikon Theatron* [...], Amsterdam, 1710 (new edition of the Greek text ed. Ch.A. Mēnaoglou, *Ho Anastasios Michaël kai ho Logos peri Hellēnismou*, Athens, 2013, γ΄- κ΄)

Alexander Helladius, *Status praesens Ecclesiae Graecae* [...], [Altdorf], 1714; H.eccl. 472 (digitised version available through *MDZ*)

[Antōnios Gkikas], *Iketēria tou Genous tōn Graikōn pros pasan tēn Christianikēn Eurōpēn*, St Petersburg [?], 1771 or 1772; new edition ed. P.Ē. Ēliou, *Prosthēkes stēn Ellinikē Vivliographia. I. Ta vivliographika kataloipa tou É. Legrand kai tou H. Pernot* (1515-1799), Athens, 1973, 290-300

[Eugenios Voulgaris], *Stochasmoi eis tous parontas krisimous Kairous, tou Kratous tou Othōmanikou*, St Petersburg [?], 1771 or 1772 (further editions, Corfu, 1851 and 1854; Athens, 1996)

Eugenios Voulgaris, 'Genealogikos katalogos tōn Othōmanōn Soultanōn', in J.-N. Duponcet, *Epitomē tēs historias Geōrgiou tou Kastriōtou tou eponomasthentos Skentermpey, Vasileōs tēs Alvanias*, trans. from the French by E. Voulgaris, Moscow, 1812, 293-348

STUDIES

On Eugenios Voulgaris

Ch. Karanasios (ed.), *Eugenios Voulgarēs. Ho homo universalis tou Neou Hellēnismou. 300 chronia apo tē gennēsē tou*, Athens, 2018

I. Carras, 'Understanding God and tolerating humankind. Orthodoxy and the Enlightenment in Evgenios Voulgaris and Platon Levshin', in P.M. Kitromēlides (ed.), *Enlightenment and religion in the Orthodox world*, Oxford, 2016, 73-139

S. Reichelt, 'Griechische Gelehrte in Deutschland im 18. Jahrhundert. Evgenios Vulgaris - Thomas Mandakasis - Nikiforos Theotokis in Halle und Leipzig und die orthodoxe Gemeinde zu Leipzig', *Ostkirchliche Studien* 61 (2012) 177-99

E. Angelomatē-Tsougarakē (ed.), *Eugenios Voulgarēs. Praktika Diethnous Synedriou, Kerkyra, 1-3 Dekemvriou 2006*, Athens, 2009

I. Carras, '"Topos" and utopia in Evgenios Voulgaris' life and work (1716-1806)', *The Historical Review* 1 (2004) 127-56

D. Stiernon, 'Eugène Boulgaris', in C.G. Conticello and V. Conticello (eds), *La théologie byzantine et sa tradition*, vol. 2, Turnhout, 2002,

721-848

G.L. Bruess, *Religion, identity and Empire. A Greek archbishop in the Russia of Catherine the Great*, Boulder CO, 1997

G. Podskalsky, *Griechische Theologie in der Zeit der Türkenherrschaft (1453-1821). Die Orthodoxie im Spannungsfeld der nachreformatorischen Konfessionen des Westens*, Munich, 1988, 344-53 (rich bibliography)

N. Camariano, 'Hepta spania hellēnika phylladia dēmosieumena stēn Petroupolē (1771-1772)', *Ho Eranistēs* 18 (1986) 1-34

S.K. Batalden, *Catherine II's Greek prelate. Eugenios Voulgaris in Russia, 1771-1806*, Boulder CO, 1982

On Iketēria tou Genous tōn Graikōn

Camariano, 'Hepta spania hellēnika phylladia dēmosieumena stēn Petroupolē'

P. Kanellopoulos, 'Poios synegrapse tēn *Iketērian tou Genous tōn Graikōn pros pasan tēn christianikēn Eurōpēn?*', *Nea Hestia* 106 (1979) 908-16

P.Ē. Ēliou, *Prosthēkes stēn Ellinikē Vivliographia*, vol. 1. *Ta vivliographika kataloipa tou É. Legrand kai tou H. Pernot (1515-1799)*, Athens, 1973, pp. 290-300

See also:

Paroikiakos Ellēnismos (150s -190s ai.) / *Greek migration to Europe (15th-19th c.)*;   http://www.ime.gr/projects/migration/15-19/gr/v2/russia.html

I. Maïer and S.M. Shamin, 'Otbor informatsii dlia "kurantov" i tekhnika perevoda v Kollegii inostrannykh del v 1720-e gody', *Vestnik Volgogradskogo Gosudarstvennogo Universiteta. Seriia 4, Istoriia. Regionovedenie. Mezhdunarodnye otnosheniia* 23 (2018) 71-88

Y. Boycheva and A. Drandakē (eds), *Thrēskeutikē technē apo tē Rōsia stēn Hellada (160s-190s aiōnas)*, Athens, 2017

J. Leikin, '"The prostitution of the Russian flag". Privateers in Russian admiralty courts, 1787-98', *Law and History Review* 35 (2017) 1049-81

Y. Boycheva (ed.), *Routes of Russian icons in the Balkans (16th-early 20th centuries)*, Seyssel, 2016

I. Carras, 'Connecting migration and identities. Godparenthood, surety and Greeks in the Russian Empire (18th-early 19th centuries)', in O. Katsiardi-Hering and M.A. Stassinopoulou (eds), *Across the Danube. Southeastern Europeans and their travelling identities (17th-19th c.)*, Leiden, 2016, 65-109

V. della Dora, 'Light and sight. Vasilij Grigorovich Barskij, Mount Athos and the geographies of eighteenth-century Russian Orthodox Enlightenment', *Journal of Historical Geography* 53 (2016) 86-103

J. Hennings, *Russia and courtly Europe. Ritual and the culture of diplomacy, 1648-1725*, Cambridge, 2016

Ch.A. Mēnaoglou, *Historia tou Rōsikou Kommatos. Dōdeka meletes gia tis aparches*, Athens, 2016

V. Taki, *Tsar and sultan. Russian encounters with the Ottoman Empire*, London, 2016

K. Zanou, 'Imperial nationalism and Orthodox Enlightenment. A diasporic story between the Ionian islands, Russia and Greece, ca. 1800-30', in I. Maurizio and K. Zanou (eds), *Mediterranean diasporas. Politics and ideas in the long nineteenth century*, London, 2016, 117-34

E. Sifnaiou and G. Harlaftē (eds), *Oi Hellēnes tēs Azophikēs. Nees prosengiseis stēn istoria tōn Hellēnōn tēs notias Rōsias*, Athens, 2015

E.B. Smilianskaia, *Grecheskie ostrova Ėkateriny II. Opyty imperskoĭ politiki Rossii v Sredizemnomor'e*, Moscow, 2015

E.B. Smilianskaia, 'Catherine's liberation of the Greeks. High-minded discourse and everyday realities', in M. Di Salvo, D.H. Kaiser and V.A. Kivelson (eds), *Word and image in Russian history. Essays in honor of Gary Marker*, Boston MA, 2015, 71-89

V. Taki, 'Limits of protection. Russia and the Orthodox coreligionists in the Ottoman Empire', *The Carl Beck Papers in Russian and East European Studies* 2014 (2015), University of Pittsburgh, April 2015; http://carlbeckpapers.pitt.edu/ojs/index.php/cbp/issue/view/174

V. Tchentsova, 'Le clergé grec, la Russie et la Valachie à l'époque de Constantin Brâncoveanu. Le témoignage des archives russes', in P. Guran (ed.), *Constantin Brâncoveanu et le monde de l'Orthodoxie*, Bucharest, 2015, 96-104

Iu. Priakhin, *Geroi pamiatnykh sobytiĭ XVIII-XIX vekov. Istoricheskie ocherki*, St Petersburg, 2014

D.N. Ramazanova, 'Perevody sochineniĭ ierusalimskogo patriarkha Xrisanfa Notary v russkikh spiskakh XVIII v.', in B.L. Fonkich (ed.), *Spetsial'nye istoricheskie distsipliny. Sbornik Stateĭ*, vol. 1, Moscow, 2014, 317-47

W. Smiley, 'The burdens of subjecthood. The Ottoman state, Russian fugitives, and interimperial law', *International Journal of Middle East Studies* 46 (2014) 73-93

W. Smiley, '"After being so long prisoners, they will not return to slavery in Russia". An Aegean network of violence between empires and identities', *Osmanlı Araştırmaları / The Journal of Ottoman Studies* 44 (2014) 221-34

E.B. Smilianskaia, 'Russian warriors in the land of Miltiades and Themistocles. The colonial ambitions of Catherine the Great in the Mediterranean', *Higher School of Economics Research Paper* WP BRP 55/ HUM (2014) 1-17; https://ssrn.com/abstract=2436332

Ch.A. Mēnaoglou, *Ho Anastasios Michaēl kai ho Logos peri Hellēnismou*, Athens, 2013

E.B. Smilianskaia, '"Protection" or "Possession". How Russians created a Greek principality in 1770-1775', in M. Baramova et al. (eds), *Power and influence in south-eastern Europe, 16th-19th century*, Berlin, 2013, 209-17

D. Klein (ed.), *The Crimean Khanate between East and West (15th-18th century)*, Wiesbaden, 2012

W. Smiley, 'Let whose people go? Subjecthood, sovereignty, liberation, and legalism in eighteenth-century Russo-Ottoman relations', *Turkish Historical Review* 3 (2012) 196-228

W. Smiley, 'The meanings of conversion. Treaty law, state knowledge, and religious identity among Russian captives in the eighteenth-century Ottoman Empire', *The International History Review* 34 (2012) 559-80

G.A. Tiurina, *Iz istorii izucheniia grecheskikh rukopiseĭ v Evrope v XVIII-nachale XIX v. Kristian Fridrikh Mattei (1744-1811)*, Moscow, 2012

B.L. Davis, *Empire and military revolution in Eastern Europe. Russia's Turkish wars of the eighteenth century*, London, 2011

M.Iu. Gosudareva, 'Russkaia diplomaticheskaia missiia v Stambule v 20-30-e gody XVIII veka', *Vestnik Riazanskogo Gosudarstvennogo Universiteta im. S.A. Esenina* 1/30 (2011) 97-106

O. Katsiardē-Hering et al. (eds), *Rōsia kai Mesogeios*, 2 vols, Athens, 2011

C. Papoulidēs, *Hoi Hellēnes tēs Hagias Petroupolēs*, Thessaloniki, 2011

Iu. Priakhin, *Lambros Katsonis. Lichnost', zhizn' i deiatel'nost'. Arkhivnye dokumenty*, St Petersburg, 2011

S.M. Shamin, 'Izvestiia o grekakh v kurantakh v period Moreĭskoĭ voĭny', *Kapterevskie Chteniia. Sbornik Stateĭ* 9 (2011) 144-61

S.M. Shamin, *Kuranty XVII stoletiia. Evropeĭskaia pressa v Rossii i vozniknovenie russkoĭ periodicheskoĭ pechati*, Moscow, 2011

I.M. Smilianskaia, M.B. Velizhev and E.B. Smilianskaia, *Rossiia v Sredizemnomor'e. Arkhipelagskaia ėkspeditsiia Ėkateriny II*, Moscow, 2011

V. Taki, 'Orientalism at the margins. The Ottoman Empire under Russian eyes', *Kritika. Explorations in Russian and Eurasian History* 12 (2011) 321-51

N.P. Tchesnokova, *Khristianskiĭ Vostok i Rossiia. Politicheskoe i kulturnoe bzaimodeĭstvie v seredine veka (Po dokumentam Rossiĭskogo Gosudarstvennogo Arkhiva Drevnikh Aktov)*, Moscow, 2011

G.L. Arsh, 'Rossiĭskie ėmissary v Peloponese i Arkhipelagaskaia ėkspeditsiia 1770-1774', *Novaia i Noveĭshaia Istoriia* 6 (2010) 60-72

I. Carras, 'Emporio, politikē kai adelphotēta. Rōmioi stē Rōsia 1700-1774', Athens, 2010 (PhD Diss. University of Athens)

S.M. Shamin, 'Izvestiia "grecheskoĭ" tematiki v kurantakh 1687 g.', *Kapterevskie Chteniia. Sbornik Stateĭ* 8 (2010) 182-95

S.M. Shamin, 'Grecheskaia zemlia v Kurantakh XVII v.', in *Istoriia rossiĭsko-grecheskikh otnosheniĭ i perspektivy iz razvitiia v XXI veke. Materialy konferentsii*, Moscow, 2010, 158-62

S.K. Chrēstou, *Hoi Hellēnes stē Notia Rōsia*, Thessalonika, 2009

S.M. Shamin, 'Izvestiia grecheskikh informatorov o deĭstviiakh Osmanskoĭ imperii i eë soiuznikov v Rechi Pospolitoĭ v 1672-1673 gg. (Po materialam fonda 155 RGADA)', *Kapterevskie Chteniia. Sbornik Stateĭ* 7 (2009) 202-8

T. Fedorova, 'Grecheskaia Gimnaziia v Sankt-Peterburge i eë vospitanniki', in F.A. Eloeva and D. Letsios (eds), *Sankt-Peterburg i Gretsiia. Proshloe i nastoiashchee*, St Petersburg, 2008, 48-53

P.V. Gusterin, *Pervyĭ rossiĭskiĭ vostokoved Dmitriĭ Kantemir*, Moscow, 2008

K.K. Papoulidēs, *To politiko kai thrēskeutiko kinēma tou Hieroethnismou kai oi prōtoporoi tou. Serapheim o Mytilēnaios (ci. 1667-ci. 1735)*, Thessaloniki, 2008

N. Pissis, 'Investments in the Greek merchant marine (1783-1821)', in S. Faroqui and G. Weinstein (eds), *Merchants in the Ottoman Empire*, Paris, 2008, 151-64

Iu. Priakhin, *Greki v istorii Rossii XVIII-XIX vekov*, St Petersburg, 2008

D.C. Waugh, 'News sensations from the front. Reportage in late Muscovy concerning the Ottoman wars', in C. Dunning, R. Martin and D. Rowland (eds) *Rude and barbarous kingdom revisited. Essays in Russian history and culture in honor of Robert O. Crummey*, Bloomington IN, 2008, 491-509

Rōsoi diplōmates to 180 ai. sto Archipelagos. I ēmerida tou Kentrou
Hellēno-Rōsikōn Istorikōn Erevnōn. Ta Praktika, Santorini, 2007
Russian-Ottoman relations online. 1, Primary Sources, Leiden, 2006
P. Stathē, 'Grammata kai prosōpa sto 180 aiōna. Allēlographia apo tē
syllogē tou Metochiou tou Panagiou Taphou Kōnstantinoupolēs',
Mesaiōnika kai Nea Hellēnika 8 (2006) 91-108
M. David-Fox, P. Holquist and A. Martin (eds), *Orientalism and empire
in Russia*, Bloomington IN, 2006
G. Arsh, 'The Aegean world of the second half of the 18th century in
the eyes of the Russian consuls', in E. Konstantinou (ed.), *Ägäis
und Europa*, Frankfurt am Main, 2005, 261-8
B.L. Fonkich, 'Popytka sozdaniia grecheskoĭ tipografii v Moskve v kontse XVII v.', *Rossiia i Khristianskiĭ Vostok* 2-3 (2004) 466-71
B.L. Fonkitch, G.V. Popov and L.M. Evseeva (eds), *Mount Athos treasures in Russia. Tenth to seventeenth centuries. From the museums,
libraries and archives of Moscow and the Moscow region*, Moscow,
2004 (exhibition catalogue, 17 May-4 July 2004)
D.A. Yalamas, 'Ierusalimskiĭ Patriarkh Dosifeĭ i Rossiia. 1700-
1706 gg. Po materialam Gosudarstvennogo Arkhiva Drevnikh
Aktov. Chast 2 (1701 g.)', *Rossiia i Khristianskiĭ Vostok* 2-3 (2004)
472-92
Iu.V. Ivanov (ed.), *Greki Rossii i Ukrainy*, St Petersburg, 2004
J.A. Mazis, *The Greeks of Odessa. Diaspora leadership in late imperial
Russia*, Boulder CO, 2004
C. Papoulidēs, *Rōsoellēnika. Oktō meletes rōsoellēnikōn politikōn,
politismikōn kai epistēmonikōn scheseōn*, Thessaloniki, 2004
W. von Scheliha, *Rußland und die orthodoxe Universalkirche in der
Patriarchatsperiode, 1589-1721*, Wiesbaden, 2004
B.L. Fonkich, *Grecheskie rukopisi i dokumenty v Rossii v XIV-nachale
XVIII v.*, Moscow, 2003
C. Papoulidēs, *Anatolios Meles (1722-;). Hē zōē kai to ergo tou. Symvolē
sto hellēniko schedio tēs Megalēs Aikaterinēs*, Thessaloniki, 2003
V.N. Makridēs, 'Symplērōmatika peri tōn *Stochasmōn* tou Eugeniou
Voulgarē', *Ho Eranistēs* 23 (2001) 316-23
V. Aksan, 'Breaking the spell of the Baron de Tott. Reframing the
question of military reform in the Ottoman Empire, 1760-1830', *The
International History Review* 24 (2002) 253-77
F. Yannitsi, *Grecheskiĭ mir v kontse 18-nachale 20 vv. po rossiĭskim
istochnikam (k voprosu ob izuchenii samosoznaniia Grekov)*, Mos-
cow, 2002

K.-P. Todt, 'Dositheos von Jerusalem', in C.G. Conticello and V. Conti-cello (eds), *La théologie byzantine et sa tradition*, vol. 2, Turnhout, 2002, 659-720

G. Bruess, 'The Chesme Church. The construction and commemo-ration of empire', *Modern Greek Studies Yearbook* 16/17 (2000-1) 225-42

V. Kardasis, *Diaspora merchants in the Black Sea. The Greeks in south-ern Russia, 1775-1861*, Lanham MD, 2001

V.N. Makrides, 'Orthodoxie und Politik. Die russisch-griechischen Beziehungen zur Zeit Katharinas II.', in C. Scharf (ed.), *Katharina II., Rußland und Europa. Beiträge zur internationalen Forschung*, Mainz, 2001, 85-119

V.N. Makridēs, 'Hē gallikē metafrasē kai ekdosē tōn *Stochasmōn* tou Eugeniou Voulgarē', *Ho Eranistēs* 22 (1999) 263-70

A. Zorin, *Kormia dvuglavogo orla. Russkaia literatura i gosudarstven-naia ideologiia v poslednei treti XVIII - pervoi treti XIX veka*, Mos-cow, 2001

O. Alexandropoulou, 'Hē hellēnikē monē Hagiou Nikolaou stē Moscha. Stoicheia apo tēn historia tōn hellēnorōsikōn scheseōn sto deu-tero miso tou 17ou aiōna', *Mesaiōnika kai Nea Hellēnika* 6 (2000) 111-54

T. Kaiser, 'The evil empire? The debate on Turkish despotism in eigh-teenth-century French political culture', *Journal of Modern History* 73 (2000) 6-34

O. Alexandropoulou, 'To rōsiko taxidi tou Athanasiou Patellarou kai o "protreptikos logos" tou pros ton Tsaro Alexio (1653)', *Mnēmōn* 21 (1999) 9-35

G.L. Arsh (ed.), *Grecheskaia kult'ura v Rossii XVII-XX vv. / Ho Hellēnikos Politismos stē Rōsia 17-20. ai.*, Moscow, 1999

S. Conermann, 'Das eigene und das Fremde. Der Bericht der Gesand-schaft Mustafa Rasihs nach St. Petersburg 1792-4', *Archivum Otto-manicum* 17 (1999) 249-70

K. de Herdt, 'Greeks about Turks in the age of Enlightenment. From illumination to denigration', in A. Argyriou et al. (eds), *Ho hellēnikos kosmos anamesa stēn Anatolē kai tē Dysē 1453-1981*, vol. 2, Athens, 1999, 381-93

D.A. Ialamas, 'Arkhimandritou Kallinikou "Periēgēsis eis to Eueseve-staton Imperion tōn Orthodoxōn Moskhovōn" (1754-1761). Spania martyria apo tēn historia tōn Hellenorōssikōn scheseōn tou 18ou aiōnos', in A. Argyriou et al. (eds), *Ho hellēnikos kosmos anamesa stēn Anatolē kai tē Dysē 1453-1981*, vol. 2, Athens, 1999, 199-206

A.E. Karathanassēs, *Ho hellēnikos kosmos sta Valkania kai tēn Rōsia*, Thessalonika, 1999

I.V. Sapozhnikov and L.G. Belousova, *Greki pod Odessoĭ. Ocherki istorii poselka Aleksandrovka s drevneĭshikh vremen do nachala XX veka*, Odessa, 1999

P. Stathē, *Chrysanthos Notaras, Patriarchēs Hierosolymōn. Prodromos tou Neoellēnikou Diaphōtismou*, Athens, 1999

A. Pippidi, 'La décadence de l'Empire ottoman comme concept historique, de la Renaissance aux Lumières', *Revue des Études Sud-Est Européennes* 35 (1998) 5-19 (repr. in A. Pippidi [ed.], *Byzantins, Ottomans, Roumains. Le Sud-Est européen entre l'héritage impérial et les influences occidentales*, Paris, 2006, 339-58)

D.A. Ialamas (ed.), *Atlas Arkhipelaga i rukopisnye karty Pervoĭ Arkhipelagskoĭ ékspeditsii russkogo flota 1769-1774 gg.*, Katalog vystavki, Moscow, 1997

C. Kafadar, 'The question of the Ottoman decline', *Harvard Middle Eastern and Islamic Review* 4 (1997/8) 30-75

V. Kardasēs, *Ho Hellēnismos tou Euxeinou Pontou. Odēssos - Taiganio - Rostoph - Marioupolē*, Athens [1997]

O.R. Khromov and D.A. Ialamas (eds), *Gravura Grecheskogo mira v moskovskikh sobraniiakh*, Katalog vystavki, Moscow, 1997

V.N. Makridēs, 'Stoicheia gia tis scheseis tou Alexandrou Helladiou me tē Rōsia', *Mnēmōn* 19 (1997) 9-39

P.M. Kitromēlidēs, *Neoellēnikos Diaphōtismos. Hoi politikes kai koinōnikes idees*, Athens, 1996

G. Podskalsky, 'Die Rolle der griechischen Kirche und Theologie innerhalb der Gesamtorthodoxie in der Zeit der Türkenherrschaft (1453-1821)', in R. Lauer and P. Schreiner (eds), *Die Kultur Griechenlands in Mittelalter und Neuzeit*, Göttingen, 1996, 222-41

O.R. Borodin and D.A. Ialamas (eds), *Russkie puteshestvenniki po grecheskomu miru (XII-pervaia polovina XIX vv.)*, Moscow, 1995

B.L. Fonkich (ed.), *Grecheskie dokumenty i rukopisi, ikony i pamiatniki prikladnogoiskusstva moskovskikh sobranii*, Moscow, 1995

D. Spathēs, 'Phanariōtikē koinōnia kai satira', in G.N. Soutzos, *Alexandrovodas o asyneidētos. Kōmōdia syntetheisa en etei 1785*, Athens, 1995, 207-429 (annotated edition by D. Spathēs)

T.C. Prousis, *Russian society and the Greek revolution*, DeKalb IL, 1994

M. Cazacu, 'Familles de la noblesse roumaine au service de la Russie, XVe-XIXe siècle', *Cahiers du Monde Russe et Soviétique* 34 (1993) 211-26 (repr. in E.C. Antoche and L. Cotovanu [eds], *Des Balkans à la Russie médiévale et moderne. Hommes, images et réalités*, 2017, 145-62)

O.A. Belobrova, 'O rukopisnoĭ traditsii proizvedeniĭ Nikolaia Spafariia', in *Nikolae Milescu Spafarĭ i problemy kul'tury Moldovy*, Chişinău, 1991, 67-74 (repr. O.A. Belobrova, 'Tableau des ouvrages manuscrits de Nikolaj Spafarij conservés dans les bibliothèques de Russie', in Z. Mihail [ed.], *Nicolae le Spathaire Milescu à travers ses manuscrits*, Bucharest, 2009, 143-50)

B.L. Fonkich, 'Russia and the Christian East from the sixteenth to the first quarter of the eighteenth century', *Modern Greek Studies Yearbook* 7 (1991) 439-61

N.C. Pappas, *Greeks in Russian military service in the late eighteenth and early nineteenth centuries*, Thessaloniki, 1991

R. Clogg, 'The Byzantine legacy in the modern Greek world. The *Megali Idea*', in L. Clucas (ed.), *The Byzantine legacy in Eastern Europe*, Boulder CO, 1988, 253-81 (repr. R. Clogg, *Anatolica. Studies in the Greek East in the 18th and 19th centuries*, Aldershot, 1996, 253-81)

D.A. Howard, 'Ottoman historiography and the literature of "decline" of the sixteenth and seventeenth centuries', *Journal of Asian History* 22 (1988) 52-77

G. Podskalsky, 'Der Beitrag der Griechen zur geistigen Kultur Russlands nach dem Fall Konstantinopels (1453-1821)', in J. Chrysostomides (ed.), *Kathēgētria. Essays presented to Joan Hussey for her 80th birthday*, Camberley, Surrey, 1988, 527-43

H. Ragsdale, 'Evaluating the traditions of Russian aggression. Catherine II and the Greek Project', *The Slavonic and East European Review* 66 (1988) 91-117

T.C. Prousis, 'The Greeks of Russia and the Greek awakening, 1774-1821', *Balkan Studies* 28 (1987) 259-80

N. Camariano, 'Hepta spania hellēnika phylladia dēmosieumena stēn Petroupolē (1771-1772)', *Ho Eranistēs* 18 (1986) 1-34

V. Karidis, 'The Mariupol Greeks. Tsarist treatment of an ethnic minority ca. 1778-1859', *Journal of Modern Hellenism* 3 (1986) 57-74

Z. Mihail, 'La diffusion des écrits orientaux de Nicolas le Spathaire (Milescu)', *Revue des Études Sud-Est Européennes* 23 (1985) 117-30 (repr. in Mihail, *Nicolae le Spathaire Milescu*, 77-93)

J. Nicolopoulos, 'Résultats du dépouillement du *Russkij biografičeskij slovarj*. Analyse de 130 biographies de Grecs ayant exercé une activité importante en Russie entre 1750 et 1850 dans le service public et les professions libérales', *Balkan Studies* 25 (1984) 21-30

A.E. Karathanassis, 'Pierre le Grand et l'intelligentsia grecque (1685-1740)', in *Les rélations gréco-russes pendant la domination turque et la guerre d'indépendance grecque*, Thessalonika, 1983, 43-52

Les relations gréco-russes pendant la domination turque et la guerre d'indépendance grecque, Thessaloniki, 1983 (colloquium of the Institute of Balkan Studies, Thessaloniki, 23-5 September 1981)

A. Argyriou, *Les exégèses grecques de l'Apocalypse à l'époque turque (1453-1821). Esquisse d'une histoire des courants ideologiques au sein du peuple grec asservi*, Thessaloniki, 1982

A. Argyriou, 'L'attitude des Grecs face à la Russie orthodoxe et aux États occidentaux (1767-1821), telle qu'elle apparait à travers les textes eschatologiques de l'époque', *Cahiers de l'Institut des Langues Vivantes* 30 (1982) 9-28

A.E. Karathanassis, 'Contribution à la connaissance de la vie et de l'oeuvre de deux Grecs de la diaspora. Athanasios Kondoïdis et Athanasios Skiadas (18e siècle)', *Balkan Studies* 19 (1978) 159-87

S K. Batalden, 'A further note on Patriarch Serapheim II's sojourn to Russia', *Balkan Studies* 18 (1977) 409-11

R.H. Davison, '"Russian skill and Turkish imbecility". The Treaty of Kuchuk–Kajnardji reconsidered', *The Slavic Review* 35 (1976) 463-83

C. Papoulidis, 'Le patriarche œcuménique Sérapheim II et les Russes', *Balkan Studies* 17 (1976) 59-66

A.M. Stanislavskaia, *Rossiia i Gretsiia v kontse XVIII-nachale XIX veka. Politika Rossii v Ionicheskoĭ Respublike: 1798-1807 gg.*, Moscow, 1976

P. Cernovodeanu, 'Pierre le Grand dans l'historiographie roumaine et balkanique du XVIIIe siècle', *Revue des Études Sud-Est Européennes* 13 (1975) 77-95

A. Camariano-Cioran, *Les académies princières de Bucarest et de Jassy et leurs professeurs*, Thessalonika, 1974

J. Cracraft, *The church reform of Peter the Great*, London, 1971

A.E. Vakalopoulos, 'Ho Megas Petros kai hoi Hellēnes kata ta telē tou 17. kai tis arches tou 18. ai.', *Epistēmonikē Epetēris tēs Philosophikēs Scholēs tou Panepistēmiou Thessalonikēs* 11 (1971) 247-59

A.W. Fisher, *The Russian annexation of the Crimea 1772-1783*, Cambridge, 1970

N. Itzkowitz and M.E. Mote (eds), *Mubadele. An Ottoman-Russian exchange of ambassadors*, Chicago IL, 1970

N.E. Saul, *Russia and the Mediterranean, 1797-1807*, Chicago IL, 1970

G.L. Arsh, 'Grecheskaia ėmigratsiia v Rossiiu v kontse XVIII-nachale XIX v.', *Sovetskaia Ėtnografiia* 3 (1969) 85-94

A. Camariano-Cioran, 'Les Îles Ioniennes de 1797 à 1807 et l'essor du courant philofrançais parmi les Grecs', in *Praktika Tritou Panioniou Synedriou*, Athens, 1967, 83-117 (repr. in L. Rados (ed.), *Relaţii româno-elene. Studii istorice şi filologice (secolele XIV-XIX)*, Bucharest, 2008, 543-68)

A. Camariano-Cioran, 'La guerre russo-turque de 1768-1774 et les Grecs', *Revue des Études Sud-Est Européennes* 3 (1965) 513-47 (repr. Rados, *Relaţii româno-elene*, 429-60)

E. Hösch, 'Das sogenannte "griechische Projekt" Katharinas II', *Jahrbücher für Geschichte Osteuropas* 12 (1964) 168-206

D. Dvoichenko-Markov, 'Russia and the first accredited diplomat in the Danubian Principalities', *Slavic and East European Studies* 8 (1963) 200-22

B.G. Spiridonakis, 'Le consulat russe dans les principautés danubiennes', *Balkan Studies* 4 (1963) 289-314

B. Lewis, 'Ottoman observers of Ottoman decline', *Islamic Studies* 1 (1962) 71-87

A.K. Sverchevskaia and T.P. Cherman, *Bibliografiia Turtsii*, Pt 1. *1713-1917*, Moscow, 1961

B. Lewis, 'Some reflections on the decline of the Ottoman Empire', *Studia Islamica* 9 (1958) 111-27

K.Th. Dēmaras (ed.), *Neoellēnikē epistolographia*, Athens, [1955]

E. Turdeanu, 'Le livre grec en Russie. L'apport des presses de Moldavie et de Valachie (1682-1725)', *Revue des Études Slaves* 26 (1950) 67-87 (repr. E. Turdeanu, *Études de littérature roumaine et d'écrits slaves et grecs des Principautés roumaines*, Leiden, 1985, 297-316)

B.H. Sumner, *Peter the Great and the Ottoman Empire*, Oxford, 1949

G.I. Zaviras, *Nea Hellas ē hellēnikon theatron*, Athens, 1872 (repr. with an introduction by T. Gritsopoulos, Athens, 1972)

H.L. Bacmeister, *Russische Bibliothek, zur Kenntniß des gegenwärtigen Zustandes der Literatur in Rußland*, vol. 2, St Petersburg, 1774

Vasilios N. Makrides

Poland and Lithuania

Andreas Acoluthus

Andreas Akoluth

DATE OF BIRTH   1654
PLACE OF BIRTH   Bernstadt an der Weide, Silesia (now Bierutów, Poland)
DATE OF DEATH   1704
PLACE OF DEATH   Breslau, Silesia (now Wrocław, Poland)

BIOGRAPHY

Andreas Acoluthus (or Akoluth) was born in Bernstadt an der Weide close to Breslau, the capital of Silesia, in 1654. His family was Lutheran in an area that was largely Catholic. He attended the St Elisabeth Gymnasium in Breslau and then proceeded to the University of Leipzig, where he was taught Eastern languages by August Pfeiffer. He went on to study theology at the University of Wittenberg, returning to Leipzig in 1675. In the following year, he was appointed Lutheran pastor in Breslau, where he also taught Hebrew at the St Elisabeth Gymnasium, and where he acquired a high reputation in the Republic of Letters, corresponding with Gottfried Wilhelm Leibniz, Mathurin Veyssière de La Croze, Louis Picques and many other scholars.

In Leipzig, Acoluthus appears to have learnt many of the more than 20 languages that he claimed to know. They included Persian, Turkish, Arabic, Ethiopic (Ge'ez), Coptic, Chinese and Armenian. He learnt Armenian from a native speaker, Jacob de Gregoriis, and went on to concentrate on that language (at that time known by hardly anyone in Europe outside the Armenian communities), publishing the Armenian version of the biblical Book of Obadiah in 1680. He also reached the remarkable conclusion that Armenian was the language of the ancient Egyptians. He based this theory on what he believed was a striking similarity between hieroglyphs and Armenian capital letters. The idea initially appealed to some of his learned acquaintances such as Leibniz, but it did not take long for them to find his arguments unconvincing and to come round to the far more plausible supposition advanced by Athanasius Kircher (and which Acoluthus was determined to combat), namely that the key to the hieroglyphs was Coptic.

Acoluthus refused invitations to the universities of Leipzig, Greifswald, Erfurt and Halle, but in 1696 he was persuaded by the influential
scholar and diplomat Ezechiel Spanheim to describe the Eastern manuscripts and coins in the electoral library in Berlin. Even though he seems
to have devoted less time to Arabic than to Armenian, Acoluthus had
in fact already started to toy with the idea of translating the Qur'an in
the late 1670s. Noted for his obstinacy and his eccentricity, Acoluthus
astonished his fellow citizens with the assurance that the locusts that
devastated local crops in 1693 had Arabic characters on their wings – a
persuasion that was attributed to his having immersed himself to excess
in the Qur'an.

Acoluthus managed to assemble a large collection of Qur'an manuscripts. These were mainly the fruits of war, and they increased after the
Ottoman defeat by the Poles and Austrians at the gates of Vienna in 1683.
They amounted in all to some 40 codices, many of them fragments, and
included a bilingual Arabic-Persian version from the spoils of Buda and
an Arabic-Turkish version given to Acoluthus by Franz Mesgnien Meninski, the imperial interpreter in Istanbul and the compiler of the first great
Turkish (and Persian) dictionary to appear in Europe. Meninski, from
Lorraine, was another of Acoluthus's admirers and had proposed him
as chief interpreter in Vienna, but the Jesuits objected for confessional
reasons. A further result of the war with the Ottomans was an abundance
of prisoners-of-war, who seem to have supplied Acoluthus with information about terms in the Qur'an. They included the wife of an imam in Belgrade, who was given as a slave to Acoluthus by some officers returning
from the front. She was apparently well educated, with excellent Turkish
and good Arabic, and was treated with respect by Acoluthus and his wife.
They emancipated her, but six months after her arrival she absconded.

Acoluthus was regarded in scholarly circles as well equipped to undertake a translation of the Qur'an, and Leibniz, who had first heard about
his efforts in 1692, hoped that he might indeed provide a Lutheran alternative to Ludovico Marracci. Acoluthus, who had still made little progress with his own project, read Marracci's *Prodromus* (1691) with a critical
eye and put together a number of objections. He wrote to Marracci, with
whom he seems to have sustained a correspondence, most of which has
yet to come to light, and received from him a sample of his translation.
Only a part of one letter, written by Marracci in 1694, was published at
the time (in Wilhelm Ernst Tentzel's *Monatliche Unterredungen* of 1695),
but from that alone we have an idea of Marracci's modesty, his readiness

to admit his mistakes, and his affectionate treatment of a rival for whom he evidently had some esteem.

Aware of Marracci's use of a large number of *tafsīr* works, or Muslim commentaries, and of his own all but total lack of similar texts, Acoluthus decided to produce a polyglot Qur'an in imitation of the polyglot Bibles that had appeared in the 16th and 17th centuries. For this purpose he turned to the two treasures in his own library, his Arabic-Turkish Qur'an and the Arabic-Persian one. On the basis of these, he issued the specimen that appeared in 1701, the *Tetrapla Alcoranica, sive Specimen Alcorani quadrilinguis, Arabici, Persici, Turcici, Latini*. The bold plan, however, got no further than the first sura. Acoluthus died in Breslau three years later.

MAIN SOURCES OF INFORMATION

Primary

MS Erfurt, Forschungsbibliothek Gotha – Chart. A 1199 (correspondence with Gottlieb Milich)

W.E. Tentzel (ed.), *Monatliche Unterredungen einiger guten Freunde*, Leipzig, December 1695, pp. 1009-10

A. Acoluthus, *Tetrapla Alcoranica, sive Specimen Alcorani quadrilinguis, Arabici, Persici, Turcici, Latini*, Berlin, 1701, pp. 5-9

A. Bernd, *Eigene Lebens-Beschreibung*, Leipzig, 1738

J.D. Wincklerus, *Sylloge anecdotorum*, Leipzig, 1750

G.W. Leibniz, *Allgemeiner politischer und historischer Briefwechsel*, vol. 7, Berlin, 1964; vol. 9, Berlin, 1975; vol. 10, Berlin, 1979; vol. 11, Berlin, 1982; vol. 12, Berlin, 1990; vol. 13, Berlin, 1987; vol. 14, Berlin, 1993; vol. 15, Berlin, 1998; vol. 17, Berlin, 2001; vol. 18, Berlin, 2005; vol. 20, Berlin, 2006; vol. 21, Berlin, 2012

Secondary

A. Hamilton, 'After Marracci. The reception of Ludovico Marracci's edition of the Qur'an in northern Europe from the late seventeenth to the early nineteenth centuries', *Journal of Qur'anic Studies* 20 (2018) 175-92 (which includes Marracci's letter to Acoluthus, pp. 188-9; special issue: *The Qur'an in Europe*, ed. J. Loop)

A. Hamilton, '"To rescue the honour of the Germans". Qur'an translations by eighteenth- and early nineteenth-century German Protestants', *Journal of the Warburg and Courtauld Institutes* 77 (2014) 173-209

B. Liebrenz, *Arabische, Persische und Türkische Handschriften in Leipzig. Geschichte ihrer Sammlung und Erschließung von den Anfängen bis zu Karl Völlers*, Leipzig, 2008, pp. 13-15

A. Hamilton, 'A Lutheran translator for the Quran. A late seventeenth-century quest', in A. Hamilton, M.H. van den Boogert and B. Westerweel (eds), *The Republic of Letters and the Levant*, Leiden, 2005, pp. 197-221

K. Migoń, 'Der Breslauer Orientalist Andreas Acoluthus (1654-1704). Seine Beziehungen zu Leibniz und zur Akademie in Berlin', *Sitzungsberichte der Leibniz-Sozietät* 53 (2002) 45-58

K. Migoń, 'Wrocławski orientalista Andrzej Akolut (jego życie, prace, księgozbiór)', *Przegląd Orientalistyczny* 4/56 (1965) 325-35

K. Tautz, *Die Bibliothekäre der Churfürstliche Bibliothek zu Cölln an der Spree im siebzehnten Jahrhundert*, Leipzig, 1925, pp. 216-18

C.H. Tromler, 'Leben und Schriften des Hern. Andreas Akoluth, weil. Predigers und Professors zu Breßlau, und der Königl. Preuß. Akad. der Wissenschaften Mitglieds', *Neue Beyträge von alten und neuen Theologischen Sachen, Büchern, Urkunden, Controversen, Anmerkungen, Vorschlägen etc.*, Leipzig, 1761, 414-71

WORKS ON CHRISTIAN-MUSLIM RELATIONS

Tetrapla Alcoranica
'Qur'anic tetrapla'

DATE   1701

ORIGINAL LANGUAGE   Latin

DESCRIPTION

Acoluthus's *Tetrapla Alcoranica, sive Specimen Alcorani quadrilinguis, Arabici, Persici, Turcici, Latini* ('Qur'anic tetrapla, or quadrilingual specimen of the Qur'an in Arabic, Persian, Turkish and Latin [...]'), a quarto volume, was published in Berlin by the Vidua Salfeldiana in 1701. It starts with the text of the opening sura of the Qur'an, printed in three parallel columns on p. 2 – from right to left, Arabic, Persian and Turkish. Opposite, on p. 3, are Latin translations of the three different versions. At the bottom of each page are footnotes, those on p. 3 running over to p. 4. On p. 4 is the beginning of the long introduction, which runs to p. 54. From p. 55 to p. 57 is a 'Corollarium', a dissertation on the two names of the Ottoman capital, Constantinople and Istanbul. The work ends on p. 58 with anonymous congratulatory verses dedicated to Acoluthus.

SIGNIFICANCE

When the *Tetrapla Alcoranica* appeared it seemed to be a highly original publication. No other scholar in Europe had attempted to publish

Illustration 13. Andreas Acoluthus, *Tetrapla Alcoranica*, p. 2, giving the text, from right to left, in Arabic, Persian and Ottoman Turkish, with notes in Latin below

a polyglot edition of the Qur'an. Nevertheless, within a few years of its publication, the French Orientalist Antoine Galland told the Dutch scholar Gijsbertus Couperus that he was planning to use Turkish and Persian versions in a translation of his own (Bevilacqua, 'Qur'an transla-tions', p. 129). Whether he had Acoluthus's example in mind we do not know, but Georg Jacob Kehr, the future professor of Oriental languages at Leipzig, announced his intention of following Acoluthus by including Turkish and Persian versions of the Qur'an in the collection of qur'anic excerpts he hoped to publish (but never did) (Preissler, 'Orientalische Studien', p. 37).

Acoluthus's interest in the Qur'an was closely connected with his wish to establish a Protestant missionary centre to rival the Propaganda Fidei in Rome. The German Arabists Christian Ravius and Matthias Wasmuth had planned to found an 'Oriental college' with the same objectives in 1670, and Acoluthus hoped that he might put their ideals into practice, preparing Lutheran preachers to be dispatched to the formerly Muslim territories reconquered by the Christian imperial armies.

But Acoluthus's decision to produce a multilingual Qur'an must also be seen in the light of his reaction to Marracci's translation. Already in his *Prodromus* Marracci had shown that he had at his disposal in Rome a vast number of *tafsīr* works. Thanks mainly to the missionaries, the Roman libraries had assembled impressive collections of such com-mentaries. This meant that Marracci could offer various interpretations of the more difficult qur'anic passages and supply meanings to words that would otherwise have been almost impossible to find. The German libraries, on the other hand, had very few of these *tafsīr* works. As for Acoluthus, the only Islamic works other than the Qur'ans that he admit-ted possessing were two 16th-century Turkish texts on Muslim beliefs, *Kirk su-āl* attributed to Mevlana Furati and *Vasīyet-nāme* by Birgili Mehmed Efendi. Acoluthus, however, believed that he could dispense with *tafsīr* works by using Persian and Turkish translations of the Qur'an which were obviously produced by scholars who had just as good an understanding of the Arabic text as the commentators. What he may also have realised is that the Persian and Turkish translators had themselves used *tafsīr* in order to produce their own versions. This emerges even from the few lines that he actually published. Q 1:6-7, 'Direct us in the right way, in the way of those to whom thou hast been gracious, not of those against whom thou art incensed, nor those who go astray' is turned into Turkish with 'those against whom thou art incensed' and 'those who go astray' explicitly identified as the Jews and the Christians.

The introductory text that follows the first sura is Acoluthus's most important contribution to Christian-Muslim relations. It starts with an appeal to Christians to abandon their 'torpor' in studying Oriental languages and to undertake the task of converting the Muslims. The missionary objective, as a reason for translating the Qur'an, remains the principal theme, and, in a more general survey of earlier Qur'an translations, Acoluthus emphasises the Lutheran contribution, from Luther's own involvement in the first published version that had been translated by Robert of Ketton in the 12th century and edited by Theodor Bibliander in Basel 1543, to the more recent plans for founding a missionary college elaborated by Ravius and Wasmuth. But even if his tone is fundamentally anti-Islamic it is clear both from his footnotes and from the manuscripts in his library that Acoluthus was interested in the recitation of the Qur'an and sensitive to the beauty of the text in Arabic.

Acoluthus intersperses his appeal and his attacks on Islam with the tale of his own beginnings as an Orientalist, his long interest in the Qur'an – he refers to his vast manuscript collection and describes the Persian and Turkish versions he has used – and the history of Arabic studies in Europe (in which he criticises many of his predecessors, both Protestant and Catholic). Marracci is constantly called to account. Acoluthus taxes him with too feeble an attack on Islam and laments the Catholic objections to the laity reading the Bible and thus depriving prospective missionaries of one of their most valuable weapons. But he also criticises Marracci's actual translation. Marracci, he claims, has failed to convey the polyvalence of many of the words, and is also guilty of certain errors. The first sura, al-Fātiḥa, should not be translated as 'the opening sura' as if al-fātiḥa were an adjective, but as 'the sura of the opening', al-fātiḥa, according to Acoluthus, being a genitive noun. Acoluthus also maintains that the title of the second sura, al-Baqara, should not be translated as 'the sura of the cow' but as 'the sura of amplitude or greatness' and that the title of the 48th sura, al-Fatḥ, should not be rendered as 'the sura of victory' but as 'the sura of the decree'.

However eccentric Acoluthus's criticisms of Marracci may be, he was one of the few translators of the Qur'an to engage with him. He was consequently quoted with reverence in a series of dissertations on the Qur'an dictated by the professor of theology at the University of Altdorf, Johann Michael Lange, in 1703 and 1704. Later still, in 1721, the biblical scholar Christian Reineccius, rector of the gymnasium in Weissenfels, who republished Marracci's Latin version (*Mohammedis Filii Abdallae pseudo-prophetae fides islamitica, i.e. Al-Coranus*, Leipzig, 1721), referred in a note to Acoluthus's ideas about the title of the first sura and actually adopted his title of the 48th sura. Although Acoluthus would continue to be quoted in Germany, particularly as a critic of Marracci, it was not long before nearly all qur'anic scholars in Europe acknowledged Marracci's achievement. It was his translation that dominated subsequent versions well into the 19th century.

PUBLICATIONS

> Andreas Acoluthus, *Tetrapla Alcoranica, sive specimen Alcorani quadrilinguis, Arabici, Persici, Turcici, Latini*, Berlin, 1701; 2 A.or. 38 (digitised version available through *MDZ*)
>
> [Johann Michael Lange, praeses], Michael Conrad Ludwig, *Dissertatio historico-philologico-theologica de Alcorani prima inter Europaeos editione arabica*, Altdorf, 1703; 4 L.as. 33#Beibd.7 (digitised version available through *MDZ*)
>
> [Johann Michael Lange, praeses], Johann Conrad, *Dissertatio historico-philologico-theologica de Alcorani versionibus variis, tam orientalibus, quam occidentalibus*, Altdorf, 1704; 4 L.as. 33#Beibd.9 (digitised version available through *MDZ*)

STUDIES

> Hamilton, 'After Marracci'
>
> Hamilton, '"To rescue the honour of the Germans"'
>
> A. Bevilacqua, 'The Qur'an translations of Marracci and Sale', *Journal of the Warburg and Courtauld Institutes* 76 (2013) 93-130
>
> Hamilton, 'Lutheran translator for the Quran'
>
> H. Preissler, 'Orientalische Studien in Leipzig vor Reiske', in H.-G. Ebert and T. Hanstein (eds), *Johann Jacob Reiske. Leben und Wirkung. Ein Leipziger Byzantinist und Begründer der Orientalistik im 18. Jahrhundert*, Leipzig, 2005, 29-43
>
> H. Bobzin, 'Von Venedig nach Kairo. Zur Geschichte arabischer Korandrucke (16. bis frühes 20. Jahrhundert)', in E. Hanebutt-Benz, D. Glass and G. Roper (eds), *Sprachen des Nahen Ostens und die Druckrevolution. Eine interkulturelle Begegnung*, Westhofen, 2002, 151-76

Alastair Hamilton

Mikołaj Chwałkowski

DATE OF BIRTH   Unknown
PLACE OF BIRTH   Wschowa (western Poland)
DATE OF DEATH   Shortly after 1700
PLACE OF DEATH   Unknown

BIOGRAPHY

Not much is known about Mikołaj Chwałkowski's youth. He came from a Lutheran family, studied law in Frankfurt am Oder and became a courtier of the Duke of Courland in Mitau (present-day Jelgava in Latvia). From 1670, he was the duke's representative at the royal court in Warsaw, first during the reign of King Michał Korybut Wiśniowiecki (r. 1669-73) and then under Jan III Sobieski (r. 1674-96), who held his legal and historical knowledge in esteem. Chwałkowski was apparently in close contact with the royal family.

He sent the Duke of Courland weekly reports about events at the royal court and in parliament, and he published on legal and historical matters. His works sparked extreme reactions (either high praise, or severe criticism – most probably his position as a close attendant of the Duke of Courland and at the same time of King Jan Sobieski contributed to this). The parliament confirmed his family's noble status in 1676. His brother Samuel was an adviser at the court of the Prince-Elector of Brandenburg.

Chwałkowski was probably not the author of *Historya Turecka o Mahomecie*, though this work was published a few years after his death as an attachment to a longer publication with his name on the title page.

MAIN SOURCES OF INFORMATION

Primary
J.A. Załuski, *Biblioteka historyków, prawników, polityków i innych autorow polskich lub o Polsce piszących*, Kraków, 1832

Secondary
K. Piwarski, art. 'Chwałkowski Mikołaj', in *Polski Słownik Biograficzny*, vol. 4, Kraków, 1938, 8-9
L. Łukaszewicz, *Rys dziejów piśmiennictwa polskiego*, Kraków, 1836, pp. 47-8; 1838[2], pp. 50-1 (then in several amended editions published in Poznań, 1859, p. 210; 1860, p. 110; 1866, p. 273; the *Historia* was not included in the 1858 edition)

WORKS ON CHRISTIAN-MUSLIM RELATIONS

Historya Turecka o Mahomecie
'A Turkish story about Muḥammad'

DATE   1712
ORIGINAL LANGUAGE   Polish

DESCRIPTION

Jan Tobiasz Keller, a publisher and printer from Poznań (Posen), published a compilation of several works in 1712. Chwałkowski, who had
most probably died some 10 years earlier, was named on the title page
as its author. *Historya Turecka o Mahomecie* (in full, *Historya Tvrecka o
Mahomecie y potomkach iego a to ku Obronie y na przestroge Chrzescianom iako tym Nieprzyiacielom Krzyza Swietego ile podeyrzanym ufac nie
trzeba Ktora od iednego Vniata, z lacinskiego na Polski przetlumaczona,
y Drukiem Christopolitanskim swiatu pokazana: W Stragonii stolecznym
miescie roku panskiego 1712. dnia 24 lipca*, 'A Turkish story about Mahomet
and his descendants given to Christians for protection and as a warning
that one should not trust those suspicious enemies of the Sacred Cross;
given by an Eastern-rite Catholic Christian, translated into Polish from
Latin and with the Christopolitan print shown to the world. In the capital
city of Stragonia AD 1712, on 24th July') appeared after *Pamietnik albo Kronika Pruskich Mistrzow y Kxiazat Prvskich Tudziesz Historya Inflandzka
y Kurlandya: Z przydanemi rzeczy Pamięci godnych, zrozmaitych Kronikarzow, zebrana / Przez Mikolaia z Chwałkowa Chwalkowskiego. Oraz iest
Szwedzka y Moskiewska Woyna za Panowania […] Augusta w Torego [!],
krotkiem stylem wyrazona y do Druku dana […]* ('Memoir or chronicle of
Prussian masters and princes of Prussia. Including the history of Livonia
and Courland. With the addition of things worthy to be remembered
gathered from various chroniclers. Compiled by Mikolaj from Chwalkow
Chwalkowski. And the Swedish and Moscovian war during the reign
of […] Augustus the Second is briefly presented and submitted to
print[…]').

Both works are compilations of material from various sources (some
are named at the end of the publication, others omitted, as e.g. a work
called *Kronika mistrzów pruskich*, 'Chronicle of the Prussian Masters'
(Toruń/Thorn, 1582), written by Marcin Murinius, a former Dominican
friar turned Lutheran, in 1573, though it appears in Keller's edition in
amended form).

Historya Tvrecka o Mahomecie consists of the title page, 20 pages of text in prose, a three-page poem against the Jews attributed to Jan Dantiscus, a 16th-century bishop of Ermland (Warmia), and the list of sources (*Regestr Avtorow z ktorych ta Historia Tvurecka y Pruska zebrana iest*). A single statement attributed to Cornelius Lapide (from a commentary on the books of the biblical Lesser Prophets) is printed on the reverse of the title page, declaring that the Turks know a prophecy about the fall of their state at the hands of the Poles and Ruthenians.

The work begins with a biography of 'Mahomet' (son of Abdala and Hennina, a Jewess), who was born in 562, captured as a boy by Arab nomads and sold to a Persian merchant. He earned such respect that, after the merchant's death, his widow saw nothing wrong in marrying Mahomet. He used a period of political tumult to write his (religious) law (*napisał zakon*), which offered something to all who were disenchanted with the Byzantines. He was helped by two apostate Jews and two heretics, Ioannes, a Nestorian, and Sergius, an Arian. The religion he created denied the divinity of Christ.

First, Mahomet convinced his wife that, during the physical fits he suffered, he was conversing with the Angel Gabriel. She spread word about this. Mahomet gave permission for all the urges of the flesh to be gratified and promised liberty to slaves who would join him, forcing him to flee from the slave owners. He moved to 'Median Talnabi', the event from which Muslims 'took the beginning of Hegira'. He defeated the Persians, became the master of Arabia and expelled the Romans from Syria. His followers expanded the state from the Euphrates to the Atlantic Ocean and from the Black River to the Pyrenees.

After an excursus, the compiler resumes his account of Mahomet, saying that he introduced the practice of circumcision to attract the Jews, and the denial of Christ's divinity to attract the then powerful Arians. The new religion accepted many novelties and fables in order to be attractive to heathens, and permitted indulging in carnal urges in order to attract the majority of people.

Machomet (*sic*) began preaching his ungodly message in Turkey in the reign of the Emperor Heraclius, then raided Arabia for three years as a brigand, captured 'Jetrib' and 'Mecha', and finally became the leader of rebel soldiers with whose help he conquered Arabia, Syria and Egypt. Made arrogant by his sudden luck, he raided Persia but was defeated and wounded (his face was cut with a sword). However, when many soldiers who had not received pay from Heraclius joined his forces, he fought again against the Persians, defeated them and became the ruler of Persia.

The compiler adds that some ascribe this victory to 'Homar' ('Umar ibn al-Khaṭṭāb), Machomet's successor.

Over a period of nine years, Machomet led 19 raids for plunder. He died poisoned by his wife's kin at the age of 40 in 603. Many of his followers started a war after his death. Homar, his immediate successor (according to some, 'the third'), was particularly important, killing the Persian king, defeating his army and conquering Persia in 640.

On 'Odyner', Machomet's fourth successor, the compiler admits to having no information. 'Haly' ('Alī ibn Abī Ṭālib), the fifth, assumed the title 'king' in place of 'Califa' ('deputy' [of Machomet]), and also 'the Prophet of the Saracens', greater than Machomet because God had originally sent Gabriel with 'Alkoran' to Haly but Gabriel lost his way, came upon Machomet and mistakenly gave him the book.

The Saracen lords ran the Machometan state until the time of 'Mauget' the Persian king, and left Persia to Machomet from the Turkish nation, who defeated them by betrayal.

During that time, in the year 634, the Machometan Saracens captured Rhodes and brought down the famous copper column, the Colossus, carrying the copper away on 900 camels. The Saracens were chased out of Asia by the Turks, who were also Machometans. They captured Africa, Sardinia and other islands in the Mediterranean.

The compiler goes on to give an outline history of the Ottoman Empire, again in a mixture of correct and incorrect information, showing clear traces of his makeshift compilation from various sources. He goes into a brief condemnation of the Ottomans as untrustworthy opponents and allies (even peace agreements with them are unreliable), followed by a short section listing a few victories over Ottoman armies with the conclusion that the Ottomans are not invincible. He repeats this line of argument later, naming a different set of battles.

Historya is followed by a three-page poem against the Jews attributed to Bishop Jan Dantyszek (Dantiscus), and finally the compiler attempts to summarise his argument in seven points, the gist of which is a call to be ready for war with the enemies of the cross: victory will be praiseworthy and defeat will bring redemption.

The list of sources the compiler provides at the end of the publication is incomplete and quite sketchy, while references are only sparingly indicated in the text and, when they do appear, they are rather general. Some works, e.g. *Turcograeciae*, are explicitly referred to several times, while others, e.g. Murinius's chronicle, are not mentioned. The selection provided in the short list at the end is idiosyncratic: Anonymus

Siedmiogrodzianin ['Anonymous Transylvanian']; Author Kazania na pogrzebie Xiazecia Zbarazkiego ['The author of the sermon during the burial of the Prince of Zbaraż']; Author o Panstwie Tureckim ['The author of *On the Turkish state*']; Cantacuzenus; Caufinus w Ephemeridach, abo Dzienniku ['Caufinus in Ephemerides or Diary']; Krzysztof Warszewicki; Cromer; Henricus Stephanus; Historia Vniversalis; Honorius; Jacobus Gordon; Jan Baptista Montanus; Ludwik Vives; Petavius; Simon Starowolski; *Summa Chrzescianskiey Chronologiey* ['Summa of Christian chronology']; *Tablica chronologiczna* ['Chronological table']; Theatrum Historiczne ['Historical theatre']; Turcograecia M. Cruziusza.

Another curiosity appears in the title. The reader is told that the information in the book comes from an Eastern-rite Catholic (*od iednego Uniata*) and has been translated from Latin into Polish. However, no original written source is mentioned. If this was an attempt to give credibility to the contents, indicating a Uniate Christian as the source might not have been helpful. Even though Eastern-rite Catholics lived within the borders of the Commonwealth, the troubled history of the Uniate church (as being always somehow between Roman Catholic and Orthodox Christianity) might have cast a shadow over the veracity of such an account. It is also not clear why an Eastern-rite Christian would write in Latin (and particularly at this time), when even some Orthodox Christians living in the Commonwealth were already writinge in Polish in the second half of the 17th century (such as J. Galatowski).

SIGNIFICANCE

The compilation has often been dismissed for containing too many inaccuracies to be taken seriously by scholars of Islam and historians, and it appears to have had only limited circulation and impact on readers in the Polish-Lithuanian Commonwealth. What can be said about it is that the contents show the state of knowledge about Islam and Muslims possessed by some scholars and members of the nobility at the beginning of the 18th century. It also shows awareness of a changing political situation. Though the scars from wounds inflicted during clashes with the Ottomans were still fresh, there were people ready to see the Ottomans as a possible ally against common enemies, especially the Habsburgs and the Russians, as the rapidly weakening Commonwealth faced neighbours who were growing in strength and displaying a predatory attitude towards the weakening state. In the face of these changes in attitude, the compiler of the publication reiterates the old notion of mistrust against the Ottomans.

PUBLICATIONS

[Mikolaj Chwałkowski], *Historya Tvrecka o Mahomecie y potomkach iego a to ku Obronie y na przestoge Chrzescianom Iako tym Nieprzyiacielom Krzyza Swietego ile podeyzanym ufac nie trzeba Ktora Od iednego Vniata, z lacinskiego na Polski przetlumaczona, y Drukiem Christopolitanskim Swiatu pokazana: W STRAGONII STOLECZNYM MIESCIE ROKU PANSKIEGO 1712. dnia 24 Lipca,* in *Pamietnik albo Kronika Pruskich Mistrzow y Ksiazat Prvskich Tudziez Historya Inflandzka y Kurlandya Z przydanemi rzeczy Pamieci godnych, zrozmaitych Kronikarzow, zebrana, przez MIKOLAJA z Chwalkowa Chalkowskiego oraz iest Szwedzka y Moskiewska Woyna za Panowania Naiasnieyszego KROLA Iego Mosci AUGUSTA w Torego, krotkiem stylem wyrazona, y do Druku dana. Roku Krola Krolow 1712 w Poznaniv. Superiorum permissu,* Posen, 1712 (it is the second item in the volume); Nr inw. 410-000052 (digitised version available through Warmińsko-Mazurska Biblioteka Cyfrowa)

STUDIES

J. Reychman, *Znajomość i nauczanie języków orientalnych w Polsce XVIII wieku,* Wrocław, 1950, p. 76 (a reference; there are no studies)

For changes in the general attitude towards the Ottomans at the end of the 17th and during the 18th century, see e.g.

M. Bałczewski, 'Zmiany w ocenie Turcji w opinii polskiej XVIII w.', *Acta Universitatis Lodziensis. Folia Historica* 22 (1985) 91-108

K. Maliszewski, 'Problematyka turecka w polskich gazetach pisanych w czasach panowania Jana III Sobieskiego', in K. Matwijowski (ed.), *Studia z dziejów epoki Jana III Sobieskiego,* Wrocław, 1984, 97-109

Stanisław Grodź

Michał Bogusław Ruttich

DATE OF BIRTH 1686
PLACE OF BIRTH Vilnius (Wilno)
DATE OF DEATH 16 or 17 February 1729
PLACE OF DEATH Toruń (Thorn)

BIOGRAPHY

Coming from a Polonised German Lutheran family – his father, a pharmacist, settled in Vilnius – Michał was educated in Vilnius and Königsberg (Królewiec; present day Kaliningrad). He moved to Halle (1702-5), where he studied philology, learning Hebrew and Arabic (the latter from Salomon Negri of Damascus), philosophy and Lutheran theology. August Hermann Francke (1663-1727), a professor of Greek and Oriental languages and of theology at Halle University and a famous German Pietist, was among his teachers. He spent a year studying in Leipzig (1704). Through Francke's recommendation, he obtained a post as teacher ('knowledgeable in Oriental languages') in a school founded by Tsar Peter I in Moscow.

Ruttich travelled to Moscow via Hamburg and Archangel, and spent three years in Russia (1705-8). He then returned to Vilnius and Königsberg, where he worked as a private teacher. In 1714, again thanks to his patrons from Halle, he took up a teaching post as *professor extraordinarius* in a school in Toruń (Thorn), though his teaching career lasted only a few years as circumstances required him to concentrate on his ministry as a preacher. His 1714 inaugural lecture at Thorn, *De machiavellismo Mahumedis in excogitanda et propaganda religione sua* ('The Machiavellianism of Muḥammad in inventing and spreading his religion') highlighted his interest in matters relating to Islam.

Ruttich worked on a translation of the Qur'an into Latin and intended to publish it in Leipzig, though it was not completed as, in the meantime, Christian Reineccius's edition of Ludovico Marracci's translation was published there in 1721. Apparently, he also worked on translating the Qur'an into Polish, though the manuscripts of both this and his Latin translation are lost. Still another lost manuscript contained his translation into Polish of Johann Arndt's *Wahres Christentum* (*Prawdziwe chrześcijaństwo*). He took part in the work on the new Pietist edition of the Bible in Polish (in Halle in 1726 and 1728), and wrote several poems and the foreword to *Danziger polnischen Cantional*.

Ruttich was a Lutheran preacher in the city churches, St George's from 1715 to 1728, and simultaneously the Blessed Virgin Mary's from 1718 to 1724 (until that church was handed over to the Catholics after the riots). He gave the last rites to Mayor Rösner and other burghers who were executed after the religious riots of 1724.

He was known for stressing the importance of the Polish language and opened a class for studying Polish. The stress he put on the importance of using Polish in the Lutheran liturgy became a bone of contention with his clergy colleagues and with the Lutheran upper burgher class that governed Thorn, who insisted on using German exclusively. As a result of this conflict, his ministry ended abruptly in 1728. In February 1729, he committed suicide in circumstances that are not exactly known. His biographers indicate that he was known for hotheaded behaviour (apparently, he had been briefly imprisoned in Moscow for expressing his discontent with the situation he encountered there).

He married Barbara Elisabeth Balde, the daughter of a Pietist pastor from Września (Great Poland region), in 1721.

MAIN SOURCES OF INFORMATION

Primary

A number of archival sources remain to be explored:

Archiv der Hauptbibliothek der Franckenschen Stiftung in Halle (Ruttich's unpublished letters)

MMS Książnica Miejska w Toruniu (the city library in Toruń) – J.S. Sammet, *Noctium Thorunensium, pars prima*[...], rkps 125 (K 4094), and E. Praetorius, *Praesbyterologia Thorunensis ex tenebris* [...] *eruta*[...], rkps 129 (K 2025 Gm), p. 67

Als der [...] *Michael Ruttich* [...] *Prediger* [...] *Anno 1721 d.17. Juni mit der* [...] *Barbara Elisabeth des* [...] *Mattheus Balden* [...] *Tochter sein Hochzeit Festin celebrirte*, Thorn, [1721]

'Nachricht von einer Thornischen 113 Jahr alt gewordenen Frauen', *Das Gelahrte Preußen* (Thorn) 2/2 (1723) 133-4

G.G. Dittmann, *Beyträge* [*sic*] *zur Geschichte der Stadt Thorn: aus guten und zuverläßigen Quellen*, Thorn, 1789, pp. 43, 92-3

R. Heuer, *Thorn – St. Georgen. Geschichte der Georgengemeinde, ihrer alten Kirche und ihres Hospitals; Baugeschichte und Baubeschreibung der neuen Georgenkirche in Thorn-Mocker*, Thorn, 1907, p. 150

Secondary

S. Salmonowicz, art. 'Ruttich, Michał Bogusław (1686-1729)', *Polski Słownik Bio-graficzny*, vol. 33, Wrocław, 1991-2, 261-2

S. Salmonowicz, *Wybitni Pomorzanie XVIII wieku*, Wrocław, 1983, pp. 168-73

S. Salmonowicz, *Wybitni ludzie dawnego Torunia*, Warsaw, 1982, pp. 117-22

S. Salmonowicz, 'Pietyzm w Toruniu', *Rocznik Toruński* 13 (1978) 194-5

S. Salmonowicz, *Toruńskie Gimnazjum Akademickie w latach 1681-1817. Studium z dziejów nauki i oświaty*, Warsaw, 1973, pp. 52, 214

S. Salmonowicz, 'Tragiczny spór Michała Bogusława Rutticha. Z dziejów walki o język polski w Toruniu w początkach XVIII w.', *Zapiski Historyczne* 35 (1970) 37-50

J. Reychman, *Orient w kulturze polskiego Oświecenia*, Wrocław, 1964, pp. 236-8

J. Reychman, *Znajomość i nauczanie języków orientalnych w Polsce XVIII w.*, Wrocław, 1950, p. 112

T. Wotschke, 'Der Pietismus im alten Polen', *Deutsche Blätter in Polen* 4/9 (1927) 429-52; 6/10 (1929) 461-86

Z. Mocarski, 'Plakat prof. Rutticha z 1714 r.', *Zapiski Towarzystwa naukowego w Toruniu* 6/2-3 (1923) 38-43, pp. 40-3

WORKS ON CHRISTIAN-MUSLIM RELATIONS

De machiavellismo Mahumedis in excogitanda religione sua
'The Machiavellianism of Muḥammad in inventing and spreading his religion'

DATE 1714
ORIGINAL LANGUAGE Latin (with Arabic)

DESCRIPTION

Ruttich delivered his inaugural lecture in the Academic Gymnasium in Toruń on 19 April 1714. It was published by the rector of the school, Piotr Jaenichen (Jaenichius, 1679-1739), in *Orationes duae auspicales in introductionis actu die XIX. April. an. 1714 in gimn. Thor. recitate* (Thorunii, 1714), pp. 39-84. For this reason it is sometimes listed in catalogues and bibliographies under the name Jaenichen (K. Estreicher, *Bibliografia polska. Stólecie [sic] XV-XVIII*, vol. 18, Kraków, 1901, p. 376). The text is in Latin with short quotations in Greek and four verses from the Qur'an in Arabic with Latin translations (Q 12:8, p. 71; 13:38, p. 75; 2:21-2, p. 76, 2:24, p. 78).

Biographical sources (see above) indicate that Ruttich began translating the Qur'an into Latin, but because of the publication of Reineccius's edition of Marracci's translation in 1721 his work was unnecessary (the manuscript is considered lost). As the text of Ruttich's inaugural lecture has not gone under the scrutiny of the specialists, it remains to be established whether the Latin translations of these four quotations are from Ruttich's own translation or Marracci's, or someone else's. Neither is it known whether Ruttich quoted these verses in Arabic during his lecture, or whether they were only introduced into the printed text. Jan Reychman (*Znajomość*, p. 114, n. 89) mentions that Johann Nicolai, the printer, made the wood cuts of the Arabic sentences for printing.

Presenting the outline of Muḥammad's biography, Ruttich makes direct references to Johann Heinrich Hottinger (1620-67), and shows awareness of various opinions concerning the year of Muḥammad's birth (p. 42). He also lists the qur'anic references to a number of biblical figures and discusses the contents of several Qur'an verses and events from the biography of Muḥammad (pp. 46-7).

Jaenichen's *De impedimentis circa convertendos Mahumedanos* ('The impediments regarding Muslims who are to be converted'; pp. 5-38), most probably served as an introduction of the new teacher to the audience (the city authorities, teaching staff and the students), highlighting his interest in 'Oriental matters' and his linguistic competence. No other text by Jaenichen on Christian-Muslim issues is known, though this essay shows his erudition and his knowledge of a number of contemporary sources on Islam.

SIGNIFICANCE

Ruttich's lecture appears to be his only surviving work on Christian-Muslim issues. In Toruń, his Oriental interests were probably only a curiosity, and the results of his work on the qur'anic material had no possibility of being published. He became increasingly involved in pastoral ministry in the city, and the conflict with the Lutheran Church and the city authorities must have marginalised him. In addition, his suicidal death probably also contributed to his heritage being left unread in archives.

Ruttich's works and actions as preacher and promoter of the use of the Polish language in the Lutheran worship in Toruń were brought to scholarly attention in the second part of the 20th century. However, his work on Islamic themes was almost completely forgotten. It receives only brief acknowledgement by Reychman and Jerzy Nosowski: the former mentions him in an overview of the state of knowledge of Oriental languages in the 18th-century Polish-Lithuanian Commonwealth, reproducing a page from his published text with one of the four quotations in Arabic (Q 2:21-2), but referring to it as though it was the only one (Reychman, *Znajomość*, pp. 112-14, with the Arabic on p. 113), while the latter gives only scant information about him (Nosowki, *Polska literatura*, vol. 1, pp. 426-7) and wrongly ascribes to him another work (vol. 2, pp. 309-10; this is Teofil Rutka's translation and amendment of Filippo Guadagnoli's work, on which see Reychman, *Znajomość*, p. 26).

PUBLICATIONS

Michał Ruttich, 'De machiavellismo Mahumedis in excogitanda et propaganda religione sua', in P. Jaenichen (Jaenichius), *Orationes duae auspicales in introductionis actu d. XIX April. A. MDCCXIIII in Gymnasio Thorun*, Thorunii, 1714, 39-84; 75296677 (digitised version available through Polona/)

STUDIES

J. Nosowski, *Polska literatura polemiczno-antislamistyczna XVI, XVII i XVIII w. Wybór tekstów i komentarze*, Warsaw, 1974, vol. 1, pp. 426-7 (and vol. 2, pp. 309-10, for the wrongly ascribed work)

J. Reychman, *Znajomość i nauczanie języków orientalnych w Polsce XVIII w.*, Wrocław, 1950, pp. 112-14 (p. 113 contains a facsimile of p. 76 from *Orationes duae auspicales* with the quotation in Arabic of Q 2:21-2)

Stanisław Grodź

Michał Ignacy Wieczorkowski

DATE OF BIRTH   3 October 1673
PLACE OF BIRTH   Gdańsk
DATE OF DEATH   26 February 1750
PLACE OF DEATH   Jarosław

BIOGRAPHY

Most authors give 1674 and 1751 as the years for Wieczorkowski's birth and death, the dates found in the oldest study (Załęski, *Jezuici w Polsce*, p. 1095), but recent works, based on new critical source studies, give 1673 and 1750 (Grzebień et al., *Encyklopedia wiedzy o jezuitach*, p. 733).

Michał Ignacy Wieczorkowski was born in Gdańsk in 1673 (Sygański, 'Z notatek podróżnych', p. 505, establishes this from his letters, contradicting earlier opinions that he was born in Russia). He joined the Jesuit Order in Krakow as a teenager, and on completion of his first studies he went on to study philosophy and theology, and then, in 1704-15, he taught poetics at Jesuit schools and colleges in Lviv and Lublin, as well as rhetoric in Rawa and Kalisz, philosophy in Lviv, polemical theology in Krakow, and Greek in Jarosław, where he also served as a parish priest.

In 1715, he was sent to Persia as a missionary and envoy by the Polish King Augustus II the Strong (r. 1709-33) to look after the Catholic residents there. Carrying a letter from Augustus to the shah, Wieczorkowski decided to travel through Yerevan to Isfahan, the Persian capital. However, as he was not considered a sufficiently important personality, he did not manage to deliver the letter until 1717. At that point, he was given a promise of the shah's support for the Jesuit mission in Yerevan and returned to Poland in 1720. He presented the king with a letter from the shah and with his own account of his mission, in which he described the difficult situation of the Catholics in Persia. Although he explained the need to send someone of greater significance than a simple priest, the king commissioned him to make a second journey to Persia, but did not fund him for the task.

It took Wieczorkowski nearly two years to collect funds for this second trip, and he set out again in 1722. His new efforts brought the same poor results as before, so less than a year later he decided to move from Isfahan to Istanbul, before finally returning to Poland in 1724. He carried out missionary work along the eastern Polish border until 1730, in Zhytomyr, Kamianets-Podilskyi, Sharhorod and Markowice, and spent the final 20 years of his life (1730-50) as a confessor at monasteries in Sandomierz, Brest, Lviv and Jarosław.

Between his travels to Persia, Wieczorkowski published two of his most important literary works in Poland, *Breve compendium* (1721) written in Turkish and Latin, and *Katechizm* (1721, 1727[2]) written in Turkish and Polish. They are bilingual catechetical handbooks, written to facilitate evangelisation. Apart from lectures on faith and a set of prayers, they also contain references to other religions, including Islam (especially *Katechizm*). Wieczorkowski probably learnt the basics of Turkish in Poland, and later improved his skills during his years in Persia, the area where the Jesuit mission centres were located being Turkish-speaking.

Wieczorkowski went on to publish four more works, two of his own compositions, *Słońce na dziesięć linyach*[...] (1715) and *Jasne promienie imienia Jezusowego*[...] (1740), and two translations into Polish of J. Drews' *Na wiekszą Pana Boga naszego chwałę i dusz obfite zbawienie*[...] (1720) and P. Segneri's work *Manna duszy albo ćwiczenia się duchowne łacne*[...] (1731). These four are different in character from the two catechetical books. They contain teachings for Christians, with calls to pray for the evangelisation of pagans and infidels.

MAIN SOURCES OF INFORMATION

Primary

S. Załęski, *Jezuici w Polsce*, vol. 3, Lviv, 1902, pp. 882-94, 1095

J. Sygański, 'Z notatek podróżnych o. Michała Ignacego Wieczorkowskiego T.J. misyonarza apostolskiego w Persyi 1715-1720', *Nasze Wiadomości. Pamiętnik Prowincyi Galicyjskiej Towarzystwa Jezusowego* 3 (1910-12) 504-14

Secondary

L. Grzebień et al. (eds), *Encyklopedia wiedzy o jezuitach na ziemiach Polski i Litwy 1564-1995*, Krakow, 2004, p. 733

H.E. Wyczawski (ed.), *Słownik polskich teologów katolickich*, vol. 4, Warsaw, 1983, pp. 418-19

T. Kowalski, 'O ks. Michała Wieczorkowskiego T.J. misjonarza perskiego, pracach tureckich', *Rocznik Orjentalistyczny* 12 (1936) 1-28

T. Kowalski, 'O. Michał Wieczorkowski T.J. i jego prace tureckie', *Misje Katolickie* 54 (1935) 65-70

WORKS ON CHRISTIAN-MUSLIM RELATIONS

Breve compendium fidei catholicae turcico textu, de verbo ad verbum in latinum converso
'A brief digest of the Catholic faith written in Turkish, translated into Latin word for word'

DATE   1721
ORIGINAL LANGUAGE   Latin

DESCRIPTION

The *Breve compendium*, 60 pages long, with Turkish on odd-numbered pages and Latin on even-numbered pages, was published in 1721 (its full title is *Ad M. D. G. et animarum salutem plurimam. Breve compendium fidei catholicae turcico textu, de verbo ad verbum in latinum converso in gratiam Catholicorum nationis turcicae in Polonia versantium, aut turcicum idioma discentium et missiones orientales ingredientium. Ex missionariorum persicorum, Catechismus turcicis excerptum et auctum. Contra turcicos, judaicos, & haereticos errores conscriptum,* 'For the greater glory of God and for the salvation of many souls. A brief digest of the Catholic faith written in Turkish, translated into Latin word for word, for Catholics of Turkish origin residing in Poland and for learners of the Turkish language setting out on missionary work in Oriental countries. Selected and extended contents from Turkish catechisms of Persian missionaries. Written down to combat Turkish, Jewish and heretical mistakes'). It is a practical guide for missionaries working in Turkish-speaking areas.

The work is divided into three lectures. It starts with basic prayers, which are followed by an exposition of the Catholic faith. Wieczorkowski explains the principles of the faith and argues that it is superior to other religions, giving examples of practices followed by infidels that are meant to prove the Catholic faith is the right choice as the only true religion. There are seven brief references to Muslim Turks in the first and second sections, though it is evident that Wieczorkowski had Muslims very much in mind throughout what he wrote.

He does not engage in discussion and does not look for arguments to support his position. He only refers to the advantages of his own religion, deprecating other faiths and their followers. He states *a priori* that: 1. the superiority of Catholicism is obvious, as all other religions derive from it; 2. Turks are incapable of understanding the uniqueness of the Holy Trinity; 3. false prophets appeared after Christ (there is no mention of Muḥammad); 4. circumcision is redundant because it has been replaced by baptism.

The European tradition of writing practical missionary guidebooks in Turkish (in non-Arabic alphabets) dates back to the end of the 13th century. Several such works were quite popular in Wieczorkowski's time, and the title and contents of the *Breve compendium* indicate that he knew some of them and modelled his own creation on them. However, the only source referred to in the text (p. 8) is *Manuductio ad conversionem Mahumetanorum*[...] by Thyrsus Gonzalez (1687), and it has not been possible to identify others.

The *Breve compendium* has the character of a compilation, as is apparent in the terminology used. There are variations, such as *apostolos* (Gr.) or *resul* for 'apostle', *patri* (Lat.) or *kahana* for 'priest', and *vaftismos* (Gr.) or *sebfat* for 'baptism'. These prove that Wieczorkowski must have relied on the works of more than one predecessor. He may also have drawn some information from the oral traditions of Turkish-speaking Christian communities of the East, such as Greeks, Armenians and the Gagauz.

What distinguishes Wieczorkowski's *Breve compendium* from other similar works is the care he shows over the syntax of Turkish in the prayers. Earlier authors copied the Latin word order when writing in Turkish, but he decided to follow the Turkish order. This was a brave move, and showed that he evidently wanted converts to be able to understand the essentials of their new faith.

SIGNIFICANCE

The *Breve compendium* praises Catholicism and attempts to discourage readers from choosing another religion. This attitude was embedded in the character of Polish Catholicism of the time, which directly combatted non-Catholic beliefs in Poland.

In comparison with similar works, the *Breve compendium* can be singled out for linguistic correctness in its prayers, texts which non-Catholics could find especially challenging to understand. As it is a Turkish-Latin guidebook, it could be used more widely than by Polish missionaries alone. It is possible that it was written to facilitate work among Turkish-speaking Armenians and Greeks living in Persia and Turkey. However, there is no evidence to suggest that the work reached a wider audience.

PUBLICATIONS

Michał Ignacy Wieczorkowski, *Ad M. D. G. et animarum salutem plurimam. Breve compendium fidei catholicae turcico textu, de verbo ad verbum in latinum converso in gratiam Catholicorum nationis turcicae in Polonia versantium, aut turcicum idioma discentium et missiones orientales ingredientium. Ex missionariorum persicorum, Catechismus turcicis excerptum et auctum. Contra turcicos, judaicos, & haereticos errores conscriptum AP. Michaele Ignatio Wieczorkowski Soc: Jesu missionario persico. Cum facultate Superiorum*, Typis clari Coll. Posnaniensis Soc: Jesu., 1721

G. Hazai (ed.), 'Die Türkischen Texte von M.I. Wieczorkowski', *Acta Orientalia Academiae Scientiarum Hungaricae* 41 (1987) 173-210 (edition of the Turkish part)

B. Podolak (ed.), 'Der Transkriptionstext von Michał Ignacy Wieczorkowski "Breve compendium fidei Catholicae Turcico textu[...]" (1721)', *Studia Turcologica Cracoviensia* 1 (1995) 23-89 (complete edition)

STUDIES

B. Podolak, 'Przekłady chrześcijańskich tekstów religijnych na język turecki', in A. Krasnowolska, B. Mękarska and A. Zaborski (eds), *Języki orientalne w przekładzie*, Kraków, 2003, 253-8

B. Podolak, 'Die türkische Sprache in "Breve compendium fidei catholicae turcico textu" (1721) von Michał Ignacy Wieczorkowski. Wörterbuch', *Zeszyty Naukowe Uniwersytetu Jagiellońskiego. Prace Językoznawcze* 120 (2000) 151-78

B. Podolak, 'Die türkische Sprache in "Breve compendium fidei catholicae turcico textu" (1721) von Michał Ignacy Wieczorkowski. Wortschatz', *Zeszyty Naukowe Uniwersytetu Jagiellońskiego. Prace Językoznawcze* 113 (1993) 75-93

B. Podolak, 'Die türkische Sprache in "Breve compendium fidei catholicae turcico textu" (1721) von Michał Ignacy Wieczorkowski', *Zeszyty Naukowe Uniwersytetu Jagiellońskiego. Prace Językoznawcze* 101 (1990) 97-114 (orthography, phonetics, inflection)

Kowalski, 'O ks. Michała Wieczorkowskiego T.J. misjonarza perskiego, pracach tureckich'

Kowalski, 'O. Michał Wieczorkowski T.J. i jego prace tureckie'

Katechizm
'Catechism'

DATE 1727
ORIGINAL LANGUAGE Ottoman Turkish

DESCRIPTION

The first version of the *Katechizm* published in 1721 in Poznań has not survived. All that is known is its title, *Katechizm z okazyi Tatarzyna Budziackiego nic po polsku tylko po turecku nieumiejącego wydany*, and that it comprised 51 pages (Estreicher, *Bibliografia polska*, p. 442). We cannot be sure whether the suggestion is correct that this first edition was, in fact, the text of *Breve compendium* in Latin and Polish (Wyczawski, *Słownik polskich teologów*, p. 419; Słowiński, *Katechizmy katolickie*, pp. 358-9). The second edition (with the full title *Na większą p. B. naszego chwałę y dusz iak naywięcey, nawrocenie katechizm z okazyi Tatarzyna budziackiego, nic po polsku nie umieiącego, tylko po turecku w Warszawie r. p. 1720. 25. d. grudnia. ochrzczonego, z polskiego ięzyka na turecki ięzyk przetłumaczony y tureckie niektore błędy zbiiaiący, dla podobnego przypadku y wygody ochrzczenia Turków albo Tatarów, y ich że w wierze s. katholickiey ćwiczenia, powtore do druku podany, y rozszerzony, od x. Michała Jgnacego Wieczorkowskiego, Societatis Jesu missionarza perskiego*, 'For the greater glory of our God and for the salvation of as many souls as possible. A catechism entirely in Turkish for the Budjak Tatar who does not speak Polish at all, baptised in Warsaw on 25 December 1720 AD. Translated from Polish into the Turkish language, and contesting some Turkish mistakes for the sake of similar cases and for the simplicity of baptising Turks or Tatars and for their learning of the Catholic faith, submitted for publication for the second time and expanded by Father Michał Ignacy Wieczorkowski, a Persian missionary of the Jesuit Order') was published in 1727 in Lviv. At 119 pages, it is significantly longer than the first edition.

The immediate reason for writing the *Katechizm* was to prepare a Tatar for baptism. He was probably a prisoner of war who intended to live in Poland and wanted to change his religion. The *Katechizm* is a practical missionary guidebook that briefly describes everything a missionary working in a Muslim environment would need: guidelines for encounters with Muslims, arguments defending Christianity, necessary teachings for the convert, prayers, the rite of baptism and advice on strengthening the new believer's faith. The work is comprised of a doctrinal and polemical part (pp. 4-43), and a ritual and catechetical part (pp. 43-119).

The doctrinal part, which takes the form of a dialogue between the catechumen, who asks questions and expresses his concerns, and the catechist, who answers them and provides explanations, is the core of the work. The conversation concerns four main issues: 1. Catholicism v. Islam; 2. the Trinitarian formula and the monotheism of Islam; 3. Muḥammad v. Christ; 4. circumcision v. baptism. Thus, the issues discussed are similar to those in the *Breve compendium*, though here they take a different form and are described in a much broader context. Wieczorkowski contrasts Christianity and Islam, provides arguments to prove the superiority of his own religion, and refutes the allegations of the other party.

He questions the validity of Islam (sometimes also referring to other religions), but by denying it any value he avoids substantial discussion with the curious Tatar. In general he upholds his own position purely with simple statements (making the logical mistake of asserting claims that themselves require justification). In his opinion, affirmation of the distinctiveness of the Catholic religion is a sufficient criterion for its validity and uniqueness, and therefore for its superiority over Islam.

Wieczorkowski explains that baptism is superior to circumcision, as the former has replaced the latter and has the power to take away sin. He denies that Christianity teaches the existence of three gods, and suggests that Catholics are able to understand the doctrine of the Holy Trinity, which Muslims cannot (on p. 90 there is an ingenious comparison of the Holy Trinity to the human intellect, memory and will), and he explains the relationship between the Father and the Son by the example of a man who recognises himself in the mirror.

He devotes a large part of the work to contrasting Christ and Muḥammad. He says nothing about the teachings of Muḥammad contained in the Qur'an, but denies he was a prophet because he had no halo, did not perform miracles and did not prophesy. He also denigrates the person of Muḥammad by showing that he did not come from a worthy family, and calling him impure, an adulterer and a sodomite.

The second part describes the sacrament of baptism and post-baptismal teachings. It contains prayers, catechismal phrases and a description of the ceremony. This part is not polemical, but on pp. 88-90 there is a short section in which the catechist explains that the words spoken while making the sign of the cross are hidden in the Muslim *basmala*. Wieczorkowski did not speak Arabic, so he was probably repeating what he had read in similar works by other authors (e.g. Bartholomaeus Georgievicz (Georgius), *Rozmowa z turczynem o wierze krzesciyańskiey*[...], Kraków, 1548; Marcin Paszkowski, *Dzieie tureckie*[...], Kraków, 1615).

The character of the *Katechizm* is clearly one of confrontation. Wieczorkowski makes numerous offensive statements about Islam, and he contrasts the spiritual values of Christianity with the materialistic and sensory values of Islam.

SIGNIFICANCE

The *Katechizm* is a rare record of Polish missionary work among Muslims. The publication of a second edition could be construed as a response to demand, but it is difficult to assess this properly in the absence of the first, and the difference in size may indicate that the first edition was significantly different from the second. We should therefore not overrate the significance of *Katechizm*. No evidence can be found to suggest that it was in fact used in missionary work among the Muslim community in the Commonwealth.

Wieczorkowski's two works have a lot in common: both are guidebooks for missionaries, both contain translations into Turkish, and some of the same prayers are found in both. However, there are also significant differences: 1. The *Breve compendium*, which was most probably created first, takes the form of lectures directed not only at followers of Islam, while *Katechizm* is a dialogue with a Muslim wishing to be baptised; 2. The *Breve compendium* is much shorter than the *Katechizm*, and does not contain many of the elements in the longer work; 3. when compared with the compilation character of the *Breve compendium*, the *Katechizm* is undoubtedly a more original work.

PUBLICATIONS

Michał Ignacy Wieczorkowski, *Na większą p. B. naszego chwałę y dusz iak naywięcey, nawrocenie katechizm z okazyi Tatarzyna budziackiego, nic po polsku nie umieiącego, tylko po turecku w Warszawie r. p. 1720. 25. d. grudnia. ochrzczonego, z polskiego ięzyka na turecki ięzyk przetłumaczony y tureckie niektore błędy zbiiaiący, dla podobnego przypadku y wygody ochrzczenia Turków albo Tatarów, y ich że w wierze s. katholickiey ćwiczenia, powtore do druku podany, y rozszerzony, od x. Michała Jgnacego Wieczorkowskiego, Societatis Jesu missionarza perskiego. Z dozwoleniem starszych*, W drukarni Collegii Leopoliensis Societatis Jesu, r. p. 1727; pl:57007 (digitised version available through Wielkopolska Biblioteka Cyfrowa)

G. Hazai (ed.), 'Die Türkischen Texte von M. I. Wieczorkowski', *Acta Orientalia Academiae Scientiarum Hungaricae* 41 (1987) 173-210 (edition of the Turkish part)

Michał Ignacy Wieczorkowski, *Katechizm z okazyi ochrzczenia Tatarzyna Budziackiego*, ed. M. Czachorowski, Wrocław, 2012 (complete edition)

STUDIES

B. Podolak, 'XVIII-wieczny "Katechizm" jako przykład tureckiego tekstu transkrybowanego o tematyce religijnej', in M. Czachorowski (ed.), *X. Michał Ignacy Wieczorkowski. Katechizm z okazyi ochrzczenia Tatarzyna Budziackiego*, Wrocław, 2012, 17-22

J.Z. Słowiński, *Katechizmy katolickie w języku polskim od XVI do XVIII wieku*, Lublin, 2005, pp. 358-69

J. Nosowski, *Polska literatura polemiczno-antyislamistyczna XVI, XVII i XVIII w.*, Warsaw, 1974, pp. 126-41

Kowalski, 'O ks. Michała Wieczorkowskiego T.J. misjonarza perskiego, pracach tureckich'

Kowalski, 'O. Michał Wieczorkowski T.J. i jego prace tureckie'

Barbara Podolak

Franciszek Gościecki

DATE OF BIRTH   3 October 1668
PLACE OF BIRTH   Region of Greater Poland
DATE OF DEATH   1 May 1729
PLACE OF DEATH   Sambor (present-day western Ukraine)

BIOGRAPHY

Not much is known about Franciszek Gościecki, particularly his boyhood and education. He joined the Society of Jesus in Kraków on 28 February 1684. This choice of career in a religious order suggests that he was born into a noble family without means as one of the younger sons with no prospects for his share in the family inheritance. In the Jesuits, he was at first mainly a school teacher. He taught rhetoric in Jesuit colleges in Łuck, Sandomierz and Toruń, among others, and served as prefect of a boarding-school in Rawa. Around 1700, the Jesuit authorities appointed him to the new Jesuit house in Sambor near Lwów, which had been founded by Marcin Chomętowski in 1698. He remained closely linked to this house for the rest of his life, serving several times as its superior (1710-12, 1714-16 and 1722-28).

He was held in esteem by Stanisław Chomętowski, son of Marcin and voivode of the Mazovia region, who was protector and benefactor of the Jesuits – he founded the Jesuit church in Sambor. In accordance with Chomętowski's wishes, Gościecki accompanied him on his missions and his pilgrimage to Rome and assisted him during the meeting of Commonwealth senators with Tsar Peter the Great (r. 1682-1725) in Żółkwia in 1708. He was the chaplain to the diplomatic mission from King Augustus II (r. 1694-1733) to Sultan Ahmed III (r. 1703-36; mistakenly named as Ahmed IV in the title of Gościecki's work) in 1712-14. The mission was conducted in adverse political circumstances, and Chomętowski was even threatened with imprisonment. In a moment of despair, he made a vow to make a pilgrimage to Rome, which he fulfilled after concluding the talks with reasonable success. Gościecki accompanied Chomętowski on his pilgrimage, in autumn 1717, and a little later on his mission to St Petersburg in 1719-20.

It is possible that Gościecki is the author of an anonymous *Krótkie opisanie miasta Petersburga* ('Short description of the city of Petersburg')

that has survived to the present. This is a description of the city written
in prose in 1720.

MAIN SOURCES OF INFORMATION

Secondary

L. Grzebień (ed.), *Encyklopedia wiedzy o jezuitach na ziemiach Polski i Litwy 1564-
      1995*, Kraków, 2004, p. 190

R. Pollak, *Wśród literatów staropolskich* [Among old Polish writers], Warsaw,
      1966, pp. 515-17

J. Poplatek, 'Gościecki Franciszek', in *Polski słownik biograficzny*, Wrocław, 1960,
      vol. 8, pp. 378-9

A. Kuczera, *Samborszczyzna*, vol. 1, Sambor, 1935, pp. 384-5, 390; vol. 2, Sambor,
      1937, pp. 299-300

W. Konopczyński, 'Chomętowski Stanisław', in *Polski słownik biograficzny*,
      Kraków, 1937, vol. 3/1, pp. 412-14

S. Załęski, *Jezuici w Polsce*, vol. 3/2, Kraków, 1900, pp. 839, 1164; vol. 4/4, Kraków,
      1906, pp. 1626-7

J. Brown, *Biblioteka assystencyi polskiej Towarzystwa Jezusowego*, Poznań, 1862,
      p. 182

WORKS ON CHRISTIAN-MUSLIM RELATIONS

Poselstwo wielkie Jaśnie Wielmożnego Stanisława Chomętowskiego
'The great mission of Stanisław Chomętowski'

DATE   1732
ORIGINAL LANGUAGE   Polish

DESCRIPTION

Franciszek Gościecki's *Poselstwo wielkie Jaśnie Wielmożnego Stanisława
Chomętowskiego* (in full *Poselstwo wielkie Jaśnie Wielmożnego Stanisława
Chomętowskiego, wojewody mazowieckiego, od Najjaśniejszego Augusta
II, króla polskiego, książęcia saskiego, elektora, i Rzeczypospolitej, do
Achmeda IV [sic], sołtana tureckiego, wielkiego z pełną mocą posła, z
szczęśliwym skutkiem przez lata 1712, 1713, 1714 odprawione*, 'The great mis-
sion of Stanisław Chomętowski, esquire, voievode of Mazovia, from the
Most Enlightened Augustus II, the Polish king, Saxon prince and elector, and from the Commonwealth to Ahmed IV [sic], the great Turkish
sultan, carried out with the full strength of the envoy and with a happy

end through the years 1712, 1713, 1714') is a long epic poem of almost 9,000 lines, containing an account of the mission sent to the Sublime Porte with the aim of ratifying the resolutions of the Treaty of Karlowitz (1699) and of finding a solution to continuing difficulties between the Commonwealth and the Ottoman Empire. The mission, which started from Lwów on 24 September 1712, was conducted in difficult political circumstances, with the Ottoman state not wishing to recognise Augustus II's right to the throne, and Swedish and French diplomats, together with the Polish opposition to the Saxon party, trying to undermine it. It was detained in Edirne until November 1713, and Chomętowski himself was threatened with imprisonment. All this resulted in the prolongation of the mission until September 1714, though it did end with success. The long stay in Ottoman lands allowed its members to acquire knowledge about Turkish affairs.

It is difficult to say exactly when the poem was composed. Gościecki probably began only in the 1720s, when he settled in Sambor, and he must have finished before mid-1728, because the censor approved the poem on 18 August 1728. Stanisław Chomętowski, the work's main protagonist, died in that year, and Gościecki himself a year later. The poem was published through the efforts of the Jesuits of Lwów, who had commissioned him to commemorate the mission. The autograph of the work was still extant before the Second World War (see E. Maliszewski, *Bibliografia pamiętników polskich* [Bibliography of Polish memoirs], Warsaw, 1928, p. 359). It was burnt, together with the other items from the collection of the Krasiński Library in Warsaw, by German soldiers.

Poselstwo wielkie consists of five parts of different lengths, each following stages in the progress of the Polish mission. It bears clear signs of influence from Samuel Twardowski's 17th-century *Przeważna legacyja*, which was extremely popular in the Commonwealth in the Baroque period. But Gościecki's work differs in the lack of hostility it shows towards the Ottoman state and its people.

Part 1 describes the events leading up to Chomętowski's mission. Swedish successes against Poland in the early 18th century had led to a civil war in the Commonwealth, the deposition of King Augustus II, and the accession of Stanisław Leszczyński in 1705. These successes encouraged the Swedes to attack Russia, but at the battle of Poltava (in present-day eastern Ukraine) in 1709 they were defeated and King Charles XII (r. 1697-1718) was forced to flee into Ottoman territory. The sultan, who was interested in regaining the territories lost to the Commonwealth and Russia after the Treaty of Karlowitz, gave support to the Swedish king and pressed him to renew hostilities against the Commonwealth, which had been weakened by the civil war. In an attempt to soothe the situation, the Polish parliament, at its session in April 1712, decided to send Chomętowski as an envoy to Istanbul. Part 1 ends with a description of the preparations and the first part of the journey.

Part 2 describes the journey through Moldova and Bulgaria (the latter now a part the Ottoman Empire) to Edirne, where the mission was halted while its legitimacy was questioned. Gościecki's description of the subsequent legs of the journey is accompanied by observations on the new conditions surrounding the travellers. The Muslims they met were disgusted by the 'infidels' and gave them hospitality only grudgingly, though this did not apply to Christian women, whose beauty incurred the risk of them being carried off to the harem.

Parts 3 and 4 contain an account of the mission's time in Edirne and later in Istanbul. Initially Chomętowski was treated with reserve because the sultan was mobilising an army against the Commonwealth, and only after great efforts was there any change among the Ottomans. Regular talks began, and at last he was invited to Istanbul for further talks. Complications continued to cause difficulties, but eventually a peace treaty was signed and the mission was allowed to return home.

In these two Parts, Gościecki's description of diplomatic matters is accompanied by wider observations. While there is some appreciation for Turkish society, his comments about religion show scepticism. He regards Islam as a false religion and 'accursed faith', though he notes the piety and mercy shown by the Turks, and the submission of Muslims throughout the empire to the sultan as the religious leader: a mission from Uzbekistan arrives to assure the sultan as 'head of Islam' of their obedience. He also observes that the muftis of Istanbul serve only as advisors to the sultan in religious law, and can be dismissed from office as the sultan decides. These are pertinent observations in light of the divisions within Christianity after the Reformation.

Gościecki does not devote much space to dogmatic issues. He only notes Muslim faith in one God, adding that they are unable to grasp the Christian concept of the Divine as one in three Persons. He quotes the *shahāda* in Polish, explaining that pronouncing it is the only condition for converting to Islam, and observing that there are many new Muslims in Istanbul, who are really attracted to the faith by its promises of moral dissipation. On the other hand, he does give some attention to various forms of religiosity. He mentions the call to prayer, the Turkish practice of performing the compulsory prayers in public, and even during travel, and the constant use of prayer beads (*subḥa*), with individual beads symbolising the 99 attributes of God. He mentions sermons preached by dervishes on the streets and their dances, mockingly pointing out that one of the dancers gets in touch with Muḥammad and then communicates what has been revealed to him.

During his stay in Edirne, Gościecki witnessed the celebration of *kurban bayram* and *ramadan bayram*. He does not have much to say about the former, and only mentions it because it was marked by the firing of cannons and illuminations because of the sultan's presence in the city. He describes what is involved in fasting during Ramaḍān, though in his view it is no more than a pretext for debauchery each night.

Gościecki writes with admiration about the Turks' generosity in various forms of charity. Numerous and well-equipped hospitals (he is particularly intrigued by an asylum), resting places for the poor, caravanserais and shelters for animals (he saw one for cats in Istanbul) witness to their great generosity.

Gościecki is interested in Turkish education because of his own profession. He admires the large number of schools in mosques where competent teachers can be found, though he doubts the worth of qur'anic teachings, which he regards as no more than strange 'fables'. He tells his readers with some sadness about a new academy being set up mainly for boys culled in the *devşirme*, who were condemned to abandon the 'true' faith.

He is interested in the way Christians practise their religion in Istanbul. He notes the tolerance of the Ottomans towards Christian ceremonial (processions, public singing by groups of believers), though he complains that the city authorities do not allow the use of bells, and that there is no music during the celebrations.

The last part of the poem recounts Chomętowski's farewell visit to the grand vizier, and his return to Poland. It describes how he redeemed compatriots from slavery, and how impoverished Christians survived in Istanbul after being freed from slavery but without the means to get home.

SIGNIFICANCE

The poem was published only once, and for a long time it did not attract interest. It has only come to notice since the mid-20th century, mainly as an example of change in the negative attitude towards the Muslim East that prevailed earlier in Polish literature, and as a work that documents Ottoman culture of the Tulip Era (*Lâle Devri*). Unfortunately, the lack of any critical edition makes research on how it was received in the period that produced it difficult.

PUBLICATIONS

F. Gościecki, *Poselstwo wielkie Jaśnie Wielmożnego Stanisława Chomętowskiego, wojewody mazowieckiego, od Najjaśniejszego Augusta II, króla polskiego, książęcia saskiego, elektora, i Rzeczypospolitej, do Achmeda IV, sołtana tureckiego, wielkiego z pełną mocą posła, z szczęśliwym skutkiem przez lata 1712, 1713, 1714 odprawione*, Lwów, 1732; SD W.1.2409 (digitised version available through Polona/)

STUDIES

R. Krzywy, *Obraz Turcji i jej mieszkańców w 'Poselstwie wielkim' Franciszka Gościeckiego na tle staropolskiego dyskursu antytureckiego* [The image of Turkey and its inhabitants in 'Poselstwo wielkie' by Franciszek Gościecki in the context the old Polish anti-Turkish discourse], in G. Czerwiński and A. Konopacki (eds), *Wschód muzułmański w literaturze polskiej. Idee i obrazy*, Białystok, 2016, 17-39

H. Dziechcińska, *Świat i człowiek w pamiętnikach trzech stuleci: XVI-XVII-XVIII* [The world and man in the memoirs of three centuries: 16th-17th-18th], Warsaw, 2003, pp. 53-7, 71-3

M. Bałczewski, *Gry i zabawy Turków osmańskich* [Games and pastimes of the Ottoman Turks], Warsaw, 2000

R. Krzywy, 'Muzy – poetów boginie'. Późnobarokowy suplement do staropolskiego mitoznawstwa (o "Poselstwie wielkim" Franciszka Gościeckiego)' [Muses – poets' goddesses. Late baroque supplement to the old Polish study of myths (on 'Poselstwo wielkie' by Franciszek Gościecki)], *Ruch Literacki* 40 (2000) 95-107

R. Krzywy, *Od hodoeporikonu do eposu peregrynackiego. Studium z historii form literackich* [From *hodoeporicon* to peregrination epic. A study in the history of literary forms], Warsaw, 2001, pp. 202-29, 242-3

M. Prejs, *Egzotyzm w literaturze staropolskiej. Wybrane problemy* [Exoticism in old Polish literature. Selected issues], Warsaw, 1999, pp. 215-57

Pollak, *Wśród literatów staropolskich*, pp. 508-27

A. Sajkowski, *Nad staropolskimi pamiętnikami* [On old Polish memoirs], Poznań, 1964, pp. 107-14

Roman Krzywy

Anti-Turkish literature in the Polish-Lithuanian Commonwealth, 1575-1733

DATE   1575-1733
ORIGINAL LANGUAGE   Polish

DESCRIPTION

This entry examines anti-Turkish works written between about 1575 and 1733, when the last known (it is still in manuscript form) appeared. The period has been divided into two parts, with the years 1622-3 chosen as the dividing line. The period between 1575 and 1622 was characterised by growing hostilities that led to the first direct large-scale military confrontations between the Commonwealth and the Ottoman Empire (for over a century the Commonwealth had avoided any confrontation). The tense, threatening stalemate that followed the first outburst finally erupted with other major military clashes in the 1670s and 1680s and ended with the gradual weakening of both states at the beginning of the 18th century.

General characteristics

Anti-Turkish works in the Polish-Lithuanian Commonwealth were written mainly in reference to: 1. constant tension in the borderland area caused by regular Tatar raids and military incursions of the nobility from present-day western Ukraine into Moldova and Wallachia, and armed raids by the Cossacks on the shores of the Black Sea, including an attack on the outskirts of Istanbul; 2. renewed propaganda campaigns and plans aimed at forming so-called pan-Christian anti-Islamic 'sacred leagues', with the goal of removing the Turks from Europe and recapturing Jerusalem; 3. military conflicts (the lost battle at Țuțora/Tsetsora/Cecora, 1620; two battles at Khotyn/Chocim, 1621 and 1673; the victory at Vienna, 1683), ceasefires and peace treaties (e.g. Busza, 1618; Buczacz, 1672).

These works were written in both poetry and prose. They include treatises describing the Ottoman Empire and proposing plans for war against it, exhortations or 'wake-up calls' (*exhorty, pobudki*), envoys' reports and war reports, memoirs, heroic epics, works written for particular occasions, prognostications (*prognostyki*), and patriotic lyrics and songs (*canti*). Some works heralded military confrontations, while others followed them as their echo. Some of their contents found more endurable forms as entries in chronicles, textbooks and encyclopaedias published after 1730.

The image of Islam in the Commonwealth was part of a fuller image of the Ottoman Empire that was based on works of decorative art and commonly used everyday objects, as well as popular ideas about the way the Turks lived and organised their society. People encountered Ottoman objects and works of art through trade and war spoils, and found them attractive (see, for example, the Ottoman-inspired clothes worn by the nobility). But the religion of Islam itself was nevertheless perceived as false and inimical to Christianity, although writers hardly ever made it the centre of their attention. Comments on Islam, if they came at all, were marginal to their arguments, or functioned in the background of hate speech directed against the 'pagan'. The strongly unfavourable presentation of Islam in wake-up calls and treatises on war was made through references to culture, customs and laws that were considered religiously inspired, but not through direct references. Thus, as part of the effort to make Muslims repulsive, thoughtless and blunt cruelty (often experienced in encounters with the Tatars and Turks) was treated as an integral part of Muslim culture and mores.

No systematic presentation of the beliefs and practices of Muslims is to be found in this literature. Rather, they deal with the details of what the Commonwealth nobility faced when they encountered the Tatars and Turks, which were often dramatic: a sudden confrontation with a Tatar raiding party; a direct clash on the battlefield; experiences of slavery. In addition, information was drawn from Christian communities that found themselves under Muslim rule, in which scorn for Islam as a religion was often expressed. Though stemming from the same Abrahamic roots as Judaism, it was seen as worse than Judaism because Muslims were considered the offspring of Abraham and his slave woman Hagar, not Sarah.

Imaginary perceptions of Islam in Polish culture were based on strongly held stereotypical beliefs about Muslims: their unimaginable cruelty (murders of the elderly and children, rapes, torture of people and animals, material destruction during Tatar raids); the kidnapping and enslavement of Christian children in regions under Ottoman rule, who after forced conversion to Islam and Muslim indoctrination were conscripted into the ranks of the Janissaries and fought under the influence of narcotics (*mastok*); the drive to eradicate Christianity from the world through military expansion; desecration and destruction of Christian churches and their conversion into mosques; the harsh life of slaves;

scorn for circumcision; the perception of Islam as a false religion that was a patchwork of various beliefs; memories of the fall of Constantinople and the defeat at Varna (1444) as a warning.

When they were writing about Tatar and Turkish Muslims, the authors typically used abusive language; for example, Muslims, especially Tatars, were compared to dogs. Such abuse was applied not only to the religious sphere, but also to the entire cultural realm of the Ottoman Empire and other Muslim states. Tatars were perceived as a cruel military formation whose sole purpose was destructive raiding. They and the Turks were called 'pagans'. However, all comments and allusions to Islam are linked to the Turks, who, together with the Arabs, were the real bearers of Muslim teachings (present only minimally in the literature described here), culture and mores.

Analogies were also constructed between current Christian-Muslim relations (the Commonwealth or all Christian countries versus the Ottoman Empire) and the struggles of the biblical Israel and its leaders against their enemies (e.g. the battles of Moses and Gideon with the Midianites; Judith killing Holofernes; the fall of Jericho to Joshua). The 17th-century idea of Sarmatian Messianism grew out of the analogy between God's chosen people and the people of the Commonwealth. (Some of the Commonwealth nobility held the conviction that their nation played a messianic role in withstanding anti-Christian or/and anti-Catholic forces. Resistance against Muslim Ottomans and Orthodox Muscovites/Russians played a redemptive role for Catholic Christendom).

Anti-Turkish and anti-Tatar utterances in the texts written between 1575 and 1733, and referring always, if only indirectly, to Muslims as invaders, are restricted to conveying the notion of defending home territory and the Christian religion. The concept of *antemurale Christianitatis* develops only gradually (in the cultural and religious sense, i.e. a military defeat by the Ottomans would be equated with the fall of Christian civilisation in the conquered area). However, the term *antemurale* was initially used in a variety of meanings. Sometimes it referred to the armed nobility defending the borders against the Tatars and Turks; sometimes to the Virgin Mary, who was appealed to by the poets Maciej Kazimierz Sarbiewski (1595-1640), who called her 'the *antemurale* of the Commonwealth army' (*Ioanni Carolo Chodkiewicz palatino Vilnensi et Magni Ducatus Lithuaniae exercituum duci, contra Turcas, Dei Optimi Maximi et Beatae Virginis Mariae auxilium spondet*, p. 4), and Wespazjan Kochowski (1633-1700), who in Canto 3 of his *Taratantara albo pobudka do rycerstwa polskiego z Niepróżnującego próżnowania*, called her a

Sarmatian *antemurale*: 'Poland is yours, You have defended it ages long, and also now You will shelter it', vv. 81-2. Only Józef Wereszczyński (1530-98) in his *Ekscytarz* (1592) clearly calls the Commonwealth the *antemurale* of the whole Christian world. The early perception of the messianic (defending/redemptive) role of the Commonwealth, which is present in the works of Marcin Paszkowski (c. 1560-1621), springs from this understanding of *antemurale* at the beginning of the 17th century and matures into Sarmatian Messianism in the second half of the 17th century (cf. W. Kochowski, W. Potocki).

A prediction ascribed to Sultan Süleyman the Magnificent (r. 1520-66) and known from the works of Bartholomeo Georgius (1505-after 1566), which foretold that the might of the Ottoman Empire would fall because of the intervention of a 'ruler from the north', was constantly recalled by Polish authors. Polish authors of anti-Turkish wake-up calls identified this unnamed individual as the ruler of the Commonwealth, and for that reason said that the Turks should avoid any war with their northern neighbour. Marcin Paszkowski, who drew on Georgius's works, knew these prophecies well (see his *Minerwa*), and they are also present in the works of Wawrzyniec Chlebowski (d. after 1626), who inserted *Praktyka stara turecka o upadku mocy i wyniszczeniu państwa ich* from Paszkowski's *Minerwa* into his own *O Królów i cesarzów tureckich dziełach albo sprawach*. The prophecy was recalled by most authors until the end of the 17th century.

A prophecy along the same lines by a 15th-century philosopher, Antonius Torquatius Ferrariensi, who foresaw the fall of the Ottoman Empire in 1596 and the conversion of the Turks to Christianity, was translated by Jan Smolik (c. 1560-after 1599). Paszkowski also referred to a similar prophecy published by Marcin of Kleck in a calendar for 1608, while Jan Gawiński recalled Cornelius Lapide's *Prophetas duodecim minores* from 1625 (which was also recalled in the 1712 book attributed to Mikołaj Chwałkowski, on whom see the entry in this volume, pp. 445-50).

1575-1622

Laments on the cruelty and brutality of the Tatars, especially against the common people are found from the beginning of this period. Authors such as Bartosz Paprocki, in his *Historyja żałosna*, mourn those killed and enslaved, and villages and small towns plundered and destroyed. They consider Muslims as enemies of Christianity, which is threatened with grave danger.

In the poem *Na postrach turecki nenia*, Kacper Miaskowski uses a set of topical images that were to incite the anger and pity of the armed nobles, building an analogy between the position of the biblical Gideon, who with God's help defeated the Midianites, and the Sarmatian knights, the nobility of the Commonwealth, who with God's support would defeat the Muslims (called here *bisurmans*). In *Pieśń żałobna na klęskę ukrainną i niebezpieczeństwo Kamieńca etc.*, Miaskowski uses offensive language against the Muslim practice of circumcision.

Treatises and exhortations (wake-up calls) appear in abundance only in the years 1594-8. Their authors search for an efficient solution to the problem of the Tatar raids and the threat to Christianity in the Commonwealth (and to the state itself) posed by Islam. They base their own images of Islam and Muslim culture on Georgius's *Rozmowa z turczynem o wierze chrześcijańskiej* (translated into Polish and published in Krakow in 1548), reports from travellers (e.g. Mikołaj Krzysztof Radziwiłł), chronicles (e.g. by Marcin Bielski and Aleksander Gwagnin), and on 16th-century anti-Turkish works published in Western and Central Europe. The authors take the basic knowledge about Islam and Muslim culture that they have received without question or qualification, and only make use of frequently occurring negative stereotypes, adding their own personal forms of hate speech.

1623-1730

The reasoning in anti-Turkish literature does not change significantly during the 17th century, when compared to the situation after the Chocim campaign of 1621, though there is a change from expressly religious to political and social motivations for fighting the Ottomans.

During the second half of the 1640s, a plan for an offensive war against the Ottomans was developed and supported eagerly by King Władysław IV Vasa (r. 1632-48). The project was sternly opposed by the nobility, however, who feared that a victorious war could strengthen the position of the king in the Commonwealth and it was completely abandoned after Władysław's death in 1648. The plan gave rise not to any supporting wave of anti-Turkish literature, but rather to works condemning it, among them the anonymous *Zaciąg nowy za objęciem buławy nowego hetmana*. A number of important military events belong to this period: the Treaty of Buczacz (1672) and the handing over of Podolia region to the Ottomans, the second battle at Chocim (1673), the victory at Vienna (1683) and the Treaty of Karlowitz (1699).

The writings of Maciej Kazimierz Sarbiewski (1595-1642), bearing echoes of the Chocim campaign of 1621, have a strong anti-Turkish but not necessarily anti-Islamic character. Apart from exhortatory calls to war and to the defence of Christianity, and abusive words directed against a 'pagan' and a 'Scythian', there are hardly any clear anti-Islamic references. Sarbiewski must have had some basic knowledge about Islam, but he evidently assumed his readers would have it too, so he did not refer to it.

Commenting on the capture of Podolia by the Turks and on the Treaty of Buczacz (1672) that confirmed their possession, Wacław Potocki in *Braterska admonicya do ichmościów wielmożnych panów braci starszych* criticised this failure to defend the region, stating that the Muslims ('pagans') had taken over the area and erected a mosque there, thus Islamising it, and making it their own by collecting a tax (*kharaj*) from ancient Christian lands for the upkeep of the mosque.

In his description of the fighting at Vienna in 1683, Jan Chryzostom Pasek (1636-1701) in his *Pamiętniki* ('Memoirs') depicts the Ottoman vizier exhorting his army to be stern in battle, and recalling the authority of the Prophet Muḥammad. The usual polemical terms appear: the vizier is called 'a traitor', the Turkish army are 'heathens', the Polish-Lithuanian army fight in order to earn favour with God, and their defeat is part of God's will as a punishment for their sins. Pasek also refers to an alleged alliance between the Muslims and Protestants. (This carried its own significance in the context of the hostility towards non-Catholics that had been growing from the mid-17th century; the 1658 Parliament Act gave the Polish Brethren a choice between conversion and banishment. The hostility had its roots partly in the 'bad conscience' of many nobles, who initially backed the Swedes during the invasion of 1655-6 and then had to return to their original allegiance to the king of the Commonwealth.) Pasek emphasises that the Lutherans in Danzig prayed for a Turkish victory at Vienna, and that the German Protestants planned to support the Ottomans both financially and militarily, while the Protestant Prince Emre Tököly (1657-1705) was on the side of the Turks. The Lutherans later claimed that the Turkish defeat of the Catholics would lead to the introduction of Protestantism in Europe.

Anti-Turkish works gradually disappeared after 1700, though some (unfounded) fears of further Ottoman territorial expansion were still present in the 18th century. The gradual Orientalising of the Baroque-Sarmatian culture of the Commonwealth nobility, which reached its apogee in the second half of the 17th and first half of the 18th century, worked to increase acceptance of Turkish culture and the Ottomans. However, even though no new anti-Turkish works appeared, the negative image of the Ottoman Empire persisted in Polish literature until the mid-18th century, in contrast to the actual state of Polish-Ottoman relations. This stereotype was based on the attitudes that had been formed under the influence of the military confrontations of the 17th century, reinforced by anti-Turkish propaganda. Abuses in the form of habitual epithets were directed against Muḥammad and all Muslims, a tendency that continued until the late 18th century, accompanied by the climax of the Sarmatian-Baroque form of religion in which to be Polish automatically meant to be Roman Catholic. The anonymous *Dyskurs, jeżeli sprawiedliwa wojna przeciwko Turczynowi* of 1733, which is preserved only in manuscript form (MS Krakow, Biblioteka Książąt Czartoryskich – rkps. 210, fols 909-923), is the latest work of this kind, although traces of stereotypical anti-Turkish thinking are present in the model letter books (*listowniki*) of Kazimierz Wieruszewski (*Fama polska*, 1720) and Wojciech Bystrzonowski (*Polak sensat w liście*, 1730).

Józef Wereszczyński (1530-98)

Józef Wereszczyński was born in Zbaraż (in present-day Ukraine). He was ordained a Roman Catholic priest, was appointed as the Benedictine abbot of Sieciechów, and in 1592 was made bishop of Kiev. He was a political writer, preacher and moralist, and supported the election of Sigismund III Vasa as king of the Commonwealth. Most of his works appeared in the last 20 years of the 16th century: sermons for Lent ('Passion sermons') and for Sundays, on the themes of confession, Purgatory, the sacrament of marriage, a polemical work with the aim of convincing the Jews that Jesus Christ was their long awaited Messiah, moralistic works stigmatising drunkenness, descriptions of the characteristics of a ruler, writings conveying encouragement, and clear indications on how to rebuild the economy in Ukraine following Tatar raids, works expressing concern for the safety of the state borders, and anti-Turkish exhortations. These latter comprise *Ekscytarz* (1592), *Publika* (1594), *Pobudka* (1597) and *Votum* (1597).

In *Ekscytarz*, Wereszczyński blames the Turks and Arabs ('Saracens') for the continuing Passion of Christ. He urges the recapture of the Holy Land and refers to a prophecy that the Ottoman Empire will be brought down by the Poles. He proclaims the need to exterminate the 'Machometan sect' (*sekta mahometańska*), expects the conversion of Muslims to Christianity, and advocates a holy war. He argues that, according to the

Qur'an, Muslims are not to recognise the authority of the written word or reason, or to get involved in religious disputes, because the sword is the only argument in discussion. For this reason, he judges that, instead of discussions and rational arguments, Christians should resist Muslims with force. The result will be that Islam will fall, in accordance with Muslim prophecy and the findings of astrologers. As arguments for war against 'circumcised Bisurmans', he cites Muslim tyranny expressed in the harsh conditions inflicted on Christian slaves, the raping of women (both wives and daughters), murders, thefts, beating of Christians, financial burdens, the mandatory conversion of Christian children to Islam and their forced conscription into the Janissaries, the desecration of churches and their conversion into mosques, and the desecration of Christian graves (p. 27). In Wereszczyński's view, Islam came into being when Muḥammad, who was a former Christian, was chosen by Arab fugitives as their chief and prophet. The essence of Islam was to fight the Christians, to conquer the Holy Land, and to pursue religious and military expansion.

Wereszczyński habitually uses abusive words about Islam. He considers the Qur'an nefarious (p. 76) and contrasts it with the Gospel. For him, the Qur'an is a set of laws that, faced with the threat of a Muslim attack, Christians should learn in order to adapt more quickly to the rules imposed by the aggressor, who are known for their tactic of binding enemies with treaties. The Commonwealth is for him the *antemurale Christianitatis* (p. 98). Contrasting the figures of Christ and Muḥammad, he tries to show that Christ, as Son of the living God, has given Christians an example and the hope of resurrection, while Muḥammad lies in the grave offering no hope of resurrection but only the decomposition of the body (p. 73).

In *Publika*, Wereszczyński proposes the creation of a military school (*szkola rycerska*) in Ruthenia (Ukraine), where the Knights of St John (the Knights of Malta), who protect the Holy Sepulchre in Jerusalem and follow their vocation to fight against the 'pagans', might be established. He also wants to recruit foot soldiers from among willing peasants (*piechota wybraniecka*) to protect Ruthenia against the Tatars, the Ottomans and the Muscovites. He accuses the Jews and the Armenians of transferring money away from the Commonwealth under the pretext of conducting trade with the Ottoman Porte, and says that, according to the Talmud, it is a lesser evil for a Jew to serve Turks than to serve Christians, so the Jews supported the Turks, who were pagans, and Jewish priests prayed in the synagogues cursing Jesus Christ. He sees the war against the Ottoman Empire as a religious war, so that to settle a military order in Ruthenia would be the best protection against the 'godless' Turks, who sign treacherous peace treaties, are the 'enemies of the Holy Cross', and force their captives to convert to Islam.

Pobudka[...] *do podniesienia wojny świętej spolną ręką przeciw Turkom i Tatarom* is addressed to all Christian rulers, including Sigismund III Vasa and the tsar of the Grand Dutchy of Muscovy. Here Wereszczyński describes Muslims as 'Mahometowie' (Muḥammadans) and again uses abusive terms for them, pointing out the paradox in sultans such as Selim (r. 1512-20) performing their prayers but also using the most refined cruelty. Wereszczyński supports a holy war, and underlines the deceptiveness of Muslims whose intention is to exterminate Christianity (he uses a comparison with the complete removal of the vine together with its roots) and replace it with the specious and abhorrent faith of Muḥammad, following the teachings of Islam (*Pobudka*, k. D).

Wereszczyński considers that Islam inevitably gives rise to self-interest in making alliances, treachery in dealing with potential allies, enmity against peace and friendship in relations between states, hatred of Christianity, enslaving and murdering people, desecration of churches and converting them into mosques. It is a false and eclectic religion in which God's message and human religious fantasising are horrendously mixed together. It is a religion that uses fear as the basic instrument in dealing with its adherents, and in which their behaviour lacks trustworthiness, because it is an age-old custom of Muslims to cheat, destroy and engage in treachery since they treat their faith as no more than an instrument for their own ends (*Pobudka*, k. Dv). He argues that Islam is the legacy of Hagar, who was only Abraham's slave woman, so it is basically inferior to Christianity. Christians have been particularly chosen by God, and Muslims should learn about this fact and accept it.

In *Votum*, Wereszczyński calls for a collection of taxes for a war against the Ottoman Empire. He depicts the Ottoman Empire as the 'enemy of the Holy Cross', and reminds his readers of people suffering in Ottoman slavery. Prayer and penance for sins will help in gaining victory because fighting against Muslims is a religious duty and a proof of love for God, Christ and the homeland. He appeals for a league of Christians against the Muslims (pagans), and recommends the Christianisation of Muslim lands.

Bartosz Paprocki (c. 1540/3-1614)

Bartosz Paprocki was an expert in heraldry, an occasional poet, a political writer and a moralist. As a courtier of Andrzej Taranowski, he accompanied him during a mission to Istanbul in 1572. In 1587, he supported Maximilian Habsburg as a candidate for the throne of the Polish-Lithuanian Commonwealth. When the Habsburgs' supporters lost the battle at Byczyna, and Sigismund III Vasa was elected king, Paprocki fled to Moravia and lived in Kromież at the court of the Olomouc bishop Stanisław Pawłowski. He returned to the Commonwealth in 1610.

In his *Historyja żałosna o prędkości i okrutności tatarskiej a o srogim mordowaniu i popsowaniu ziemi ruskiej i podolskiej, które się stało księżyca października roku 1575* (Kraków, 1575) he uses religiously motivated hate speech and abusive words when he describes the Ottoman invaders. While he notes the alien nature of their dress and headgear, the essence of his description is their religion. In his view, the main goal of the Tatars is to instil fear in Christian hearts and minds, and their raids are a punishment for Christians' sins. He admires the achievements of the 15th-century Albanian hero Skanderbeg, who inflicted heavy losses on Muslims ('Jako gnębił tę niecną mahomecką wiarę', k. Aiijv), whose slain bodies were an 'offering' to the devil. He reviles the deceptiveness of Muslims who make treaties when they serve their own interests and then break them without remorse, and he also underlines the hostility of Muslims to everything Christian. A particular evil is that kidnapped and enslaved children are converted to Islam and indoctrinated into Muslim ways, adopting Muslim dress and customs.

In a word, in Paprocki's writings Islam appears as a hostile, aggressive and predatory religion. Its adherents are ruthless, cruel, vicious and hostile to Christians, whom they want to annihilate or force to accept Islam.

Marcin Paszkowski (c. 1560-1621)

Minerwa [...] z ligi chrześcijańskiej zebrana [...] is a poetic compilation in two parts, in which Marcin Paszkowski makes use of K. Daminaeus's *Liga z zwadą koła poselskiego*, K. Warszewicki's *Wenecya*, S.F. Klonowic's *Pożar*, M.K. Radziwiłł's *Peregrynacya* and M. Stryjkowski's *O wolności Korony Polskiej*. He includes an old Turkish prophecy that the Christians will invade the Holy Land on a Friday during the time when Muslims go to congregational prayer, for fear of which the Muslims of the Holy Land lock up Christians every Friday.

Paszkowski treats Islam with contempt. He calls the prayers conducted in mosques and in Mecca superstition, and describes Muslim teachings as no more than fables of Muḥammad. He presents Islam as a religion geared towards the eradication of Christianity, and a cursed religion in comparison to the holy Christian faith. As he sees it, Muḥammad created a syncretistic religion that mixes the divine and human order and holds its adherents in fear. They fear the fulfillment of the prophecy about Christians recapturing the Church of the Holy Sepulchre, and of a prophecy about Christians getting the upper hand and destroying Muslim culture and religion.

In *Apostrophe do wszystkich panów chrześcijańskich*, Paszkowski treats this prophecy seriously, and encourages the nobles to plan military action in order to fulfil it. He enumerates several reasons for undertaking such a crusade: the weakening of the Ottoman Empire, concern that the sons of Hagar should not take Isaac's heritage, revenge for wrongs committed against co-believers, the breaking of peace treaties, hopes for spoils, and gaining fame on the battlefield. He maintains that Muslims are afraid of the 'whip of God' with which they are to be punished, and asserts that, while the Janissaries may be the kernel of Ottoman strength, they often fight under the influence of drugs (he calls them *masłocznicy*). He rejects the fear that Christians have for turbaned heads, because when this is struck away the cause of fear has been removed and the Muslim can easily be overpowered.

Jan Gawiński (c. 1622-84)

The main theme of Gawiński's anthology *Clipaeus Christianitatis, to jest tarcz chrześcijaństwa* (a collection of opinions from the authors F. Kallimach, J. Kochanowski, K. Warszewicki, O.G. de Busbecq, S. Twardowski, M.K. Sarbiewski, W. Kochowski, and M. Winkler) and also of his *Ekscytarz*, written in verse, is incitement to wage war against the Ottoman Empire after the humiliating Treaty of Buczacz, of 1672, which gave the Ottomans part of the south-eastern territories of the Commonwealth and also required an annual settlement to be paid to the sultan. The subsequent war of 1672-6 ended with the Ottomans retaining the fortress of Kamieniec Podolski and part of Podolia (until the new Treaty of Karlowitz in 1699).

Gawiński decided to write his work following a discovery in 1679 during renovation work in St Hedwig's chapel in Wawel Cathedral, Krakow, of a gold quilted shield that had probably been hidden there during the time of the Swedish invasion in 1655. The picture on the shield represented the battle between Constantine and Maxentius in 312, in which Constantine was victorious after seeing Christ in a vision. This discovery was taken as a sign of victory over Islam, and, like many before him, Gawiński refers to the prophecy about the fall of the Ottoman Empire at the hand of the ruler from the north.

For him, the Turks are oath-breakers and untrustworthy people, who strive as inveterate enemies of Christianity to eradicate it according to the teachings of the Qur'an. He refers to Q 76, where, according to him, it is written: 'You, O Prophet, go and raid and take spoils from the unbelievers, attack them so that they fear you.' He also writes that Muḥammad said: 'I am sent with the power of the sword, and the one who does not accept my message should be either killed or must pay a tribute for his disbelief' (p. 38). Gawiński argues that Muslims are required to wage war on Christians, and he calls Muḥammad 'the main arch-robber of kingdoms'. He appeals to his readers' emotions, highlighting the harm done by Muslims to women and children, and their desecration of churches. He sees Christian fighting against the Ottomans as just because it is defensive.

Wespazjan Kochowski (1633-1700)

Wespazjan Kochowski's *Dzieło Boskie albo pieśni Wiednia wybawionego* treats the theme of confrontation between the Christian and Islamic worlds. In the opening dedication, he declares that the very appearance of Prince Alexander Sobieski, son of King John III Sobieski (r. 1674-96), would arouse fear in the sultan, and a Christian army would be able to advance as far as Mecca itself. The Christian victory at Vienna serves the defence of the Christian world against Islam, with which the Muslim army wanted to replace Catholic Christianity. Kochowski sees the Muslim invasion as God's punishment for sins. He recognises the defence of the Habsburg Empire as the duty of all Christians, though only the Poles, who constantly struggle with Muslims, are serious about fighting for their faith against the Turks.

It is clear that the authors of these treatises and anti-Turkish poems composed between 1575 and the mid-18th century do not show any thorough knowledge of the teachings of Islam, apart from occasional references to the Qur'an and incidents from the life of Muḥammad. Instead, they base their view on their own immediate experiences of Muslims, such as acts of cruelty, rape, enslavement and murder during Tatar raids, and on the opposition between Islam and Christianity.

These popular anti-Turkish works were written in response to public demand. They originate from the need to mobilise decision makers, in the persons of the king, members of the parliament, *hetmans* and the nobility trained in fighting, to defend people who were exposed to raids from Ottoman territory, and they were written by authors, who might be called agitators, commissioned by the higher nobility concerned for the safety of their estates (where they often maintained private armies). The works were also written by individuals who were sincerely concerned with the fate of local populations and economic conditions of particular parts of the country.

Religious motivation is understandably discernible in works by the clergy. These give prominence to the religious character of war, while works by lay writers stress more civic and class virtues, especially bravery and emulation of the merits of ancestors. All the writers argue that the nobility should fight in defence of their families, their wives and children, especially their daughters, so they can be spared from rape, slavery and death.

The image of Islam in these works of the period 1575-1733 changes little, though by the end of the 17th century remarks that are to be found scattered through earlier works tend to appear in a more coordinated fashion. This suggests that, by this time aims in writing had become clearer, and writers had become more familiar with traditional images of condemnation. Knowledge of Islam did not increase, even though there were noticeable influences from the material culture of the Islamic world on the society of the Commonwealth, seen in the dress of nobles, types of weapons, armour and military decorations employed, saddles and horse trappings. Islam as a religion was looked on as unchangingly hostile, which explains why the texts are full of abusive language about Muslims.

Most lay writers of the 17th century did not conduct religious debates, but aimed to produce anti-Muslim and anti-Turkish propaganda under slogans of liberating the Holy Land, freeing slaves and captives, and regaining lost territory. However, some writers hinted at alliances between Protestants and Muslims. They also made frequent references to the prophecy about 'the ruler from the north' who would bring an end to Islam, identifying this figure as the king of the Polish-Lithuanian Commonwealth.

The image of Islam gradually changed after the Treaty of Karlowitz. The work by Franciszek Gościecki (1668-1729), *Poselstwo wielkie* (1732), provides an excellent example of this, although the negative stereotypes persist in public awareness, as is attested in *Nowe Ateny* (1745-6), the encyclopaedia by Benedykt Chmielowski (1700-63), and in 18th-century calendars and newspapers that readily perpetuated them. There was a growing awareness that the Ottoman Empire could become an ally of the weakening Commonwealth against the growing might of the Russian and Habsburg Empires. The text published at the beginning of the 18ᵗʰ century with Chwałkowski named as its author, *Historya turecka o Mahomecie* (Poznań, 1712; see the entry in this volume), contains a baffling combination of the old conviction that the Turks are treacherous and the new possibility of seeing them as allies against the more dreadful enemies, who are the Russians, the Habsburgs, and the Prussians.

SIGNIFICANCE

These works are responses to the acute danger brought on by Tatar raids and Ottoman attempts to expand their empire. Their reactions, in the form of condemnation of the debased lifestyle and inhuman cruelty of the aggressors, and the evil of their intent to destroy Christian civilisation, are the predictable contents of works aimed to galvanise a general readership. They were nearly all published only once, especially those composed in response to particular events, indicating that their importance did not extend far beyond their immediate readership.

PUBLICATIONS

Bartosz Paprocki, *Historyja żałosna o prętkości i okrutności tatarskiej, a o srogim mordowaniu i popsowaniu Ziemie Ruskiej i Podolskiej. Które się stało Księżyca Października roku 1575*, Kraków, 1575; 309021 (digitised version available through PAN Biblioteka Kórnicka)

Józef Wereszczyński, *Ekscytarz księdza Józefa Wereszczyńskiego z Wereszczyna, z łaski Bożej nominata biskupstwa kijowskiego a opata sieciechowskiego do podniesienia wojny ś[więtej] przeciwko Turkom i Tatarom, jako głównym nieprzyjacielom wszystkiego chrześcijaństwa*, [Kraków], 1592; 14210 (digitised version available through Lower Silesian Digital Library)

I[an] S[molik], *Otucha na pogany wszystkim potentatom chrześcijańskim. I[ana] S[molika]. Z przydaniem Praktyki Antoniusa Torquaciusa ferarskiego filozofa medyka i astrologa sławnego: którą o odmianie niektórych k[rajów] chrześcijańskich Mathiaszowi królowi węgierskiemu roku 1480 uczynił. A teraz nowo z łacińskiego na polskie przełożona przez tegoż I[ana] S[molika]*, Kraków, 1594; 287603 (digitised version available through PAN Biblioteka Kórnicka)

Józef Wereszczyński, *Publika księdza Józefa Wereszczyńskiego z Wereszczyna z łaski Bożej biskupa kijowskiego a opata sieciechowskiego Ich M[ościów] Rzeczyposp[olitej] na sejmiki przez list objaśniona, tak z strony fundowania szkoły rycerskiej synom koronnym na Ukrainie, jako też krzyżaków według reguły malteńskiej w sąsiedztwie z pogany i z Moskwą na wszystkim Zadnieprzu dla snadniejszego ochronienia koronnego od niebezpieczeństwa wszelakiego*, Kraków, 1594; 10820 (digitised version available through Lower Silesian Digital Library)

Józef Wereszczyński, *Pobudka na Jego Cesarską Miłość wszytkiego krześcijaństwa. Jako też na Jego K[rólewskiej] M[ości] Króla Polskiego. Tudzież też na Jaśnie Oświeconego Kniazia Wielkiego Moskiewskiego do podniesienia wojny świętej spólną ręką przeciw Turkom i Tatarom trąbiona*, Wilno, 1594; Kraków, 1597; 4086 (digitised version available through Lower Silesian Digital Library)

Bartosz Paprocki, *Gwałt na pogany ku wszem chrześcijańskiem panom, królom i książętom, a osobliwiej ku niezwyciężonego Królestwa Polskiego obojga stanom duchownemu i świeckiemu uczyniony roku 1595*, [s.l.], 1595; 2256 (digitised version available through Lower Silesian Digital Library)

Piotr Grabowski, *Zdanie syna koronnego, o piąciu rzeczach Rzeczpospolitej Polskiej należących*, [Parnawa], 1595; 10248 (digitised version available through Lower Silesian Digital Library)

Piotr Grabowski, *Polska niżna albo osada polska na cześć i chwałę Panu Bogu wszechmogącemu i na wiele zacnych ozdób i pożytków Rzeczypospolit[ej] Polskiej. A osobliwie na ochronienie pogranicznych państw od Tatar i na uczciwe opatrzenie rozpłodzonych synów koronnych, pachołków chudych, podana Ich Mościom Panom Braciej swej P[anom] Stanom i Rycerstwu Rzeczypospol[itej] Polskiej*, [Parnawa], 1596; 4358 (digitised version available through Lower Silesian Digital Library)

Krzysztof Daminaeus [Dzierżek], *Liga z zawadą koła poselskiego spólnego narodu K[orony] P[olskiej] i W[ielkiego] K[sięstwa] L[itewskiego] authore Christophino Daminaeo peregrino Polono. Gromadą zawsze przodkowie chodzili naszy na wilka i tak go łowili. Tymże sposobem na Turka społecznie idźcie, chcecieli w pokoju żyć wiecznie, roku Pańskiego, 1596*, [s.l.], 1596; 39718 (digitised version available through Lower Silesian Digital Library)

Sebastian Fabian Klonowic, *Pożar. Upominanie do gaszenia i wróżka o upadku mocy tureckiej*, [Kraków], 1597; 43790 (digitised version available through Lower Silesian Digital Library)

Józef Wereszczyński, *Votum ks. Józefa Wereszczyńskiego z łaski Bożej biskupa kijowskiego a opata sieciechowskiego z strony podniesienia wojny potężnej przeciwko cesarzowi tureckiemu bez ruszenia pospolitego; a iżby każdy gospodarz zostawszy w domu swoim, mógł bezpiecznie zażywać gospodarstwa swego Ich M[ościom] Panom posłom na sejmie warszawskim w roku 1597 na piśmie podane*, Nowy

Wereszczyn, 1597; 4770 (digitised version available through Lower Silesian Digital Library)

Wawrzyniec Chlebowski, *Trąba pobudki ziemie perskiej, do wszystkich narodów chrześcijańskich przeciwko mahometanom*, Kraków, 1608

Wawrzyniec Chlebowski, *Wolność prawdziwa Korony Polskiej*, Kraków, 1608

Adam Władysławiusz, *Pieśni nowe pamięci godne o przypadkach koronnych*, Kraków, 1608; 95347393 (digitised version available through Biblioteka Jagiellońska)

Wawrzyniec Chlebowski, *Historyja i wywód narodu cesarzów Tureckich i walki ich z chrześcijany*[...], Kraków, 1609

Wawrzyniec Chlebowski, *Wolność złota Korony Polskiej nad insze pod Słońcem narody; przytym Utrapienie i srogie zniewolenie narodów chrześcijańskich pod jarzmem tureckim*, Kraków, 1611; 286272 (digitised version available through University of Warsaw Library)

Wawrzyniec Chlebowski, *Królów i cesarzów tureckich dzieła abo sprawy i żywotów ich dokończenie: począwszy od Otomana pierwszego aż do sułtana Ahmeta dzisiejszego według ich własnej kroniki w Konstantynopolu będącej pismem arabskim i łacińskim pisanej. Przy tym Prognosticon o upadku ich monarchijej przez pana północnego*, Kraków, 1612

Wawrzyniec Chlebowski, *Chronologia o wywodzie narodu cesarzów tureckich i walki ich z chrześcijany aż do dnia dzisiejszego. Przy tym upominanie do wszystkich, a mianowicie Sarmatów, którym pod pretekstem przymierza tak wiele szkód przez Tatary wyrządzają, żeby zdradliwemu przymierzu tureckiemu nie ufając, wczas o sobie radzili i bronić ojczyzny gotowemi byli*, Kraków, 1613

Mikołaj Chabielski, *Pobudka narodom chrześcijańskim w jedność miłości chrześcijańskiej na podniesienie wojny zgodnie, przeciwko nieprzyjacielowi Krzyża Świętego. Do tego przydany jest sposób obrony, jaki ma być przeciwko nieprzyjacielom Krzyża Świętego i wierszem wyznanie niewymownego dobrodziejstwa Bożego, i pienie chwały Bożej*, Kraków, 1615; NDIGSTD003998 (digitised version available through Biblioteka Jagiellońska)

Wojciech Kicki, *Dialog o obronie Ukrainy i pobudka z przestrogą dla zabieżenia inkursyjom tatarskim przez persony rozmawiające. Naprzód przedmowa do łaskawego czytelnika. Prologus, Szlachcic, Ukraina, Żołnierz, Satyr, Epilogus*, Dobromil, 1615

Jan Krajewski, *Ucisk koronny Jana Krajewskiego i wtargnięcie tatarskie do Podola roku Pańskiego 1615*, [s.l.], 1615; NDIGSTDR001801 (digitised version available through Biblioteka Jagiellońska)

Jan Francisciades, *Pobudka na ekspedycyją wojenną J[aśnie] W[ielmożnego] P[ana] Stanisława hr[abie] na Wiśniczu Lubomirskiego sandomierskiego, spiskiego, dobczyckiego starosty, którą Czynił z szlachetnym żołnierstwem swoim przeciw pogranicznym nieprzyjaciołom Turkom, Tatarom itd. z Pilzna. Przez ks. Jana Francisciadesa z Pilzna plebana Dembickiego A. P. NN. WW. sławnej Akad [emijej] Krak[owskiej] mistrza. W Pilźnie r[oku] P[ańskiego] 1618 iunii 29 czyniona*, Kraków, [1618]; NDIGSTDR017287 (digitised version available through Biblioteka Jagiellońska)

Piotr Gorczyn, *Tren abo Lament żałosny więźniów koronnych do hord tatarskich w roku 1618 zabranych[...] uczyniony*, [s.l.], 1618

Krzysztof Palczowski, *O Kozakach, jeśli ich znieść czy nie dyskurs*, Kraków, 1618; 360918 (digitised version available through PAN Biblioteka Kórnicka)

Wawrzyniec Chlebowski, *Krwawy Mars narodu otomańskiego, z królmi i cesarzmi chrześcijańskiemi aż do dnia dzisiejszego. Przy tym upominanie do wszytkich, a mianowicie Sarmatów, którym pod pretekstem przymierza tak wiele szkód przez Tatary wyrządzają, żeby zdradliwemu przymierzu tureckiemu nie ufając, wczas o sobie radzili i bronić ojczyzny gotowemi byli*, Kraków, 1620; 360918 (digitised version available through PAN Biblioteka Kórnicka)

Wojciech Rakowski, *Pobudka zacnym synom Korony Polskiej do służby wojennej na ekspedycyją przeciwko nieprzyjaciołom koronnym roku Pańskiego 1620*, Kraków, 1620; 47498 (digitised version available through Dolnośląska Biblioteka Cyfrowa)

Grzegorz Czaradzki, *Pobudka na wojnę turecką rycerskim ludziom polskim ku pociesze z listy tureckimi i konstytucyjami tegorocznymi o rządzie wojennym przydanym*, Poznań, 1621; 65070 (digitised version available through PAN Biblioteka Kórnicka)

Anonymous, *Poseł z Wołoch z obozu polskiego roku 1621*, Kraków, 1621

Anonymous, *Rozmowy świeże o nowinach z Ukrainy, z Węgier i z Turek*, Kraków, 1621

Jacek Kołakowski, *Powab wojenny na Turka z krojnikarzów niektórych polskich, osobliwie z Kromera biskupa warmińskiego. Napisany przez[...] sławnej Akademijej Krakowskiej studenta. Numerorum XXXI. Mówił Pan Bóg do Mojżesza, rzekąc: Pomści się pierwy*

*krzywdy synów izraelskich nad Madyjanitami i tak zebran będziesz
od ludu twego, i wnet Mojżesz: Uzbrojcie z was męże ku bitwie, którzy by mogli uczynić pomstę Pańską nad Madyjanity; tysiąc mężów
z każdego pokolenia niech będzie wybranych, z Izraela, którzy by byli
posłani na wojnę i wyprawili po tysiącu z każdego pokolenia, to jest
dwanaście tysięcy gotowych do bitwy, które posłał Mojżesz z Fine-
esem syna Eleazara kapłana, naczynie też święte i trąby na trąbienie
dał mu*, Kraków, 1621

Stanisław Witkowski, *Pobudka ludzi rycerskich przez nawalność
pogańską w małej kupie z żałością chrześcijaństwa zniesionych. Ku
czułości i przestrodze dalszej wojny tureckiej panom chrześcijańskim
nowo uczyniona*, Zamość, 1621; NDIGSTDR005459 (digitised version
available through Biblioteka Jagiellońska)

Adam Jan Komorowski, *Triumphus Christianus, sive de insigni prin-
cipium christianorum, Selimano Turcarum tyranno ad Naupactum
caeso, victoria, oratio publice frequentia celebri in aede S[anctissi]
mae Trinitatis, dominica 1 Octobr[is] ab [...] eloquentiae apud profes-
sorem Tylicianum in Acad[emiae] Crac[oviensis] Stud[iosi] habita*,
Cracoviae, 1630

Samuel Twardowski, *Władysław IV, król polski i szwedzki*, Leszno, 1649;
ed. R. Krzywy, Warsaw, 2012; 102084487 (digitised version available
through Biblioteka Jagiellońska)

Rafał Leszczyński, *Zwycięstwo niezwyciężonego narodu polskiego nad
hardym Turczynem na polach chocimskich w r. 1673*, [s.l., s.a.]

Wespazjan Kochowski, 'Taratantara albo pobudka do rycerstwa
polskiego, żeby ufności w Bogu pełni pospieszali na odsiecz
Kamieńcowi Podolskiemu' (Epodon, 3), 'Do monarchów chrześcijańskich sąsiedzkie quanquam' (Epodon, 16), in Wespazjan
Kochowski, *Liryka polskie w niepróżnującym próżnowaniu napisane*,
[s.l.], 1674, pp. 310-14, 343-5; NDIGSTDR000126 (digitised version
available through Biblioteka Jagiellońska)

Zbigniew Morsztyn, *Sławna wiktoryja nad Turkami od wojsk koronnych i Wielkiego Księstwa Litewskiego pod Chocimiem otrzymana
w Dzień Świętego Marcina 1673*, [s.l.], 1674; 56241 (digitised version
available through PAN Biblioteka Kórnicka)

Jan Ślizień, *Haracz krwią turecką Turkom wypłacony*, Wilno,
1674; 12041347 (digitised version available through Biblioteka
Jagiellońska)

Mateusz Ignacy Kuligowski, *Dźwięk Marsa walecznego z walnej
ekspedycyi chocimskiej i z otrzymanego w roku 1673 nad Turkami*

zwycięstwa, Wilno, 1675; 74121636 (digitised version available through Biblioteka Narodowa)

Anonymous, *Dyskurs, jeżeli sprawiedliwa wojna przeciwko Turczynowi*, 1733 (MS Kraków, Biblioteka Książąt Czartoryskich – rkps 210, k. 909-923)

[Jan Ponętowski], *Deliberacyja o spółku i związku Korony Polskiej z pany chrześcijańskimi przeciwko Turkom*, [*1595, 1596, 1646*], ed. K.J. Turowski, Kraków, 1858; 30704 (digitised version available through Biblioteka Uniwersytecka im. Jerzego Giedroycia w Białymstoku)

Anonymous, *Szpieg polski z Turek, który wiele rzeczy przejrzawszy swoim na przestrogę oznajmuje. Przy tym o wojsku tureckim, które jest zebrane z dziesiąci prowincyj azyjskich, którego jest liczba pewna po pięciokroć sto tysięcy*, [s.l., s.a.]; 48914 (digitised version available through PAN Biblioteka Kórnicka)

Wacław Potocki, *Wojna chocimska*, ed. A. Brückner, Kraków, 1926

Maciej Kazimierz Sarbiewski, 'Ioanni Carolo Chodkiewicz palatino Vilnensi et Magni Ducatus Lithuaniae exercituum duci, contra Turcas, Dei Optimi Maximi et Beatae Virginis Mariae auxilium spondet' (oda Pp. 4), in *Lyrica quibus accesserunt Iter Romanum et Lechiados fragmentum*, trans. T. Karyłowski, ed. M. Korolko and J. Okoń, Warsaw, 1980, pp. 528-31

Wespazjan Kochowski, *Dzieło Boskie albo Pieśni Wiednia wybawionego i inszych transakcyjej wojny tureckiej w roku 1683 szczęśliwie rozpoczętej*, ed. M. Kaczmarek, Wrocław, 1983; 105121272 (digitised version available through Biblioteka Narodowa)

Jan Chryzostom Pasek, *Pamiętniki*, ed. R. Pollak, Warsaw, 1987

Wacław Potocki, 'Braterska admonicyja do ichmościów wielmożnych panów braci starszych', in Wacław Potocki, *Wiersze wybrane*, ed. S. Grzeszczuk, intro. J.S. Gruchała, Wrocław, 1992, 137-41

Jan Białobocki, 'Brat Tatar abo liga wilcza ze psem na gospodarza', in Jan Białobocki, *Poematy rycerskie*, ed. P. Borek, Kraków, 2004, 139-46

Jan Gawiński, *Clipaeus Christianitatis, to jest tarcz chrześcijaństwa*, ed. D. Chemperek and W. Walecki, Kraków, 2003

Stanisław Makowski, *Relacyja Kamieńca wziętego przez Turków w roku 1672*, ed. P. Borek, Kraków, 2008

Samuel Twardowski, *Władysław IV, król polski i szwedzki*, ed. R. Krzywy, Warsaw, 2012; 83153 (digitised version available through Muzeum Narodowe w Krakowie)

Marcin Paszkowski, 'Ukraina od Tatar utrapiona, książąt i panów pogranicznych o ratunek z żałosnym lamentem prosi', in Marcin

Paszkowski, *Utwory okolicznościowe*, ed. M. Kuran with R. Krzywy, Warsaw, 2017, part 1, pp. 51-77 (Biblioteka Dawnej Literatury Popularnej i Okolicznościowej – BDLPO 36)

Marcin Paszkowski, 'Minerwa Marcina Paszkowskiego z ligi chrześcijańskiej zebrana i cytowaniem zacnych a rozmaitych autorów konfirmowana: o upadku mocy tureckiej, o wyswobodzeniu Ziemie Ś[więtej] z ręku ich przez narody chrześcijańskie, tudzież też prześladowanie chrześcijan w jarzmie tych pogan stękających', in Marcin Paszkowski, *Utwory okolicznościowe*, ed. M. Kuran with R. Krzywy, Warsaw, 2017, part 1, pp. 149-87 (BDLPO 36)

Marcin Paszkowski, *Rozmowa Kozaka Zaporoskiego z perskim gońcem o sprawach wojennych pogan z chrześcijany, do których się więzień Polak z Turek uciekający nagodził przez Marcina Paszkowskiego teraz świeżo w roku Pański[m] 1617 in Septembre naprędce złożona, a wszytkim synom koronnym panom a dobrodziejom swoim miłościwym, którzy się do Proszowic zjechali na elekcyją ich mościów panów deputatów, chętliwie ofiarowana*, in Marcin Paszkowski, *Utwory okolicznościowe*, ed. M. Kuran with R. Krzywy, Warsaw, 2017, part 2, pp. 65-79 (BDLPO 36)

Marcin Paszkowski, *Podole utrapione z państwy przyległemi, książąt i panów pogranicznych o społeczny ratunek prosi*, in Marcin Paszkowski, *Utwory okolicznościowe*, ed. M. Kuran with R. Krzywy, Warsaw, 2017, part 2, pp. 81-100 (BDLPO 36) 325421 (digitised version available through Biblioteka Jagiellońska)

Marcin Paszkowski, *Bitwy znamienite tymi czasy na różnych miejscach mężnych Polaków z nieprzyjacioły Krzyża Świętego. W roku teraźniejszym 1620, przez Marcina Paszkowskiego opisane. Na ostatek nieszczęsny przypadek ich za niezgodą*, in Marcin Paszkowski, *Utwory okolicznościowe*, ed. M. Kuran with R. Krzywy, Warsaw, 2017, part 2, pp. 115-49 (BDLPO 36); 239516 (digitised version available through Biblioteka Jagiellońska)

Marcin Paszkowski, *Posiłek Bellony słowieńskiej. Na odpór nieprzyjaciołom Krzyża Ś[więtego] na sejm warszawski teraźniejszy w roku 1620 wydany. Tudzież umowa niemiecka z różnymi nacyjami chrześcijańskiemi na Turka i na Tatary*, in Marcin Paszkowski, *Utwory okolicznościowe*, ed. M. Kuran with R. Krzywy, Warsaw, 2017, part 2, pp. 103-13 (BDLPO 36); 97804 (digitised version available through Biblioteka Jagiellońska)

STUDIES

W. Pyłypenko, *W obliczu wroga. Polska literatura antyturecka od połowy XVI do połowy XVII wieku*, Oświęcim, 2016

A. Maśko, 'Obraz islamu w Rzeczpospolitej w XVIII w.', *Przegląd Orientalistyczny* 3-4 (2015) 191-206

R. Ryba, *Literatura staropolska wobec zjawiska niewoli tatarsko-tureckiej. Studia i szkice*, Katowice, 2014

D. Dolański, *Trzy cesarstwa. Wiedza iI wyobraźnia o Niemczech, Turcji i Rosji w Polsce XVIII wieku*, Zielona Góra, 2013, pp. 143-70

M. Kuran, *Marcin Paszkowski. Poeta okolicznościowy i moralista z pierwszej połowy XVII wieku*, Łódź, 2012

M. Kuran, 'Między Cecorą a Chocimiem. Stanisława Witkowskiego "Pobudka ludzi rycerskich". O strukturze tekstu i jego specyfice genologicznej', in K. Płachcińska and M. Kuran (eds), *Miscellanea literackie i teatralne (od Kochanowskiego do Mrożka)*, vol. 1, Łódź, 2010, 249-74

T. Ulewicz, *Sarmacja. Studium z problematyki słowiańskiej XV i XVI w. Zagadnienie sarmatyzmu w kulturze i literaturze polskiej*, Kraków, 2006

K. Maliszewski, *W kręgu staropolskich wyobrażeń o świecie*, Lublin, 2006, pp. 157-67, 202-13

J. Kroczak, *'Jeśli mię wieźdźba prawdziwa uwodzi[...]'. Prognostyki i znaki cudowne w polskiej literaturze barokowej*, Wrocław, 2006

A. Sitkowa, *O pisarstwie Józefa Wereszczyńskiego. Wybrane problemy*, Katowice, 2006

D. Skorupa, *Stosunki polsko-tatarskie 1595-1623*, Warsaw, 2004

J. Tazbir, *Polska przedmurzem Europy*, Warsaw, 2004

D. Chemperek, 'Jana Gawińskiego spraw tureckich tezaurus, czyli *Tarcz Chrześcijaństwa*. Konwencje i eksperymenty literackie', in J. Gawiński, *Clipaeus Christianitatis to jest Tarcz Chrześcijańska*, ed. D. Chemperek and W. Walecki, Kraków, 2003, 7-23

I. Czamańska, 'Traktaty karłowickie. Problemy badawcze', *Balcanica Posnaniensia* 13 (2003) 7-14

M. Jačov, *Europa i Osmanie w okresie Lig Świętych. Polska między Wschodem a Zachodem*, Kraków, 2003

P. Borek, *Ukraina w staropolskich diariuszach i pamiętnikach*, Kraków, 2001

M. Prejs, *Egzotyzm w literaturze staropolskiej. Wybrane problemy*, Warsaw, 1999

B. Majewska, 'Wschód w kulturze i piśmiennictwie', in T. Michałowska et al. (eds), *Słownik literatury staropolskiej*, Wrocław, 1998, 1042-5

D. Kołodziejczyk, *Podole pod panowaniem tureckim. Ejalet Kamieniecki 1672-1699*, Warsaw, 1994

B. Rok, 'Obraz Turcji w kalendarzach czasów saskich', *Acta Universitatis Wratislaviensis* 75 (1990) 115-22 (no. 1108, 'Historia')

J. Tazbir, *Polska jako przedmurze chrześcijańskiej Europy. Mity a rzeczywistość historyczna*, Warsaw, 1987

T. Chrzanowski, 'Orient i orientalizm w kulturze staropolskiej', in *Orient i orientalizm w sztuce. Materiały Sesji Stowarzyszenia Historyków Sztuki Kraków, grudzień 1983*, Warsaw, 1986, 43-69

M. Bałczewski, 'Zmiany w ocenie Turcji w opinii polskiej XVIII w.', *Acta Universitatis Lodziensis. Folia Historica* 22 (1985) 91-108

J. Woliński, *Z dziejów wojen polsko-tureckich*, Warsaw, 1983

H. Olszewski, 'Ideologia Rzeczypospolitej. Przedmurza chrześcijaństwa', *Czasopismo Prawno-Historyczne* 35 (1983) 7-19

M. Bogucka, 'Szlachta polska wobec wschodu turecko-tatarskiego. Między fascynacją a przerażeniem (XVI–XVIII w.)', *Śląski Kwartalnik Historyczny Sobótka* 3 (1982) 185-93

S. Herman, 'Antyturecka publicystyka Józefa Wereszczyńskiego (lata 1592-1597)', *Wyższa Szkoła Pedagogiczna w Zielonej Górze. Studia i Materiały. Nauki Filologiczne* 7 (1981) 15-31 (no. 111)

J. Nowak-Dłużewski, *Okolicznościowa poezja polityczna w Polsce. Dwaj królowie rodacy*, Warsaw, 1980, pp. 49-85, 119-57

L. Podhorodecki and N. Raszba, *Wojna chocimska 1621 roku*, Kraków, 1979

J. Pajewski, *Buńczuk i koncerz. Z dziejów wojen polsko-tureckich*, Warsaw, 1978

J. Tazbir, 'Problem nietolerancji religijnej w Polsce XVI i XVII wieku', *Przegląd Humanistyczny* 19 (1975) 13-15

J. Nosowski, *Polska literatura polemiczno-antyislamistyczna XVI, XVII, XVIII w. Wybór tekstów i komentarzy*, 2 vols, Warsaw, 1974

J. Tazbir, *A state without stakes. Polish religious toleration in the sixteenth and seventeenth centuries*, New York, 1973

J. Nowak-Dłużewski, *Okolicznościowa poezja polityczna w Polsce. Dwaj młodzi Wazowie*, Warsaw, 1972, pp. 69-77

J. Nowak-Dłużewski, *Okolicznościowa poezja polityczna w Polsce. Zygmunt III*, Warsaw, 1971, pp. 233-310

R. Majewski, *Cecora rok 1620*, Warsaw, 1970

S. Cynarski, 'Sarmatyzm. Ideologia i styl życia', in J. Tazbir (ed.), *Polska XVII wieku. Państwo – społeczeństwo – kultura*, Warsaw, 1969, 220-43

J. Nowak-Dłużewski, *Okolicznościowa poezja polityczna w Polsce. Pierwsi królowie elekcyjni*, Warszawa, 1969, pp. 70-5

A. Krzewińska, *Pieśń ziemiańska, antyturecka i refleksyjna. Studia nad wybranymi gatunkami staropolskiej liryki XVI i XVII wieku*, Toruń, 1968, pp. 85-105

B. Baranowski, *Znajomość Wschodu w dawnej Polsce do XVIII wieku*, Łódź, 1950

Michał Kuran

Tadeusz Juda Krusiński

DATE OF BIRTH   15 May 1675
PLACE OF BIRTH   Jarantowice, Cuyavia (Poland)
DATE OF DEATH   27 August 1757
PLACE OF DEATH   Zabrzeże, near Kamieniec Podolski (today
    Ukraine)

BIOGRAPHY

Tadeusz Juda Krusiński was born into a noble family. He studied at a
Jesuit college, and joined the Society of Jesus in Krakow in 1691, changing his first name Jan to Tadeusz Juda. He spent the following 13 years
studying and teaching in Jesuit schools and colleges in Krakow, Jarosław,
Brześć and Lublin. In 1704, the head of his province sent him as a missionary to Persia, together with another Jesuit named Jan Reuth. They
travelled through Moscow and Astrakhan to Ganja probably in spring
1705, and reached their destination in autumn 1706.

Between 1706 and 1712, Krusiński was probably active in Mesopotamia, Syria, Palestine, Greece, Anatolia, Turkish and Persian Armenia, and
western Iran. He usually made a living as a physician, though it is known
that at least once he hired himself out as a camel drover. He returned to
Poland in 1712 to persuade King Augustus II (r. 1697-1704/6, 1709-33) to
send an envoy to Persia. He went back to Yerevan in 1714, via Istanbul,
where he served as an interpreter for a Polish envoy, Chomętowski. In
1715, he obtained restitution of some Jesuit property that had been seized
in Yerevan, probably due to the conflicts between Catholic and Eastern
Armenian Christians. The same year, he was appointed chaplain to the
Georgian prince Vakhtang VI of Kartli (r. 1716-24).

In 1720, Krusiński was appointed by the Sacred Congregation for the
Propagation of the Faith as a procurator for the bishop of Isfahan, Barn-
aba Fedele OP, and all Catholic missionary orders in Persia. He obtained
seven decrees from the Persian shah, Sultan Ḥusayn (r. 1694-1722), in
favour of the Jesuits, as well as decrees in favour of other orders (Domini-
cans in Nakhichevan, Capuchins in Ganja) after 11 July 1721. The following year, he survived the Afghan siege of Isfahan, and served briefly as a
physician to one of the Afghan leaders.

Thanks to his linguistic skills (he spoke Polish, Latin, Italian, Persian,
Turkish and Armenian, and understood French and Russian), Krusiński

served occasionally as a translator at the Persian court (he supposedly translated a letter from Louis XIV of France (r. 1643-1715) to Sultan Ḥusayn, as well as various other documents and reports).

He left Persia together with Persian diplomats sent to Istanbul in 1726. En route, he may have spent some time in Palestine. He arrived in France in 1728, from where he returned via Italy to Poland. From 1728, he served as administrator, director or chaplain in various educational institutions in Kamieniec Podolski, Jarosław, Krosno, Ostróg and Brześć Litewski, and as preacher at the courts of the local nobility. He died in Zabrzeże near Kamieniec Podolski in 1757.

Krusiński's major work is *Tragica vertentis bellis Persici historia* ('The history of the late revolutions in Persia'), a description of the downfall of Safavid rule in Iran, which he witnessed. This work was published in many languages under various titles, and with slightly different contents.

MAIN SOURCES OF INFORMATION

Primary

MS Rome, Archives of the house of the Superior General – Polonica 45-6 (*Catalogus personarum et oficiorum provinciae Poloniae S.I. 1691-1756*); Polonica 49 (*Catalogus personarum et oficiorum provinciae Poloniae Minoris S.I. 1756-1758*); Polonica 20-7 (*Catalogus triennalis primus, years 1693, 1700, 1711, 1714, 1717, 1723, 1727, 1730, 1737, 1743, 1746*); Polonica 89, fol. 9 (*Defuncti in Collegio Camenecensi S.I.*); Polonica 78 fol. 294r-v (*Informationes*, Tomus 131, fols 349-62); Epist. NN. 47, fol. 21 l. v (brulion); Polonica 63 fol. (nr) 62 (*Annuae Litterae collegii Ostrogiensis S.I. 16 Junii 1737*)

[Krusiński Tadeusz Juda], *The history of the late revolutions in Persia*, 2 vols, London, 1728, vol. 1, pp. II-XI

T.S. Wolski, *Ilustris Hierosolymitana peregrinatio*, Leopolis, 1737, p. 273

F. Zieliński, 'Xiądz Krusiński. Wiadomość historyczna', *Biblioteka Warszawska* 4 (1841) 375-97

C. Sommervogel, *Bibliothèque de la Compagnie de Jésus*, vol. 4, Brussels, 1893, pp. 1262-5

B. Natoński, art. 'Krusiński Jan Tadeusz', in *Polski słownik biograficzny*, vol. 15, Warsaw, 1970, 426-2

Secondary

R. Matthee, 'Introduction', in Judas Thaddeus Krusinski, *The history of the revolutions in Persia*, ed. R. Matthee, London, 2018, vol. 1, pp. IX-XIII

I. Ciborowska-Rymarowicz, 'Orientalista Tadeusz Juda Krusiński (1675-1757) i egzemplarze jego prac w bibliotekach klasztornych i prywatnych XVIII wieku', *Bibliotekarz Podlaski* 30 (2015) 11-34

B. Składanek, *Historia Persji*, Warsaw, 2007, vol. 3, p. 83

D. Kolbaja, 'Juda Tadeusz Krusinski SJ – misjonarz, uczony, dyplomata. Życie i dzieło', *Pro Georgia* 2 (1992) 19-25

J. Reychman, *Znajomość i nauczanie języków orientalnych w Polsce XVIII w.*, Wrocław, 1950, pp. 32-7

S. Brzeziński, *Misjonarze i dyplomaci polscy w Persji XVII i XVIII wieku*, Potulice, 1935, pp. 48-71

S. Zaleski, *Jezuici w Polsce, w skróceniu*, vol. 5, Kraków, 1908, pp. 83, 147-9

A. Muchliński, 'Materiały do dziejów Kościoła polskiego z języków wschodnich', *Przegląd Religijno-Moralny* 8 (1861) 136-51

WORKS ON CHRISTIAN-MUSLIM RELATIONS

Tragica vertentis bellis Persici historia
'The history of the late revolutions in Persia'

DATE 1740

ORIGINAL LANGUAGE Latin

DESCRIPTION

Tragica vertentis bellis Persici historia (in full, *Tragica vertentis bellis Persici historia per repetitas clades ab anno 1711 ad annum 1728 cum continuata post Gallicos, Hollandicos, Germanicos, ac demum Turcicos, authoris typos auctior authore Patre Thadaeo Krusinski Societatis Jesu Missionario Persico accesit ad eandem historiam Prodromus iteratis typis subjectus*) is the last, and probably the most extended, version of Krusiński's treatise on the downfall of the Safavid dynasty. Various parts of the material contained in the work had previously been published several times in many languages and under various titles. For this reason it seems pertinent to describe briefly all the known editions, and then to discuss the contents of only the most complete 1740 Latin edition published in Lviv (all the quotations in Latin come from this edition unless stated otherwise).

Histoire de la dernière révolution de Perse, a French translation of an unknown Latin source, published in Paris in 1728, is the first printed work that may be attributed with certainty to Krusiński. The French editor, a Jesuit, Jean Antoine du Cerceau, named Krusiński as the author, but changed the original order of the chapters. This change was later accepted by Krusiński and included in the Leopolitan (Lviv) Latin edition.

The book is in two volumes (their content is generally included in the Leopolitan *Tragica vertentis bellis Persici historia*). The edition also contains a map of western Iran. It should be noted that the spelling of Oriental proper nouns in both editions is typical of Polish (*Aszraff*, instead of *Achraffe*, *Vachtanga* instead of *Vahtanga*). Haydari and Ne'mati, which in the Leopolis edition of 1740 (see below) are called 'Hayderi' and 'Nematullachi' (p. 44), are here for unknown reasons referred to as 'Felenk' and 'Pelenk'. The spelling suggests that the translator of the French edition based it on an original by Krusiński. Bronisław Natoński suggests that this work was written by Krusiński in 1726, and entitled *Relatio de mutationis regni Persarum*. Some other Polish authors suggest that this was printed in Rome in 1727, but there is no evidence that any of them (Natoński included) had seen this manuscript or any printed edition of it (and its very existence is doubted by Natoński).

The first English edition of Krusiński's work, *The history of the late revolution in Persia*, based on the French edition, was published in London in 1728. In 1728-9, an Ottoman Turkish translation, *Tārīḫ saiyāḥ*, was published in Istanbul. It was probably made by Krusiński himself at the request of the grand vizier, and was not based on the French edition. In the main, it covers the same issues as *Tragica vertentis*.

Tārīḫ saiyāḥ, hoc est: Chronicon peregrinantis seu historia ultimi belli Persarum cum Agvanis, published in Leipzig in 1731, was a Latin translation from the Ottoman Turkish edition by a German Orientalist, Johann Christian Clodius, who was apparently unaware of the previous European translations or versions of the work. This is the source of a later English translation by George Newnham Mitford, published in London in 1840. In this edition, the reasons for the decline of the Safavid state are only briefly mentioned.

The only complete Polish version, *Wiadomości o rewolucyi perskiey*, has never been printed (the manuscript is kept in Biblioteka Kórnicka in Kórnik, Poland). Its translator or author knew the Leipzig edition as well as another unidentified one, probably French (it contains some information on the Armenians that is absent from the Leipzig edition). Since he apparently had not read any of the Leopolitan editions (neither *Prodromus* nor *Tragica vertentis*), the work was probably written before the publication in Poland of any of Krusiński's works.

Prodromus ad tragicam vertentis belli Persici historiam (Leopolis, 1733), a work in Latin with one short letter in French, was designed by Krusiński as a supplement to his earlier works. (It contains a report of Durry Effendi, an Ottoman envoy to Persia in 1720, which Krusinski translated from Persian into Latin during his stay in Istanbul.) It is also one of the least known printed editions of his works that trace the fall of the Safavids. Probably only the 1740 Leopolitan edition, *Tragica vertentis bellis Persici historia per repetitas clades* (taken in this entry as the point of reference), is less known than *Prodromus*. The author of the 1840 English translation of the Leipzig edition refers to the *Prodromus* as 'an extremely rare book', and was also unsure whether Leopolis, where it was published, was the same city in which 'one of the two principal Universities of Poland' was located at that time.

Prodromus contains the history of Polish-Persian diplomatic relations, as well as some letters from Polish kings to Persian shahs. It does not therefore focus on Islamic doctrine, though it does provide some information on Muslim religious practices. Probably the most interesting statement included in it deals with the assertion that both Persians and Ottomans were influenced by the philosophy of Plato, whom they called Eflatus (pp. 36, 86). It also comments on the care the Ottomans took of the religious foundations of their past sultans, even those long dead, and recite or write the *basmala* as a form of *incipit* (p. 106), and that the Persians revere the alleged tomb of Esther and Mordechai in Hamadan (pp. 127-8). There is also a short explanation of the term *szehit* (*shahīd*, martyr) and of the various kinds of martyrs in Islam: 'Those who are killed in a duel, or by accident are called by the Turks *maktul*, those who are sentenced to death because of justice are called *katl*, those who have died of natural causes are called *merhum*, and those who have died in war against the infidels (as Turks call Christians and also Persians) are granted a palm of martyrs by the Turks, and called *szehit*. Whoever dies fighting against the infidels, by his death will confirm his faith' (*Qui casu vel in duello mactatus Turcis dicitur Maktul, qui a iustitia morti addictus Katl, qui naturali morte obiit: Merhum contra (uti, qui in bello Christianos Turcae vocant & etiam Persas) infideles, illis martyrii palmam tribuunt & vocant Szehit, qui scilicet contra infideles pugnando fidem morte sua contestatus fuerit*) (p. 151).

Another book attributed to Krusiński by George Newnham Mitford, the author of the 1840 edition of 'Chronicles of the traveller', called *An historical account of the revolutions in Persia. In the years 1722, 1723, 1724, and 1725. Wherein the rise and progress of those fatal broils, are set in a true light*, was published (apparently as a translation from French) in London in 1727. It does not mention Krusiński and contains several statements that contradict information given in later publications whose authorship can be far more certainly attributed to him; for example, an Afghan leader Mirwais Hotak is described here as 'born of mean parents' (p. 3), while elsewhere Krusiński staunchly opposes such views, claiming that Mirwais's family was of great importance in Kandahar province; the

Illustration 14. Tadeusz Juda Krusiński, *Prodromus ad tragicam vertentis belli Persici historiam*, title page, listing Ahmed Efendi Dürri (Ahmed III) as author

sack of New Julfa by the Afghans, which is an important episode in all Krusiński's other accounts, is mentioned very briefly and also contradicts details in them.

Tragica vertentis bellis Persici historia (Leopolis, 1740), written in Latin, is the last and probably the most extended version of Krusiński's treatise on the downfall of the Safavid dynasty. This edition also contains *Prodromus*. Biographers refer to Krusiński's constant interest in Persian affairs, confirmed by the publication of his *Analecta ad tragicam belli persici historiam* (Lviv, c. 1755; copies are rare).

Even though he was a missionary in Muslim countries, Krusiński never wrote any work that focused mainly on Islam as a religion. Nevertheless, there are many references to it in the works about the fall of the Safavid dynasty. He understands the division between Sunnīs and Shīʿīs (he calls the latter 'Rafi', presumably from the Arabic *Rāfiḍa*, a term of abuse often used by Sunnīs for Shīʿīs), and so he is able to see the religious aspect of the wars between the Afghans, who were Sunnīs, and the Persians, and also the role of fatwas against Persian rule that were obtained by Mirwais in Mecca. He knows that fatwas usually end with the formula 'Allāh knows best', which suggests that he had seen such documents (English edition of 1728, vol. 1, p. 172).

Krusiński also understands the religious dimension of the rule of the Safavid shahs. He describes the coronation ceremonies, which involved whipping the in-coming shah with 12 rods of chaste-tree (*agnus castus*) 'in memory of the twelve martyrs of the Raphasi, i.e. Persian, sect, whom Persians call Imam' (*in memoriam duodecim sectae Raphasi, seu Persicae, martyrum, quos Persae Iman* [scil. *Imam*] *vocant*) (p. 14), after which shahs were considered to be sinless (*impeccabilis*) and every one of their deeds would be seen as just, or at least justifiable. It was this sense of *impeccabilitas* (sinlessness) that played an important part in the attempt by Sultan Ḥusayn's grandmother to persuade him to drink alcohol (English edition of 1728, vol. 1, pp. 72-5).

Although Krusiński thinks Islam is false, he has some respect for pious Muslims unless they are hostile towards Christians and Christianity. He praises the Shī'ites for the respect they show to the Blessed Virgin Mary, and reports that Persian kings, unlike the iconoclastic Sunnīs, hold the pictures of Mary and Jesus sent to them by European rulers in high esteem. In fact, Persian Muslims insult Jews by calling them 'those who hate Mary', and Persian girls are frequently named Mary. He also notes the respect that Persian rulers have for the pope.

Krusiński contrasts the situation during the reign of Shah 'Abbās (r. 1588-1629), whom he considers a political genius, with that under Sultan Ḥusayn. He severely criticises the sentence imposed on a Persian Muslim who had murdered an Armenian woman and her six children: he was only to have his little finger amputated (p. 83), and he applauds Shah 'Abbas' policy of applying the *lex talionis* to every murder case, regardless of the religion of the victim or perpetrator. During the reign of Sultan Ḥusayn, executing a Muslim for murdering an Armenian was virtually impossible, although the murderer was made to pay all the taxes that would have been paid by his victim (p. 86), which provided Armenians with some protection against murder.

He also praises Shah 'Abbās for making it possible for Armenians who had converted to Islam to return to Christianity (pp. 78-9), and for encouraging his subjects to make a pilgrimage to Mashhad instead of Mecca, though he sees this as a means of stopping Persians from enriching Ottoman-controlled Mecca and Medina.

SIGNIFICANCE

As a Catholic priest, Krusiński regarded Islam as a false religion. Nevertheless, his works are accounts of political events in Safavid Persia, together with explanations of their historical and sociological background, without evidence of polemical bias. He has much compassion for Christian Armenians and Georgians who are persecuted by Muslims, or even forced to convert, but he also has much sympathy for Muslim Persians and Afghans and he is able to see some moral or religious values in Islam and to approve of them.

The Leopolitan edition, which was generally unknown in Western Europe, was used by Benedykt Chmielowski in *Nowe Ateny albo Akademia wszelkiej scyencyi pełna* (1745-6), regarded as the first Polish encyclopaedia. It was also translated into various European languages, as well as Ottoman Turkish, and was republished and commented upon in the 18th and 19th centuries. It was also borrowed from without acknowledgement (e.g. by Louis-Andre de la Mamie de Clairac in *Historie de Perse depuis le commencement de ce siècle*, 1750), and plagiarised (e.g. by Charles Picault in *Historie des révolutions de Perse*, 2 vols [1810], and Jonas Hanway, *An historical account of the British trade over the Caspian Sea* [1753], who mentions Krusiński in a footnote and no more). Later historians, such as John Malcolm in *A history of Persia* (1815), give due praise to Krusiński. His history also became known among Persian historians from the middle of the 19th century.

Several editions are referred to that cannot be traced, partly because their titles are not given. For example, Natoński mentions a Dutch translation that was published in Amsterdam in 1728, and two new editions of Du Cerceau's translation that appeared under various titles in 1741 and 1742, and adds that the 1741 edition appeared also in Spanish and English.

PUBLICATIONS

This list contains information on the editions of the works by Krusiński, or attributed to him, that are referred to in the entry; a comprehensive list of all the editions and various modifications of the text(s) still remains to be compiled.

MS Rome, Archivum Romanum Societatis Iesu – Fondo Gesuitico, 720 II, no. 9 [P. Tadeusz Juda Krusinski, SJ], *Informatio de missionibus persicis* [1727]

MS Vienna, Staatsbibliothek Wien – 8855 (Judas Krusinsky, *Historia revolutionis Persicae*; probably brought from Istanbul, and could have been used by Stöcklein for the German trans.)

MS Kórnik, Poland, Biblioteka Kórnicka – BK 00140 (*Wiadomość o rewolucji perskiej*)

[Attributed to Krusiński], *An historical account of the revolutions in Persia. In the years 1722, 1723, 1724, and 1725. Wherein the rise and progress of those fatal broils, are set in a true light*, London, 1727 (English trans.); ESTC T116485 (digitised version available through *ECCO*)

Tadeusz J. Krusiński, *Histoire de la dernière révolution de Perse*, 2 vols, Paris, 1728 (French trans.); 009314223 and 224 (digitised version available through Hathi Trust Digital Library)

Tadeusz J. Krusiński, *The history of the late revolutions in Persia*, 2 vols, London, 1728, Dublin, 1729 (English trans., with amendments); ESTC T116485 (digitised version available through *ECCO*)

Tadeusz J. Krusiński, *The history of the late revolutions in Persia*, 2 vols, London, 1733² (English trans., printed for J. Pemberton); ESTC T122309 (digitised version available through *ECCO*)

Tadeusz J. Krusiński, *The history of the late revolutions in Persia*, 2 vols, London, 1740² (English trans., printed for J. Osborne; repr. New York: Arno Press, 1973); ESTC N017888 (digitised version available through *ECCO*)

Tadeusz J. Krusiński, *Tarǵumā tārīḫ sijāḥ dur ẓuhūr 'Efǵānajāin*, trans. Ibrahim Effendi, Istanbul, 1728-9 (Ottoman Turkish trans.); Res/4 A.or. 3410 (digitised version available through *MDZ*)

Tadeusz J. Krusiński, *Ta'rīḫ-i saiyāḥ, hoc est, Chronicon peregrinantis seu Historia ultimi belli Persarum cum Aghwanis gesti, a tempore primae eorum in regnum persicum irruptionis ejusque occupationis, usque ad Eschrefum Aghwanum, Persiae regem continuata, ex codice turcico, in officina typographica recenti constantinopolitana impresso, versa ac notis quibusdam illustrata, cum Tabula imperatorum familiae othmanicae, ex codice manuscripto turcico, in fine adjecta*, trans. J.Ch. Clodius, Lipsiae, 1731 (Latin trans.); 4 A.or. 3411 (digitised version available through *MDZ*)

Neuer Welt-Bott oder Allerhand So Lehr-als Geist-reiche Brief, Schrifften und Reis-Beschreibungen, Welche von denen Missionariis der Gesellschaft Jesu aus Weit-entfernten Ländern biß Anno 1730. in Europa angelangt seynd. Jetzt zum erstenmal verteutscht/ und vielfältig verbessert von P. Josepho Stöcklein, gedachter Societät Priestern. Achtzehnder Theil von numero 394. biß numero 410. Begreifft in sich R.P. Judae Thaddaei Krusinski's. und des Herrn Durri Effendi, Nachrichten von der letzten Unruhe in Persien, Augsburg: in Verlag

Philips, Martins, und Joh. Veith seel. Erben, 1732, pp. 1-159 (German trans., probably from the Vienna MS)

Tadeusz J. Krusiński, *Prodromus ad tragicam vertentis belli Persici historiam: Seu Legationis a fulgida porta ad Sophorum regem Szah Sultan Hussein anno 1720, expedita autentica relatio* [...]: *Ex Turcico Latine facta opera Judæ Krusinski: Accessit ejusdem De legationibus Polono-Persieis dissertativ*, Leopolis [Lvov], 1733, 1734², 1740³; 4 A.or. 3314 (digitised version available through *MDZ*)

Tadeusz J. Krusiński, *Tragica vertentis belli persici historia per repetitas clades ab anno 1711 ad annum 1728vum continuata post Gallicos, Hollandicos, Germanicos ac demum Turcicos authoris typos. Auctior authore patre Thadeo Krusinski Societatis Jesu misionario persico accesit ad eandem historiam prodromus iteratis typis subjectus*, Leopolis [Lvov], 1740

Tadeusz J. Krusiński, *The chronicles of the traveller, a history of the Afghan wars with Persia in the beginning of the last century from the commencement to the ascension of sultan Ashruf* [...], trans. G. Newnham Mitford, London, 1840 (English trans.); 13960 (digitised version available through Hathi Trust Digital Library)

Basirat-nama dar gozaresh-o estila-ye Afghan bar Esfahan dar zaman-e dowlat-e Shah Soltan Hoseyn [Book of insight into the Afghan occupation of Isfahan during the reign of Shah Soltan Hoseyn] (a condensed Persian trans. made by 'Abd al-Razzāq Donboli 'Maftun'; some 10 MSS are available in Persian libraries, the oldest dated 1860-1)

Hasan Khan E'temad al-Saltana, *Montazam-e Naseri*, 3 vols, Tehran, 1880-2, vol. 2, pp. 240-79 (Maftun's translation integrated into a Qajar historiography)

'Abd al-Razzaq Donboli 'Maftun', transl., *Safarnama-ye Krusinski. Yaddasht-ha-ye kashish-e Lehestani-ye 'asr-e Safavi*, ed. Maryam Mir-Ahmadi, Tehran, 1984-5 (Persian trans.)

D. Kolbaja, 'Tadeusz Krusiński, Tragica vertentis belli Persici historia', *Pro Georgia* 2 (1992) 25-7 (Polish trans. of passages concerning Georgia)

Suqūṭ-i Iṣfahān bah rivāyat-i Krūsīnskī, ed. Javād Ṭabāṭabā'ī, Tehran, 2005-6 (Persian trans.)

Judas Thaddeus Krusinski, *The history of the revolutions in Persia*, 3 vols, ed. R. Matthee, London, 2018 (this edition includes the 1733 English trans. and Clodius's Latin trans.)

STUDIES

R. Matthee, 'Introduction', in Judas Thaddeus Krusinski, *The history of the late revolutions in Persia*, vol. 1, pp. vii-xvii

M.P. Borkowski, 'Wewnętrzne przyczyny upadku monarchii Safawidów w dziełach o. Tadeusza Krusińskiego SJ', *Przegląd Orientalistyczny* (2017) 357-66

M.P. Borkowski, 'Tadeusz Juda Krusiński's works and the image of Iran in 18th century Polish printed geographical compendia', in D. Kołodziejczyk and H. Kazemzadeh (eds), *Irān va Lahestān. Munāsabāt-e farhangi va tamaddoni / Historical and cultural interactions of Poland and Iran*, Tehran, 2016, 15-25

Ciborowska-Rymarowicz, 'Orientalista Tadeusz Juda Krusiński'

R. Matthee, *Persia in crisis. Safavid decline and the fall of Isfahan*, London, 2012, ch. 8, pp. 197-241

J. Fedirko, 'Afganistan w polskich badaniach naukowych. Zarys chronologii i problematyki', *Krakowskie Studia Miedzynarodowe* 4 (2007) 211-38, pp. 212-14

D. Kolbaja, 'Etnograficzne i historyczne wiadomości w Tragica belli Persici historia polskiego misjonarza Tadeusza Krusińskiego', *Pro Georgia* (1994) 5-14

C. Ghani, *Iran and the West. A critical bibliography*, London, 1987, pp. 213-15

L. Lockhart, *The fall of the Safavi dynasty and the Afghan occupation of Persia*, Cambridge, 1958, pp. 516-25

Reychman, *Znajomość i nauczanie języków orientalnych*, pp. 24, 32-9, 72, 98, 102

T.H. Weir, *The revolutions in Persia at the beginning of the 18th century*, Cambridge, 1922, p. 490

S. Załęski, *Missye w Persyi w XVII i XVIII w. pod protektoratem Polski. Szkic historyczny*, Kraków, 1882, pp. 91-119

Zieliński, 'Xiądz Krusiński'

Mikołaj Piotr Borkowski

Benedykt Chmielowski

DATE OF BIRTH   1700
PLACE OF BIRTH   The diocese of Łuck, Volhyn (present-day north-western Ukraine)
DATE OF DEATH   7 April 1763
PLACE OF DEATH   Firlejów (present-day Lipivka, western Ukraine)

BIOGRAPHY

Benedykt Chmielowski was born in 1700, possibly on 20 or 21 March, assuming the practice of the time of naming newborns after the patron saint of the day of their birth. He came from a noble family that used the *Nałęcz* coat of arms. He studied at a Jesuit academy in Lwów (Lviv), and then entered the diocesan seminary in Lwów in 1722. He worked for some time at the court of Jan Jabłonowski as teacher to his son, Dymitr. In 1725, on his employer's recommendation, he was appointed to the parish of Firlejów. In 1733, he was nominated parish priest of Leszno by King Stanisław Leszczyński (d. 1766), but never entered the parish due to the victory of Augustus III (r. 1734-63) in the War of the Polish Succession of 1733-4. Chmielowski became dean of Rohatyn before 1740, and in 1743 he became domestic chaplain to Mikołaj Gerard Wyżycki, archbishop of Lwów. He was later promoted to the rank of canon by Józef Jędrzej Załuski, bishop of Kijów (now Kiev). He died of natural causes in 1763.

Chmielowski is best known as the author of *Nowe Ateny, albo akademia wszelkiej scyencyi pełna*[...] (New Athens, or an Academy full of science of any kind[...]), a work regarded as the first Polish encyclopaedia. He also wrote on heraldry and on devotional matters, with the language of the latter significantly less saturated with Latin vocabulary than the *Nowe Ateny*.

It is possible that he never travelled abroad, and it is highly unlikely that he ever visited a non-Christian country. All his knowledge of Islam was gained through reading. His works are generally compilations from other authors whose works were published in Polish and Latin. It is uncertain whether he knew any other languages but the number of books he read is nevertheless impressive.

MAIN SOURCES OF INFORMATION

Primary

Benedykt Chmielowski, *Nowe Ateny albo Akademia wszelkiey scyencyi pełna, na różne tytuły, iak na classes podzielona mądrym dla memoryału, Idiotom dla nauki, politykom dla praktyki, melancholikom dla rozrywki Erigowana, część wtóra*, Lwów, 1746

J.D. Janocki, *Polonia literata nostri temporis*, Breslau (Wrocław), 1750, p. 14

J. Jabłonowski, *Musaeum Polonum*, Lwów, 1752, pp. 38, 89

J.J. Załuski, *Bibliotheca poetarum polonorum*, Warsaw, 1754, pp. 32-3

J.D. Janocki, *Lexicon derer itztlebenden Gelehrten in Polen*, Wrocław, 1755, vol. 1, p. 21, vol. 2, pp. 174-5

F. Bentkowski, *Historia literatury polskiej*, 2 vols, Warsaw, 1814, vol. 2, pp. 679-81

Ł. Gołębiowski, *O dziejopisach polskich, ich duchu, zaletach i wadach*, Warsaw, 1826

J.J. Załuski, *Biblioteka historyków, prawników, polityków i innych autorów polskich lub o Polsce piszących*, Kraków, 1832, pp. 58, 66, 142

Secondary

E. Kotarski, 'Benedykt Chmielowski'; http://literat.ug.edu.pl/autors/chmiel.htm

M. Wichowa, 'Ksiądz Benedykt Chmielowski jako uczony barokowy', *Napis* 5 (1999) 45-56

Art. 'Chmielowski Joachim Benedykt', in R. Pollak (ed.), *Bibliografia literatury polskiej. Nowy Korbut*, Piśmiennictwo staropolskie, Warsaw, 1964, vol. 2, 80-1

W. Ogrodziński, 'Joachim Benedykt Chmielowski', in *Polski słownik biograficzny*, Kraków, 1937, vol. 3, p. 341-2

WORKS ON CHRISTIAN-MUSLIM RELATIONS

Nowe Ateny albo Akademia wszelkiey scyencyi pełna

'New Athens or an Academy full of all (kinds of) science'

DATE 1745-56

ORIGINAL LANGUAGE Polish

DESCRIPTION

Nowe Ateny is known as the first Polish encyclopaedia. Its full title is: *Nowe Ateny albo Akademia wszelkiey scyencyi pełna, na różne tytuły, iak na classes podzielona mądrym dla memoryału, Idiotom dla nauki, politykom dla praktyki, melancholikom dla rozrywki Erigowana*, ('New Athens

or an Academy full of all [kinds of] science, divided into various chapters as into classes, issued for the wise to remember, for the uneducated
to learn, for politicians [or the polite/civilised ones] to practise, for the
melancholy as entertainment'). The first edition comprises two volumes
(published 1745-6), the second edition (published 1754-6) four volumes
(two volumes of the first edition without any major changes, plus two
further volumes). The contents are presented by topic, rather than in
alphabetical order. The work was written in Polish and Latin, with very
occasional words from other languages (e.g. French or German). *Nowe
Ateny* contains a variety of information, but focuses mainly on geography, history and Greek and Latin literature. The first volume consists of
924 pages in its first edition (all references here are to the pagination
used in this edition), and 850 pages in the second edition, although the
two editions do not appear to vary in content. The second volume consists of 807 pages in the original edition, with the second edition a few
pages shorter, as it does not include the *errata* to the first volume at the
end. The third volume covers 736 pages, and the fourth 660 pages. Material relating to Islam, Muslims and Christian-Muslim relations is scattered through various parts of the work.

Chmielowski was a compiler, and he tends not to judge the authors
he quotes, generally preferring to present their statements rather than
make his own. However, he notes contradictions between statements,
and sometimes shows his preference for one over another, and is far
from assuming them to be flawless. At times, he provides conflicting
information from different authors; for example, the date of the *hijra*
is given incorrectly as 591 (p. 196) and then, on the very same page,
as 622.

The first chapter (*tytuł*) discusses the concept of one God, and the
various characteristics attributed to Him in the Old and the New Testaments and in ancient philosophy. Various polytheistic religions, both
ancient and current (such as Hinduism, Zoroastrianism, the beliefs of
some of the indigenous peoples encountered by Europeans around the
world) are described in four of the following chapters. Islam is not mentioned in any of these, because it is neither polytheistic, nor part of the
tradition that Chmielowski considered as his own, such as the Old Testament of Judaism or ancient philosophy. Islam is both too exotic to be
part of orthodoxy and too similar to Christianity to be treated as another
pagan religion.

Muḥammad is first mentioned in the eighth chapter, entitled *Dubitantius lub kwestye dotychczas bez response albo sciencya potrzebne dubia
solwuiąca* ('Dubitantius, or questions having so far no answers or the

knowledge to solve doubts'). These doubts include the questions 'The body of Muḥammad the pseudo-prophet: does it still exist? Where is it?' (pp. 133-4). This section quotes various authors on the location of Muḥammad's tomb in Mecca. It is said to be one of the holiest places for Muslims, and it fascinated, for example, Mikołaj Krzysztof Radziwiłł 'Sierotka', whose description Chmielowski quotes for his allegation that the coffin was suspended in the air, achieved through skilful use of magnetism (which was false, and denied by Radziwiłł's informers).

Among the opinions about Muḥammad's death and burial, Chmielowski also quotes those of the Italian scholar, Cardinal Cesare Baronio, according to whom Muḥammad claimed that he would not be buried, because he would rise again after three days, although his corpse was instead eaten by dogs. However, Chmielowski identifies the difficulties in determining the ultimate fate of Muḥammad's body as stemming from the fact that 'learned and more polished Mahometans, in order not to confound their religion, do not reveal to the world what happened with this corpse [...] has it decayed or has it been burned by a thunderbolt. And other Mahometans, being very stubborn, dogged in their religion and overly zealous, consider any inquiry into it to be sinful' (pp. 133-4).

In a chapter on politics, Chmielowski states that religious intolerance and conversion by force are generally unacceptable. In a passage on just and unjust war, he claims that it would be an 'unjust war if Christian monarchs on the pretext of spreading the Holy Faith, took realms from Turks and other barbaric nations; as St Thomas [Aquinas], Concilium Toletanum [the Council of Toledo], all Canonistae [canonists] and jurists teach that they [i.e. Christian monarchs] would be obliged *ad restitutionem* [to restore (lands to the previous owners)]' (p. 250). Chmielowski's view on actual Christian-Muslim wars, both past and present, is, however, ambiguous. On the one hand, he criticises the Polish and Hungarian king, Władysław III Jagiellon (r. 1434-44), for breaking a truce with the Ottomans in 1444, while on the other, he believes the crusades to the Holy Land and the *Reconquista* of the Iberian Peninsula to be just wars. His views on the subject are clearly very complex, and it is difficult to ascertain what criteria determined his attitude towards particular Christian-Muslim wars.

The first volume of *Nowe Ateny* also contains a chapter on various religions and beliefs entitled *Taran ale nie tyran Volens non valens, mocne fale, ale nie Piotrowej Skale Albo Przeciwne Wierze S. Chrześcijańsko-Katolickiej Błędy i sekty ią iak złoto poleruiące* ('Battering ram, but not tyrant, *volens non valens* (willing but not strong enough), strong waves, but not against Peter's Rock or sects and errors opposing the holy Catholic-Christian faith, and polishing it as gold'). The title itself proves that, for Chmielowski, writing about the errors of Islam, as well as other non-Catholic beliefs, was a way of showing the reader the perfection of Catholicism as compared with other beliefs.

The subchapter on Islam (pp. 750-68) is positioned between those on Judaism and various Christian heresies. It begins with a short biography of Muḥammad (pp. 750-4), based on the writings of Baronio, Filippo Guadagnoli, and possibly others. According to this biography, which contains several inaccuracies, Muḥammad was born in 592 or 629 to a Jewish mother named Imina and an Arabian father of noble origin, called Abdalla. After his father's death, he was brought up in his mother's house, and at the age of 16 started working for the merchant Abdemonas (or Minofi), whose widow Hadyga he later married. He travelled to Persia and to the Byzantine Empire and met some Christians, in particular two Arians: a monk named Sergius and a certain John, both of whom later became his followers. There were also among his followers some Jews who believed he was the Messiah. They left him later, however, upon realising that, despite being circumcised, Muḥammad continued to eat camel meat, which is forbidden in Judaism.

Essentially, Chmielowski considers Islam to be a mixture of (heterodox) Christianity, Judaism, from which he derived circumcision, and Arab paganism. Chmielowski also writes that Muḥammad claimed to be a descendant of Sarah rather than Hagar. From Christianity, Muḥammad is said to have drawn reverence for Jesus and Mary. In the section on Judaism, a Latin quotation is attributed to the Qur'an: *Dedimus JESUM Filium MARIAE, ut faceret miracula & prodigia manifesta & fecimus eum per Spiritum Sanctum & insusstavimus in eum de spiritu nostro & conceptus est Christus ex virtute DEI & Matre Sanctissima & purissima supra omnes Mulieres* ('We [i.e. God] gave them JESUS Son of MARY, so that he made miracles and gave signs; and we made him by the Holy Spirit and breathed into him from our Spirit and he was conceived from GOD'S virtue of Mother most Holy and Pure among all other women'; pp. 742-3).

On the other hand, Chmielowski accuses Muḥammad of following heretical Christological doctrines such as the claim that only a shadow of Jesus was crucified (considered by Chmielowski to be originally a Manichean concept), and the Arian denial of the divinity of Jesus.

Chmielowski believed that Muḥammad invented the story of his receiving Divine revelation in order to deceive others. He lied to his wife, saying that his dreams were divine revelations, and convinced her that his seizures were his reaction to seeing the Archangel Gabriel. His wife became the first to believe in his revelations. He also supposedly kept a trained pigeon, which he fed with a pea placed in his ear; he claimed that this pigeon was the Holy Spirit revealing to him the truths of faith.

Chmielowski also provides information about the Qur'an, but it is not consistent. In one place he writes that the Qur'an was written during the reign of 'Umar, while in another he assumes that the first parts of this book were part of Muḥammad's deceit and attributed by Muḥammad to the Archangel Gabriel himself. He provides the number of letters and words in the Qur'an (323,015 and 77,639, respectively), and derives the term *Alkoran* from Alfulian, i.e. 'chapters'. When he writes on the contents of the Qur'an, he sometimes refers to suras (*Azory*), even mentioning their numbers, but the correspondence of these numbers to the actual text of the Qur'an is dubious.

He also refers to other Muslim scriptures, such as 'the Book of Sonnat' (Sunna) and an unidentified 'Book of Agar'.

Chmielowski writes that Muḥammad died of poison or intoxication (*struty*), and afterwards repeats some of the stories about the fate of his body mentioned above. He knows that Muḥammad was succeeded by caliphs, who were political as well as religious leaders. He knows the names of the four *rāshidūn* (rightly-guided) caliphs as well as the fact that they are inscribed in Ottoman (i.e. Sunnī) mosques. He is also aware that the division between Sunnīs and Shī'īs was the result of the conflict between 'Umar and 'Alī. Chmielowski writes (incorrectly) about the latter that he claimed to be a greater prophet than Muḥammad and that the Qur'an was to be revealed to him, but by mistake it was received by Muḥammad . He also knows that the Turks accuse Persians of distorting the Qur'an.

The following subsection, *Regestr niezregestrowany baśni Machometa y sektarzów iego z Alkoranu y różnych Autorów z refutacyą gdzie nie gdzie Autora tey xięgi* ('An unregistered register of the fairy tales of Muḥammad and his sectarians taken from Alcoran and other authors with [their] occasional refutation by the author of this book [i.e. Chmielowski]'; pp. 755-60), contains various accusations against the teaching ascribed by Chmielowski to Muḥammad. These may be divided into the following categories: 1. That it justifies violence against non-Muslims and spreading Islam by fire and sword; 2. That Islamic soteriology is materialistic: Chmielowski is scandalised by the Islamic idea of Paradise as a place of carnal pleasure (as he writes, 'By God's providence, the delights of Paradise, are not in the carnal ecstasies, but in seeing HIM'). This materialism is also present in Muslim angelology: he finds the idea that the angels Hārūt and Mārūt were seduced by a woman ridiculous; 3. That Muḥammad usurped some prophetic and even messianic attributes: the story of stones greeting Muḥammad and calling him a prophet and a divine messenger, or trees protecting him from the sun (a surprisingly accurate description of al-isrā' wa-l-mi'rāj, Muḥammad's Night Journey) can be perceived as belonging to this category. Chmielowski was probably most scandalised by Muḥammad's supposed role in the last judgement: Muslims are said to believe that he will be given the keys to Paradise. A story about devils, freed from Hell because they listened to Muḥammad's preaching, is similarly criticised; 4. That some Muslim beliefs are ridiculous, such as the claim that the world is positioned on the horn of a giant ox, or the description of some angels encountered by Muḥammad during the mi'rāj.

The next section, Ceremonie religii Mahometowej ('The ceremonies of Muḥammad's religion'; pp. 760-4), includes a description of various Muslim religious practices. Chmielowski knows the concept of the Five Pillars of Islam, although he omits the shahāda, replacing it with ablutions. He nevertheless quotes the shahāda at least four times but frequently in a distorted form: Nie iest BÓG ieno BEG i Machomet Apostoł iego ('There is no God but Beg [probably a distorted form of the Polish word Bóg – God] and Muḥammad is his Apostle'). However, more correct translations also appear in the encyclopaedia (pp. 766, 85).

Other Pillars are referred to correctly. Moreover, Chmielowski praises the idea of the five daily prayers, as well as the humility shown by Muslims during prayer. He writes that, 'it would all be good, had it not been for their false faith'. He also gives a short description of bayram in a passage concerning the ḥajj.

The rest of the subsection about Muslim ceremonies, as well as the last two subsections, Sekty w Machometańskiej religii ('Sects of Muḥammad's religion') and Teraźniejsze herezye Machometanów ('Present heresies of Mahometans') deal with various Muslim 'sects'. Among them are mentioned the four madhāhib of Sunnī Islam (he even gives fairly accurate information on madhāhib popularity by region), as well as some non-Muslim religions, e.g. Bogomilism (Potarowie) and Munazychy, a sect that believed in reincarnation (possibly the Alawites or Druze). There is also a short description of some Sufi ṭuruq, such as Mevlevis or Bektashis, the latter associated with the Janissaries and depicted as the most militant. He says that there are 72 Muslim sects, though elsewhere he mentions that Muḥammad said that 73 sects would emerge from his teaching, of which only one would be the true faith, and that even Muslims consider some of the content of the Qur'an to be false. The best Muslim sects, in his view, are those similar to Catholicism, i.e. which believe in the Trinity, have less materialistic views of salvation (*Eszreff*), or hold Christ in high esteem (*chep Meszajchlar*).

The primary source of Chmielowski's knowledge about Islam was a Polish translation of one of Filippo Guadagnoli's works made by Teofil Rutka. He also used a Polish edition of *The history of the present state of the Ottoman Empire* by Paul Rycaut, which was the source for various Muslim 'sects'. Some details in the description of the *ḥajj* are taken from *Hierosolymitana peregrinatio* by Mikołaj Krzysztof Radziwiłł 'Sierotka' ['the orphan'], a Commonwealth magnate who lived in the 16th century. These are certainly not all the sources used by Chmielowski, who was extremely well-read but did not always mention the origin of his information.

The content of the second volume of *Nowe Ateny* is mostly homogeneous, focusing entirely on geography (in the broadest sense). It consists of only five chapters, the first discussing travel and the geography of the world (in a very wide sense), the second, various peoples, and the third, the languages of the world. The last two chapters are very short *errata* to the first volume, and do not mention Islam.

The first chapter of this volume includes various information on Islam and Islamic peoples. Chmielowski mentions, for example, that Ottomans abstain from wine and pork, and consider death in war against Christians to be a divine grace. He also reports that Turks consider the Christian cult of icons as idolatry (p. 493). However, descriptions of the Safavid coronation ceremonies, taken directly from *Tragica vertentis belli Persici* by Tadeusz Krusiński, are the most interesting (pp. 582-3).

'Saracens' are among the peoples described in the second chapter (pp. 717-29). The term refers generally to white Muslims who are neither Turks (or at least not Ottomans) nor Persians. The section about Saracens consists of a brief outline of the history of Christian-Muslim relations (or rather Christian-Muslim wars) prior to the emergence of the Timurid and Ottoman empires in the east, and the fall of the Emirate of Granada in the west, as well as a short passage on the 'Abbasid caliphs.

There are several interesting references to Islam in the third volume of *Nowe Ateny*. The first chapter, being in fact a continuation of *Dubitantius* from the first volume, contains a section about various types of headgear. The red turbans of the Qizilbash are mentioned among them.

Short biographies of Avicenna and Averroes (Ibn Sīnā and Ibn Rushd), found in the chapter *Katalog osób wiadomosći o sobie godnych* ('A catalogue of persons worth being known about'), are the most interesting items in this volume (pp. 583-4). Chmielowski had serious difficulties in placing both authors in time and place. He is unsure whether Avicenna lived in the Middle East or Spain. He also claims that he died in 1151 (actually 1037), and considers it possible that Averroes was his disciple. Chmielowski is aware that Avicenna was 'a sectarian of Muḥammad's errors' (*błędów Machometańskich Secator*), but he nevertheless has great respect for him, calling him 'the prince of Arabian physicians' (*Xiążęciem medyków arabskich*). Chmielowski is also aware of Avicenna's other intellectual pursuits, such as metaphysics and alchemy. He mentions his manuscripts, written in Arabic and kept in the Jesuit Library in Collegio Romano and in the church library in Toledo. He accuses Averroes of many foul deeds: poisoning Avicenna, apostasy from Christianity to Judaism, and later conversion to Islam. Chmielowski finds it likely that he was in fact an atheist who denied God's omnipotence, omniscience and infinity, as well as human free will. For that reason, states Chmielowski, his teachings were condemned by the Council of Vienna.

The fourth and last volume of *Nowe Ateny* again mentions Islam in the sections describing various Muslim countries. The section about Persia (pp. 519-27) contains some new information from *Tragica vertentis belli persici* by Tadeusz Krusiński, mentioning, for example, the reverence shown by Persians for the Virgin Mary.

Chmielowski clearly believes Islam is a mixture of Christian heresies, Judaism and Arab paganism, and generally despises it. He calls Muḥammad a 'pseudo-prophet' and claims that his 'revelations' were an effect of epilepsy. Nevertheless, he praises Muslims for their devotion in prayer. He is also aware of the difference between Islamic and Talmudic views on Jesus and Mary.

SIGNIFICANCE

Benedykt Chmielowski's work was harshly criticised by Polish advocates of the Enlightenment and, more recently, by some Polish philologists. This criticism was, however, generally based on a *pars pro toto* reasoning, with arguments focusing mainly, if not exclusively, on the few chapters about magic and demonology (regardless of the fact that these chapters appear quite late, in the third volume), and Chmielowski's baroque language, which is saturated with Latin macaronics. The intensity of this criticism, together with the fact that *Nowe Ateny* was published in a number of editions, suggests that in the late Wettin period the encyclopaedia was widely read.

PUBLICATIONS

Benedykt Chmielowski, *Nowe Ateny albo Akademia wszelkiey scyencyi pełna, na różne tytuły, iak na classes podzielona mądrym dla memoryału, Idiotom dla nauki, politykom dla praktyki, melancholikom dla rozrywki Erigowana*, Lwów, 1745, 1755[2]; SD.XVIII.2.2905 I (digitised version available through Polona/)

Benedkt Chmielowski, *Nowe Ateny albo Akademia wszelkiey scyencyi pełna, na różne tytuły, iak na classes podzielona mądrym dla memoryału, Idiotom dla nauki, politykom dla praktyki, melancholikom dla rozrywki Erigowana, część wtóra*, Lwów, 1746, 1756[2]

Benedykt Chmielowski, *Nowe Ateny albo Akademia wszelkiey scyencyi pełna, na różne tytuły, iak na classes podzielona mądrym dla memoryału, Idiotom dla nauki, politykom dla praktyki, melancholikom dla rozrywki Erigowana, część trzecia albo suplement*, Lwów, 1754; SD XVIII.2.2905 III (digitised version available through Polona/)

Benedykt Chmielowski, *Nowe Ateny albo Akademia wszelkiey scyencyi pełna, na różne tytuły, iak na szkolne classes podzielona mądrym dla memoryału, Idiotom dla nauki, politykom dla praktyki, melancholikom dla rozrywki Erigowana, część czwarta a drugi suplement*, Lwów, 1756

Benedykt Chmielowski, *Nowe Ateny, albo Akademia wszlekiey scyencyi pełna*, ed. M. and J.J. Lipscy, Kraków, 1966 (edition of selected passages; a still shorter selection from this edition, by M. Hanczkowski, was published in Kraków, 2003)

Benedykt Chmielowski, *Nowe Ateny traktat dubitantius*, ed. J. Kroczak, Wrocław, 2009 (partial edition, including only the *Dubitantius*)

Benedykt Chmielowski, *Nowe Ateny albo Akademia wszelkiey scyencyi pełna, na różne tytuły, iak na classes podzielona mądrym dla memoryału, Idiotom dla nauki, politykom dla praktyki, melancholikom dla rozrywki Erigowana*, 2 vols, Warsaw, 2018

STUDIES

M.P. Borkowski, 'Obraz Arabów w osiemnastowiecznej Rzeczypospolitej w świetle *Nowych Aten* Benedykta Chmielowskiego i *Świata we wszystkich swych częściach większych i mniejszych*[...] Władysława Aleksandra Łubieńskiego', *Przegląd Orientalistyczny* 1-2 (2016) 31-43

W. Paszyński, 'Czarna legenda *Nowych Aten* Benedykta Chmielowskiego i próby jej przezwyciężenia', *Zeszyty Naukowe Uniwersytetu Jagiellońskiego. Prace Historyczne* 141 (2014) 37-59, 196

J. Axer, 'Dyskusja o roli łaciny w "Nowych Atenach" Benedykta Chmielowskiego jako świadectwo republikańskiej świadomości narodu szlacheckiego', in I.M. Dacka-Górzyńska and J. Partyka (eds), *Staropolskie kompendia wiedzy* [Old Polish compendia of knowledge], Warsaw, 2009, 33-45

H. Rybicka-Nowacka, *Nowe Ateny Benedykta Chmielowskiego. Metoda, styl, język*, Warsaw, 1974

Mikołaj Piotr Borkowski

Salomea Regina Pilsztynowa

Salomea Regina z Rusieckich Pilsztynowa; Regina Pichelsteinowa;
Regina von Pichelstein; Regina Makowska; Regina Salomea Makowska;
Regina Halpirowa; Regina Salomea Rusiecka; Regina S. Rusiecka;
Salomée Halpir; Solomanida Yefimovna

DATE OF BIRTH   1718
PLACE OF BIRTH   Nowogródek (today, Navahrudak, Belarus)
DATE OF DEATH   After 1763
PLACE OF DEATH   Probably Bakhchisarai, Crimea

BIOGRAPHY

Salomea Regina Rusiecka was born in Nowogródek in the Polish-Lithuanian Commonwealth in 1718. Her father's name was Joachim (this
proved vital in identifying her in the Russian sources), and it is possible
that she came from a family of Jewish converts to Christianity (Grosfeld,
'Pichelsteinowa [Pilsztynowa] z Rusieckich Salomea Regina', pp. 30-2).
When she was 14, her parents married her to Jakub Halpir, a Lutheran
physician. She went with him as his assistant to Istanbul, where he had
his medical practice, learning from him and also from an Italian doctor
from Malta (Lubamersky, 'Unique and incomparable', p. 97). Her husband left her after three years (he himself died soon afterwards) and she
continued in the medical practice herself. Then, she took lessons from
a Turkish ophthalmologist from Baghdad and developed her skills, also
using intuition and her observational ability combined with systematic
note-taking about the cases she treated.

She led the life of an itinerant physician, travelling through the Ottoman Empire, the Commonwealth, Russia, Austria and Prussia, in order to
earn enough to keep her children. She also made two journeys to collect
funds for the captives she had redeemed. She married one of the captives, an Austrian called Josef Fortunat Pichelstein (the name was later
Polonised to Pilsztyn), an infantry officer (*chorąży*). That marriage was
not happy either and caused her much trouble. Pilsztynowa had three
children, one of whom, Stanisław Pilsztyn (Pichelstein), later became a
translator of Oriental languages in the service of the Polish King Stanisław
August Poniatowski (r. 1764-95) (J. Reychman, *Znajomość i nauczanie
języków orientalnych w Polsce XVIII wieku*, Wrocław, 1950, p. 57).

As a woman, Pilsztynowa had easier access to harems and specialised in treating the women there. She healed Ayşe Sultan (1718-76), a pregnant sister of Sultan Mustafa III (r. 1757-73), and women in the harem of the Beylerbey of Rumelia in Sofia. She specialised in treating cataracts, and acted as ophthalmologist at the court of the Tatar khan in Bakhchisarai (Crimea) and at the court of the tsar in St Petersburg. She employed Oriental healing practices, advising her patients about hygiene, diet and exercise (Kuchowicz, *Wizerunki niepospolitych niewiast*, pp. 303-4). As a woman she had no opportunity to obtain a formal education, let alone medical qualifications. However, she studied medical books, and her openness to various healing practices may be attributed to her lack of formal medical education, which might have prejudiced her against unconventional methods (Pluta, 'Osiemnastowieczne metody leczenia', p. 155).

She also read about Islam, and in Istanbul she was taught about the Qur'an (Pilsztynowa, *Proceder podróży*, p. 243). In all, she spent about 12 years in Turkey (1732-9, 1741-3, 1757-60), and learnt Turkish, getting to know the country and its inhabitants through her medical work and extensive travels. She recorded her experiences in her memoir, *Proceder podróży i życia mego awantur*, which is in part a guidebook for travellers and pilgrims, and describes beliefs, customs and incidents she witnessed.

After completing her memoir, she left Istanbul for Poland but was stopped on the way by order of the Crimean khan and brought to Bakhchisarai to be his physician. The first Russian consul in Crimea, Alexander Nikiforov, narrated a conversation he had had in 1763 with a certain Salamanida Yefimovna (i.e. Salomea, the daughter of Joachim – the wife of the tsar had called her by this same name during her stay earlier in St Petersburg). Maybe she provided him with information about Turkey, thanks to her knowledge of the language, country and the sultan's court (Kołodziejczyk, 'Na tropach Salomei Reginy Pilsztynowej', pp. 226-27). Her whereabouts after this are unknown.

MAIN SOURCES OF INFORMATION

Primary
L. Glatman, 'Doktorka medycyny i okulistka polska w XVIII wieku w Stambule', *Przewodnik Naukowy i Literacki* 24/9 (1896) 856-61; 24/10 (1896) 926-46
M. Lipińska, 'Une femme médecin polonaise au XVIII siècle. Mme Halpir', in M. Lipińska, *Histoire des femmes médecins*, Paris, 1900, 218-41

B. Grosfeld, art. 'Pichelsteinowa (Pilsztynowa) z Rusieckich Salomea Regina', in *Polski słownik biograficzny*, vol. 26, Wrocław, 1981, 30-2 (contains primary biographical details)

D. Kołodziejczyk, 'Na tropach Salomei Reginy Pilsztynowej: glosa do życiorysu', in U. Kosińska, D. Dukwicz and A. Danilczyk (eds), *W cieniu wojen i rozbiorów. Studia z dziejów Rzeczypospolitej XVIII i początków XIX wieku*, Warsaw, 2014, 215-29 (contains new primary biographical material)

Secondary

J. Puchalska, 'Salomea Regina z Rusieckich Pilsztynowa. Jejmość doktorki przygody nie tylko tureckie', in J. Puchalska, *Polki, które zadziwiły świat. Historia 13 niezwykłych Polek*, Warsaw, 2016, 26-55

M. Ożarska, 'Beyond the Old Polish "hic mulier". Regina Salomea née Rusiecka, secundo voto Pilsztynowa, and her memoir', *Studia Filologiczne Uniwersytetu Jana Kochanowskiego* 29 (2016) 141-56

K. Zielińska, 'Polka w osiemnastowiecznym Stambule. Rzecz o Reginie Pilsztynowej i jej postrzeganiu Imperium Osmańskiego', *Turystyka Kulturowa* 6 (2016) 108-20

J. Partyka, 'Overpassing state and cultural borders. A Polish female doctor in 18th-century Constantinople', in A. Sanz, F. Scott and S. van Dijk (eds), *Women telling nations*, Amsterdam, 2014, 371-82

L. Lubamersky, 'Unique and incomparable. The exceptional life of the first female doctor in Poland, Regina Salomea Pilsztynowa', *The Polish Review* 59 (2014) 87-100

A. Piotrowska, 'Zapiski Reginy Salomei z Rusieckich Pilsztynowej na tle XVIII-wiecznego pamiętnikarstwa – uwagi wstępne natury literackiej i językowej', *Językoznawstwo* 1 (2009) 75-82

M. Bahadziazh, 'Lekarka manarhaŭ', in I. Maslianitsyna and M. Bahadziazh (eds), *Zhanchyny, naïbol'sh znakamityia ŭ historyi Belarusi*, Minsk, 2008, 48-55

J.S. Łątka, *Słownik Polaków w Imperium Osmańskim i Turcji*, Kraków, 2005, pp. 247-8

M. Pluta, 'Osiemnastowieczne metody leczenia nieprofesjonalnego w pamiętniku Reginy Salomei z Rusieckich Pilsztynowej', *Medycyna Nowożytna* 10 (2003) 153-68

M.K. Bahadziazh, 'Rusetskaia Salameia Rėhina (1718-paslia 1760)', in M.K. Bahadziazh (ed.), *Myslitseli i asvetniki Belarusi, X-XIX stagoddzi. Ėntsyklapedychny davednik*, Minsk, 1995, 285-7

Z. Kuchowicz, *Żywoty niepospolitych kobiet polskiego baroku*, Łódź, 1989, pp. 298-319 ('Pierwsza lekarka polska – Regina Salomea Rusiecka')

V.P. Hrytskevich, *Adyseia navahradskaï lekarki. Salameia Rusetskaia*, Minsk, 1989

Z. Kuchowicz, *Wizerunki niepospolitych niewiast staropolskich XVI-XVIII wieku*, Łódź, 1974

Art. 'Pilsztynowa Regina Salomea', in *Bibliografia literatury Polskiej. Nowy Korbut, Piśmiennictwo staropolskie*, vol. 3, Warsaw, 1965, 107-8

R. Pollak, 'Wstęp', in S. z Rusieckich Pilsztynowa, *Proceder podróży i życia mego awantur*, ed. R. Pollak and M. Pełczyński, Krakow, 1957, 5-26 (the first important modern source)

M. Gadomska, 'Polska doktorka i okulistka w wieku XVIII w Stambule', *Medycyna i Przyroda* 3 (1939), 28-30

M. Lipińska, *Les femmes et le progrès des sciences médicales*, Paris, 1930, pp. 91-5

WORKS ON CHRISTIAN-MUSLIM RELATIONS

Proceder podróży i życia mego awantur
'An account of my journeys and life's adventures'

DATE 1760
ORIGINAL LANGUAGE Polish

DESCRIPTION

Proceder podróży i życia mego awantur is a memoir written by Salomea Regina Pilsztynowa in Polish in Istanbul in about 1760 (its title in full is *Echo na Swiat podane procederu Podróży y Życia mego Awantur. Na Cześć y Chwałe P. Bogu w Świętey Truycy Jedynemu y Naświęszey Matce Chrystusa Pana mego y Wszystkim Świętym. Przezemnie Same Wydana ta Ksiąszka Salomei Reginy de Pilsztynowey Medycyny Doktorki i Okulistki W Roku 1760 W Stambule*, 'Echo of the proceedings of my journey and adventures of my life given to the world. To the glory and praise of one Triune God and the most holy Mother of Christ, my Lord and all the saints. The book of Salomea Regina Pilsztynowa, a physician and ophthalmologist by herself edited in Istanbul in 1760'). The autograph, which is preserved in the National Museum (*Muzeum Narodowe*), Kraków, has a red morocco cover with gold ornaments in an Oriental style, possibly made in Istanbul (Pollak, 'Wstęp', p. 25). It is 388 pages long, numbered 1-368 by the author herself, and 369-88 by another hand. The title page bears the words, *Ex cathalogo librorum Joannis de Witte Colonelli Art. Reg.* Jan de Witte was most probably a spy in Istanbul, from where he brought the memoir to Poland. It is not known how he acquired it (Pollak, 'Wstęp', p. 25). The printed text of the memoir, which was published only in 1957, is 270 pages long.

The memoir consists of seven chapters, the last unfinished, a poem-song composed by the author. The 1957 publication includes a letter from Pilsztynowa to Prince Michał Radziwiłł, complaining against the injustices she experienced in Przemyśl (a town in present-day south-east Poland), endnotes and an index.

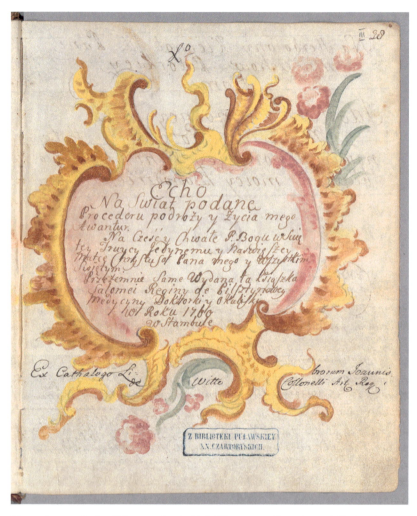

Illustration 15. Regina Salomea z Rusieckich Pilsztynowa, *Proceder podróży i życia mego awantur*, first MS page

Ch. 5 contains details about Islam, with subtitles such as *O sekcie tureck-iej* ('On the Turkish sect'), *Zachwycenie Mahmeta do nieba* ('Mahmet's mystical journey to heaven'), *Skromność w modleniu turecka* ('Turkish modesty in prayer'), *Post turecki* ('The Turkish fast'), *Zwyczaj wesela tureckiego* ('The custom of a Turkish wedding-party'), *Ślub turecki* ('A Turkish wedding'), *Ceremonie pogrzebu tureckiego* ('Turkish burial ceremonies'), *Cześć Turków Najśw. Panny* ('Turkish reverence for the Virgin

Mary'), *Różne z Alkoranu powieści* ('Various stories from the Qur'an'), *Dlaczego Turcy wina nie piją* ('Why the Turks do not drink wine'), *Turków do Mekki droga* ('The journey of the Turks to Mecca'), and *Grób Mahmeta* ('Mahmet's sepulchre'). In addition, other observations about Islam are included at other points in the memoir when the author describes her experiences and events from her stay in Turkey, or among the Muslims in general.

As these subtitles indicate, Pilsztynowa considered Islam the 'Turkish religion', which was not unusual, as earlier works on Islam from the Commonwealth show. The image of Islam in most of these was clearly negative, their polemically anti-Muslim character arising from recurring military clashes with the forces of the Ottoman Empire (N. Jord, *Koran rękopismienny w Polsce*, Lublin 1994, p. 28). The memoir contains fewer elements borrowed from other works than Pilsztynowa's own observations. Regarding warfare (*qitāl*), she shows a correct understanding: 'War is forbidden for the Turks by the Qur'an, i.e. they themselves should not intend to wage war, unless someone wages it against them' (*Proceder podróży*, ed. Pollak and Pełczyński, p. 248). She also comments that there is no compulsory conversion of Christians to Islam: 'They force no one to accept their faith, only a Turk should three times a day say to a slave or a Christian neighbour: "Become a Turk" (i.e. accept Islam)' (p. 249). She observes that the Turks treat their animals well: 'No Turk should eat or drink before he feeds his animals' (p. 251). She describes the reverence with which the Muslims address the Virgin Mary: 'The Turks, when they speak about the Virgin Mary while sitting, they stand up and say that she was truely virgin before giving birth, during it and after' (p. 252). They also revere Jesus: 'They consider the Lord Jesus as the greatest prophet and believe that the Jews never killed him – could God possibly permit it that the ugly Jews were able to kill such a good and innocent man?' (p. 252). She avoids insulting Muḥammad, and writes that God calls him God's friend (p. 246) and that the Qur'an was sent to him in a miraculous way, making no comment on these details. Concerning the Ramaḍān fast, she states: 'They have a custom that, during those days, they give alms generously and invite guests to supper, especially the poor' (p. 247). It is clear that, as she describes the religious beliefs and practices of Muslims, she does not judge them but tries to describe what she has heard or seen, all the time, of course, creating an image according to the standards of her time.

Pilsztynowa briefly describes Arabs, portraying them unfavourably as nomads and barbarians, far less civilised than the Turks, almost savages who wear hardly any clothes, do not marry and rob pilgrims on their way to Mecca (pp. 256-7). She does not consider them to be Muslims.

The language of Pilsztynowa's memoir is simple, based on everyday language, and it shows her lack of formal education. She does not use the then fashionable references to Greek or Roman mythology, or Latin quotations (Pollak, 'Wstęp', p. 20), and her style is sometimes awkward with occasional mistakes.

SIGNIFICANCE

The memoir is unique in 18th-century Polish travel literature and among works on the Ottoman Empire and Muslims. Since Pilsztynowa had received no formal education in her homeland, she had had no exposure to the biased stereotypes of the Turks and Islam that the educated found in their European reading material, so she describes Islamic religion and customs as she sees them, without dislikes and prejudices (though she was also a child of her time). One can sense a liking for the Turks in her memoir and understand that she felt comfortable in Istanbul. After all, her material status and social position in Turkey was better than at home because the earning prospects in Turkey were better for her and as a physician she was treated with some esteem. The fact that she was a woman did not hinder her in effectively functioning in Turkish-Muslim society, and even in winning a court case against a high-ranking Janissary, or in discussions with men about faith and customs: 'I can talk with women and with men' (p. 42).

Until it was printed in 1957, the memoir exercised hardly any influence on the perception of Islam, Muslims or the Turks in Polish society. Few researchers who came across the single manuscript in which it remained commented on it, focusing rather on Pilsztynowa's medical activities. After it was published, the memoir provided a witness to the fact that a person without a formal education had acquired none of the current stereotypes about Islam and Muslims, and was thus able to develop a positive image of both and describe them according to her own observations and experiences. The memoir also attests to the strength of prejudiced stereotypes that people acquire during their formal education.

PUBLICATIONS

MS Kraków, National Library – Princess Czartoryski collection 1482 (around 1760)

Regina Salomea z Rusieckich Pilsztynowa, *Proceder podróży i życia mego awantur*, ed. R. Pollak and M. Pełczyński, Kraków, 1957

Salameia Pilshtynova, *Avantury maĭho zhytstsia*, trans. M. Khaŭstovich, Minsk, 1993, 2008², 2015³ (Belarussian trans.)

Salameia Pilshtynova, 'Avantury maĭho zhytstsia', trans. M. Khaŭstovich, *Chasopis perekladnoĭ litaratury*, Minsk, 2013 (Belarussian trans.); http://prajdzisvet.org/storehouse/authors/Pilsztynova,%20Salamieja/Pilsztynowa_avantury.pdf

P.D. Dominik (ed.), *The Istanbul memories in Salomea Pilsztynowa's diary 'Echo of the journey and adventures of my life'* (1760), intro. S. Roszak, Bonn, 2017 (English trans., selections from chs 1, 4 and 5, containing details on the Ottoman Empire); http://menadoc.bibliothek.uni-halle.de/menalib/download/pdf/3190439

STUDIES

P.D. Dominik, 'Editor's preface', in Dominik, *Istanbul memories*, 5-10

D. Chemperek, '"Echo na świat podane procederu podróży i życia mego awantur" Salomei Pilsztynowej w świetle geopoetyki. Miejsce autobiograficzne', in P. Borek, D. Chemperek and A. Nowicka-Struska (eds), *Memuarystyka w dawnej Polsce*, Kraków, 2016, 187-201

D. Dźwinel, 'O kategorii obcości w "Procederze podróży i życia mego awantur" Reginy Salomei Pilsztynowej', in B. Mazurkowa (ed.), *Światy oświeconych i romantycznych*, Katowice, 2015, 133-54

R. Krzywy, 'Pragnienie pamięci i "białogłowski koncept". Kilka uwag o świadomości warsztatowej pierwszych polskich pamiętnikarek (Anna Zbąska, Regina Salomea Pilsztynowa)', *Śląskie Studia Polonistyczne* 2 (2013) 119-40

M. Czarnecka, 'Die Reise- und Lebensbeschreibung von Regina Salomea Pilsztyn geb. Rusiecka (1718-1760). Einer polnischen Orientreisenden im Kontext der Kulturgeschichte der Frauenreisen im 18. Jahrhundert', in M. Czarnecka, C. Ebert and B. Szewczyk (eds), *Der weibliche Blick auf den Orient. Reisebeschreibungen europäischer Frauen im Vergleich*, Bern, 2010, 13-30

A. Piotrowska, 'Zapiski Reginy Salomei z Rusieckich Pilsztynowej na tle XVIII-wiecznego pamiętnikarstwa – uwagi wstępne natury literackiej i językowej', *Językoznawstwo* 1 (2009) 75-82

W. Roczniak, 'Power in powerlessness. The strange journey and career of Regina Salomea Pilsztynowa', *Polish Review* 53 (2008) 25-51

M. Hawrysz, 'Portret kobiety nowoczesnej w świetle pamiętnika "Proceder podróży i życia mego awantur" Reginy Pilsztynowej', in E. Woźniak (ed.), *Tradycja a nowoczesność* [Tradition and modernity], Łódź, 2008, 583-94

I. Maciejewska, 'Kobiecym piórem o miłości, małżeństwie i erotyce (Regina Salomea z Rusieckich Pilsztynowa, Elżbieta Drużbacka, Franciszka Urszula Radziwiłłowa)', in I. Maciejewska and K. Stasiewicz (eds), *Kobieta epok dawnych w literaturze, kulturze i społeczeństwie*, Olsztyn, 2008, 213-23

D. Kołodziejczyk, 'Die Frau, die mit Männern handelte. Eine Polin am Bosphoros', in S. Prätor and C.K. Neumann (eds), *Frauen, Bilder und Gelehrte. Studien zu Gesellschaft und Künsten im Osmanischen Reich / Arts, women and scholars. Studies in Ottoman society and culture. Festschrift Hans Georg Majer*, vol. 1, Istanbul, 2002, 159-65

J.M. Konczacki and K. Aterman, 'Regina Salomea Pilsztynowa. Ophthalmologist in 18th-century Poland', *Survey of Ophthalmology* 47 (2002) 189-95

I. Maciejewska, 'Jak to z obyczajnością Reginy Salomei z Rusieckich Pilsztynowej bywało? ("Proceder podróży i życia mego awantur")', in K. Stasiewicz, S. Achremczyk (eds), *Między barokiem a oświeceniem*, vol. 3. *Obyczaje czasów saskich*, Olsztyn, 2000, 118-24

I. Maciejewska, 'Specyfika relacji pamiętnikarskiej "Procederu podróży i życia mego awantur Reginy Salomei z Rusieckich Pilsztynowej"', in K. Stasiewicz (ed.), *Pisarki polskie epok dawnych*, Olsztyn, 1998, 141-52

J. Partyka, 'Kobieta oswaja męską przestrzeń. Polska lekarka w osiemnastowiecznym Stambule', in K. Stasiewicz, *Pisarki polskie epok dawnych*, Olsztyn, 1998, 153-62

T. Ciecierska-Chłapowa, 'Table de l'onomastique orientale dans les mémoires de R.S. Pilsztyn, née Rusiecka (XVIIIe s.)', *Folia Orientalia* 29 (1992/3) 65-9

A. Cieński, *Pamiętnikarstwo polskie XVIII wieku*, Wrocław, 1981, pp. 153-6

J. Rytel, 'Dwa pamiętniki – w czasach króla Jana i później', *Przegląd Humanistyczny* 4 (1960) 157-65

J. Reychman, *Życie polskie w Stambule w XVIII wieku*, Warsaw, 1959, pp. 154-62

Pollak, 'Wstęp'

Agata S. Nalborczyk

Franciszek Bohomolec

DATE OF BIRTH   29 January 1720
PLACE OF BIRTH   Near Vitebsk (present-day Belarus)
DATE OF DEATH   24 April 1784
PLACE OF DEATH   Warsaw

BIOGRAPHY

Franciszek Bohomolec was born on 29 January 1720 in the region of Vitebsk (present-day Belarus). In 1737, he joined the Society of Jesus, followed by a period of study of philosophy at the Vilnius Academy, then work as a teacher. In 1747-9, he moved to study theology and rhetoric in Rome. After his return, he was appointed to teach Polish-Latin rhetoric at the Vilnius Academy. Then, in 1751, he moved to Warsaw, where he first became a teacher in the Gymnasium Zaluscianum, and then a professor of rhetoric at the Collegium Nobilium. He held the latter post until 1762. During this period, he gained recognition in Polish Enlightenment society thanks to his defence of the Polish language in schools in his orations (*Pro ingeniis Polonorum oratio*, 1752; *De lingua Polonica colloqium*, 1752), attempts at the revival of Polish poetry in the collection of his students' rhetorical exercises (*Zabawki oratorskie*, 1755), and plays written for the Jesuit school theatre (*Komedye*, vols 1-2, 1755-60; see also Gołąbek, *Komedie*; Stenden-Petersen, *Die Schulkomödien*; Kott, 'Wstęp'; van Der Meer, 'Some remarks').

In 1762, Bohomolec was appointed a prefect of the Jesuit printing house, and continued to hold that position after the dissolution of the Jesuit order (1773), as a prefect of the Printing House of His Royal Majesty. He founded and published the following periodicals: *Wiadomości Uprzywilejowane Warszawskie* (1761-3), *Wiadomości Warszawskie* (1765-74), *Kurier Warszawski* (until 1773), and *Monitor* (1765-84), which was modelled on *The Spectator*. In 1765, he started participating in the so-called Thursday Dinners, meetings of intellectuals, artists and politicians held by King Stanisław II August Poniatowski (r. 1764-95; Łukaszewicz, *Rys dziejów*, pp. 60-3; Bednarski, 'Bohomolec Franciszek'; art. 'Oświecenie', pp. 273-4; art. 'Bohomolec Franciszek'). During this period, he also wrote many plays for the court theatre (*Komedye na theatrum*, 1766-83), some of which, like those written for the Jesuit school theatre, were inspired by the plays of Molière and other Western dramatists (Bełcikowski, 'Pierwszy sceniczny pisarz'; Strusiński, 'Komedia ks. Franciszka'; Kott, *Bohomolec w terminie*, pp. 223-34; Kadulska, *Komedia w polskim teatrze*, pp. 148-78). In addition, he initiated the publishing of Old Polish historical works (*Zbior dzieiopisow polskich we czterech tomach zawarty*, vols 1-4, 1764-8), biographies of prominent Polish military commanders (*Zycie Tarnowskiego*, 1773; *Zycie Jana Zamoyskiego*, 1775; *Zycie Jerzego Ossolińskiego*, 1777), and the collections of famous Polish poets of the 16th and 17th centuries (*Jana Kochanowskiego Rymy Wszytkie*, 1768). During the last years of his life, Bohomolec received a royal pension. He died in Warsaw on 24 April 1784, bequeathing all his possessions to the poor citizens of Warsaw (Szczepaniec, *Testament*, pp. 62-78).

Franciszek Bohomolec is considered to be one of the most distinguished men of the Enlightenment in the Polish-Lithuanian Commonwealth in the 18th century; he contributed to the development of education, theatre, journalism and printing (Batowski, *Rajnold Hajdenstein*, pp. 18-20). The full list of his works in these fields is impressive (Biegeleisen, 'Żywot', pp. 645-7; Estreicher, art. 'Bohomolec Franciszek', pp. 223-30), and there are many academic studies on them (Gramatowski, 'Franciszek Bohomolec', pp. 531-72; Kryda, *Szkolna i literacka działalność*; Mazurkowa, *Weksle prawdy*, pp. 93-160, 203-62).

MAIN SOURCES OF INFORMATION

Primary

L. Łukaszewicz, *Rys dziejów piśmiennictwa polskiego*, Krakow, 1838, pp. 60, 63, 75

A. Batowski, *Rajnold Hajdenstejn i Franciszek Bohomolec. Pisarze żywota Jana Zamoyskiego Kanc. i Hetm. W. K.*, Lviv, 1854

H. Biegeleisen, 'Żywot ks. Jezuity Franciszka Bohomolca', in *Album uczącej się młodzieży polskiej poświęcone J.I. Kraszewskiemu*, Lviv, 1879, 646-7

A. Bełcikowski, 'Pierwszy sceniczny pisarz polski ks. Franciszek Bohomolec S.J.', *Ateneum* 1 (1885) 385-420

K. Estreicher, art. 'Bohomolec Franciszek', in *Bibliografia polska*, vol. 13 (stulecie XV-XVIII), Krakow, 1894, 223-30

W. Strusiński, 'Komedia ks. Franciszka Bohomolca w stosunku do teatru francuskiego i włoskiego', *Pamiętnik Literacki* 4 (1905) 246-60

J. Gołąbek, *Komedie konwiktowe ks. Franciszka Bohomolca w zależności od Moljera*, Krakow, 1922

A. Stender-Petersen, *Die Schulkomödien des Paters Franciszek Bohomolec S.J.*, Heidelberg, 1923

S. Bednarski, art. 'Bohomolec Franciszek', in *Polski słownik biograficzny*, vol. 2, Krakow, 1936[1] (1989), 224-5

Secondary

B. Mazurkowa, *Weksle prawdy i nieprawdy: studia literackie o książce oświeceniowej*, Warsaw, 2011, pp. 93-160, 203-62

Art. 'Bohomolec Franciszek', in *Wielka encyklopedia PWN*, Warsaw, 2001, 231

J. van Der Meer, 'Some remarks on the literary sources of Bohomolec's Arlekin na świat urażony', *Russian Literature* 37 (1995) 535-59

I. Kadulska, *Komedia w polskim teatrze jezuickim XVIII wieku*, Wrocław, 1993

B. Kryda, *Szkolna i literacka działalność Franciszka Bohomolca. U źródeł polskiego klasycyzmu XVIII w.*, Wrocław, 1979

W. Gramatowski, 'Franciszek Bohomolec. Wydawca, prefekt drukarni i redaktor "Wiadomości Warszawskich"', *Roczniki Biblioteczne* 3-4 (1970) 531-72

Art. 'Oświecenie', in *Bibliografia literatury polskiej. 'Nowy Korbut'*, vol. 4, Warsaw, 1966, 273-82

J. Szczepaniec, 'Testament Franciszka Bohomolca i jego losy do roku 1794', in *Miscellanea z doby Oświecenia*, vol. 2, Wrocław, 1965, 62-78

J. Kott, 'Bohomolec w terminie u Moliera', in *Księga pamiątkowa ku czci S. Pigonia*, Krakow, 1961, pp. 223-34

J. Kott, 'Wstęp', in F. Bohomolec, *Komedie. Komedie konwiktowe*, Warsaw, 1960, 7-87

WORKS ON CHRISTIAN-MUSLIM RELATIONS

Opisanie krotkie panstwa tureckiego
'A brief description of the Turkish state'

DATE 1770

ORIGINAL LANGUAGE Polish

DESCRIPTION

Opisanie krotkie panstwa tureckiego, comprising 215 pages, was published in the Printing House of His Royal Majesty in Warsaw in 1770. There is no information about any other editions.

The main part of the work is preceded by a dedication to Kazimierz Karaś, the king's court marshal, Stanisław II August Poniatowski, and a preface to the reader. In the preface, Bohomolec indicates that 'the present circumstances of the war', that is the Russo-Turkish war of 1768-70, which broke out because of Ottoman support for the Bar Confederation against Russian influence, was the immediate impulse to write the work. He wants to provide information on the neighbouring country. He emphasises that he has written a medium-sized compilation on the basis of a number of other works, indicating their authors and shortened versions of their titles. These are (in full version): *Monarchia*

*turecka opisana przez Ricota Sekretarza Posła Angielskiego u Porty
Ottomańskiej residuiącego z francuskiego ięzyka na polski przetłumaczona
przez szlachcica polskiego y do druku podana w roku 1678* (a Polish translation of Rycaut's *The present state of the Ottoman Empire*), *Geografia
czasow teraznieyszych, albo opisanie naturalne y polityczne królestw,
panstw, stanow wszelakich, ich rządu, praw, rzemiosł [...] ku pożytkowi
narodowey młodzi wydana* ('Geography of the present times. It is the
natural and political description of kingdoms, countries, and different
estates, their governments, rights, crafts [...] published for the benefit of
the nation's youth', 1768) by Karol Wyrwicz, *La science du gouvernement,
ouvrage de morale, de droit et de politique* (1762-4) by Gaspard de Réal
de Curban, and *Le droit public de l'Europe fondé sur les traités conclus
jusqu'en l'année 1740* by Gabriel Bonnot de Mably (Mazurkowa, *Weksle
prawdy*, pp. 222-3). The importance of the first of these works will be
discussed below. At this point, it is worth mentioning that the second is
a source of information on the geography and population of the Turkish
state; the third is on the foundation of the Ottoman Empire, its development and decline, as well as its government offices and military forces;
the fourth is on the treaties of the Sublime Porte with other countries.

The main part of the work consists of 38 chapters on the following
topics: the history of the Turkish state (its origins, development and
causes of its diminution), the current political and geographical conditions of the Ottoman Porte (its political situation, customs of the Turks,
its expansion, nations under its influence, Turkish provinces near the
Polish border, the Tatars), the administration of the Turkish state (government, courts, the vizier and other public officials and courtiers, the
Grand Mufti and other representatives of the Muslim clergy, education
of youth and science, the army and its various branches), Islam (its principles, Bayram, religious endowments and mosques, dervishes, marriage
and divorce, various sects), and Turkish diplomacy (receiving foreign
representatives, instructions for deputies arriving at the sultan's court,
Polish-Turkish treaties). This is followed by a table of contents and an
index.

Islam is treated in eight chapters in the work (chs 27-34), although
comments on it and its followers can also be found in other chapters.
Thus, in ch. 2 Bohomolec points out that the Qur'an is the reason for the
expansion of the Turkish state because Muḥammad spread Islam by the
sword, promising rewards for those who fought, and threatening with
hell those who did not participate in the struggle. Furthermore, other
laws established by the Prophet, such as the prohibition against drinking

alcohol and permission for polygamy, as well as belief in fate, contributed to the militarisation of Islamic society (*Opisanie krotkie*, pp. 7-10).

In ch. 3, Bohomolec emphasises that Islam led to the weakening of the Ottoman Porte, since it did not promote public education or development of crafts and trade, and its adherents focused on the pleasures of the harem and spilling blood in wars (pp. 10-13). In ch. 5, he mentions Muslims' contempt for Christians, though he describes them as abstemious and hospitable, as is prescribed in the Qur'an (pp. 23, 25). In ch. 10, he notes that the sultan is obliged to observe the laws of the Qur'an, though these laws give him an unlimited, despotic power (pp. 46-7). In ch. 11, the *'ulamā'* are called 'a tribunal of the Grand Mufti' who settle not only religious matters, but also some secular ones (pp. 50, 52). In ch. 16, the responsibilities of the Grand Mufti, qadis, imams (designated as 'heads of the private mosques'), muezzins and emirs are described (pp. 75-80).

Turning to the main treatment of Islam, in ch. 27 Bohomolec describes the Five Pillars of Islam as ablution (he lists its three types), prayer, fasting (he uses the term *ramaḍān*), almsgiving (he uses the term *zakāt*) and pilgrimage to Mecca (he indicates the number of its participants and its origins, and describes some rituals) (pp. 127-32). In ch. 28, he mentions two Muslim customs: belief in fate and its consequences, which are fearlessness in battle and inaction in the face of epidemics, and circumcision, its origins and the course of the ceremony (pp. 132-6). Ch. 29 includes descriptions of the Feast of Breaking the Fast and the Feast of the Sacrifice, and traditions related to these two festivals (pp. 137-8). Ch. 30 features Islamic injunctions, such as fasting, abstaining from eating pork and drinking wine, and recommendations, such as charitable treatment of the poor and animals (pp. 141-3). Ch. 31 deals primarily with religious endowments and the income of mosques, but it also contains references to helping the poor and the prohibition of usury in the Qur'an (pp. 144-6). In ch. 32 (*O derwisach* ['On dervishes']), he mentions several Sufi brotherhoods, including the Khalwatiyya, Naqshbandiyya, Qadiriyya, Qalandariyya, Baktashiyya and Mawlawiyya, describes their way of life (the practice of patience, humility, abstinence, fasting and chastity) and the *dhikr* ceremony (without giving its name). He notes, however, that not all dervishes follow the rules of their brotherhoods, especially those who belong to the Qalandariyya order, who 'should rather be called Epicureans than monks' (pp. 147-50). In ch. 33, there are descriptions of a wedding ceremony and comments about polygamy (*wielożeństwo*), as well as information on temporary marriage, the acceptance of marriage with non-Muslim women belonging to the People of the Book and duties

of husbands towards their wives. This chapter also stresses that polygamy – contrary to what Muslims believe – is not conducive to higher
fertility. It closes with definitions of the three types of divorce (pp. 151-6).
In ch. 34, Bohomolec writes about 'various Mahommetan sects'. According to the Muslims themselves, there are 72 sects, which one can associate with 72 nations 'that were there before the confusion of the tongues
during the construction of the Tower of Babel'. The number of Islamic
sects is greater than the numbers of Jewish and Christian sects (70 and 71,
respectively) because Islam is the God's final revelation to humankind.
Then, Bohomolec describes the two major sects, the followers of the
Prophet Muḥammad and the supporters of ʿAlī, followed by Turks and
Persians, respectively. He also cites their accusations about each other,
and stresses that the hatred of Turks for Persians is greater than the
animosities between Christians and Jews (pp. 157-60). Finally, in ch. 38,
devoted to how the Turks do not abide by their treaties with Christians,
Bohomolec reiterates that this is the result of following the example of
Muḥammad, who did not keep his agreement with the inhabitants of
Mecca and attacked the city treacherously. As for the contemporary wars
of the Turks, they are justified by the Grand Mufti whose verdicts are
often unfairly issued (pp. 178-80).

Rycaut's *The history of the present state of the Ottoman Empire* is evidently the main source of Bohomolec's information on Islam. In the
preface, Bohomolec states that Rycaut's work may be too daunting for
most readers due to its sheer volume, and this is why he has decided to
shorten it (*Opisanie krotkie*, p. VIII).

SIGNIFICANCE
Opisanie krotkie panstwa tureckiego was written at the command of
Stanisław II August Poniatowski, the last king of the Polish-Lithuanian
Commonwealth, who, as an enlightened reformer, interested in establishing new relations (particularly commercial ones) with the Turkish
state, saw the need to provide the nobility of the Commonwealth with
up-to-date information on the neighbouring country. Bohomolec was to
summarise Rycaut's work, which had been reprinted several times as the
main source of knowledge about the Ottoman Porte in the Polish-Lithuanian Commonwealth before the 1770s (Reychman, *Życie polskie*, p. 90).
Until then, the nobles had not been ready to change their views about
the Turkish state, which they still perceived through the prism of the old
stereotypes formed in earlier centuries when their ancestors had fought
'the pagans' in defence of Christianity. However, this stance began to

change gradually during the Russo-Turkish War of 1768-74 (Bałczewski, 'Zmiany w ocenie', pp. 91-7).

Opisanie krotkie panstwa tureckiego, as a compilation of Rycaut's work and later geographical, historical and political works written by Wyrwicz, Réal de Curban and de Mably, does not provide any new, substantial information on Islam. Rather, Bohomolec tries to use it to refocus the perspective of the Commonwealth nobles on the Ottoman Empire.

There was only one edition of the work, and it did not enjoy the same popularity as Bohomolec's other works. Biegeleisen concludes: 'It seems that it was not bought despite frequent announcements' ('Żywot', p. 649). There is no information about its possible impact on later works devoted to Christian-Muslim relations (Maśko, 'Obraz islamu', pp. 191, 200-3).

PUBLICATIONS

Franciszek Bohomolec, *Opisanie krotkie panstwa tureckiego*, Warsaw, 1770; NDIGSTDR010275 (digitised copy available through Jagiellońska Biblioteka Cyfrowa)

J. Nosowski, *Polska literatura polemiczno-antyislamistyczna XVI, XVII i XVIII w.*, vol. 1, Warsaw, 1974, pp. 27-47 (excerpts on pp. 29-45, intermingled with Nosowski's own comments)

STUDIES

A. Maśko, 'Obraz islamu w Rzeczpospolitej w XVIII w.', *Przegląd Orientalistyczny* 3-4 (2015) 191-206

Mazurkowa, *Weksle prawdy*

M. Bałczewski, 'Zmiany w ocenie Turcji w opinii polskiej XVIII w.', *Acta Universitatis Lodziensis. Folia Historica* 22 (1985) 91-108

J. Reychman, *Życie polskie w Stambule w XVIII wieku*, Warsaw, 1959, pp. 50-4, 90, 118-19

Biegeleisen, 'Żywot'

Adrianna Maśko

Kajetan Chrzanowski

DATE OF BIRTH   About 1748
PLACE OF BIRTH   Unknown
DATE OF DEATH   1793
PLACE OF DEATH   Pera, Istanbul

BIOGRAPHY

Much about the life of Kajetan Chrzanowski remains unknown. None of the Polish studies that mention him specify the place or the date of his birth. The date given in this entry, about 1748, is based on a comment by Jan Reychman in his study of Poles living in Istanbul in the 18th century, where he cites the words on Chrzanowski's tombstone in the Church of St Mary Draperis in the district of Pera (present-day Beyoğlu): *Gaetanus Chrzanowski, negotiatorius Polonae Reipublicae agens, aetatis suae circiter 45* ('Kajetan Chrzanowski, a businessman and agent for the Polish state, his age was about 45'; Reychman, *Życie polskie*, p. 262). We have no information about Chrzanowski's education.

It is certain that Chrzanowski was a secretary to the Polish legation in the Ottoman Empire in 1776-7, and wrote letters about Turkey given to King Stanisław II August Poniatowski (r. 1764-95) in 1780 (Konopczyński, *Polska a Turcja*, p. 249). Later, he served as a counsellor in the Department of Foreign Interests of the Permanent Council, and in 1782 was working for the newly established Eastern Trade Company (*Kompania Handlów Wschodnich*), also known as the Black Sea Trade Company (*Kompania Handlu Czarnomorskiego*). In 1785, he was sent on a trade mission to the city of Kherson in the Ukraine, which belonged at that time to the Russian Empire. From there, he travelled to Istanbul, where he became a royal correspondent.

He was appointed by King Stanisław II, with Russia's consent, as the royal resident in Istanbul, with the task of negotiating free trade agreements with the Ottoman Empire. He held this post during the Russo-Turkish War (1787), trying not to fall into disfavour with either party. In 1788, he was an adviser to the great legation of Piotr Potocki in Istanbul, representing the Four-Year Sejm [Parliament] (1788-92), which aimed to regain the Commonwealth's independence from the Russian Empire. Chrzanowski not only made arrangements with the Turkish side for the reception of the great legation, but also encouraged Potocki to work intensively on a commercial treaty with the Sublime Porte (Waliszewski, *Ostatni poseł*, vol. 1, pp. 104, 110, 112, 131-2; vol. 2, p. 56; Dutkiewicz, 'Ambasada Piotra Potockiego', pp. 69-75; Łątka, art. 'Kajetan Chrzanowski', p. 72).

In 1789-91, he was warning King Stanisław II August in his reports about arrangements between various powers that were conspiring against the Polish-Lithuanian Commonwealth (Żychliński, *Złota księga*, p. 35). In 1791, he sent to the king his memorandum entitled *Sur l'administration de l'économie politique de l'État*, in which he proposed establishing a *Collège de Commerce* (Konopczyński, art. 'Chrzanowski Kajetan', p. 460). However, in 1792 he was dismissed from the post of adviser as a result of the victory of the Targowica Confederation, which aimed to restore the old political order in the Commonwealth under the auspices of the Russian Empire (Reychman, *Życie polskie*, p. 54). He died during a cholera epidemic in Pera in 1793, and was buried in the Church of St Mary Draperis.

MAIN SOURCES OF INFORMATION

Primary

MS Krakow, The Princes Czartoryski Library – 632, fols 601-724 (Correspondence particuliére de la Majesté avec Constantinople, 1785-7; *Listy zawierayące nowe relacye podróży przez prowincye Mołdawij, Bulgaryi y dawney Thracyi czyli Rumilij tudzież opisanie sposobem geograficznym topograficznym y historycznym Stambułu* [...], 'Letters containing new accounts of a journey through the provinces of Moldova, Bulgaria and the ancient Thrace, that is Rumelia, with geographical, topographical and historical description of Istanbul [...]')

MS Krakow, Polish Academy of Learning – 1651, fol. 58 (Chrzanowski's correspondence in Constantinople with the royal office in 1789-91)

Kajetan Chrzanowski, *Wiadomosci o Panstwie Tureckim: przez iednego Polaka, w listach do Przyiaciela pisanych, przesłane. To iest: podroż przez Prowincye Tureckie: Opisanie Sztambułu, Seraiu, Rząd, Stan Porty, Religia, Obyczaie, Charakter Turków, etc.*, Warsaw, 1786, 1797[2]

T. Żychliński, *Złota księga szlachty polskiej*, vol. 1, Poznań, 1879, pp. 35-6

K. Waliszewski (ed.), *Ostatni poseł polski do Porty Ottomańskiej. Akta legacyi stambulskiej Franciszka Piotra Potockiego, Starosty Szczerzeckiego*, Paris, 1894, vol. 1 (1789-90), pp. 3-4, 22, 24, 32, 40, 42, 68, 74-5, 83, 102, 104-5, 110, 112, 119-25, 131-2, 161-3, 173-4, 188, 214, 216, 234; vol. 2 (1791-2), pp. 56, 66-7, 94-7, 126, 135, 149, 180, 182-3, 186, 193-5, 200, 227-8, 233, 245, 251, 255

W. Konopczyński, art. 'Chrzanowski Kajetan', in *Polski słownik biograficzny*, vol. 3, Krakow, 1937, 460

Secondary

J. Łątka, art. 'Kajetan Chrzanowski', in *Słownik Polaków w Imperium Osmańskim i Republice Turcji*, Krakow, 2005, 72

J. Reychman, *Życie polskie w Stambule w XVIII wieku*, Warsaw, 1959, pp. 50-4, 56, 65, 68, 88, 90, 92, 118-19, 192, 220-1, 262

W. Konopczyński, *Polska a Turcja 1683-1792*, Warsaw, 1936 (repr. Krakow, 2013), pp. 237, 249-50, 262, 264, 270-1

J. Dutkiewicz, 'Ambasada Piotra Potockiego', *Przegląd Historyczny* 12 (1934-5) 66-116, pp. 69-75, 80, 100, 108-9, 111

WORKS ON CHRISTIAN-MUSLIM RELATIONS

Wiadomosci o Panstwie Tureckim
'News of the Turkish state'

DATE   1786
ORIGINAL LANGUAGE   Polish

DESCRIPTION

The first edition of the work (its title in full is *Wiadomosci o Panstwie Tureckim: przez iednego Polaka, w listach do Przyiaciela pisanych, przesłane. To iest: podroż przez Prowincye Tureckie: Opisanie Sztambułu, Seraiu, Rząd, Stan Porty, Religia, Obyczaie, Charakter Turków, etc.,* 'News of the Turkish state: written in letters by a Pole to a friend. It is a journey through the Turkish provinces: a description of Istanbul, the *saraglio*, the government, the state of the Porte, religion, customs, the character of Turks, etc.') was published anonymously in Warsaw in 1786, followed by a second edition, also published in Warsaw, in 1797. The author was not correctly identified until the second half of the 20th century because some scholars in the late 19th century and the first decades of the 20th century identified another Polish counsellor in Istanbul as the author (Reychman, *Życie polskie*, p. 118), and others did not associate Chrzanowski's name with the authorship of this work (Konopczyński, *Polska a Turcja*, p. 249). It was the expert on Polish-Turkish relations, Jan Reychman, who stated that 'the mystery of the authorship of *Wiadomosci o Panstwie Tureckim* can be solved by comparing the contents of this work with the contents of the manuscript work entitled (in translation) 'Letters containing new accounts of a journey through the provinces of Moldova, Bulgaria and the ancient Thrace, that is Rumelia, with a geographical, topographical and historical description of Istanbul', which was included in volume 632 of the manuscript collection in the Princes Czartoryski Library in Krakow (Reychman, *Życie polskie*, pp. 118-9. p. 54 n. 63). This comparison indicates that the work was probably written by Kajetan Chrzanowski, the Polish resident in Istanbul and the author of the accounts included in the above-mentioned volume. The identity of the letters and the anonymous editions of *Wiadomosci o Panstwie Tureckim* was then recognised by other Polish researchers (Bałczewski, 'Zmiany w ocenie Turcji', p. 99).

Chrzanowski wrote these letters to the Polish King Stanisław II, who, as Reychman suggests, entrusted to him the preparation of a new description of Turkey, because there was a lack of up-to-date studies in the Polish-Lithuanian Commonwealth in the second half of the 18th century (Reychman, *Życie polskie*, pp. 88-90).

The first edition, on which this description is based, contains 197 pages (there are some mistakes in pagination), and consists of 18 letters preceded by a preface. The second edition totals 168 pages and does not differ from the first in its contents. In the preface, the editor stresses that the work will improve understanding of the functioning of the Ottoman government and administration, and of the customs and character of the Turks. Thus, in his opinion, it will assist in commercial dealings with the empire. In addition, the editor expresses his conviction that there was a need for reliable descriptions of foreign nations, not based on superficial prejudices.

Letters 1-5 comprise the author's accounts written during his journey, which he began in the Khotyn Fortress on the Polish-Turkish border and continued through such towns as Iassy and Galatz in Moldova and Aidos in Rumelia. Letters 6-18, which were written in Istanbul, contain descriptions of: the topography of Istanbul, the structure of the great *seraglio*, the sultan's despotic rule, the importance of the vizier and other civilian authorities, the military, the authority of the great admiral, the position of foreign ministers residing at the sultan's court, audiences given to foreign legations at the sultan's court, trade and the activities of European merchants in Turkey, the religion of Islam, the morals and character of the Turks, Turkish women and the behaviour of Muslims toward their wives and slave girls, the situation of Greeks, Armenians and Jews settled in Turkey, and finally, the form of the sultan's letters addressed to European courts. Comments on Islam and its followers are scattered throughout all the chapters, though particularly in letters 14-16.

In letter 14, the author provides a general description of Islam by listing its basic tenets (monotheism, belief in an afterlife, Muḥammad as Seal of the Prophets, Jesus Son of Mary as a prophet who was not crucified), religious duties (attendance at Friday sermons, the five daily prayers, fasting during Ramaḍān, feasts, ablutions, pilgrimage, almsgiving, circumcision – although Chrzanowski does not think that the last is mentioned in the Qur'an), the rights and obligations of marriage (polygamy, conditions of divorce), and finally the Sunnī-Shīʿī conflict. These issues are described briefly and largely correctly, with one exception: the Shīʿa are identified as members of a sect that follows the prophet Omar. In letter 15, on the morals and character of the Turks and the impact of Islam on them, Chrzanowski addresses such issues as the prohibition of alcohol, the Muslim attitude towards the conversion of Christians and Jews to Islam, the treatment of Christians held captive by Muslims, and belief in fate. However, the information given is not comprehensive. In letter 16, in which the position of Turkish women in the family and society is described, Chrzanowski devotes much attention to Muḥammad's

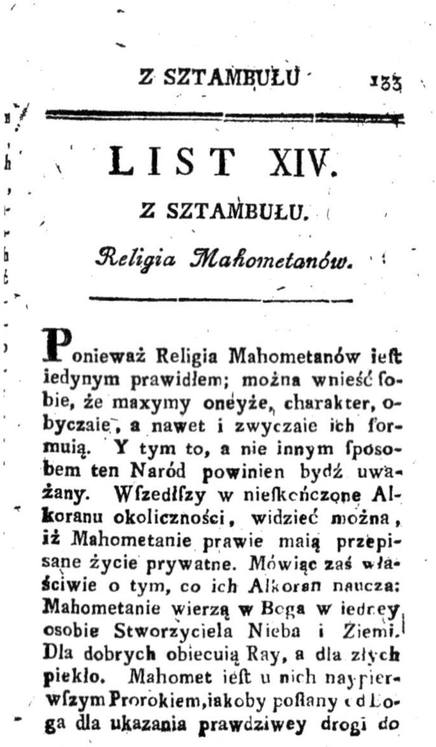

Z SZTAMBUŁU 133

LIST XIV.

Z SZTAMBUŁU.

Religia Mahometanów.

Ponieważ Religia Mahometanów iest iedynym prawidłem; można wnieść sobie, że maxymy oneyże, charakter, obyczaie, a nawet i zwyczaie ich formuią. Y tym to, a nie innym sposobem ten Naród powinien bydź uważany. Wszedłszy w nieskończone Alkoranu okoliczności, widzieć można, iż Mahometanie prawie maią przepisane życie prywatne. Mówiąc zaś właściwie o tym, co ich Alkoran naucza: Mahometanie wierzą w Boga w iedney osobie Stworzyciela Nieba i Ziemi. Dla dobrych obiecuią Ray, a dla złych piekło. Mahomet iest u nich naypierwszym Prorokiem, iakoby posłany od Boga dla ukazania prawdziwey drogi do

Illustration 16. Kajetan Chrzanowski, *Wiadomości o państ-wie tureckim*, p. 133, List XIV (Letter XIV), where Islam is first discussed

relationships with his wives. He cites the passages of the Qur'an (without specific references) that relate to the personal life of the Prophet and governed the behaviour of his wives. Muḥammad's conduct towards his women – as Chrzanowski states – was then imitated by Muslim men in later centuries.

Of the other letters, it is worth pointing out letter 6, which includes comments on the functions of mosques (especially Aya Sophia), their internal features (*miḥrāb, qibla*, lack of images), their surroundings (wells for ablutions in courtyards, minarets nearby), and the separation of the sexes during prayer. In letter 8, there are references to the relationship between secular and spiritual powers (the requirement on the sultan to obey the precepts of the Qur'an, the status of the *'ulamā'*) and the various Muslim religious functionaries (the duties of the Grand Mufti, the importance of emirs, the duties of imams and muezzins).

Chrzanowski also presents an Islamic point of view on a number of issues that were controversial for Europeans at the time. In this, he does not only rely on his own observations, but also cites the words of a Muslim serving at the sultan's court. For example, in his description of the sultan's authority, Chrzanowski questions the concept of Oriental despotism that had been popular in the West for centuries. He stresses that every Turkish sovereign, like any other Muslim, is obliged to obey the Qur'an's teachings. Then he quotes his Muslim friend, who expresses his surprise at the attention this issue aroused among Christians. The Muslim says that Islam requires its followers to obey their rulers, but also imposes on monarchs many duties towards their subjects (*Wiadomosci*, pp. 81-4). Similarly, Chrzanowski completes his description of polygamy in Islam with the opinion of his Muslim friend, who explains this custom by saying that a Christian man is allowed to marry only one woman, but he can know who he is going to marry. Muslims do not have the same chance to know the appearance and character of their wives-to-be and that is why they often marry other women if the first wife does not meet their expectations (*Wiadomosci*, p. 185). Regarding the Qur'an and its laws, the Muslim friend states that Christians should not disapprove of Islamic rites, given that there are also many misinterpretations and misunderstandings concerning religious ceremonies among various Christian factions. What is most important, in his Muslim friend's view, is not the way of worshipping but living a virtuous life (*Wiadomosci*, pp. 166-7).

Despite this objectivity, Chrzanowski's work includes some elements of the traditional European perception of Islam and Muslims, which was still common in the Polish-Lithuanian Commonwealth in the second half of the 18ᵗʰ century (Bałczewski, 'Zmiany w ocenie Turcji', pp. 93-6), including an opinion about the Prophet Muḥammad. He is depicted as a debauched and lecherous man, driven by his immoderate passions (*Wiadomosci*, p. 176-80). The Qur'an is described as a peculiar collection that has held 'almost the greater part of the world in a superstition' (*Wiadomosci*, p. 166; Maśko, 'Obraz islamu', pp. 197-201). Dervishes are described as living in promiscuity and despised by other Muslims (*Wiadomosci*, p. 96), while all Muslims are characterised as inactive, effeminate and passive during plague epidemics because of their belief in fate (*Wiadomosci*, pp. 33, 53, 168, 173).

SIGNIFICANCE

The aim of *Wiadomosci o Panstwie Tureckim* was to provide Polish nobles, especially those who sympathised with the reformist camp of King Stanisław II, with the latest information about a neighbouring country (Reychman, *Życie polskie*, pp. 88, 90). It was a product of a process of changing Polish opinions about Turkey, its government and its Muslim inhabitants, throughout the 18ᵗʰ century. In previous centuries, until the Treaty of Karlowitz (1699), the nobility of the Polish-Lithuanian Commonwealth had been proud to fight against the old 'pagan' enemy, and considered their country as *antemurale Christianitatis*. However, in the second half of the 18ᵗʰ century, new prospects of economic cooperation with the Sublime Porte were taken into consideration by Enlightenment reformers (Bałczewski, 'Zmiany w ocenie Turcji', pp. 97-108). This is clearly pointed out by the editor of the work, as mentioned above. The same attitude is represented by Chrzanowski, who not only writes down his observations on the inhabitants of Turkey, but also tries to find justifications for certain social and religious practices of Muslims by listening to their own voices.

Nevertheless, even though he presents an Islamic point of view and writes some favourable words on Muslims, his work does not differ much from other works on Turks and Islam that were widely read in the Polish-Lithuanian Commonwealth at the time. These were works such as the Polish translations of *The present state of the Ottoman Empire* by Paul Rycaut (translated from French into Polish probably by Hieronim Kłokocki, and published in Słuck in 1678) and *Histoire de l'Empire ottoman, depuis son origine jusqu'à la paix de Belgrade en 1740* by Vincent Mignot (translated into Polish by Dominik Szybiński, published in Warsaw in 1779) (Reychman, *Życie polskie*, p. 90; Bałczewski, 'Zmiany w ocenie Turcji', p. 94).

It is very likely that Chrzanowski's work was read among the Commonwealth enlightened circles of nobles in the first few years after its publication in 1786. Nevertheless, the victory of the Targowica Confederation in 1792 and the Second Partition of Poland in 1793 prevented the implementation of reforms planned by the king, including the establishment of trade relations with Turkey. Thus, the purpose that had prompted the author to write the work ceased to exist. Despite this, as has already been mentioned, the work was republished in 1797.

PUBLICATIONS

Kajetan Chrzanowski, *Wiadomosci o Panstwie Tureckim: przez iednego Polaka, w listach do Przyiaciela pisanych, przesłane. To iest: podroż przez Prowincye Tureckie: Opisanie Sztambułu, Seraiu, Rząd, Stan Porty, Religia, Obyczaie, Charakter Turków, etc.*, Warsaw, 1786

Kajetan Chrzanowski, *Wiadomosci o Panstwie Tureckim: przez iednego Polaka, w listach do Przyiaciela pisanych, przesłane. To iest: podroż przez Prowincye Tureckie: Opisanie Sztambułu, Seraiu, Rząd, Stan Porty, Religia, Obyczaie, Charakter Turków, etc.*, Warsaw, 1797[2]; 1298.a.13. (digitised version available through British Library)

P.P. Panaitescu (ed.), *Catalori polonii in tarile romine*, Bucharest, 1930, pp. 224-32 (Romanian trans. of excerpts)

STUDIES

A. Maśko, 'Obraz islamu w Rzeczpospolitej w XVIII w.', *Przegląd Orientalistyczny* 3-4 (2015) 191-206

Łątka, 'Kajetan Chrzanowski'

M. Bałczewski, 'Zmiany w ocenie Turcji w opinii polskiej XVIII w.', *Acta Universitatis Lodziensis. Folia Historica* 22 (1985) 91-108

Reychman, *Życie polskie w Stambule*, pp. 50-4, 90, 118-19

Konopczyński, 'Chrzanowski Kajetan'

Konopczyński, *Polska a Turcja*, p. 249

Adrianna Maśko

The image of Muslims and Islam in 18th-century Polish geographical and historical works

DATE   18th century
ORIGINAL LANGUAGE   Polish

DESCRIPTION

The difference between the perception of history that saw the hand of God guiding events and the perception influenced by the Enlightenment that saw events as the results of historical causes was a vital feature of intellectual life in the Polish Commonwealth in the 18th century. It found its expression particularly in geographical and historical works written in this period. The conviction that the contemporary form of the Commonwealth was almost a worldly reflection of heavenly reality and enjoyed the particular favour of Divine Providence, and that the Commonwealth had come to fulfil the role of *antemurale Christianitatis* ('bulwark of Christendom'), defending Europe from the Turks and Islam, held an important place in the Sarmatian worldview, the belief that the origins of the Polish nobility lay in the Iranian Sarmatians, who had invaded Poland in ancient times. It was dominant among the elite, especially those belonging to the clergy, until the 1760s, though it continued to have its representatives throughout the 18th century. Augustyn Kołudzki (d.1720), Władysław Łubieński (1703-67), Benedykt Chmielowski (1700-63), Gaudenty Pikulski (d.1763) and Szymon Majchrowicz (1727-83) were among its main exponents. This group drew its pattern of writing from *Annales ecclesiastici a Christo nato ad annum 1198* ('Ecclesiastical annals from the nativity of Christ to 1198', 12 vols, Rome, 1558-1607) by Cesare Baronio (1538-1607) and *Discours sur l'histoire universelle* (Mabre-Cramoisy, 1681) by Jacques-Bénigne Bossuet (1627-1704). These two works were translated into Polish in 1603 and 1772 respectively.

Enlightenment ideas gradually began to enter the Polish-Lithuanian Commonwealth from the 1730s, and enjoyed popularity after the election of Stanisław August Poniatowski (1732-95) as king in 1763. In the Commonwealth, the Enlightenment did not have an anti-religious or anti-clerical character, and among its main exponents were some of the most prominent members of the Roman Catholic clergy. Polish historical and geographical works were also influenced by the religious character of the Enlightenment. The perception of the world through religious lenses, accompanied by the mythologisation of the Polish victory at the Battle of Vienna in 1683, remained a strong element in the Enlightenment view, though simple belief in Providence was abandoned. Authors of historical and geographical works who followed Enlightenment principles tended to focus on facts and avoided religious frameworks. Representatives were Jan Wyrwicz (1717-93) and Dominik Szybiński (1730-99), among others.

Islam is generally mentioned in 18th-century Polish geographical and historical works with reference to the Ottoman Empire (commonly referred to as Turkey), the most important references being to the wars against the Turks in the 17th century and King Jan III Sobieski's (r. 1674-96) victory at Vienna in 1683. Authors usually focused on the origins of Islam rather than on contemporary developments in the Islamic world, and when the latter were mentioned the references were typically to religious structures, places of pilgrimage, and practices such as polygamy, fasting and the ban on wine.

In their descriptions of the beginnings of Islam and the life of Muḥammad, authors from the Sarmatian-religious circle followed the tradition of which the so-called 12th-century Toledan collection (and its later editions) was part, but reaching back to the Byzantine chronicler Theophanes the Confessor (c. 760-c. 818). According to this tradition, Muḥammad suffered from epilepsy and, as a way of hiding this from his wife, he invented the explanation that the fits were the result of his encounters with the Archangel Gabriel. Władysław Łubieński adds other deprecatory elements, which also appear in other accounts from the Sarmatian circle: Muḥammad's Jewish origin, his false prophecies, lies, stealing, violence, debauchery and sectarianism (Łubieński, *Świat we wszystkich swoich częściach*, p. 507). Szymon Majchrowicz writes that Muḥammad was possessed by the devil (*Trwałość szczęśliwa królestw*, part 1, p. 66), and Gaudenty Pikulski, Jan Naumański and Benedykt Chmielowski add similar descriptions. In *Krótka wiadomość o znakomitszych w świecie monarchach*, Dominik Szybiński, from the Enlightenment circle, presents a similar story about Muḥammad, though less spiced with rhetoric (part 2, p. 171). In 1779, he published a Polish translation of the history of Turkey by Vincent Mignot (c. 1725-91), which was very popular in Europe. This contains no mention of Muḥammad's epilepsy, but talks of his plan for conquest and the gaining of power.

All the Polish authors characterise Islam as an amalgam of Jewish and Christian teachings.

The Jesuit Jan Bielski (1714-68) in *Widok Królestwa Polskiego* ('A survey of the Polish kingdom') adheres to Sarmatian values, but presents the history of the Commonwealth as a process of historical development, showing the first Enlightenment influences. Islam is mentioned in connection with wars conducted against the Ottomans, and with the Commonwealth as the *antemurale Christianitatis*. The death of Władysław III Jagiellon at the Battle of Varna in 1444 and all the confrontations with the Ottomans from the 15th century onwards are depicted as the Commonwealth's contribution to the defence of Christianity, with the victory at the Battle of Vienna as the climax. References to Turkey and Islam only appear in the margins of the history of the Commonwealth.

Hilarion Karpiński's (d. before 1765) *Lexykon geograficzny* ('Geographical lexicon'), published in 1766, was the first work of its type to appear in the Commonwealth, though in Western Europe such works had already been published in the 17th century. This work opened a new chapter in Polish geography by giving an alphabetically ordered lexicon of geographical names throughout the world. On the one hand, Karpiński was a supporter of the Ptolemaic earth-centred theory of the universe, while on the other his lexicon was a sign of a new way of thinking. The work contains no entries directly dealing with Islam, though Karpiński's strongly anti-Islamic views can be detected in short entries on Mecca and Medina. He also mistakenly writes that Mecca was where the fraudulent Muḥammad 'gave up his dirty soul', and Medina was the city where he had been born and where he preached his false message.

Augustyn Kołudzki (d. 1720) was a state official and soldier who enjoyed the support of Jan III Sobieski. He wrote a synthesis of Polish history (republished a number of times) called *Tron ojczysty* ('The native throne'), told through the biographies of the country's rulers. It fully adheres to the Sarmatian ideology of the nobility, treating history as a series of rewards and punishments given by God for human conduct on earth. Thus, Kołudzki treats the death of Władysław III Jagiellon during the Battle of Varna as punishment for perjury and breaking the treaty he had concluded with the Ottomans, which was an insult to God. He also underlines the role of Sobieski as the deliverer of Christian Europe from the Islamic threat. In the 300 or so pages of the work, references to Turkey and Islam appear only as details in the story of the Commonwealth.

Szymon Majchrowicz (1727-83), a Jesuit who published political and religious treatises, was one of the followers of the Sarmatian-religious trend. This is evident in the 474 pages of his politico-historical synthesis of world history, *Trwałość szczęśliwa królestw* ('Happy stability of kingdoms'), published in 1764. The views it expresses were seen as anachronistic as soon as it was published. It portrays history as a pattern of rewards from God for doing good and punishments for doing evil. Freedom is God's reward, so when nations have abandoned Catholicism, God has punished them by taking it away. Hence, Orthodox Christianity was a break from the true Catholic faith, and the fall of the Byzantine Empire to the Ottomans was punishment for the sins of emperors and patriarchs. This was all the more harsh because Islam was 'a dirty Mahometan heresy', 'a pest' and 'heathendom', and the sultans were treacherous rulers allowing 'lascivious pagan insubordination', violence and cruelties, greed and crimes. Islam was also a punitive tool in God's hands against African kingdoms, where magnificent temples were changed into 'dirty mosques'. 'Mahometan rage' reached the Holy Land, and more recently Hungary, which was punished with Ottoman domination for joining the Reformation.

Jan Naumański was a mysterious figure in 18th-century Polish intellectual life, about whom little is known except that he was active between 1729 and 1733. During this period, he produced *Nowiny Polskie* ('Polish news'), renamed *Kurier Polski* ('Polish herald'), considered the first Polish newspaper to include news and political commentaries. In this newspaper, he published the history of Poland in instalments. The contents of his narrative adhered to all the Sarmatian values, including the conviction that religious and moral thinking was supreme over all other areas of knowledge, and that the Poles had been raised up over other nations because of their staunch defence of Roman Catholicism. In 1732, he published *Historya politico-universalis*, a general history in which he separates human history from divine influence and, unlike contemporary Polish historians, limits its determination by Providence. In this work, he was ahead of his time, as in his unfinished *Geografia novissima* in which he acquaints readers with the new understanding of geography.

Like most other authors, in *Historya politico-universalis* Naumański only refers to Islam and Muḥammad briefly, in a short note on Turkey, where he says that Islam is a mixture of heathen, Jewish and Christian (mainly Nestorian) teachings. In *Geografia novissima*, which is unfinished, the Commonwealth is the defender of Christianity against the Ottomans, with the Battle of Vienna as the climax of confrontation; the Muslims are described as 'unpleasant guests' (*nieprzyjemni goście*).

Władysław Łubieński (1703-67), the primate of Poland, was one of the leading representatives of the Sarmatian religious trend. He wrote a general geography entitled *Świat we wszystkich swoich częściach* [...] *określony* ('The world in all its parts [...] described'), published in 1740. Accompanied by many maps, it includes much dubious and even fabulous information in addition to accounts of the author's own travels and foreign books. The parts on Poland were later twice republished as *Historia polska z opisaniem rządu i urzędów polskich* ('Polish history with a description of the Polish government and offices'). The geography contains numerous references to Turks in the context of battles fought in the Middle Ages and the present, though Łubieński does not ascribe any particular religious significance to them. Names such as 'pagans', 'heretics' appear only rarely, though 'Turk' is often used as a synonym for 'Muslim'. Some wars against the Turks are described as 'holy wars', and with regard to the Battle of Vienna, Łubieński writes about the 'great danger for the whole of Christianity'.

Łubieński includes a one-and-a-half-page-long description of the history of Islam in his account of the European part of the Turkish Empire. This contains a detailed (at least, in comparison with other Polish writers) biography of Muḥammad, a general outline of the history of his successors and the spread of Islam, and the internal disputes between the caliphs that led to the creation of the Ottoman state. He writes that Muḥammad was of the lower class and was sold by his parents to a rich Jewish merchant. His wife Chadidża (Khadīja) married him after the death of her husband, although because of the convulsions he suffered at first she was not well-disposed towards him (*był przez nią zbrzydzony*). In order to gain her favour, Muḥammad began explaining that he suffered from fits every time the Archangel Gabriel revealed himself to him. Chadidża believed this lie and started to circulate her husband's prophecies. After his wife's death, Muḥammad intensified his preaching and caused dissension among the people. They set out to apprehend him but he fled to Medina. He won over a group of Arabs, mainly thieves and robbers, with whom he started visiting the neighbouring towns and winning over their inhabitants. Soon he gathered an army, which he used to convert the cities he conquered to Islam. He allowed the followers of his sect to have many wives and enjoy debauchery, but he forbade wine, which was to be their award in paradise. Muḥammad died in Medina.

Łubieński devotes one page of his work to the principles of Islam. It is based on six main imperatives: circumcision, prayer, fasting, alms-giving, pilgrimage to Muḥammad's grave and abstinence from wine. On the basis of the lavish ceremonies that accompany circumcision he compares it to a Christian wedding ceremony, and for its religious significance he likens it to baptism. He points out that prayer is short but frequent, and he refers to the accompanying rituals. The fast, he says, is strictly observed, especially during Ramaḍān, and failure to observe it may even be punished with death. In the description of Turkey, there are a few references to the Muslim treatment of Christians. Christians are forced to be executioners, and are impaled if they contravene Islamic law or marry Muslim women; Muslims who become Christians are burned alive with a sack of gunpowder above their head.

The description of Persia and the Shī'a also contains about a page of details about Islam. The Persians are adherents of the sect of 'Alī, a false prophet who won people over with cunning miracles and an ascetic way of life. Shī'īs pray three times a day, for which they turn to the south and kneel on a carpet under which they put a stone, and on which they put prayer beads, a Qur'an and a comb with which they comb their beards before prayer. The carpet is spread to commemorate the grave of Muḥammad. They read the Qur'an with their head bowed in order to praise the name of God. They follow the custom of cleansing themselves from their sins prior to prayer, a practice borrowed from the Jews; they carry out circumcision and are idolaters. The highest-ranking clergy take places near the king's throne and influence state affairs.

Gaudenty Pikulski (d. 1763), a Franciscan friar and a teacher of theology in the major seminaries of religious orders, a religious writer and historian, was one of the main representatives of the Sarmatian trend. His monumental work called *Sukcess świata* ('The success of the world'), published in 1763 at the dawn of the Polish Enlightenment, followed a radically providential view of history. Despite (or perhaps because of) this, it was republished and was still used in some monasteries of the Franciscans and the Brothers of St John of God until the 20th century. Pikulski believed in the action of God's providence through history, and identified the role of morality in human actions. In what he wrote about Turkey, he describes Islam and Muḥammad, seeing Islam as an amalgam of Judaism and Christianity, and says that Muḥammad taught about the flaws in Christianity and Judaism, which he was entrusted to mend. Muḥammad forbade discussion about religion under pain of death, so that his frauds should not be exposed.

Jan Poszakowski (1684-1757), a Jesuit, was a professor at the Academy in Vilnius and head of the Jesuit schools in Słuck and Nieśwież (in present-day Belarus). Although he subscribed to the Sarmatian worldview, he also accepted some Enlightenment ideas. In 1748, he published *Summa historii uniwersalnej* ('Summa of universal history'), a reprint of works he had earlier published in the *Kalendarz polityczny* ('Political calendar') 1739-47. It consists of lists of popes, patriarchs, eastern and western emperors, and rulers from biblical times to the present. Information about rulers is usually brief, consisting mainly of dates of accession and death, occasionally with some other details. A significant feature is that he treats the Ottoman rulers as the heirs to the Byzantine emperors and crusader rulers of Jerusalem (though during the 13th and 14th centuries they are listed partly in parallel, partly in succession).

In 1749, he published *Summa historii cesarzów* ('Summa of the history of emperors'). Here, the Ottoman sultans are included, with details about the life and main activities of each. These are preceded by a three-page biography of Muḥammad, in which Poszakowski mentions Muḥammad's low social status and Jewish origins, and says that he created a false teaching under Nestorian influence – an 'obscenity' (*sprośność*).

Dominik Szybiński (1730-99), a priest of the Piarist teaching order and teacher at the Collegium Nobilium in Warsaw, the first Polish school to offer a programme inspired by Enlightenment thinking, was a translator (mainly from French) and author of geography and history schoolbooks. Among others, his *Atlas dziecinny* ('Children's atlas'), published in 1772, and *Krótka wiadomość o znakomitszych w świecie monarchiach* ('Brief information about the more prominent monarchies of the world'), published in 1773, were addressed to the youth. In the first, as part of his description of Turkey, he devotes half a page to Islam, presenting it as an amalgam of various Jewish, Christian and Greek articles of faith and Oriental rites, and calling Muḥammad a heretic and false prophet. He adds that the Catholic Church in some parts of Turkey enjoys freedom of worship, though all religions have to pay tribute money to the Turks. Further information about Islam is included in the second book, where he states that Islam is characterised by conversion through force, by torture and by religious wars. Muḥammad's followers call themselves Muslims ('having the right faith'), and consider followers of other religions as pagans. Szybiński includes a brief account of the spread of Islam and its acceptance by the Tatar Hordes, from which, he says, the Turks originated, and gives longer accounts of the Turkish conquests and the introduction of Islamic law in the conquered territories. He considers the Ottoman wars against the European states as a threat to Christendom, though he abstains from a polemical narration and focuses rather on facts. Thus, the Christian victory in the Battle of Vienna is not presented in religious terms, apart from a brief mention of rescuing the city from the hands of *bisurmans*. Issues related to Islam in this long work cover only about five pages, together with scattered details in descriptions of wars with European rulers.

Szybiński also translated into Polish *Histoire de l'Empire ottoman, depuis son origine jusqu'à la paix de Belgrade en 1740* (1771) by Vincent Mignot (c. 1725-91). This is an extensive history of Ottoman Turkey, preceded by the longest description of Muḥammad's life, the teachings of Islam, and the split between the Sunnīs and Shīʿa that was available at that time in Polish. Islam is presented as a religion of violence.

Karol Wyrwicz (1717-93), a Jesuit, was a teacher in Jesuit schools and a close collaborator of King Stanisław August Poniatowski (r. 1764-95), and in addition he was one of the main representatives of the Polish Enlightenment. He authored two geography textbooks. Of the first, *Geografia czasów teraźniejszych* ('Geography of the present times'), published in 1768, only the first volume appeared owing to Russian diplomatic interference. The work contains general geographical information and a description of Europe. A few years later Wyrwicz published *Geografia powszechna czasów teraźniejszych* ('General geography of the present times') in one volume. It eventually reached four editions and served as a textbook in the schools of the National Education Commission (first Ministry of Education, 1773-94).

In *Geografia czasów teraźniejszych*, there is a chapter of 37 pages on religions, *O wiarach i sektach* ('On faiths and sects'), in which one page is devoted to Islam called *wiara /religia/ muzułmańska lub mahometańska* ('Muslim or Muḥammedan faith /religion'); in the general classification of religions at the beginning of the chapter it is also called the Turkish faith. Wyrwicz explains that its core is faith in one God, who had Muḥammad as his prophet, and that it is the dominant religion in Arabia, Asian Turkey, Persia, the eastern side of the Ganges in India, the Maldives, North Africa, Sudan and Ethiopia, the European part of Turkey and the Tatar lands. Wyrwicz also explains that the division into Sunnīs and Shīʿīs comes from the division between the opponents and supporters of ʿAlī, and shows in which regions the adherents of the two divisions live. There is nothing about Christian-Muslim relations in his description of the Holy Land, though issues related to Islam reappear in the description of Turkey, where Wyrwicz writes that the Turks are proud and haughty towards Christians, but at the same time they are helpful towards foreigners regardless of their faith. One page is devoted to religious functionaries (whom he calls 'clergy'). He identifies the position of mufti as the religious leader of the Turks, and explains that even the sultan cannot go against his decisions. He briefly goes on to describe various religious functions and groups in Turkey, e.g. explaining the role of imams, dervishes and others.

The second of Wyrwicz's textbooks, *Geografia powszechna czasów teraźniejszych* (dated 1770 on the title page, but according to the *imprimatur* dated December 1772), repeats the earlier work with slight modifications.

SIGNIFICANCE

None of these works deals exclusively with Islam. Issues related to the faith are treated among many other elements of knowledge about the world, and are seen as minor in importance. Nevertheless, the works of Szybiński and Wyrwicz, which served as textbooks in schools run by the Piarists and by the National Education Commission, were often the only source of objective knowledge about Islam for the majority of children of the nobility who were growing up during the second half of the 18th century. Calendars, whose texts were later collected into separate publications, as in the case of Poszakowski's *Summa historii uniwersalnej*, that were present in many houses of the nobility also exercised a wide influence. Chmielowski's *Nowe Ateny* played a very particular role in this respect, as did, to a lesser extent, Łubieński's *Świat we wszystkich swoich częściach* [...] *określony* and Pikulski's *Sukces świata*. These works aimed to offer geographical and historical knowledge about the world, and they claimed a particular role for the Commonwealth in defending Christianity against Islam.

This view was shared by representatives of both the Sarmatian (Kłobudzki) and the Enlightenment (Bielski) circles. It found its full form in Majchrowicz's *Trwałość szczęśliwa królestw*, published at the request of the archbishop of Lviv, Wacław Hieronim Sierakowski (1700-80), which was a covert polemic against the proponents of Enlightenment reforms in the Commonwealth. Some of Majchrowicz's views later influenced the formation of Polish Messianic ideology, while the linguistic and compositional qualities of the work earned the author the title of the 'Polish Bossuet'.

With the influx of Enlightenment ideas into the Commonwealth and (under the threat of the political partition of the country) the increase of positive attitudes towards Ottoman Turkey – regarded by some as a guardian of Polish independence and caretaker of the 'golden freedom' of the nobility – the way of writing about Islam was changing, and anti-Islamic polemic was being abandoned. Nevertheless, the attitude towards Islam and Muslims was not completely free from elements of the old perception. This is apparent in such elements as the recurring motif of Islam as the religion of violence.

PUBLICATIONS

Listed alphabetically by author:

J. Bielski, *Widok Królestwa Polskiego z wszystkimi województwami, xięstwami i ziemiami, monarchami i monarchiniami jako też monarchów tychże i monarchiń prawami, Rzeczpospolitej stanami i tychże stanów urzędami* [...] *wystawiony*, Poznań, 1763, 1873[2] (vol. 1), 1879[2] (vol. 2); 6980 (digitised version available through Elbląska Biblioteka Cyfrowa)

H. Karpiński, *Lexykon geograficzny dla gruntownego pojęcia gazet i historii z różnych autorów zebrany*, Vilnius, 1766

A. Kołudzki, *Tron ojczysty albo pałac wieczności w krótkim zebraniu monarchów, książąt i królów polskich różnych aprobowanych autorów, od pierwszego Lecha aż do teraźniejszych czasów, zupełną w sobie z życia i dzieł ich nieśmiertelnych zamykający historią*, Poznań, 1707, Supraśl 1727[2], Poznań 1727[3]; 2452 (digitised version available through Zielonogórska Biblioteka Cyfrowa)

W. Łubieński, *Świat we wszystkich swoich częściach większych i mniejszych to jest: w Europie, Azji, Affryce y Ameryce, w monarchiach, królestwach, xięstwach, prowincjach, wyspach y miastach geograficznie, chronologicznie y historycznie określony. Opisaniem religii, Rządów, rewolucji, praw, zwyczajów, skarbów, ciekawości y granic każdego kraju z autorów francuskich, włoskich, niemieckich y polskich zebranym przyozdobiony*, Breslau, 1740; bsb10897024 (digitised version available through *MDZ*)

W. Łubieński, *Historia polska z opisaniem rządu i urzędów polskich*, Vilnius, 1763; 132747 (digitised version available through Google books)

Sz. Majchrowicz, *Trwałość szczęśliwa królestw albo ich smutny upadek wolnym narodom przed oczy stawiona na utrzymanie nieoszacowanej szczęśliwości swojej*, Lwów, 1764, Kalisz, 1783[2]; 4460 (digitised version available through Podlaska Digital Library)

J.X. Mignot, *Historya turecka czyli państwo Ottomanskie od początku aż do pokoju Belgradzkiego zawartego w roku 1740*, trans. D. Szybiński, 5 vols, Warsaw, 1779 (Polish trans.); 22364 (digitised version available through Hieronim Łopaciński Lublin Provincial Library)

J. Naumański, *Historya politico-universalis, zawierająca w sobie co osobliwego od stworzenia świata aż do teraźniejszego czasu działo się dla lepszego pojęcia przez pytania ułożona*, Warsaw, 1732

J. Naumański, *Geographia novissima albo wielce pożyteczne a przez pytania sporządzone opisanie świata, ziem i miast, w którym cztery części świata Europa, Azja, Afryka i Ameryka geograficznie, fizycznie, politycznie i historycznie objaśnione z przydatkiem o sferze i XIII objaśnieniami i ilustrowanemi mappami na pożytek kwitnącej młodzi wydane*, Warsaw, s.d.

G. Pikulski, *Sukcess świata czyli historia uniwersalna o pierwszych Rodzicach Adamie i Ewie, początku monarchij, krolestw i miast sławniejszych, zaczązwszy od stworzenia pisarzów zebrana*, Warsaw, 1748, Lvov, 1763; 79862892 (digitised version available through Polona/)

J. Poszakowski, *Summa historii uniwersalnej na dwie części rozłożona abo index Kalendarzyków seu Kolend, które w Wilnie corocznie się wydają*, Vilnius, 1748; 11711482 (digitised version available through Polona/)

J. Poszakowski, *Summa historii cesarzów zachodnich jako też wschodnich i sułtanów ottomańskich, różne potym w sobie ciekawe rewolucje zawierająca przez cztery lata kontynuowana, a teraz roku 1749 zakończona*, Vilnius, 1749

D. Szybiński, *Atlas dziecinny czyli nowy sposob do nauczenia dzieci geografii, krótki, łatwy i najdoskonalszy przez przyłączone nowej inwencji XXIV kart geograficznych z wykładem onychże, zawierający dokładniejsze opisanie Polski i Litwy tudzież naukę o sferze, w której obroty gwiazd i planet, systemata czyli rozporządzenie świata, używanie globu, wymiar dróg geograficznych dawny i teraźniejszy są opisane z francuskiego przełożony, powiększony i poprawiony*, Warsaw, 1772; 70285979 (digitised version available through Polona/)

D. Szybiński, *Krótka wiadomość o znakomitszych w świecie monarchiach, starodawnych królestwach, rzeczachpospolitych, tudzież o cesarzach państwa rzymskiego, jego podziale, upadku i wznowieniu na Zachodzie, powitaniu tureckiego na Wschodzie i rewolucjach w nich zachodzących aż do naszych czasów. Dla pożytku Młodzi uczącej się zebrana*, 2 vols, Warsaw, 1773, repr. 1790, Vilnius, 1813; 92893529 (digitised version of 1813 edition available through Polona/)

K. Wyrwicz, *Geografia czasów teraźniejszych albo opisanie naturalne i polityczne Królestw, Państw, Stanów wszelakich, ich rządu, praw, rzemiosł, handlu, przemysłu, przymiotów, obyczajów etc. ku pożytkowi narodowej młodzi wydana*, vol. 1, Warsaw, 1768

K. Wyrwicz, *Geografia powszechna czasów teraźniejszych albo opisanie krótkie krajów całego świata, ich położenia, granic, płodu ziemskiego, skłonności obywatelów, handlu, obyczajów etc. etc. z najświeższych wiadomości, Krajopisarzów i Wędrowników zebrana ku pożytkowi Młodzi Narodowej na szkoły publiczne wydana,* Warsaw, 1770, 1773[2], Warsaw 1794[3], Vilnius, 1794[4]; 69349284 (digitised version available through Polona/)

STUDIES

M.P. Borkowski, 'Obraz Arabów w osiemnastowiecznej Rzeczypospolitej w świetle Nowych Aten B. Chmielowskiego i Świata we wszystkich częściach większych i mniejszych [...] W.A. Łubieńskiego', *Przeglad Orientalistyczny* 1-2 (2016) 31-43

A. Maśko, 'Obraz islamu w Rzeczpospolitej w XVIII wieku', *Przegląd Orientalistyczny* 3 (2016) 191-206

J. Żukowska, *Jan Poszakowski. Historyk czasów saskich,* Słupsk, 2016

K. Puchowski, art. 'Szybiński Gabriel, w zakonie Dominik od św. Aleksandra', in *Polski słownik biograficzny,* vol. 49, Warsaw, 2014, 516-18

D. Dolański, *Trzy cesarstwa. Wiedza i wyobrażenia o Niemczech, Turcji i Rosji w Polsce XVIII wieku,* Zielona Góra, 2013

S. Roszak, *Koniec świata sarmackich erudytów,* Toruń, 2012

W. Decyk-Zięba, *'Lexykon geograficzny' bazylianina Hipariona Karpińskiego. Studium historycznojęzykowe (wybrane zagadnienia),* Warsaw, 2009

D. Kołodziejczyk, 'Obraz sułtana tureckiego w publicystyce staropolskiej', in F. Wolański and R. Kołodziej (eds), *Staropolski ogląd świata. Rzeczpospolita między okcydentalizmem a orientalizacją,* vol. 1. *Przestrzeń kontaktów,* Toruń, 2009, 11-19

F. Wolański, 'Staropolskie podręczniki i kompendia geograficzne jako źródło wiedzy o świecie w XVIII wieku', in I.M. Dacka-Górzyńska and J. Partyka (eds), *Staropolskie kompendia wiedzy,* Warsaw, 2009, 195-202

D. Dolański, 'Jan Naumański. W kręgu prekursorów polskiego oświecenia', *Wiek Oświecenia* 21 (2005) 59-72

D. Kołodziejczyk, 'Rola islamskiego sąsiedztwa w kulturze i polityce Rzeczpospolitej', in A. Kaźmierczyk et al. (eds), *Rzeczpospolita wielu wyznań. Materiały z Międzynarodowej Konferencji, Kraków 18-20 listopada 2002,* Kraków, 2004, 441-8

D. Dolański, *Zachód w polskiej myśli historycznej czasów saskich. Nurt sarmacko-teologiczny,* Zielona Góra, 2002

M. Bałczewski, *Znajomość edukacji Turków osmańskich w Polsce od schyłku średniowiecza do końca oświecenia*, Warsaw, 2001

S. Lipko, 'Podręczniki geografii w szkołach polskich w XVIII wieku', *Rozprawy z Dziejów Oświaty* 9 (1996) 3-33

J. Kozłowski, 'Erudyci epoki saskiej', *Wiek Oświecenia* 10 (1994) 115-34

P. Komorowski, *Historia powszechna w polskim piśmiennictwie naukowym czasów stanisławowskich i jej rola w edukacji narodowej*, Warsaw, 1992

B. Rok, 'Obraz Turcji w kalendarzach czasów saskich', in J. Pietrzak (ed.), *Z dziejów i tradycji srebrnego wieku*, Wrocław, 1990, 115-22

M. Bałczewski, 'Zmiany w ocenie Turcji w opinii polskiej XVIII w.', in Z. Libiszowska (ed.), *Kultura elit XVIII w.*, Łódź, 1985, 91-108

M. Bogucka, 'Szlachta polska wobec Wschodu turecko-tatarskiego: między fascynacją a przerażeniem (XVI-XVIII w.)', *Śląski Kwartalnik Historyczny* 3-4 (1982) 185-94

J. Lorenz, art. 'Pikulski Gaudenty', in *Polski słownik biograficzny*, vol. 26, Wrocław, 1981, 225-6

T. Słowikowski, 'Pijarskie podręczniki do nauczania historii w Polsce w XVIII w.', *Nasza Przeszłość* 54 (1980) 181-229

K. Bartkiewicz, *Obraz dziejów ojczystych w świadomości historycznej w Polsce doby oświecenia*, Poznań, 1979

M. Tyrowicz, art. 'Jan Naumański', in *Polski słownik biograficzny*, vol. 22, Wrocław, 1977, 622

A.F. Grabski, *Myśl historyczna polskiego oświecenia*, Warsaw, 1976

S. Grzybowski, 'Majchrowicz Szymon', in *Polski słownik biograficzny*, vol. 19, Wrocław, 1974, 157

J. Nosowski, *Polska literatura polemiczno-antyislamistyczna XVI, XVII i XVIII w. Wybór tekstów i komentarze*, 2 vols, Warsaw, 1974

S. Lipko, *Nauczanie geografii w szkołach Komisji Edukacji Narodowej*, Warsaw, 1973

E. Rostworowski, art. 'Łubieński Władysław Aleksander', in *Polski słownik biograficzny*, vol. 18, Wrocław, 1972, 505-11

K. Zglińska, art. 'Kołudzki Augustyn', in *Polski słownik biograficzny*, vol. 13, Wrocław, 1967-8, 365

K. Augustowska, 'Karol Wyrwicz jako geograf', *Zeszyty Geograficzne WSP w Gdańsku* 9 (1967) 77-137

J. Reychman, 'Dzieje orientalistyki w Polsce do końca XVIII w.', *Studia i Materiały Dziejów Nauki Polskiej*, Seria A 9 (1966) 87-105

S. Grzybowski, 'Z dziejów popularyzacji nauki w czasach saskich', *Studia i Materiały z Dziejów Nauki Polskiej*, Seria A 7 (1965) 11-173

S. Bednarski, art. 'Bielski Jan', in *Polski słownik biograficzny*, vol. 2, Warsaw, 1936, 60-1

J. Bartoszewicz, 'Xiążę Władysław Aleksander Łubieński, prymas, arcybiskup gnieźnieński', in J. Bartoszewicz, *Znakomici mężowie polscy w XVIII wieku*, vol. 2, St Petersburg, 1856, 1-114

Dariusz Dolański

Russia

Andrei Andreevich Vinius

DATE OF BIRTH   4 June 1641
PLACE OF BIRTH   Uncertain; The Netherlands or Moscow
DATE OF DEATH   8 November 1716
PLACE OF DEATH   Moscow

BIOGRAPHY

Andrei Andreevich Vinius was a Russian statesman of Frisian descent originating from an old merchant clan of the Dutch Republic. He was a close associate of Tsar Peter I (r. 1682-1725) and a nobleman with the rank of *dumnyi d'iak* (Duma secretary). He spoke Dutch and Russian fluently from childhood, and was home-schooled in English, German, Greek and Latin, as well as geography, drawing, mathematics, chemistry and theology.

Vinius was raised as a Calvinist, but in 1655 he converted to Orthodoxy. He lived in the Moscow Foreigners' Quarter (*Nemetskaia sloboda*), obtaining a position as translator in the Foreign Affairs Chancellery (*Posol'skii prikaz*) in 1664 and visiting France, Spain and England as a member of several diplomatic missions. Upon his return to Russia, he was raised to the nobility and subsequently held various important governmental positions, notably head of the Postal Service and the Pharmaceutical (*Aptekarskii prikaz*), Siberian (*Sibirskii prikaz*) and Artillery (*Artilleriiskii prikaz*) Chancelleries. He was a member of an organisation called the Most Comical and All-Drunken Council, which brought together Peter I's reformers and parodied the structure and rituals of the Catholic and Orthodox Churches.

In 1703, Vinius was dismissed on charges of corruption and delays in army supplies, though the death sentence imposed on him was commuted to flogging and a large fine. In 1706, he fled to the Dutch Republic, but sought Peter I's pardon and returned to Russia two years later.

In addition to state service, Vinius is known as a translator of military and technical literature. He owned a large library of foreign books and an art collection. After his death, Peter ordered his library to be handed over to the Academy of Science, where it is still preserved; a section is held at the University Library in Helsinki.

MAIN SOURCES OF INFORMATION

Primary

I.P. Kozlovskii, *Andrei Vinius, sotrudnik Petra Velikogo (1641-1717)*, St Petersburg, 1911

Secondary

K. Boterbloem, *Moderniser of Russia. Andrei Vinius, 1641-1716*, Basingstoke, 2013

I.N. Iurkin, '*Ot pervoprestol'nogo grada Moskvy*[...]' *A.A. Vinius v Moskve i Podmoskov'e*, Moscow, 2009

E.A. Savel'eva (ed.), *Knigi iz sobraniia Andreia Andreevicha Viniusa. Katalog*, St Petersburg, 2008

I. Wladimiroff, *De kaart van een verzwegen vriendschap. Nicolaes Witsen en Andrej Winius en de Nederlandse cart ografie van Rusland*, Groningen, 2008

I.N. Iurkin, *Andrei Andreevich Vinius, 1641-1716*, Moscow, 2007

S.G. Miliukov, 'Dumnyi d'iak Andrei Andreevich Vinius. Gosudarstvennyi deiatel' Rossii vtoroi poloviny XVII-nachala XVIII vekov', Moscow, 2000 (PhD Diss. Moscow State University)

I. Wladimiroff, 'Andries Winius and Nicolas Witsen. Tsar Peter's Dutch connection', in C. Horstmeier, H. van Koningsbrugge and I. Nieuwland (eds), *Around Peter the Great. Three centuries of Russian-Dutch relations*, Groningen, 1997, 5-28

G.N. Moiseeva, art. 'Vinius Andrei Andreevich', in A.M. Panchenko (ed.), *Slovar' russkikh pisatelei XVIII veka*, vol. 1. A-I, Leningrad, 1988, 152

N.A. Kazakova, 'A.A. Vinius i stateinyi spisok ego posol'stva v Anglii, Frantsiii i Ispaniiu v 1676-1774 gg.', *Trudy Otdela Drevnerusskoi Literatury* 39 (1985) 348-64

WORKS ON CHRISTIAN-MUSLIM RELATIONS

O stolitsakh narochitykh gradov, i slavnykh gosudarstv, i zemel'
'On the capitals of particular cities, glorious states, and lands'

DATE   1667
ORIGINAL LANGUAGE   Russian

DESCRIPTION

Vinius composed *O stolitsakh* ('The description') in 1667, while serving as a translator at the Foreign Affairs Chancellery during the reign of Tsar

Fedor Alekseevich (r. 1676-82). Due to similarities in its contents and approach, it was often bound together with *Kniga bol'shomu chertezhu* ('Book of the great map'), the 1627 handbook for couriers and emissaries that included a description of Russian rivers and cities, and *Poverstnaia kniga* ('The book of distances measured in *versty*'), a 1630s reference book of the distances between Russian cities that was used for calculating travel expenses. *O stolitsakh* was used to plan the routes for embassies and commercial missions. It had become necessary as a result of the increase in Russia's contacts with other countries; the same year in which Vinius composed it, Russia signed the Truce of Andrusovo with Poland, bringing to an end the long Russo-Polish war. *O stolitsakh* ranges in length between 10 and 15 pages, depending on the edition. It contains information on 54 large foreign cities, countries and islands in the Christian and Muslim worlds, in equal proportions, with information on the distances and routes between each of them and Moscow. This information is arranged alphabetically, with some copies giving it in table format.

Vinius used as sources: *De zee-atlas ofte Water-Wereld*[...] ('The sea-atlas of the water world', Amsterdam, 1666), *Poverstnaia kniga*, European newspapers (*kuranty*), information from the employees of the Foreign Affairs Chancellery and its archive, and his own personal experience.

The title of *O stolitsakh* varies from copy to copy, and some include the full title *O stolitsakh narochitykh gradov i slavnykh gosudarstv, i zemel' i ostrovov, i prolivov i znatnykh mest sukhimi i vodnymi putiami koliko imut razstoianie Rossijskogo gosudarstva ot [...] grada Moskvy, po alfavitu raspisano perevodchikom* or *Opisanie razstoianiu stolits narochitykh gradov, slavnykh gosudarstv i zemel', takozh de i znatnykh ostrovov i prolivov, vodnym i sukhim putem po rozmeru knigi, imenuemyia Vodnyi Mir i inykh, prinadlezhashchikh k tomu opisanii Rossiiskago gosudarstva, ot pervoprestol'nago ego tsarskago velichestva grada Moskvy skol'ko do kotorogo goroda i prolivy verst, po alfavitu*. The name of the author and the date of copying are usually given at the end of the text.

The work includes information about places in the Orthodox Middle East, Greece and Crimea that were not known in Europe at the time. In particular, it mentions cities 'in the domain of the Turkish sultan': Adrianople, 'the great city in Egypt' Alexandria, Antioch, Belgrade 'in Hungarian land', Smyrna in Anatolia on the shore of the White (Mediterranean) Sea, Jerusalem, Constantinople and the Cyprian Island (Cyprus). It also describes cities of the 'Persian land': Baghdad or Babylon, Ispagan' or Isfahan, Mount Athos, and Bakhchisarai 'the Crimean capital'.

The route to Turkish lands 'passes through Kiev, while the route to Persia lies through Astrakhan'.

SIGNIFICANCE

O stolitsakh is a short handbook that demonstrates the increased interest in geography in Russia at the time, as well as the geographical orientation of the work of the Foreign Affairs Chancellery clerks. The fact that the work does not contain any ethnic or religious observations suggests many felt that it was possible or necessary to separate religious attitudes towards Muslims and Ottomans as followers of error and believers in wrong from more pragmatic approaches to them as neighbours and trading partners with whom a form of *modus vivendi* was unavoidable. This action of compartmentalising religion from the realities of living may indicate an incipient secular outlook.

PUBLICATIONS

O stolitsakh gained great popularity due to its concise form and informative content. At least 26 manuscript copies are known, preserved in collections in St Petersburg and Moscow. One copy is in Uppsala, Sweden, MS Uppsala, University Library – Slav 2014.

For a list of the Russian editions of *O stolitsakh* see Olena Pashnyk, *Upsal'skii spisok geograficheskogo spravochnika A.A. Viniusa. Istoriko-paleograficheskoe issledovanie i izdanie teksta*, Uppsala, 2014, 50-2; http://www.diva-portal.org/smash/get/diva2:715578/FULLTEXT01.pdf

> P.G. Butkov, *Zhurnal Ministerstva Vnutrennykh del* 10 (1840) 1-6 (three articles, connected to *Knige bol'shogo chertezha Rossii, rukopisi XVII veka, o Rezstoianii ot Moskvy glavnykh gorodov, inostrannykh i inykh russkikh, i o chisle tserkvei v Rossii* [Book of the great map of Russia, manuscripts of the 17th century, about the distance from Moscow to several foreign and other Russian towns, and about the number of churches in Russia])

STUDIES

> S.M. Shamin, 'Politiko-geograficheskii krugozor chlenov pravitel'stva tsaria Fedora Alekseevicha', *Drevniaia Rus'. Voprosy Medievistiki* 1 (2004) 16-31
>
> N.A. Borisovskaia, *Starinnye gravirovannye plany XV-XVIII vv. Kosmografii, karty zemnye i nebesnye, plany, veduty, batalii*, Moscow, 1992
>
> A.A. Zimin, 'Russkie geograficheskie spravochniki XVII v.', *Zapiski otdela Rukopisei Gosudarstvennoi Biblioteki im. V.I. Lenina* 21 (1959) 220-31

V.A. Petrov, 'Geograficheskie spravochniki XVII veka', *Istoricheskii Arkhiv* 5 (1950) 74-165

K.N. Serbina, *Kniga bol'shomu chertezhu*, Moscow, 1950

P.P. Pekarskii, *Nauka i literaura v Rossii pri Petre Velikom*, St Petersburg, 1862, vol. 1, p. 201

Liudmila Sukina

Nikita Zotov

Nikita Moiseevich Zotov

DATE OF BIRTH   About 1644
PLACE OF BIRTH   Moscow
DATE OF DEATH   December 1717-January 1718
PLACE OF DEATH   Uncertain

BIOGRAPHY

Nikita Moiseevich Zotov, the son of a *duma* clerk, became the personal secretary and financial advisor to Tsar Peter I (r. 1682-1725). Relatively well educated for his time, he began as a clerk in the tax department, where he became known for his knowledge of the Bible. Around 1677, he was selected as tutor to the five-year-old tsarevich Peter Alekseevich. Zotov proved to be a skilful instructor, and combined lessons on writing, religion and history with amusement and an abundant supply of picture-books with engravings, woodcuts and maps. Although not a scholar, Nikita Moiseevich instilled a love of learning in the young Peter. The future tsar, in turn, developed a deep affection for his tutor and, for as long as Zotov lived, the two were nearly always together.

In August 1680, Peter's half-brother, Tsar Fyodor III (r. 1676-82), sent Zotov on a major mission to conclude an armistice with Khan Murad Giray of Crimea and the Ottoman Sultan Mehmed IV (r. 1648-87). The negotiations culminated in the Treaty of Bakhchisarai of 1681, which brought an end to the Russian-Ottoman war of 1676-81 and designated the River Dnieper as the demarcation line between the two empires. As a member of Tsar Peter's inner circle, Zotov participated in the torture and execution of the *streltsy* (musketeers) regiments in 1689. During the Azov campaign in 1695-6, he managed the tsar's travelling chancellery. In 1701, he became director of financial affairs of the privy chancellery, and in 1703 he was among the elite selected to supervise the foundation of St Petersburg. The recipient of numerous gifts from the ruling family, he was named a count in 1710-11 and awarded the titles privy councillor and general-president of the privy chancellery.

Many of the primary sources on Zotov's life recount the tsar's so-called all-mad, all-jesting, all-drunken assembly, where Nikita Moiseevich acquired the titles 'prince-pope', 'great sovereign' and 'most holy patriarch', along with a suite of mock priests, deacons and nuns. One famous story concerns the tsar's decision to force the 70-year-old Zotov to marry a young widow. In 1715, the wedding took place in St Petersburg during a masquerade, described by the German traveller F.C. Weber as an event 'the world never had heard of before'.

Zotov was a beloved companion of Peter, to whom he did not hesitate to air his views, which in turn made others fear him. Zotov's sons served the state with distinction, and in 1803 the family received the title of count from Tsar Alexander I (r. 1801-25).

MAIN SOURCES OF INFORMATION

Primary

F.C. Weber, *The present state of Russia*, vol 1, London, 1722, pp. 89-90

P.N. Krekshin, *Kratkoe opisanie slavnykh i dostopamiatnykh del Imperatora Petra Velikogo*, St Petersburg, 1788

'Zapiski Zheliabuzhskago i Krekshina', in I.P. Sakharov, *Zapiski russkikh liudei, sobytiia vremen' Petra Velikogo*, St Petersburg, 1841

N. Murzakevich (ed.), *Stateinyi spisok stol'nika Vasiliia Tiapkina i d'iaka Nikity Zotova, posol'stva v Krym v 1680 gody, dlia zakliucheniia Bakchisaraiskogo dogovora*, Odessa, 1850

A.A. Preobrazhenskii et al., *Pis'ma i bumagi imperatora Petra velikogo*, 11 vols, St Petersburg, 1887-1907, vols 1, 2, 10, 11/1, 11/2

Just Juel, 'Iz zapisok datskogo poslannika Iusta Iulia', *Russkii Arkhiv* 30 (1892), pp. 21-2

Secondary

E.A. Zitzer, *The transfigured kingdom. Sacred parody and charismatic authority at the court of Peter the Great*, Ithaca NY, 2004

M.M. Bogoslovskii, *Petr I. Materialy dlia biografii*, Moscow, vol. 1, 1940, pp. 34-7, 55-6

M.M. Bogoslovskii, 'Detstvo Petra velikogo', *Russkaia Starina* 1 (1917) 27-9

S. Liubimov, art. 'Zotovy', in S.V. Liubimov (ed.), *Opyt istoricheskikh rodoslovii. Gundorovy, Zhizhemskie, Nesvitskie, Sibirskie, Zotovy i Ostermany*, Petrograd, 1915, 80-90

N. Murzakevich, 'Introduction', in Murzakevich (ed.), *Stateinyi spisok stol'nika Vasiliia Tiapkina i d'iaka Nikity Zotova*, iii-vi

B. Korsakova, art. 'Zotov, Nikita Moiseevich', *Russkii biograficheskii slovar'*, vol. 7, St Petersburg, 1897, 476-81

N.P. Pavlov-Sil'vanskii, art. 'Zotov, Nikita Moiseevich', *Entsiklopedicheskii slovar'. Brokgauza i Efrona*, vol. 12a, St Petersburg, 1894, 688

WORKS ON CHRISTIAN-MUSLIM RELATIONS

Stateinyi spisok stol'nika Vasiliia Tiapkina i d'iaka Nikity Zotova, posol'stva v Krym v 1680 gody

'The official journal of stol'nik Vasilii Tiapkin and d'iak Nikita Zotov, embassy to Crimea in 1680'

DATE   1680-1
ORIGINAL LANGUAGE   Russian

DESCRIPTION

This work is Zotov's account of his journey across the Pontic steppe and his negotiations with Khan Murad Giray in Crimea. His embassy included Vasilii M. Tiapkin, the Russian ambassador to Poland, and Semen Rakov-ich, an envoy of Ivan Samoilovich, the pro-Russian *hetman* of left-bank Ukraine. The talks formed the basis for the Treaty of Bakhchisarai, which brought an end to the Russian-Ottoman war of 1676-81. The published edition of the journal is 284 pages long, while the manuscript consists of 335 notebook pages written in four different hands and stitched together in a small binding. Zotov signed each page of the manuscript and made numerous corrections and revisions. Direct references to Christian-Muslim relations are abundant, though these are mainly descriptive accounts of the ways in which the local population kept a balance between min-gling together and maintaining differences based on belief. There are no accounts of Muslim religious teachings, and no signs of any direct criti-cisms or disparagement of Islam.

The journal covers the period from 15 August 1680 to 4 June 1681, with a postscript dated 25 December 1681. It begins with Zotov's trip from Moscow south-west to Tula, Orel, Kursk and Sumi, where he met Tiap-kin and Rakovich, accompanied by Cossack troops. On 25 September, Crimean Tatar messengers arrived with letters from the khan guarantee-ing safe passage. Zotov remarks that the Tatars had recently devastated the town of Valki, enslaving many thousands of Orthodox Christians. People in Valki greeted him in tears, and Zotov assured them that the tsar would be told of their suffering. As he travelled south-west, Zotov noted the apprehension of Crimean and Nogai Tatars. He praised the natural resources of the Zaporozhian Sech and emphasised its advan-tages for Russia. The text includes descriptions of Muslim dwellings and the fortifications of Perekop, where the Muscovites met with Tatar com-manders.

The embassy entered Crimea on 20 October, and Zotov did not feel welcome when passing Muslim villages. Tatar officials delayed his request for a formal audience with the khan. In late October, Zotov recorded the setting in Bakhchisarai, where meetings with the khan's representatives took place. After the opening formalities, the Russian legation made statements about past agreements and an end to hostilities. Both sides made claims about population, borders and recent events. Religious boundaries were described in geographical terms, and the Muscovites supplied a European map of the region with place-names in Latin and Polish.

Cordial moments occurred, but generally the negotiations were difficult. Nevertheless, Khan Murad Giray sought to limit conflict with Muscovy and, on 26 November, he invited the embassy to the palace. The khan's emissaries insisted that the River Dnieper must be the boundary because no concessions could be given where the troops of the sultan had once trod. The Russian delegates remained firm in their demands and they were detained while awaiting a response from the sultan. On 3 January, the sides agreed to a 20-year armistice. The sultan and khan formally acknowledged Kiev and left-bank Ukraine as Muscovite possessions. Two Russian nobles incarcerated in the Crimean fortress, Vasilii B. Sheremetev and Andrei G. Romodanovskii, were released under the agreement, which included clauses about Cossacks, Nogais, Kipchaks, Tatars and other populations in the wilderness of the right bank, a buffer zone between states at the turn of the century, and the tribute that Moscow would pay the khan.

Once the talks were concluded, the Muscovites visited the village of Marino, where they viewed a miracle-working icon of the Holy Mother. Zotov's travel-log contains material about the other members of the Russian mission and the final diplomatic exchanges in Crimea. On 21 March, the legation returned to the Zaporozhian Sech, where they were welcomed by Cossacks. On his journey north back to Moscow, Zotov took note of churches and recorded that clergy met the mission with crosses and holy water, while the population greeted them with joy, love and tears in all the towns of Ukraine (Malorossiia). While he was recording the arrival of a letter from the sultan in Turkish emphasising peace and good relations, Zotov emphasised the need for the religion of the ruled to be that of the ruler. The final passages of the journal relate the return to Moscow and the payment for the embassy.

SIGNIFICANCE

Zotov's journal provides the main record of a landmark treaty in 17th-century relations between two major Christian and Islamic empires. It contains invaluable material for political, diplomatic and military history, and the description of civilian populations illuminates the complexity of these borderland encounters. The Russian-Ottoman war ended on terms advantageous to Moscow, and the tsar achieved his primary objective of the war: the protection of Kiev and the left bank. Khan Murad Giray played a crucial role in subsequently inducing Sultan Mehmet IV to ratify these same terms.

Zotov's notes contain a great deal of geographical and ethnographic material, and the embassy provided important logistical information for subsequent Russian travellers to the region. The text also reveals that legations such as that of Zotov paved the way for the Russian state to continue its expansion across the steppe and towards the Black Sea. An aggressive Russian policy of colonisation and fortification followed.

PUBLICATIONS

The current location of the MS of the journal is uncertain. According to Murzakevich's Introduction (p. vi), in 1850 it was in the library of the President of the Odessan Society of History and Antiquity named after Prince Mikhail Semenovich Vorontsov. It may now be in St Petersburg, Odessa or Moscow, but this has not been verified.

>N. Murzakevich (ed.), *Stateinyi spisok stol'nika Vasiliia Tiapkina i d'iaka Nikity Zotova, posol'stva v Krym v 1680 gody, dlia zakliucheniia Bakchisaraiskogo dogovora*, Odessa, 1850; 10079 (digitised version available through runivers.ru)

STUDIES

>B. Boeck, *Imperial boundaries. Cossack communities and empire-building in the age of Peter the Great*, Cambridge, 2009, pp. 84-5

>B.L. Davies, *Warfare, state and society on the Black Sea steppe, 1500-1700*, London, 2007, pp. 170-2, 176-80, 190, 193-4

>V.E. Vozgrin, *Istoricheskie sud'by krymskikh tatar*, Moscow, 1992, pp. 229-30

>A.W. Fisher, *Crimean Tatars*, Stanford CA, 1978, pp. 52-3

>Bogoslovskii, *Petr I*, vol. 1, pp. 34-7

>R. Nisbet Bain, *The first Romanovs, 1613-1725. A history of Moscovite civilization and the rise of modern Russia under Peter the Great and his forerunners*, New York, 1905, pp. 208, 220

>Murzakevich, 'Introduction'

Lucien Frary

Iov

DATE OF BIRTH   Second half of the 17th century
PLACE OF BIRTH   Unknown
DATE OF DEATH   1721
PLACE OF DEATH   Khutynskii monastery, Novgorod

BIOGRAPHY

Iov was a monk at the Chudov Monastery in the Kremlin, Moscow, later becoming archdeacon, archmonk, teacher, writer and translator. From about 1680 to 1690 he attended the school run by Ioanniki and Sofronii Likhud, and in 1694 he spent a few months as instructor at the Slavic-Greek-Latin Academy. In 1696, Iov fell into disgrace and was sent to the Novospasskii Monastery, where he claimed to be living in the poorest and most miserable conditions ('Proshenie', p. 143), writing a petition (*Proshenie*) to the tsars to request a subsidy. In 1700, he moved to the Solovetskii Monastery, further to the north.

In 1713, his namesake Iov, the Novgorod metropolitan, sent for him to organise the episcopal school, together with Ioannikii Likhud. He then became its director in 1716, although by then he was suffering from old age and weakness. In 1718, he was admitted to the Khutynskii monastery infirmary, where he died in 1721.

For a Russian of his time, Iov was highly educated, knowing Latin, as well as ancient and modern Greek. After his death, 20 manuscripts and 85 printed books were found among his possessions, including some in languages such as Hebrew, German and Italian.

The monasteries where Iov initially lived, Chudov and Novospasskii, were closely associated with the Romanov dynasty, with Chudov situated in the Kremlin near the palace, and Novospasskii being the dynastic burial place of the Romanovs.

MAIN SOURCES OF INFORMATION

Primary

MS St Petersburg, Gosudarstvennaia publichnaia biblioteka – Q.I.48

F. Polikarpov, 'Istoricheskoe izsvestie o Moskovskoi Akademii', in N.I. Novikov (ed.), *Drevniaia Rossiiskaia Vivliofika*, Moscow, 1771², vol. 16, p. 298

Iov, 'Proshenie monakha Iova k tsariam Ioannu i Petru Alekseevicham', *Strannik* 1 (1861) 143-5

Secondary

M.D. Kagan, art. 'Iov', in D.S. Likhachev (ed.), *Slovar' knizhnikov i knizhnosti Drevnei Rusi*, St Petersburg, 1993, vol. 3, part 2, pp. 82-5 (contains additional secondary literature)

E.M. Prilezhaev, 'Novgorodskie eparkhial'nye shkoly v Petrovskuiu epokhu', *Khristianskii Chitatel'* 1 (1877) 338, 343-7

WORKS ON CHRISTIAN-MUSLIM RELATIONS

Beseda molebnaia o blagochestivom gosudare i o pobede na vragi
'Te Deum for the pious ruler and for victory over the enemy'

DATE   April 1695
ORIGINAL LANGUAGE   Old Russian

DESCRIPTION

Iov wrote his *Beseda molebnaia* in April 1695, in anticipatory praise of Peter the Great's victory over the Ottomans at Azov, which was to take place in the summer of that year. Consisting of 44 manuscript pages, it is written in prose and syllabic verses, and is composed of 15 parts. The first two consist of a petition to the former Metropolitan Iov of Novgorod, now archimandrite at the Monastery St Sergius, asking him to pray for the author.

The text ends with four prayers asking God to crush the Muslims, here referred to as the sons of Hagar, and to help the tsar. In the final prayer, Iov, using metaphorical terms, asks God to punish the enemy by, for example, darkening their eyes so that they cannot see, petrifying their ears so they cannot hear.

The original text is extant in only one manuscript, which is not easily accessible. The description given here is based on more widely available secondary material, which provides only a very small portion of the work.

SIGNIFICANCE

Iov's *Beseda molebnaia* is a rare work by an intellectual in Muscovite Rus' on the topic of Peter the Great's victory in Azov, clearly also flatteringly anticipatory. It derives significance from the author's proximity to the ruling family, as evidenced by his biography. Although it was undoubtedly written – as was his petition – to secure himself a good income within the state apparatus, it also provides a new genre in Old Russian writing.

Iov resorts to well-known clerical stereotypes in referring to the Muslims as the sons of Hagar, although here employing these stereotypes in a text written in his personal capacity rather than as an official statement of the church. The work is also notable for the colourful language he employs in his pleas to God to punish the tsar's foes.

The extent to which his polemics differ from the standard Orthodox condemnation of Muslims, and the uniqueness of his argument, cannot be assessed without a thorough investigation of the text of the original manuscript, which at present remains a desideratum.

PUBLICATIONS

MS St Petersburg, Rossiiskaia natsional'naia biblioteka – Sofiiskoe sobranie, no. 1514 (listed in P.M. Stroev, *Bibliologicheskii slovar' i chernovye k nemu materialy*, St Petersburg, 1882, repr. Leningrad, 1966, pp. 145-6, includes a small section of the text)

STUDIES

Kagan, art. 'Iov'

Cornelia Soldat

Povest' o zhenitbe Ivana Groznogo na Marii Temriukovna

Povest' o zhenit'be Ivana Groznogo na Marii Temriukovne

'The tale of the marriage of Ivan the Terrible and Mariia Temriukovna'

DATE   End of the 17th century or early 18th century
ORIGINAL LANGUAGE   Russian

DESCRIPTION

Only one manuscript copy of this text exists: part of a miscellany from the late 17th or early 18th century (judging from watermarks and other paleographical features). The *Tale* consists of 15 folios, while most published editions are approximately six pages in length. Its paleographic and textological features, together with its belles-lettrist style, have suggested to R.K. Rosovetskii, the leading scholar on the *Tale*, that it was produced in the provinces, perhaps in Yaroslavl or Astrakhan (Rosovetskii, 'Povest'' [1989], p. 585). The work is entirely fictional, with numerous factual inaccuracies and imagined scenes and texts, including correspondence between Ivan IV and the Muslim Shahghali Khan (Shakhalei) of Kasimov, and between Ivan IV and his future bride, Mariia Temriukovna. The *Tale* clearly draws upon a number of other literary sources, including the *Pesni o Kostriuke* ('Songs of Kostriuk'), the Serbian 'Alexandrine' epics and the *Kazanskaia istoriia* ('History of Kazan').

The *Tale* opens in the year 7072, or 1564, with Tsar Ivan IV (r. 1533-84) sending Khan Shakhalei of Kasimov at the head of a joint Muscovite and Kazan force to capture the city of Astrakhan, located in the Volga River delta. According to the *Tale*, Astrakhan is ruled by the Muslim *murza* Tevriug Iun'gich (Temir-Guki, or, as better known in Russian sources, Temriuk Aidarovich), who is able to withstand the siege of his city. Shakhalei decides to send a letter to Tevriug, urging him to submit to Ivan IV as he himself had earlier. Tevriug responds that he is willing to do so, but only if Ivan agrees to marry his 'only daughter, the beautiful and kind Mariia Tevriugovna'.

Buoyed by the prospects of a successful end to the campaign against Astrakhan, Shakhkalei writes a letter to Ivan, sending it with envoys who arrive in Moscow on Easter Sunday and appear before the tsar and his uncle (by marriage), Nikita Ivanovich Romanov. At the end of the service, during which the tsar receives holy communion, he retires to his palace with his uncle and reads the letter. Ivan is receptive, even pleased, by the idea of the marriage and the surrender of the city to him, but asks in his reply to Shakhalei for a portrait of the young Mariia to be made and sent to him first.

On learning the tsar's demand, Tevriug commissions a portrait, which is completed in three days. When Shakhalei and his highest-ranking commanders see it, they are stunned at Mariia's beauty. Tevriug then suggests that Shakhalei meet his daughter in person but he resists, thinking that no one should behold the young maiden before the tsar does. After some urging, Shakhalei finally agrees to meet her, and affirms that she has 'beauty worthy of our sovereign, Tsar Ivan Vasil'evich'. The portrait is placed in a chest along with an ornamental handkerchief (*shirinka*) sewn by Mariia herself, with gold thread, precious stones and pearls.

When the chest arrives in Moscow, Ivan hurries to open it. He looks at the portrait and is stunned at Mariia's beauty, telling his uncle, N.I. Romanov, 'Do you see how beautiful she is? There were more than 100 beautiful maidens, the daughters of my courtiers, at the bride-show (*v vybore*) but not one is even half as beautiful and pleasing as she is.' He also examines the handkerchief and marvels at its workmanship as a sign of Mariia's character and virtue. Ivan then sends for Metropolitan Filipp, and the two discuss the marriage at length. Finally, the metropolitan blesses the tsar to marry, and a banquet and gift exchange take place before the metropolitan returns to his palace.

Ivan then dispatches a large embassy to Astrakhan made up of many of the great magnates (*velmozhi*) of the court dressed in the finest court costumes. The embassy stops first in Kazan to pick up more servants, as well as soldiers and arms to escort the embassy to Astrakhan, which still lies in the hands of the Muslim *murza*, Tevriug.

After weeks of travelling by land and by barge down the Volga River, the embassy, now headed by Shakhalei, arrives at Astrakhan and ceremonially enters the city. They are met by Tevriug, who inquires after the tsar's health and announces that he will quit the city, retiring to an estate located on the other side of the Iaik River. Members of the tsar's embassy enter Tevriug's palace and meet Mariia, who is arrayed in a magnificent royal costume that illuminates the entire hall and whose beauty is unmatched among women. The Muscovites fall to the ground before her, and then present her with a diadem (*venets*) and ring. She is attended by her mother and brother, Mastriuk. Mariia then orders three barges to be fitted for her trip up the Volga to Kazan, which would be the first leg of her journey to Moscow. All her personal possessions and what amounts to her dowry are placed in the barges. Mariia bids a tearful farewell to her parents, boards one of the barges, and departs from Astrakhan for the last time.

Shakhalei sends an envoy ahead to Moscow to report on the happenings in Astrakhan. Ivan receives the news of the city's surrender and the oaths of allegiance of its inhabitants to him with enormous joy, because 'without bloodshed the Astrakhan khanate (*tsarstvo*) has pledged itself, and joined itself, to Muscovy'. He is also pleased to learn that Mariia has left Astrakhan and, after a consultation with Metropolitan Filipp, decides that Mariia should be baptised in Kazan en route to Moscow by Metropolitan (*sic*) Gurii of Kazan. Ivan instructs Gurii to construct a new chapel on the water's edge where the baptism will take place, and he further orders that none of those accompanying her on this journey should enter the chapel, but only Gurii, who will perform the baptism himself. Ivan warns Gurii to guard against any possible conspiracy or evildoing that might foil the marriage plans. When Gurii receives the tsar's instructions, he rejoices and gathers the leaders of the city and reads Ivan's letter to them. Workmen and craftsmen begin construction of the chapel immediately.

Here, at the climax of the narrative, Mariia is baptised. The *Tale* pauses to mark the moment by situating it (incorrectly, as it turns out) chronologically in Ivan's reign: in the eighth year (*sic*) of his accession, in the fourth year of his taking Kazan (*sic*), at the age of 20 (*sic*). Mariia is said to be 19 years old. The date, according to the *Tale*, is 22 July.

In a letter sent from Ivan to Mariia, he tells her to agree to the baptism by Archbishop Gurii and to obey him as a father. Ivan urges her to 'rejoice, for you go from one kingdom to another kingdom'. Shakhalei reads Ivan's letter to Mariia, who 'having heard the letter, rejoiced greatly, that she is to be baptised'. In a separate letter, the tsar warns his Muslim servant Shakhalei on pain of death to ensure that every detail of this journey and the baptism go off without a hitch.

When Mariia's party arrives in Kazan, they are greeted with a cannon salute so massive that the smoke from it 'obscured the sun' and so loud that no one could hear anyone speak. Mariia is overwhelmed by the size of the tsar's retinue sent to receive her and marvels at the power the tsar must command. Arriving at the newly-constructed chapel, she is greeted by a throng of townsfolk, but enters the chapel alone with Gurii, as instructed, saying, 'Make me a Christian, honourable father, for such my soul desires.' She is baptised in private, with no one inside the chapel to witness her nakedness as she enters the baptismal font. There is a banquet and gift exchange afterwards, and as she is escorted back to her barge for the remainder of her journey to Moscow, Mariia adapts the words of the tax collector in the Gospel: 'Father, great Archbishop Gurii! Pray to God for me a sinner!' (Luke 18:13). Gurii presents Mariia with gem-encrusted icons and offers his blessing on her. She then departs for Moscow.

On her arrival in Moscow, Mariia is immediately taken to the tsar's palace, escorted by the wives of his senior courtiers (*velmozhi*). Entering the hall, she venerates the holy icons, turns and prostrates herself before the tsar, and is seated on the throne by his side. The tsar is enthralled by her beauty and commands the entire assembly to bow down before her. The couple change into their finest royal regalia, and Metropolitan Filipp arrives to bless their marriage, saying to the tsar that he has 'gained a mate equal to his own majesty'. They all then go in procession to the Dormition (Uspenskii) Cathedral, where the couple are betrothed and crowned, followed by a divine liturgy where they both receive holy communion. After the service, a procession led by the metropolitan returns to the tsar's palace, where he serves a *moleben* (intercessory prayer service). At the palace, the tsar distributes gifts to his court, including the metropolitan, and he accepts the 'treasure' brought by Mariia in her barges. Shakhalei is richly rewarded for his dutiful service by being placed to rule over Kazan and Astrakhan. The marriage is the beginning of a shining moment in Ivan's reign, when 'the Tsar and Grand Prince Ivan Vasil'evich began to rule justly with his Tsaritsa and Grand Princess Mariia Tevriugovna'.

However, according to the last lines of the *Tale*, this did not last very long: 'And Ivan and his wife lived together in this way for one year and six months. She was given poison by traitors, by the tableman (*stolnik*) Vasilii Khomutov and his co-conspirators. He was killed, thrown into a boiling cauldron, and his family and all their wives and children were hanged.'

Very few of the details in this tale align with historical facts and chronology. The inaccuracies begin in the first line of the text. By 1564, the year in which the events of the *Tale* take place, Astrakhan had been part of Muscovy for eight years, having been conquered (not unified via a dynastic marriage) in 1556. Shakhalei (Shahghali Khan) was Khan of Kasimov in 1564, as the *Tale* reports (he ruled on and off in Kasimov and Kazan between 1516 and 1567), but Tevriug (Temriuk/Temir-Guki) was never the ruler (*murza*) of Astrakhan. The last khan of Astrakhan was Dervish Ali (d. c. 1558), and Tevriug was a ruler among the Circassian people of Kabardia on the northern slopes of the Caucasus Mountains. All of the correspondence mentioned and quoted in the *Tale* is entirely fictitious. Tevriug's daughter was named Kochenei, and was known as Mariia only after her baptism. The claim Tevriug makes in the *Tale* that she is his only (*edinorodnuiu*) daughter is untrue: he had one other known, older daughter. Mariia/Kochenei was baptised in the Cathedral of the Dormition in Moscow on 20 July 1561 (not 22 July 1564, in Kazan) by Metropolitan Makarii (not Archbishop Gurii of Kazan). She had been brought to Moscow before 7 July 1561, as a potential second bride for the tsar (his first wife, Anastasiia Iur'eva, had died on 7 August 1560), and was installed in the Terem (the female apartments of the Kremlin palace complex), where Ivan was able to view her from afar. He selected her to be his bride and married her after her conversion to Orthodoxy, on 21 August 1561. The *Tale* suggests that a bride-show had been arranged for Ivan's second wedding and that Mariia/Kochenei outshone all the other contestants, but no evidence survives for a bride show in 1560 or 1561. The wedding was performed by Metropolitan Makarii, not Metropolitan Filipp, who was metropolitan later, from 1566 to 1568 (and was murdered in 1569). Archbishop (inconsistently also called in the *Tale* 'metropolitan') Gurii of Kazan, who, according to the *Tale*, baptised Mariia/Kochenei in Kazan, was archbishop from 1555 to 1563, that is, before the events described and dated in the *Tale*.

The *Tale* significantly mentions a Romanov relative of the tsar, 'Nikita Ivanovich Romanov', who is certainly the boyar Nikita Romanovich Iur'ev, the brother of Ivan's first wife, Anastasiia. The prominent position assigned to this royal relative is probably a reflection of the fact that, by the time the *Tale* was composed around the end of the 17th century, the Romanovs had become the ruling dynasty in Russia. Nikita was the grandfather of the first Romanov tsar, Mikhail Feodorovich (r. 1613-45).

The portrait of Mariia/Kochenei is also an unlikely element in the narrative. Mariia and her father were Muslims, and Islam forbids the creation of depictions of people and other sentient beings, especially God and Muḥammad, but the prohibition applies generally to all people.

In addition, portraits were unknown in Muscovite matrimonial negotiations in the 16th and 17th centuries, though not for doctrinal reasons. Descriptions of bridal candidates from around European Russia were used instead, written and sent to Moscow by envoys who had been dispatched to the provinces to find contestants for the tsars' bride-shows. Portraits were never included with these reports (though extensive physical descriptions, medical histories, and genealogies were), and only became commonplace in Russia (as elsewhere) from the 18th century.

Finally, Ivan's marriage to Mariia lasted longer than the year and a half reported in the *Tale*. Mariia died on 1 September 1569, eight years after she and the tsar married. The union produced only one known child, Vasilii, who died in May 1563, shortly after his birth. It was not, by some accounts, a particularly happy union, and Mariia in both contemporary and later sources is depicted as a poor influence on her husband, and as possessing a savage and cruel temperament. The conspiracy led by Vasilii Khomutov mentioned in the *Tale* is entirely fictitious, though Ivan did believe that Mariia (as well as two of his other wives) had been victims of poisonings by his enemies at court.

SIGNIFICANCE
The Tale of the marriage of Ivan the Terrible and Mariia Temriukovna is a well-known and important example of belletristic literature of the 18th century, with textual and literary ties to other important epics and tales of the 17th and 18th centuries. It therefore occupies a central place in the literary history of the period and in the development of the literary Russian language in the decades following the reign of Peter the Great (1682-1725).

The *Tale* also provides important insights into Christian-Muslim relations in the 18th century. First, diplomatic and dynastic relations between Muscovy and its Muslim neighbours are portrayed as operating on a level similar to relations between Russia and the states of western Europe. Embassies travel back and forth, correspondence is exchanged, treaties are negotiated and honoured. Muscovy in the *Tale* may have been on the war path against Astrakhan, but is otherwise portrayed as acting nobly and honourably towards the ruler and inhabitants of the city. A bloodless, negotiated annexation is preferred over a war of pillaging and looting. Astrakhan is an equal, and Mariia is reminded in the text that she should 'rejoice, for you go from one kingdom to another kingdom'.

Second, Mariia is deemed worthy of Ivan because of both her royal background and her stunning beauty. She is made the daughter of

a Chinggisid ruler of Astrakhan, a member of one of the most important lineages in all Eurasia, even though in reality her father was neither Chinggisid nor the ruler of Astrakhan, nor even a resident of the
city or the khanate. Her beauty is also vital to the narrative action.
She is described as having 'beauty worthy of our sovereign, Tsar Ivan
Vasil'evich', which is to say that her looks were as much a qualification
to be tsaritsa as anything else, including her illustrious background. In
Mariia, beauty and pedigree co-mingle to make her uniquely suited to
be a Muscovite tsaritsa.

Third, religion is no obstacle to this match nor even a factor in Muscovite diplomacy in the Pontic Steppe. Ivan IV did not require Shakhalei
to convert before he accepted him as his servant, even entrusting him,
a Muslim ruler of the subservient Kasimov khanate, with the command
of a Muscovite and Kazan-combined army charged with the mission of
conquering Astrakhan. Nor does Ivan require Tevriug and his family to
abandon their Muslim faith and convert to Orthodoxy as part of the deal
that brings Astrakhan into the Muscovite tsardom. Here the *Tale* correctly depicts the practical-mindedness of Muscovy's rulers – Ivan IV,
and his ancestors and successors – about interactions with their Muslim
neighbours, which does not, in the main, privilege Orthodoxy over het-
erodoxy or Christianity over Islam. Orthodox Muscovy both warred and
allied with Catholic (Lithuania, Poland) and Muslim (Kazan, Kasimov,
Crimea, Astrakhan) neighbours across the Pontic Steppe. Diplomacy
trumped religion in the west Eurasian space.

Even so, conversion is a prerequisite for the marriage between Ivan
IV and Mariia. She must convert from Islam to Christianity in order for
her to participate in the Christian sacrament of marriage and play the
role assigned to tsaritsas in the 16th century: that of pious and faithful
intercessors to heaven for their royal husbands and children. In fact, it
is so fully assumed in the *Tale* that Mariia must convert that the subject
is never even brought up as a matter of debate. Mariia (and her father)
accept the need for her conversion without comment or complaint, and
indeed, Mariia is depicted as fully desiring her conversion: she 'rejoiced
greatly, that she is to be baptised', and pleads with Archbishop Gurii to
'make me a Christian [...] for such my soul desires'. Any and all expressions of regret or resistance at the thought of leaving the faith of her
childhood and converting to Orthodox Christianity are entirely absent
from the *Tale*. Nor is Mariia's sad death attributed to her non-Russian
or Muslim background. Her murder is depicted as a case of court politics, the resistance of one courtier and his faction against the tsar, and

therefore an episode in the history of Ivan's tumultuous reign rather than an example of inter-confessional hostility.

PUBLICATIONS

MS St Petersburg, Russian National Library (Rossiiskaia natstional'naia biblioteka, St Petersburg) – Collection of the Society of Ancient Literature (Sobranie Obshchestva liubitelei drevnei pis'mennosti, OLDP), Q.155, fols 204-19 (late 17ᵗʰ or early 18ᵗʰ century)

S.K. Rosovetskii (ed.), 'Povest' o zhenit'be Ivana Groznogo na Marii Temriukovne', *Pamiatniki kul'tury. Novye otkrytiia. Ezhegodnik 1975*, Moscow, 1976, 27-37 (text on pp. 31-7)

S.K. Rosovetskii (ed.), 'Povest' o zhenit'be Ivana Groznogo na Marii Temriukovne', in R.P. Dmitrieva and D.S. Likhachev (eds), *Pamiatniki literatury drevnei Rusi. XVII vek. Kniga vtoraia*, Moscow, 1989, 5-15 (commentary on pp. 585-7)

S.K. Rosovetskii (ed.), 'Povest' o zhenit'be Ivana Groznogo na Marii Temriukovne', in D.S. Likhacheva (ed.), *Biblioteka literatury drevnei Rusi*, St Petersburg, 2010, vol. 16, 21-30 (commentary on pp. 544-6)

STUDIES

A.V. Shunkov, 'Dokumental'nyi tekst v literaturnoi traditsii perekhodnogo vremeni (k voprosu ob evoliutsii dokumental'nykh zhanrov v istoriko-literaturnykh usloviiakh vtoroi poloviny XVII v.)', *Vestnik Tomskogo gosudarstvennogo universiteta* 388 (2014) 42-6

S.K. Rosovetskii, 'Odno iz stilevykh techenii russkoi belletristiki vtoroi poloviny XVII – nachala XVII v. i provintsial'nyi knizhnik Fedor Zlobin', in R.P. Dmitrieva and D.S. Likhachev (eds), *Knizhnye tsentry drevnei Rusi, XVII vek. Raznye aspekty issledovaniia*, St Petersburg, 1994, 315-79

S.K. Rosovetskii, 'Ustnaia proza XVI-XVII vv. ob Ivane Groznom – pravitele', *Russkii fol'klor* 20 (1981) 71-95 (repr. as 'Oral prose of the 16*th*-17*th* centuries about Ivan the Terrible as a ruler', *Soviet Anthropology and Archeology* 23 (1984) 3-49)

Rosovetskii (ed.), 'Povest' o zhenit'be Ivana Groznogo na Marii Temriukovne', 1976

Kh.M. Loparev, *Opisanie rukopisei imperatorskogo Obshchestva liubitelei drevnei pis'mennosti*, St Petersburg, 1893, vol. 2, p. 227

Russell Martin

Povest' o tsare Vasilii Konstantinoviche

'The tale of Tsar Vasilii Konstantinovich'

DATE   Unknown; probably the end of the 17th or first half of the 18th century

ORIGINAL LANGUAGE   Russian

DESCRIPTION

Povest' (*skazanie*) *o tsare Vasilii Konstantinoviche* ('The tale of Tsar Vasilii Konstantinovich', who is named after the city of Kostentin) is by an unknown author. It is relatively short, consisting of only seven handwritten pages, and has the flavour of a fable or legend. It is about the dramatic struggle between Christians and Muslims in the former Byzantine territories, though all the characters, events and facts are fictional. Thus, while Tsargrad was a name given in Russia for Constantinople, in the Tale these names designate two separate cities, Constantinople, the seat of the Christian Tsar Vasilii Konstantinovich, and Tsargrad, the seat of the Turkish sovereign Saltan Saltanovich. The author employs fantastical images and writes in a poetic folk style, though historians of literature assert that the story is not an oral folk tale that has been written down but the work of an individual who was familiar with book culture.

The Tale connects the fall of Constantinople to Vasilii Konstantinovich's betrayal. In order to hold on to power, he agrees to abandon Christianity and surrender his city to the ruler of the 'infidels', who is named Dolmat Evseevich and is acting in agreement with a khan. However, Prince Konstantin, the Christian son of Tsar Vasilii, defeats and kills the Turkish ruler Saltan and liberates both Constantinople and Tsargrad. Two former criminals, Persha and Ivashka, assist the prince, risking their lives in the process.

In its detailed description of the diplomatic and military processes employed in relations between Christian and Muslim rulers, the Tale sets a realistic tone. For instance, Prince Konstantin bestows the rank of boyar on Persha and Ivashka before he sends them to the Turkish ruler, because only high-status people could act as ambassadors. Although Tsar Saltan behaves rudely towards them, even throwing his shoe at them, the

Christian ambassadors maintain their dignity and in what they say firmly uphold the Christian faith and their sovereign's interests. In contrast, the Turkish ambassadors at Prince Konstantin's court are portrayed as servile and deceitful, showing reverence for the image of Christ that is there in order to gain the trust of the Christians.

Tsarina Irina and Prince Konstantin are deceived by the Turkish ambassadors' flattering speeches, and send to Tsargrad an image of the crucified Christ that is greatly revered in Constantinople. In Tsargrad, its head is cut off, put on a stake and set up in one of the squares, while the two ambassadors Persha and Ivashka are thrown into prison for refusing to convert to Islam. But God hears the prayers of the faithful Christians and appoints Prince Konstantin to be his avenger.

An angel appears before Konstantin and gives him a magic horse with the head of an ox and a star between its eyes – both symbols of Christ. He comes to Tsargrad and single-handedly defeats the Turks, frees his ambassadors, and removes the head of Christ from the stake. Tsar Saltan begs for mercy, saying: 'I have sinned before your Lord God!', but driven by Christ's will Konstantin cuts off his head. He also cuts off the heads of the Turkish idols, that are called Iraklii and Bokhmet.

Konstantin discovers in Saltan's palace Tsar Dolmat's wife and daughter. Charmed by the princess's beauty, he marries her and adds Dolmat's kingdom to his own.

The purpose of the Tale was to use a legendary form to tell its readers about the origins and essence of the military conflicts between Orthodox Christians and Muslims. The intensity of the Russo-Turkish wars in the era of Tsar Peter I (r. 1682-1725) gave it urgency. It resembles the 'Tale of the capture of Constantinople by the Turks', which was popular in Russia at this time.

SIGNIFICANCE

The plot of the story enshrines the principle that the conflict between Christians and Muslims is irreconcilable. Thus, because Tsar Vasilii Konstantinovich is an apostate who abandoned Christianity in the face of the Muslim threat, he deserves the most severe retribution. His opposites are Tsarina Irina Dmitrievna, Persha and Ivashka, and above all Prince Konstantin, who were ready to defend Jesus Christ and the Christian faith at the cost of their own lives. The Turks and Tatars are godless, while the Turkish ruler Saltan is 'unfaithful and evil-spirited'. His main crime is not capturing cities and killing people but his denial of the Christian God.

The climax of the story illustrates this perfectly: after Saltan's ambassadors bring him Prince Konstantin's image of the crucified Christ, he urges the Christian ambassadors, Persha and Ivashka, to take part in its desecration and accept 'our idols and saints, Rakhliia and Bakhmet'. As a reward, he promises them the domains of Tsar Dalmat and the Tatar khan, but they staunchly maintain loyalty to their faith.

The author emphasises that it is Jesus Christ himself who is active in defence of His own image by choosing pious and brave Konstantin as his instrument and making him invulnerable and powerful. In contrast, the Muslim 'idols and saints' can neither protect themselves nor save Tsar Saltan's life, and none of Saltan's subjects attempts to defend either the ruler or the images. The Tale presents Prince Konstantin's victory over Tsar Saltan as a triumph of Christianity over Islam, an event when 'God our Lord worked a miracle over the godless Turks and Tatars'.

PUBLICATIONS

MS Moscow, Rossiiskaia gosudarstvennaia biblioteka – 236 (Sobranie A.N. Popova), no. 71, pp. 9-15 (1750; part of the collection entitled *Sbornik povestei*, previously located in Muzeinoe sobranie RGB, no. 2432)

V.V. Sipovskii (ed.), *Russkie povesti XVII-XVIII v.*, vol. 63, St Petersburg, 1905, pp. 288-93

D.S. Likhachev and L.A. Dmitriev (eds), *Pamiatniki literatury Drevnei Rusi. XVII vek*, vol. 1, Moscow, 1988, pp. 442-50

D.S. Likhachev, L.A. Dmitriev and N.V. Ponyrko (eds), *Biblioteka literatury Drevnei Rusi*, vol. 15. *XVII vek*, St Petersburg, 2006, pp. 390-4

STUDIES

N.F. Droblenkova, 'Povest' o tsare Vasilii Konstantinoviche', in D.M. Bulanin (ed.), *Slovar' knizhnikov i knizhnosti Drevnei Rusi*, vol. 3, St Petersburg, 1998, 219-21

N.S. Demkova, 'Stilisticheskaia "pestrota" narodnoi belletristiki rubezha XVII-XVIII vekov ("Skazanie o tsare Vasilii Konstantinoviche")', in N.S. Demkova, *Srednevekovaia russkaia literatura. Poetika, interpretatsii, istochniki: sbornik statei*, St Petersburg, 1997, 182-92

N.F. Droblenkova, 'Povest' o tsare Vasilii Konstantinoviche', in *Trudy otdela drevnerusskoi literatury*, vol. 41, Leningrad, 1988, 96-8

M.N. Speranskii, 'Povest' o vziatii Tsar'grada turkami v "Skifskoi istorii" A.Lyzlova (Iz istorii russko-pol'sko-bolgarskikh sviazei na rubezhe

XVII-XVIII vv.)', in M.N. Speranskii, *Iz istorii russko-slavianskikh literaurnykh sviazei. Sbornik statei*, Moscow, 1960, 211-24, p. 227

V.P. Adrianova-Peretts and V.F. Pokrovskaia, *Drevne-russkaia povest'*, vol. 1, Moscow, 1940, pp. 248-9

S.P. Rozanov, 'Retsenziia na knigu V.V. Sipovskogo', in *Izvestiia otdeleniia russkogo iazyka i slovesnosti Imperatorsko Akademii nauk*, vol. 9, kn. 4, St Petersburg, 1904, pp. 272, 277

Liudmila Sukina

Ioann Luk'ianov

DATE OF BIRTH   Second half of the 17th century
PLACE OF BIRTH   Kaluga
DATE OF DEATH   First half of the 18th century
PLACE OF DEATH   Unknown

BIOGRAPHY

Of merchant background, Ioann Luk'ianov was a priest from the *pokrov* of the Mother of God (St Nicholas on the Yellow Sands [*na zheltykh peskakh*]) Church in Moscow, and most possibly, a crypto-Old Believer (that is, belonging to one of the several groups of Russian Orthodox believers who had rejected the reforms of Patriarch Nikon in the mid-17th century and faced various degrees of persecution as a result). According to some scholars, he went to Jerusalem in order to examine the possibility of having a hierarchy of Old Believer bishops installed by Eastern Orthodox arch-hierarchs.

In the late 19th century, M.I. Lileev proposed the identification of Luk'ianov with the Elder (*starets*) Hieromonk Leontii, an Old Believer from the island of Vetka on the Sozh River. Present-day scholars do not necessarily agree on this identification (Kirillina, '*Ocharovannye stranniki*', pp. 27-31; Seemann, *Die altrussische Wallfahrtsliteratur*, 366-8; L.A. Ol'shevskaia and S.N. Travnikov, 'Zhitie i khozhdenie Ioanna Luk'ianova', in Ol'shevskaia, Reshetova and Travnikov, *Khozhdenie v Sviatuiu zemliu*, 396-481, pp. 400-1).

MAIN SOURCES OF INFORMATION

Primary
L.A Ol'shevskaia, A.A. Reshetova and S.N. Travnikov (eds), *Khozhdenie v Sviatuiu zemliu moskovskogo sviashchennika Ioanna Luk'ianova, 1701-1703*, Moscow, 2008, pp. 371-92

Secondary
S.A. Kirillina, '*Ocharovannye stranniki*'. *Arabo-osmanskii mir glazami rossiiskikh palomnikov XVI-XVIII stoletii*, Moscow, 2010, esp. pp. 407-66 (chapter on approaches to Islam)
Ol'shevskaia, Reshetova and Travnikov, *Khozhdenie v Sviatuiu zemliu*

T.G. Stavrou and P.R. Weisensel, *Russian travelers to the Christian East from the twelfth to the twentieth century*, Columbus OH, 1986, pp. 55-7

K.D. Seemann, *Die altrussische Wallfahrtsliteratur. Theorie und Geschichte eines literarischen Genres*, Munich, 1976, pp. 366-76

WORKS ON CHRISTIAN-MUSLIM RELATIONS

Opisanie puti ko sviatomu gradu Ierusalimu Khozhdenie

'Description of the route to the holy city of Jerusalem'

DATE 1701–03

ORIGINAL LANGUAGE Russian

DESCRIPTION

Presented in diary form, Luk'ianov's account (its full title is *Opisanie puti ko sviatomu gradu Ierusalimu ot Moskvy do Kieva, ot Kieva do Volozhskoi zemli, ot Volozhskoi zemli do Dunaia, velikiia reki, i ot Dunaia do Tsaria-grada, i ot Tsaria-grada do sviatogo grada Ierusalima – to vse khozhde-nie morem. Tokmo poltara dni zemleiu. Leta sem tysiach' dveste desiatogo godu mesiatsa dekemvriia v semyinadesiat' den khozhdenie vo Ierusalim s Moskvy startsa Leontiia*, 'Description of the route to the holy city of Jeru-salem from Moscow to Kiev, from Kiev to the Wallachian land, from the Wallachian land to the Danube, the great river, and from the Danube to Constantinople, and from Constantinople to the holy city of Jerusalem. All this itinerary by sea. Only a quarter of the distance by land. In the year 7,210, month of December on the 17th day itinerary to Jerusalem from Moscow of the Elder Leontii') follows the fairly typical tripartite division of pilgrim accounts to Jerusalem: the journey there, the sojourn in Jerusalem and the return trip. Luk'ianov set out in December 1701 and returned in January 1703. He says he spent 14 weeks in Jerusalem. His trip was meant to allow him to see the promised land and as a way of atoning for his many sins.

Scholars usually distinguish between three versions (redactions) of the work. (On the differences between them, see Ol'shevskaia, Reshetova and Travnikov, *Khozhdenie v Sviatuiu zemliu*, pp. 482-533, and especially the conclusions on pp. 530-2.) The present discussion is based on the third redaction.

The most recent publication with commentary is that by Ol'shevskaia, Reshetova and Travnikov, who consider Luk'ianov's account to be an example of what was called in Soviet times 'democratic baroque', an account by a not highly-placed person which exhibits elements of baroque travel literature.

There is no attempt to treat any theological matters in this pilgrim account. Rather, Muslims are present in the form of Turks and Arabs, as the conquerors of Constantinople and the Byzantine Empire, as administrators and guards, as tax and toll collectors, and finally as guides and providers of transport intent on fleecing pilgrims by exploiting their desire to walk where Christ had walked. There is also a marked and emphatic penchant towards detailed criticism of the failings of the co-religionist Greeks, probably a result of the Old Believer leanings of the author.

SIGNIFICANCE

The element of human interaction is more pronounced here than in other pilgrim accounts of the time. Thus, the reader finds more episodes of Muslim-Christian interaction, with much detail and even actual dialogue, sometimes in Turkish in Cyrillic transliteration.

Muslims are regularly referred to as dogs (*sobaki*). Luk'ianov exposes a particularly venomous streak when referring to Arabs, whether they are Muslims or Christians, starting with their external appearance (which he finds frightening) and ending with their everyday and religious practices. That said, there are good Muslims and bad Muslims. A faith such as Islam may be bad and devilish, but certain individuals can exhibit good traits and there are some good Arab Christians. Conversely, Orthodoxy is the only true faith, but there are also good Orthodox and bad Orthodox, the latter normally being the Greeks. (One wonders whether the nature of Luk'ianov's mission led him to highlight the perceived Greek defects.) The Greeks come across as less than stellar: they are money grabbing, they do not follow established practice in their religious services, they have a weaker faith because of their subjection to the Turks, and they expect salvation from the Russian tsar. But there are also examples of good Greeks, usually abbots in monasteries who provide Luk'ianov and his group with shelter and food. Similarly, the Armenian faith is heretical and accursed, but there are examples of good Armenian behaviour, especially among Armenian women, who are models of devotion to the Holy Sepulchre.

The image projected of the Ottomans/Turks is a decidedly mixed one. The Ottomans have good judges, for example, but their prayers are devilish. On the other hand, in Istanbul order is scrupulously maintained and there is no tolerance of public drunkenness. Even the Greeks do not drink in public.

Such observations, and also the beauty and lushness of the environment, together with the productivity of the land, make Luk'ianov exclaim repeatedly: 'How can it be that God has allowed this land to be taken over and mocked by the Muslims? How can such beauty have been given to the Turks?'

PUBLICATIONS

For earlier publications of the text (or excerpts from them), see Ol'shevskaia, Reshetova and Travnikov, *Khozhdenie v Sviatuiu zemliu*, p. 623; for a discussion of the manuscript tradition of the three redactions, see pp. 482-533.

<blockquote>

Ol'shevskaia, Reshetova and Travnikov, *Khozhdenie v Sviatuiu zemliu*, pp. 7-124 (first redaction), 124-242 (second redaction), 243-372 (third redaction)

</blockquote>

STUDIES

I.V. Fedorova, *'Puteshestvie v Sviatuiu Zemlu i Egipet' kniaz'ia Nikolaia Radzivilla i vostochnoslavianskaia palomnicheskaia literatura XVII-nachala XVIII v. Issledovanie i tekst*, St Petersburg, 2014, pp. 62-84 (on the genre)

Kirillina. *'Ocharovannye stranniki'*, esp. pp. 407-66 (chapter on approaches to Islam)

Ol'shevskaia, Reshetova and Travnikov, *Khozhdenie v Sviatuiu zemliu*

Art., 'Ioann Luk'ianov', in *Slovar' knizhnikov i knizhnosti Drevnei Rusi, vyp. 3, XVIII v.*, St Petersburg, Dmitrii Bulanin, 1993, pt 2, 71–2

Seemann, *Die altrussische Wallfahrtsliteratur*, pp. 366-76

B.M. Dantsig, *Russkie puteshestvenniki na blizhnem vostoke*, Moscow, 1965, pp. 53-7

Nikolaos Chrissidis

Petr Andreevich Tolstoi

P.A. Tolstoi

DATE OF BIRTH   1645
PLACE OF BIRTH   Moscow
DATE OF DEATH   1729
PLACE OF DEATH   Solovetskii monastery

BIOGRAPHY

Born in 1645, Petr Andreevich Tolstoi began his service career in 1676 as a *stol'nik* (lord-in-waiting) to the future tsar Ivan V (r. 1682-96), who was to rule jointly with his half-brother Peter. In 1693, Tolstoi was appointed governor of the province of Velikii Ustiug. In 1697, at the age of 52, he joined the group of courtiers whom Tsar Peter I (r. 1682-1725) sent to Europe. A two-year sojourn in Italy exposed him to modern technology, medicine, Italian city culture and classical art, though he remained a man of traditional piety who believed in the miraculous powers of relics and icons. His detailed daily journal recording his visit to Europe is perhaps the best travel account by a Russian of this era.

For the remainder of his career, Tolstoi devoted himself to Peter's reforms. In 1701, Peter selected him as Russia's first permanent ambassador to Constantinople, a post of major significance. His first four years as ambassador coincided with a series of intense crises within the Ottoman government, while longstanding tensions between the tsar and the sultan prevented him from achieving much success. The Ottoman declaration of war on Russia in 1710 led to his incarceration for four years in the Yedikule Fortress, where he feared imminent death. He was released from prison and left Constantinople in 1714. Tolstoi's reports and letters from Constantinople provide an invaluable Russian record of the Ottoman Empire during this period.

After his return to Russia, Tolstoi became a senator, minister in the Council on Foreign Affairs, and the first president of the Commerce College. He accompanied Tsar Peter to Warsaw, Copenhagen, Amsterdam and Paris in 1716, and he travelled abroad again in 1717 on a mission to entice the errant heir, Aleksei Petrovich, to return to Russia and to his angry father. He received promotion and awards from Peter for participating in the tsarevich's prosecution. From 1718 to 1722, Tolstoi served in diplomatic positions in Berlin, Riga and Astrakhan. In 1724, the octogenarian accompanied Peter to Persia.

After the tsar's death in 1725, Tolstoi planned the coronation of Catherine I (r. 1725-7), who made him a count. He played a major role on the Supreme Privy Council. Upon Catherine's death, he clashed with the mighty Prince A.D. Menshikov, and ended his remarkable life in exile at the Solovetskii monastery (on the Solovetskii Islands in the White Sea in northern Russia). Petr Andreevich's legendary fortune was pivotal to the great family's history.

MAIN SOURCES OF INFORMATION

Primary

'Instruktsiia grafu P.A. Tostomu pri otpravlenii ego chrezbychainym i polno-mochnym poslom k Porte Ottomanskoi v 1702 gody', *Otechestvennye Zapiski* 10-12 (1822) pt 10, 258-72, 410-20; pt 11, 370-8; pt 12, 33-42

N.A. Popov (ed.), 'Puteshestvie v Italiiu i na o. Mal'tu stol'nika P.A. Tolstogo v 1697 i 1698 godakh', *Atenei* 7-8 (1859) 300-39, 421-57 (Polish trans. 1859)

A.A. Preobrazhenskii et al., *Pis'ma i bumagi imperatora Petra velikogo*, vols 1-5, St Petersburg, 1887-1907

'Putevoi dnevnik P.A. Tolstogo', *Russkii Arkhiv* 26 (1888) pt 1, 161-204, 321-68, 505-52; pt 2, 5-62, 113-56, 225-64, 369-400 (Italian trans., Geneva, 1983; English trans., DeKalb IL, 1987; Polish trans., Wrocław, 1991; Russian ed., Moscow, 1992)

A.A. Sergeev (ed.), *Sostoianie naroda turetskago v 1703 godu*, Simferopol, 1914

Secondary

Iu.A. Petrosian, *Rossiiskaia istoriografiia Osmanskoi imperii XVIII-XX vv.*, Moscow, 2012, pp. 46-52

A. Kollakidi and A. Sever, *Spetssluzhby Rossiiskoi imperii*, Moscow, 2010, pp. 44-50

A.P. Viatkin, S.F. Oreshkova, and I.V. Zaitseva (eds), *Opisanie Chernogo moria, Egeiskogo arkhipelaga i osmanskogo flota*, Moscow, 2006

N.I. Pavlenko, *Ptentsy gnezda Petrova*, Moscow, 1994, pp. 197-279

L.A. Ol'shevskaia and S.N Travnikov, 'Umneishaia golova v Rossii', in L.A. Ol'shevskaia and S.N. Travnikov (eds), *Puteshestvie stol'nika P.A. Tolstogo po Evrope, 1697-1699*, Moscow, 1992, 251-91

M.J. Okenfuss, 'Translator's introduction', in *The travel diary of Peter Tolstoi. A Muscovite in early modern Europe*, DeKalb IL, 1987, xi-xxviii

G. Munro, art. 'Tolstoi, Petr Andreevich', in J.L. Wieczynski (ed.), *The modern encyclopedia of Russian and Soviet history*, Gulf Breeze FL, 1985, vol. 39, pp. 110-14

M.S. Lazarev et al. (eds), *Russkii posol v Stambule. Petr Andreevich Tolstoi i ego opisanie Osmanskoi imperii nachala XVIII v.*, Moscow, 1985

M.J. Okenfuss, 'Petr Tolstoi in Rome. The hydraulics of mystery and delight', *Newsletter. Study Group on Eighteenth-Century Russia* 12 (1984) 35-41

M.J. Okenfuss, 'The cultural transformation of Petr Tolstoi', in A.G. Cross (ed.), *Russia and the West in the eighteenth century*, Newtonville MA, 1983, 228-37

N. Tolstoy, *The Tolstoys*, New York, 1983, pp. 20-88

N.P. Pavlov-Sil'vanskii, 'Graf Petr Andreevich Tolstoi (prashchur grafa L'va Tolstogo)', in *Sochineniia, II. Ocherki po russkoi istorii XVIII-XIX vv.*, St Petersburg, 1910, 1-41 (repr. The Hague, 1966; includes a three-page bibliography; first published in *Istoricheskii Vestnik* [June 1905]; earlier version in *Russkii biograficheskii slovar'*, vol. 27, Moscow, 1896-1918, 77-91)

WORKS ON CHRISTIAN-MUSLIM RELATIONS

Russkii posol v Stambule 'A Russian ambassador in Istanbul'

DATE   1703

ORIGINAL LANGUAGE   Russian

DESCRIPTION

Russkii posol v Stambule (in full, *Russkii posol v Stambule: Petr Andreevich Tolstoi i ego opisanie Osmanskoi imperii nachala XVIII v.*, 'A Russian ambassador in Istanbul. Petr Andreevich Tolstoi and his description of the Ottoman Empire at the beginning of the 18th century') consists of Tolstoi's dispatches from his post in Constantinople and instructions to him from the *Posol'skii Prikaz* (Foreign Office). The modern edition (Moscow, 1985) covers 77 pages. The manuscript is held in the Russian State Archive of Ancient Acts. Direct references in the dispatches to Christian-Muslim relations are scattered, but fascinating.

The work is divided into two parts: questions from Moscow followed by the author's responses, and six of his letters to the tsar's chief of foreign affairs, F.A. Golovin.

In a serious examination of various aspects of Ottoman life, Tolstoi underscores the proud and independent character of Muslims, who ruthlessly exploit the Christian masses and subject them to unfair taxes and sumptuary restrictions. He expresses frustration that his Janissary guards prevent him from meeting with Christians, including the Patriarch of

Jerusalem. Lavish gifts are required when dealing with Muslim officials, but Tolstoi's bribes secure vital information from muftis and dragomans (interpreters).

Tolstoi is impressed by the mosques in Constantinople, and by the monasteries and hostels, and the amount of resources devoted to religion. He notes that Arabs take advantage of Turkish Muslims on pilgrimage to Mecca and Medina, and that great sums are spent on the maintenance of pilgrimage routes. He notes that Turkish people are resistant to adopting European ways.

Christians are generally referred to as 'Greeks', but the author makes passing references to Serb, Vlach, Armenian and Arab Christians, and to their relations with Muslims. At times Tolstoi criticises 'Greeks' for corruption, greed and other un-Christian behaviour. He expresses great fear that his Russian attendants will waver in their belief, 'because the Muslim faith is very attractive to simple people'.

In his dispatches, Tolstoi notes that the Ottomans are suspicious of Christians native to the empire, because they consider the tsar as their future deliverer. The Russian capture of Azov sparked the expectation among them that Muscovite ships would arrive at any time.

Tolstoi details the daily life of the Turkish Muslim peasantry, and also of Arabs living in Syria, Iraq and Yemen, their interactions with Christians, and their overlords. During his period of service in Constantinople, a major Arab uprising took place in Syria and Iraq, and Tolstoi remarks that the government discriminated between Egyptian Arab Muslims and Iraqi Arab Muslims. Tolstoi also describes the close ties between the Turks and the Muslims of the Crimean Khanate.

SIGNIFICANCE

While Tolstoi's main interests are naval, military, commercial and political, his reflections on the Muslim treatment of Christians set the groundwork for Russian policy at the Sublime Porte in the centuries that followed.

Although portions of these writings were not published until the 19th century, they provided crucial information for Russian statesmen and diplomats in unpublished form and the dispatches feature prominently in histories of Tsar Peter I, Russian foreign policy, and Russian military and naval history.

PUBLICATIONS

MS Moscow, Russian State Archive of Ancient Acts – Russian Relations with Turkey, F.89, Index 1 (1512-1719) (1703)

Tolstoi, *Sostoianie naroda turetskago v 1703 godu*

M.S. Lazarev et al. (eds), *Russkii posol v Stambule. Petr Andreevich Tolstoi i ego opisanie Osmanskoi imperii nachala XVIII v.*, Moscow, 1985

M.S. Lazarev et al. (eds), *Tolstoy'un gizli raporlarında Osmanlı İmparatorluğu: İstanbul'daki Rus büyükelçi Pyotr Andreyevic Tolstoy ve onun Osmanlı İmparatorluğu'na dair hatıraları (XVIII. yüzyılın ilk çeyreği)*, ed. and trans. İbrahim Allahverdi and İlyas Kamalov, Istanbul, 2009 (Turkish trans. of Lazarev edition)

STUDIES

Pavlenko, *Ptentsy gnezda Petrova*, 210-43

M.P. Arunova and S.F. Oreshkova, 'Osmanskaia imperiia v nachale XVIII v. i ee opisanie P.A. Tolstym', in Lazarev et al. (eds), *Russkii posol v Stambule*, 5-36

Tolstoy, *The Tolstoys*, pp. 54-67

E. Schuyler, *Peter the Great, Emperor of Russia. A study of historical biography*, New York, 1884, vol. 2, pp. 172-82, 191, 203

N. Popov, 'Iz zhizni P.A. Tolstago, odnogo iz sledovatelei po delu tsarevicha Alekseia Petrovicha', *Russkii Vestnik* 27 (1860) 323-9

Pis'ma (Gr.) P.A. Tolstago iz Turtsii k bratu ego I.A. Tolstomy
'Letters of Count P.A. Tolstoi from Turkey to his brother I.A. Tolstoi'

DATE   1703
ORIGINAL LANGUAGE   Russian

DESCRIPTION

This group comprises four letters from P.A. Tolstoi to his older brother I.A. Tolstoi, who was the Russian governor of Azov and the former Russian ambassador to the Ottoman Empire. The first two were written from Adrianople in 1703; the place and date of the third and fourth are not specified, although they clearly post-date the first two letters.

Tolstoi details his first encounters with the Ottoman viziers and the sultan. The ceremonial exchanges of gifts and greetings indicate that both sides were interested in maintaining peaceful and friendly ties, though the Ottoman officials were evidently suspicious of his presence and a corps of janissaries kept him under constant surveillance. He remarks that the bellicose spirit of the Tatars in Crimea is restrained by the Ottoman government, and he complains that Greek merchants are being robbed by Zaporozhian Cossacks. Amicable relations with the Ottomans promised to facilitate Russian trade in the Black Sea and eastern Mediterranean.

SIGNIFICANCE

These letters provide insight into the nature of tsarist relations with the Ottoman state at a crucial moment in history, when Russia was facing potential enemies on two fronts: Sweden to the north, and the Ottomans to the south. The letters highlight the geostrategic importance of the Sea of Azov, which was a borderland between Muslims and Christians. In this respect, the Crimean Tatars, who were vassals of the Ottoman sultan, played an important role in the nature of Muslim-Christian relations in the region. The letters also indicate the importance of diplomacy for the Russian state in maintaining peaceful relations with the Muslims of the Ottoman Empire.

PUBLICATIONS

According to a footnote in the published version on p. 273, the letters exist(ed) in the personal archive of the great author, Lev Petrovich Tolstoi.

'Pis'ma (Gr.) P.A. Tolstago iz Turtsii k bratu ego I.A. Tolstomy', *Russkii Arkhiv* 5-6 (1864) 473-93

Lucien Frary

Povest' o vziatii Azova Petrom I v 1696

'The tale of the siege of Azov by Peter I in 1696'

DATE 1701-4 and 1707
ORIGINAL LANGUAGE Russian

DESCRIPTION

Povest' o vziatii Azova Petrom I v 1696 is connected to the founding of
the port of Taganrog by Peter I (r. 1682-1725) in 1698, which ultimately
forced the Ottoman Empire into the Treaty of Karlowitz (1699). The second Azov campaign began in 1695 with the aim of capturing the Turkish
fortress of Azov and its 7,000 men, which had been blocking Russia's
access to the Sea of Azov and the Black Sea, and impeded the establishing of any new port.

The story was written in two versions in 1701-4 and 1707, both anonymous. According to M.D. Kagan's archival investigations, neither was initially published and the manuscripts are in the Russian National Library
in St Petersburg. The first, GPB, Q.XVII.46, dating to 1701-4, was acquired
from the Diplomatic Mission in Ukraine, found among documents relating to the Great Northern War. Its contents are secular and historical-
geographical in character. The second, GPB, F.XVII.10 (RGADA, F. 340,
Op. 1, D. 7, no. 13981), written in 1707, was originally held in Arkhangelsk
in the library of Prince Dmitri Mikhailovich Golitsyn, who was sent to
Constantinople in 1701 to claim Russian control over the Black Sea. He
acquired the manuscript from the Diplomatic Mission during his travels in Ukraine (Kagan, 'Povest' o vziatii Petrom I', p. 52). In 1737-8, this
manuscript was confiscated and placed in the central archive in Moscow.
Its contents are eschatological in nature.

Both versions were included in a later 18th-century history of the siege
of Azov, in the entry 'Skazanie o vziatii Azova', in Nikolai Novikov's *Drevniaia rossiiskaia vivliofika*, vol. 16, which also gives a number of other
accounts of the siege.

The *Povest'* expressly declares that, if Turks and their foreign and
schismatic allies seek to make war against Russia, they are warring
against God himself. God is on the side of Christian nations, especially
Orthodox nations, and definitely not on the side of Muslims, who will
find no peace by invading foreign lands (Novikov, 'Skazanie', p. 258). It

recalls natural disasters that have wreaked havoc not only on the Turkish sultan and his forces, but also on towns with Muslim, Christian and Jewish populations that were controlled by the Turks. Following the Battle of Zenta (1697) and the desertion of the French fleet from the side of Sultan Mustafa II (r. 1695-1703), 'we heard in a letter today that God so ordained that the earth consumed three towns along with its inhabitants, and that flames from the mountains came and took another town, and in still another town an earthquake so frightened its people that they fled [...] and the sultan's vizer could not help them' (Novikov, 'Skazanie', p. 257). Mirroring the narrative historical tradition, the *Povest'* uses natural phenomena – earthquakes, floods, solar and lunar eclipses – to reflect God's wrath, which assists the Christian righteous and deals death to the Muslim evildoers.

SIGNIFICANCE

The *Povest'* and other essays about the siege of Azov have been described by Nikolai Novikov and Alexander Radishev as the 'enlightened realism' of a modernising Russian Empire. However, it should be recognised as a return to older literary forms and themes that can be found in traditional Orthodox chronicles. By replacing the Cumans (Polovtsi), pagan, Turkic-speaking nomadic warriors of the Eurasian steppe, who appear in works of the 15th-17th centuries, with Tatars and Turks in an international setting in the 18th century, the *Povest'* displays the continuity of the Orthodox religious struggle. Likewise, its depiction of the struggle between the Christian Russian Empire and the Muslim Ottoman Empire as the struggle between good and evil, with God assisting the Christian side, recalls a world-view whose dominance was waning.

PUBLICATIONS

MS Moscow, Rossiiskaia Natsional'naia Biblioteka – GPB, Q.XVII.46 (1701-4)

MS Moscow, Rossiiskaia Natsional'naia Biblioteka – GPB, F.XVII.10 (1707)

N.I. Novikov, 'Skazanie o vziatia Azova', in N.I. Novikov, *Drevniaia rossiiskaia vivliofika*, vol. 16, Moscow: Tip. Kompanii Tipograflcheskoi, 1788-91, repr. The Hague, 1970, 171-282

STUDIES

M.D. Kagan, 'Povest' o vziatii Petrom I Azova v 1696', in *Slovar' knizhnikov i knizhnosti drevenei Rusi xvii vek*, vol. 3, St Petersburg, 1998, 49-52

P.N. Krasnov, 'Vziatie Azova tsarem Petrom 1696 g.', in *Kartina bylogo Tikhogo Dona*, Moscow, 1992; https://history.wikireading.ru/15713

A.V. Pozdneev, 'Pesn' o vziatii Azova v 1696 godu', *Trudy Otdela Drevnerusskoi Literatury* 10 (1954) 353-7

D.V. Sen', 'Iz istorii bor'by Rossii za Azov v 1695-1696 godakh. Uchastie akhreian v zashchite osmanskoi kreposti', *Menshikovskie Chtenie* 5/13 (2014) 160-8

Gwyn Bourlakov

Semen Ulianovich Remezov

DATE OF BIRTH 1642
PLACE OF BIRTH Tobolsk
DATE OF DEATH About 1715 or after 1720
PLACE OF DEATH Tobolsk

BIOGRAPHY

Semen Ulianovich Remezov was a Russian historian, geographer, cartographer and architect, who lived most of his life in Tobolsk, where he was a serviceman ('sluzhyly chelovek') with the rank of boyar's son ('syn boyarski'), equivalent to an officer's rank. The Remezovs were well-known among Siberian service people; Semen's father and grandfather were both prominent figures. During his military service, Remezov himself performed duties ranging from engagements against the indigenous population to the control of lime production.

MAIN SOURCES OF INFORMATION

Secondary
A.R. Ivonin, art. 'Remezov, Semyon Ulyanovich', in *Istoricheskaia entsiklopediia Sibiri*, Novosibirsk, 2009, vol. 2, 763-4
L.A. Gol'denberg, 'Semen Ul'ianovich Remezov', in V.A. Esakov (ed.), *Tvortsy otechestvennoj nauki. Geografy*, Moscow, 1996, 50-2
L.A. Gold'enberg, *Izograf zemli sibirskoj. Zhizn' i trudy Semena Remezova*, Magadan, 1990
V.K. Ziborov, art. 'V.K. Remezov Semyon Ul'ianovich', in D.S. Likhachev (ed.) *Slovar' knizhnikov i knizhnosti Drevnej Rusi*, vol. 3, part 3, St Petersburg, 1988, 195-6
E.I. Dergacheva-Skop, 'S.U. Remezov. Sibirskii prosvetitel' kontsa XVII veka', in *Ocherki russkoi literatury Sibiri*, Novosibirsk, 1982, vol. 1, 95-106
L.A. Go'ldenberg, *O pervom istorike Sibiri, in Russkoe naselenie Pomor'ia i Sibiri*, Moscow, 1973
A.I. Martynenko, 'Pioner russkoj kartografii', *Geodeziia i Kartografiia* 4 (1971) 65-7
L.A. Gol'denberg, *Semen Ul'ianovich Remezov. Sibirskij kartograf i geograf. 1642-1720*, Moscow, 1965

WORKS ON CHRISTIAN-MUSLIM RELATIONS

Istoria sibirskaia, Khorographicheskaia chertezhnaia kniga, *and* Chertezhnaia kniga Sibiri

'Siberian history', 'Topographical sketchbook' and 'Sketchbook of Siberia'

DATE 1689-1711
ORIGINAL LANGUAGE Russian

DESCRIPTION

Semen Remezov recorded the history and geography of various areas of Siberia. Three of his works reveal his attitudes towards the Muslim communities he interacted with. The first is the *Istoria Sibirskaia* ('Siberian history'), also known as the *Remezovskaia Letopis* ('Remezov's chronicles'), the second is *Chertezhnaia Kniga Sibiri* ('Sketchbook of Siberia'), and the third is *Khorographicheskaia Chertezhnaia Kniga* ('Topographical sketchbook of Siberia').

Istoria Sibirskaia was written between 1689 and 1703. It differs from earlier Siberian chronicles in citing local sources such as folk tales, and setting out historical facts in a systematic way. The book has 157 articles. It contains more than 100 paragraphs with illustrations and the explanatory text above, giving a short description of the colonisation of Siberia at the end of the 16th century under the voevoda Ermak. Miniatures make the work unique for its time.

The work reveals a strong bias against Muslims, when they were direct enemies. For example, in his first description of Kuchum, the Mongol khan of Siberia, Remezov calls him:

> Of Muslim faith, an idolater, eating filth lived without law: he was not embarrassed to have 100 wives and youths, as well as girls, as is the custom for the sons of Hagar, as many as they want to have. But the all-seeing God was soon to make an end to his reign.

Remezov also makes clear the hierarchy between the faiths when, in another paragraph, he says that a certain indigenous people were pagans, but God punished them by sending the Muslim Mongols to defeat them and to force them to become Muslims. Christianity, he concludes, is the means of saving the indigenous peoples of Siberia. So, apart from being a region where trade relations were to be secured and natural resources sought, Siberia was a locus for missions by state and church officials.

Chertezhnaia kniga Sibiri, published in 1701, describes the diversity of Siberia and its population, and its economic and colonial development at the end of 17th century. It outlines the territory controlled by the Russian state and shows its relations with neighbouring countries, including China.

Remezov compiled *Khorographicheskaia Chertezhnaia kniga*, the third book, between 1697 and 1711. It is dedicated to Tsar Peter I (r. 1682-1725), but it was never presented to him and is almost unknown in Russia. The original was only discovered at the beginning of the 20th century. Then, it was thought for many years to have been destroyed during the Revolution, but it was taken from Russia in 1918, and has been kept in the Houghton Library of Harvard University since 1956. *Khorographicheskaia Chertezhnaia kniga* contains very valuable information on the cartography and archaeology of Siberia, and on the history of its population. The introductory part, which discusses problems of theoretical geography, is followed by more than 100 pages of maps representing major Siberian rivers and the population along their banks.

SIGNIFICANCE

These three books were highly influential and also exceptionally useful for the government of Russia under Peter the Great as part of his expansion policies. Their systematic descriptions of Siberia made possible the exploration of the land for mining, and also the enforcement of law and collection of taxes.

Remezov's maps reflect the ethnic and confessional situation in Siberia, but in a rather one-sided way because Christianity is over-represented, mostly through the pictures of churches and monasteries. His descriptions tend to be biased against Muslims rather than against the pagan indigenous peoples, surely because he felt that the organised Muslim government of Kuchum was an obstacle to the colonisation of Siberia. As the state increasingly interfered in church matters, and in fact subjugated the church to state authority in the first quarter of the 18th century, Remezov's books and drawings played a key role in the Christianisation which urged the aboriginal population of Siberia to become loyal, tax-paying subjects of the tsar.

PUBLICATIONS

MS Cambridge MA, Houghton Library, Harvard University – MS Russ 72 (6) *Khorograficheskaia kniga* (1697-1711; 172 fols)

G.I. Spasskii, *Letopis' sibirskaia, soderzhashchaia povestvovanie o vziatii Sibirskie zemli russkimi, pri tsare Ioanne Vasil'eviche Groznom; s kratkim izlozheniem predshtstvovavshikh odnomu sobytij. Izdana s rukopisi XVII veka*, St Petersburg, 1821

S.U. Remezov, *Chertezhnaia kniga Sibiri, sdelannaia synom Tobol'ska boiarom Semenom Remezovym*, St Petersburg, 1882

S.U. Remezov, *Istoriia sibirskaia*, [npd], [nd]; http://vbook.nsu.ru/?int=VIEW&el=8&templ=title

S.U. Remezov, *Atlas of Siberia*, ed. L.V. Bagrov, The Hague, 1958 (facsimile of *Khorograficheskaia kniga*)

T. Armstrong (ed.), *Yermak's campaign in Siberia. A selection of documents translated from the Russian*, trans. T. Minorsky and D. Wileman, London, 1975, pp. 87-277 (English trans. of *Istoriia sibirskaia*, includes copies of original miniatures)

S.U. Remezov, *Chertezhnaia kniga Sibiri, sdelannaia synom Tobol'ska boiarom Semenom Remezovym*, Moscow, 2003 (facsimile of 1882 edition)

S.U. Remezov, *Remezovskaia letopis'. Istoriia sibirskaia, letopis' sibirskaia kratkaia kungurskaia*, ed. V. Guminskii, E. Dergacheva-Skop and V. Alekseev, 2 vols, Tobolsk, 2006 (vol. 1, facsimile of *Istoriia sibirskaia*, vol. 2, modern Russian trans. and commentary)

S.U. Remezov, *Khorographicheskaia chertezhnaia kniga*, ed. V.E. Bulatov, Tobolsk, 2011

STUDIES

S. Smit-Piter, 'S.U. Remezov i sibirskaia identichnost' v kontse XVII – nachale XVIII v.', *Sibirskie Istoricheskie Issledovaniia* 3 (2014) 7-23

V.A. Kivelson, 'Exalted and glorified to the ends of the earth. Imperial maps and Christian spaces in seventeenth and early eighteenth century Russian Siberia', in J.R. Akerman (ed.), *The imperial map. Cartography and the mastery of empire*, Chicago, 2009, 47-91

Guminskii, Dergacheva-Skop and Alekseev (eds), *Remezovskaia letopis'. Istoriia sibirskaia, letopis' sibirskaia kratkaia kungurskaia*, vol. 2

E.I. Dergacheva-Skop, 'Sibirskie letopisi v istoricheskoj proze XVII veka. Tekst-kontekst', in *Vestnik Novosibirskogo gosudarstvennogo universiteta. Serija Istoriia, filologiia*, vol. 1, *Filologiia*, Novosibirsk, 2002, 3-12

E.I. Dergacheva-Skop, *Genealogiia sibirskogo letopisaniia. Kontseptsiia. Materialy*, Novosibirsk, 2000

V.N. Alekseev, 'Rukopis' "Istorii Sibirskoj" S.U. Remezova. K probleme khudozhestvennogo edinstva', in *Materialy i soobshcheniia po fondam Otdela rukopisnoj i redkoj knigi*, Leningrad, 1987, 94-112

V.N. Alekseev, 'Kungurskaia letopis' v sostave "Istorii Sibirskoj" S.U. Remezova', in *Stanovlenie sistemy bibliotechnogo obsluzhivaniia i knizhnogo dela v Sibiri i na Dal'nem Vostoke*, Novosibirsk, 1977, vol. 37, 80-2

V.N. Alekseev, 'Rusinki "Istorii Sibirskoj" S.U. Remezova. Proemy atributsii', in O.I. Podobedova and G.V. Popov (eds), *Drevnerusskoe iskusstvo. Rukopisnaia kniga*, vol. 2, Moscow, 1974, 175-96

V.V. Kirillov, 'Metody proektirovaniia Semena Remezova', *Arkhitekturnoe Nasledstvo* 22 (1974)

F.A. Shibanov, 'O nekotorykh aspektakh kartografii Rossii dopetrovskogo vremeni (XVI-XVIIvv.) i roli S. U. Remezova v istorii russkoj kartografii', *Vestnik Leningradskogo Universiteta* 18 (1969) 127-130

E.I. Dergacheva-Skop (ed.), '"Pokhvala" Sibiri S.U. Remezova', in *Trudy Otdela drevnerusskoy literatury* 21 (1965) 266-74; http://lib2.push-kinskijdom.ru/Media/Default/PDF/TODRL/21_tom/Dergacheva-Skop/Dergacheva-Skop.pdf

L. Bagrow [Bagrov], 'Semyon Remezov. A Siberian cartographer', *Imago Mundi* 11 (1954) 111-25

Ivan Sokolovsky

Feofan Prokopovich

Feofan, Theophan, Eleazar Prokopovich,
Prokopovych, Prokopowicz

DATE OF BIRTH   18 June 1681 (Old Style   8 June 1681)
PLACE OF BIRTH   Kiev, Ukraine
DATE OF DEATH   19 September 1736 (Old Style   8 September
    1736)
PLACE OF DEATH   St Petersburg

BIOGRAPHY

Feofan Prokopovich was a Russian-Ukrainian churchman, statesman, educator, theologian, writer and poet of the early 18th century. He was probably the most influential and best-known Orthodox cleric of the era.

Born Eleazar Prokopovich in Kiev in 1681, he received his initial ecclesiastical education at the Kiev-Mohyla Academy. To gain access to further education, he became a Uniate, a Roman Catholic practising Eastern Orthodox rites in accordance with the Union of Brest (1596). Such conversions were common practice for Ruthenians of the Eastern Orthodox faith who wished to advance their education in the Catholic West. Eleazar studied rhetoric, poetry, philosophy, theology, history and other disciplines in various Jesuit colleges in Poland, and eventually entered the College of St Athanasius in Rome. In 1702, he returned to Kiev, reverted to Eastern Orthodoxy, and accepted monastic vows under the name of Feofan.

From 1704, Feofan taught a number of subjects at the Kiev-Mohyla Academy and eventually became rector of the academy. During this time, he started to write treatises in Latin on poetics and rhetoric. Feofan also revealed himself to be a talented author of literary works, and his tragicomedy 'Vladimir' (1705) is considered one of the masterpieces in Russian-Ukrainian literature of the 18th century.

In 1708, the Russian Tsar Peter I (r. 1682-1725) attended a church service in Kiev in which Feofan praised the tsar's victory over the Swedes at Poltava. This occasion demonstrated his remarkable talents and determined his spectacular future career in the imperial capital.

In 1716, Feofan moved to St Petersburg at the request of Peter I, and soon became one of the tsar's close associates. He was appointed bishop of Pskov in 1718 and later, in 1725, archbishop of Novgorod. During these years, Feofan authored the first Russian catechism, political and theological treatises and sermons, along with other works. Together with Peter I, he designed the 'Spiritual regulation' (1721), which defined a new, rather submissive position of the Russian Orthodox Church in the empire – patriarchy was abandoned and the collegial Holy Synod became the church's highest authoritative body. As the synod's primary member of many years, Feofan used political manoeuvring and intrigue to remain the most influential churchman in the Russian Empire until his death in 1736.

MAIN SOURCES OF INFORMATION

Primary

[Dmitrii Semenov-Rudnev], 'Vita Auctoris', in Theophanis Procopowicz, *Tractatus de Processione Spiritus Sancti*, Gothae, 1772, no pagination

'Vita Theophanis Procopovitsch', in J.B. Scherer (ed.), *Nordische Nebenstunden. Das ist, Abhandlungen über die alte Geographie, Geschichte und Alterthümer des Nordens*, Frankfurt, 1776, 249-70 (for a Ukrainian trans. see *Zhyttepys Teofana Prokovycha*, in *Filosofs 'ka dumka* 3 (1970) 94-107)

'Feofan Prokopovich', in Evgenii (Bolkhovitinov) (ed.), *Slovar' istoricheskii o byvshikh v Rossii pisateliakh dukhovnago china, Grekorossiiskoi tserkvi*, St Petersburg, 1818, part 2, 668-702

'Delo o Feofane Prokopoviche', *Chteniia v Imperatorskom Obshchestve Istorii i Drevnostei Rossiiskikh pri Moskovskom Universitete*, 1 (1862) 1-92

'Pis'ma Feofana Prokopovicha', *Trudy Kievskoi Dukhovnoi Akademii* 1 (1865) 139-59, 287-310, 595-613

Secondary

R. Collis, *The Petrine instauration. Religion, esotericism and science at the court of Peter the Great, 1689-1725*, Leiden, 2012, pp. 271-354

T.E. Avtukhovich, 'Prokopovich', in A.M. Panchenko et al. (eds), *Slovar' russkikh pisatelei XVIII veka*, St Petersburg, 1999, 488-96

S.P. Luppov, *Kniga v Rossii v poslepetrovskoe vremia (1725-1740)*, Leningrad, 1976, pp. 253-65

J. Cracraft, 'Feofan Prokopovich. A bibliography of his works', *Oxford Slavonic Papers* 8 (1975) 1-36

J. Cracraft, *The church reform of Peter the Great*, Palo Alto CA, 1971, pp. 49-62

R. Stupperich, 'Feofan Prokopovič in Rom', *Zeitschrift für Osteuropäische Geschichte* 5 (1931) 327-39

I.A. Chistovich, *Feofan Prokopovich i ego vremia*, St Petersburg, 1868

WORKS ON CHRISTIAN-MUSLIM RELATIONS

Za Mogiloiu Riaboiu
'Near the [place called] Riabaia Mogila'

DATE 1711

ORIGINAL LANGUAGE Old Russian

DESCRIPTION

In the summer of 1711, during the so-called Pruth Campaign, Russian forces led by Tsar Peter I marched into the territory of Moldavia, a dominion of the Ottoman Empire. In July of the same year, a decisive battle between the Russian and Turkish armies took place on the River Pruth, lasting several days and resulting in thousands of casualties on both sides. The Russian forces were defeated, and negotiated a peace treaty with Ottoman Turkey. Commissioned by Tsar Peter to the army's headquarters for the period of the campaign, Feofan became a witness to the bloody battle and dedicated a poem to this tragic event.

The poem is known by its first line, 'Za Mogiloiu Riaboiu', which is translated as 'Near the [place called] Riabaia Mogila' (the latter literally meaning 'the speckled grave'). Written in baroque manner, the poem, 45 lines long, follows the style of a folkloric soldiers' song. It describes the battle, adhering closely to actual events, and its general mood is gloomy, characterising the battle as 'dreadful' (*v strashnom boiu*). Feofan depicts the Russian forces, which also include Cossack and Wallachian regiments, in their battle against the 'numerous Turks' (*turchin mnogoli-udnyi*). This allows him to demonstrate the numerical advantage of the enemy forces and thereby stress the heroism of the warriors on the Russian side. The poem ends with a promise of vengeance on the enemy.

The last six lines of the poem carry a messianic, anti-Islamic message. Feofan does not use the word Islam, but instead the term 'paganism' (*poganstvo*), a traditional Russian polemical label for all non-Christians. The poet portrays the battle between the Russian and Turkish forces as a clash between Christianity and Islam, won by the Turks through the mysterious work of Providence. He exclaims about the defeat of Tsar Peter's forces:

> God did not grant Christianity
> To be freed from paganism,
> [He] had not yet allowed paganism to be brought down.

Feofan insists that the triumph of the Turkish forces is temporary. Further, he addresses Islam, personified in the Prophet Muḥammad, with the promise of the ultimate victory of Christianity:

> Muḥammad, [you] foe of Christ,
> The future will show,
> Who will fall from whose hands.

SIGNIFICANCE

The final lines of 'Za Mogiloiu Riaboiu' refer to a Messianic idea that had been prevalent in Russian state ideology for centuries. The fall of the 'second Rome', Constantinople, in 1453 symbolised the ultimate disappearance of the Orthodox Byzantine Empire at the hands of the Muslim Ottoman Turks. This event had a profound impact on the worldview of Russian rulers, resulting in their adoption, from the 15th century onwards, of the concept of Moscow as the last stronghold and protector of Orthodoxy in the world. This image became especially vivid in the second half of the 17th century. According to Paul of Aleppo's travelogue, the Russian Tsar Alekseĭ Mikhailovich himself promised to emancipate the Orthodox lands from 'the hands of the enemies of our religion', the Muslim Turks (Paul of Aleppo, *The travels of Macarius, Patriarch of Antioch*, trans. F.C. Belfour, vol. 2, London, 1836, p. 292).

Tsar Aleksei's successors perpetuated Russia's imperial claim to be a chief guardian of Orthodox Christianity against the infidel. Therefore, Russia's wars against Ottoman Turkey had strong religious undertones. For example, in the spring of 1711, before the Pruth Campaign was begun, the Russian government distributed in the Balkans leaflets declaring the tsar's commitment to 'deliver the Christian peoples from the tyranny of the pagans' (*tiranstva poganskogo*) and to drive 'Muḥammad's heirs' back to the Arabian Peninsula (*Pis'ma i bumagi*, pp. 117-19, 153). Prokopovich's poem refers directly to the religiously Messianic attitude of the growing Russian Empire.

'Za Mogiloiu Riaboiu' circulated widely during the 18th century in manuscript songbooks. Its lyricism and messianic message apparently contributed to the poem's popularity.

PUBLICATIONS

Chistovich, *Feofan Prokopovich i ego vremia*, vol. 1, pp. 16-17 (in footnote); PSU 589 (digitised version available through Hathi Trust digital library)

Feofan Prokopovich, *Sochineniia*, ed. I.P. Eremina, Moscow, 1961, pp. 214-15

STUDIES

O.M. Buranok, *Feofan Prkopovich i istoriko-literaturnyi protsess pervoi poloviny XVIII veka*, Moscow, 2014, pp. 278-84

Pis'ma i bumagi imperatora Petra Velikogo, vol. 11, part 1, Moscow, 1962, pp. 117-19, 153

N.V. Sinitsyna, *Tretii Rim. Istoki i evoliutsiia russkoi srednevekovoi kontseptsii (XV-XVI vv.)*, Moscow, 1998

H. Smorczewska, 'Bóg - człowiek - naród. Z obserwacji nad problematyka religijna w pjezji Teofana Prokopowicza', in *Roczniki Humanistyczne* 42 (1994) 180-1

E.V. Anisimov, *The reforms of Peter the Great. Progress through coercion in Russia*, trans. J.T. Alexander, Armonk NY, 1993, pp. 127-34

Feofan Prokopovich, *Sochineniia*, vol. 1, pp. 480-1

A. Kochubinskii, 'Snosheniia Rossii pri Petre I s iuzhnymi slavianami i rumunami', *Chteniia v Imperatorskom Obshchestve Istorii i Drevnostei Rossiiskikh pri Moskovskom Universitete* 2 (1872) 1-98

Evgeny Grishin

Pyotr Vasilevich Postnikov

DATE OF BIRTH   About 1670
PLACE OF BIRTH   Russia
DATE OF DEATH   1710
PLACE OF DEATH   Russia

BIOGRAPHY

Pyotr Vasilevich Postnikov was the son of a secretary who worked for the diplomatic department of the 17th-century Russian state, and even travelled abroad, a rare circumstance for a Russian at that time. In the late 1680s, Pyotr Postnikov was among the first Russians to enter the newly-formed Slavo-Greco-Latin Academy (founded 1685) in Moscow, where he studied languages. Between 1692 and 1694, he was abroad studying medicine at the University of Padua. This further education was paid for by the Russian state.

On his return to Russia in 1698, he worked briefly for both the Apothecary Chancery (the Russian palace medical department) and the Slavo-Greco-Latin Academy, but ultimately his ability in languages was deemed his most valuable skill, even above his medical training. He was transferred to the diplomatic department, where his father had worked earlier, and then on to a series of assignments in Western Europe, both fulfilling diplomatic missions and sourcing desirable foreign commodities such as medicines and books. He was abroad from 1698 until 1700, for some of this time as a member of Peter the Great's Grand Embassy. When he returned to Moscow, he brought with him the books and other goods he had collected, before being sent abroad yet again in 1701.

Postnikov then remained primarily in Paris as a diplomat. When he returned to Russia in 1710, he began translating a selection of the various texts he had acquired abroad, which covered a huge range of subjects. He died later the same year.

MAIN SOURCES OF INFORMATION

Secondary

A.B. Bogdanov, *Materialy dlia biografichekogo spravochnika russkikh vrachei XVII-XX vv.*, St Petersburg, 2014, p. 327

P.V. Gusterin, 'Pervyi perevodchik i pervoe izdanie Korana na russkom iazyke', *Islamovedenie* 1 (2011) 89-97

E. Shmurlo, 'Postnikov, Pyotr Vasilevich', in *Russkii biografichekii slovar'*, St Petersburg, 1905, vol. 14, pp. 634-5

D. Tsvetaev, *Mediki v Moskovskoi Rusi i pervyi russkii doktor. Istoriko-biografichekii ocherk*, Warsaw, 1896

WORKS ON CHRISTIAN-MUSLIM RELATIONS

Alkoran o Magomete
'The Qur'an on Muḥammad'

DATE   1716
ORIGINAL LANGUAGE   Russian

DESCRIPTION

This translation of the Qur'an, made from André du Ryer's mid-17th-century French translation, *L'Alcoran de Mahomet, translaté d'arabe en françois par le Sieur du Ryer, Sieur de la garde Malezair* (1647), is now generally agreed to have been made by Pyotr Postnikov. It was previously ascribed to Dmitrii Cantemir, a former governor of Ottoman Moldavia who defected to Russian service in the 1710s. Cantemir composed his own work on Islam, *Kniga sistima ili Sostoianie muhammedanskiia religii* (published in 1722; see in this volume, pp. 317-22), which led scholars also to ascribe the *Alkoran* to him. However, P.V. Gusterin has established Postnikov's authorship of the work ('Pervyi perevodchik'). As Postnikov died no later than 1710 and the work was printed only in 1716, it is likely that there was an earlier manuscript version.

According to Robert Crews (*For prophet and tsar*, p. 37), the 1716 edition was printed on the orders of Peter the Great (r. 1682-1725) while he was marching towards Astrakhan. It certainly fits into Peter's broader policy of gathering information on the Ottoman Empire and Islam, which included recruiting Cantemir.

The *Alkoran*, which is 350 pages long, is rather simply printed, with no illustrations and no contents list, although it is paginated and contains some marginal notations, highlighting the themes of certain paragraphs. Preceding the Qur'an text itself is a two-page introduction titled 'On the Turkish faith', which has led some scholars to refer to this as a part of the title of the main work (see, for example, Crews, *For prophet and tsar*, p. 37, who refers to the work as 'The Al-Koran on Muḥammad, or the Turkish creed'). 'On the Turkish faith' serves to contextualise the text of the *Alkoran*, briefly explaining the key beliefs and practices of Islam. It starts from the basics, that Muslims believe in a single God who protects the good and punishes sinners, and briefly covers prayers and rituals, fasts and feasts, marriage and children, and the sacred geography of the Arab lands, in particular the importance of Mecca and Medina. It also links Islam to Christianity by mentioning Muslim thought on Jesus, highlighting that he is seen as a great prophet but not as divine.

The *Alkoran* consists of 110 chapters, each beginning with the title and number of verses, and whether it is Meccan or Medinan. A number of chapters are glossed with a brief explanation as to their meaning and significance. Since the text is a translation of a translation, and since du Ryer's French text has been accused of inaccuracy, its exact relationship to the canonical Qur'an remains questionable.

SIGNIFICANCE

The *Alkoran* is the first official Russian translation of the Qur'an, and indeed may be the first ever attempt to translate the Qur'an into Russian. It is significant as being a part of Peter the Great's approach to Islam and his Muslim subjects and neighbours. Peter was very interested in expanding his empire to the south, and in taking on the Ottoman Empire. In order to do so effectively, he felt it was important to gather knowledge not simply on the Ottoman state, but also on the Muslim religion. The *Alkoran* was thus effectively a tool for defeating and ruling Muslims.

The *Alkoran* is also significant for the way it portrays Muslim thought on Christians. The marginal notes most commonly mark places where the Qur'an makes a statement about Christians. The text of the *Alkoran* discusses Latinate Christianity in the same breath as Judaism and 'Ethiopians', presumably meaning Coptic Christians, and so puts Christians together with the other Abrahamic faiths whose adherents were commonly to be found within Muslim lands. These sections are not adversarial or negative, but see Christians as fellow followers of Abraham.

PUBLICATIONS

P.V. Postnikov, *Al-koran o Magomete*, Moscow, 1716

STUDIES

R.D. Crews, *For prophet and tsar. Islam and empire in Russia and Central Asia*, Cambridge MA, 2009, p. 37
Gusterin, 'Pervyi perevodchik'
Shmurlo, 'Postnikov, Pyotr Vasilevich'

Clare Griffin

Matvei Gavrilov Nechaev

Matvei Gavrilovich Nechaev

DATE OF BIRTH   Last quarter of the 17th century
PLACE OF BIRTH   Iaroslavl', Russia
DATE OF DEATH   1752
PLACE OF DEATH   Unknown

BIOGRAPHY

Matvei Gavrilov Nechaev was a merchant from Iaroslavl', living in the settlement (*sloboda*) of Tolchkovsk. According to his account of his pilgrimage to Jerusalem, he was involved in trading with Greek merchants. He is referred to as a witness in an October 1722 trial in his native city, after his return from his pilgrimage. Not much else is known about his life, or any other writings by him.

MAIN SOURCES OF INFORMATION

Primary

Matvei Gavrilov Nechaev, *Puteshestvie posadskogo cheloveka Matveia Gavrilova Nechaeva v Ierusalim (1719-1720 goda)*, ed. N.P. Barsov, Warsaw, 1875

Secondary

T.G. Stavrou and P.R. Weisensel, *Russian travelers to the Christian East from the twelfth to the twentieth century*, Columbus OH, 1986, pp. 67-9

K.-D. Seemann, *Die altrussische Wallfahrtsliteratur. Theorie und Geschichte eines literarischen Genres*, Munich, 1976, pp. 396-401

WORKS ON CHRISTIAN-MUSLIM RELATIONS

Khozhdenie
'Itinerary'

DATE   1721–2
ORIGINAL LANGUAGE   Russian

DESCRIPTION

Nechaev's *Khozhdenie* (in full, *Kniga khozhdenie vo sviatyi grad Ierusalim Iaroslavtsa Tolchkovskoi slobody posadskogo cheloveka Matveia Gavrilova syna Nechaeva*, 'A book called Itinerary to the Holy City of Jerusalem of the merchant Matvei Gavrilov Nechaev, of the Tolchkovsk settlement in Iaroslavl') is a short work, following the structure of a diary, and survives only in incomplete form. It covers pp. 3-34 in the 1875 publication edited by N.P. Barsov (*Puteshestvie posadskogo cheloveka Matveia Gavrilova Nechaeva v Ierusalim (1719-1720 goda)*; all references are to this edition). The work describes how, after joining a Greek merchant caravan, Nechaev arrives in Constantinople, from where he travels to Jerusalem.

His main emphasis is on the shrines he visits there. Reference to Christian-Muslim relations follows the usual form, namely, observations that Muslims are administrators and toll and tax collectors, as well as guards. There is a marked reticence to demonise Muslims, a stance that is highly uncharacteristic of the genre, and is probably related to Nechaev's being a merchant rather than a cleric. There are occasional attacks on Muslim practices, but Nechaev is generally fairly matter-of-fact in his descriptions of the 'other'. Even in references to the story of Evdokiia, a woman who refuses the advances of a Turk and is falsely accused of promising to become a Muslim, and then incarcerated for many years in Adrianople, his account lacks direct criticism of the Turks but instead expresses considerable admiration for her persistence (p. 9). He expresses jealousy of the Turks for having control of such a great city as Constantinople (p. 11). The rare critical remarks he does make relate to what he calls the wild noise (*skvernaia molba*) of the Islamic call to prayer (p. 11), or the 'wild, disorderly Muslim calls to the god-opposing gathering' (p. 15). Nechaev also laments the problems faced by prisoners-of-war, but without adding any particular criticism of the Turks (p. 16): he emphasises that Maltese pirates do harm to both Greeks and Turks. Furthermore, Nechaev does not exhibit any particular animus towards other Christian denominations, a stance that further distances his from other pilgrim accounts of the time. His account also includes information about the imprisonment of Varlaam Lenitskii in Cyprus in 1712-14.

SIGNIFICANCE

Nechaev's *Khozhdenie* is important for the light it potentially sheds on the mentality of a provincial Russian merchant and his approach to Christian-Muslim relations. Rarely does he openly attack or engage in insulting Muslims. Moreover, the Greeks, another favourite target of many, but not all, Russian clerical authors of pilgrim accounts at the time, also come off reasonably well. There is very little information about Arabs in this account, and the references to Turks have to do primarily with administrative formalities and tolls that need to be paid, which is overall to be expected given Nechaev's merchant identity.

PUBLICATIONS

Matvei Gavrilov Nechaev, *Puteshestvie posadskogo cheloveka Matveia Gavrilova Nechaeva v Ierusalim (1719-1720 goda)*, ed. N.P. Barsov, Warsaw, 1875, pp. 3-34 (Barsov gives a slightly earlier date than the modern consensus)

For other 19th-century editions, see art. 'Nechaev, Matvei Gavrilovich', in D.S. Likhachev (ed.), *Slovar' knizhnikov i knizhnosti Drevnei Rusi*, vol. 3, XVIII v., St Petersburg, 1993, part 2, 376–8, p. 378

STUDIES

I.V. Fedorova, '*Puteshestvie v Sviatuiu Zemlu i Egipet' kniaz'ia Nikolaia Radzivilla i vostochnoslavianskaia palomnicheskaia literatura XVII-nachala XVIII v. Issledovanie i tekst*, St Petersburg, 2014 (useful for information about the genre)

S.A. Kirillina, '*Ocharovannye stranniki'. Arabo-osmanskii mir glazami rossiiskikh palomnikov XVI-XVIII stoletii*, Moscow, 2010, pp. 407–66 (chapter on approaches to Islam)

B.M. Dantsig, *Russkie puteshestvenniki na blizhnem vostoke*, Moscow, 1965, pp. 57–9

Nikolaos Chrissidis

Opisanie tseremoniala

'Description of the ceremonial'

DATE   13 May 1741
ORIGINAL LANGUAGE   Russian

DESCRIPTION

This *Opisanie* (in full, *Opisanie tseremoniala s kotorym Ee Imperatorsk-ogo Velichestva cherezvychainyi i polnomozhnyi posol gospodin general Rumiantsev v Konstantinopol' svoi torzhestvennyi z'ezd imel i sperva u Verkhovnogo Viziria na vizite a potom u Turetskogo Sultana na audient-sii byl*, 'Description of the ceremonial with which her Imperial Majesty's extraordinary and plenipotentiary ambassador Lord General Rumiant-sev had his congress in Constantinople first on a visit with the Grand Vizier and then at an audience with the Turkish sultan') is a published extract from a report composed by an unnamed member of the Russian diplomatic mission to Constantinople led by Aleksandr Ivanovich Rumiantsev that was sent to the court of the Regent Anna Leopol'dovna (r. 8 November 1740-6 December 1741), detailing the diplomatic mission they had undertaken to the Ottoman Empire. It was delivered in St Petersburg on 13 May 1741.

As the document notes, Rumiantsev's mission was occasioned by the concluding of a peace treaty with the Ottoman Empire in 1739, which stipulated the mutual exchange of diplomatic delegations (the document mentions in its prologue that a description of the Turkish mission to St Petersburg was published in 1740).

The *Opisanie* describes the mission's progress through various Turkish towns, such as Bender and Adrianople (Edirne), en route to Constantinople. At each stop, the delegation was greeted with ceremonial cannon fire, music and other kinds of welcome. The document lists in detail the various members of the Russian and Ottoman delegations, including Janissaries, *dīwān*s, officers, musicians, and so forth.

On 26 March 1741, General Rumiantsev had a meeting with the Ottoman grand vizier in order to gain a formal audience with the sultan. The general gave a speech in which he stated his purpose for this proposed meeting, namely to reaffirm the peace concluded the previous year. He was to make this reaffirmation on behalf of Russia's new regent, Anna Leopol'dovna, and Count Andrei Ivanovich Osterman, acting in the name of the infant Tsar Ivan VI (r. 1740-1). The general also lamented the recent passing of Empress Anna Ioannovna. He then presented the grand vizier with an imperial charter as confirmation. Upon receipt of the charter, the vizier thanked the general and granted him a formal audience with the sultan.

On 31 March, the retinue moved in a carefully choreographed procession to the sultan's palace, where the vizier's note of admission was sent to the sultan, and the delegation had lunch while waiting for the sultan's formal invitation. When it arrived, 15 members of the retinue along with a translator were dressed in special clothes and given entry to the sultan. When they met, Aleksandr Ivanovich and Sultan Mahmud I (r. 1730-54) recited speeches in which they pledged mutual friendship and the preservation of the peace.

The document gives only formal details of Rumiantsev's mission, merely stating that both sides reaffirmed the peace concluded at the end of the war in 1739. In fact, there were several specific questions left to be decided, such as the recognition of the Russian imperial title, the status of fortifications at Azov, and prisoner exchanges. General Rumiantsev would remain in Constantinople conducting negotiations through most of 1741. The conditions that emerged as a result of the treaty and the subsequent agreements were to last until the next outbreak of war with the Ottomans in 1768.

The only direct reference to religion in the *Opisanie* comes when it notes that General Rumiantsev was awakened by the call to prayer at 5.00 am on the morning he met with the sultan. This lack of religious references is not surprising, as the document is a simple account of the diplomatic delegation's journey and meeting with the sultan, and is generally lacking in commentary. It emphasises the pleasantries of the visit and not the thorny diplomatic issues to be resolved. Any detailed account of religious practices might have seemed potentially divisive, and thus out of place in a document that sought to highlight the peace that had been concluded.

SIGNIFICANCE

While it is almost silent on matters of religion, the *Opisanie* nevertheless attests to a realistic attitude on the part of the Russian government with regard to its political relationship with Russia's traditional enemies. It points to a pragmatism that recognised the relative importance of religion and the demands of mutual co-existence, and the awareness that coming to terms with religious opponents could not be avoided.

This *Opisanie* can be taken as representative of a whole succession of similar documents, both Russian and Ottoman, that arose from diplomatic exchanges between the two powers, whose attitudes towards the actual political and religious realities prevailing at the time require careful assessment.

PUBLICATIONS

Opisanie tseremoniala s kotorym Ee Imperatorskogo Velichestva cherez-vychainyi i polnomozhnyi posol gospodin general Rumiantsev v Konstantinopol' svoi torzhestvennyi z'ezd imel i sperva u Verkhovnogo Viziria na vizite a potom u Turetskogo Sultana na audientsii byl, St Petersburg, 1741

STUDIES

B.L. Modzalevskii (ed.), *Russkii biograficheskii slovar'*, Petrograd, 1918, vol. 17, pp. 471-3

Glen Johnson

Mikhail Lomonosov

Mikhail Vasilievich Lomonosov, Mikhailo Vasilievich Lomonosov

DATE OF BIRTH   Autumn 1711
PLACE OF BIRTH   Denisovka, Russia
DATE OF DEATH   4 April 1765
PLACE OF DEATH   St Petersburg, Russia

BIOGRAPHY

Mikhail Lomonosov was born sometime in the autumn of 1711 in the village of Denisovka, near Kholmogory on the White Sea, to a small merchant family of peasant origin. At the age of 19, he left his home and walked to Moscow in order to enrol in the Slavo-Graeco-Latin Academy. In order to be admitted, he had to conceal his peasant origins; they were later discovered, but by then he had proved to have such a prodigious academic talent that, instead of being expelled or even arrested, he was chosen to be sent to study natural sciences in Marburg. On completing his studies, he returned to Russia and became a professor of chemistry.

Although Lomonosov's primary focus during his lifetime was natural science, his greatest influence has been on the development of the Russian language and Russian literature. In the mid-18th century, Russian writers were just beginning to experiment with modern European literary forms and how they should be adapted for the Russian language. Lomonosov contributed to this discussion with his *Short guide to rhetoric* (1748) and his *Foreword on the utility of ecclesiastical books* (1757), in which he outlined various stylistic levels and their relationship to Church Slavonic. Lomonosov also introduced the use of syllabotonic verse in Russian poetry, an innovation that was widely adopted, used by all the major poets of the Golden Age (e.g. Pushkin, Lermontov, Baratynsky), and continues to be used today.

Along with odes dedicated to rulers and great occasions, Lomonosov wrote a number of poems about natural phenomena and their relation to religion. One of his best-known is the 'Evening meditation upon the greatness of God', inspired by viewing an aurora. Although religious, Lomonosov also engaged in polemics against the official church teachings of the time, arguing for the idea of multiple worlds and, in his 1761 poem 'Two astronomers happened to come together at a feast', for a Copernican heliocentric conception of the solar system.

Lomonosov was recognised as one of the great thinkers of his age, and continues to hold an important position in the pantheon of Russian writers and academics. Apart from his introduction of the syllabotonic versification system to Russian poetry, his most significant contribution was probably his involvement in the creation of a university in Moscow; Moscow State University still bears his name in its official title.

MAIN SOURCES OF INFORMATION

Primary

M.V. Lomonosov, *Polnoe sobranie sochinenii,* vol. 10. *Sluzhebnye dokumenty. Pis'ma. 1734-1765 gg,* Moscow, 1952

Secondary

Art. 'Lomonosov, Mikhailo Vasilievich (1711-65)', in V. Terras (ed.), *The handbook of Russian literature,* New Haven CT, 1985, 264-5

G.E. Pavlova and A.A. Federov, *Mikhail Vasilievich Lomonosov. His life and work,* trans. A. Aksenov, ed. R. Hainsworth, 2nd rev. edition, Moscow, 1984

W. Huntington, 'Michael Lomonosov and Benjamin Franklin. Two self-made men of the eighteenth century', *The Russian Review* 18 (1959) 294-306

B.B. Kudryavtsev, *The life and work of Mikhail Vasilyevich Lomonosov,* Moscow, 1954

B.N. Menshutkin, *Russia's Lomonosov. Chemist, courtier, physicist, poet,* Princeton NJ, 1952

WORKS ON CHRISTIAN-MUSLIM RELATIONS

Oda na vziatie Khotina
'Ode on the capture of Khotin'

DATE 1739
ORIGINAL LANGUAGE Russian

DESCRIPTION

Lomonosov composed his *Oda na vziatie Khotina* (an alternative, more formal title is *Oda blazhennyia pamiati gosudaryne imperatritse Anne Ioannovne na pobedu nad turkami i tatarami i na vziatie Khotina 1739 goda,* 'Ode to the blessed memory of the Empress Anna Ioannovna on her victory over the Turks and Tatars and on the capture of Khotin in the year 1739') in the autumn of 1739, while living abroad in Germany.

He sent it to the Russian Academy of Sciences along with his *Epistle on the rules of Russian versification*. Written in iambic tetrameter, it is one of the first examples of the syllabotonic verse that Lomonosov championed and that would quickly become the norm in Russian poetry. It comprises 28 ten-line stanzas of iambic tetrameter with alternating masculine and feminine rhymes.

The ode describes in vivid detail the Russian victory over Turkish forces at Khotin, modern-day Khotyn in south-western Ukraine, during the Russo-Turkish war. Although it glorifies a Russian victory over the Muslim Ottoman Empire, the conflict is not portrayed as primarily religious; indeed, the main mythological elements are taken from the Graeco-Roman pantheon, not Christianity or Islam. The focus is not on a clash of cultures but on the glory of Anna Ioannovna's reign and the inevitable victory of Russia over all other countries. While it is jingoistic, it is more 'pro-Russia' than 'anti-Turk/Tatar', and is more concerned with praising the empress and the empire than with criticising Russia's enemies. Therefore, although it directly depicts an armed clash between Christians and Muslims, it does not emphasise the Muslim character of Russia's enemies or Russia's Christian character, but rather Russia's predestined path to greatness.

SIGNIFICANCE

The greatest significance of the work is that it launched the literary career of Lomonosov and also introduced to Russian poetry the iambic tetrameter, soon to become the favourite metre of Russian poets. The influential critic Vassarion Belinsky (d. 1848) commented that it was the beginning of modern Russian literature.

At the same time, it also set a tone for Russian 'imperial' writing. The Turks are not the enemy because of Islam (which hardly figures at all in the poem), but because they are standing against Russian imperial ambition. They are advised to concede their inevitable defeat and 'kiss the hand that with a bloody sword / Showed you fear', for, if they do so, 'Great Anna's terrible gaze / Is quick to give joy to supplicants'. Russia's imperial designs are depicted as divinely mandated but also benevolent, and those who surrender or are defeated can expect merciful treatment, an attitude that prefigures Pushkin's 'imperial' verse with its compassion for the vanquished standing side-by-side with its belief in the righteousness of Russia's actions.

In a way, *Ode on the capture of Khotin* suggests the possibility of a multi-ethnic, multi-confessional nation under the umbrella of Russia's imperial power. Russia's Muslim enemies do not need to be destroyed root and branch, but rather to be assimilated into the growing empire, where they will add to its glory and international fame.

PUBLICATIONS

The poem was originally written in 1739. The oldest surviving version is in the 1751 collected works.

M.V. Lomonosov, *Oda blazhenyia pamiati Gosudaryne Imperatritse Anne Ionnovne na pobedu nad Turkami i Tatarami i na vziatie Khotina 1739 goda*, St Petersburg, 1747

M.V. Lomonosov, 'Oda blazhennyia pamiati gosudaryne imperatritse Anne Ioannovne [...]', in *Sobranie raznykh sochinenii v stikhakh i proze* [Collected works of poems and prose], vol. 1, St Petersburg, 1751, repr. 1759, 1765, 1803

M.V. Lomonosov, 'Oda blazhennyia pamiati gosudaryne imperatritse Anne Ioannovne [...]', in *Polnoe sobranie sochinenii*, vol. 8. *Poeziia, oratorskaia proza, nadpisi, 1732-1764*, Moscow, 1959, 16-30 (annotated edition); http://feb-web.ru/feb/lomonos/texts/loo/lo8/lo8-0162.htm

M.V. Lomonosov, *Izbrannoe*, Moscow, 1976

M.V. Lomonosov, *Izbrannye proizvedeniia*, Leningrad, 1986, pp. 61-9; http://rvb.ru/18vek/lomonosov/01text/01text/010dy_t/001.htm

M.V. Lomonosov, 'An ode in blessed memory of Her Majesty the Empress Anna Ivanovna on the victory over the Turks and Tatars and the taking of Khotin, 1739', in I. Kutik and A. Wachtel (eds), *From the ends to the beginning. A bilingual anthology of Russian poetry*, Evanston IL (English trans. of the first 14 stanzas); http://max.mmlc.northwestern.edu/mdenner/Demo/texts/ode_to_anna.htm (online publication)

STUDIES

E. Kazartsev, *A comparative study of the early Dutch, German, and Russian iambic tetrameter*, Bloomington IN, 2014

I. Berson, 'Iazykovaia transformatsiia russkoi ody. Dva "Khotina"', *Toronto Slavic Quarterly* 13 (2005); http://sites.utoronto.ca/tsq/13/berson13.shtml (online journal)

Harsha Ram, *The imperial sublime. A Russian poetics of empire*, Madison WI, 2003

Demetrios Dvoichenko-Markov, 'Lomonosov and the capture of the fortress of Khotin in 1739', *Balkan Studies* 8 (1967) 65-74

Tamira i Selim. Tragediia
'Tamira and Selim. A tragedy'

DATE   1750

ORIGINAL LANGUAGE   Russian

DESCRIPTION

Lomonosov composed the verse play *Tamira and Selim* in 1750 at the behest of Empress Elizabeth (r. 1741-62), who ordered Lomonosov and Vasily Trediakovsky, another leading man of letters of the era, to each compose a tragedy. It was performed that year by the St Petersburg Cadet Corps.

The play is a fictionalised love story set against the backdrop of the Battle of Kulikovo in 1380, the first major Russian victory against the Golden Horde. However, it features not Russian, but Tatar and Middle Eastern characters. The heroine is Tamira, princess of the Crimean Tatars. Her father Mumet, the tsar of the Crimean Tatars, has promised her hand in marriage to the great Khan Mamai, but Tamira has secretly fallen in love with Selim, prince of Baghdad, who is leading a siege against Tamira's city. Struck by her beauty after catching a glimpse of her, he offers peace in exchange for her hand in marriage but, against Tamira's express wishes, Mumet feels honour-bound to insist on the marriage to Mamai. Tamira attempts to flee the city and escape to Baghdad with Selim, but she is captured. Meanwhile, Mamai returns proclaiming a great victory at Kulikovo Field. His deception about Tamira is dramatically revealed, Tamira and Selim are able to marry, and everyone except Mamai lives happily ever after.

SIGNIFICANCE

Tamira and Selim was an early attempt to write Western-style plays in verse, at a time when Russian literature was being revolutionised by writers such as Lomonosov, Trediakovsky and Alexander Sumarokov. Although modern readers may find it contrived and melodramatic, the introduction of historical dramas in verse into the Russian literary milieu paved the way for later masterpieces such as Pushkin's *Little tragedies* and especially his *Boris Godunov*.

Tamira and Selim presents Muslim characters, and specifically Tatars, as sympathetic and worthy of being the subject of serious works of literature. The reader or viewer is expected to agonise over Tamira's desperate situation and Selim's heartbreak, and Tamira's relatives are also depicted as people of feeling and honour. While the Muslim Tatars and Middle Easterners in the play are exotic, they are also presented as worthy of admiration and romantic. At the same time, a happy end to the play is supplied by a great Russian military victory over the Tatars. As in the *Ode on the capture of Khotin*, Russia's military victories and imperial domination are depicted as both inevitable and right: Mamai is a lying scoundrel who deserves the defeat and dishonour that strike him down, not because he is a Tatar or a Muslim, but because he attempts to defeat the Russian forces and uphold their subjugation to the Golden Horde. Mumet, Tamira and Selim, however, who have no desire to conquer Russia, are positive and sympathetic characters who are rewarded at the end of the play. The implication is that cultural assimilation of Tatars or Muslims is unnecessary, as long as they recognise the military and imperial might of the Russian state.

The multicultural acceptance hinted at in *Tamira and Selim* is thus also another way in which it prefigures the works of later, greater poets such as Pushkin, who included Gypsies, Jews and Tatars, often as sympathetic characters, in his verse. While Lomonosov and most of the Golden Age poets who inherited and developed his innovations were imperialists and Russian nationalists, they were also interested in other cultures and seemed to support the idea of a multicultural empire rather than a totalitarian state requiring complete assimilation into the dominant Russian culture.

PUBLICATIONS

M.V. Lomonosov, *Tamira i Selim. Tragediia*, St Petersburg, 1750

M.V. Lomonosov, *Polnoe sobranie sochinenii*, vol. 8. *Poeziia, oratorskaia proza, nadpisi, 1732-1764*, Moscow, 1959, pp. 292-364; http://feb-web.ru/feb/lomonos/texts/loo/lo8/lo8-292-.htm

Lomonosov, *Izbrannoe proizvedeniia*

STUDIES

N. Grantseva, *Lomosov. Sopernik Shekspira?*, St Petersburg, 2011

G.N. Moiseeva, 'K voprosu ob istochnikakh tragedii M.V. Lomonosova "Tamira i Selim"', in *Literaturnoe tvorchestvo Lomonosova*, Moscow, 1962, 253-7

Elena Pedigo Clark

Russian travellers to Jerusalem in the first half of the 18th century

BIOGRAPHY

Makarii and Sil'vestr were both hieromonks of the Novgorod Severskii Monastery.

The priest Andrei Ignat'ev served in the Russian embassy in Constantinople under Ambassador P.A. Tol'stoi in the early 18th century and returned to Russia in 1714. He entered the Voskresenskii Novo-Ierusalimskii Monastery and assumed the monastic habit under the name of Aaron.

Varlaam (Lenitskii, Linitskii, Levitskii; d. 1 January 1741) was a hieromonk of the Kievo-Pecherskaia Lavra and domestic priest (chaplain) to Field Marshall Boris Petrovich Sheremet'ev during the Pruth campaign in 1711. He came from the gentry and studied in the Kiev Mohyla Academy. After Pruth, he served in the Russian legation in Istanbul, under P.P. Shafirov and Count M.B. Sheremet'ev. In 1712, he travelled to the Holy Land. As he recounts in his travelogue, when the Russian representatives were arrested in Istanbul following the breakdown in negotiations after the Pruth campaign, he escaped to Cyprus but was arrested and sent to Istanbul. He was freed and returned to Russia, where he became an abbot and later a bishop.

Serapion (Serapion Mnozhinskii Kaiakov) was a monk of the Matronitskii Troitskii Monastery, near Chigirin, Ukraine.

MAIN SOURCES OF INFORMATION

Secondary

T. Stavrou and P.R. Weisensel, *Russian travelers to the Christian East from the twelfth to the twentieth century*, Columbus OH, 1986, pp. 59–60, 60–1, 65–6, 78–9

K.-D. Seemann, *Die altrussische Wallfahrtsliteratur. Theorie und Geschichte eines literarischen Genres*, Munich, 1976, pp. 377–83, 392–6

WORKS ON CHRISTIAN-MUSLIM RELATIONS

Accounts by Russian travellers to Jerusalem in the first half of the 18th century

ORIGINAL LANGUAGE Mainly Russian

DESCRIPTION

These four Russian accounts of Jerusalem and the pilgrimage to it are treated together because they come from roughly the same period, the first half of the 18th century. Also, while each of them alone only makes relatively brief references to Islam and Muslims, together they shed light on Russian Orthodox views about the other faith at a time of direct military confrontation between the Ottoman and Russian Empires.

Makarii and Sil'vestr's trip lasted from 1704 to 1707. Their account, *Put' nam ieromonakham Makariiu i Selivestru iz Monastyria Vsemilostivogo Spasa Novgorodka Severskogo do Sviatogo grada Ierusalima poklonitisia grobu Gospodniu 1704 godu* ('The itinerary of us, the hieromonks Makarii and Sil'vestr from the Monastery of the All-Merciful Saviour of Novgorod Severskii, to the holy city of Jerusalem in order to bow in front of the Holy Sepulchre, in the year 1704'), covers 24 pages in Leonid [Kavelin], 'Palomniki-pisateli'. Its structure is typical of the genre, made up of three parts: the trip to Jerusalem, the stay in Jerusalem, and the return to Russia. The authors pay particular attention to the problems generated by demands of Ottoman officials for payment (*garach, harac*) to allow them passage. Another theme is the dangers of sea travel, both in the Black Sea and the Eastern Mediterranean, due to storms and piracy. They describe the Christian shrines in Istanbul, and pay particular attention to the local flora. They also describe the defensive capabilities of Istanbul, a city whose size and population inspired awe in them, and also Alexandria, and note certain parallels in celebrations between Christians ('us') and Muslims.

They visited Christian shrines on the way to Jerusalem, but they also engaged in some of what could be called tourism, with visits south to the River Nile. The main part of the travelogue is, of course, devoted to Jerusalem and other places in the Holy Land. Relations with Muslims (distinguished between Arabs and Turks) are presented mainly through the prism of restrictions, prohibitions and entry fees. Particular criticism is addressed towards Western Christians (dubbed 'Franks') and Armenians, who were the main competitors of the Greeks (and, by extension, the Russians) for control of the Holy Land shrines. Orthodoxy is throughout presented as the only true Christianity, as evidenced by the emphasis on the 'miracle' of the descent of the Holy Fire on Holy Saturday. In this sense, the account portrays a united front of 'us', the Orthodox (Greeks and Russians), versus 'them', other Christians (who are at best heretics, and at worst pagans) in the Holy Land, where the authors spent one year. The account is published in Leonid [Kavelin], 'Palomniki-pisateli', pp. 1-26.

Andrei Ignat'ev and his brother Stefan travelled to the Holy Land in 1707 from Constantinople, in fulfilment of a promise they had made to themselves. The account describing their journey, *Puteshestvie iz Konstan-tinopolia v Ierusalim i Sinaiuskuiu Goru, nakhodivshagosia pri Rossiiskom Poslannike, Grafe Petre Andreeviche Tolstom, Sviashchennika Andreia Ignat'eva i brata ego, Stefana, v 1707 godu* ('A journey from Constantino-ple to Jerusalem and Mt Sinai by the Priest Andrei Ignat'ev, who served the Russian emissary Count Peter Andreevich Tolstoi, and by his brother Stefan, in the year 1707'), pays special attention to the hazards of travel at sea, and the farming methods and products of Egypt in particular. It also expresses wonderment at the underground network of Alexandria's water system. The united Greek-Russian Orthodox front is evident, with the main enemies being other Christians who were competitors of the Orthodox.

As befits a priest, Ignat'ev also describes in detail the order and prac-tices of services he witnesses in various churches and monasteries. His account is punctuated by outbursts of pride for the way in which the Orthodox Church in Jerusalem still 'shines' despite constant persecution from both Muslims and 'heretical' Christians. Ignat'ev acknowledges the existence of Arab Christians, but does not spend much time on them, and describes them as noisy in church. He offers a detailed description of the descent of the Holy Fire on Holy Saturday and also includes their journey to Sinai, where the sight of an ostrich is noted, and a detailed description is given of a reliquary gifted to the monastery by the Russian monarchs in the 1680s for the remains of St Catherine. Troubles because of storms at sea on the way back, and his arrest and release by the Otto-mans close the account. A note at the end informs the reader that this 'book' was written (*pisal*) in 1732 by Pakhomii Agapov, the treasurer (*kaz-nachei*) of the Voskresenskii Novo-Ierusalimskii Monastery. The account is published in Leonid [Kavelin], 'Palomniki-pisateli', pp. 27-54.

The account by the Hieromonk Varlaam, *Peregrinatsiia ili Putnik, v nem zhe opisuetsia put' do sviatogo grada Ierusalima i vse sviatye mesta*

Palestinskie, ot ieromonakha Varlaama, byvshogo tamo v 1712 g ('Peregrination or travelogue, in which is described the route to the holy city of Jerusalem and to all the holy places of Palestine, by Hieromonk Varlaam, who was there in 1712'), is rather shorter, and visibly so in its coverage of the various shrines, which in some cases are presented as simple listings. Given his service as a priest in diplomatic circles, Varlaam understandably emphasises the entries regarding pilgrimage in Russian-Turkish treaties. He particularly targets Armenians, who are attacked venomously throughout the work, and also the 'evil' Muslim faith (*zloverie*). He makes occasional references to historical events in modern, ancient and Byzantine times, indicating the level of his education.

Like other contemporary and later pilgrim authors, Varlaam emphasises the emotions of pilgrims on their first sight of Jerusalem and their first visit to the Church of the Holy Sepulchre. He provides a detailed description of the ritual of the washing of pilgrims' feet (of men; only the hands of women were washed), which was part of the welcome to pilgrims practised by the staff of the Greek Orthodox Patriarchate.

Varlaam spent six weeks in Jerusalem, and on the way back he had to pretend to be a Serb or Bulgarian (i.e. an Ottoman subject) because of the breakdown in the negotiations between Russians and Ottomans after the war of 1711. He was betrayed by his servant, and was arrested and brought to Cyprus, where he spent some time in jail. He was saved by the intervention of the British consul in 1714 (his knowledge of Latin helped him in this regard), but his unfortunate servant, who had converted to Islam, was captured by Maltese pirates and immediately killed. The account is published in Leonid [Kavelin], 'Palomniki-pisateli', pp. 55-77.

Serapion's account, entitled *Putnik ili puteshestvie vo Sviatuiu Zemliu Matroninskogo monastyria inoka Serapiona 1749 goda* ('Travelogue or journey to the Holy Land by the monk Serapion of the Matroninskii Monastery in the year 1749'), is in some ways the most detailed of all these four accounts. He provides a consise but adulatory description of Istanbul and its wonders (the *stelae*, and the lighthouses on its sea approach), exclaiming that it is an 'exquisite, wonderful, glorious, enormous and very populous' city (*prechuden, prekrasen, preslaven, prevelik i mnogonaroden*, the prefix pre- denoting something akin to 'extremely') (Leonid [Kavelin], 'Palomniki-pisateli', p. 81). Serapion also recounts the various shrines of Istanbul, noting that from one of them even the Ottoman sultan drinks holy water (p. 82).

He continues with a description of Mt Athos and Smyrna. He pays particular attention to the organisation of pilgrim visits put in place by the

Brotherhood of the Holy Sepulchre, and emphasises what he regards as administrative or practical problems, including Arabs and Turks forcing travellers to accept their services. Much like the other authors discussed here, he reports on the constant conflict between the various denominations for control of Holy Land shrines, although he emphasises that the Greek churches are decorated the best. He includes the longest and most detailed description of the visit to the River Jordan, and provides the most detailed description of the ritual of the descent of the Holy Fire on Holy Saturday. The account is published in Leonid [Kavelin], 'Palomniki-pisateli', pp. 78-129.

All these authors were clerics, either priests or monks, or priest-monks (hieromonks), so a tolerant attitude towards Muslims (at least openly) should not be expected from them. But there is no attempt to engage in theological or polemical arguments. In fact, they do not appear to have been interested in engaging with their opponents at all, because the main emphasis is on Jerusalem as the centre of Christianity and following in the steps of Christ.

References to interactions with Muslims are primarily about bureaucracy and procedure. If the authors had everyday interactions with Muslim guides or guards, they say very little about them in their accounts, but instead complain about restrictions imposed by Ottoman officials, even when there is an edict (*firman*) allowing travellers to proceed without impediments. They also regularly emphasise the need for bribes to secure access even to otherwise normally accessible areas of the Holy Land. Indeed, if anything characterises the Muslim Other in these accounts, it is their rapacity and their capacity to exact payment even when none is due. Special attention is paid to the Arab robbers who regularly attacked travellers between Jaffa and Jerusalem, and there are references to or even detailed descriptions of the ways in which Arab guides and guards fought for customers and forced them to accept their services.

The Ottomans are depicted as all-powerful, but they are not invincible. On occasion the authors explain that the wrath of God is seen as bringing them into humility and submission (Leonid [Kavelin], 'Palomniki-pisateli', p. 101).

Curiously little emphasis is placed on any Ottoman persecution of Christians, except for individual cases of forced conversion. Other than that, the authors regard their main enemies, other than Muslims, to be other Christians and in particular the Armenians. Venomous attacks against them pepper all these accounts, where the 'accursed' Armenians have either wrested control of shrines from 'us' or from 'our' patriarch through bribery (e.g. Leonid [Kavelin], 'Palomniki-pisateli', pp. 60, 106), or they have miserably failed to do so. Special attention is given to the 'miracle' of the Holy Fire on Holy Saturday, and the story of the one occasion when the Armenians, who controlled the Church of the Holy Sepulchre, tried to replicate the miracle but spectacularly failed to do so, leading the Ottomans to make them eat human pus, as one of our authors rather gleefully reported (Leonid [Kavelin], 'Palomniki-pisateli', p. 98).

Other Christians, the Franks, as they are collectively dubbed (but also the Copts and Syrians), are not much less dangerous. Beyond cases when their control of holy shrines is noted, they are also called a number of derogatory names: heretics, accursed, pagans, sons of Origen, fake Christians (the last in Serapion's account (Leonid [Kavelin], 'Palomniki-pisateli', p. 91).

Throughout the accounts, two particular marks of holiness are emphasised: the presence of relics and the connection of a given place to the biblical scenario of salvation. Particular attention is given to miracles. The authors regularly note that in some cases these benefit both Christians and Muslims, but they are reluctant to elaborate further. This is the one instance of an insight into the everyday 'lived' religion of the Ottoman Empire, where Christians and Muslims appear to share some common practices. But our authors do not elaborate, perhaps because to do so would not be appreciated by their readers. The one exception is the occasion of the Ottoman authorities sending greetings to the Christians on Holy Saturday (Leonid [Kavelin], 'Palomniki-pisateli', p. 124).

Open and direct attacks against Muslims do not often appear in the accounts beyond name-calling, although in one account there is a reference to *bogomerzkii prorok Mahomed* ('the unholy prophet Mohamed'). Interestingly, the presence of Arab Christians is noted occasionally, but without much elaboration as to their beliefs. Instead, we are told that they are noisy in church.

SIGNIFICANCE

While these works exemplify contempt for Islam and some disdain for Muslims, the main impression they convey is of indifference towards the faith of the Ottomans and Arabs and towards the people themselves. This can be explained by the nature of the works, of course, as memoirs of time spent in the holy places of Christianity and descriptions of these places and the rites performed there. But the authors show little explicit concern about the faith of individuals they must have met throughout their stays in the Holy Land, such as guides they must have come to know. It is as though, for them, Muslims (like Christians from other Churches) were so obviously in the wrong and so evidently destined for God's wrath that they hardly needed to be mentioned, beyond the occasional reference to them as 'accursed'.

PUBLICATIONS

Arkhimandrit Leonid [Kavelin] (ed.), 'Palomniki-pisateli petrovskogo i poslepetrovskogo vremeni ili Putniki vo sviatoi grad Ierusalim, s ob'iasnitel'nymi k tekstu primechaniiami', in *Chteniia v Imperatorskom Obshchestve Istorii i Drevnostei Rossiiskikh pri Moskovskom Universitete*, Moscow, 1873, book 3, pp. 1-129

STUDIES

On Makarii and Sil'vestr:
Stavrou and Weisensel, *Russian travelers to the Christian East*, pp. 59-60
Seemann, *Die altrussische Wallfahrtsliteratur*, pp. 377-80

On Andrei Ignat'ev:
Stavrou and Weisensel, *Russian travelers to the Christian East*, pp. 60-1
Seemann, *Die altrussische Wallfahrtsliteratur*, pp. 380-3

On Varlaam Lenitskii:
Art., 'Varlaam', in *Pravoslavnaia entsiklopediia*, vol. 6, Moscow, 2009, 594-5; http://www.pravenc.ru/text/154195.html
V.V. Sheremetevskii, art. 'Varlaam (Levitskii)', in *Russkii Biograficheskii Slovar'*, Moscow, 2000, 109–13
Stavrou and Weisensel, *Russian travelers to the Christian East*, pp. 65-6
Seemann, *Die altrussische Wallfahrtsliteratur*, pp. 392-6

On Serapion:
'Palomnichestvo na Afon Serapiona, monakha Matroninskogo Troitskogo monastyria, v 1749-1751 godakh', in *Istoriia Russkogo Sviato-Panteleimonova monastyria na Afone s 1735 do 1912 god*, vol. 5, Mt Athos, Greece, 2015, 98-101
E.Iu. Diukova, 'Vnov' naidennyi spisok "Putnika" ili "Puteshestviia v Sviatuiu Zemliu inoka Serapiona" i kontseptsiia obshchevostochnoslavianskogo podkhoda k izucheniiu zhanra khozhdenii', in *Slavianskiia litaratury ŭ kantėkstse susvetnaĭ: Matėryialy IX Mizhnar. Navuk. Kanf., prysvech. 70-goddziu filalagichnaga fakul'tėta*

Belaruskaha dziarzhaŭnaha universitéta, Minsk, 15-17 kastr. 2009 h.),
Minsk, 2010, vol. 2, pp. 79-85

Stavrou and Weisensel, *Russian travelers to the Christian East*, pp. 78-9

W [P. Gorlenko], 'Na puti v Ierusalim', *Kievskaia Starina* 18/5 (1887)
204-6

See also:

V. Izmirlieva, 'Christian hajjis. The other Orthodox pilgrims to Jerusalem', *Slavic Review* 73 (2014) 322-46

I.V. Fedorova, *'Puteshestvie v Sviatuiu Zemlu i Egipet' kniaz'ia Nikolaia
Radzivilla i vostochnoslavianskaia palomnicheskaia literatura XVII–
nachala XVIII v. Issledovanie i tekst*, St Petersburg, 2014 (useful for
the genre)

S.A. Kirillina, *'Ocharovannye stranniki'. Arabo-osmanskii mir glazami
rossiiskikh palomnikov XVI-XVIII stoletii*, Moscow, 2010, especially
pp. 407-66

P. Bushkovitch, 'Orthodoxy and Islam in Russia, 988-1725', in
L. Steindorff (ed.), *Religion und Integration im Moskauer Russland.
Konzepte und Praktiken, Potentiale und Grenzen* (Forschungen zur
osteuropäischen Geschichte 76), Wiesbaden, 2010, 117-44

Nikolaos Chrissidis

Johann Georg Gmelin

Ioanne Georgio Gmelin

DATE OF BIRTH	8 August 1709
PLACE OF BIRTH	Tübingen
DATE OF DEATH	20 May 1755
PLACE OF DEATH	Tübingen?

BIOGRAPHY

Johann Georg Gmelin (Ioanne Georgio Gmelin), a German naturalist, botanist and geographer, was born in Tübingen on 8 August 1709, the son of Johann Georg Gmelin the Elder (d. 1728), a renowned Swabian apothecary and professor of chemistry at the University of Tübingen. The young Johann entered the University at the age of 13 and received a degree in medicine in 1728. In the same year, at the age of 18, he was appointed lecturer in natural history at the Academy of Sciences in St Petersburg. Two years later, in 1731, he was appointed professor of natural history and chemistry.

In 1731, as professor at the Russian Imperial Academy of Sciences, he was recruited as a member of the Second Kamchatka Expedition (1733-43). His task was to record and classify the flora and fauna he encountered across the wide spans of Siberia.

In 1747, he went back to Tübingen and became professor of medicine at the university, and in 1751 director of the university's botanical garden. He died on 20 May 1755.

His *Flora sibirica* ('The flora of Siberia'), published posthumously in 1760, remains one of the most comprehensive studies of Siberian plant life to the present day. A lesser-known publication *Reise durch Sibirien* ('Travels in Siberia') was published in Germany in 1751-2. The contents provide an early ethnographic sketch of the spiritual life of the peoples Gmelin encountered in his trek across Siberia. As noted by the 21st-century Russian scholar Aleksandr Elert, these observations clearly fell outside his purview as a botanist, as the task of ethnography was that of G.F. Müller, the expedition historian. However, Gmelin provides an informal and nuanced view of the virtues and uprightness of Tatar Muslims, as compared to Müller's formal observations of the loosely-held belief in Islam in 18th-century Siberia.

MAIN SOURCES OF INFORMATION

Primary

Polnoe Sobranie Zakonov Rossikoi imperii, St Petersburg, 1885-1916, vol. 8 (1728-32), nos 6023, 6041, 6042, 6291, 6351 (instructions to the Kamchatka Expedition under the command of Captain Vitus Bering)

Secondary

Puteshestvie v Sibir', Otv. red. E.V. Smironov (trans. from the German by D.F. Krivoruchko), Solikamsk, 2012

F.N. Egerton, 'A history of the ecological sciences. Part 27: Naturalists explore Russia and the north Pacific during the 1700s', *The Bulletin of the Ecological Society of America* 89 (2008) 39-60

A.K. Elert, 'Puteshestvie po Sibiri, Tiurki Krasnoiarskogo uezda i ikh shamany', *Nauka iz Pervykh Ruk* 6 (18) 2007; http://cyberleninka.ru/article/n/puteshestvie-po-sibiri-tyurki-krasnoyarskogo-uezda-i-ih-shamany

V.A. Grishev, *Issledovateli Sibirs Iogann Georg Gmelin i Gerard Fredrikh Müller*, Kraevedcheskie zapiski , #11. Irkutsk: Irkut. obl. kraev. Muzei, SO RAN, 2004

O. Gmelin, *Johann Georg Gmelin, 1709-1755. Der Erforscher Siberiens*, Munich, 1911

WORKS ON CHRISTIAN-MUSLIM RELATIONS

Reise durch Sibirien
'Travels through Siberia'

DATE   1751-2

ORIGINAL LANGUAGE   German

DESCRIPTION

From the time of its publication Gmelin's *Reise durch Sibirien* was condemned for its lack of academic merit, and characterised as a sentimental travelogue. It has not been included in scholarly observations of Siberia dating from the 18th century. The reasons behind this are twofold. One is what was judged as the work's want of scholastic expertise, and the other is Gmelin's indifference to the conditions of the expedition of which he was part. All expedition members took an oath of secrecy in which they undertook only to send reports back to the Russian Senate, and on their return to resume work at the St Petersburg Academy and not return to their native land, and they were only to publish their findings, in Latin, with the permission of the Russian Senate. Gmelin, however, returned to Tübingen in 1747, and published *Reise durch Sibiren* in German at Göttingen. However, his associates M.V. Lomonosov and G.F. Müller supported him by acting as guarantors, and repaid 715 roubles of his 1,000 rouble salary for 1748-9. This enabled Gmelin to remain in Tübingen until his death in 1755 (M.V. Lomonosov, *Zhizneopisanie*, St Petersburg, 1911, pp. 39-40).

During the expedition, as he travelled through Siberia en route to Kamchatka, Gmelin recorded the cultural practices and everyday life of the native peoples he came across, including Muslim Tatars from Kazan to Irkutsk. Religious rituals, particularly marriage ceremonies, fascinated him. For example, while he was attending a wedding in Tobolsk in 1734, he describes the similarities between Muslim and Russian Orthodox weddings he had witnessed:

> It is best to tell of this, as I was a bit surprised. The evening before the marriage ceremony the bride was in the house, there were a lot of women and young girls from the side of the bride, and it seemed as though they were mourning her maidenhood, as is also common and tends to take place with Russians. (*Reise*, p. 139)

Gmelin continues to note that in the ceremony the welfare of the bride is given consideration should the husband marry a second wife. At this time, Russian Orthodox clergy on the Siberian frontier were expressing concern about the immorality of polygamy, and advocated the conversion of Muslims and pagans as a means to combat this. Yet Gmelin's description presents a picture of the encouragement given to the husband to remain faithful to his wife, and to honour the institution of marriage, but, if other wives are taken, to ensure the bride will not be abandoned and left without resources. This is a very different picture from the one painted by the Russian Orthodox Church and Gmelin's colleagues of the tendency among Tatar men to abandon and deceive their wife when they took another.

SIGNIFICANCE

Gmelin's *Reise durch Sibirien* provides a counterpoint to conventional histories and administrative writings concerning encounters with Muslims in Siberia. His words are not constrained by the Russian context, and freely reflect the humanity and inquisitiveness of a first-hand observer, rather than the rhetoric of the anti-Muslim sentiments that were common in popular and scholarly writings in 18th-century Russia.

PUBLICATIONS

Johann Georg Gmelins, *Reise durch Sibirien, von dem Jahre 1733 bis 1743*, 4 vols, Göttingen, 1751-2; Gs 3324 -3/4 (digitised version available through *MDZ*)

Johann Georg Gmelin, *Reize door Siberiën naar Kamtschatka, van't jaar 1733 tot 1743*, trans. H. van Elvervelt, 4 vols, Haarlem, 1752-7 (Dutch trans.); KW 661 K 8 [-9] (digitised version available through Koninklijke Bibliotheek)

Johann Georg Gmelin, *Reiser gjennem Sibirien: uddragne af Gmelins og Muellers beskrivelser* [Copenhagen], 1760 (Danish trans.)

Johann Georg Gmelin, *Voyage en Sibérie: contenant la description des moeurs & usages des peuples de ce pays, le cours des rivieres considérables, la situation de chaines de montagnes, des grandes forêts, des mines, avec tous les faits d'histoire naturelle qui sont particuliers à cette contrée*, trans. M. de Keralio, Paris, 1767 (French trans.); It.sing. 1446 e-1 [2] (digitised version available through *MDZ*)

Johann Georg Gmelin, *Reise nach Kamtschatka durch Sibirien. 1733-43*, [s.l.], 1769

J.G. Gmelin et al., *Jenseits des Steinernen Tores Reisen deutscher Forscher des 18. und 19. Jahrhunderts durch Sibirien*, Berlin, 1973 (selections)

J.G. Gmelin et al., *Die Grosse nordische Expedition von 1733 bis 1743. Aus Berichten der Forschungsreisenden Johann Georg Gmelin und Georg Wilhelm Steller*, Munich, 1990

J.G. Gmelin, *Expedition ins unbekannte Sibirien*, ed. D. Dahlmann, Sigmaringen, 1999

Gwyn Bourlakov

Matvei Mironov

DATE OF BIRTH   Unknown; early 18th century
PLACE OF BIRTH   Unknown
DATE OF DEATH   Unknown; presumably late 18th century
PLACE OF DEATH   Unknown

BIOGRAPHY

Few details about Matvei Mironov's life are known. He came from a Russian noble family based in Chernigov. During the 17th century, members of the family performed reconnaissance missions for Muscovy in the Zaporozhian Sech and the Crimean Khanate. In 1749, Mironov was a captain stationed in Kiev; six years later he was a second-major in the Russian infantry. In August 1755, the vice-governor of Kiev, I.I. Kostiurin, sent Mironov to the Crimean Khanate to congratulate the khan, Arslan Giray, on the accession in Istanbul of the new sultan, Osman III (r. 1754-7). In addition, he was ordered to discuss various border issues, and to negotiate the establishment of a Russian resident in the Crimean capital, Bakhchisarai. To accomplish this assignment, he was given 50 roubles and the command of a small team of Cossacks who had knowledge of Turkish and Tatar.

The results of the undertaking were mixed: although the khan rejected the request for a Russian resident, Mironov was able to collect information about the internal structure of the khanate.

MAIN SOURCES OF INFORMATION

Primary

A. Andr. (ed.), 'K istorii pogranichnykh nashikh snoshenii s krymskim khanstvom. (Putevoi zhurnal sekund-maiora Matveia Mironova, v komandirovky ego k krymskomy khanu, 1755 goda)', *Kievskaia Starina* 9 (1885) 339-56, pp. 344-56

Secondary

Andr., 'K istorii pogranichnykh nashikh snoshenii s krymskim khanstvom', pp. 340-1

WORKS ON CHRISTIAN-MUSLIM RELATIONS

K istorii pogranichnykh nashikh snoshenii s krymskim khanstvom
'On the history of our border relations with the Crimean khanate'

DATE 1755
ORIGINAL LANGUAGE Russian

DESCRIPTION

This work, divided into dated journal entries (21 August-10 September 1755) and an undated postscript from Kiev, describes Matvei Mironov's journey through Crimea and his negotiations with the Crimean khan (its full title is *K istorii pogranichnykh nashikh snoshenii s krymskim khanst-vom. Putevoi zhurmal' sekund-maiora Matveia Mironova, v komandirovke ego k krymskomu khanu 1755 goda*, 'On the history of our border relations with the Crimean khanate. Travel journal of second-major Matvei Mironov, during his mission to the Crimean khan, in the year 1755'). The 1885 edition is 13 pages long. Direct references to Christian-Muslim relations are frequent.

In a logbook of his journey from the Zaporozhian Sech (also referred to as Malorossiia) into Tatar territory, Mironov describes his encounters with various peoples living within the Crimean khanate, including Cossacks, Tatars, Turks, Poles, Greeks and Armenians. When entering the khanate, he makes passing reference to Tatar soldiers, who seem ambivalent about the presence of Russians. In Perekop, he meets a Crimean *kaymakam* (regional governor), with whom he discusses the benefits of friendly Russian-Ottoman relations and the problem of Cossack raids into Crimean territory. As the group nears the Crimean capital, Muslim-Tatar interpreters greet them and discuss details of their travel. At one point, Mironov relates the experience of an interpreter named Mehmed who, in 1737, learned to read and write Russian while stationed in Ochakov. An anecdote from a Greek named Ianakii (who accompanied the Russian legation into the Crimean capital) concerns the marriage between a Muslim, Khali-khadzhi, and a beautiful Greek widow. According to Ianakii, after his marriage Khali-khadzhi secretly converted to Christianity, purchased palms, candles and wine for liturgies, and donated money for the upkeep of Christian churches.

Once in Bakhchisarai, Mironov describes his encounters with Crimean interpreters and officials, including the khan, Arslan Giray. As both sides exchange letters, the general mood of negotiations is amicable: the legations wish each other good health and prosperity over coffee and pipes of tobacco. The ostensible occasion for Mironov's visit is to congratulate the khan on the accession of a new Ottoman sultan; the men also discuss the status of fugitive Ukrainians, who apparently prefer to live in the khanate.

It becomes apparent that the khan is not interested in welcoming a permanent Russian representative, in part because of the paltry economic exchange between the two states, and in part due to confrontations between Tatars and Cossacks. The latter, according to the khan, are guilty of stealing Tatar horses. The khan informs Mironov of the 50,000 Muslims who recently fled to Crimea from Russian-controlled Kuban and Cherkessia. In sum, Arslan Giray is suspicious and wary of the Russian presence in Crimea.

Mironov also records discussions with the Greek, Ianakii, about military affairs, including the quantities of cannon balls and gunpowder in cities such as Yenikale, the condition of churches and fugitive Russian criminals, and the possibility of employing locals as spies. Mironov's final journal entries summarise the last days of his trip and his return to Russian territory.

SIGNIFICANCE

Mironov's notes contain rare historical information about relations between Russia and the Crimean Khanate during the period between the Russian-Ottoman wars (1739-68). His comments emphasise the multiethnic nature of the region. The description of audiences with the khan in Bakhchisarai and with Crimean notables sheds light on the diplomacy involved in these encounters, and on economic and military issues.

Mironov's account seems to suggest that the Russians no longer considered the Tatars to be a hostile infidel force on the frontier. The Crimean khan is approached with respect and deference, like the leader of a Christian power. The text also reveals that Russian achievements in Crimea were due, in part, to the astute policies of Tsarina Elizabeth (r. 1741-62), whose periodic embassies fostered closer relations with the Tatars.

PUBLICATIONS

Andr., 'K istorii pogranichnykh nashikh snoshenii s krymskim khanstvom, pp. 344-56

STUDIES

V.E. Vozgrin, *Istoricheskie sud'by krymskikh tatar*, Moscow, 1992, pp. 250-7

A. Fisher, *Crimean Tatars*, Palo Alto CA, 1978, pp. 51-3

A. Fisher, *The Russian annexation of the Crimea*, Cambridge, 1970, p. 25

Lucien Frary

Batyrsha Aliev

Abdulla Aleev; Gabdulla Galiev; Abdulla Miazgaldin;
Gubaidulla Miagziadlin; Batyrsha Gubaidulla; Bahâdur Shah

DATE OF BIRTH   Around 1710
PLACE OF BIRTH   Karyshbash village, Bashkiria
DATE OF DEATH   1762
PLACE OF DEATH   Shlisselburg fortress

BIOGRAPHY

According to the majority of sources, Batyrsha was born in Bashkyria in a Mishar family. His father was possibly a Muslim scholar, and gave him his primary education in the village of Karyshbash. In the 1730s and 1740s, Batyrsha attended madrasas in the Kazan region, travelling extensively in the Orenburg, Kazan and Tobolsk regions.

In 1749, the by now Mullah Batyrsha Aliev returned to Karyshbash to become an imam and a teacher in a madrasa there. In 1755, he was nominated to be an official Islamic cleric (*akhund* or *akhoond*) of the Siberian khanate, but never accepted the position. Early in 1755, Batyrsha wrote an appeal, calling upon the Bashkirs, Tatars, Kazakhs and Uzbeks to rise against the unjust rule of the Russians in their khanates. Acting on this call, the Bashkirs in the south started a premature rebellion against the authorities.

Before the uprising could spread, it was easily crushed by the imperial authorities, who dispatched 1,300 troops to deal with the disturbances. While he was not a formal leader of the uprising, Batyrsha nonetheless took responsibility for its ideological basis and went into hiding. He was finally captured in August of 1756. Transported via Moscow and St Petersburg, he was imprisoned in Schlisselburg fortress in the Baltic. There, he wrote a letter to the Empress Elizabeth (r. 1741-62) explaining the principle of the legitimacy of authority based on Islamic political thought, and the issue of just rule. In 1762, he was killed in prison during an escape attempt that left four guards dead.

MAIN SOURCES OF INFORMATION

Primary

Batyrsha Aliev, 'Vozzvanie misharskogo mully Batyrshi Ali-ully k bashkiram, misharam i drugim musul'manskim narodam Priura'lia', in V.N. Vitevskii (ed.), *I.I. Nepliuev i Orenburgskii krai, v prezhnem ego sostave do 1758 g.*, Kazan, 1897, vol. 3, pp. 93-100

Batyrsha Aliev, *Pis'mo Batyrshi imperatritse Elizavete Petrovne*, ed. and trans. G.B. Khusainov, Ufa, 1993

Secondary

C. Steinwedel, *Threads of empire. Loyalty and tsarist authority in Bashkiria, 1552-1917*, Bloomington IN, 2016, pp. 62-3

M. Tepeyurt, 'Bashkirs between two worlds, 1552-1824', Morgantown WV, 2011 (PhD Diss. West Virginia University)

Vosstanie pod predvoditel'stvom Batyrshi i obshchestvenno-kul'turnaia situatsia v tatrskom obshchestve v XVIII v. Materialy konferentsii [The uprising under the leadership of Batyrsha and the social and cultural situation in the Tatar society in the eighteenth century], Kazan, 2007

Art. 'Batyrsha', in *Bashkirskaia encyclopedia*, Ufa, 2005, vol. 1, p. 331

S.U. Taimasov, 'Batyrsha i Bashkirskoe vosstanie 1755 goda' [Batyrsha and the Bashkir uprising in 1755], *Vestnik Bashkirskogo Universiteta* 4 (2005) 71-3

F. Islaev, *Vosstanie Batyrshi, god 1755* [Batyrsha's uprising, 1755], Kazan, 2004

A.J. Frank, *Muslim religious institutions in imperial Russia. The Islamic world of Novouzensk District and the Kazakh Inner Horde, 1780-1910*, Leiden, 2001, p. 24

A.J. Frank, *Islamic historiography and Bulghar identity among the Tatars and Bashkirs of Russia*, Leiden, 1998, p. 45

S.M. Vasil'ev, 'Rol' Batyrshi v vosstanii 1755 g. v Bashkirii' [The role of Batyrsha in the uprising of 1755 in Bashkiria], in *Stranitsy istorii Bashkirii*, Ufa, 1974, 25-32

Art. 'Batyrsha', in *The great Soviet encyclopedia*, 1970[3], vol. 3

A.P. Chuloshnikov, *Vosstanie 1755 g. v Bashkirii* [The uprising of 1755 in Bashkiria], Moscow, 1940

WORKS ON CHRISTIAN-MUSLIM RELATIONS

Donoshenie misherskogo mully Batyrshi Ali-uly imperatritse Elizavete
'The report of the Mishar Mulla Batyrsha Ali-uli to Empress Elizabeth'

DATE   24 November 1756
ORIGINAL LANGUAGE   Turkic

DESCRIPTION
Written as a letter to the Empress Elizabeth while Batyrsha was in a Moscow prison, the original document spanned 140-50 pages (its full title is *Donoshenie misherskogo mully Batyrshi Ali-uly imperatritse Elizavete o prichinakh vosstaniia v Bashkirii v 1755-kh g. i ego sobstvennoi roli v podgotovke volnenii na Osinskoi, Sibirskoi i Nogaiskoi dorogakh*, 'The report of the Mishar Mulla Batyrsha Ali-uli to Empress Elizabeth on the causes of the uprising in Bashkiria in 1755, and about his own role in the causing of unrest on the Osin, Siberian and Nogai doroga'). Written in a conversational, autobiographical form, the letter features vignettes reflecting the life of the people, their social situations and relationships, legends, customs, languages, festivals and practices. Batyrsha often uses dialogue to relay stories about the imperial officials' oppressive policies and dismissive attitudes towards the Bashkirs and Tatars.

Batyrsha offers many practical reasons for the Bashkirs' revolt. He describes in detail the difficult socio-economic situation of the Bashkirs and Mishars in the provinces in the mid-18th century, and pointedly criticises tsarist officials for their abuse and harassment of the local population. He writes about the people's dissatisfaction with a tax on the purchase of salt, the forced baptisms of Muslims and military conscription.

These facts serve as a basis for a well-developed argument about the illegitimacy of the empress's authority from the standpoint of just rule in Islamic political thought. Batyrsha postulates that as long as the empress respects Muslim religious practices, protects all her subjects, and fulfils her obligations, his fellow Muslims are bound to uphold her authority. But he did not see any of this happening in reality, and so he advocated an uprising.

SIGNIFICANCE

This document not only describes the culture, traditions and life-conditions of the Bashkirs and Tatars in the mid-18th century, but also provides moving criticism of the imperial administration on the basis of the Islamic notion of justice. According to Mehmet Tepeyurt, the rebellion, followed by Batyrsha's extensive letter, pointed to the ineffectiveness of forced conversions, which ultimately led to the dissolution of the Office of New Converts in 1764.

PUBLICATIONS

MS Moscow, Russian State Archive of Ancient Acts (RGADA) – fond 7 (1781)

MS Ufa, Scientific Archive at the Ufa Scientific Centre of the Russian Academy of Sciences (Nauchnyi Arkhiv UNTs RAN) – fond 3, op. 12, d. 31

Batyrsha Aliev, 'Vozzvanie misharskogo mully Batyrshi Ali-ully k bashkiram, misharam i drugim musul'manskim narodam Priura'lia', in V.N. Vitevskii (ed.), *I.I. Nepliuev i Orenburgskii krai, v prezhnem ego sostave do 1758 g.*, Kazan, 1897, vol. 3, 93-100

Batyrsha Aliev, *Pis'mo Batyrshi imperatritse Elizavete Petrovne*, ed. and trans. G.B. Khusainov, Ufa, 1993

STUDIES

Steinwedel, *Threads of empire*, pp. 62-3

Tepeyurt, 'Bashkirs between two worlds'

Vosstanie pod predvoditel'stvom Batyrshi

Taimasov, 'Batyrsha i Bashkirskoe vosstanie'

G.B. Khusainov, 'Introduction', in Khusainov (ed. and trans.), *Pis'mo Batyrshi imperatritse Elizavete Petrovne*

Natalie Bayer

Gerhard Friedrich Müller

Fyodor Ivanovich Miller

DATE OF BIRTH   29 October 1705
PLACE OF BIRTH   Herford, Duchy of Westphalia
DATE OF DEATH   22 October 1783
PLACE OF DEATH   Moscow

BIOGRAPHY

Gerhard Friedrich Müller (Russianised to Fedor Ivanovich Miller) was born in Herford, Duchy of Westphalia, on 29 October 1705, and died in Moscow on 22 October 1783. He co-founded the Russian Imperial Academy of Sciences in 1725 and was professor of history there, and he was a member of the Second Kamchatka Expedition (1733-43).

Müller's father was a minister, and his mother was the daughter of Gerhard Bode, professor of law, theology and eastern languages in Minden. He was educated at the University of Leipzig in philosophy and history. At the age of 20, he was invited to be a founding member of the St Petersburg Academy of Sciences. As professor of history and Latin, he was one of the first foreign scholars to be involved in realising Gottfried Leibniz's proposal to Peter the Great (r. 1682-1725) to establish an Academy of Sciences in St Petersburg. One of his first notable works was a collection of articles concerning Russia, *Sammlung russischer Geschichte* (1732-65), the first major publication to acquaint foreign audiences with the territory of Russia and its history. He became editor of *Sankt-Peterburgskie Vedomosti*, one of Russia's first domestic newspapers, which featured scholarly commentary intended for a general audience. Following his return from Siberia, he became one of the highest-ranking state officials (Active State Councillor), and directed the Main Moscow Archive (*Moskovskii Glavni Arkhiv*) from 1766 until his death in 1783. Today this archive is known as the Russian State Archive of Ancient Acts, and is used by researchers from around the world.

In March of 1733, at the age of 27, Müller was appointed by the Ruling Senate of Empress Anna Ioannovna as one of the leaders of the Second Kamchatka, or 'Great Northern', Expedition. The other members included the naturalist J.G. Gmelin, the astronomer Louis de l'Isle de la

Croyér, and the navigator Vitus J. Bering, who had led the First Kamchatka Expedition (1725-30). As a newly appointed professor of history, Müller was to report on the manners, customs, religions and histories of the inhabitants of Siberia. He was also to observe and comment upon its geography, its commerce, its military and political institutions, and the history of Russian geographical discoveries in Siberia, and the Arctic and Pacific oceans. As dictated by the Ruling Senate, all of his findings were to be recorded in Latin and kept secret, only to be published with permission by the Ruling Senate.

In 1750, accounts of his travels in Siberia were published as the *Opisanie sibirskogo tsarstva* ('Description of the Siberian realm'). Some official documents of the expedition were also published in *Ezhemesiachnyia Sochineniia* 7, in 1758, although Müller's full account of the trip, 'Zur Geschichte der Akademie der Wissenschaften Petersburg', was not published until 1890. In the 20th century, the Soviet historians S.V. Bakhrushin, and A.I. Andreev republished Müller's original 1750 work, together with a commentary, as *G.F. Miller: Istorii Sibiri* (vol. 1, 1937; vol. 2, 1941; vol. 3, 2005).

One of the most recent and significant works on the Second Kamchatka Expedition was published in 2009 by Aleksandr Elert and Wieland Hintzsche, who collaborated on the Russian and German multi-volume *Opisanie sibirskikh narodov* and *Beschreibung sibirscher Völker* ('Description of the Siberian peoples'). These materials provide an early ethnic history and ethnography of Siberian peoples, as well as cataloguing dozens of unique vocabularies of the languages and dialects of nearly all Siberian Muslims, Buddhists and other inhabitants of Siberia.

The G.F. Müller collection is one of the largest archival collections, numbering in the hundreds of thousands of documents from unique written sources on the history of Siberia from the 16th to the 18th centuries.

MAIN SOURCES OF INFORMATION

Secondary

'G.F. Miller. Rossiskaia akademiia nauk. Institut etnologii i antropologii', in N.N. Mikluho-Makaia, *G.F. Miller. Istorii Sibiri*, vol. 3, Moscow, 2005; http://drevlit.ru/texts/m/Miller_7/index.php

P. Hoffmann, *Gerhard Friedrich Müller (1705-1783). Historiker, Geograph, Archivar im Dienste Russlands*, Frankfurt, 2005

A.K. Elert, *Ekspeditsionnye materialy G.F. Millera kak istochnik po istorii Sibiri*, Novosibirsk, 1990

J.L. Black and D.K. Buse, *G.F. Müller and Siberia, 1733-1743*, Kingston, Ontario, 1989

S.V. Bakhrushin and A.I. Andreev, *G.F. Miller: Istorii Sibiri*, 2 vols, Moscow, 1937, 1941, 2005

F.K. Russov, *Beiträge zur Geschichte der Ethnographischen und Anthropologischen Sammlungen der Kaiserlichen Akademie der Wissenschaften zu St.-Petersburg*, St Petersburg, 1900

WORKS ON CHRISTIAN-MUSLIM RELATIONS

Opisanie sibirskikh narodov
'Description of the Siberian peoples'
Opisanie sibirskogo tsarstva
'Description of the Siberian realm'

DATE   1750
ORIGINAL LANGUAGE   German

DESCRIPTION

Among Müller's collected writings are two foundational works that describe Muslim everyday life, belief and practices, and the history of the missionary work of the Russian Orthodox Church in the Siberian administrative district in the mid-18th century. The first, *Opisanie sibirskikh narodov* ('Description of the Siberian peoples'), contains his eye-witness accounts of Muslim beliefs and practices. He outlines his encounters with large groups of Tatars in western Siberia, describing marriage practices, child-rearing, diet, trade and travel, and their pastoral and agrarian economies, observing that their literacy and education derives directly from their study of the Qur'an. As a quasi-ethnographer, he lists the names and lengths of religious holidays, and the months and signs of the zodiac adhered to by the 'Mohammadean Tatars'. But even though he had extensive interactions with followers of Islam throughout his travels in Siberia, for specific religious practices he relies heavily on the writings of the 17th-century Persian historian Abulgazi.

Abulgazi's two historical works *Shajare-i Tarakime* ('Genealogy of the Turkmen'), finished in 1661, and *Shajare-i Türk* ('Genealogy of the Turks'), finished in 1665, were widely read in Europe during the 18th century. Russian and European scholars came to know of Abulgazi's works when Swedish officers, detained in Russian captivity in Siberia, purchased a manuscript of the *Shajare-i Türk* from a Bukhara merchant in Tobolsk. Using local Tatars, the officers first translated the book into Russian and then into various other languages. A French translation was first published in Leiden in 1726, and this served for a Russian translation published in 1768-74, and for German and English translations in 1780.

Müller's observations of religious practices among the Muslim Tatar populations are directly related to Abulgazi's writings, with the exception of the inclusion of the mystical features of Sufism that appealed to the animist native population. Unlike Abulgazi, Müller makes little distinction between the Siberian Tatars and the Volga Tatars. He most often refers to all Tatars he encounters in Siberia as 'Mohammadean Tatars' or 'pagan Tatars'.

The second of Müller's accounts that deal with Muslims in Siberia, *Opisanie sibirskogo tsarstva* ('Description of the Siberian realm'), provides a narrative of how Kuchum, the leader of the Khanate of Sibir', sought to spread Islam among the native peoples of western Siberia in cross-border raids. Many of Müller's descriptions contradict accounts of the spread of Islam in Siberia produced by Russian military governors (*voevody*) and Orthodox churchmen that appeared in earlier 17th-century sources. Müller shows that the Russian chronicler Semyon Remezov was inaccurate in his descriptions of the lineage of Kuchum, his wives, and the regional influence of his khanate, which originated in Bukhara and spread to the Bashkir tribes in the Ural Mountains. As Müller read and re-copied the local archives of Tobolsk, Tiumen, Tomsk and other Siberian cities, he echoed and affirmed the ultimate Christian and military victory of the Cossack *ataman* Ermak Timofeovich over Islam and Kuchum, the Khan of Sibir'.

Disregarding Semyon Remezov's assertion that Islam was introduced and spread to Siberia from Kazan by Volga Tatars, he references Abulgazi and conversations with Tobolsk Tatars and Bukharans, and writes, 'The Mohammadean belief was brought to Siberia by Bukharan holy men who martyred themselves during their attempts to spread Islam' in the time of Kuchum (*Istorii Sibiri*, pp. 198-9). Despite claiming an alternative version of the extent of Islam in Siberia, he chooses to relate Russian declarations of the brutal methods used by Muslims to convert native Siberian peoples to Islam:

> The Tobolsk chronicle recalls that Kuchum brought with him many spiritual people from Kazan, who according to Mohammedan law did not want to be circumcised voluntarily. They were strongly coerced, but some

in their stubbornness were condemned to death. (*Opisanie sibirskogo tsarstva*, ch. 1, para. 80, p. 55)

In accepting the accounts by local Muslims and the genealogical history by Abulgazi, Müller exhibits the spirit of the Enlightenment that sought alternatives to Eurocentric historical accounts and the tales of conquerors. And yet he also stresses the ruthlessness of Muslim Tatars and their willingness to transgress Islamic law.

Throughout his writings, Müller exhibits a sense of urgency to create a Christian spiritual and secular order to contend with the spread of Islam in Siberia. In an attempt to underscore the need for missionary work, he emphatically details Kuchum's ties to Sufism through one of his marriages to the daughter of a Bukharan shaykh, and Kuchum's attempt to supplant Islam among the native populations. Although he provides little detail and an incomplete understanding of Sufism or Islam in general, Müller concludes that Orthodox Christianity was more acceptable to native populations because it was compatible with their own cosmology and spiritual practices. In his notes published in 1900, Müller observes that 'Muhammedianism is weakly rooted, and is lukewarmly held onto in many places in Siberia' (*Beiträge zur Geschichte*, p. 78). In his eyes, the continuing effort of Orthodox missionary activities was paramount to the settlement of Siberia.

As Müller records the establishment of monasteries throughout Siberia, he remarks that 'the spiritual fathers/monastic elders sought to introduce people to the monastic life as a path to salvation of the soul' (*Istorii Sibiri*, vol. 3, para. 55). No distinction is made between the native Siberian peoples in Tatar settlements and the Christian (primarily Orthodox) settlers and service people migrating from lands west of the Urals. Müller notes that from the establishment of the Tobolsk archbishopric under Kiprian in 1621, monasteries and churches were founded not only for the salvation of souls but in fact to establish order concerning the baptism of pagan and Tatar women and men on the frontier (*Istorii Sibiri*, vol. 2, pp. 86-7). The missionary activities of the Russian Orthodox Church in the 18th century did not seek a wholesale conversion of pagan and Tatar peoples, but were rather based on the practical needs of baptism for a growing number of interconfessional marriages, and the baptism of men as a way to get round imperial regulations against slavery in Siberia. As a contemporary observer in 18th-century Siberia, Müller most frequently mentions existing secular relationships between Christian and Tatar populations that sought the protection and support of the Russian state, rather than relating the real dilemma Russia faced with a broadening state policy concerning the non-Orthodox confessions in Siberia.

SIGNIFICANCE

As a renowned academician and influential voice in the imperial courts of 18th-century Russia, Müller's influence provided Europe and Russia with a lasting perception of its history and peoples. Serving nearly all his professional life in Russia, Müller appears to have embraced Russian Orthodoxy as a 'civilising' force for the expanding the Russian Empire. His ethnographic work and vast collection of manuscripts copied or collected throughout Siberia became the authoritative source for the history of the Siberian frontier and the peoples who lived in this vast territory during the second half of the 18th century.

Müller's work and that of his colleagues on the expedition continues to be referenced and studied to the present day. Not only did Müller influence and provide the foundations for imperial and Soviet ethnographical studies, but also his impressions of Islam and its followers in Siberia contributed to controversial policies and practices of Russification and 'Sovietization' in the 19th and 20th centuries.

PUBLICATIONS

G.F. Müller, *Opisanie sibirskogo tsarstva i vsekh proizshedshikh v nem del, ot nachala a osobivo ot pokoreniia evo Rossiiskoi derzhave po sii vremena*, St Petersburg, 1750; (http://www.runivers.ru/lib/book 8356/473863/ (digitised version available through Runivers)

G.F. Müller, 'Opisanie morskikh puteshestvii po Ledovitomu i po Vostochnomu moriiu s Rossiiskoi storony uchinennykh', *Ezhemesiachnyia Sochineniia* 7 (January 1758) 3-37; (February) 99-120; (March) 201-18; (April) 299-334; (May) 405-26; 8 (July 1758) 9-34; (August) 99-124; (September) 195-232; (October) 309-36; (November) 393-425

G.F. Müller, *Sammlung russischer Geschichte*, vol. 3, St Petersburg, 1761, pts 5-6, pp. 1-381 (German trans.); Bibl.Mont. 3490-9,1/6 (digitised version available through *MDZ*)

G.F. Miller, *Voyages from Asia to America, for completing the discoveries of the north west coast of America: to which is prefixed, a summary of the voyages made by the Russians on the frozen sea, in search of a North East Passage: serving as an explanation of a map of the Russian discoveries, published by the Academy of Sciences at Petersburgh*, London, 1761, 1764² (English trans. from the German edition, a summary of Müller's journey through Siberia); 0665389027 (digitised copy available through Hathi Trust Digital Library)

G.F. Miller, *Voyages et découvertes faites par les Russes le long des côtes de la mer Glaciale & sur l'océan Oriental, tant vers le Japon que vers l'Amérique: on y a joint l'histoire du fleuve Amur et des pays adjacens, depuis la conquête des Russes: avec la nouvelle carte qui précouvertes & les cours de l'Amur, dressée sur les mémoires authentiques, publiée par l'Académie des sciences de St. Pétersbourg*, trans. C.G.F. Dumas, 2 vols, Amsterdam, 1766, 1768² (French trans. from the German edition, a summary of Müller's journey through Siberia); 099395770 (digitised version available through Universiteits Bibliotheek Gent)

G.F. Müller, 'Zur Geschichte der Akademie der Wissenschaften Petersburg', in *Materialy dlia istorii Imperatorskoi Akademii nauk* 6 (1890) 1-638; http://books.e-heritage.ru/book/10074709

S.V. Bakhrushin and A.I. Andreev, *G.F. Miller: Istorii Sibiri*, 3 vols, Moscow, 1937, 1941, 2005 (facsimile of the 1750 edition)

G.F. Müller, *Opisanie sibirskikh narodov*, trans. A.K Elert and W. Hintzsche, Moscow: Pamiatniki istoricheskoi mysli, 2009 (Russian trans. from German edition)

STUDIES

Bakhrushin and Andreev, *G.F. Miller: Istorii Sibiri* (see the commentary)

Gwyn Bourlakov

Aleksandr Sumarokov

Aleksandr Petrovich Sumarokov; A.P. Sumarokov

DATE OF BIRTH   25 November 1717 (Old Style: 14 November 1717)
PLACE OF BIRTH   Villmanstrand (present-day Lapeenranta,
    Finland)
DATE OF DEATH   12 October 1777 (Old Style: 1 October 1777)
PLACE OF DEATH   Moscow

BIOGRAPHY

Aleksandr Petrovich Sumarokov contributed enormously to modern Russian literature during its early stages in the 18th century. Widely recognised as the father of Russian theatre and the nation's first professional writer, he initially gained attention for his tragedies, *Khorev* (1747) and *Gamlet* (1748, a loose adaptation of Shakespeare's *Hamlet*), and his 1748 *Dve epistoly* (*v pervoi predlagaetsia o russkom iazyke, a vo vtorom o stikhotvorstve*) ('Two epistles'; 1748). He eventually composed a total of nine tragedies, an equal number of comedies, two operas, two ballet-operas and a religious drama. In recognition of this devotion to the stage, he was appointed director of the newly established Russian National Theatre in 1756. A devout Christian, his Russian Orthodoxy was infused with Masonic beliefs developed after joining a Masonic lodge in 1756.

Although his career predates the late 18th-century fashion for 'the Orient', a few of his works do treat Christian-Muslim relations, most notably the commentary on Voltaire's *Zaïre* in his 1774 *Mnenie v snovidenii o frantsuzskikh tragediiakh* ('Opinion in a dream about French tragedies'), and his 1769 ode to Catherine II *Oda na vziatie Khotina i pokorenie Moldavii* ('On the taking of Khotin and conquest of Moldavia'). That same year, he penned the opening 28 lines of a planned epic poem, *Dimitriady*, in honour of Dimitrii Donskoi, the first Russian leader directly to challenge Tatar rule. The poem was never completed and the fragment appeared only posthumously, in his 1781 complete works. Sumarokov wrote numerous other poems alluding to Russia's wars with the Ottoman Empire, but without giving specific emphasis to religion.

Sumarokov was born on 25 November 1717 (Old Style: 14 November 1717), near Villmanstrand (present-day Lapeenranta, Finland). His father claimed Peter the Great as his godfather, and served under him during the Great Northern War, after which he transferred to state service in St Petersburg. Sumarokov's father tutored him at home between 1726 and 1732, and then enrolled him and his older brother Vasilii in the Noble Infantry Cadet Corps in St Petersburg. The school had just opened its doors as a training ground for officers and was considered the most prestigious institution for young Russian noblemen. Sumarokov graduated in 1740 and went on to a series of official posts, but focused increasingly on literary pursuits from the late 1740s.

Sumarokov's personal life proved tumultuous. In 1746, he cemented his status at court by marrying a German lady-in-waiting to the future Catherine II, Johanna Khristiforovna Ballior. They had two daughters, Ekaterina and Praskovia, but divorced in 1766. He was married twice more, first to Vera Prokhoruva, the daughter of a coachman, with whom he lived for almost a decade before officially marrying her in 1774. This period of his personal life was complicated by family quarrels related to his wife's non-noble status and the division of his father's estate. When Vera died in May 1777, Sumarokov almost immediately married her niece, Elena Gavrilovna. He died in Moscow just a few months later, on 12 October 1777 (Old Style: 1 October 1777). Sumarokov's final years were marked by poverty, illness and alcoholism. He was buried in the cemetery at Moscow's Donskoi Monastery in an unmarked grave whose location was soon forgotten.

MAIN SOURCES OF INFORMATION

Primary

N. Novikov, *Opyt istoricheskago slovaria o rossiiskikh pisateliakh*, St Petersburg, 1772, pp. 207-9

'Sokrashchennaia povest' o zhizni i pisaniiakh gospodina statskago deistvitel'nago sovetnika i Sviatyia Anny kavalera, Aleksandra Petrovicha Sumarokova', *Sanktpeterburgskii Vestnik* 1 (1778) 39-49

A.P. Sumarokov, 'Dimitriady', in *Polnoe sobranie vsekh sochinenii*, St Petersburg, 1781, vol. 1, p. 293

N. Struiskii, *Apologiia k potomstvu ot Nikolaia Struiskogo ili nachertanie o svoistve nrava Aleksandra Petrovicha Sumarokova i o nravouchitel'nykh ego poucheniiakh, pisana 1784 goda v Ruzaevke*, St Petersburg, 1788

I. Dmitrevskii, *Slovo pokhval'noe Aleksandru Petrovichu Sumarokovu, chitannoe v Imperatorskoi Rossiiskoi Akademii v godovoe torzhestvennoe eia sobranie 1807 goda chlenom onyia Ivanom Dmitrevskim*, St Petersburg, 1807

A.F. Merzliakov, 'Sumarokov', *Vestnik Evropy* 12 (1817) 258-281; 'Sumarokov: Prodolzhenie', *Vestnik Evropy* 13 (1817) 26-54; 'Sumarokov: Okonchanie', *Vestnik Evropy* 14 (1817) 106-40

'Stat'ia dlia biografii Sumarokova', *Severnaia Pchela* 72 (1833) 287

'Pis'mo k izdateliu', *Severnaia Pchela* 76 (1833) 302-3

'Biograficheskaia popravka', *Moskovkskii Telegraf* 6 (1833) 266-70

S. Glinka, *Ocherki zhizni i izbrannye sochineniia A.P. Sumarokova*, St Petersburg, 1841

P. Sumarokov, 'Otryvok iz biografii Aleksandra Petrovicha Sumarokova', *Moskovskii Gorodskoi Listok* 79 (1847) 317-18

N.N. Bulich, *Sumarokov i sovremennaia emu kritika*, St Petersburg, 1854

V.A. Stouinin, *A.P. Sumarokov*, St Petersburg, 1856

'Otryvki iz perepiski Sumarokova (1755-1773)', *Otechestvennye Zapiski* 2 (1858) 579-98

M.N. Longinov, 'Poslednye gody zhizni Aleksandra Petrovicha Sumarokova (1766-1777)', *Russkii Arkhiv* 10 (1871) 1637-1717; 'Popravki i dopolneniia. K stat'e M.N. Longinova o Sumarokove', *Russkii Arkhiv* 11 (1871) 1956-60

Secondary

V.P. Stepanov, art. 'Sumarokov, Aleksandr Petrovich', in N.D. Kochetkova et al. (eds), *Slovar' russkikh pisatelei XVIII veka*, St Petersburg, 2010, vol. 3; http://lib.pushkinskijdom.ru/Default.aspx?tabid=10377

E.P. Mstislavskaia, 'Zhizn' i tvorchestvo A.P. Sumarokova', in E.P. Mstislavskaia and E.V. Ivanova (eds), *Aleksandr Petrovich Sumarokov 1717-1777: Zhizn' i tvorchestvo. Sbornik statei i materialov*, Moscow, 2002, 8-41

V.P. Stepanov, 'Sumarokov v shliakhetnom korpuse', *Russkaia Literatura* 4 (2000) 83-7

V.M. Zhivov, 'Pervye russkie literaturnye biografii kak sotsial'noe iavlenie. Trediakovskii, Lomonosov, Sumarokov', *Novoe Literaturnoe Obozrenie* 25 (1997) 24-83

I.A. Vishnevskaia, *Aplodismenty v proshloe. A.P. Sumarokov i ego tragedii*, Moscow, 1996

M. Levitt, 'A.P. Sumarokov', in M. Levitt (ed.), *Early modern Russian writers, late seventeenth and eighteenth centuries*, Detroit, 1995, 370-81

G.A. Lapkina (ed.), *Sumarokovskie chteniia. Iubileinye torzhestva k 275-letiu so dnia rozhdeniia A.P. Sumarokova*, St Petersburg, 1993

G.P. Makagonenko (ed.), 'A.P. Sumarokov', in *Pis'ma russkikh pisatelei XVIII veka*, Leningrad, 1980, 68-181; http://rvb.ru/18vek/letters_rus_writers/01text/02sumarokov/letter_index.html

P.N. Berkov, 'Neskol'ko spravok dlia biografii A. P. Sumarokova', *XVIII Vek* 5 (1962) 364-75

P.N. Berkov, 'Zhiznennyi i literaturnyi put' A. P. Sumarokova', in P. Berkov (ed.), *A.P. Sumarokov, Izbrannye proizvedeniia*, Leningrad, 1957, 5-46

A.P. Sumarokov, 'Dmitriady', in P. Berkov (ed.), *A.P. Sumarokov, Izbrannye proiz-vedeniia*, Leningrad, 1957, 108-9; http://rvb.ru/18vek/sumarokov/01text/01versus/04ep_poem/036.htm

P.N. Berkov, *Aleksandr Petrovich Sumarokov. 1717-1777*, Leningrad, 1949

WORKS ON CHRISTIAN-MUSLIM RELATIONS

Oda Eia Imperatorskomu Velichestvu Gosudaryne Ekaterine Alekseevne [...] na vziatie Khotina i na pokorenie Moldavii
'Ode to her imperial Majesty and Sovereign the Empress Catherine Alekseevna [...] on the taking of Khotin and on the conquest of Moldavia'

DATE　1769
ORIGINAL LANGUAGE　Russian

DESCRIPTION

Sumarokov composed his *Oda na vziatie Khotina i pokorenie Moldavii* in Moscow in late October 1769 to commemorate the Russian victory over the Ottomans at the fort of Khotin. He published it shortly afterwards in St Petersburg. Sumarokov's odes were probably presented directly to the addressee, in this case the Empress Catherine II (r. 1762-96), either personally or through an intermediary.

The original 1769 edition comprises 12 ten-line stanzas, which follow the classic ode pattern of iambic tetrameters. The better-known 1774 edition reflects some minor revisions to word choice as well as the more striking change of the omission of the entire final stanza, which significantly alters the message and tone of the poem. There are no extant manuscript copies of this or any of Sumarokov's other odes.

This poem marks a polemical response to the famous 1739 *Oda na vziatie Khotina* ('Ode on the taking of Khotin') by Sumarokov's rival, Mikhail Lomonosov. That work, commemorating the capture of Khotin by Russian forces, which helped end a three-year war with the Ottoman Empire, was Lomonosov's first ode. It not only launched his career, but also marked the beginning of modern Russian prosody.

In an elevated register that relies heavily on biblical allusions rather than on the pagan mythology most typical of the genre, Sumarokov's

Oda na vziatie Khotina depicts the horrors of battle and the intense fear that Russians instil in their enemy, which the poet claims will lead to the end of Ottoman rule, and describes how the world will take notice of Russian power. Amid the emphasis on violence and horror, the opening two stanzas and the concluding twelfth stanza (the one omitted in the 1774 edition) are notable for their religious imagery that pits Christians against Muslims.

In the opening stanza, Sumarokov lifts his gaze to the distant heavens and sees the angels entreating God to 'wrench the sceptre from the Ottoman' in favour of the worthy Catherine. In the next stanza, God complies by sending the archangels to the empress. That same stanza suggests that Byzantium will rise up and the 'Palaeologue' (the last Byzantine dynasty) will be victorious. Finally, 'The Greeks' – the Russians' Eastern Orthodox brothers – will 'chase Hagar from the gates', an allusion to the expulsion in Genesis of Hagar, the mother of Ismāʿīl (Ishmael) and a key figure in Islam. Sumarokov adopted this traditional Russian reference to Hagar as a symbol for Muslims in at least two other poems of this same period: a panegyric ode to Catherine on her name day in 1769, and the 1774 revision of the ode celebrating the cessation of hostilities.

The *Oda na vziatie Khotina* thus opens by framing the Russian victory as the happy result of divine intervention on behalf of Christians over Muslims, who are being rightfully expelled, like Hagar before them. After the opening stanzas, however, the religious imagery recedes to make way for the terror and awe of raging battle. Notably, the revised 1774 edition ends on a note of military triumph, whereas the original 1769 edition concludes with a prayer to God for peace.

SIGNIFICANCE

As would be expected, given the wars between Russia and the Ottomans throughout the 18th century, Sumarokov's oeuvre contains several poems that anticipate or reprise the theme of Russian military might tempered by a call for peace. Yet, perhaps reflecting the increasing atmosphere of relative tolerance toward Muslims under Catherine II, Sumarokov only occasionally singles out his enemies' Islamic faith. In place of this, most of his odes focus on military exploits. This reserve is actually quite striking, given that Sumarokov frequently wrote on Christian themes, including in his best known work, the play *Dimitri Samozvanets* ('Dimitry the Pretender') completed in 1771, in which Russian Orthodoxy is placed directly in conflict with Roman Catholicism rather than with Islam.

PUBLICATIONS

There is no extant manuscript of this ode.

A.P. Sumarokov, *Oda eia imperatorskomu velichestvu gosudaryne Ekaterine Alekseevne Imperatritse i Samoderzhitse Vserossiiskoi na vziatie Khotina i na pokorenie Moldavii*, St Petersburg, 1769 (original publication as a separate booklet)

A.P. Sumarokov, 'Oda Gosudaryne Imperatritse Ekaterine Vtoroi na vziatie Khotina i pokorenie Moldavii', in *Ody torzhestvennyia*, St Petersburg, 1774, 75-9 (revised version of the ode omitting the final stanza)

A.P. Sumarokov, 'Oda Gosudaryne Imperatritse Ekaterine Vtoroi na vziatie Khotina i pokorenie Moldavii', in P. Berkov (ed.), *A.P. Sumarokov, Izbrannye proizvedeniia*, Leningrad, 1957, 71-4 (Soviet edition based on the revised 1774 version); http://rvb.ru/18vek/sumarokov/01text/01versus/010des/008.htm

A.P. Sumarokov, 'Oda Eia Imperatorskomu Velichestvu Gosudaryne Ekaterine Alekseevne Imperatritse i Samoderzhitse Vserossiiskoi na vziatie Khotina i na pokorenie Moldavii', in R. Vroon (ed.), *Aleksandr Sumarokov, Ody torzhestvennyia i elegii liubovnyia*, Moscow, 2009, 142-6 (reprint of the 1769 edition with extensive critical apparatus and notes indicating changes made to the poem for the 1774 edition)

STUDIES

V. Proskurina, *Creating the Empress. Politics and poetry in the age of Catherine II*, Brighton MA, 2011, pp. 165-6 (includes brief translated passages from the poem)

R. Vroon, 'Ody torzhestvennye i elegii liubovynyia: Istoriia sozdaniia, kompozitsiia sbornika', in R. Vroon (ed.), *Aleksandr Sumarokov, Ody torzhestvennyia i elegii liubovnyia*, Moscow, 2009, 387-468, pp. 334-7, 430-2

R. Vroon, 'Aleksandr Sumarokov's *Ody torzhestvennye*. Toward a history of the lyric sequence in eighteenth-century Russia', *Zeitschrift zur Slavische Philologie* 55 (1995/6) 223-63, pp. 226, 249-50, 257

W. Gleason, 'Sumarokov's political ideals. A reappraisal of his role as a critic of Catherine II's policies', *Canadian Slavonic Papers/Revue Canadienne des Slavistes* 18 (1976) 415-26, pp. 424-5

Amanda Ewington

The 1773 decree on religious toleration

DATE   1773
ORIGINAL LANGUAGE   Russian

DESCRIPTION

The document known as 'The 1773 decree on religious toleration' ('The edict of religious toleration', or 'Toleration of all faiths edict') was a resolution (*vysochaishii otzyv*) issued by the Empress Catherine II (r. 1762-96) in response to a report dated 29 May 1773 by Russia's Chief Prosecutor, Aleksandr Viazemskii, concerning the Kazan Muslims. It constituted part of the Holy Synod's official order of 17 June 1773, restricting the powers of church hierarchs to interfere in the affairs of non-Orthodox subjects.

The decree was prompted by Archbishop Veniamin of Kazan's (r. 1762-85) complaint to the Holy Synod, the highest institution of the Russian Orthodox Church, about mosques being constructed in the city of Kazan. The archbishop disputed the official permission that the governor of Kazan province, Andrei Kvashnin-Samarin, had granted in 1767 for local Muslim Tatars to construct two stone mosques. On receiving the complaint, the Holy Synod raised the issue before the Ruling Senate, the highest civil administrative body in the Russian Empire. The synod stressed two problems: first, the mosques were being built close to Orthodox churches; second, the area was inhabited not only by Muslims, but also by Tatars who had chosen to convert from Islam to Orthodox Christianity, the *novokreshcheny* ('newly baptised'), a term used for non-Orthodox imperial subjects who converted to Orthodox Christianity in the first half of the 18th century, as opposed to the *starokreshcheny* ('baptised a long time ago'), those who had converted to Orthodoxy in the 16th century. Thus, the argument went, the construction of the mosques was an offence to Orthodoxy as well as a potential obstruction to the church's missionary efforts.

After consulting with the empress, the Ruling Senate replied to the Holy Synod using the words of Catherine herself, who was unequivocal in her support for her Muslim subjects: 'As Almighty God tolerates all faiths, tongues, and creeds on earth, Her Majesty, starting from the same principles, and in accordance with His Holy Will, has proposed to follow in the same path, desiring only that Her subjects always be in love and peace with each other' (*Polnoe sobranie postanovlenii*, p. 31). As a result, on 17 June 1773, the Holy Synod issued a decree prohibiting the local Orthodox hierarchy from interfering in the construction of religious buildings by the so-called 'foreign faiths' (*inovernye ispovedaniia*). Henceforth, this matter would not rest with the Church but would fall within the competence of the civil administration.

The 1773 decree was an important manifestation of the Russian government's commitment to religious toleration. However, rooted in the principles of the European Enlightenment and cameralist ideals, toleration in the 18th-century Russian Empire was characterised by profound conceptual assumptions and practical limitations.

From the end of the 17th century, the non-Orthodox subjects of the emerging empire experienced growing pressure to convert to Orthodox Christianity. Particularly prominent was the state-supported missionary campaign of the 1730-50s to the Volga region, where the population was largely Muslim and animist. Numerous instances of physical violence and other coercive practices on the part of the Orthodox clergy accompanied the campaign. At the time, the Russian authorities considered Muslims not only a target of the church's missionary work, but also a threat to its success (*Polnoe sobranie zakonov*, t. 8, p. 100). In the first half of the 18th century, while there were no complete bans on Muslim activities, there were serious restrictions on the construction of mosques, arising from concerns about Muslims proselytising among Christian and non-Christian imperial subjects (*Polnoe sobranie zakonov*, t. 12, pp. 157-8).

From the time of her enthronement in 1762, Catherine clearly displayed her dedication to the principles of enlightened toleration. Notably, in 1764 the senate abolished the notorious Office of New Converts (*Kontora novokreshchenskikh del*), a state institution that assisted the Church in its missionary campaign. The missionaries would have to content themselves with words alone or, as phrased in the senate's decree, they should spread Orthodox Christianity 'in likeness to Apostolic preaching – with all possible meekness, peacefulness, and gentleness' (*Polnoe sobranie zakonov*, t. 16, pp. 705-6).

The most profound demonstration of Catherine's commitment to enlightened toleration was the 'Instruction' (*Nakaz*) she compiled for the Legislative Commission. This commission brought together deputies from different regions and strata of Russian society in Moscow in 1767 to compose a legal code for the new empire. The 'Instruction' was based almost entirely on the works of enlightened thinkers such as Montesquieu, Cesare Beccaria and Jacob Bielefeld, and, among other things, praised the merits of religious tolerance for the Russian Empire (articles

Illustration 17. Dmitry Levitzky, 'Portrait of Catherine II [...]' Catherine burns an offering
of poppies to the statue of Justice

494-6). In accordance with the expressed principles, the Legislative
Commission also included Muslim delegates from the Tatar and Bashkir
communities.

In the 'Instruction', of particular relevance are articles 494, 495, and
496. These state:

Art. 494: 'In so vast an Empire which extends its dominion over such a variety of people, the prohibiting, or not tolerating of their respective religions would be an evil highly detrimental to the peace and security of its subjects.'

Art. 495: 'And truly, there is no other method than a wise toleration of such other religions as are not repugnant to our own Orthodox faith and policy, by which all these wandering sheep may be reconducted to the true flock of the faithful.'

Art. 496: 'Persecution incenses the human mind; but permitting each to believe the tenets of his own doctrine, softens even the most obdurate hearts, and keeps them from implacable obstinacy, quenching those contentions which are contrary to the peace of government and to the unity of the citizens' (cited in Dukes, *Russia under Catherine the Great*, p. 104).

In 1767, the governor of Kazan province, Kvashnin-Samarin, based his decision to allow local Tatars to construct mosques on these articles in the 'Instruction'. Therefore, contrary to common assumption, the 1773 decree, rather than creating a new legal norm, in fact reinforced the existing governmental commitment to religious toleration, in a specific case concerning Kazan Muslims.

SIGNIFICANCE

Religious toleration as pronounced in both the 1767 'Instruction' and the 1773 decree should not be confused with freedom of conscience. The former was restricted to the granting of limited religious rights to minority groups in the name of social tranquillity and the common good, as understood by the adherents of cameralism (German, *Kameralwissenschaft*). Mark Raeff has famously dubbed their ideal a 'well-ordered police state' (Raeff, *The well-ordered police state*). Confessional uniformity in such a state was highly desirable, though achieving this was a long-term goal, to be attained through peaceful and educational measures, rather than coercion.

Policy-makers in Russia did not question the primacy of the Orthodox Church in society, neither during nor after the reign of Catherine II. However, in the rapidly growing empire it was important to win the loyalty of both new and old non-Orthodox subjects, including Muslims, Jews and Catholics. The Russian authorities therefore made a consistent effort to institutionalise these confessions. In the case of Russia's Muslim subjects, this meant establishing 'a churchlike organisation among a population that had previously known no such institutions': in a word, creation of 'a church for Islam' (Crews, *For Prophet and Tsar*, p. 33). The pinnacle of this process was the establishment of the 'Muslim Spiritual

Assembly' in 1788-9 in the Orenburg province. Functioning in a similar way to the Holy Synod of the Russian Orthodox Church, the Assembly monitored Islamic teaching, as well as managing appointments of mullahs, supervising Muslim schools and handling divorce cases.

PUBLICATIONS

Details of editions and translations are given in W.E. Butler, 'Printed editions of Catherine's Nakaz. A bibliography', in W.E. Butler and V.A. Tomsinov (eds), *The Nakaz of Catherine the Great. Collected texts*, Clark NJ, 2010, 521-31 (for countries of publication, see page numbers as follows: Russia, 523-5; France, 525-6; England, 527; Germany, 527-8; Holland, 528; Italy, 528-9; Latvia, 529-30; Poland, 530; Sweden, 530; Switzerland, 530-1; United States, 531).

Nakaz Kommissii o sostavlenii proekta novago ulozheniia, Moscow: [pech. pri Senate], 1767, pp. 128-9

Polnoe sobranie zakonov, vol. 8 (1728-32), St Petersburg, 1830, p. 100, no. 5333

Polnoe sobranie zakonov, vol. 12 (1744-8), St Petersburg, 1830, pp. 157-9, no. 8978

Polnoe sobranie zakonov, vol. 16 (1762-4), St Petersburg, 1830, pp. 705-6, no. 12126 and others

Polnoe sobranie zakonov, vol. 19 (1770-4), St Petersburg, 1830, pp. 775-6, no. 13996

Polnoe sobranie postanovlenii i rasporiazhenii po vedomstvu pravoslavnago ispovedaniia Rossiiskoi imperii, vol. 2 (1773-84), St Petersburg, 1915, p. 31, no. 691

P. Dukes (ed.), *Russia under Catherine the Great*, vol. 2. *Catherine the Great's Instruction (Nakaz) to the legislative commission, 1767*, ed. and trans. P. Dukes, Newtonville MA, 1977 (English trans.)

W.E. Butler and V.A. Tomsinov (eds), *The Nakaz of Catherine the Great. Collected texts*, Clark NJ, 2010 (texts in Russian, French, Latin, German and English)

STUDIES

G.M. Hamburg, 'Religious toleration in Russian thought, 1520-1825', in *Kritika. Explorations in Russian and Eurasian History* 13 (2012) 539-43

R.D. Crews, *For Prophet and Tsar. Islam and empire in Russia and Central Asia*, Cambridge, 2006, pp. 31-60

P. Werth, 'Coercion and conversion. Violence and the mass baptism of the Volga peoples, 1740-55', *Kritika. Explorations in Russian and Eurasian History* 4 (2003) 543-69

M. Raeff, *The well-ordered police state. Social and institutional change through law in the Germanies and Russia, 1600-1800*, New Haven CT, 1983, pp. 222-50

I. de Madariaga, *Russia in the age of Catherine the Great*, New Haven CT, 1981, pp. 503-4, 508-10

A.W. Fisher, 'Enlightened despotism and Islam under Catherine II', in *Slavic Review* 27 (1968) 542-53

N. Chechulin, 'Vvedenie', in *Nakaz imperatritsy Ekateriny II, dannyi Kommissii o sochinenii proekta novago Ulozheniia*, St Petersburg: Tipografiia Imperatorskoi Akademii Nauk, 1907, cxxix-cliv

Evgeny Grishin

Vasilii Mikhailovich Dolgorukov

DATE OF BIRTH   1 July 1722
PLACE OF BIRTH   Moscow
DATE OF DEATH   30 January 1782
PLACE OF DEATH   Volynshchina-Poluektovo

BIOGRAPHY

Born in 1722, Vasilii Mikhailovich Dolgorukov came from an eminent Russian noble family. His father, Prince Mikhail Vladimirovich, was a senator and the governor of Siberia. However, under Empress Anna Ioannovna (r. 1730-40), the family fell into disgrace, because of their intrigues against Tsar Peter II (r. 1727-30), making Vasilii Mikhailovich's childhood difficult. In 1735, at the age of 13, he enrolled as a private in the dragoons. He experienced combat in Crimea, during the Russian-Ottoman war of 1735-9, and was promoted to lieutenant after distinguishing himself at the siege of Perekop. Dolgorukov progressed rapidly through the ranks as his fortune improved under the reign of Elizabeth Petrovna (r. 1741-62). He fought in the Russian-Swedish war in 1741-3, and was made full colonel in 1747, with command over the Tobolsk infantry regiment.

Dolgorukov participated in several major operations during the Seven Years' War, attaining the rank of major-general. For valour at the siege of Küstrin (1758) he received the order of Aleksandr Nevskii. Although wounded several times, he continued to lead infantry in battles and sieges. Upon the coronation of Catherine II (r. 1762-96), he became general-in-chief. In 1767, at the age of 45, he was awarded the order of St Andrei.

During the Russian-Ottoman war of 1768-74, Dolgorukov continued to serve with distinction. In 1770, he commanded the second army, which defeated the forces of the Crimean khan, Selim III Giray, and occupied the Crimean peninsula. His successful negotiations with the khan, which separated the khanate from the Ottoman sultan, earned him the order of St Georgii and the honorary title, 'Krymskii'.

In 1780, having retired to his country residence after the war, Dolgorukov was appointed general commander of Moscow. Entering into civil service, he oversaw the construction of the Petrovskii Theatre (later the Bol'shoi Theatre), and performed various services that advanced the urban development of Moscow. He died in 1782, a year before Crimea was formally annexed by the Russian Empire.

MAIN SOURCES OF INFORMATION

Primary

Ukaz imperatritsy Anny Ioannovny o prestupleniiakh kniazei Dolgorukovykh, St Petersburg, 1739

V.G. Ruban, *Nadpisi na zavoevanie Krymskikh gorodov i na pororenie ikh pod Rossiiskuiu derzhavu, armii glavnym predvoditelem generalom i kavalerom kniazem Vasil'em Mikhailovichem Dolgorukovym v 1771 god*, (s.l.), 1771

E. Trytov, *Istoriia o kniaze Ia. F. Dolgorukove s pribavleniem svedenii o drugikh znamenitykh muzhakh slavnoi familii kniazei Dolgorukikh*, Moscow, 1807

V.G. Ruban, *Skazaniia o rode kniazei Dolgorukovykh*, St Petersburg, 1840

P.V. Dolgorukov, *Skazaniia o rode kniazei Dolgorukovykh*, St Petersburg, 1842

A. Bokk, *Vospominaniia o kniaze Vasilii Mikhailoviche Dolgorukov-Krymskom*, Moscow, 1855

A.R. Andreev, *Kniaz' Vasilii Mikhailovich Dokgorukov-Krymskii. Dokumental'noe zhizneopisanie. Istoricheskaia khronika XVIII veka*, Moscow, 1997

Secondary

B.L. Davies, *The Russo-Turkish war, 1768-1774. Catherine II and the Ottoman Empire*, London, 2016, pp. 172-7, 284-5

A.R. Andreev, *Istoriia Kryma. Kniaz' Dolgorukov-Krymskii*, Moscow, 2001

M.V. Nogteva, *Vasilii Mikhailovich Dolgorukov-Krymskii i Moskva*, Moscow, 2000

A.B. Shirokorad, *Russko-turetskie voiny 1676-1918 gg.*, Moscow, 2000, pp. 176-7

A.W. Fisher, *Crimean Tatars*, Stanford CA, 1978, pp. 51-7

A. Fisher, *The Russian annexation of the Crimea*, Cambridge, 1970, pp. 40-52

L.G. Beskrovnyi, *Russkaia armiia i flot v XVIII veke (ocherki)*, Moscow, 1958, pp. 460-509

P. Simanskii, art. 'Dolgorukov Krymskii, kniaz', Vasilii Mikhailovich', *Russkii biograficheskii slovar'*, vol. 6, 1905, 522-5

WORKS ON CHRISTIAN-MUSLIM RELATIONS

Podennaia
'Travelogue'

DATE   1773
ORIGINAL LANGUAGE   Russian

DESCRIPTION

The published edition of Dolgorukov's travelogue (its full title is *Podennaia zapiska puteshestviia ego siiatel'stva kniazia Vasiliia Mikhailovicha Dolgorukova v Krymskii poluostrov, vo vremia kompanii 1773 goda,*

'Travelogue of his Excellency Prince Vasilii Mikhailovich Dolgorukov in the Crimean Peninsula, during the campaign of 1773') is made up of six pages, consisting of his notes during his trip through Crimea in July 1773. Direct references to Christian-Muslim relations are scarce.

The work is divided into dated journal entries, from 10 to 23 July 1773. Dolgorukov describes his travels across the peninsula to meet the Crimean khan at the Bakhchisarai Palace. He makes passing reference to Muslim villages, noting that Tatar officials are pleased with the Russian presence. In Balaklava, he briefly describes interviews, on sofas, with hereditary Tatar nobility (*murzas*), over coffee and refreshments. On arrival in Bakhchisarai, Dolgorukov meets the Crimean khan in the audience hall of the palace. Dolgorukov observes that the khan is grateful to accept Russian protection. The Tatar capital and its environs are briefly described. The remainder of the text details his return from the peninsula.

SIGNIFICANCE

Dolgorukov's notes contain valuable historical information about the encounter between Russian officials and the khan on the eve of the Russian annexation of Crimea. His brief comments emphasise the Crimean khan's readiness to accept Russian control; during their audience, the Muslim leader recognised the authority of the Russian leaders without objection. The account of the Russian embassy's procession into Bakhchisarai and Dolgorukov's audiences with Crimean notables sheds light on the protocol of these Christian-Muslim encounters.

PUBLICATIONS

Vasilii Mikhailovich Dolgorukov, 'Podennaia zapiska puteshestviia ego siiatel'stva kniazia Vasiliia Mikhailovicha Dolgorukova v Krymskii poluostrov, vo vremia kompanii 1773 goda', *Zapiski Odesskogo Obshchesvta Istorii i Drevnostei* 8 (1872) 182-7

STUDIES

V.E. Vozgrin, *Istoricheskie sud'by krymskikh tatar*, Moscow, 1992, pp. 258-64

A.W. Fisher, *Crimean Tatars*, Stanford CA, 1978, pp. 51-7

Lucien Frary

Treaty of Küçük Kaynarca

Kiuchuk-Kainardzhiiskii mirnyi dogovor mezhdu Rossiei i Turtsiei
'Treaty of Küçük Kaynarca between Russia and Turkey'

DATE   21 July 1774 (Old Style: 10 July 1774)
ORIGINAL LANGUAGE   Russian

DESCRIPTION

The Treaty of Küçük Kaynarca marked the end of the Russo-Turkish war of 1768-74, sealing 'an everlasting peace' between the two countries. It was concluded between Catherine II (the Great), Empress of Russia (r. 1762-96), represented by General-Fel'dmarshal Graf Petr Rumiantsev, and Sultan Abdul Hamid I (r. 1773-89), represented by his High Vizier Musa Zade Mehmed Pasha.

The treaty contains 28 articles, seven of which deal specifically with religion.

Article 3 deals with all Tatar peoples, stipulating that they shall be free and have their own government according to their customs, without interference from either of the two parties. The two parties acknowledge the Tatar peoples as rightful and free political entities. The sultan, as the highest authority in the Muslim world, may only issue rules and laws in religious matters that do not affect the Tatars' political affairs. The Russian Empire gives the Tatar peoples all the territory in Kuban and Crimea, except for the fortresses in Kerch and Enikol. The Sublime Porte likewise will not interfere in these territories.

In Article 7, which is very short, the Porte promises to defend the Christian law and churches, and to permit ministers of the Russian Empire to give alms to the churches in Constantinople (mentioned in Article 14) and to clergy working there.

Article 8, likewise short, stipulates that Russian clergy and lay people may visit the Holy City of Jerusalem and other holy places without paying any fees or taxes on their way. They can obtain special passports for this undertaking and, during their stay in the Ottoman Empire, nobody shall give them offence and they will be protected by the law.

Article 14, which is even shorter, grants Russian ambassadors permission to build a church of the Greek-Russian confession in the Galata quarter of Constantinople (Bei Oglu Street). The church will be under the protection of the ambassador, without any hindrance.

Article 16 is very long and consists of ten numbered paragraphs. As restitution to the Ottoman Porte, the Russian Empire offers Bessarabia, Moldavia and the lands on the Volga. In return, the Porte guarantees full freedom of faith to Christians there and will build new churches in compensation for old ones that had been destroyed (§2). The Porte gives land and estates to the monasteries (§3), and acknowledges the rights of the clergy (§4). The 'princes of the principalities' will act as the *chargés d'affaires* in Greek-Christian matters at the Ottoman Porte (§9).

Article 17 consists of five paragraphs, stipulating that the Russian Empire will restore all Aegean islands to the Porte. The Porte in return promises (§2) to uphold the Christian law there and not to oppress the churches and people living and serving there.

Article 25 concerns prisoners of war. All captives, men and women, shall be freed immediately without ransom and returned to their respective countries. The same applies to people from third countries, such as Poland and Moldova. All Russian subjects who had fallen into Ottoman captivity shall be freed, except those who embraced the Islamic faith.

SIGNIFICANCE

The Treaty of Küçük Kaynarca was concluded after the defeat of the Ottomans at the Battle of Kozludzha, and ended the Russo-Turkish war of 1768-74. It provided for the nominal independence of Crimea, with Russia gaining Kabardia in the Caucasus and unlimited sovereignty over the ports of Azov, Kerch and Enikale as well as parts of other regions. While the Russian Empire had to restore Wallachia and Moldavia to the Ottoman Empire, they gained more from the treaty than the Ottomans. The treaty features prominently in the Russian history curriculum of most schools in Russia.

Crimea was annexed by Russia in 1783. Recently, the treaty has been used in the Russian media to justify the annexation of Crimea in 2014, with diverse arguments that do not always derive from the treaty.

Concerning religion, the authority of the Ottoman caliph over Muslim affairs among the Tatar peoples was recognised. This was the first time that a European power formally acknowledged the authority of the caliph outside Ottoman borders.

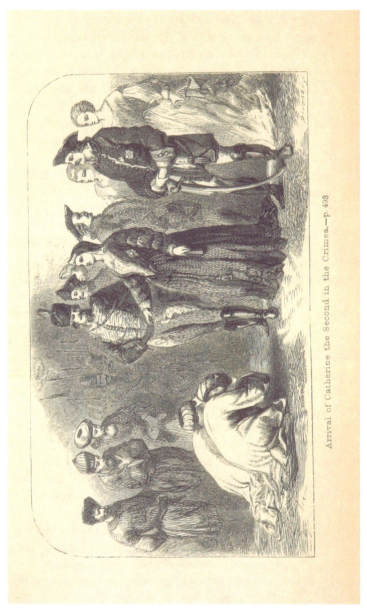

Arrival of Catherine the Second in the Crimea.—p. 493

Illustration 18. Arrival of Catherine II in Crimea

Similarly, the articles on religion suggest that Russia nominated itself as the protector of Orthodox people living under the rule of the sultan. Russia gained assurance that Orthodox Christians in the Ottoman Empire were free to practise their religion, that monasteries were returned with lands and rights, and that pilgrims from Russia would be able to go to the Holy Land without having to make excessive payments. In the aftermath, the Greeks made extensive use of the privileges and rights offered, resulting in improvements to their social and economic life.

In the following century, the treaty was interpreted by Russia to mean that the tsar was responsible for the sultan's Orthodox subjects, and Russia began to protect Orthodox Christians throughout the Ottoman Empire. The consequences of this approach can be seen in the Crimean war in 1854, when the protectors of Christian minorities in the Holy Land (Russia, France and the British Empire) ostensibly struggled over their prerogatives in this respect. As the treaty was a first indication of the decline of the Ottoman Empire, the European powers in 1854 competed for territorial gains rather than over religion; the religious argument had been settled before the war began.

The Treaty of Küçük Kaynarca was not only a peace treaty that sealed Ottoman defeat in a long-lasting conflict. For Russia, it also formed the basis for a new interpretation of their responsibilities towards Orthodox Christians living in the Ottoman Empire, as well as a means of gaining territory from a declining empire on religious grounds.

PUBLICATIONS

F. Pitteri, *Storia dell'anno 1774*, Venice, [1774], pp. 248-64 (Italian trans.; see Parry for digitised version)

G.F. Martens, *Recueil des principaux traits*, Göttingen, 1791, vol. 1, entry 44, pp. 507-22 (French trans.); J.publ.e. 242,1-1 (digitised version available through *MDZ*)

G.F. Martens, *Recueil des principaux traits*, Göttingen, 1817², vol. 2/1, pp. 286-322 (French trans.; see Parry for digitised version)

Great Britain, 'Treaties (Political and Territorial) between Russia and Turkey 1774-1849', in *Parliamentary papers*, London, 1854, vol. 72, pp. 171-9 (French text with English trans.); 1735 (digitised version available through UK Parliamentary papers)

T. Juzuefovich (ed.), *Dogovory Rossii s Vostokom, politicheskie i torgovye*, St Petersburg, 1869, pp. 24-41

J.C. Hurwitz (ed.), *Diplomacy in the Near and Middle East. A documentary record*, New York 1956, pp. 54-61

C. Parry, *The consolidated treaty series*, vol. 45. *1772-1775*, Dobbs Ferry NY, 1969, entry 349 (Italian text, from Pitteri, pp. 351-68; French text, from Martens, 1817[2], pp. 368-401); 45 CTS 349 (digitised version available through Oxford Historical Treaties)

A.A. Sazonov et al. (eds), *Pod stiagom Rossii. Sbornik arkhivnykh dokumentov*, Moscow, 1992, pp. 78-92 (full Russian text); http://web.archive.org/web/20030117234356/http://hronos.km.ru/dokum/1700dok/1774ru_tur.html

B. Geffert and T.G. Stavrou (eds), *Eastern Orthodox Christianity. The essential texts*, New Haven CT, 2016, pp. 354-6 (English trans.; extract)

STUDIES

S.L. Schwarz, *Despoten – Barbaren – Wirtschaftspartner. Die Allgemeine Zeitung und der Diskurs über das Osmanische Reich 1821-1840*, Vienna, 2016, p. 110

J. Hort, *Architektur der Diplomatie. Repräsentation in europäischen Botschaftsbauten 1800-1920. Konstantinopel – Rom – Wien – St. Petersburg*, Göttingen, 2014, pp. 67-8

B.L. Davies, *Empire and military revolution in Eastern Europe. Russia's Turkish wars in the eighteenth century*, London, 2011

O. Schulz, *Ein Sieg der zivilisierten Welt? Die Intervention der europäischen Großmächte im griechischen Unabhängigkeitskrieg (1826-1832)*, Berlin, 2011, pp. 158-60

K. Hitchins, 'Wallachia and Georgia confront the Eastern Question, 1767-1802', in I. Biliarsky, O. Cristea and A. Oroveanu (eds), *The Balkans and Caucasus. Parallel processes on the opposite sides of the Black Sea*, Newcastle, 2012, 12-28

G. Ágoston and B. Masters, *Encyclopedia of the Ottoman Empire*, New York, 2009, p. 126

D. Schorkowitz, *Postkommunismus und verordneter Nationalismus. Gedächtnis, Gewalt und Geschichtspolitik im nördlichen Schwarzmeergebiet*, Frankfurt am Main, 2008, pp. 63-5

G. Jenkins, *Political Islam in Turkey. Running West, heading East?*, New York, 2008, pp. 45-6

H. Kramer and M. Reinkowski, *Die Türkei und Europa. Eine wechselhafte Beziehungsgeschichte*, Stuttgart, 2008, pp. 75-9

O. Selekou, art. 'Treaty of Küçük Kaynarca', in *Encyclopaedia of the Hellenic world* (electronic resource), http://www.ehw.gr/l.aspx?id=11605

M. Marcinkowski, *Die Entwicklung des Osmanischen Reiches zwischen 1839 und 1908. Reformbestrebungen und Modernisierungsversuche im Spiegel der deutschsprachigen Literatur*, Berlin, 2007, pp. 13-15

O. Köse, *1774-Kücük Kaynarca andlaşmasi*, Ankara, 2006

R. Crews, *For prophet and tsar. Islam and empire in Russia and Central Asia*, Cambridge MA, 2006, pp. 39-45

D. Arapov, *Sistema gosudarstevnnogo regulirovaniia Islama v Rossiiskoi Imperii*, Moscow, 2004, p. 45

A.I. Tret'jak, *Severnoe Prichernomor'e v politiko-pravovom prostranstve Evropy kontsa XVIII veka*, Odessa, 2004, pp. 8-13

E.V., art, 'Kücük Kainarca, Friede von', in K. Clewing and E. Hösch (eds), *Lexikon zur Geschichte Südosteuropas*, Vienna, 2004, 549

H.-J. Torke, *Einführung in die Geschichte Russlands*, Munich, 1997, pp. 136-7

B. Lewis, *The Middle East. 2000 years of history from the birth of Christianity to the present day*, London, 1995, pp. 273-85

E.I. Druzhinina, *Kiuchuk-Kainardzhskii mir*, Moscow, 1995

K. Zernack (ed.), *Handbuch der Geschichte Russlands*, Stuttgart, vol. 2/2, 1988

A.V. Vitol, *Osmanskaia tsivilizatsiia*, Moscow, 1987

R.H. Davison, 'The "Dosografa" Church in the Treaty of Küçük Kaynarca', *BSOAS* 42 (1979) 46-52

R.H. Davidson, 'Russian skill and Turkish imbecility. The Treaty of Kuchuk Kainardji reconsidered', *Slavic Review* 35 (1976) 463-83

I.S. Dostian, 'Znacheniia Kiuchuk-Kainardzhiiskogo dogovora 1774 g. V politike Rossii na Balkanakh kontsa XVIII i XIX vv.', *Etudes Balkaniques* 11 (1975) 97-107

M.I. Harvey, 'The development of Russian commerce on the Black Sea and its significance', Berkeley, 1938 (PhD Diss. University of California)

A. Sorel, *The Eastern Question in the eighteenth century. The partition of Poland and the Treaty of Kaindardji*, Edinburgh, 1969

V.G. Gadzhiev, *Istoriia Dagestana*, Moscow, 1967, vol. 1, p. 393

A.F. Miller, *Mustafa pasha Bairaktar*, Moscow, 1947, pp. 64-7

F.A. Byuler et al. (eds), *Politicheskaia perepiska imp. Ekateriny II.*, part 7. *1772-3*, St Petersburg, 1904

O. Zhuravev, *Russkaia politika v vostochnom voprose (Ee istoriia v XVI-XIX vekakh, kriticheskaia ottsenka i budushchie zadachi). Istoriko-iuridicheskie ocherki*, Moscow, 1896, vol. 1, pp. 171-223

V.A. Ulianitskii, *Dardanelly, Bosfor i Chernoe more v XVIII veke. (Ocherki diplomaticheskoi istorii vostochnogo voprosa)*, Moscow, 1883, pp. 106-484, LXVIII-CCLVIII

'Kainardzhiiskii mir. Bumagi, otnosiashchiesia do zakliucheniia etogo mira (s 17 ianv. Po 19 iiunia 1775 g.)', *Russkii Arkhiv* 3/10 (1879) 137-69

J. Hammer, *Histoire de l'Empire ottoman*, Paris, 1839, vol. 16, pp. 209-400

Cornelia Soldat

Vasilii Iakovlevich Baranshchikov

DATE OF BIRTH   1756
PLACE OF BIRTH   Nizhnii Novgorod
DATE OF DEATH   Unknown
PLACE OF DEATH   Unknown

BIOGRAPHY

A *meshchanin* (an individual belonging to the lower middle-level social rank in the Russian Empire), Vasilii Baranshchikov catapulted to fame in the 1780s and 1790s, after his travelogue became a bestseller of the time. Until 1900, some doubts persisted regarding his real existence; indeed, some thought he was a *nom de plume*, an invention. But after 1900, it became clear that Baranshchikov had not only existed, but may well also have undertaken a journey filled with unfortunate adventures, and survived it. Baranshchikov was a merchant of the second guild from Nizhnii Novgorod. According to documents uncovered in 1900, consisting of testimony in front of the city's governor (*namestnik*), in 1786 he was 30 years old, so he must have been born in 1756, one of three brothers. He received a basic education and, like his father, went into trade, visiting various provincial fairs. In 1780, he travelled to St Petersburg, where he boarded a ship as a sailor. He arrived in Copenhagen in December 1780. He was lured onto a ship by Danish soldiers, and ended up on the island of St Thomas in the Caribbean, where he was forced to become a soldier in the local army. As a soldier, he was both unsuccessful and linguistically challenged, so he found himself travelling on a Spanish ship to Puerto Rico. There, he served a Spanish field marshal, until he was allowed to leave for Venice on an Italian ship. He worked in Venice, and subsequently ended up as a sailor on an Italian ship bound for Jerusalem. After further travels he ended up in Constantinople, with the aim of returning to Russia. He set out from Constantinople on foot to Russia, through Wallachia and Moldavia.

The above is a summary of events that are much more colourfully and adventurously recounted by Baranshchikov himself (for a number of factual and chronological discrepancies, see Vigasin, 'Neshchastnye prikliucheniia', pp. 104-6; Taki, *Tsar and sultan*, pp. 67-70). It appears that, once he returned to Russia, Baranshchikov had to face his creditors, and he resorted to the publication of his *Neshchastnye prikliucheniia* ('The unfortunate adventures') so as to attract donations to help him. His work went through three editions (two in 1787, and a third in 1793, with a reprint in 1788), becoming a bestseller, and including in the second and third editions a list of the names of high-ranking individuals who came to his 'rescue' from his creditors. The present entry is based on the second edition, published in 1787.

MAIN SOURCES OF INFORMATION

Primary

'Review', *Zertsalo Sveta* 97 (5 November 1787) (cited in B.W. Maggs, 'Fedor Karzhavin and Vasilii Baranshchikov. Russian travellers in the Carribean and Colonial America', in R.P. Bartlett et al. (eds), *Russia and the world of the eighteenth century*, Columbus OH, 1988, 604-14, p. 612 n. 3)

V.I. Sreznevskii, 'Opis' zhurnalam nizhegorodskogo namestnicheskogo pravleniia 1784 g", *Nizhegorodoskaia Gubernskaia Uchenaia Arkhivnaia Komissiia, Sbornik Statei, Soobshchenii, Opisei i Dokumentov* 4 (1900) 81-146

Secondary

V. Taki, *Tsar and sultan. Russian encounters with the Ottoman Empire*, London, 2016, pp. 66-73

A.A. Vigasin (ed.), 'Neshchastnye prikliucheniia Vasil'ia Baranshchikova, meshchanina Nizhnego Novgoroda, v trekh chastiakh sveta: v Amerike, Azii i Evrope s 1780 po 1787 god', in A.A. Vigasin and S.K. Karpiuk, *Puteshestviia po Vostoku v epokhu Ekateriny II*, Moscow, 1995, 101-33, pp. 101-6

Maggs, 'Fedor Karzhavin and Vasilii Baranshchikov. Russian travellers in the Carribean and Colonial America'

Th.G. Stavrou and P.R. Weisensel, *Russian travelers to the Christian East from the twelfth to the twentieth century*, Columbus OH, 1986, pp. 108-9

WORKS ON CHRISTIAN-MUSLIM RELATIONS

Neshchastnye prikliucheniia
'The unfortunate adventures'

DATE   1787

ORIGINAL LANGUAGE   Russian

DESCRIPTION

The assumption among scholars is that Baranshchikov did not write his own work, but employed somebody else to record his story and embellish it. Some argue that this could have been Fedor Karzhavin, another traveller to the Caribbean. The account fits into the genre of the popular tale (Maggs, 'Fedor Karzhavin and Vasilii Baranshchikov', p. 605).

Unlike the biographical sketch outlined above, which is based on Baranshchikov's deposition to the authorities in 1786, his account, written in the third person, is infinitely more colourful and entertaining (its title in full is *Neshchastnye prikliucheniia Vasil'ia Baranshchikova, meshchanina Nizhnego Novgoroda, v trekh chastiakh sveta: v Amerike, Azii i Evrope s 1780 po 1787 god*, 'The unfortunate adventures of Vasilii Baranshchikov, a *meshchanin* from Nizhnii Novgorod, in the three parts of the world: in America, Asia and Europe from 1780 to 1787'). In it, he recounts that in December 1780 he was in Copenhagen, and after making the rounds for various provisions he entered a tavern ('as is characteristic', he adds, 'of a Russian person') where he was befriended by two Danes. They started drinking and soon a third individual, pretending to be a Russian from Riga, joined them, speaking Russian and praising the two Danes. The night of drinking resulted in Baranshchikov being chained on a boat together with other unfortunate individuals of various ethnicities, sailing to the Americas. This unwilling sailor on the Danish ship was rather unconvinced that his prospects in the New World were bright. In 1781, they arrived in St Thomas, where Baranshchikov ended up serving as a soldier, having to deal with issues such as the fact that his name was unpronounceable, and so he was named Michel Nikolaev. His account is full of fascinating details relating to comparisons between Russian and American food (for example, the banana is like a cucumber, he notes) and he repeatedly refers to coffee. Having failed to get used to the Danish language, he is allowed to leave, and finds himself in Puerto Rico. There, he works as a servant in the kitchen of a field marshal until the latter's wife takes pity on him and lets him go.

He then sails on an Italian ship to Genoa, and in 1784 is captured by Tunisian or Egyptian pirates. Ending up as booty, he is forced to convert to Islam, given the Muslim name 'Isliam', and branded with a sun on his right hand. He then travels to Bethlehem, where he works as a servant in the house of the captain of the pirate ship. Among his duties is the astonishing task of preparing coffee up to 15 times a day. When he prepares and eats so much porridge (*kasha*) that the four wives of his captor think he will burst, they are amazed and tell their husband, who is also amazed and starts comparing him to the Russians who at the time were fighting the Ottomans. In a discussion with the captain, he is asked why the Russians are so strong, to which he lyingly says that the Russians look down on death, and also use a number of herbs that give them strength.

Baranshchikov tries to escape but is caught and beaten. He resigns himself to his fate, until some Greeks enter the story, helping him to travel to Jerusalem on pilgrimage disguised as one of them. He is not able to visit the Holy Sepulchre, but does go to other shrines. His 'good natured' Greek helper takes him to some Greek Orthodox clerics, who secretly receive him back into Orthodoxy so that he can save his soul. This latest conversion is marked by yet another tattoo. Finally, he leaves for Venice where he receives yet another passport, Venetian this time, and embarks for Constantinople, where the Russian ambassadorial authorities do not believe his story and refuse to help him. He unsuccessfully seeks help from other Russian merchants, until finally a compatriot by the name of Gusman, an apostate from Orthodoxy and convert to Islam, befriends him. He pretends to convert to Islam, and through his compatriot's services he marries and ends up working as a shoemaker, all the while under the unflinching scrutiny of his wife and father-in-law in their attempt to verify his sincerity in the faith. He also starts working as a Janissary. Finally, his longing for his homeland and family lead him to escape, which he does on foot after gleaning information from a Russian courier about the various roads to Russia from Istanbul.

He puts on Greek clothes and sets off. The courier had assured him that the beloved Empress Catherine II (r. 1762-96) offered her pardon to everyone who returned home, especially if they settled in the newly-acquired territories around Kherson. On 23 February 1786, he returns to Nizhnii Novgorod and to his debts, which lead him into a number of difficulties from which he can only free himself with the help of highly-placed individuals in St Petersburg, both laymen and clergy. It would appear that what Baranshchikov essentially did was to try to sell his story in order to cover his debts (Maggs, 'Fedor Karzhavin and Vasilii Baranshchikov', pp. 603-4).

Neshchastnye prikliucheniia was composed against the backdrop of the Russo-Turkish wars of the second half of the 18th century, and especially the war of 1787-92. It touches on issues relating to pilgrimage to the Holy Land, Russo-Greek relations, and the condition of captivity.

Baranshchikov's first encounter with Muslims was as a captive after being seized by pirates in the Mediterranean. He was forcibly Islamised and given the name 'Isliam' – a process the narrative presents matter-of-factly. His period as a servant for the captain in Bethlehem does not appear to have been particularly onerous, apart from the beatings he was subjected to when he tried to escape. His *kasha* stunt served him well, as did the stories he told the wives of his captors. In his narrative,

Baranshchikov presents himself as the clever and inventive Russian who manages (or almost manages) to make his captors believe his tall tales about Russian valour and use of magical herbs. He comes across as the quintessential survivor.

In his account, the image of Muslims is one of conquerors and masters, who are also capable of showing their human side, as in the case of Baranshchikov's entertaining his captain with his stories about Russians and the *kasha* trick. If anything, those who fare worse in their portrayal are the Russian authorities who refuse to accept his explanations and stories in Istanbul, forcing him to resort to apostate Russians for help. Indeed, of the characters portrayed as the least trustworthy and most complex are the Russian apostates, such as Gusman. If Gusman is taken as representative of such converts to Islam, his case indicates the support networks available to apostates. It was through him that Baranshchikov managed to find a wife and a job, and establish a life for himself in Istanbul. Baranshchikov went along with the ruse and played the game (as, for example, when reciting correct Muslim prayers in order to receive some money allocated to new converts). On the other hand, Gusman was also money-loving and crafty, in spite of all the help he provided.

The narrative describes in a matter-of-fact way Baranshchikov's life as a Janissary, with a particular focus on how Janissaries would share their food with others out of philanthropy. On the other hand, Baranshchikov's wife turns him in for not washing or performing the appropriate prayers. If the narrative portrays anybody as an evil person, it is his wife. It appears to be precisely his unwillingness to follow certain Turkish habits and customs that were different from Russian ones that eventually gave him the impetus to escape. In particular, he missed the elaborate decoration of Russian churches, which he could not find in mosques. The final straw was when he was told to take a second wife, as a guarantee that he was sincere in his Muslim faith; at this point, he resolved to act and escape all of Islam's 'vanities'.

Baranshchikov's account includes an appendix which covers various subjects, including descriptions of Constantinople, the sultan's harem, marriage practices, the leadership of the Ottomans in military and civilian matters, and dervishes. It remains an open question as to whether he himself could and did write this appendix, as it contains a number of items that he would not necessarily have been familiar with (such as a listing of officials in lay and clerical positions in the Ottoman administration). Vigasin suggests that P.A. Levashov's *Tsaregradskie pis'ma* could have provided a source (see Vigasin, 'Neshchastnye prikliucheniia',

p. 106); this would, however, presuppose, as Vigasin readily admits, Baranshchikov's having advance knowledge of Levashov's manuscript, which was published later than his.

The appendix itself is matter-of-fact, a form of presentation that, without much commentary or offensive remarks, continues into the final section, which is entitled 'On the strange Turkish habits'. The habits listed are Muslim concepts of paradise, the permitted number of wives and concubines, the sultan's harem, the use of eunuchs in the administration, the use of *otroki* (presumably meaning the *icoglan*, boy servants) in the sultan's administration, and Turkish respect for the fiscal system. There are occasional critical comments; for example, full castration (different from that practised in Italy, the author notes, where only the testicles are removed) is mentioned as a custom that consolidates ignorance and superstition. Also, the Ottomans do not focus on much detail in criminal matters, unlike the Russians. Nevertheless, the author does not present all their habits as strange in his exposition in the appendix. The section ends with reference to Muslim piety, with the author distinguishing between varieties of Muslim piety in fasting. He also argues that the rich rarely give charity, unlike those of lesser means. Finally, he claims that Turkish piety is such that it would lead the faithful not to interrupt their prayers in the mosque even if their houses were on fire. The section closes with the remark that Turkish funeral habits are similar to Russians ones.

SIGNIFICANCE

According to Taki (*Tsar and sultan*, p. 72), contemporary and later reviews of the work were mixed. Still, Taki argues that Baranshchikov's narrative reflects a step in a process that allowed the Russian reading public (and not just the ecclesiastical authorities) a say in the way in which captivity and forced conversion to Islam were dealt with once captives had managed to escape and make their way home (p. 73).

Overall, both in the work and the appendix (if it was authored by him), Baranshchikov's representation of the other, the Muslim, is characterised by a matter-of-fact approach. While he occasionally refers to the vanity of Islam, this is a far cry from attacking it for its principles or practices. The exception is polygamy, which he criticises.

PUBLICATIONS

V.I.A. Baranshchikov, *Neshchastnye prikliucheniia Vasil'ia Baranshchikova, meshchanina Nizhnego Novagoroda, v trekh chastiakh sveta: v Amerike, Azii i Evrope s 1780 po 1787 god*), St Petersburg, 1787

V.I.A. Baranshchikov, *Neshchastnye prikliucheniia Vasil'ia Baransh-chikova, meshchanina Nizhnego Novagoroda, v trekh chastiakh sveta: v Amerike, Azii i Evrope s 1780 po 1787 god)*. *Vtoroe izdanie s dopolneniem i figurami*, 2nd edition, St Petersburg, 1787; nyp.33433051574337 (digitised version available through Hathi Trust Digital Library)

V.I.A. Baranshchikov, *Neshchastnye prikliucheniia Vasil'ia Baransh-chikova, meshchanina Nizhnego Novagoroda, v trekh chastiakh sveta: v Amerike, Azii i Evrope s 1780 po 1787 god)*. *Novoe izdanie, s dopol-neniem i figurami*, St Petersburg: [Tipografiia Bogdanovicha?], 1788

V.I.A. Baranshchikov, *Neshchastnye prikliucheniia Vasil'ia Baransh-chikova, meshchanina Nizhnego Novagoroda, v trekh chastiakh sveta: v Amerike, Azii i Evrope s 1780 po 1787 god)*. *Tretie izdanie s dopolneniem, izhdiveniem I.G.*, 3rd edition, St Petersburg: V tipo-grafii B.L. Geka, 1793

Vigasin, 'Neshchastnye prikliucheniia'

STUDIES

Taki, *Tsar and sultan*, pp. 66-73

W. Smiley, 'The meanings of conversion. Treaty law, state knowledge, and religious identity among Russian captives in the eighteenth-century Ottoman Empire', *The International History Review* 34 (2012) 559-80

C. Evtuhov, *Portrait of a Russian province. Economy, society and civili-zation in nineteenth-century Nizhnii Novgorod*, Pittsburgh PA, 2011

E.B. Smilianskaia (ed.), *Rossiia v Srednizemnomor'e. Arkhipelagskaia ekspeditsiia Ekateriny Velikoi*, Moscow, 2011

D.L. Ransel, *A Russian merchant's tale. The life and adventures of Ivan Alekseevich Tolchënov, based on his diary*, Bloomington IN, 2009

Vigasin, 'Neshchastnye prikliucheniia'

Maggs, 'Fedor Karzhavin and Vasilii Baranshchikov'

Stavrou and Weisensel, *Russian travelers*, pp. 108-9

B.M. Dantsig, *Russkie puteshestvenniki na blizhnem vostoke*, Moscow, 1965, pp. 92-4

N.I. Konrad, 'Posleslovie', in R.A. Shtil'mark (ed.), *Povest' o strannike rossiiskom*, Moscow, 1962, 230-7

Nikolaos Chrissidis

Von Raan

Second Major von Raan

DATE OF BIRTH   Unknown
PLACE OF BIRTH   Possibly Germany
DATE OF DEATH   Unknown
PLACE OF DEATH   Unknown

BIOGRAPHY

Although Von Raan's precise origins are not known, he referred to himself as a foreign national (*chuzhestranets*), indicating he was not a native of the Russian Empire. Details from his letters suggest that he was not Austrian, and that he read German, so he may have been from one of the German states.

Despite his aristocratic appellation, Von Raan entered Russian service because, as he put it, he 'possessed neither friends nor prospects' (*Perechen'*, p. vii). During the 1787 Russo-Turkish War, he held the rank of second major in the Russian Army. He fought in the corps of Count Rumiantsev in Moldavia in 1787 and 1788, and then in Bessarabia in 1789 under the overall command of Prince Potemkin. Although he saw combat in several skirmishes, Von Raan was not present at any of the major sieges or battles of the war, but his correspondents did provide first-hand accounts of several of these actions.

In 1790, Von Raan suffered a severe illness, and an extended period of recuperation kept him from active service for the remainder of the conflict. In 1792, he published his wartime correspondence as a record of the Russian Army's conduct of the war.

Although multiple secondary sources give Von Raan's full name as 'M.L. von Raan', it is unclear where this was originally sourced, and it may represent a misattribution from the initials of one of Von Raan's correspondents, 'M.L.R.' (*Perechen'*, p. 13).

MAIN SOURCES OF INFORMATION

Primary
Sek. Maior Fon Raan, *Perechen' iz sobstvennago svoego zhurnala v prodolzhenie proshedshei voiny Pri zavoevanii Moldavii i Bessarabii C 1787 po 1790 god*, St Petersburg, 1792

WORKS ON CHRISTIAN-MUSLIM RELATIONS

Perechen' iz sobstvennago svoego zhurnala
'Compendium from his own journal'

DATE 1787-90
ORIGINAL LANGUAGE Russian

DESCRIPTION

Von Raan's *Perechen'* (in full, *Perechen' iz obstvennago svoego zhurnala v prodolzhenie proshedshei voiny pri zavoevanii Moldavii i Bessarabii S 1787 po 1790 god*, 'Compendium from his own journal, kept over the course of the recent war during the conquest of Moldavia and Bessarabia, from 1787 to 1790') is a collection of his personal correspondence from the 1787 Russo-Turkish war. It has appeared in two editions, the first (128 pages) published in 1792, and including a map, the second (99 pages) produced in 1891, and including an introduction and notes by Avksentii Standitskii, but lacking the map.

In his introduction, Standitskii wrote that the text of the 1891 edition was based on a handwritten manuscript in his possession, and that, while he knew of the earlier publication, he did not have access to it. Both versions are, however, virtually identical. His analysis of the text led Standitskii to theorise that Von Raan's correspondence had originally been conducted in German and later translated.

The bulk of Von Raan's *Perechen'* consists of 30 letters. One of these (no. 16) is a translation from a short letter sent by a Crimean Tatar noble named Mehmed Giray, a commander in the Ottoman army, relating to the death of his son. Four letters (nos. 4, 10, 17 and 26) were received by Von Raan from other officers in Russian service. The authors are not named (although one is identified as an engineering officer with the initials M.L.R.). These messages detail important events that Von Raan did not witness, including the campaign against Kherson, naval actions in the Black Sea, the capture of Ochakov, and the Battle of Focşani. The other 25 letters describe Von Raan's experiences during the Moldavia campaign. In large part, these outline periods of encampment and manoeuvre, punctuated by occasional skirmishes. They also include much information on the army's organisation and command staff at various points in the war. Von Raan's intention in publishing the letters was to provide a more complete picture of military operations during the war, particularly with respect to the Russian Army.

Religion is not a topic in which Von Raan demonstrated much interest. However, information pertaining to confessional relations can be
found scattered throughout the letters. Themes of particular importance include the way Von Raan conceived the war against the Ottoman Empire, his framing of ethnic categories, and his views on the
depredations that both sides inflicted on the residents of the contested
region.

The most significant aspect of Von Raan's *Perechen'* is his Orientalist interpretation of the Russo-Turkish war as just one part of a much
larger civilisational conflict. While the idea is only occasionally given
prominence in his letters, it is clear that Von Raan saw himself as a soldier fighting to protect and advance civilised Europe against the backward East. He was stirred to give voice to these feelings most eloquently
at the beginning of the war, when he witnessed a meeting between
Catherine II of Russia (r. 1762-96) and Joseph II of Austria (r. 1765-90):
'Would it be possible [...] to forget the moment when the two foremost
Lords of Europe came together with a single humanitarian purpose for
the great undertaking of saving an entire people from barbarianism?'
(*Perechen'*, p. 3).

Von Raan reveals his Orientalist perspective not only by overt statements, but also through the subtext of his wartime narrative. This is true,
for example, in the sweeping ethnic categories he uses to describe the
enemy. The hypothetical or abstract foes he anticipates encountering
included the 'courageous Tatar', the 'bearded Turk', and the 'naked Arab'
(*Perechen'*, pp. 54, 91). This broad array of enemies, understood in essen-
tialised ethnic terms, suggests a conflict with roots that went beyond
mere political rivalry with the Ottoman Empire. Similarly, Orientalism
shaped Von Raan's interpretation of the atrocities of war. He witnessed
many instances in which one side or the other destroyed or depopu-
lated villages and towns in Moldavia and Bessarabia, and he portrays
these events through an unabashedly Orientalist frame of reference. The
Turks, he claims, 'habitually incinerated all the villages through which
they travelled'; 'desolation and destruction were uniquely characteristic
of this barbaric enemy' (*Perechen'*, pp. 28, 47-8). When the Russian army
committed similar acts, however, Von Raan passes over them as military
necessities or inevitable side-effects of war – as when the Russian army
burned down the city of Galați and its surrounding villages 'for the reason of denying the enemy the means to again position themselves on
this side of the Danube' (*Perechen'*, p. 75). These themes came together

in the striking incident of the Russian army's ethnic cleansing of the city of Bender, where, Von Raan relates without comment, 'Asiatic residents were allowed to sell their property before leaving', while 'European residents were to remain' (*Perechen'*, p. 108).

Despite all his prejudices, it should be acknowledged that Von Raan was not incapable of respecting and humanising his opponents. He often attributes qualities of bravery and steadfastness collectively to the Ottoman troops, despite their military ineffectiveness. The inclusion of the letter from Mehmed Giray in the collection provides a particularly striking piece of evidence for shared humanity – detailing the pain of the Tatar commander at the loss of his son, the son's honour and patriotism in defence of his homeland, and the civility that could exist between officers of opposing sides in the conflict. However, in its ability to reconcile moments of humanity with broad cultural stereotypes, Von Raan's style of Orientalism was in no way exceptional.

SIGNIFICANCE

What is noteworthy about Von Raan's views is that they were not at all typical within the Russian army of the time. Most Russian officers of the late 18th century would have agreed with him that Russia was a European country; however, the westernisation programme of Peter the Great was still within living memory, and Russia's place in the European order remained a matter of debate. Moreover, as the administrators of empire, Russian officers tended to resist broad civilisational categories, for reasons of both experience and necessity. The Russian Empire had long been made up of a variety of faiths and ethnicities, and non-Christian and non-European ethnic groups were seen as intrinsic parts of the state. Meanwhile, European Christians had frequently been imperial adversaries, most alarmingly in Poland. As a result, Russian officers generally tended to view conflicts through the lenses of imperial politics and pragmatic decision-making, rather than those of ethnic and religious identity or civilisational affinity.

Von Raan's significance, then, lies in showing how Western European patterns of thought – derived from a binary view of a world divided between Christians and heathens – could be introduced into elite Russian society by foreign retainers, and gradually take hold. Von Raan's style of Orientalist discourse would never predominate in the Russian Empire but, aided by the influence of figures such as him, it would gain a much higher profile over the course of the 19th century.

PUBLICATIONS

Sek[und] Maior Fon Raan, *Perechen' iz sobstvennago svoego zhurnala v prodolzhenie proshedshei voiny Pri zavoevanii Moldavii i Bessarabii S 1787 po 1790 god*, St Petersburg, 1792

Sekund-maior fon Raan, *Materialy dlia istorii Bessarabii, o voine pri zavoievanii Moldavii i Bessarabii v 1787, 1788, 1789 i 1790 godakh*, Kishinev, 1891

Sekund-maior fon Raan, 'Materialy dlia istorii Bessarabii, o voine pri zavoievanii Moldavii i Bessarabii v 1787, 1788, 1789 i 1790 godakh', *Kishinevskiia Eparkhal'nyia Vedomosti* 1/2-12 (1892) 1-99 (supplement to the unofficial section)

Eric Johnson

Contributors

Name	Affiliation	Entries
Ian Almond	Professor of World Literature, Georgetown University (Qatar)	Gottfried Wilhelm Leibniz
Asterios Argyriou	Professor emeritus, University of Strasbourg	Anastasios Gordios
Natalie Bayer	Associate Professor of History, College of Arts & Sciences, Drake University, Des Moines IA	Batyrsha Aliev
Asaph Ben-Tov	Researcher, School of History, University of Kent; Fellow, Herzog August Bibliothek, Wolfenbüttel	Central European encounters with the Muslim world in the 18th century; Matthias Friedrich Beck
Zrinka Blažević	Associate Professor, History Department, Faculty of Humanities and Social Sciences, University of Zagreb	Josip Ruđer Bošković
Maurits van den Boogert	Publishing Director, Middle East, Islam and African Studies, Brill, Leiden	Heinrich Myrike
Mikołaj Piotr Borkowski	Doctoral candidate, Faculty of History, University of Warsaw	Benedykt Chmielowski; Tadeusz Juda Krusiński
Gwyn Bourlakov	Doctoral candidate, Department of History, University of Kansas, Lawrence KS	Johann Georg Gmelin; Gerhard Friedrich Müller; *Povest' o vziatii Azova Petrom I v 1696*

Name	Affiliation	Entries
Neven Budak	Professor, Humanities and Social Sciences, University of Zagreb	Pavao Ritter Vitezović
John Chesworth	Research Officer CMR1900, Department of Theology and Religion, University of Birmingham	Johann Jakob Brucker; Johann Heinrich Callenberg; Johann Salomo Semler
Nikolaos Chrissidis	Professor of Russian History, Department of History, Southern Connecticut State University, New Haven CT	Vasilii Iakovlevich Baranshchikov; Eighteenth-century Russian travellers to Jerusalem; Ioann Luk'ianov; Matvei Gavrilov Nechaev
Daniel Cyranka	Professor, Faculty of Theology, Martin Luther University, Halle-Wittenberg	David Nerreter
Evguenia Davidova	Professor, Department of International and Global Studies, Portland State University, Portland OR	Parteniĭ Pavlović
Dariusz Dolański	Professor, Head of Department of History of Science and Culture, Institute of History, University of Zielona Góra	The image of Muslims and Islam in 18th-century Polish geographical and historical works
Marek Dospěl	Association for Central European Cultural Studies, Prague; Associate Editor, Biblical Archaeology Review	Remedius Prutký; Jakub Římař
Ralf Elger	Professor, Oriental Institute, Martin Luther University, Halle-Wittenberg	Jonas Korte; Johann Traugott Plant
Amanda Ewington	Professor, Department of Russian Studies, Davidson College, Davidson NC	Aleksandr Petrovich Sumarokov

Name	Affiliation	Entries
Lucien Frary	Professor, Department of History, Rider University, Lawrenceville NJ	Vasilii Mikhailovich Dolgorukov; Matvei Mironov; Pietr Andreevich Tolstoi; Nikita Zotov
A. Yunus Gencer	Assistant Professor, Department of Music, Mimar Sinan Fine Arts University, Istanbul	Ottoman influences on European music. Part II
Clare Griffin	Assistant Professor, History, Philosophy, and Religious Studies Department, Nazarbayev University, Republic of Kazakhstan	Pyotr Vasilevich Postnikov
Evgeny Grishin	Professor, School of Advanced Studies, University of Tyumen	Feofan Prokopovich; The 1773 decree on religious toleration
Stanisław Grodź	Director, Anthropos Institute, Sankt Augustin, Germany	Introduction; Gottfried Arnold; Mikołaj Chwałkowski; Constantinopolitan- oder Turckischer Kirchen-Staat; Johann Christoph Döderlein; Johann Leonhard Froreisen; Gottfried Less; Johann David Michaelis; *Neu-eröffnetes Amphitheatrum*; Michał Bogusław Ruttich

Name	Affiliation	Entries
Alastair Hamilton	Senior Research Fellow, The Warburg Institute, University of London	Andreas Acoluthus; Friedrich Eberhard Boysen; David Friedrich Megerlin; Sebastian Gottfried Starck
Marios Hatzopoulos	Adjunct Lecturer, Hellenic Open University / Research Fellow, Centre of Modern History Research (KENI), Panteion University of Social and Political Sciences, Athens	Eighteenth-century Greek prophetic literature
Eric Johnson	Lecturer, Department of History, University of Washington, Seattle WA	Von Raan
Glen Johnson	Independent Scholar	*Opisanie tseremonial*
Chariton Karanasios	Senior Researcher, Research Centre for Medieval and Modern Greek Hellenism, Academy of Athens	Anastasios Gordios
Roman Krzywy	Researcher, The Faculty of Polish Studies, University of Warsaw	Franciszek Gościecki
Michał Kuran	Professor, Institute of Polish Philology, University of Lodz	Anti-Turkish literature in the Polish-Lithuanian Commonwealth, 1575-1733
Vjeran Kursar	Assistant Professor, Department of History and Department of Hungarian, Turkish, and Judaic Studies Faculty of Humanities and Social Sciences, University of Zagreb	Nikola Lašvanin

Name	Affiliation	Entries
Jan Loop	Associate Professor of History, Faculty Director of Internationalisation, University of Kent	Johann Jacob Reiske
Vasilios N. Makrides	Professor of Religious Studies (Orthodox Christianity), Department of Religious Studies, Faculty of Philosophy, University of Erfurt	Eighteenth-century Greek Orthodox contacts with Russia
Iva Manova	Assistant Professor, Institute of Philosophy and Sociology, Bulgarian Academy of Sciences, Sofia	Krsto Pejkić
Russell Martin	Professor, Department of History, Westminster College, New Wilmington PA	*Povest' o zhenitbe Ivana Groznogo na Marii Temriukovna*
Adrianna Maśko	Adjunct Lecturer, Faculty of Modern Languages and Literatures, Adam Mickiewicz University, Poznań	Franciszek Bohomolec; Kajetan Chrzanowski
Agata S. Nalborczyk	Head of the Department for European Islam Studies Faculty of Oriental Studies, University of Warsaw	Salomea Regina Pilsztynowa
Ovidiu-Victor Olar	Researcher, N. Iorga Institute of History of the Romanian Academy, Bucharest	Dimitrie Cantemir
David Do Paço	Assistant Professor, Sciences Po, Centre for History (CHSP), Paris, France	The political agents of Muslim courts in Central Europe in the 18th-century

Name	Affiliation	Entries
Radu G. Păun	Researcher, Centre d'Études des Mondes Russe, Caucasien et Centre-Européen, CNRS-EHESS, Paris	Introduction; Ianache Văcărescu
Elena Pedigo Clark	Associate Professor of Russian, Department of German and Russian, Wake Forest University, Winston-Salem NC	Mikhail Lomonosov
Barbara Podolak	Senior Lecturer, Faculty of Philology, Jagiellonian University, Kraków	Michał Ignacy Wieczorkowski
Birgit Röder	Associate Lecturer, School of Modern Languages, University of St Andrews	Engelbert Kaempfer
Çetin Sarıkartal	Professor of Theatre, Department of Theatre, Kadir Has University, Istanbul	Josef Franz
Kostas Sarris	Research fellow, SFB 980 'Episteme in Bewegung. Wissenstransfer von der Alten Welt bis in die Frühe Neuzeit', Freie Universität Berlin	Meletios of Athens
Ivan R. Sokolovsky	Research Fellow, Institute of History of the Russian Academy of Sciences, Siberian Branch, Novosibirsk	Semen Ulianovich Remezov
Cornelia Soldat	Research Associate, Cologne-Bonn Centre for Central and Eastern Europe (CCCEE), University of Cologne	Introduction; Treaty of Küçük Kaynarca; Iov

Name	Affiliation	Entries
Paul Strauss	Assistant Professor of History, Department of History, College of the Arts, Humanities and Social Sciences, California State University, Stanislaus, Turlock CA	Abraham a Sancta Clara
Liudmila Sukina	Professor, Head of the Department of training highly qualified personnel, Programme Systems Institute of the Russian Academy of Sciences, Pereslavl-Zalessky	*Povest' o tsare Vasilii Konstantinoviche*; Andrei Andreevich Vinius
Christian Tauchner	Director, Steyler Missionary Institute, Sankt Augustin, Germany	Gotthold Ephraim Lessing
Andrei Timotin	Director, Institute for South-East European Studies, Romanian Academy, Bucharest	Theoklytos Polyïdis; *Vision of kyr Daniel*
Mihai Ţipău	Researcher, Institute for South-East European Studies, Romanian Academy, Bucharest	Vasilios Vatatzes
Klaus-Peter Todt	Privat-Dozent, History Department, Byzantine Studies, Johannes Gutenberg-University, Mainz	Dositheos of Jerusalem

.

Index of Names

Numbers in italics indicate a main entry.

Index of Titles

Numbers in italics indicate a main entry.

Printed in the United States
By Bookmasters